Pirates

Pirates

ROSS KEMP

MICHAEL JOSEPH

Published by the Penguin Group
Penguin Books Ltd, 80 Strand, London WC2R 0RL, England
Penguin Group (USA) Inc., 375 Hudson Street, New York, New York 10014, USA
Penguin Group (Canada), 90 Eglinton Avenue East, Suite 700, Toronto, Ontario, Canada M4P 2Y3
(a division of Pearson Penguin Canada Inc.)
Penguin Ireland, 25 St Stephen's Green, Dublin 2, Ireland
(a division of Penguin Books Ltd)
Penguin Group (Australia), 250 Camberwell Road, Camberwell, Victoria 3124, Australia
(a division of Pearson Australia Group Pty Ltd)
Penguin Books India Pvt Ltd, 11 Community Centre, Panchsheel Park, New Delhi – 110 017, India
Penguin Group (NZ), 67 Apollo Drive, Rosedale, North Shore 0632, New Zealand
(a division of Pearson New Zealand Ltd)
Penguin Books (South Africa) (Pty) Ltd, 24 Sturdee Avenue,
Rosebank, Johannesburg 2196, South Africa

Penguin Books Ltd, Registered Offices: 80 Strand, London WC2R 0RL, England

www.penguin.com

First published 2009

2

Copyright © Ross Kemp, 2009
Photography courtesy of British Sky Broadcasting Limited

The moral right of the author has been asserted

Set in 13.5/16pt Monotype Garamond Std
Typeset by Penguin Books Ltd
Printed in Great Britain by Clays Ltd, St Ives plc

A CIP catalogue record for this book is available from the British Library

ISBN: 978–0–718–15443–1

www.greenpenguin.co.uk

Penguin Books is committed to a sustainable future
for our business, our readers and our planet.
The book in your hands is made from paper
certified by the Forest Stewardship Council.

This edition produced for The Book People Ltd,
Hall Wood Avenue, Haydock, St Helens WA11 9UL

'Where there is a sea, there are pirates.'
Greek proverb

'It is when pirates count their booty that
they become mere thieves.'
William Bolitho

'The sea was so vast. The vessels they sailed in were
small. Yet still the [pirates] tracked them down . . .'
Linda Colley, *Captives*

Contents

vii

PART 4
Djibouti

PART I
The Gulf of Aden

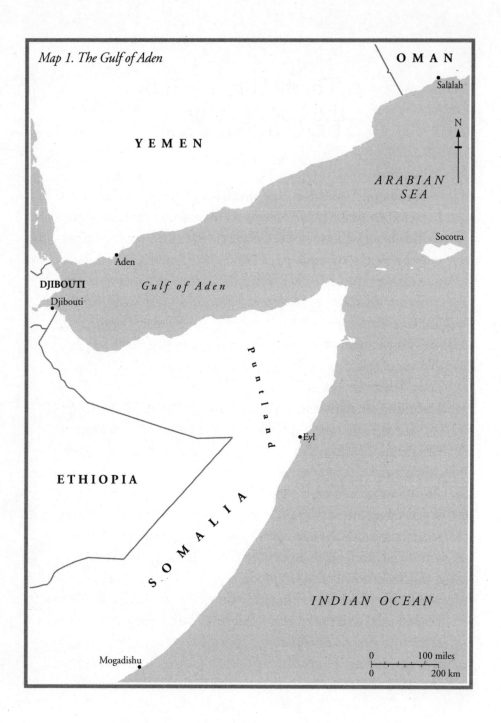

Map 1. The Gulf of Aden

OMAN

Salalah

N

YEMEN

ARABIAN
SEA

Socotra

Aden

Gulf of Aden

DJIBOUTI

Djibouti

Puntland

Eyl

ETHIOPIA

SOMALIA

INDIAN OCEAN

Mogadishu

| 0 | 100 miles |
| 0 | 200 km |

1. Them That Die'll Be the Lucky Ones . . .

Why pirates?

It is a good question, and one a lot of people asked me as I started to make preparations to investigate this dangerous world about which I knew almost nothing. I'd seen the newspaper reports, of course. I knew piracy was on the up. But I was also fresh out of Afghanistan. Over the previous couple of years I'd spent time in that dangerous war zone; I'd had Taliban snipers zeroing in on me, doing their best to kill me. I'd probably have been forgiven for taking it a bit easy.

Life doesn't work out like that, unfortunately. In January 2009 I was in Kajaki – one of the northern outposts of Helmand Province and scene of some of the fiercest fighting in Afghanistan. While I was there, a Marine by the name of Travis Mackin lost his life in an improvised explosive device strike near where I was accompanying his colleagues during an attack on a major Taliban stronghold. I suppose it goes without saying that I was impressed with the professionalism and tenacity of the Marines I met on that trip, and honoured to be accepted into their confidence. What I didn't know at the time was that in another part of the world the final act of a crime on the high seas was being played out, where the Royal Marines had been deployed in a very different conflict to that which the men at Kajaki were enduring. That crime was the hijacking of an oil tanker, the MV *Sirius Star*.

The *Sirius Star* is a big boat. A *very* big boat. It's classed as a VLCC – a very large crude carrier. You can say that again: well over 300 metres long, it can carry 2.2 million barrels of crude oil. How much that amount of black gold is worth depends on the value of oil, but even back then, with the world economy in free fall, the *Sirius Star*'s cargo would have been worth at least $100 million. As it set out from Saudi Arabia in November 2008, it was carrying about a quarter of that country's daily output of oil.

On 15 November 2008 the *Sirius Star* was heading south, 400 nautical miles from the coast of Kenya. Its destination: the United States. Its route: round the southern tip of Africa, past the Cape of Good Hope and then north-west across the Atlantic. It's easy to imagine that as the vessel passed through the waters off the eastern coast of Africa, its crew, while not being blasé, would at least have been reasonably confident of the ship's security. Sure, piracy was already a problem, but the incidents had generally taken place further north, in the Gulf of Aden. Moreover, ships of this size were generally safe. Surely just getting onto the boat would be nigh-on impossible. You'd need a brass neck, balls of steel and a very long ladder to attempt to hijack such a massive vessel. Wouldn't you?

If these were the thoughts of the *Sirius Star*'s owners and crew, they were mistaken. Because on that Saturday morning, at about 08.55, the boat was boarded by Somali pirates. They didn't mess around. By 09.02 the pirates had control of the bridge. The *Sirius Star* was so weighed down by its massive load of oil that its freeboard – the height between the deck and the waterline – was low. The crew, including two Britons, were taken hostage and the ship was

4

diverted from its original course, back up towards the Somali coastline. A couple of days later the pirates opened up communications with the ship's owners. They demanded a ransom of $25 million. The hijackers clearly knew the value of their haul, and were prepared to milk it for every last cent.

The eyes of the world were on the *Sirius Star*, but the hijackers held their nerve. They even released an audio tape to Al-Jazeera, the Middle Eastern news network. 'Negotiators are located on board the ship and on land. Once they have agreed on the ransom, it will be taken in cash to the oil tanker. We assure the safety of the ship that carries the ransom. We will mechanically count the money and we have machines that can detect fake money.' These pirates, then, were well organized and professional. They knew what they were doing.

The hostages were not mistreated. One of the Britons, Peter French, even managed to conduct an interview by phone. 'Our families don't have too much to worry about at the moment,' he said. 'Apart from the inconvenience of being locked up, our life is not too bad.' Nothing like a good British stiff upper lip. But if I were in his position, I imagine I'd be giving a great deal of thought to what would happen if the ransom *wasn't* paid. Would the pirates continue to be quite so considerate, or would they find a use for the automatic weapons they were carrying? As one of the pirates stated when they captured the vessel, 'We do not want long-term discussions to resolve the matter. The Saudis have ten days to comply, otherwise we will take action that could be disastrous.'

Disastrous for whom, I wonder . . .

The British government announced that there was no way they'd pay the ransom: giving in to hostage-taking was just an encouragement for people to do it again. The *Sirius Star*'s Saudi owners took a more pragmatic view. Not only were the 25 crew members their responsibility, they also had 100 million bucks to protect. And so the ransom negotiations started. They were long and drawn-out. On 25 November the pirates reduced their demand to $15 million. By January, it had come down even further. On 9 January 2009 the ship was released after the pirates received 3 million dollars. Sounds like a lot of money, but just think about what the shipowners had to lose . . .

A small plane dropped the ransom onto the deck of the *Sirius Star* by parachute. The pirates presumably checked the notes using the machines of which they had boasted, then they left the ship as swiftly as they had boarded it. The ending, however, was not a happy one for the Somali hijackers. Days after they left, their small boat apparently got into trouble in a storm. It capsized and five of the eight were drowned. A rumour later stated that the body of one was washed ashore with $150,000 in cash shoved into a plastic bag. What happened to the remaining three isn't clear. I guess they wouldn't be parading their presence any more than they had to – stepping into Somalia and announcing you have hundreds of thousands of dollars can't be good for your health. But I would later be told – totally unofficially, of course – that a team of private mercenaries had followed the hijackers, retrieved a large proportion of the money, capsized their boat and left the pirates for the fishes. Fact or rumour? Who knows . . .

The hijacking of the *Sirius Star* was significant for lots

of reasons. It was the first time such a big ship had been successfully pirated. It also marked an escalation in the pirates' field of operations – previously they had been confined to a much smaller area. The Somali pirates now roamed an area of about 1.1 million square miles, and there simply aren't enough military vessels in the world to patrol that amount of sea successfully.

I knew none of this in January 2009. I was busy with other worries, like how to avoid rocket-propelled grenade attacks from the local Taliban in Helmand Province – a very good way of keeping your mind occupied. But when the time came for me to say goodbye to 45 Victor Commando in Afghanistan and return home to London, it was clear that the piracy problem was current. It was happening now. There was no time for me to put my feet up. If I wanted to investigate pirates, to find out what was behind these attacks occurring in various hot spots and maybe even meet some of these people who were wreaking havoc and terror all round the world, the legwork would have to be done immediately.

And one thing was sure: the pirates weren't going to come to me. *I* was going to have to go to *them*.

All little boys want to be pirates. Why wouldn't they? The pirates of our imagination are romantic figures. They engage in acts of great daring. They seek out buried treasure and make their enemies walk the plank. If they're the Johnny Depp kind of pirate, they might even get the girl. And then they disappear, ready to plunder another day. The pirates we read about in books are villains, certainly. We know that. But, like highwaymen, perhaps we imagine that they're the acceptable face of villainy. That's why people don't mind their children dressing up with eyepatches and cutlasses.

I knew, of course, before I set out on my quest to track down some real-life pirates, that they aren't like that any more. That the pirates hijacking ships around the world armed with the kind of weaponry I'd previously seen in major war zones were not going to be of the yo-ho-ho-and-a-bottle-of-rum kind. But in fact they never *were* like that. Not in the real world. Successful pirates have always relied on the threat of force to achieve their ends, and the threat of force is only effective if people know you're willing to carry those threats out. Before I set off to learn about and meet modern-day pirates, I decided to learn something about the reality of their predecessors. Maybe if I knew something of the past, I'd learn something about the present. The stories I came across were unsettling, to say the least.

Our image of historical pirates is massively influenced by one book, huge in its time – a bestseller of the day. Robert Louis Stevenson's *Treasure Island* (1883), with its well-known anti-hero Long John Silver, is probably the most important source of all our ideas of what pirates used to be like, if not of the reality. The story of Jim Hawkins, the treasure map and Long John Silver's piratical mutiny aboard the *Hispaniola* is probably the most famous pirate story of all time. It's thanks to this book that we think of treasure maps, parrots, wooden legs and desert islands; it's thanks to this book that little boys grow up under the misapprehension that X always marks the spot . . . As with many writers, Robert Louis Stevenson allowed himself plenty of licence in the story's telling. Real-life pirates were no more disposed to search for chests of buried treasure than anyone else – in fact they would steal whatever they could get their hands on, and their loot was as likely to be made up of cargos of rope or sugar as it was pieces of eight and gold doubloons.

That said, Stevenson knew what he was talking about, and we can learn a lot about the real pirates of the day by reading his story. Take Long John Silver, the ship's cook with a wooden leg. It was commonplace for old sailors and those who had been wounded at sea to join expeditions as the ship's cook, a role that required a working knowledge of the vessel if not the physical ability to sail it. And for a sailor to be wounded – even to lose a limb – was a pretty regular occurrence. There are plenty of examples of pirates losing arms and legs during skirmishes at sea. Perhaps the most eye-watering is that of a man called William Phillips. He sustained a bad wound to his left leg during a fight between two pirate ships. Unfortunately there was no doctor or surgeon on board. There was, however, a carpenter, and it was decided that he was the man for the job. He used his largest saw to cut William Phillips' leg from his body – history doesn't record how long it took, or what sort of inhuman noises the patient made as the saw's teeth cut through his gristle and bone. We do know, however, that once the leg was removed, the carpenter heated his axe in a flame and used the flat side of it to cauterize the bleeding stump. He burned off more flesh than he intended, but somehow William Phillips survived the operation. When Long John Silver promised, 'Them that die'll be the lucky ones,' perhaps the tortures he had in mind were derived from the day he lost *his* leg.

Silver's parrot, Cap'n Flint, is almost as famous as he is, and while the idea of a talking bird on his shoulder sounds fanciful, sailors regularly brought back exotic birds and other animals from their trips abroad. Parrots, it seems, were especially popular, not only because they were colourful and could be taught how to speak, but also because they were a low-maintenance pet on board ship.

And of course *Treasure Island* is the archetypal story of an inside job. When I conducted my investigation into modern-day piracy, I learned that while many aspects of the story might belong to another age, Long John Silver's modus operandi is very much alive and well.

Piracy, however, has been around for a lot longer than *Treasure Island*. Ancient Greek mosaics show images of ships being attacked by pirates, and the Vikings were a piratical nation. The pirates that spark our imagination the most, however, arrived in the seventeenth and eighteenth centuries, and they were a rum bunch. Take Edward 'Ned' Low. He was a real-life pirate of the Caribbean, and a man with a reputation. He was born in London in 1690 in abject poverty. His family were thieves and pickpockets, and he soon fell into the family business. At the age of about 30, however, Low decided on a career change, joining a sloop – a one-masted sailing boat – bound for Honduras. Low worked honestly as a rigger on that first voyage, but he didn't stay honest for long. When the captain of the ship told him one day that he would have to wait for his food, Low took exception. He picked up a loaded musket and fired it, missing the captain but shooting a shipmate through the throat. Messy.

Low and his friends – unsurprisingly – were kicked off the boat, and it was then that they turned pirate, taking over another sloop off Rhode Island. It was a short career, but a brutal one. He became noted for his acts of viciousness and torture. On one occasion, when the captain of a Portuguese ship allowed a substantial quantity of money to fall into the sea rather than let it be stolen, Low cut off the man's lips with his cutlass, fried them in front of him then forced him to eat them while they were still hot. For pudding, he murdered the entire crew.

It's said that Low once announced that one of his victims was 'a greasy fellow, who would fry well'. To prove his point, he burned him alive. One of Low's crew later wrote of his time under the pirate's command. 'Of all the piratical crews that were ever heard of, none of the English name came up to this in barbarity. Their mirth and their anger had much the same effect, for both were usually gratified with the cries and groans of their prisoners; so that they almost as often murdered a man from the excess of good humour as out of passion and resentment; and the unfortunate could never be assured of safety from them, for danger lurked in their very smiles.' All in all, he made Captain Hook look like a pussycat.

Ned Low was one of the better-known pirates to emerge from what has been dubbed the Golden Age of Piracy, a period that spanned the 1650s to the 1720s. There were many others, some of whose names have passed into myth. Edward Teach was more commonly known as Blackbeard. Teach was born in Bristol, took to the seas at an early age and spent the first part of his career on privateers. These were armed ships which had permission – recognized by international law – to attack the ships of an enemy nation. A proportion of the loot was handed over to the crown; the rest was kept by the privateers. Originally, privateer licences were intended to allow ships to recoup any losses they sustained as a result of attack by enemy vessels; in time, though, they became a cheap way of boosting a country's naval forces. Perhaps the most famous privateer was Sir Francis Drake, who during the sixteenth century was the scourge of Spanish shipping. He shared his booty with Elizabeth I, and received a knighthood for his efforts. Privateers could not be arrested for piracy, but in practice many of them were simply official pirates. And it was not beyond the scruples of many of them to turn their hand to acts of genuine piracy.

Teach was a privateer during England's ongoing war with Spain, targeting Spanish ships, but when Britain withdrew from the war, many privateers turned pirate. Teach was among them. He drew his nickname, of course, from his enormous black beard, which he decorated with ribbons and slung over his ears. Traditional pictures of Blackbeard show him carrying several pistols hanging from his clothes – not entirely fanciful as the weapons of the day were unreliable, especially if they got wet, which was an occupational hazard. In Blackbeard's line of work, you really wanted to make sure you had a backup if that happened. You wanted, quite literally, to keep your powder dry.

Blackbeard's reputation was fearsome, and rumours of his barbarity travelled far. It was said that he once shot his first mate just to remind the crew of his position, and that he would allow his fourteenth (yes, fourteenth) wife to be raped by up to six members of his crew in a single night – once he had had his own way with her. In fact, although he was, financially speaking, a very successful pirate, there is little actual evidence of all this barbarity. The same can't be said for his somewhat gruesome death. A price was put on Blackbeard's head and he was hunted down by a Lieutenant Maynard. They fought with swords and pistols, and it took Maynard five bullets and twenty slashes with a sword to kill the pirate. Either Maynard's weapons were dodgy, or Blackbeard was a hard bastard. Once he was dead, his head was cut off and hung from the side of Maynard's ship – a reminder to anyone who saw it what fate pirates could expect if they were brought to justice.

Ned Low and Blackbeard were buccaneers – pirates who operated around the Caribbean and off the coast of South America. Nowadays 'buccaneer' has connotations of swashbuckling romance. The original buccaneers were actually French settlers on the Caribbean island of Hispaniola (now split into Haiti and the Dominican Republic). They looked after herds of livestock and for food used to smoke strips of meat over open fires. The French word for this method of cooking is *boucaner*, and these herders were a pretty wild and unsavoury bunch. When they realized there was a better living to be made pirating the Spanish galleons returning home laden with treasures from Mexico and South America, they lost their enthusiasm for livestock farming, underwent a quick career change and the original buccaneers were born.

Some buccaneers were privateers; others were out-and-out pirates. In many cases, the distinction between the two became a bit hazy. Sometimes they joined forces and attacked entire cities. Even those on the more criminal side, however, lived a weirdly democratic existence. Plunder was shared out according to an established system, and a ship's captain could be voted out by his crew – a novel way of doing things in the seventeenth century. Perhaps that was why, even back then, stories of buccaneers became popular with landlubbers.

Life on pirate ships was no cosy utopia, however. Rules were strict, and if you broke them you were flogged or killed. Any pirate found stealing from his shipmates or deserting during battle would be marooned on a desert island – a slow and agonizing way to meet your death. An extremely popular book at the time, written by a Dutchman called Alexander Exquemelin, was called *The Buccaneers of America*. Exquemelin knew what he was talking about because he spent 12 years travelling on buccaneer ships as a surgeon. His book had a pretty colourful cast of characters, such as the French buccaneer Francis L'Ollonais. 'It was the custom of L'Ollonais,' he tells us, 'that, having tormented any persons and they not confessing, he would instantly cut them in pieces with his anger, and pull out their tongues.' On one occasion, when L'Ollonais wanted to gain entry to a Caribbean town, some Spanish soldiers made an unsuccessful attempt at ambushing him. The buccaneer captured the ambushers and forced them to tell him how to get into the town without being seen. According to Exquemelin, 'he drew his cutlass, and with it cut open the breast of one of those poor Spaniards, and pulling out his heart with his sacrilegious hands, began to bite and gnaw it with his teeth, like a ravenous wolf, saying to the rest: I will serve you all alike, if you show me not another way.'

L'Ollonais wasn't the only one with a penchant for torture. A Dutch buccaneer called Roche Brasiliano derived his kicks from getting blind drunk and roasting Spanish prisoners alive over a spit. Whatever turns you on . . .

The Caribbean provided rich pickings for the buccaneers because of the trade routes that took a huge amount of commercial shipping to that part of the world. Merchant boats would load up in Europe with manufactured goods and weapons, then sail to Africa, where they would trade these goods for slaves. The slaves would then be taken to the Caribbean to be exchanged for commodities such as sugar, tobacco and cocoa, and the ships would return to Europe. This triangular trade route, however, was not the only one, and the buccaneers of the Caribbean were not the only pirates. The Mediterranean also played host to them, and those pirates that operated there were known as corsairs. There were some European corsairs, but they were far outnumbered by those from the northern coast of Africa, operating especially from Tunis, Tripoli, Algiers and Salé. This was known by Europeans as the Barbary Coast. The pirates that originated from these ports were known as the Barbary corsairs.

The Barbary corsairs terrorized the Mediterranean, the West African coast and the North Atlantic long before the so-called Golden Age of Piracy. As early as the eleventh century, when the Christian countries of Europe were waging war on Islam and other faiths in the Crusades, many Barbary pirates were given permission by the rulers of Muslim North Africa to attack European ships. The effect of these pirates was massive. They wouldn't just attack ships, but also coastal towns. Huge lengths of the Spanish and Italian coasts remained unoccupied for hundreds of years because of the piracy threat. In 1631 almost all the inhabitants of a town on the south coast of Ireland were captured by pirates and taken to the Barbary coast, where an unpleasant fate awaited them. Between 1580 and 1680, around 850,000 European captives of the Barbary pirates were sold into slavery in North Africa. White slaves in North Africa were not nearly as numerous as black slaves elsewhere – nothing like – but thanks to the Barbary corsairs there were still a hell of a lot of them.

The Barbary pirates kept a proportion of their slaves for themselves, and the lives of these unfortunate captives could be miserable, especially if – as often happened – they were used to row the pirates' galleys, the light winds of the Mediterranean being less suited to sailing ships. This was brutal work. The slaves were chained to their oars, and anyone not pulling their weight was whipped. Many died from exhaustion or went mad. If it became clear that they were no longer any use, it didn't take long to throw them over the side (the idea that pirates forced people to walk the plank is just a myth – these brutal men had no patience for such ceremonial methods). The slaves ate where they were chained, they slept where they were chained, they even went to the toilet where they were chained. An Englishman called Francis Knight wrote of his stint as a galley slave in the early seventeenth century, 'The stroke regular and punctual, their heads shaved unto the skull, their faces disfigured with disbarbing, their bodies all naked, only a short linen pair of breeches to cover their privities . . . all their bodies pearled with a bloody sweat.' In around 1670, the families of some of these captives wrote an appeal to the House of Commons: 'The [slave owners] do frequently bugger the said captives, or . . . run iron into their fundaments, rip open their bellies with knives, cut their britches across, and washing them with vinegar and salt, and hot oil, draw them in carts like horses.'

16

Some slaves were consigned to a life of rowing for decades without ever leaving their ships. Others would return to land during the winter months, when it was too treacherous for the Barbary pirates to be on the high seas. Here they were set to work building harbour walls or constructing new ships. They were given very little to eat or drink, and if they collapsed their masters would beat them until they got up again. They were given a change of clothes once a year.

The Barbary pirates didn't limit themselves to taking men. Christian women were fair game too. They were sold to the rulers of the Barbary coast and became part of their harems. If they were lucky, they'd be engaged only as harem attendants on the off chance that they might attract a ransom. Male slaves could also be bought out of slavery through payment of a ransom. But most of them came from poor backgrounds, so this rarely happened – unless they were the lucky recipients of money from charities back home set up for this purpose.

The most famous of the Barbary corsairs were two brothers who went by the name of Barbarossa, though only one of them – Aroudj – had the red beard from which they derived their name. His brother Hayreddin, however, became the more famous seaman, and in later years he died his beard red with henna out of respect for his brother. The Barbarossas came from the Ottoman empire, and Hayreddin was a hugely successful privateer around the Mediterranean. But he was more than that. He became admiral in chief of the Ottoman sultan's fleet, and thanks to his exploits the empire controlled the Mediterranean for many years. Barbarossa was a national hero – in modern-day Istanbul there is a boulevard named after him.

Another well-known Barbary corsair happened, peculiarly, to be an Englishman. His name was John Ward and he spent his early career as a privateer for Queen Elizabeth, plundering Spanish ships under licence from her. When Elizabeth died and James came to the throne, he ended the war with Spain. Ward, like many privateers, was put out of business. And so he turned pirate. Having stolen an enormous 32-gun warship, he spent two years terrorizing merchant shipping around the Mediterranean. In about 1606 he arranged with the ruler of Tunisia to use Tunis as a base in return for a proportion of his spoils. He converted to Islam and changed his name to Yusuf Reis. Ward's actions made him ever so slightly unpopular in his home country. One contemporary report described him as being 'very short with little hair, and that quite white, bald in front; swarthy face and beard. Speaks little and almost always swearing. Drunk from morn till night . . . the habits of a thorough salt. A fool and an idiot out of his trade.' The English ambassador to Venice called him 'the greatest scoundrel that ever sailed from England' – and in a country that wasn't short on pirates, he was up against some pretty stiff competition. Still, he lived out the rest of his life in Tunis, and died a rich man.

The Western powers were ready to condemn the action of these Muslim corsairs, but they weren't exactly lily-white themselves. There were Christian corsairs too, who targeted North African shipping. The Knights of St John, for example, were based in Malta and regularly hit Muslim vessels – so much so that in 1720 there were around 10,000 Muslim slaves in Malta alone. Many Mediterranean galleys were manned by Muslim slaves, and while it was true that there were an eye-watering number of white slaves in North Africa at the time, it was by no means a one-sided evil. In 1714 a British naval officer wrote that 'amongst the several towns situated on the coast of Spain, there may be moors purchased at very reasonable rates, such as are aged, blind or lame. It's no matter, all will pass so they have life.' A charming sentiment, and not an infrequent one in those sad days of slavery. As is always the case, every coin has two sides.

But the Barbary pirates were a major risk to Western shipping. In order to minimize the risk, France and other countries started paying bribes – they called them tributes – to the Barbary states. These tributes took the form of gold, jewels and other goods, and meant that the attentions of the corsairs were directed towards the weaker powers of Europe and, after the American War of Independence, the United States (until independence American ships had been under the protection of the mighty Royal Navy). In 1800, 20 per cent of the American government's annual spending was on ransoms to the Barbary corsairs, and it was this that caused the fledgling United States to build its first navy and engage the Barbary nations in the First and Second Barbary Wars – the US's first, but often forgotten, brush with Islamic nations. The newly formed United States Marines fought in these wars, and wore thick leather collars to protect them from the cutlass swipes of the corsairs. To this day, US Marines are known as leathernecks. (Interestingly, Royal Marines are sometimes called bootnecks because they would wrap their leather gaiters around their necks to stop themselves being slashed by mutinous crews.)

Despite this anti-piracy effort, it was not until 1816 that the threat of the Barbary corsairs was eliminated. The British navy achieved this by crushing the might of Algiers, killing about 8,000 men and destroying every building in the city. A British warship would not be called upon to fight the threat of piracy for another two centuries. When that happened, it would have the dubious honour of carrying me on board . . .

The real world of pirates, then, was a brutal one. Unlike the pirates of fiction, who are often portrayed as roguish adventurers, the pirates of history were hard, mean men. Violence and cruelty were second nature to them and their lives were tough and dangerous: for every John Ward who ended his days a rich man, there were many more Ned Lows and Blackbeards, gruesomely beheaded or hanged for their crimes after only a couple of years of plundering on the high seas.

In short, encountering pirates was one of the most frightening things that could happen at sea. They were heavily armed, determined and, surrounded by mile upon mile of water, there was nowhere the victims could go to escape them.

Many things have changed since those days. But some things haven't. Seventy per cent of the earth's surface is covered with water. Ninety per cent of all goods are transported by sea. Just look around your house. Tea bags? They came here by boat. Sugar? By boat. Ikea furniture? By boat. The clothes on your back and the car on your driveway? You guessed it. As has been the case for hundreds and hundreds of years, from the days of the Greek pirates, through the Golden Age of Piracy, where there's trade, there's crime. And just like in the days of Ned Low and Blackbeard, coming under attack in the middle of the ocean is not like coming under attack on land, because there's nowhere to run and there are no police stations out at sea.

Modern-day pirates, I realized as I prepared to go out and find them, were not so different from the pirates of history. They were ruthless. They were daring. They were heavily armed — not with cutlasses and pistols but with automatic weapons and rocket-propelled grenades. And if my experiences in the past had taught me nothing else, they had taught me this: when someone is carrying that kind of weaponry, chances are they're prepared to use it . . .

2. Pirate Alley

On 6 January 2009, just as the hijacking of the *Sirius Star* was coming to an end and while I was still in Kajaki, a 44-year-old Somali man by the name of Ibrahim Hussein Duale was going about his business, monitoring a school in the Gedo region of Somalia, near the Kenyan and Ethiopian borders. Duale worked for an organization called the World Food Programme. His role was to monitor the feeding of the schoolchildren in this ravaged country. A worthwhile occupation, I'd say. A good man.

Three masked gunmen entered the school. Duale happened to be sitting down at the time. The gunmen told him to get to his feet. He obeyed. And then, without explanation or hesitation, the gunmen shot him dead. Duale had a wife and five children, and was the third World Food Programme staff member to be killed in three months. Two days later, the total went up to four.

A shocking story. But where Ibrahim Hussein Duale came from, crimes like this are commonplace. In a weird kind of way, they're not even crimes. Somalia has no functioning government. Lawlessness is the norm. I've been to some tough places in the world, but the thought of going there made me a bit green around the gills. And the more I learned about that troubled place, the more nervous I became.

The modern history of the country we now think of as Somalia, like the history of most African countries, is deeply complicated. In the late nineteenth century a number of European powers attempted to establish themselves in the area. One look at the map is enough to understand why. The country's northern coastline is along the Gulf of Aden. If you want to transport goods from the Middle East up through the Red Sea and along the Suez Canal to the Mediterranean, your route has to take you through the Gulf of Aden – unless you want the expense of sailing south around the tip of Africa. To control the ports along the Somali coast would be to have a great economic advantage.

The British made treaties with a number of Somali chiefs, guaranteeing them security in return for establishing the protectorate of British Somaliland. The protectorate was bordered on three sides by Ethiopia, French Somaliland and Italian Somaliland, and covered the area around the northern coast. The colonialists were not universally popular. In fact, that's a bit of an understatement: between 1899 and 1920, British Somaliland came under regular, brutal attack from the forces of a religious leader called Sayyid Muhammad Abdullah Hassan. A bit of a mouthful – no wonder the British nicknamed him the Mad Mullah. Hassan was eventually suppressed, but 20 years later things were shaken up again with the arrival of the Second World War, when for a short while the Italians took British Somaliland. It was reconquered a few months later.

In 1960 British Somaliland gained independence and unified with Italian Somaliland to form the Somali Republic. What followed was the internal strife common to many post-colonial African states, culminating in a devastating civil war that started in 1991. The repressive Siad Barré fell from power, sparking a spiral of revolution and counter-revolution as some factions tried to reinstate him and others did whatever they thought necessary to stop this happening. The result was total anarchy. The northern region of Somaliland declared itself independent of the rest of the country, but the international community refused to recognize it.

The humanitarian situation became dire. Fighting raged between warlords, starting in the capital Mogadishu but soon spreading throughout the country; in the meantime, the ordinary people starved. From all over the world, governments sent food aid to help the starving. It's estimated, however, that the warlords stole 80 per cent of the food that reached Somalia and sold it to other countries in order to raise money for weapons. And so both the starvation and the violence worsened. By the end of 1992, approximately 500,000 Somalis were prematurely dead and 1.5 million displaced.

The UN approved the insertion of a United States-led peacekeeping force. It was called Operation Restore Hope. If only. Anyone who has seen the movie *Black Hawk Down* will know something of the Battle of Mogadishu. A force of approximately 160 American soldiers, with 19 aircraft and 12 vehicles, was dispatched to capture a high-ranking accomplice of one of the warlords on the outskirts of the capital. A lot of muscle to pick up one guy. During the operation, however, militants shot down two Black Hawk helicopters with rocket-propelled grenades. A number of wounded American soldiers were trapped at the crash site and came under attack during the night in a fierce firefight on the streets of Mogadishu. A task force was dispatched the next day to rescue them, but the casualties had been high: 19 American soldiers and more than 1,000 Somali militia dead.

The Battle of Mogadishu was a bloodbath, and it blunted the Americans' appetite for involvement in Somalia. By 1995, all UN personnel had been withdrawn from the region, but Somalia was as volatile as ever, and its people were suffering just as badly.

Fast-forward to now. After years of internal strife there is a transitional government of sorts, backed by Ethiopian troops, but it has very little in the way of actual authority. Most of the country is a violent mess and, as ever, it is the ordinary people who suffer the most. Killing, looting and gang rape are rife, instigated both by insurgent and government forces. One Amnesty International report tells of a 17-year-old girl being raped by Ethiopian troops. When her two brothers – aged 13 and 14 – tried to intervene, the soldiers gouged out their eyes with bayonets. Others tell of men having their testicles removed, and of people having their throats cut and being left to die in the street. They even have their own word for this method of slaughter, which roughly translates as 'to kill like a goat'. Without a proper functioning government, nobody is held accountable for these crimes. And nobody stops them.

The dire situation in Somalia is made even more difficult – and probably unsolvable – by the complicated system of clan loyalties and family groupings that exists there. Somalis themselves barely understand these loyalties; for a foreigner they're almost impossible. The most prominent clans are the Hawiye, the Darod, the Ishaak and the Rahanwein, but within each clan there is a fiendish network of sub-clans with complex hierarchies and impenetrable webs of loyalties.

The clan system has been an essential part of Somali politics for as long as anyone can remember. Any new leader will ensure all the plum jobs go to members of his own clan at the expense of others while inter-clan rivalries and arguments are constantly escalating into violence. Moreover, one of the characteristics of the clan system is the payment of any earnings to those further up the hierarchy of your clan – a kind of African Cosa Nostra.

The result is a country ripped apart. Around 3.25 million people are in need of humanitarian assistance in Somalia – that's about a third of the population. One in six children under the age of five suffers acute malnourishment; one in four dies before this age. Life expectancy at birth is 42. So if I lived there, I'd probably be dead. (Don't say it.)

The World Food Programme provides food aid to more than 2 million people a month. That's a lot of food. It's got to get there somehow. Like almost everything else in the world, most of the WFP's supplies arrive in Somalia by sea. Ninety per cent, to be precise. But cargo ships are increasingly reluctant to make the dangerous voyage to the coast of Somalia. Why? Because just as the staff of the WFP – men like Ibrahim Hussein Duale – are not immune from the danger and unpredictability of the region, so their ships are not immune from the country's other great problem.

And that problem, as you might have guessed, is the pirates.

Piracy is not new in the Gulf of Aden. It's not for nothing, then, that sailors have nicknamed it Pirate Alley. The reason pirates, historically, have been drawn to this waterway is the same reason the colonialists were drawn to it centuries ago: it forms a vital passage for trade. Each year 23,000 vessels pass through this waterway. And where there are trade ships, there's money to be made – legally or illegally.

Off the coastline of Somalia lies the island of Socotra. Socotra falls under Yemeni jurisdiction, but in many ways it is its own place. A UNESCO natural world heritage site, Socotra has an amazing abundance of plant life. It is one of the few places in the world where you'll find the dragon's blood tree, whose bright red sap was once thought of as a powerful medicine and became a valuable commodity. In addition, Socotra was always rich in frankincense, myrrh and aloe. During the first century AD these commodities made Socotra an important staging post and a destination for ships from all over the world.

Times changed. Global demand for frankincense and myrrh reduced; better medicines than dragon's blood came along. Between the tenth and fourteenth centuries the beautiful island of Socotra, situated as it was in the centre of an important trade route, became notorious as a haven for pirates instead. From here they could run riot across the Indian Ocean and even up the Red Sea. Merchant ships often had to resort to the use of an ancient incendiary weapon known as Greek fire to keep them away. Greek fire was a mixture of chemicals that could be sprayed, burning, towards nearby ships, with the advantage that it continued to burn even on water. Really not what you want when your boat is made of wood.

In 1507 Socotra was colonized by the Portuguese, followed by the British in the nineteenth century. At the start of the Second World War an RAF airfield was built, and following British withdrawal there were rumours that the Soviet Union maintained a naval base there. Nowadays its reputation as a pirate haven is firmly part of its history, but the Gulf of Aden hasn't stopped being very important to a lot of people, and the pirates have found other havens on the Somali coastline from which to operate. Somalia, with its lack of anything remotely resembling law and order, is an obvious choice. Recently, the number of recorded pirate attacks has gone up dramatically. In 2004 there were five; in the first nine months of 2008 there were more than sixty. In 2008 Somali pirates raised an estimated $30 million in ransoms. Insurance premiums for cargo ships travelling through the Gulf of Aden have increased ten-fold.

When my team and I make a documentary film, there's a lot of work that goes on behind the scenes. We are given safety briefings and have to commission detailed risk assessments (I do sometimes wonder if I must be a risk assessor's worst nightmare). We try to find local fixers in the countries to which we're travelling, people with a knowledge of the area and a book of contacts that will help grease the wheels and make the shoot run smoothly and – with a bit of luck – safely. The process has served us well. It's got us into some dangerous parts of dangerous countries, and facilitated interviews with dangerous men. It's allowed us to meet paramilitaries in Colombia who'd kill you without a second thought; it's taken us into slums as far apart as Rio and Kenya where you run a very real risk of having your throat cut for a handful of coins; it's taken us into the most dangerous war zone in the world.

Somalia, though, was a different matter. We were told that if we so much as set foot on Somali soil, we would be killed or kidnapped.

Not might. *Would.* All the journalists to have set foot outside the port of Mogadishu in recent years have been shot.

This point of view was reinforced when I went to meet a guy in London who freelances for MI6, the CIA and other intelligence agencies. His job title? Special Operations Operative. To you and me, he's a spook, and I can't reveal his name or anything else about him. His work regularly takes him into Somalia, and as we sat down to chat I asked him what it was, exactly, that he did for a living.

'I fix problems,' he told me.

What sort of problems?

'Pretty much anything. It could be issues between tribes, issues between certain persons, political issues . . .' He didn't seem too keen to elaborate, and I didn't push it.

I asked the spook what it was like to walk down the street in Mogadishu.

'It can have its moments.' He explained that there is a standing kill order against Caucasian people in Somalia, and I asked him exactly what that meant. 'A kill order is where different tribes, different groups or different factions decide they're not going to allow certain people or an individual into an area. Word will spread on the streets that if this person, or type of person, is seen, then get rid of them. It might be that they take them and throw them in the back of a van somewhere, or it could be quite simply that they open fire.'

But surely if you're with the right people . . .

'The problem with somewhere like Somalia is that there's no right people. You can be on one side of the fence and the other side will always be after you. You take your chances. It's 50-50 either way.'

Was the spook armed when he walked around the streets of Somalia?

'Most definitely.'

And did he have close protection?

'No. The more people you have, the more chance there is of drawing attention to yourself.'

I asked what I thought might sound like a ridiculous question, but he didn't seem to think it was ridiculous at all: did he wear a disguise?

He nodded. 'Depends on where I am, but yes, I can wear a disguise.'

I wondered if our man had ever had a kill order placed specifically on him. He looked a bit uncomfortable. 'There's been people that have been unhappy with me,' he conceded.

From everything I'd learned about Somalia, I was intrigued to know how he got into the country – presumably he didn't just turn up at the airport with his suitcase and passport. He explained that the methods of entry varied: a four-by-four across the border, small planes or a small boat across from Yemen. So how difficult would it be, I wondered, for myself and a camera team to get onto the mainland?

'Getting there,' the spook explained, 'is not your hardest or biggest problem. It's what's going to happen when you're there. Word would spread quickly – a film crew turns up with a famous presenter. There's a good chance you could become another asset. At the same time there's a good chance you could upset a few severe people and you'll never leave the place.'

I could tell by the look on his face and the sound of his voice that he wasn't exaggerating. 'Because of the work you do,' I said, 'you travel to a lot of dangerous places. How would you rate this on a scale of one to ten?'

'It's certainly up there as one of the worst places in the world at this moment in time.'

Our spook knew his onions, and I was more than happy to believe everything he told me about Somalia. More to the point, his information was backed up by the other investigations we undertook. There was no chance of the camera team and me getting any kind of insurance to go there, and no matter how hard we tried, we couldn't find a fixer willing to set things up for us – not for any money. We tried to arrange to join a World Food Programme ship taking food aid into Mogadishu. Nothing doing. If we set foot on land, it was explained to us, we'd be shot. Everyone said the same thing: risk going there and we'd barely last a few hours. No matter who we asked, the reply was identical: stay away. Somalia is just too damn dangerous.

It was clear that we couldn't even think about venturing into Somalia and I had mixed feelings about that. Half of me was disappointed: I knew that searching for a Somali pirate out at sea would not be straightforward. Unlike some of the gang members I'd met in the past, who often had a drum to bang or just liked the idea of being on TV, these guys would have absolutely no reason to talk to me and would be distinctly camera shy. The other half of me – the more sensible side, I suppose – couldn't help thinking, Thank fuck for that. I'd had a pretty exciting couple of years, got myself into some hairy situations, and I didn't fancy rounding them off by becoming another dismal statistic of the Somali civil war.

However, instead of setting foot on Somali soil, if we

were to track down some pirates there was no getting away from the fact that we'd need to spend a good deal of time in Somali waters, and that, as anyone who had been reading or listening to the news over the past couple of months knew, would be no picnic. It was some comfort that when the *Sirius Star* had been taken, the pirates had chosen not to mistreat their prisoners, but we all knew that hostage situations could have a very different outcome. Somali pirates were armed, dangerous and desperate. It's not a good combination.

Dangerous it might be, but if I was going to meet any pirates it was clear that I couldn't avoid these waters. Our investigation did not start there, however. It started in London, at the sleek offices of the International Maritime Bureau – ironically just metres from the former site of Execution Dock, where pirates, smugglers and mutineers were hanged. Their bodies were not removed from the gallows when they were dead; rather they were left swinging there until the tide of the Thames had covered their heads three times. The corpses of the worst criminals were then tarred to preserve them and taken to Graves Point at the mouth of the Thames. Here they were gibbeted – strung up – as a warning to other sailors of what might happen if they were tempted by a life of piracy. (One of history's most famous pirates, Captain Kidd, had his body displayed there for three years.)

Attitudes have changed somewhat in the couple of hundred years since Execution Dock was abolished in 1830. The IMB is a non-profit-making organization whose role is to combat maritime fraud and suppress piracy. They've got their work cut out. The IMB has links with

Interpol and was instrumental in the creation of the IMB Piracy Reporting Centre in Kuala Lumpur. Before this organization was established in 1992, ships that had been hit by pirates had nowhere to turn as more often than not local law-enforcement agencies would simply ignore the fact that they even had a problem with piracy. Now, acts of piracy can be described to the Reporting Centre, and the result is an ongoing live database of incidents that warns shipping exactly where the current hot spots are. Anyone can read it on the Internet, and it's a pretty eye-opening source of information.

At the IMB's headquarters I met Captain Mukundun, a mild-mannered but no-nonsense former sailor. I asked him if he had any idea how many pirates were currently operating in the Gulf of Aden. The figures were as bad as I expected. 'We are told,' Mukundun said, 'that there are many hundreds of young Somalis seeking a career in piracy. It's one of the most sought-after careers in a country where there is no proper economy.'

I wanted to know, from the mouth of an expert, how violent these pirates were. Mukundun explained to me that they were very well armed with automatic weapons and rocket-propelled grenade launchers (like I hadn't seen enough of those over the past few months). 'In trying to board the ships,' the captain said, 'they will use as much violence as they can.'

Captain Mukundun's words really brought it home to me that while this trip might not present the more immediate dangers of Helmand Province, it still had the potential to be perilous. And where most people who travel through the area go out of their way to *avoid* pirates, we intended to do the very opposite: to seek out these dangerous, unpredictable and often desperate individuals. If we were going to spend time around the Gulf of Aden, we would have to take some pretty serious precautions.

For my previous travels I had been on what are known as Hostile Environment Courses. Generally run by experienced former members of the military, these courses teach you techniques that to some people might sound like common sense, but which you'd be glad you knew if you found yourself in trouble. They teach you what to do if your vehicle finds itself in a minefield. (Answer: get out of the back of the vehicle and walk away along the tracks that it's made. That way, you know you're not going to step on a pressure plate.) They teach you how to ascertain who has the most serious injuries if your car is involved in a crash. (Answer: check the pulses and breathing of the injured passengers.) They teach you whether or not to move a seriously injured person. (Answer: only if their life is going to be put at greater risk if you don't. If you can keep them still, do. You really don't want to move someone with, say, a punctured lung if you can help it, but if there are bullets flying through the windscreen and he's going to get hit in the head, get him the hell out of there.) They teach you how to make a makeshift neck brace out of a shirt or jacket, and how to make a tourniquet if someone is losing blood at a ferocious rate. They teach you how to identify anti-personnel mines and where the best place is to take cover; they give you the low-down on some common weapons and show you how they work. And the most important thing they teach you? The closer you get to the front, the more chance you have of getting shot . . .

Like I say, all useful stuff in its way, and of course I'd spent time in a highly hostile land environment anyway, which teaches you more than you can ever learn from any training course. But being at sea is different from being in the desert. Not necessarily more dangerous, but different. There might not be any anti-personnel mines in the Gulf of Aden; but equally it's difficult to take cover when you're surrounded by miles of open ocean. We could take certain precautions – each member of the crew was issued with a tracking device, for example, and a means of alerting London if we ran into trouble – but our first trip in search of pirates still had the potential to be a very hazardous operation. If the pirates were willing to board a vessel the size of the *Sirius Star*, just where would they stop? What we needed was a bit of protection. A bit of muscle. We wanted to be on board a boat that even the pirates of Somalia wouldn't consider raiding.

And that was where HMS *Northumberland* came in.

3. Action Stations

I wouldn't be the first member of the family to step on board a Royal Navy warship. I could only hope, however, that I wouldn't have the maritime luck of some of my forebears.

I come from a family of seafarers. My mum's grandfather was known to everyone – including my mum – as Pop. That was short for Popeye the Sailor Man. In the little village in Norfolk where he lived the final years of his life he was the only man to have gone to sea. He joined the merchant navy at the age of 12, and spent the last 17 years of his career, up to the age of 72, as a quartermaster on a pleasure cruiser called the *Andes*. (A quartermaster at sea is different from an army quartermaster. In the British merchant navy this was the person who actually steered the ship, and was so called because the duty was divided into four shifts. On pirate ships during the Golden Age of Piracy the quartermaster ranked just below the captain, and could even veto the captain's decisions under certain circumstances. I'm pleased to report, though, that Pop kept entirely to the straight and narrow during his long years at sea.)

Pop was shipwrecked several times, but survived them all. On one of these occasions he was marooned on a Pacific Island with members of the United States navy. He was missing for several months, eventually turning up on his home doorstep in a US uniform. During his time at sea he was involved in the transportation of troops all over the world. He watched the bombing of the Suez Canal, just north of the Gulf of Aden; he took troops to Korea; and during the Second World War he was involved in the 'Russian run', taking supplies out to the Russian troops. My mum still remembers him bringing her back a pair of fur-lined leather Russian boots. They must have seemed very exotic to a little girl all those decades ago . . .

Pop's brothers were also naval men. Two of them jumped ship in Canada, which was a serious offence – they had to wait for the monarch to die and the resulting amnesty to be declared before they could even write back to their families. A third brother was a submariner. He died just after the First World War from brain damage, probably caused by lack of oxygen in the submarines. He left four children, two of whom – Arthur Buck and his younger brother Bertie – joined the navy at the start of the Second World War. They were posted to HMS *Hood* – an Admiral-class battle-cruiser, the largest warship the British possessed and the pride of the Royal Navy.

This was early in the war, and Britain was in a precarious situation. France – her closest ally – had fallen, and although the Americans had been helping out with weapons and other supplies, they were still months away from entering the fray. As an island nation, Britain relied heavily on foreign imports to keep going and the only way these imports could arrive was by sea. The German navy – the Kriegsmarine – pulled out all the stops to ensure that these goods never made it. And the best way for them to do that was through the use of their submarines, or U-boats. The U-boats did their work with ruthless efficiency. Between September 1939 and May 1941 they sank something in the region of 3 million tonnes of shipping and it hit the country hard.

Hitler had realized for a long time that sea assets were essential in a war against Britain and ordered the construction of a modern fleet made up of a new type of ship. To this end the Germans launched the famous battleship *Bismarck* on 14 February 1939. Happy Valentine's Day, everyone. *Bismarck* was a mean machine. Sixty thousand tonnes of pure naval power, a symbol of German strength, and by the late spring of 1941 she set out on her first mission.

When the war arrived, *Hood* had been in service for 20 years. When she had first been built, she had been state-of-the-art. During the interwar period, she had even been sent on a round-the-world tour, ostensibly to thank the Commonwealth nations for their help during the First World War, but also to remind the world that Britain still ruled the waves. She was world famous, a symbol of Britain's maritime might, but had spent so much time showing the flag that she hadn't been maintained, updated and repaired as well as she should. By the time of the Second World War she was out of date, and although still a fine ship wasn't a match for vessels such as the *Bismarck*. In May 1941 the *Bismarck* was engaged by the *Hood* in the Denmark Strait between Greenland and Iceland. The *Hood* was sunk. Only three members of the crew survived; Arthur and Bertie were not among them. (The incident famously caused Churchill to order, 'Sink the *Bismarck*.' A few days later she was crippled by aircraft launched from HMS *Ark Royal*, and then sunk by Royal Navy ships.)

As I prepared to embark on HMS *Northumberland*, I

couldn't help thinking about Pop, and about Arthur and Bertie. Would they have been surprised that seven decades after their deaths the transport of goods by sea continued to be of such importance? Probably not. Would they have been surprised that the British navy was once again hunting pirates? Perhaps. And what would they have made of the new breed of warship, with all its sophisticated and advanced weaponry, that was being tasked to patrol these waters?

Ever since the risk of piracy in the Gulf of Aden started to increase, there has been a concerted international effort to curb the number of incidents. This effort has taken the form of several operations, including Combined Task Force 151 and Operation Atalanta. It was as part of Operation Atalanta that HMS *Northumberland* was patrolling these waters. It was the first time that a Royal Navy warship had been tasked to fight pirates since 1816, when the British finally quelled the threat of the Barbary corsairs.

When the Somali pirates started hitting the headlines, the trouble was this. International military vessels patrolling the Indian Ocean would hear news of an attack and make chase. The pirates, though, were cute to the intricacies of international diplomacy. They would speed back into Somali waters knowing that, without permission from the interim Somali government, foreign naval vessels were unwilling to follow. The pirates would be home and dry before they were either home or dry. If the international community was to be of any help at all, the Somali government needed to make an official request, and allow military vessels from other nations to enter its waters. That request finally came in June 2008.

Operation Atalanta is a joint naval patrol comprising around 20 ships from several member nations of the European Union, although it has its headquarters in Northwood, England. It operates alongside Combined Task Forces 151 – an American-led patrol – and 150. CTF-150 had in fact been patrolling these waters for some years in an anti-terrorist action. Large quantities of weapons are illegally transported through the Gulf of Aden; moreover, Somalia and Yemen are suspected hideouts for al-Qaeda, and Pirate Alley is their escape route. So that was another thing to worry about. Between them, Operation Atalanta and CTF-150 and -151 had put a lot of naval might in the Gulf of Aden, but there's a hell of a lot of water to patrol, and the pirates still slip through the net.

HMS *Northumberland* is a Type 23 frigate. There are 13 Type 23s in the Royal Navy, each of them named after British dukes, which is why they're also known as Duke-class vessels. Originally designed as anti-submarine warships, they are now the mainstay of the navy's surface fleet and can operate anywhere in the world. Type 23 frigates have two Rolls-Royce engines not unlike those that once powered Concorde, which are used to get the ship from A to B very quickly. They burn a lot of fuel, however, and are very noisy. If you're hunting submarines, that noise is going to give you away, so in addition they have four quieter engines mounted on rubber to absorb the throb. So these warships might look big and cumbersome, but in fact they're incredibly quiet and manoeuvrable when they need to be.

It costs well over £10 million a year to keep *Northumberland* shipshape, but you get a lot of bang for your buck. The frigate is loaded with a formidable arsenal: two quad

Harpoon surface-to-surface missile launchers, a vertical-launch Sea Wolf anti-missile system, a 4.5-inch Mark 8 naval gun, two 30-millimetre close-range guns, two anti-submarine torpedo tubes, a NATO Seagnat (a decoy system used to protect against incoming missiles) and DLF3 decoy launchers. It sounds like a lot – it *is* a lot – but the ship needs it: if she comes under attack from an enemy surface-to-surface missile, which whizzes across the water like a skimming stone, she has the grand total of four seconds to react to the incoming fire.

Northumberland also carries a Merlin Mark 1 helicopter. This helicopter is also primarily for anti-submarine operations, but its state-of-the-art sonics and sonar systems mean it's ideally suited for anti-surface ops. The Merlin is designed to be used in adverse weather and 'high-sea states'. It has a maximum speed of 167 knots (that's about 190 miles per hour) and is armed with Sting Ray torpedoes or depth charges – a kind of underwater bomb. ('Depth charges' is also naval slang for a bowl of stewed figs – gives you an idea of the sort of effect the weapons have . . .) A general purpose machine gun (GPMG) can be mounted in five different locations throughout the cabin so that it can be aimed through the doors or windows. Merlin has enough fuel to operate within a radius of 200 nautical miles. All in all, a serious piece of kit. As well as its current maritime duties, it's seen plenty of active service – both in Iraq and in the Caribbean on anti-narcotics and hurricane-support ops.

I didn't quite know what to expect when I met up with the frigate where it was docked in the port of Salalah on the coast of Oman – 100 miles from the coast of Yemen and at the eastern end of the Gulf of Aden. I'd spent plenty of time with the British army, but the navy was a new one on me. One of the first things I noticed was that the area of the port around the ship was blocked off by huge metal containers piled up on each other. This was to stop potential suicide bombers approaching the vessel. Oman might have been a low-risk location, but it brought home to me that our notions of safety are all relative: even here nobody associated with a Royal Navy frigate could fully relax.

I was welcomed on board by the captain of the *Northumberland*, Lieutenant Commander Martin Simpson – a charming man with a clipped, British way of speaking. I was soaking wet as we met on the deck – not from seawater, but from sweat. Salalah is only a few degrees south of the equator, and the heat was almost crippling.

It was explained to me how the naval hierarchy of command works. The second in command is the executive officer, or XO. He runs the ship. The captain makes all the decisions about what the ship is going to do and where it's going to go. Martin was answerable to a Greek commander as Operation Atalanta involved an international fleet. The crew were nearing the end of a six-month deployment in the area. He told me that his greatest sense of achievement came not from hunting pirates, but from escorting food aid from the World Food Programme into Mogadishu – even though *Northumberland* could not actually enter the port itself for fear of being rocketed from the mainland.

Introductions made, the camera crew and I started looking around this impressive ship. What we found was something like a floating city. *Northumberland* produces its own electricity; it can desalinate a certain amount of its own water; and, of course, it must accommodate its crew for large stretches of time. At no point, however, could you ever forget that you're on a battleship. Below decks is like something from *Blade Runner*. No windows, just a maze of tiny metal corridors with flashing lights, ladders and buttons, a constant electrical hum in the air and the distant churning of the ship's engines. There are wooden blocks all over the place. These are there in the event of water flooding into the boat and entrances needing to be blocked off. They are more effective than metal barriers because wood bends under force rather than buckles. You need to be incredibly careful and skilled at going up and down the ladders and moving around the ship – I was forever tripping up and bashing myself around, and to this day parts of me still ache from my clumsiness. Poor me. It took me four days to work out the route from our cabin up to the bridge. Those grey, metallic corridors all look the same. Some of the ladders lead somewhere, others lead nowhere – or at least nowhere I wanted to go. Or was allowed to go. I felt like the new boy at school, always getting lost on his way to class.

I was barracked with five others in a warrant officers' dorm – cramped and tiny by anyone's standards, though hardly surprising given that the ship has a crew of about 200 men and women. At least in the army when you settle down for the night you've got room to dump your Bergen and spread out a bit. Not here. One bunk, one drawer and one little cupboard is all you have each. All your belongings have to be immaculately squared away and tied down so that they take up the minimum of space and don't go walkabout should the ship hit a rough patch. Our cabin couldn't have been more than six metres by six, and we were lucky:

43

in a warrant officers' dorm the bunks are only two high. Lower-ranking sailors have to put up with three or four bunks on top of each other. It makes a tin of sardines look positively roomy.

You might be surrounded by all the water you can see, but on a ship you have to be very careful about how much you use. It's not rationed, but everyone understands that the last thing a ship wants to do is run out, especially in the burning heat just south of the equator. At the end of the corridor was the toilet, or 'head', so called because sailors would traditionally do their business at the head of the ship, where the splashing water would naturally clean away their deposits (give me a bottle of Domestos any day). Now, though, it was below deck with us, its walls curved because it's pressed up against the hull of the ship, and hot because that's what modern ships are like.

When I arrived at my bunk I found a copy of *Private* magazine under the covers. For those of you unfamiliar with this highbrow publication, it's an intimate magazine for gentlemen, put there just in case the long lonely nights should prove too much for my libido. Thanks, lads. Much appreciated. Whether the lads themselves rely on such magazines, I couldn't say. I do know, however, that although relationships certainly occur on board ship, there's a strict no-shagging policy, and anyone caught in flagrante can expect a severe reprimand. I suppose you have to make sure that the boys and girls have their minds on the job in hand.

My hosts had also stuck a picture of my former on-screen better half Sharon and Roly the dog onto the underside of the bunk above – 'so you don't get homesick'. By now, though, I was well used to the military sense of humour and while there was the same piss-taking I'd had to undergo whenever I got to know a new bunch of soldiers in Afghanistan, most of the guys and girls on *Northumberland* had seen those documentaries and had liked them. It helped to break the ice – the guys and girls on board had a great deal of respect for what the army were going through, even if there was a vague sense of rivalry between them. Unlike in Afghanistan, alcohol was allowed on the ship. There's a limit of two cans of beer a day for regular sailors on their downtime, although they managed somehow to find enough supplies on one occasion to get *me* a little merrier than perhaps I should have been. After all, there's nothing funnier than a bloke off the telly getting hammered . . .

On a massive ship like this the biggest threat is not sinking – it is, after all, very hard to down a Type 23 frigate – but fire. If a fire somehow started on board, it could be disastrous, especially if it reached the network of corridors below deck. Fire needs oxygen to burn, so it will seek it out, causing deadly fireballs down those corridors. If you happen to be between the fireball and the oxygen it needs, you fry; and you can imagine the chaos and devastation a fire could cause when so many people are crammed into such a small place with no means of escape. Trouble is, a warship is packed to the rafters with things that *cause* fire: fuel, electrics, enough weaponry to take out a substantial chunk of north London. It means that fire regulations are of paramount importance. Everyone's aware of these regulations, and they follow them to the letter. Smoking, obviously, is a no-no below deck, and every time you go above you have to seal the hatch in order to limit the possible entrance points a fire can take. Many members of the crew wore white fire-retardant suits over their uniforms.

Even in the absence of fire, temperatures could be horribly high. *Northumberland*'s cooling system was a network of pipes carrying cold water. Just before we joined the ship, this cooling system had broken down – not good in such a hot environment, and it meant that everyone was cooking in their cabins. The ship never sleeps. Everyone on board is on a continuous rotation and there is a constant hubbub of activity as the crew goes about their business of keeping this floating town operational and, at the same time, performing their crucial military task: hunting for pirates.

There was a palpable sense of tension as *Northumberland* prepared to leave the relative security of Salalah. Some of that tension derived from the fact that manoeuvring a frigate out of port is a complicated business. Get it wrong and you can do some serious damage to a very expensive ship. All hands were on deck, and anxious sailors looked nervously over the side to check that everything was going as it should. After all, scraping a Type 23 isn't like scratching your mum's car. But the tension wasn't just down to the difficulty of moving this massive but strangely delicate ship out of harbour. Everyone was well aware that as soon as we moved out of Omani waters, we'd be in Pirate Alley. It didn't matter that we were aboard a Royal Navy warship. We'd be searching for dangerous men carrying dangerous weapons and you could sense the ship was moving from a relaxed state to an operational one.

As soon as we were out of harbour, I joined Commander Simpson up on the bridge. This is the hub of the ship, and it was alive with activity. Orders were given and carried out;

information came in over the radio to be processed and disseminated; bearings were taken; and a lookout kept constant watch over the surrounding water through a set of powerful binoculars. It was a hard-working, utilitarian place, but not without its comforts. Martin Simpson had engaged a friend of his who worked at an Aston Martin garage to make a seat for him – not exactly standard navy issue, but more comfortable (and more slick) for the boss's behind than whatever arrangement it replaced. The Aston Martin accessory took centre stage in the middle of the bridge. Simpson was chuffed to bits with it.

As we stood together on the bridge, he explained to me what his operational priorities were. Number one: to protect World Food Programme ships delivering food aid into Somalia. Number two: to protect other vulnerable shipping in the Gulf of Aden. Number three: to arrest pirates.

'Is there any particular environment,' I asked him, 'that the pirates prefer to operate in?'

The captain stretched out his hands and indicated the wide open ocean that we could see through the bridge window. The water was flat. Calm. Like a millpond. A vast merchant ship chugged in the distance.

'*This* environment,' he said. 'It's easier for them to board ships when the sea state is calm. The choppier the water is, the better it is for the merchant vessels.' Made sense.

I wanted to know what ships were most at risk. 'The vessels that have been pirated have all been slow and have a low freeboard – the distance from the water to a deck they can put a ladder on.'

I learned that a ship is unlikely to be pirated if it's travelling above 14 knots. Pirates are like burglars – they will go for the house where the latch isn't secure. Like burglars, they know that there are easy pickings out there, so why make life difficult for themselves? 'All the pirates will do,' the captain told me, 'is wait until they find something that *looks* promising.' As we stared out of the window I pointed out a vessel. Its freeboard seemed pretty high to me – certainly I didn't much fancy the idea of using a ladder placed precariously on a little boat many metres below to try and board it. 'Too high?' I asked the captain.

He shook his head. 'Low enough.' Pointing to another vessel, he explained that the freeboard on that would present more difficulties – to me it looked unnaturally high. I was beginning to get the impression that there was a lot of at-risk shipping out there – I'd only been on board a few minutes and I'd already seen some. HMS *Northumberland* and the rest of the Operation Atalanta fleet had their work cut out.

Having patrolled these waters for the past six months, Lieutenant Commander Simpson obviously knew a great deal about how modern pirates operate. I asked him what usually happened once they took control of a ship. 'The pirates themselves don't hurt in any way the crew of the vessels they've pirated,' he told me. 'We want that to continue. If we start taking down vessels that have been pirated, there is a very great risk that the innocent civilians will either be caught in crossfire or, at worst, executed.'

The captain of the *Northumberland*, then, and indeed those in charge of the rest of Operation Atalanta, had a difficult balance to strike between the threat of force and actually carrying it out. It struck me that all the advanced weaponry the ship was carrying could very well be redundant when it was faced with delicate hostage situations, that in the hunt for pirates, brain could be more important than brawn. That didn't mean, though, that the weapons systems weren't at the ready. While we were in Omani waters, the guns weren't allowed to be loaded, but the moment we crossed over onto open sea and into our patrol area, that changed. Ammo was inserted; weapons systems were activated. It wasn't long before the air above me turned to thunder and all around us the water exploded as rounds slammed into the sea – the ship's guns had to be test-fired to make sure they were fully operational. It was only a short demonstration of *Northumberland*'s firepower, but it was enough to make it clear that the frigate's arsenal was as impressive as I thought it would be.

Now that we had entered dangerous waters, the ship's crew were instructed to prepare for action stations – a state of readiness that means every single member of the crew, from the cooks to the captain, is ready to enter a battle situation. Every man and woman on the *Northumberland* needed to be able to switch to action stations at a moment's notice. Should that happen, off-duty members of the crew would have to report to their posts and the weapons systems would be placed on 'hot standby', which meant they would be ready to fire. Officers would make regular checks to ensure everyone was at their posts and ready to do battle. At action stations, though, the day-to-day running of this ship still had to go smoothly – meals, for example, would still have to be produced and so *Northumberland*'s cooks would be tested regularly on their ability to do this.

Action stations is exhausting for the crew. Keep it up for too long and they'll be knackered before you know it. And so they would maintain a state of advanced readiness, just below action stations, for as long as the frigate was patrolling Pirate Alley.

The majority of the crew of HMS *Northumberland* were not armed. There was, however, a small contingent of men carrying firearms. They were highly trained, and performed constant firearms exercises. These were, of course, Royal Marines. It was the Marines who would be on the front line of the battle against the pirates. With any luck, we'd be joining them in this battle, and having spent some time with their colleagues in Afghanistan, I wanted to get to know them as soon as possible.

The Marines on the frigate were part of the Fleet Protection Group Royal Marines (FPGRM). This elite commando force is a cadre of just over 500 soldiers whose responsibility is the security of Royal Navy assets, both at home and worldwide. Once known as the Comacchio Group, they were originally responsible for the protection of Britain's nuclear weapons and for counter-terrorist operations at sea. This latter role is now the responsibility of the SBS – the Special Boat Service – but the SBS continues to be backed up by the Fleet Protection Group. The FPGRM is divided into four squadrons: HQ headquarters squadron, O rifle squadron, R rifle squadron and S rifle squadron. Each of these is divided into several units, and the lads on board *Northumberland* were from the Fleet Standby Rifle Troop (FSRT), a high-readiness unit tasked to support the Royal Navy worldwide. FSRT teams have specialist weapons skills, and are specifically trained in 'non-compliant boarding skills'. (To you and me, that means getting on a boat when the pirates don't want you to – a dangerous occupation in this part of the world, but a crucial one.) The Fleet Protection Group can find themselves almost anywhere in the world – from the Arctic Circle to the equator.

The Marines I met were as fit as a butcher's dog. These guys spent a *lot* of time on the ship working out and were, they told me, a little frustrated not to have had the chance to fire their guns in a combat situation. To a man, they wished they had been posted to Afghanistan like some of their mates. I told them they were better off where they were, but it was a testament, I think, to their professionalism that they were eager to face up to whatever anyone could throw at them. The Marines constantly had to practise close-quarter battle techniques on board the ship. Sergeant Macaffer explained to me that it was impossible to drill these techniques too often: they had to be second nature to the team because they never knew when or under what circumstances they would have to use them.

The ship's captain had explained to me the difficulties involved in engaging a vessel that had been pirated. In addition, I knew from my time in Afghanistan that the military's actions are governed by their rules of engagement – the predetermined regulations that state when, where and how they are permitted to engage an enemy. In Helmand Province it was well known that Taliban fighters would put down their RPG launchers, pick up a hoe and pretend to be innocent villagers, and when that happened, the British army couldn't touch them – even if, minutes ago, they'd been trying to take the soldiers' lives. Commander Simpson had hinted at similar problems at sea, and I wanted to know exactly what the Marines' rules of engagement were. Once pirates were on a vessel and controlled the hostages, were the Marines allowed to exercise their 'non-compliant boarding skills'?

Sergeant Macaffer shook his head. 'No. If it's effectively a hostage situation where they've adopted a defensive posture and are threatening to take the lives of the crew, that's out of our jurisdiction.'

I could well imagine that it must be frustrating for these highly trained soldiers not to be able to use their well-honed expertise to deal with dangerous hostage situations. At the same time I could see the problems involved. The pirates in the Gulf of Aden tended not to kill their captives, and as Sergeant Macaffer succinctly put it, 'We don't want to force the issue.'

It was becoming clear to me that there was only a small window of time during which the forces of HMS *Northumberland* – and therefore I – would be able to catch up with any pirates, and that was when they were actually in the process of boarding a target vessel. In order to capture them at that crucial moment, we needed to be in that part of the Gulf of Aden where they were likely to be most highly concentrated. Where the action was, and the danger.

And so it was that we set sail for the corridor.

4. The Corridor

Shipping convoys have been around for a very long time, and for very good reasons. Safety in numbers is one; ease of military protection is another. During the Second World War, the British made it compulsory for all merchant ships to travel in convoy along specific routes so the Royal Navy could more readily offer them protection against German surface ships and U-boats. The Germans soon developed anti-convoy tactics, but convoys were still better than the alternative – ships dotted willy-nilly around the ocean, easy targets for enemy strikes. When the Americans joined the war and refused to use convoys along their eastern seaboard, the German U-boats had a field day. The Americans were finally forced to follow the British example, and convoys became the norm for the remainder of the conflict.

Maritime technology might have come a long way in the intervening 60 years, but a lot of things have stayed the same, and the convoy system is one of them. Any merchant shipping travelling through the Gulf of Aden is advised to follow a particular route. They queue up at the end of this narrow corridor, then travel together through it. This stops the merchant vessels from being spread out all over a million square miles of sea and allows naval ships and air support to patrol a more concentrated area of ocean.

There is just one problem. The existence of the corridor

not only tells the warships of Operation Atalanta where the merchant vessels are congregating, it tells the pirates too, and some of them flock to the corridor like wasps to jam. It seemed to me that the corridor didn't reduce the number of Somali pirates in the Gulf of Aden, it just forced them to operate in a smaller area. And it was to that area that we were headed. (Other pirates have worked out that ships queuing up at the end of the corridor to travel through the Gulf of Aden together have to have come from somewhere and that it's impossible to police all the world's oceans. And so they simply move their area of operations. If you look at maps on which piracy hot spots have been charted from year to year, you'll see that they change location. It's like cutting the heads off the hydra – remove one and another grows somewhere else.)

As the sun set on our first day on board HMS *Northumberland*, a radio operator sent out a message to all shipping in the Gulf: 'All stations. All stations. All stations. This is coalition warship Foxtrot 23. We are conducting maritime security operations within the Gulf of Aden. Anyone witnessing any criminal or suspicious activities are to contact coalition warship on channel 16.'

Channel 16. The international distress channel. Monitored day and night by coastguards around the world and used only for broadcasting distress calls. The radio operators on *Northumberland* would be keeping constant, careful tabs on channel 16 for as long as we were in Pirate Alley, waiting for the call that meant a merchant ship was being boarded by pirates. Whether that call came or not was anyone's guess. We just had to wait and see.

*

Darkness. My first night on board. The stars above were blindingly bright, a breathtaking canopy out here in the middle of the ocean where there was no ambient light to make them dim. But out to sea it was impenetrably black. Anything could be going on out there.

The sun might have gone down, but it was still hot on deck thanks to the winds blowing off the deserts of Africa and the Arabian Gulf. I was sweating even as I peered into the gloom, wondering what was out there waiting for us. I knew that most pirate attacks took place at dawn or dusk, but I also knew that when you're dealing with dangerous, unpredictable people like this, the one thing you have to expect is the unexpected. The crew of *Northumberland*, on constant rotation, would not be letting their guard slip for a minute. And aboard the merchant ships in the Gulf of Aden the cover of darkness wouldn't bring much comfort . . .

And then word reached me that we were just about to enter the corridor. I made my way to the bridge to speak to one of the guys. He showed me a navigation screen, glowing blue in the darkness and with our position and that of the corridor clearly marked. It was 50 nautical miles to the south-west. 'As you go past Aden,' he told me, 'you get a lot of vessels that look like pirate vessels, so we'll stick to the north of the corridor because the merchant traffic does tend to get a bit nervous around there.' I bet they do.

It would take us around 40 hours to travel the length of the corridor. Two days, two nights, as near as damn it. I tried to imagine what it must be like for a merchant ship travelling that route, knowing that they could be boarded by pirates with RPGs at any moment. Not for the first time, I felt a sense of relief that I was on board a Royal Navy frigate and not one of those vulnerable vessels.

With that thought going through my head, I turned in for the night, genuinely not knowing what the next few days would bring.

In Afghanistan I had learned that war was characterized by long stretches of boredom, punctuated by moments of sudden activity (and in the Stan, blind fear). The fight against the pirates wasn't much different – acts of terror on the high seas don't tend to happen where and when you want them. In a million square miles of ocean it's difficult to be in the right place at the right time and there's a lot of nervous waiting around. So it was not until my third day on board HMS *Northumberland* that the call came in. Captain Andy Morris of the Fleet Protection Group Royal Marines was called to the bridge for a briefing and I went with him. There was a large group of Somali boats, or dhows, in the vicinity, surrounded by a significant number of skiffs – long flat boats of the type favoured both by Somali fishermen and by Somali pirates. 'My intention,' Simpson told the Marine unit leader, 'is to perform an approach-and-assist visit on that group.'

Andy Morris nodded. He had his orders, and left the bridge to brief his men.

The Fleet Protection Group congregated on deck. They wore desert camouflage gear and life jackets, along with Osprey body armour and Gecko Marine Safety Helmets. A couple of the guys carried the short version of the SA80 assault rifle. The standard version would be too long because in the event of them having to board a large ship, they would have to go round tight corners. (I learned that the shortened SA80 is also used by tank crews so that they can get in and out of their vehicles more easily.) Other members of the FPG carried Heckler & Koch MP5 submachine guns – predominantly a special forces weapon and more suited to the job in hand. The 556 round from an SA80 has more velocity behind it than the 9-millimetre from the MP5. This can be hazardous in a close-quarter battle situation: the 556 can go through a body and still bounce around the room like a rubber ball in a tin can. The rigid inflatable boats (RIBs) themselves were mounted with general purpose machine guns. All in all, everyone was pretty heavily armed.

Andy explained to me that it was commonplace in these waters for tuna fishermen to tow skiffs behind the slightly bigger dhows, and these skiffs usually had about 12 people on board. Unfortunately, this was exactly what the pirates do as well. Often the dhows will have been pirated in the first place, and the fishermen thrown overboard. The pirates will then stay out to sea for up to 40 days, watching and waiting for a suitable target to cross their path. I guess when you have the prospect of such a big payday coming your way, you don't mind hanging around for a while . . .

From a distance, the dhows we were about to approach looked just like innocent fishing boats. Fly over the Gulf of Aden and you'll see plenty of these boats, many of them sailed by legitimate Somali fishermen earning their living from the tuna-rich waters of the area. There were ways, however, of distinguishing fishermen from pirates. 'They've got equipment that they use for getting on board other vessels, and that's the key,' Andy told me. 'It's the ladders – you can't hide a ladder on a skiff.' And obviously, if you have a ladder out at sea, it's not so that you can go and clean windows. 'If we see grappling hooks,' Andy continued, 'and obviously weapons . . .'

'Fishermen don't have rocket-propelled grenades,' I suggested.

Andy grinned. 'Exactly,' he said. 'It's a bit of a giveaway.'

The Marines would approach the skiffs in their RIBs. Two members of the group would be ready to act as snipers from the Merlin helicopter, which could be called into action should things kick off. One of these snipers would be armed with an AW50 rifle. This is a serious bit of weaponry, as I had found out in Afghanistan when, more than once, its rounds flew just over my head. The sniper wouldn't use his 50-cal to take out people; instead it would be used, should the situation require it, against engine blocks, a technique that's used a lot in anti-narcotics operations out in the West Indies. Hit a small boat's engine with one of those rounds, which can have either explosive or armour-piercing tips, and there really won't be a lot left of it.

As the Marines, accompanied by some regular navy guys, prepared to disembark from *Northumberland* and speed in their RIBs towards the suspicious vessels, you could tell that this was a well-practised routine for them. There was just one small difference this time round: they'd have a couple of extra passengers, namely me and Will, the cameraman. It wasn't just the Marines that had to get their gear together. We did too. I'd been told before I left England that if I had body armour, I should bring it along, so I had it wrapped around my torso and a helmet firmly on my head. I was also carrying camera batteries and tapes so that Will had a bit less to deal with. You don't get a very stable ride travelling at 25 knots on a RIB (understatement of the decade), and it's kind of difficult to get a steady shot. I was also wearing a life jacket. I'd had it explained to me that some life jackets inflate on contact with water, which sounds like a good idea, especially if you're knocked unconscious into the water. But they have their downsides. If you're underwater and your life jacket inflates automatically, you rise to the top no matter what's above you (and in a military environment the thing above you can be sharp and dangerous). In situations like that, it's much safer, if you can manage it, to swim out of the way of any hazards on the surface and then inflate your life jacket manually. So it was that we had been equipped with toggle-inflating jackets.

I watched as a group of Marines embarked and then sped off in their RIB, and then it was my turn. To get onto the RIB from the deck of *Northumberland* involves climbing down a rope ladder. It looks easy, but it's not: as the hull of the ship curves inwards towards the bottom, you're not only going down, you're also at a precarious angle. Nothing too dramatic, but enough to make it tricky if, like me, you're unused to the process – and enough to make you look like a prize prick if you lose your footing and end up in the drink. More to the point, there are plenty of sharp, jagged bits of kit in the RIB below that you really don't want to fall on top of. (During our stay on *Northumberland*, one of our party came a cropper doing this and got such severe rope burn that it cut right through the skin of his hand.) As I struggled down the ladder from the moving deck of the *Northumberland* onto the wobbling RIB, I felt I was having a brief taster of how difficult it must be for pirates to board the ships they target.

Once the RIB was loaded, I grabbed hold of something to keep my balance in the gently billowing water, and then we were off.

We headed towards the suspect vessels at speed and the plan was this. We would approach the first dhow and one of the boats would hold off at a slight distance and offer fire support from the GPMG. The other guys would approach the sailors and ask if they could board their vessel. Nothing like the direct approach. The white foam on either side of the speeding RIB splashed and sprayed as the sun beat down from the clear blue sky. Under other circumstances, it could almost have been idyllic. Almost, but not quite – most people don't take GPMGs and MP5s on holiday with them.

The RIBs started to slow down, the spray decreased and I caught my first sight of the potential pirates. There were nine or ten of them, sitting quietly on a skiff and staring at us with unknowable, almost blank expressions on their faces. Their skin was dark and they wore an odd assortment of clothes: some had traditional headdresses and ethnic garb; others wore old sweatshirts with Western logos. A lot of them were very young, but their skiff was rickety and old. Parts of it were brightly painted, but in general it had a functional, utilitarian feel. The occupants looked poor. They looked wary. What they didn't look like was pirates. Even I could tell that without any knowledge of what pirates looked like.

Andy tried to speak to them, using basic Arabic, but they

didn't respond. One of the guys opened up a little box and held up a small plastic bag filled with a handful of tiny fish. 'We're fisherman,' he appeared to be trying to say. Well, perhaps, but it was a minuscule catch for a lot of guys. It seemed obvious to me, and to everyone else, that the fish we were being shown were food, even though the Somalis in general are not big fish-eaters. (They prefer a slice of camel meat, washed down with camel milk. I think I'll stick to cod and chips myself.) But whatever these people's foodie preferences were, we started to suspect that the boat we had encountered was run not by fishermen, nor even pirates, but by purveyors of another kind of illegality that plagues the Gulf of Aden, another community of seafarers. You'd be hard pressed to find a more desperate, treacherous bunch anywhere in the world.

I'd already learned that Somalia was a war-torn, dangerous place. What I didn't know was the lengths to which the Somali poor would go in order to get the hell out of there. Where there's a will, there's a way; and where there's a need, there's money to be made. The plight of these citizens has given rise to a booming trade in people smuggling, and the human tragedy involved in this sorry business is almost immeasurable.

Hundreds of people a week make the dangerous voyage across the Gulf of Aden to Yemen. They are not always Somalis, but also come from Ethiopia, Sudan or even further afield. Driven from their homes by drought, economic hardship, the threat of violence or – most probably – all three, these men, women and children are willing to risk everything in search of a better life in Yemen and the Middle East. Yemen, though, is hardly a refugee's paradise. On the contrary. It's one of the five remaining countries in the world where the execution of juvenile offenders is still permitted; arbitrary arrests – especially in the south – are commonplace and there is widespread judicial corruption. Freedom of speech, freedom of the press and freedom of religion are all highly restricted. In short, Yemen is a brutal, difficult place to live. But it's still better than Somalia.

A substantial proportion of the refugees, however, don't even make it as far as the Yemeni coast. The people smugglers charge a fee of around £20 per person – doesn't sound like a lot, but it's an almost impossible sum for a Somali refugee – and pack them tightly into their tiny boats. The smugglers, however, are not exactly full of the milk of human kindness. They frequently overload their boats – the more money they can earn from a crossing, the better – before setting sail. If, as often happens, they get out into the open water and the boat is too heavy on account of their greed, these enterprising businessmen simply dump part of their load. There have been reports of pregnant women and children being unceremoniously chucked into the water, and of course they have no hope of surviving.

Yemen has more than 80,000 Somali refugees. It mounts constant coastguard patrols throughout its waters in an attempt to locate the smugglers. This only has a limited effect. If the smugglers see the coastguard – or a vessel that they think *might* be a coastguard – they do what any profes-sional criminal would do: get rid of the evidence. If that means throwing a whole boatload of refugees overboard, so be it.

You'd think that the dangers involved, along with the smugglers' sense of customer service, would dissuade refugees from paying their £20 and risking everything to get to Yemen. Not a bit of it. They're queuing up to get out of Somalia. They risk it in their thousands. I'm told that if you walk along the northern coast of Somalia, it won't be long until you come across a shoe. Or a belt. Or a jacket. The non-human remains of humans long gone, drowned somewhere between the Somali and Yemeni coasts, their bodies rotted away or eaten by fish.

Were these Yemeni people smugglers that we had encountered? It was impossible to say for sure but it certainly seemed likely. From the RIB, Andy continued trying to talk to them. Without an interpreter it was difficult – none of them spoke English and his Arabic was basic – but gradually he managed to tease out some information. He pointed at a small hatch that led into the hull of the boat and indicated that he wanted a member of the skiff's crew to open it up. One of them did so, removing a piece of rush matting before he could raise the hatch.

There were people sleeping underneath. 'How many?' Andy asked.

A shuffling kind of pause. One of the passengers held up five fingers, but without boarding the skiff you couldn't say if he was telling the truth or not.

Andy radioed through to *Northumberland* and reported what we had found. 'Sixteen people on board, one child that we can see. They've got a fair amount of fuel on board and they say they're from Yemen.'

Back on the bridge of the *Northumberland*, Lieutenant Commander Martin Simpson listened carefully, all the while speaking into a Dictaphone so that he had a legal record of the encounter. Everything had to be done very strictly by the book. 'Do not board,' he instructed, 'until I give a direct order.'

'Roger,' Andy replied, and slowly the RIBs started to withdraw from the vicinity of the Yemeni boats.

As the RIBs filled with Marines and guns bobbed around the boats, Andy gave me the low-down. 'That's a lot of people,' he told me, 'for that size dhow with one skiff.'

So could they be running people?

He nodded curtly. 'Yeah,' he stated. 'That's exactly what they could be doing. This is prime space, in between Somalia and Yemen. What I'd like to do is get on board and see if they've got any ID. We've had reports in the past they've seen the coastguard coming out, they obviously don't want to be caught with people so they're fairly ruthless and just chuck them overboard.'

The Marines might have had the upper hand in terms of the force they could exert, but even with their firepower the intricacies of international diplomacy on the high seas meant they couldn't just board this tiny 'fishing' vessel at will. Royal Marines boarding a ship from another nation could cause a stink and they had to follow certain protocols. Andy and the Fleet Protection Group first needed permission from the commander of *Northumberland*; he, in turn, needed to get the go-ahead from HQ back in the UK.

While we waited for permission to board, we approached another skiff which had so much old clothing draped over its beams that it looked like a floating laundry. 'Fishermen are normally pretty proud of their catch,' Andy explained as we drifted towards them. 'Normally when we come alongside them, they'll get the fish out and show us straightaway.' But we were getting no impromptu fish counters to look at; just a wary greeting from the many desperate-looking individuals on this second boat.

'*Salam*,' they called.

'*Salam*,' we replied, in our pidgin Arabic.

They waved at us as we drew alongside them. Andy asked what they were doing. In response, one of them handed over a beaten-up old block of polystyrene with a length of knotted twine wrapped around it and, at the end, the rustiest hook I'd ever seen in my life. These people *could* have been fishermen, but you'd have more luck tickling trout than trying your luck with that kind of tackle. They weren't fooling anyone, not that it seemed to bother them. Perhaps they were emboldened by the fact that we hadn't boarded the previous skiff. I don't know. What I *do* know is that at one end of the skiff was a group of ten or eleven young men – children, really – looking exhausted in the brutal heat of the day. I later found out that the younger Somali refugees are, the more chance they have of finding work in Yemen. They are stronger and have more stamina. They can be worked into the ground for a slave's wage and are less likely to get ill or die. It seemed probable that this was the fate that awaited these youngsters when and if they finally made it across Pirate Alley.

Permission to board the skiffs never arrived, so we were unable to investigate any further. There was no sign that they were transporting drugs or arms and we couldn't prove that they were people smugglers. Even if we could, what would we do with them? Where would we take them? Dump them back on the coastline? That wouldn't be a great idea: if refugees find themselves in an area controlled by a rival clan they'll probably be killed; if not, they'll immediately be out on the water again, trying to get to Yemen. I had the impression that the crews of these boats knew that they would be dealt with softly by the British navy. Had we been the Yemeni or Omani coastguard, on the other hand, I suspect the smugglers' attitude would have been somewhat different – and possibly terminal for the refugees. I'd heard that in parts of Yemen convicted pirates could still be cruci-fied. I don't know what the punishment is for people smuggling, but I somehow doubt it's just a fine and an ASBO, and all the evidence suggests that Yemeni people smugglers will go to any lengths to avoid being caught by the wrong authorities.

That didn't include us, however. The Marines were RTB'd – returned to boat – and as we sped back to HMS *Northumberland* I had the distinct feeling that we had just witnessed one of the more unsavoury consequences of the chaos and hardship occurring in Somalia. Whatever the truth, everyone was pretty sure they weren't fishermen.

And I was also starting to realize something else, some-thing that was to become increasingly clear to me as my global search for pirates progressed. The Somali refugees I had just encountered, if indeed that is what they were, were only on the water because of what was happening in Somalia itself. If I was going to understand why piracy is so widespread, maybe I would have to look at what was happening not only out at sea, but also on land.

I didn't have much time to think about this, however, because just then a call came through. Some more suspicious boats had been reported to HMS *Northumberland*, but this time they were out of range of the RIBs. The Merlin helicopter was being prepped for flight, and if we wanted to find out what was going down, we needed to be on it.

5. Distress Call

The rotary blades of the Merlin were already spinning as I gingerly climbed out of the RIB, up the rope ladder and back onto the deck of *Northumberland*. It's only when you get up close to a helicopter on a flight deck that you realize how skilled these pilots must be. There's not a lot of room, even on a frigate of this size. Not much margin for error when you're coming in to land. I waited, a bit apprehensively, only metres away from this impressive piece of machinery while it was readied for take-off and then, when everything was prepped, Will the cameraman and I were given the thumbs up. We loaded ourselves in, and within seconds we were rising into the air.

The Gulf of Aden opened out before us, and HMS *Northumberland* disappeared from view. With the advantage of height I started to get some sense of the geographical problem facing the pirate hunters. Water as far as the eye could see and beyond the horizon, more water. Ships were dotted around below us, but even though there were many of them, they were insignificant compared to the vastness of ocean.

We sped through the skies. From up here, you can never rely on the naked eye to see what is happening on the water, but as the Merlin is primarily designed for anti-surface ship and anti-submarine warfare, tracking, surveillance and search-and-rescue missions, it's essential that the crew have good location and imaging capabilities. For this reason, the Merlin is equipped with both an over-the-horizon targeting radar and an extremely sensitive high-quality camera.

The radar is a bowl on the underside of the Merlin and is operated by a member of the crew. As soon as he picks up a vessel he assigns a track to it, and the camera operator can then target the vessel with his imaging machinery. This brings up clear images on the six high-definition colour displays in the cockpit of what is happening miles away. It needs to be powerful, of course, in order to pick up the periscope of a submarine's conning tower – little more than a dot in the ocean – and as we flew in the vicinity of a huge merchant ship, the camera operator, Tiny, showed me how he could pick out individual people on its deck using this high-tech equipment. He explained to me that this capability is particularly useful when you're going up against little fishing dhows of the type normally used by pirates, because you can get a good idea of who they are and what they're carrying, and on the basis of that information can decide whether to call for assistance from the ship, with a view to doing a boarding if necessary. Everything picked up by the camera was being recorded for the purpose of evidence.

We hadn't been in the air long when a dot came up on the radar screen. 'Left, 11 o'clock, four miles. We've got something in the water.'

'Roger. I've got a very faint radar contact but not a lot. If you can close it and try and get visuals on it . . .'

The camera zoomed in. This ship might have been some distance away, but the image on the screen was impressively clear. It was a dhow, churning through the water with four skiffs trailing behind it. And as I had already learned, that

69

was a classic pirate set-up. From our position up in the skies the camera continued to focus on the dhow. The image was crystal. We saw a canopy flapping in the wind and a sturdy metal fishing rod leaning out over the water. No ladders. No grappling hooks. No weapons. The guys on the dhow, even to my untutored eye, were pretty obviously fishermen, just out there trying to make an honest living. They were allowed to go on their way without any further interference from us. It wasn't the first time that I'd been left to reflect that hunting pirates in the Gulf of Aden wasn't the easiest way to spend your time . . .

We continued our patrol, high above the corridor where 60 merchant vessels travel through the Gulf every day. I could see them clearly from this vantage point – huge industrial chunks of metal ploughing on like enormous workhorses. The crew pointed one out to me. 'They're obviously a bit twitched about pirates in the area,' Tiny told me. 'He's got his hoses out at the moment. That's to deter them.'

From the top of the freeboard, huge streams of water were pumping out of the ship into the surrounding sea. Tiny explained to me that generators are used to suck vast amounts of seawater in before spitting it out of the side as a deterrent. I could well understand that trying to come alongside a boat with those things thundering at you could put you off your shopping trip. At the same time, I'd come to the conclusion that the pirates in these waters were nothing if not ballsy. I wouldn't put it past them to give it a go even under these circumstances.

But not today. We continued our patrol for a while longer, then returned to *Northumberland*, our pilot putting us down perfectly on the flight deck. I couldn't help marvelling at his skill at touchdown even more than when we took off – the Merlin only just fits on the deck. At the same time I was a bit disappointed that our flight had come to nothing. It had been an eventful day, but by the end of it I was left frustrated that so far our search for pirates had been unsuccessful.

We woke early the following day, though to look at the activity on the ship you'd never have known the sun had only just risen: the corridors were bustling, just as I knew they would have been all night – the mini-city that is HMS *Northumberland* doesn't go to bed just because it's dark. So too were the decks. Groups of Royal Navy sailors kept their fitness up to scratch by jogging round the ship; the guys from the Fleet Protection Group dismantled and cleaned their weapons. They may not have had call to use them, but that didn't mean their SA80s and MP5s didn't have to be in perfect working order. Mechanics were at work before the heat of the day became too intense. A warship is constantly being fixed, tampered with, twiddled and twoddled (although I'm not sure if those are the precise technical terms). It's a sensitive piece of kit that requires constant expert maintenance.

I grabbed a quick breakfast before joining Commander Simpson on the bridge for an update on what had happened overnight. Nothing in terms of piracy, he told me. We looked at his chart which mapped the flow of shipping up and down the corridor. It was a busy old place but that didn't guarantee that we'd find ourselves any pirates. I continuously had to remind myself that robberies are unpredictable events, whether you're on land or sea. I was glad, of course, that nobody had been pirated over the past couple of days, but I couldn't keep the nagging disappointment at bay that so far our search had been unsuccessful. I asked the ship's commander, straight out, what the chances were of us coming into contact with pirates.

'There's every chance,' he told me firmly, before indicating the shipping map again. 'If you're a pirate, there's a lot of trade out there.'

He was right. What none of us knew at the time, however, was that things weren't going to pan out quite the way anyone expected.

To pass the time, I decided to go and chat with some of the junior ratings, the rank and file of *Northumberland*'s crew. I wanted to know what the ordinary sailors thought about the job that they were being tasked to do. We met in the 45-man mess, so called because, surprise surprise, 45 men live in it. They were a friendly, welcoming bunch, and I asked how many of them thought, when they joined the Royal Navy, that they'd be tasked with looking for pirates. They all shook their heads – all of them, that is, apart from one bright spark. 'I did, I must admit,' he announced. 'But then again I joined in 1640.' Give that man a prize!

I pointed out to the lads that it was costing a great deal of money to keep them out here in the Gulf of Aden. Was it worth it? Weren't our resources better used elsewhere. One of them shrugged. 'You're pretty much damned if you do and damned if you don't,' he said. 'If you *do* go and investigate skiffs and it just turns out to be fishermen, you could be seen as hassling them. But if you didn't go and investigate and it turned out to be a piracy attack, then they would look and say, what's the point of you actually being here?'

A pretty succinct distillation of the problem, I thought. But what of the pirates themselves? There are two sides to every story, and was it possible, while deploring their actions, to have sympathy for their motives? The people of Somalia are, after all, very, *very* poor. Mr 1640 gave his opinion.

'I see their point of view,' he said, 'because they've got families to feed. And they think the only way they can do it, because they've had no government for 20 years and all the rest of it, is to go out and rob some vessels. But I've got a family to feed. I don't go round pointing guns at people.'

A pause.

'Well,' he added, 'I do . . .'

Everyone laughed, me included. In a funny kind of way, however, this light-hearted comment had highlighted the problem well. Piracy is a serious criminal act, and like many criminal acts it is being dealt with by the threat of force. That doesn't mean to say, however, that some pirates aren't driven by genuine necessity. The World Bank estimates that about three-quarters of Somalis live on less than two US dollars a day. One of the few industries they have is fishing. The Gulf of Aden has traditionally been rich in tuna and other valuable fish. With worldwide fish stocks plummeting as a result of overfishing, the relative riches of the Gulf of Aden have attracted illegal trawlers. Foreign ships have made a beeline for the Gulf, hoovering up the precious fish stocks – to the tune of $300 million worth a year – to sell around the world, destroying the livelihood of these Somali fishermen before their very eyes.

The destruction of Somalia's fishing industry is not the only seaborne indignity the country has had to suffer at the hands of greedy foreign nations ready to take advantage of the political upheavals in the area. Another example has been going on for many years, but did not fully come home to roost until the Asian tsunami of 2004. Somalia is almost 3,000 miles away from the epicentre of the earthquake which caused that tsunami, but the effect on the country was devastating nevertheless. Accurate official figures do not exist, but it's thought that nearly 300 people were killed by the coastal damage and more than 50,000 were displaced. The region of Puntland took the lion's share of the damage, and that is the area of Somalia from which most of the pirates originate.

The tsunami was disastrous enough in itself, but it also uncovered a dirty little secret of the Somali coast. When the waters subsided, they left behind debris carried in from the sea. This debris included rusty steel drums, barrels and a range of other containers, many of them smashed open by the force of the tides. These containers held vast quantities of toxic waste – waste that foreign countries had been dumping off the coast of Somalia for more than a decade. Why Somalia? As usual, it comes down to the green stuff. To get rid of toxic waste in Europe is expensive – around the $250-a-ton mark. To dump it off the coast of Somalia costs $2.50. You do the math.

These containers of toxic waste are more than just an eyesore. They contain all manner of harmful materials – radioactive uranium, lead, heavy metals such as cadmium and mercury, hospital waste, chemical waste . . . The list goes on, and none of it's the sort of thing you want ending up on your beaches. The effect of this waste on health is terrible. Since the containers washed ashore there have been many reports of locals falling ill with symptoms that you might reasonably expect to be associated with such substances – bleeding from the mouth and abdomen, for example. There's no real way of proving that these symptoms stem from exposure to the toxic waste, if only because there's no one brave enough to set foot in Somalia to investigate it fully, but the correlation between the waste and the illnesses seems obvious enough to me.

Although it was the Asian tsunami that highlighted this problem, both to the Somalis and to the world, there had been rumours it was happening for a number of years. In 1994 an Italian journalist by the name of Ilaria Alpi travelled to Somalia to investigate. She claimed that the Italian Mafia was behind a large chunk of the toxic waste dumping, and it has been estimated that the Mafia is behind about 30 per cent of Italy's waste disposal. It was to be the last investigation the journalist ever made. She and her cameraman were killed in Somalia. Word on the street is that they were assassinated. By the Mafia? By Somali warlords? By any of the many people with a vested interest in keeping this business alive? Who knows, but it seems clear that a major international criminal organization was polluting the Somali coast without any thought for the people of that country. And it wasn't like they didn't have enough to deal with already.

Their livelihoods taken from them, their land poisoned, it would have been naive to expect the Somali fishermen to take this sitting down. They armed themselves, took to their boats and started patrolling the area. Some of them tried to scare foreign shipping away; others tried to levy a 'tax' on them. These fishermen did not see themselves as pirates, but as an unofficial coastguard, there to stop their waters being destroyed in the same way as their land had been. From these beginnings, the piracy epidemic spread. This is not to say that there are not gangsters, opportunists and out-and-out criminals among the pirates of Somalia. There are. Many of the pirates of Somalia are, relatively speaking, wealthy men, happy to use the wrongdoings of other nations as an excuse for their actions. But the truth about the origins of piracy in the area is not black and white. As usual, it is shades of grey.

1500 hours.

What looked like being a quiet day was suddenly hotting up. Two small unidentified vessels had been picked up on the radar. Nobody knew who they were or what they were doing, and so Lieutenant Commander Simpson had ordered the Fleet Protection Group and the Merlin to go and investigate. The already busy corridors of *Northumberland* became suddenly busier as we prepared ourselves for the off.

The Marines loaded themselves into their RIBs while I joined the Merlin crew and once more took off into the skies. The two Marine snipers in the helicopter took up position by their weapons – one with a GPMG, capable of firing a lot of rounds and designed to take out people, the other with an AW50 50-cal rifle designed to take out the engine block. Each weapon had a piece of black material attached to its side, the purpose of which was to stop the casings of discharged ammunition from pinging back into the Merlin. Those casings are very hot, and you want a fire on a helicopter even less than you want a fire on a boat . . .

Down on the water, the RIBs started circling one of the two skiffs. Everyone on the boats put their hands up. They were a ragtag bunch – men, women and children, all poorly dressed and with expressions of confused despair on their faces. It was clear from a single look that these were yet more refugees, unfortunate Africans risking the dangers of being smuggled across the water to Yemen.

The Merlin circled the second skiff, but something was happening back at *Northumberland*. A channel 16 distress call. Something was going on, and it was going on nearby.

The distress call came from a vessel called the MV *Saldanha*. It had a crew of 22, including 19 Filipinos, and was registered to the Marshall Islands in the north Pacific Ocean. On the bridge of the *Northumberland* the radio operator made contact. 'Can you tell me what your situation is? What's going on now?'

A hesitant voice replied. It spoke English but with a heavy accent. 'Three speedboats on the starboard side. They send a message to slow down. The mother ship is on our port side, about one and a half to two miles.'

You didn't have to be a naval expert to twig that it sounded suspicious. The officer operating the radio turned to Commander Simpson for instructions. 'Do you want them to increase speed and start manoeuvring, sir?'

More from the *Saldanha*: 'They are still approaching us, at low speed now. We'll try to keep them astern.' He didn't sound entirely confident.

The radio operator received his instructions, then relayed them: '*Saldanha*, this is Foxtrot 23. I want you to increase speed to your maximum and start manoeuvring heavily to port and starboard.'

This was a defensive manoeuvre. If the *Saldanha* could get up speed and then start swerving, it would create a wave and make it more difficult for the pirates – if indeed that's what they were – to approach. In the meantime, Commander Simpson ordered the Merlin, with us on board, into action. 'Send the helicopter off to that bearing.' It looked like we were about to have our first taste of piracy.

The MV *Saldanha* was 60 miles from our current position. In a Merlin helicopter in clear conditions, that takes about 12 minutes. Not a long time, but we were all aware of the need for speed. If these *were* pirates, we knew that they could board the *Saldanha* extremely quickly, and once this had been completed, there was nothing we could do about it. There was a feeling of tense expectation in the helicopter as it sped towards its target; and if it was tense for us, I couldn't help wondering what it must have been like for the crew that believed itself to be under attack.

As we crossed the water as fast as the machinery would allow, the *Saldanha* kept in constant contact with *Northumberland*, relaying its precise position. But at that distance the warship was of little practical use to the merchant vessel. It was all going to be down to the Merlin. The Marine snipers took up their positions, but I couldn't help thinking that, if it came down to it and the sniper with the AW50 had to destroy the pirates' engine blocks, these would be pretty hard shots to make, being from one unstable platform to another. I pointed this out to one of the Marines and he didn't disagree.

The minutes passed. *Saldanha* appeared as a blur on the high-definition screens when we were still eight minutes away. We were approaching from the west, and word came through that an American missile cruiser in the vicinity – the USS *Vella Gulf* – had dispatched a second helicopter from the east, which was also hurrying towards the distressed ship. For both aircraft it was a race against time. We *had* to catch the pirates in the act of taking the ship. From a distance the Merlin's cameras scanned the decks of the *Saldanha*, looking for signs of boarding. So far, nothing. But we didn't know how long that would last.

Four minutes away.

GPMG prepped and ready to go.

Update from the *Saldanha*. 'The mother ship is about three miles behind me. One fast boat together with this vessel. The other three fast boats, they run away. Maybe they are now eight, nine miles far from me.'

The skiffs were retreating. Evidently the *Saldanha*'s evasive action had deterred the supposed pirates.

The American helicopter arrived at the *Saldanha* first. It circled the vessel to assess the situation. Our pilot opened up communications with the American ship and reported back to *Northumberland*. 'Just spoke to the *Vella Gulf*, sir. Their cab's [helicopter] on top. Don't assess it as a threat. They're keeping it there to monitor the situation. He says it's more likely they'll RTB their cab shortly.'

Not a threat? Well, perhaps. But I couldn't help thinking it was unlikely that those skiffs had been closing in on the *Saldanha* just for the hell of it. The same thoughts were clearly going through Commander Simpson's head. 'I want to know when he's absolutely convinced they're fishermen, not pirates,' he instructed. As we all knew, however, telling the difference between the two is not always straightforward.

The assessment was eventually made that the retreating

skiffs were fishermen chasing tuna, but we didn't have the chance to consider how likely or unlikely that was, because just then the Merlin crew received new orders. Yet another suspicious vessel ten miles back the way we'd come. The pilot performed an about turn, leaving the *Saldanha* to go on its way while we hurried to assess the new threat. The snipers remained at their stations as I gazed at the water below.

A small flotilla of yachts came into view, boats that looked like they'd be more at home off the Côte d'Azur than in Pirate Alley. I have to admit that a part of me wondered what the hell they were doing in that part of the world; it's certainly not where I'd choose to take a yachting holiday. A skiff had been chasing them, or at least had appeared to be chasing them. But now it had backed off. Once more word came through that it was just a fishing vessel. Yet again a false alarm.

The sun was beginning to set as we returned to HMS *Northumberland*. It had been an exhausting afternoon, and a frustrating one. I'd learned a lot about the job the Royal Navy is asked to do in the Gulf of Aden. I'd come to realize that although there is a formidable military presence in that waterway, the guys are still incredibly stretched in terms of responding to the distress calls when they come in. The sheer size of the ocean they have to patrol means that the odds are stacked firmly against them.

Still, it was some small comfort that the MV *Saldanha* had been allowed to continue safely on its way.

Or had it?

6. The Pirates Strike

In the centre of HMS *Northumberland* lies the command room. It's the most heavily defended part of the ship and it is from here that the captain makes all his tactical decisions should the ship go to battle stations. And it was here that we congregated for an intelligence briefing from Sub Lieutenant Simon Henderson. 'It's believed that a majority of pirates are affiliated to clans,' he explained, 'within the northern part of Somalia. These clans give logistical support to pirates, giving enough food and supplies for vessels that are held in the detention area, and their crews. Mother ships were introduced to the piracy organizations around September last year. They allow pirates to loiter at sea, operate further out in excess of 500 nautical miles and in rougher conditions, and also hold resupplies of food, ammunition and water.'

After the briefing, I approached the sub lieutenant. I was frustrated that during our time on the ship we hadn't managed to catch up with any pirates, and I wondered if, having gathered so much detailed intelligence about them, he felt the same.

'It's extremely frustrating,' he told me. 'We have a snippet of information that in this general location there may be a pirate skiff. However, we may be two or three hundred miles away. By the time we've launched the Merlin helicopter, they're long gone. A piracy attack lasts ten or fifteen minutes.

So unfortunately, unless you're in the right place at the right time, you aren't going to catch people. It's a lot to do with luck, unfortunately.'

From my small experience so far, he was spot on. Luck hadn't been on our side. And it was about to run out for a merchant ship not a million miles from where we were at that very moment.

Pirates like to attack at dusk or at dawn, when the half-light cloaks them and they can approach their targets with less chance of being seen. In this respect they are very much like their buccaneer and corsair predecessors. As dawn broke the following day, I looked out from deck to see shoals of dolphins diving through the waves. A beautiful sight. Despite others' attempts to pollute it, this remains a very clear sea. That morning we were due to come alongside an American oiler to refuel. This vessel was absolutely vast, dwarfing even the *Northumberland*, and it was an intricate operation to pull up against it. The oiler used a rifle to fire a line over; *Northumberland* reciprocated and this continued until a network of wires existed between the two ships and they could pull themselves together. Once we were close enough, an enormous pump was winched over to us, and the ship started to refuel. The whole process took a good couple of hours. We were taking receipt of 200 tonnes of oil, after all.

What none of us knew, however, was that we were not the only vessel in the vicinity to be drawing up alongside another. As *Northumberland* had its oil thirst quenched, the crew of a merchant ship 60 miles away was coming under attack. That merchant ship went by the name of the MV *Saldanha*. The same ship we had attended the previous day on account of it being followed by skiffs that had been dismissed as fishermen chasing tuna . . .

The bridge of the *Northumberland* had no idea anything was happening until it picked up something odd on the radar. *Saldanha*, which had been doggedly plotting its course along the corridor, had now changed direction. It was no longer part of the convoy. Instead, it was heading towards the coastline of Somalia.

Commander Simpson's face was grim when he realized what was happening, and a tenseness fell upon everyone in the ship. The officer operating the radio tried to make contact: 'MV *Saldanha*, MV *Saldanha*. This is coalition warship Foxtrot 23. Channel 16. Over.'

Silence on the airwaves. *Saldanha* wasn't responding.

We couldn't hear it, but we could see it – a blip on the radar travelling off route, away from the corridor and towards the coastal town of Eyl. And if it was going to Eyl, that could mean only one thing.

Eyl is situated in the Puntland region of Somalia from which most of the pirates originate. Only a few years ago it was little more than a poor fishing town – some boats, a few shacks and a population of impoverished Somalis. All in all, not much different from the rest of the country. But Eyl has undergone a transformation, and that transformation has occurred because it is a modern-day pirate town, the lair of the people wreaking havoc in the Gulf of Aden. The shacks are still there, but they are now accompanied by signs of wealth. There are restaurants, for example, and four-by-fours driven by men in suits. The number of people engaged in actual piracy is relatively small, but a whole economy has sprung up in Eyl to service their needs.

Whenever a vessel is pirated, wealthy middlemen appear. They have new weapons and shiny cars, and you can bet your bottom dollar they didn't acquire these status symbols by honest, straightforward means. Houses are being built along the coastline surrounding Eyl – not the poor places that are the mainstay of the rest of the country, but large properties for the successful practitioners of Puntland's illegal profession.

Commander Simpson immediately changed *Northumberland*'s bearing to follow the *Saldanha*. It was eight miles away and moving steadily in a south-easterly direction. There had been no distress call from the ship, but everyone knew that her drastic change in course was not a good sign. The Merlin crew was scrambled, and I took to the air with them once again. We needed to get to the merchant vessel as quickly as possible. The bridge must have been taken, but maybe other parts of the ship hadn't. Perhaps we could help the crew with covering fire, although nobody was under the illusion that the odds were in our favour.

On the bridge, *Northumberland* continued trying to contact the vessel. 'MV *Saldanha*, MV *Saldanha*. This is coalition warship Foxtrot 23. Over.'

A deafening and very meaningful silence.

The Merlin approached. Once more, the *Saldanha* appeared on the screens in the cockpit. The bridge and the upper deck were clearly visible. No sign of anyone, or anything.

And still, nothing from the captain of the ship.

Then the radio burst into life.

It was the *Saldanha*'s captain, his accented English strangely emotionless as he updated the warship on their situation.

'*Saldanha* captain speaking. We are under a hostage situation. Control of the vessel is seized by pirates.'

'How many crew do you have on board?' the radio operator requested.

'We are 22. For the moment all of them OK.'

For the moment. But you don't take hostages if you're not prepared to hurt them.

Suddenly the Merlin picked up something on the *Saldanha*'s bridge. The crew reported back to *Northumberland*, 'Captain, there is a two-person visual on the bridge roof.'

The order came through to load the GPMG. 'Load gun. Roger, load gun.' The gunner had eyes on. We were one squeeze of the trigger away from an air-to-sea battle.

More info from the *Saldanha*'s captain: 'The pirates request to stay away and not to transmit any other message to them.'

Our options had been cut short. The Merlin had some powerful weaponry trained on the enemy, but it was as good as useless. Fire on the pirates and we risked two things. First, a counter-attack, using RPGs, on the helicopter. It would have been a brave move by the pirates, but then their bravery was something nobody could call into question. Second, retaliation aimed not at us but at the hostages. So far in the Gulf of Aden pirates had refrained from harming their hostages, and they knew it was in everyone's interests to keep it that way.

Commander Simpson's options were limited. He could monitor the situation, observe the *Saldanha*'s movements. But he couldn't take any military action. He couldn't board the vessel or attempt to seize it back from the pirates. The honest truth was that he could do nothing of any practical use. It was a galling moment. There we were, the Merlin hovering above the pirated vessel, *Northumberland* a handful of miles away. All that military hardware primed and ready to do its job. But in the final analysis it was worthless.

The MV *Saldanha* had just been pirated from right under our very noses. It was on its way to a known pirate haven and there wasn't a thing we could do about it.

The frustration was tangible, not just for the Marines, who had the pirates in their sights, would have liked to have taken a shot and attempted to seize the vessel, but whose hands were tied; but also for the crew as a whole. To avoid any danger to the crew, Commander Simpson ordered the Merlin to RTB immediately. The helicopter swerved.

'How you feeling?' I asked the pilot.

'I'm pissed off.'

'How frustrating is that?'

'Fucking frustrating.'

'Roger that.'

All I could do was agree with them as the crew of *Northumberland* watched the pirated *Saldanha* sail right past them, headed for the coast of Somalia.

And what of the crew of the merchant vessel? What could they expect? I could only imagine how terrified they must be. The pirates that were now swarming over their ship would be heavily armed. But in fact bloodshed would be a worst-case scenario for the pirates just as much as for the crew. They knew that as soon as they started killing or even hurting their hostages, they could expect military reprisals. Take care of them and, as they had seen time and again, they'd be given an easy ride: coalition warships would avoid boarding them in order to maintain the bloodless status quo. Moreover, the crew was the pirates' collateral. Their bargaining chips. As the *Saldanha* slipped away into the distance, I recalled the conversation I'd had before I left with the spook whose business took him into Somalia. He had explained to me that the pirates would go out of their way to protect their assets. 'If you had a car that you wanted to sell, would you go around and smash it up? No, you'd look after it – you'd clean it, you'd make sure the engine was OK, make sure it had oil and water.'

Once the *Saldanha* reached land, the pirates would make some attempt to ensure the hostages were comfortable. They have set themselves up to provide Western food in Eyl, and while the hostages would hardly be living in the lap of luxury, they could at least expect to be kept in reasonable health. That said, every part of Somalia is dangerous and unpredictable. The pirates might want to protect their assets, but that didn't mean their safety was assured. Not by any means. I wouldn't want to be in the shoes of those hostages, no matter how much pizza and Coke my captors fed me.

Saldanha did finally make it to port and, thanks to the restraint of Commander Simpson and the Marines, without anyone getting hurt. The vessel remained there for two months, supported by the infrastructure of the pirate town. It later transpired that the lead pirate went by the name of Abdirashid Ahmed. His nickname was Juqraafi – 'Geography'. Several weeks after his escapades in the Gulf of Aden, our geographical mastermind reportedly took receipt of a ransom of $1.3 million before releasing the ship and its hostages unharmed. Not a bad fee for a few minutes' work.

His original demand was for $17 million, but Juqraafi claimed that he lowered it when it became clear that the negotiations would otherwise drag on too long. This extended period of negotiation is completely normal: as soon as the pirated ships hit land, the ransom demand becomes like any other business transaction, with one side trying to keep the price up, the other doing what they can to lower it. Once the deal is done, the money can be delivered by a variety of methods.

It is believed that until recently pirates' ransoms have been transferred using an informal Islamic system called *hawala*. This system has its origins in Islamic law and has been around since at least the eighth century. It relies on a network of brokers. If a customer wishes to transfer money to somebody in another city, they give the money to one of these brokers, along with the details of the person to whom it is to be sent. The broker will contact another *hawala* broker in the recipient's city, instruct them to make the payment and then will settle the debt at a later date. Nowadays such a payment can be completed within 24 hours.

It's a simple system, but one based entirely on trust. If a sender loses his or her money, they don't have a legal leg to stand on. Moreover, *hawala* operates entirely outside the international banking system. And it's huge. According to the United Nations, somewhere between $100 billion and $300 billion is transferred through the system each year. Of this, around $15 billion enters India, $7 billion enters Pakistan, and just under a billion goes into Somalia.

Hawala is popular for a number of reasons. It's cheaper than using a bank, for a start – *hawala* brokers charge a much smaller percentage than their bank counterparts.

Modern-day pirates: not
exactly Jack Sparrow.

Pirates off the coast of Somalia hold Skipper Florent Lemacon and the
four passengers (including his wife and three-year-old son) on board the
French yacht *Tanit* to ransom. Tragically, Lemacon later took a bullet in
the head and died during a rescue attempt.

After almost 20 years of civil war, Somalia is a country ripped apart.

One in six children under the age of five suffers acute malnourishment; one in four dies before they reach this age.

Captain Lieutenant Commander Martin Simpson welcomes me on board the HMS *Northumberland* in the port of Salalah on the coast of Oman.

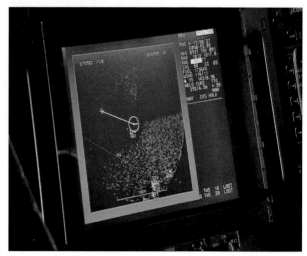

I take a look at the radar screen on the HMS *Northumberland*.

Searching for pirates 24/7: a constant watch is kept on the bridge.

This ship would be very difficult for pirates to board because of its high freeboard.

A vulnerable ship pumps sea water from its fire hoses to prevent pirates from boarding.

Captain Andy Morris gives his briefing before searching a suspicious vessel.

Aboard a Royal Marine RIB – rigid inflatable boat – speeding towards a suspicious skiff.

Drugs and guns are not the only cargo being transported across the Gulf of Aden. These are desperate people trying to leave a war-torn country.

Boarding the Merlin helicopter.

More unfortunate Africans risking the dangers of being smuggled across the water to Yemen.

To alleviate the boredom, the Marines are continually cleaning and stripping their weapon systems.

Decompressing in the 45-man mess, so called because, surprise surprise, 45 men live in it.

Northumberland makes contact with the pirated MV *Saldanha*.

This is a classic pirates' skiff. Fuel, water, food and the big giveaway, the 12-foot ladder.

Captain Andy Morris finds two RPG warheads on board, further proof that these guys aren't fishermen.

The pirates' skiff finally sinks as the mini-gunner looks on.

Each year, more than 100 oil workers are kidnapped by pirates in Nigeria.

The Niger Delta's maze of mangrove swamps makes it the perfect hiding place.

Robin Barry Hughes and Matthew Maguire, two British hostages who were kidnapped by pirates and held deep in the impenetrable Niger Delta.

Billy Graham was kidnapped by Nigerian pirates, held captive for 26 days without food and forced to dig his own grave.

Duncan Macnicol, a former ship's captain, takes me out into Lagos harbour, and explains how the merchant shipping vessels waiting to enter the harbour are sitting ducks: easy targets for pirates.

Hell on earth. Ajegunle is Lagos's biggest waterside slum. It's difficult to say how many people live here, but one thing's for sure – it's too many.

The slum is so polluted that you can't see the riverbank for the rubbish that is piled up by the side of the water. It was like crossing the River Styx.

One of the 17 or so chiefs of Ajegunle gives me a tour of the area and explains some of the effects piracy has had on his community.

Sonny takes me to see a damaged oil well head in Ogoniland in the heart of the Niger Delta.

A leaking deserted oil head, the cause of devastating pollution to the surrounding area.

The oil companies claim to have 'cleaned up' this area. It didn't look very clean to me.

I meet Ledum Mitee, a human rights campaigner for the Ogoni people.

Their exchange rates are often better and, most importantly, *hawala* brokers don't ask any questions. They also don't keep detailed records of individual transactions, just a running total of the amount owed by one broker to another. It's easy to use the *hawala* system to make anonymous payments that are difficult to trace. Pay someone by *hawala* and there's no paper trail. As such, it has often been used to finance terrorism and other illegal activites – after the 11 September attacks the United States urged greater regulations of *hawala* operators.

It is thought that some pirates in Puntland purchase weapons by sending money via *hawala* to dealers in Mogadishu. It also seems likely, as there are no banks or Western Union offices that can transfer money in and out of Somalia, that the system has been used in some instances to arrange payment of pirates' ransoms. But it is reported that the ransoms eventually grew too big for even the *hawala* system to cope with. Rumours now abound – unsubstantiated, it should be said – that teams of ex-special forces personnel are sometimes engaged to perform a cash dump onto the deck of the ship in question. I've also been told that money is simply transferred from one bank account to another in, for example, the City of London. That made me wonder just who was behind these operations, and it made me realize that the people committing these acts of piracy are nothing if not savvy.

Juqraafi the pirate has gone on record as saying that the pirates have well-organized systems for divvying up the loot. They generally have a 'financier' who sponsors them – he gets 30 per cent. The pirates themselves get 50 per cent. The remaining 20 per cent is divided out among the community and those who have helped the pirates on shore in some way – including corrupt officials who expect bribes whenever a ship is successfully taken.

How true pirates' claims of Robin Hood-like generosity are, it's impossible to say. They certainly have support among particular sections of the population, but in a part of the world that remains grindingly poor there seems little doubt that the people who benefit the most from these crimes are the pirates themselves and the Mr Bigs that support them.

Back on HMS *Northumberland*, none of us knew how long the *Saldanha* would remain in port, or whether the crew would come to any harm in the lawless town of Eyl. There wasn't a man or woman on our ship that didn't feel the frustration keenly. There was nothing anybody could do about the pirated vessel itself, but we knew that the pirates had to have gained access to the merchant ship somehow, and there had been no sign of any skiffs attached to the *Saldanha*. So it was that Merlin set off once again. Its mission this time was to scour the seas for a mother ship or any skiffs floating in the vicinity.

It didn't take long for the Merlin to pick up a faint echo on the radar in the area of ocean where the *Saldanha* was pirated. The Fleet Protection Group immediately manned the RIBs and I joined them as they sped through the waves on the bearing the helicopter had indicated. The Marines expected it to be a skiff, and they weren't disappointed: within minutes, we came across a long, solitary vessel, floating innocuously. We approached with caution, not knowing if the skiff was booby-trapped, and as Captain Andy Morris and Sergeant Macaffer gingerly boarded the empty vessel, that caution doubled. It would only take a primed hand grenade sitting under an RPG and suddenly we'd be swimming with the fishes.

The skiff was battered, old and very far from glamorous, but it contained everything necessary to carry out an act of piracy. Two Yamaha outboard motors – big enough to allow the vessel to catch up with a merchant ship – and plenty of canisters of fuel to power them, plus a 12-foot ladder, long enough to board most low-freeboard vessels. In addition, the Marines found plenty of items on board which suggested that the pirates hadn't wanted to lose this skiff. There were wrapped-up wads of Somali cash – too much for any fisherman. There were clothes and shoes – the pirates must have boarded barefoot, but in poor countries like Somalia shoes are important, so they definitely wouldn't have left them there on purpose. We found two RPG warheads, but no launcher. You wouldn't have the warheads without the launcher, which meant they must have boarded with it; and they wouldn't have boarded with a launcher and no warhead – they probably had several with them. There were shell casings from an AK-47 lying in the hull of the boat. It was impossible to say when they had been fired; all we knew was that they *had* been fired, and that the pirates were more than likely armed with assault rifles. There was the obligatory camel meat, and a large bunch of a green plant that looked a bit like basil. This was khat, an amphetamine-like stimulant indigenous to East Africa and the Arabian peninsula. It's illegal in Somalia but widely available, and it's said to be a particular favourite of the pirates. Khat keeps you awake, suppresses your appetite and gives you an addictive high. Some people chew the leaves, others the stalk, mashing it to a paste in their mouth which they keep there for a long time, sucking out all the juices before spitting it out again when it's served its purpose.

We also found an expensive sea compass that they wouldn't have wanted to lose and, bizarrely, a blue strap with the word 'Arsenal' embroidered on it. Clearly our men liked the Gunners as well as their guns. Our suspicions that the skiff had been lost rather than abandoned were confirmed when the Marines located, tied to the end of the boat, a frayed piece of rope that had clearly once been attached to something but had then snapped. It was impossible to ascertain how many people had been on this skiff and subsequently boarded the *Saldanha*; indeed, there might well have been two skiffs, with the second speeding back to some mother ship nearby, ready to go shopping again if a suitable target crossed its path. All we could say for sure was that this skiff had once been tied to something – most probably the merchant vessel itself – and that it belonged not to fishermen, but to pirates.

Captain Andy Morris jettisoned the RPG warheads over the side of the skiff. They sank without trace and it was good to know that, submerged in 2,500 feet of water, they were now harmless. But an unmanned floating skiff remained a hazard to navigation, so back on the bridge of HMS *Northumberland* the captain received permission to destroy the vessel. It was up to the Marines to bring the skiff within range of the frigate's guns, so they attached a rope and used their RIBs to bring it in. I made the return journey in the skiff. In fact, I insisted on it. I might have missed out on meeting a pirate, but I wanted at least to ride in his boat.

Once the Marines and I were safely back on board *North-umberland*, the skiff was set adrift. But it wouldn't sail for long. Already the ship's gunners had it in their sights, and as soon as the skiff was a safe distance away, one of them opened up with a Minigun, a multi-barrel machine gun that fires 7.62 mm rounds at a rate of over 3,000 a minute. The ocean around the skiff was peppered with little explosions, and as the rounds slammed into the skiff itself, the fuel canisters ignited and it burst into flame. A thick black plume of smoke billowed up from it, and still the rounds from the Minigun came, the noise from the weapon thundering into the air around us. The skiff still wasn't sinking, so the captain ordered the larger 30 mm Oerlikon guns on it.

It took a lot of firepower to sink that skiff. More than I would have expected. Or maybe the gunner was just taking out his frustrations on that tiny vessel, a lone symbol of the opportunity *Northumberland* had just narrowly missed to do what it had been put in the Gulf of Aden to do and catch a team of pirates. I wouldn't have blamed him. As the skiff burned and sank, all we could do was reflect on the fact that combating piracy off the coast of Somalia is a bit like finding a needle in a haystack. If you're not in the right place at the right time, you simply don't stand a chance.

Our time on board the Royal Navy frigate was coming to a close. HMS *Northumberland* was on a bearing towards the port of Djibouti, and it was here that we were to disembark. Djibouti is a tiny country on the northern border of Somalia: a population of half a million, a fifth of whom live below the poverty line. Like Somalia, it has come through a period of civil war, but Djibouti, at least, has a functioning government. It's not exactly a safe haven, but in this part of the world all things are relative, and it's a hell of a sight safer than Eyl, where at that moment the MV *Saldanha* was taking its place alongside 16 other pirated vessels. In addition to its crew, there were also 292 other hostages in that pirate haven.

It was disappointing that during my time on board *Northumberland* we had not managed to catch up with a pirate. I'd learned a lot about the difficulties the British navy and others face in their struggle against this seaborne menace. I'd seen at first hand just how hard it is to catch pirates, and witnessed the frustration of the men and women of the Royal Navy at how little they could do. At the same time, I could understand how careful the coalition warships in the Gulf of Aden have to be. Just a couple of months previously an Indian frigate by the name of INS *Tabar* had destroyed a deep-sea trawler which they claimed was a pirate arsenal, full to the brim with supplies of weapons and ammo. Unfortunately, they were wrong. It was in fact a Thai fishing boat that had been hijacked, which still contained the entire crew, tied up below decks. Only one of them was ever found alive. A cautionary tale of the dangers involved in using your superior military strength. Later in my investigation I met a group of former Marines and Paras. Ordinarily, they would be plying their trade as private security guards in hot spots like Iraq, but they explained to me that their livelihoods had been taken by younger lads prepared to do the same job for a lot less money. And so they had diversified, offering themselves up to merchant vessels who wanted a bit of extra insurance. These guys weren't allowed to take any weapons on board ship with them, so they had to make do with whatever they might find on a merchant vessel – fire extinguishers, hammers and the wherewithal to make Molotov cocktails. Their hands were tied, but maybe it was for the best, as later events in the Gulf of Aden would demonstrate the human cost of taking the fight to the pirates with genuine weapons.

But that was in the future. For now, I had made some good friends on the *Northumberland*, but what I really wanted to do had so far eluded me: to speak to a pirate, and to find out straight from the horse's mouth what drives them to these crimes on the high seas. Is it poverty? Is it organized crime? Is it sheer opportunism? Or is it a mixture of all three? As we said goodbye to the friends we had made on board ship, I realized that I still had a lot more to learn. What I didn't know was that my next trip, to the waters of a country many hundreds of miles from Somalia, would show me a very different side to the menace of international piracy.

PART 2
The Bight of Benin

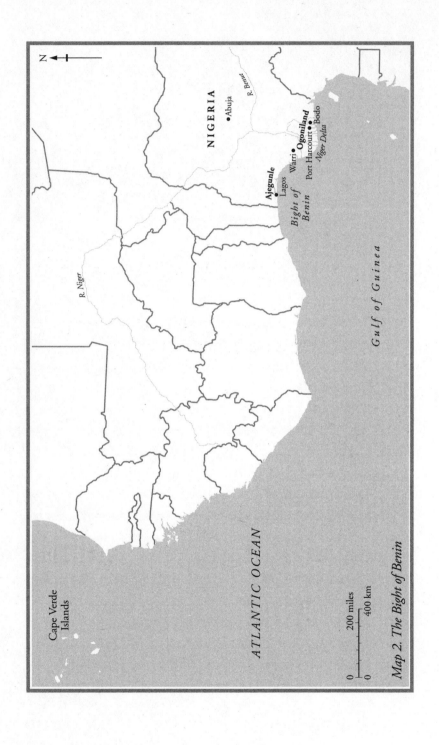

Map 2. The Bight of Benin

7. Chop-chop

There's an old sea shanty, dating from the nineteenth century, about the area I was to visit next in my quest to discover the truth about international piracy.

> Beware, beware the Bight of Benin
> There's one that comes out for forty goes in.

That cheerful little jingle was inspired by the risk of malaria to anyone venturing into that part of the world, and it's true that the illness is more of a threat in this part of Africa than almost anywhere else. But the Bight's inhospitable nature was not limited to deadly mosquitoes. It was famously a hub of the slave trade; indeed this stretch of land along the western coast of Africa was known as the Slave Coast, and as such it was a busy waterway for ships full of misery.

Nowadays, boats that travel through these waters have different cargos, some legal, some not. The Gulf of Guinea, which comprises the Bight of Benin, the neighbouring Bight of Bonny and the coastlines of the 11 countries that lie between Ghana and Angola, is a major hub for narcotics trafficking. In recent years significant quantities of high-grade cocaine have been seized in these waters because it is part of the drug-trade triangular route between the Cape Verde Islands, the Canary Islands and Madeira.

As well as being part of a drug route, since the late 1990s

the area has consistently ranked as one of the top piracy hot spots worldwide. In the two years between 2002 and 2004 there were more pirate attacks in the Gulf of Guinea than in the rest of African waters put together. Today, it is officially the world's second-biggest piracy hot spot after Somalia, but that statistic doesn't tell the whole story. A large number of pirate attacks in the Gulf go unreported. After all, if someone nicks your stash of coke, you're hardly likely to go moaning to the authorities. And if you're a fisherman whose small boat has been boarded, all your money pinched and then you've been thrown overboard and left to your own luck – well, the chances are you're not going to survive long enough to report the incident. No one knows how many ships are currently being pirated here, but it is thought the Gulf could easily knock Somalia off the top spot.

The Gulf of Guinea extends for 3,400 miles. That's about the same size as the Gulf of Mexico and in an area of coastline that size, there's bound to be bits that are less safe than others. One country along the Gulf has the dubious honour of playing host to the majority of pirate attacks in the area. That country is Nigeria, and its piracy problem is escalating. Big time. In 2003 there were four reported attacks; in 2008 there were 107. The Nigerian Trawler Owners' Association reckoned that in 2006 half of all fishing vessels in Nigerian waters had been pirated. The International Transport Workers' Federation, which represents workers in 148 different countries, has branded Nigeria's waters a war zone.

Nigerian pirates are different from Somali pirates in one important respect: they kill people. This hasn't always been the case – until a few years ago they principally targeted cash, valuables and shipping gear. Not any more. Violence is a regular occurrence, and so are killings. In one week alone, not long before I travelled to Nigeria, there were 20 attacks on ships and 10 people killed.

And I don't mind admitting that I didn't much like the sound of those odds.

Nigeria's a long way from home. But I didn't even have to leave Britain in order to discover that the effects of the country's piracy problem reached much further than the African coastline. Instead I prepared to meet the Maguire family from the Wirral. Anxious times for anxious people, as I found out when I spoke to Bernard Maguire, whose son Matthew was one of a group of British oil-rig workers who had been on a boat moored at Port Harcourt, the capital of Nigeria's Rivers State. Matthew is an electrician by trade but wasn't making the money he needed, so he retrained as a diver. Divers are important to the oil industry, which needs them to work on underwater drilling, inspecting pipes or fixing oil derricks. Diving can be well paid, and Matthew was on a ship waiting to be transported to an oil platform further out to sea so that he could earn a living for himself and his family.

Unfortunately, things didn't quite go according to plan. The ship was hijacked by 8 to 10 pirates, and 27 crew members originating from a variety of countries were forced into a smaller vessel and onto land. This area of Nigeria is characterized by a vast network of waterways and inlets. The pirates moved their hostages into a smaller speedboat still, and then ferried them to a nearby village.

Over the next few days most of the hostages were released, and each time someone was released, the pirates moved somewhere else along these complex waterways so they couldn't be tracked down. First the pirates let the Nigerian nationals go, then the various foreign nationals until they had whittled it down to their two British captives. Matthew Maguire and Robin Barry Hughes, captain of the pirated ship, were retained. It turned out that the pirates specifically wanted British hostages, for reasons I would come to understand once I got to Nigeria. The pirates took their hostages deep into the Niger Delta – 27,000 square miles of intricate, inter-twined waterways that cover nearly a tenth of Nigeria's land mass. There was some attempt by the authorities to locate them, but it was an impossible task. Hole yourself away in the Niger Delta and nobody is ever going to find you . . .

All this had happened some five months previously. Since that time neither man's family had heard from him. Matthew Maguire had a wife and three young children back home, and his father's face spoke eloquently about his worry as I sat down to talk to him. Word had reached him that one of the two hostages was seriously ill, but they didn't know which one. I could only imagine the worry the family must have been feeling. 'It's little things of a night,' he told me, trying to put a brave face on it, but not entirely succeeding, 'when you're trying to go to sleep, or you wake up early because you're thinking about the conditions he's kept in. Stupid things like shower, clothes, what food is he eating, where's he sleeping.' All the minutiae of day-to-day living, the things parents are hard-wired to worry about, no matter that their son was grown up with children of his own. Stupid things? They didn't sound stupid to me at all, especially knowing what I knew about Nigerian pirates' readiness to kill their hostages.

The question was, why had Matthew Maguire and Robin Barry Hughes been taken? Was this an opportunist attack like the one I had witnessed in the Gulf of Aden? Were the pirates looking for a sizeable monetary ransom in return for their assets? Or was there something else going on here? In order to work out the reasons for Matthew Maguire's kidnapping, I would have to learn more about the precarious political situation in Nigeria. As had been the case in the Gulf of Aden, in order to understand what was occurring on the water, I would need to gain a better grasp of what was happening on land.

The kidnapping of Matthew Maguire and Robin Barry Hughes was by no means a one-off. Until recently Nigeria was the world's eighth-biggest oil producer. Where there's oil, there are oil companies – huge multinational corporations who import workers with the expertise necessary to pump black gold from deep under the earth from around the world. In Nigeria there are an estimated 20,000 of them. These oil workers are well paid for their time and professionalism, but their rewards come at a price. Each year more than a hundred are kidnapped by pirates. If I was going to find out why this was happening, I would have to go straight to the centre of the problem. So it was that I boarded a plane for Lagos. It was the first time I had travelled to this part of Africa, and as I took to the skies I was more than a little apprehensive about what it was I would find when I got there.

In 2003 the respected magazine *New Scientist* published a survey which claimed to rank more than 65 countries in order of happiness. I don't know how you can measure happiness but Nigeria, to the surprise of many, came top. The happiest country in the world. Maybe it is. It certainly has the raw materials for happiness: sandy beaches, spectacular tropical forests, magnificent waterfalls and, perhaps most importantly, enough oil to make it one of the richest, most affluent countries on earth. You would think that the inhabitants of such a country would be very happy indeed.

But there's a flip side. Nigeria might be oil rich and beautiful, but it has some of the worst social indicators in the world. One in five children dies before the age of five; 12 million do not get to go to school; there are nearly 2 million Aids orphans; more than half the population lives below the poverty line. Life expectancy at birth is 47. Per capita income is $1,400 – that's not as bad as Somalia, but it isn't far off. Walk almost anywhere in Nigeria and you can guarantee that someone will come up and ask you for 'chop-chop' – money for food. Take a camera out, and someone will approach you, demanding to see your papers and asking for chop-chop. A lot of them are just trying it on, but plenty of Nigerians are genuinely hungry. Far be it for me to say whether these statistics should be a fly in the ointment for the Nigerian people, but I think they might take the smile off *my* face.

The Nigerians themselves have a joke. Jesus looks down from heaven and he says to God, 'Father, look at that country. They have so much. Why did you give them all this: the oil, those natural resources, the fertile soil, the beautiful landscape?' God smiles and winks at Jesus. 'Just wait,' he says, 'until you see what sort of *people* I'm going to give them.'

Perhaps the Nigerians do themselves an injustice. In my

time in their country I met some genuinely friendly, good people. But there's no way of denying that Nigeria has its fair share of rotten apples. Anyone with an email account will have received mail from scam artists claiming to be rich Nigerians, and the famous 419 scam originated in Nigeria. So called because number 419 is the article of the Nigerian criminal code pertaining to fraud, this scam involves a letter or email claiming to be from a Nigerian citizen who knows the whereabouts of a large sum of money – in the bank account of a deposed leader perhaps, or belonging to a terminally ill person with no friends or relatives. A good scammer will make some effort to ensure that the story stands up to scrutiny, so if someone decides to investigate, they don't fall at the first hurdle. The recipient of the letter – or 'investor' – is offered a substantial chunk of that money if they 'assist' the scammer in retrieving this money. If the investor bites, they are sent a load of official-looking documentation; sometimes they are asked to travel all the way to Nigeria. However the scam unfolds, you can bet your bottom dollar that at some point in the proceedings they'll be asked for money – most often to pay a tax or a bribe. And the moment they hand over any money, of course, the scammer disappears.

It might sound like a pretty obvious swindle to you and me, but if a few million such emails are sent out, it only takes a small percentage to fall for it and the exercise is made worthwhile. And worthwhile it certainly is: in Lagos, 419 scammers have proper business premises. They make money doing it. Walk around Lagos and you'll see houses and cars with the number 419 marked on them. That means, don't try to buy this house or this car: someone's already tried to do it and it doesn't really belong to the person pretending to own it.

It would be grossly unfair to paint all Nigerians with this brush, but the point is that corruption is commonplace. Every petty official will ask you for chop-chop; even the police will demand it. This corruption goes all the way up to the highest echelons of the government and, as I would find out, it's a major cause of the piracy that I was here to investigate.

Nigeria is a troubled country with a troubled history. Like so many African states, it has a history of colonization, independence and bloody civil war. The Portuguese were the first Europeans to reach the Nigerian coast, and they named the port of Lagos after the town of the same name in the Algarve. (It means 'lagoon'.) This was in the late fifteenth century, and in the 400 years that followed Nigeria became a hub of the slave trade, with millions of its people being traded, principally to the Americas but also elsewhere round the world.

The British rolled up in the nineteenth century, just after the Napoleonic wars. On 1 January 1901 the whole of Nigeria became a British protectorate, with Britain governing by 'indirect rule' through local leaders. In keeping with Britain's colonial past, the slave trade was, almost unbelievably, not banned in Nigeria until 1936. By the middle of the century, a huge wave of anti-colonial feeling was sweeping over Africa. Nigeria was no exception. Despite the fact that the country was divided into more than 200 separate tribes, there was an increase in nationalistic feeling and demands for independence became frequent. Nigeria finally gained independence in 1960, just two years after the first barrels of Nigerian crude oil left the country destined for the world market.

The first Nigerian administration – a coalition government – managed six years of power before the prime minister, the splendidly named Sir Abubakar Tafawa Balewa, was killed in a coup. There followed many years of political strife, corruption and military coups, some bloodless, others distinctly bloody. There was a three-year civil war during which a million Nigerians were killed. But throughout all this one thing kept Nigeria very firmly on the map and in the minds of major powers around the world.

Oil. Because Nigeria had, and has, a hell of a lot of it.

In the 1970s Nigeria joined OPEC – the Organization of Petroleum Exporting Countries. The densely populated Niger Delta region produced billions of dollars' worth of oil and attracted oil workers from around the world. In 1983 the government expelled over a million foreigners – mostly Ghanaians – on the basis that their visas had expired and they were taking jobs from Nigerians. It was a popular move, but of course it didn't stop people drilling for oil.

In 1991 the capital city of Nigeria was moved from Lagos on the coast to Abuja in the middle of the country. The reasons for moving the capital were numerous: Abuja was deemed to be located in territory neutral to the many tribes and clans of the country; Lagos was overcrowded and sprawling; and Lagos suffered, politically speaking, from its geographical position. It is made up of a number of islands separated by creeks, lagoons and waterways – a complicated, labyrinthine network. The main islands are connected by bridges, but are easy to defend if they're taken over in a coup. There had been so many of these since Nigeria's independence that successive governments, frightened of being deposed in the same way that they themselves had seized power, felt the need to move the capital somewhere a little more secure. Hence Abuja, which I'm told is a fantastic place with expensive buildings and manicured lawns, although you can only live there if you're in the government, the oil business or the service industries.

Truth was, however, it didn't matter how well manicured the lawns of Abuja were; from the point of view of my investigation into pirates, it was of no interest. Lagos, however – the dirty, sprawling, impoverished, busy, dirty lagoon town – was a different matter.

Lagos is the fastest-growing city on the planet. It's certainly the most chaotic I've ever been to. In the 1950s it had a population of about 250,000 people. Today, depending on who you talk to, the population is somewhere between 9 million and 18 million. It may no longer be Nigeria's capital, but it's by far the country's biggest city. Like many expanding cities, it faces certain challenges: unemployment, crime, corruption and pollution to name a few. The poverty that blights Nigeria is at its peak here: many people (though not all) live on a pittance; it has been known for armed criminals to have shoot-outs with the police in the busy streets of the city.

Now, though, it has a new problem to deal with. That problem is piracy.

Lagos is West Africa's principal and busiest port. Seventy-five per cent of all the country's goods arrive there by sea. That means a lot of shipping and, as I'd already seen, where there's lots of ships, there's lots of pirates. It was Lagos, therefore, that would be my first port of call in my attempt to hunt down the dangerous pirates of Nigeria.

Lagos is the busiest, most congested city I've ever seen. Traffic jams – or, as the Nigerians have it, 'go-slows' – sit motionless in the searing heat, the air is thick with humidity and petrol fumes and people swarm around you in their thousands. One guidebook describes it as 'chaos theory made flesh and concrete'. Elevated motorways surround the city, the ever-present go-slows on top, tin shacks underneath. I can't begin to describe how hot it is – sweat pours from your face, your eyes, and your clothes are constantly soaked. The streets are strewn with litter and the people stride around with a swaggering kind of purpose. Lagos has expanded because people come here to make money, and everyone seems to be hustling something. Millions don't succeed: you see poverty on the street corners, but I was also very aware of the divide between the haves and the have-nots. There are some very rich people in Lagos, and an expat community with its oil money and yacht clubs. As I'd seen in other parts of the world, that's never a good mix. Even though there's an expat community, white people still stick out like a sore thumb. Arrive at the port of Lagos and you can be in no doubt that you're in the heart of black Africa.

There was no luxurious accommodation for this Western film crew when we arrived in West Africa. Far from it. Our hotel, run by Christian Lebanese, was to put it mildly not nice. No concierge at the door; instead, there were grim-faced guards armed with the ubiquitous AK-47s. You only have that for one reason: because there are people out there who want to come into your hotel and steal everything you've got. The place was full of brass – prostitutes coming in and out to service the needs of the hotel's fluid population. Despite all this, there were plenty of Western faces around. Nigeria might be a tense place, but the prospect of a quick buck was enough to embolden people. A lot of these people get robbed, particularly to and from the airport and particularly if they're not with the right people (it's very rare that you see an *oyibo* – a white man – in a car by himself). But still they come.

I was doing my opening piece to camera when we came up against the difficulties of getting things done in Nigeria. I walked towards the place I'd left Will the cameraman and Kiff the sound man, unable to see them through the crowd of locals. Like all white people, we stood out, but we stood out more than most because Kiff had lost his right arm in an accident – instead of a hand he had metal pincers. Suddenly I realized the guys weren't there. I looked around. Nothing but a sea of black faces, so I used my mobile phone to call Will.

'Will, where are you?'

He almost managed to sound sheepish. 'We've been arrested,' he said.

'Arrested? Who by?'

'The port authority. For filming without permission.'

I couldn't believe what I was hearing – Will hadn't even been pointing his camera at the port. It seems that didn't matter. Day one of shooting and our camera crew had been nicked. It took ages to sort everything out, and in the end we only managed to do so by a pretty unconventional method. The guy who ran the port authority split his time between the UK and Lagos. As a result, it turned out that he was a fan. In return for a photograph with me that he could put on the Internet and a little bit of a bung, he agreed to help release Will and Kiff and give us permission to film in the port. Chop-chop, snap snap, job done. The boss man was happy and we had what we wanted, but I couldn't help wondering what would have happened if our soap opera-loving official *hadn't* recognized my face . . .

My first meeting in Nigeria was with Duncan Macnicol, a former ship's captain who now works as a shipping agent across West Africa, helping shipping operators navigate their way through the mountains of red tape, inefficiency and corruption that go with trying to get a vessel into the port of Lagos. He had lived and worked in Lagos for nearly 20 years and had promised to show me some footage of a very recent pirate attack. The captain of the targeted vessel had taken the footage from the bridge wing. It was grainy and unprofessional, but that didn't matter: you could easily make out what was going on. The pirates were using what had once been a lifeboat from a ship. I watched as the boat approached from the starboard side of the vessel. It circled round as the pirates fired heavy-calibre and automatic weapons towards the ship. You could see the flashes from the guns and hear the crack as the ammo slammed against its target. It was a violent display, full of intent and, I suppose, bravado. They clearly meant business, and you wouldn't want to be at the receiving end of an attack like that.

Duncan explained to me that piracy was on the increase in Nigeria, and the reason for this was two-fold. First, there was what was known as the Niger Delta problem. This is a political dispute which has led, among other things, to pirates attacking oil tankers in the Delta region. Second, he explained, there are so many merchant vessels lying offshore at Lagos that they are sitting ducks, easy targets for anyone of a piratical bent to hit and make a quick buck. It was the Niger Delta problem that would become the focus of my investigation into piracy in Nigeria. But before I followed that lead Duncan offered to take me out into Lagos harbour, just so I could see what he meant when he described the merchant ships out there as sitting ducks.

8. The Victims

Go-slows aren't limited to the roads of Lagos. Its port plays host to them too. The vessels might not be crunched up against each other in the same way the cars are; there may not be the shouting and the frenzy. But make no mistake about it: trying to unload your goods in Lagos means joining the mother of all traffic jams.

Extraordinary bureaucracy and a crumbling and corrupt infrastructure mean that nothing can happen at anything other than a creeping pace. To get a ship into the port of Rotterdam, which is the largest in Europe, takes something of the order of three pieces of paper. Unless anything unusual happens, you're in and out. To get a ship into Lagos harbour takes more like 70. There are layers and layers of needless bureaucracy and corruption which line the pockets of those administering the backhanders and the chop-chop and which make unloading goods a painfully slow – and potentially dangerous – occupation. At any one time there will be up to 100 ships waiting offshore to ditch their cargos. The area in which they wait is known as the quarantine anchorage, and it was around this area that I travelled with Duncan in a small boat dwarfed by the huge vessels that were laid up here.

Immobile. Valuable. Huge chunks of metal dotted around in the ocean, some of them impressive, others barely seaworthy. Ships can remain in the quarantine anchorage for many weeks. I couldn't help notice three ladies climbing the ladder of a ship. Duncan told me they were local prostitutes that did the rounds of the merchant vessels to service the needs of homesick sailors. Supply and demand . . .

I couldn't count how many ships there were, but it was absolutely clear to me that Duncan was right. The vessels I had seen in the Gulf of Aden had at least been able to perform evasive manoeuvres, could pump jets of water at attackers and had warships such as HMS *Northumberland* to patrol the waters – and still they got pirated with relative ease. These vessels had none of this. They *were* sitting ducks, clearly vulnerable to being pirated at any moment. Indeed, just four days previously, a chemical tanker had been boarded by pirates, who had beaten up the crew, stolen their money and ripped out the radio communications system, presumably so that their victims could not raise the alarm until the pirates were safely away.

We floated around the base of a vessel called the *Princess Alice*, registered in Panama. It was a long way from home, and as Duncan explained was particularly vulnerable by virtue of its fairly low freeboard. It wouldn't be too taxing to put a ladder up the side, or use a grappling hook to board the vessel. My guide explained that most attacks happen at night, the pirates using the cover of darkness to approach the ships unseen and go about their business. The smaller ships were easier to hit, he told me, because they wouldn't necessarily have 24-hour watches, and some of the bigger ships took the precaution of waiting much further out to sea, some of them not even anchored so that they could drift up and down and make it just a little bit more difficult for the pirates.

As we continued to tour the quarantine anchorage, people looked down on us from the decks of their ships. They could see the cameras we had trained on them, and I could tell that many of them were extremely edgy about that. They didn't like being filmed. They didn't like anyone taking an interest in them. I couldn't say why, but equally I couldn't help reminding myself that transporting goods by sea is a line of business that offers more opportunity for criminality than almost any other. Just because some of these ships were vulnerable to pirate attacks, that didn't mean they were entirely on the straight and narrow themselves.

I asked Duncan why it was that Nigeria imported so much. Why didn't it have any kind of manufacturing industry? He explained that it was all down to oil. When the country discovered that it was oil rich, it also discovered that it was easier to earn money from that industry than any other. 'They let the farms go,' he told me. 'They let the plantations go. In the end the Nigerians *had* to import all these goods because they couldn't produce them themselves, and they had the money to do it.' And yet, if the country was so rich, why were its people so poor? It was an important question, and one that I would have answered for me over the next few days.

As part of Duncan's guided tour of Lagos, he took us to a yacht club situated on a nearby peninsula. Drinks at the club. It sounded glamorous, but in fact the building looked like it had been built in the 1970s and was now cracking up. It felt more like an old comprehensive school than a glamorous hangout for the beautiful people. The yacht club is by a stretch of water where a river joins the ocean. You can see the brown water and the blue water mixing with each other, and they cause a wave where they meet. As the roads are so congested in Lagos, people also use boats to get around, navigating the lagoons and waterways as a means of getting from A to B. As we sat outside with our very welcome cold drinks looking out over the bustle of the water, we noticed one particular boat. It had the appearance of an old lifeboat with an outboard motor but was in fact a taxi, ferrying people round the waterways of Lagos. There must have been about 15 passengers, all of them heavily laden down with bags and belongings.

We watched it from a distance. And then, as it approached us and the fast current where the river and ocean met, it suddenly flipped over.

The boat was sinking; a lot of the passengers were struggling. The reaction from the locals was immediate and impressive. Men jumped into the water from surrounding boats and rescued all the people. A crowd of kids also jumped in. Some of them dived underneath the boat, pushing it back up; others started bailing out water quicker than it could leak into the hull so that finally it rose, phoenix-like, and righted itself. Some people then tinkered around with the engine – everything was working as it should – so the passengers got back into their taxi and off it went.

That little incident seemed to me to say a lot about Africa. If it had happened on the Thames, it would be front-page news for a week. In Nigeria they just get on with it. Far worse things happen in that part of the world, so they don't have the inclination to hang about wringing their hands. I was also struck by how ready everybody was to help out. Nigeria certainly has a criminal underbelly, but while I was there I also saw such moments of selfless kindness that put the Nigerian people in an altogether better light. In Afghanistan I had observed how the Afghan people were brilliant at recycling and reusing things; the same was true of Nigeria. Everyone talks about how bad the Third World is at recycling – and as I was soon to find out, Nigeria had more than its fair share of environmental problems. But the truth is that in poor places nobody *wants* to throw anything away if it can be fixed and has some use. There was no way anyone was going to let that boat sink. It would be patched up, put to work and no doubt earn a living for its owner for a good few years to come. I think our disposable society could learn a lot from that.

It is not just merchant shipping that is under threat from piracy. Unlike the pirates of Somalia, Nigerian pirates don't just go for big game; they hit the tiddlers too. Lagos has – or at least it had – a large deep-sea fishing fleet, but as I explored the main fishing port I saw that a large number of the trawlers had been tied up and left to rust. The world was in the middle of an economic downturn at the time, but this wasn't an economic problem. It was a criminal one. Over the last few years pirate attacks on fishermen in these waters had increased three-fold. Many of these attacks go unreported, and as they don't have much in the way of wider ramifications for the international community, the world's press has pretty well ignored the issue. One report, though, tells of an attack in which the pirates boarded a ship at 1.30 a.m., shot the ship's cook through the belly and then proceeded to eat the food that he had prepared earlier while he lay dying in agony, before looting the ship of all the money and goods they could find, including the captain's shoes. (I told you shoes were important in poor parts of the world.) The captain went on record as saying, 'There were attacks before, but it's the worst now. Formerly we had hijackings and they would steal everything, but now they attack and they are shooting and taking lives.'

The statistics show this to be true: over the past four years, 298 fisherman had lost their lives to pirates. That's more than one a week.

In response to the problem, the Nigerian Trawler Owners' Association recalled all its ships into port and led a series of demonstrations to raise awareness – in 2008 they even blockaded Lagos itself. 'The pirates have established a republic in a republic,' they announced. 'They have their own commander in chief. You have to pay to be allowed to fish. You will be given their flag before you are allowed to fish. They are a country of their own.'

The threat from pirates was so immediate and acute that we could find nobody willing to talk to us on the record about it. One man, though, agreed to be interviewed on the strict proviso that we didn't reveal his identity. He ran a fleet of 69 vessels operating out of the port of Lagos – shrimping boats, there to take advantage of the fact that the waters around Nigeria supply some of the best and most abundant shellfish in the world. His business, and the livelihoods of the men he employed, was being crippled by the effects of these attacks.

I asked him how often his 69 vessels came into contact with pirates.

'It's more or less a daily affair,' he told me.

So when was the last time one of his vessels was attacked?

'This week I've had twelve.'

Sounded more than daily to me. I wondered what had happened to the crews of these trawlers.

'They've beaten them up. I've had four or five of them hospitalized. You see, the people come on board with guns, or they come shooting. Whether they do anything to you or not, *they* are traumatized and *I* am traumatized.' Having been shot at a few times myself, I could well believe it. 'I am scared to send off my vessels,' he continued. 'I normally don't have so many vessels in port.'

It was true. His trawlers were lined up in the water, neat and useless. Elsewhere in the port I had seen a substantial number of vessels in a state of run-down disrepair, now just rusting hulls. Some of them had been left to rot in the saltwater; others had been plundered for scrap and spare parts. It was clear that no one was ever going to move these boats from the port of Lagos. They'd just be left to sink into the harbour. I couldn't help wondering if, thanks to the attention of the pirates, this was the fate that awaited my interviewee's fleet.

I wanted to know if he thought the pirates attacking his ship were just opportunist criminals, or if they were a bit more organized than that. He shook his head. 'They come in boats with bulletproof vests.'

Body armour?

'Yeah, body armour. They've got enough fuel supply to remain 40 miles offshore.'

That sounded to me like a gang that knew what it was doing.

'No place is safe,' the trawler owner told me. He explained that when a trawler is travelling with its nets down, it moves very slowly – around two and a half knots – and its freeboard is only about eight feet high. 'You're a sitting duck.'

It wasn't the first time I'd heard that phrase used in Lagos, and I was beginning to understand just what a problem piracy was in this town.

I'd heard a lot *about* pirates, but I was still no closer to speaking to one. Trouble was, I wasn't the only person who wanted to catch up with these people – who, for good reasons, didn't want to be caught up with. Even more problematically, they have a very good place to hide. The maze of waterways that surrounds Lagos is the perfect environment for them. It's huge, complicated and nigh-on impossible to police. Finding pirates among the labyrinth of backwaters and miles of open ocean was not an easy task for the authorities, and it wasn't going to be an easy task for us.

We hadn't yet got an in with a pirate, but we had received word that one of their victims was willing to talk to us. His name was Billy Graham (no relation), an American who had been in the oil business since 1991. He made his living working for a company that supplied machinery to oil platforms off the Nigerian coast. During the working week he and his colleagues lived in a gated community near the port. Not luxurious exactly, but a far cry from the pronounced poverty that exists literally just over the wall. In their downtime, however, they travelled up to a beach residence, where they could chill out away from the bustle and the dirt of Lagos.

It was a hot, uncomfortable journey of about four hours up into the network of channels behind Lagos. As we travelled, I noticed a lot of what are known as sand barges. These are long, thin boats, very low in the water. Men dive from these boats with an empty bucket, down to the bottom, where they fill their bucket with sand and bring it back to the surface. There's a global demand for sand, and it has to be collected somehow. These men are out there from dawn till dusk. That's what I call a tough way to make a living. If I ever find myself moaning about my day, I think of the sand barges of Nigeria and it puts things in perspective.

Our destination was a white enclave with a number of weekend residences of the type used by Billy and his mates. There were a bunch of black kids looking after the boats by the side of the lagoon where we moored, and a few of the locals earned a scant living fetching and carrying for the white men, but apart from these, black faces were very scarce. Billy's beachside hangout was a pretty basic place – there were no proper bedrooms and only the most basic facilities. But for a couple of days of beach, beer and barbecues – which is what the expat workers come here for – it was fine.

Billy Graham was a traumatized man. When we turned up I got the distinct feeling that he had furnished himself with a little Dutch courage, but perhaps, in the circumstances, that was to be expected. I was going to ask him to recount an event that he would no doubt rather forget. If he had hit the bottle before our arrival, I couldn't entirely blame him. Eighteen months ago Billy had been kidnapped. His abductors had stuck him on a boat, taken him to a hiding place and held him for 26 days. He went without food for ten days, and during this time they forced him to dig his own grave and made him lie down in it. The pirates who took him were young – 'fresh out of secondary school,' he told me in his southern drawl – and he claimed to have known every one of them before the kidnapping.

Billy might have been traumatized by what had happened to him, but what struck me was that he was unwilling to blame his captors fully for what they had done. 'I was a victim of it,' he told me, 'and *they* were a victim of it. Nigeria is a place with great potential. Look around you.'

I did so. I saw sandy beaches and palm trees. The sun sparkled on the lapping water. Half close your eyes and you might be looking at a holiday brochure. 'It's fantastic,' I told him.

'Well,' Billy continued, '*we* get to live this way. The rest of the country does not.'

What Billy was telling me was the time-honoured tale of the haves and the have-nots. He believed that the terrifying experience he had undergone was a direct result of the differences between the rich foreigners in Nigeria and the indigenous poor. My next trip would take me to a place that threw these differences into even sharper relief. A place that I know I will not forget for as long as I live.

The residents of Ajegunle call it the Jungle. It's a bit of a misnomer. Jungles are green and fertile. Stuff grows there. You'd be hard pressed to find anything that grows in this desperate place.

Ajegunle is Lagos's biggest waterside slum. It's difficult to say how many people live there – like the rest of Lagos, the population is fluid and expanding. Estimates vary. What-ever the true figure, one thing's for sure – it's too many.

To get to Ajegunle from our hotel we had to drive through the perpetual Lagos traffic. Once we had freed ourselves from that snarling logjam, we drove through some suburbs that weren't, by Nigerian standards, too bad. I remember passing a school not far from our destination that wouldn't have looked out of place in a less impoverished part of the world, with big bright paintings of animals on the walls. But with a population so large, I knew it was only a privileged few that received the advantage of any kind of education. We stopped our car at the end of a long thin alleyway – perhaps half the length of a football pitch – and as we unloaded our vehicle we started attracting the usual attention. Locals approached us, intrigued by the camera gear and offering to carry it. In Africa, it's easy to assume that when this happens they mean to rob you, but that would be a lazy assumption. These people were poor, and like so many others they wanted chop-chop – a small tip for services rendered.

We walked down the alleyway. There was litter on the ground, but nothing out of the ordinary for Lagos. The further I walked, though, the more I could tell that there was something round the corner. Something unpleasant. A sudden stench filled the air – the sort of stench that makes you screw up your face, and which grew stronger and stronger the further we walked down that alleyway.

And then we saw it.

Ajegunle is hell on earth, its principal waterway like the River Styx. I half imagined the Devil cruising by in his speedboat, nodding proudly at a job well done. A couple of years previously, when I had travelled to Kenya to try and meet members of the Mongiki clan, I had visited Dandora, the biggest, most toxic rubbish tip in Africa. Ajegunle was like Dandora by the sea. The slum is so polluted that you can't see the riverbank for the rubbish that is piled up by the side of the water. To get to the main drag of the slum, we had to cross the river in one of the crowded punts that ferried the inhabitants back and forth. The water that carried us was thick with debris – plastic bottles, food wrappers, all manner of day-to-day waste that you or I would put in the bin, ready for the tip. But there are no bins in Ajegunle. It *is* the tip and this rubbish covers every spare space.

A large proportion of the population of the slum originates from the interior. In the Nigerian countryside most of what the people consume comes from the ground. It doesn't matter if they throw it away because it biodegrades. But in Ajegunle it's different. Like in most cities, food comes in plastic wrappers, in cartons and tins – stuff that won't biodegrade in a thousand years, that will stay precisely where you chuck it. While I was in the slums, I heard it said that the pollution was in large part down to the Western soft-drinks factory just a couple of miles up the road. Maybe that's true, but this wasn't just packaging. This was everything – the accumulated detritus of an overpopulated hellhole.

There were other kinds of waste here too. There is no proper drainage in Ajegunle, or sewers. The people who live in the Jungle defecate in the street. They don't clear it up because there's nowhere to put it, and because to clean up one turd out of millions would be a drop in the malodorous ocean. When it rains, what drains there are overflow and yet more raw sewage is coughed up onto the streets. As I wandered around Ajegunle that day I saw a sign advertising a 'Top Class Toilet', open to anyone willing to pay the few *kobo* it cost. These exclusive facilities, though, consisted simply of a toilet seat opening out onto the water below. You might get somewhere to park your behind, but you still have to shit into the river.

There are, strangely, a few semi-decent houses in this slum, raised above the water on stilts. They still look out on to the pollution, however, and in any case they are far outnumbered by run-down shanties cobbled together from sheets of corrugated iron, where families live, 12 to a room, in subhuman conditions. The electricity supply is erratic and unpredictable; open a window from one of these squalid dwellings and more than likely you look out into a gutter crammed with human waste and clouds of mosquitoes. And yet the people who live in Ajegunle are fiercely proud of their city. Some of Nigeria's biggest music stars come from here, and though it appeared hellish to me, the slum grows by the day. They're coming to Ajegunle in droves, and it's hard, from our comfortable Western perspective, to understand why.

It wasn't the first time my camera team and I had been the only white men in a slum, and you never quite get used to it. You do, however, learn certain techniques, and for me the only way of dealing with the inevitable attention is to plough on through the streets no matter what. As I set foot in Ajegunle, that's exactly what I did. It didn't stop me being a magnet for the inhabitants pushing their wares: it might have been early in the morning, but I hadn't gone more than 20 metres before I was offered palm wine by two men and sex by three girls. Could have been a very eventful morning, and it was an immediate reminder that street crime and prostitution were rife here.

We immediately attracted attention from other sources too. I'd barely set foot in Ajegunle before seven or eight big burly young men started following us and shouting, 'What you doing here? What you doing, *oyibo*? *Oyibo*, go! You have no right to be here! *You go!*' They were screaming, excitable and aggressive, crowding round us as we stepped through the rubbish-strewn slum. I barged through, away from our unwanted companions, but they managed to stop Will the cameraman and they weren't going to let him go any further, so we had to tell them what we were doing.

Our Nigerian fixer had arranged for us to meet a man who had been described to us as the chief of Ajegunle. He had lived in the slum for many years, and we had been told he had agreed to give us a tour of the area and explain to us some of the effects piracy had had on his community.

'We're going to see the chief,' I told them, naively thinking that this might buy our passage.

'What chief?' they shouted. 'Who chief?'

Will and I looked at each other with a bit of a sinking feeling. They seemed slightly less impressed than we thought they would be. What we didn't know was that, in true Nigerian style, there were about 15 different chiefs in Ajegunle, all self-appointed and all, as far as I could tell, vying with each other for whatever tenuous authority they had. Too many chiefs, you might say, and not enough Indians . . .

We told them the name of our man and they sucked their teeth, unimpressed. They stepped back, but it was obvious this was just a temporary reprieve for us. There was nothing else for the team and me to do other than press on into the slum – I had the distinct feeling that we wouldn't be allowed to turn back in any case – so we did exactly that. We couldn't shake our trail and before long we had a massive crowd following us, like a meteor with its long tail.

It was only 8.30 in the morning but already the sweat was pouring off me. We hadn't brought any water with us and I could feel myself dehydrating, but stopping for a leisurely drink was off the menu. It was clear as we went that nobody particularly wanted to be filmed. I had the impression that they were proud of where they lived and didn't want a white man to come there and look down on them. That wasn't what we were there to do of course, but I guess they weren't to know that. As our tail got bigger, however, it became increasingly clear what our new companions wanted. Chop-chop. They sniffed money.

We walked and we walked, the stench filling our noses, our shoes covered in shit. Eventually we came to the place where our fixer had told us we could meet our chief. It was hardly grand – a room on a platform on stilts overlooking the filthy water, the squalor and the degradation. There was a second room alongside it, also on stilts, and it was possible, if you were of a mind to risk falling into the filthy water, to jump between the two. By now we must have attracted a tail of between 150 and 200 people, all of them looking at us like we were a meal ticket. By that time all I wanted to do was get the hell out of Ajegunle. The mood was getting ugly. You could forget about interviews and pirates and TV shows – we had images of being mugged, or thrown into the shitty water, or worse. All we wanted to do was get away, but it was clear by now that the locals weren't going to let that happen. Not easily.

We crowded around the edge of one of the platforms. Inside the room all the local chiefs had congregated, along with their advisers and their heavies. We were not invited inside as they argued among themselves, clearly working out exactly how much money they could rip us off for, and who should get what slice. On the other platform our followers thronged. You could see the stilts starting to sway and bend, and if too many people moved to one side, the whole platform would tilt precariously. Kids jumped from one platform to the other. I could envisage either one collapsing into the water at any moment, and I really didn't feel like a swim.

The chiefs carried on bickering. One of them was particularly lairy, and he looked like a cross between Oliver Hardy and Robert Mugabe. He was more despot than funny man, though, and he kept approaching us, telling us that *he* was the real boss and shouting that we didn't have permission to film here. He threatened to confiscate our equipment, and only backed down thanks to our fixer's attempts to smooth things over. Inside, the 'negotiations' continued, each of the chiefs saying their piece as we waited nervously outside, wishing that we were almost anywhere but there.

It was a riot of aggression and confusion, and to be honest none of us really knew what was going on. Eventually, though, they arrived at some sort of consensus and we were allowed access to *our* chief, an elderly man in traditional African garb, more quietly spoken than the others. It was clear, though, that the other chiefs were not fully satisfied with the outcome. I could tell that there was a good deal more aggro to come from them . . .

In the past, the people of Ajegunle had earned their living from fishing. The chief himself had fished the river for oysters and crayfish just 15 years ago. He took us out on a boat that chugged slowly through the polluted waters. Nothing could live here now, not in this soupy miasma of pollution. The chief echoed my very thoughts. 'There is no life in this water any more,' he said passionately. In order to find water clean enough for fish, you had to travel 20 miles out of Ajegunle. A big deal in a place whose main industry once relied on the health of the water.

As I had already learned, however, taking a boat out to sea off the Nigerian coast carried with it certain risks. The chief explained to me that many people were too scared to leave the filthy waterways of Ajegunle because of the piracy threat. 'They carry weapons,' the chief told me of the pirates. 'Sophisticated ones. They carry weapons that even our soldiers, our navy are not having in their possession.'

I wanted to know if the chief could shed any light on where these pirates were coming from. 'They migrate from anywhere,' he told me. 'Not from this community. They use masks to cover their faces. You cannot identify them.' He explained to me that if the pirates came across a fisherman, they would steal what little money he had on him. If there was no money, they would steal the fisherman's engine and net, then leave him to drift. 'Many are dying,' he told me. 'Many are wounded.'

Our chief spoke with real passion, and I didn't doubt that what he was saying was the truth. I wasn't entirely sure I believed his assertion, though, that none of the pirates came from Ajegunle. To rob a poor fisherman smacks of desperation, and I sensed that desperation was in plentiful supply in this slum.

I couldn't tell for sure if the pirates originated from places like Ajegunle or not, but I suspected that they did.

What was clear, however, was that they were having a devastating effect on an already devastated community. The people of Ajegunle were impoverished; their principal means of making a living had been taken from them on account of the astonishing levels of pollution; and now, if they tried to travel further afield to fish, they came up against the violent criminality of the pirates. It looked to me like a vicious circle, and there didn't seem to be any way out.

I couldn't wait to leave Ajegunle, but that wasn't possible. Not yet. We were still the focus of everyone's attention, and before we could get away from that godforsaken place we were told that we had to go and 'pay our respects' to the Oliver Hardy lookalike who claimed to be such an important man. Of course, we all understood what the phrase 'pay our respects' really meant. Ollie wanted chop-chop; otherwise we weren't getting out of there. It was about half past five when we arrived at his house, followed, of course, by the ever-present crowd of people. For such an important chief, it was a humble abode, although there was a whole row of people lined up outside – but Ollie was nowhere to be seen. It turned out that he was inside, having a kip – he'd hit the palm wine earlier that afternoon, got absolutely sozzled and was now sleeping it off.

When he finally made his appearance he certainly looked the worse for wear. He slurred his words, which didn't make it at all easy for us to understand him as his English was heavily accented anyway. As he demanded once more who we were and why we were here, he was a pretty comical figure. Under other circumstances we might have just laughed at him, or simply walked away, but that wasn't possible here. He might have been ridiculous, but we were surrounded by people who seemed to take him seriously. We weren't getting out of there until Ollie gave us the thumbs up, and for that to happen we needed to do some fast talking.

I stepped forward. The chief and his stooges fell quiet. And then, in a voice that made me sound like something between Captain Cook and General Custer, I spoke. 'We have come from far away,' I said.

Behind me, I could sense the guys suppressing their giggles.

'We have travelled many miles across Africa to search for pirates,' I improvised. 'To the Sudan.' (No, I don't know where that came from either – as the crew took great pleasure in pointing out to me later, Sudan is landlocked.) 'And now here.' I waffled on for a couple of minutes with my grandiose, over-the-top speech. And when I had finished there was a heavy silence.

I looked at the chief.

The chief looked at me.

And then he spoke.

'What?' he said. 'I am not understanding you.'

I blinked. And then, because he hadn't appeared to understand a word I'd said, I repeated the whole thing again.

My piece finished, the chief demanded to see the identity cards that we had been issued by the Nigerian government. He made a great show of scrutinizing these documents, looking us up and down as if we were obviously presenting him with forgeries, before revealing that he used to work as a passport control officer at the airport. So much for being the big chief of Ajegunle. Once he had satisfied himself that we were who we said we were, he started on a speech of his own. A long speech, telling us what an important man he was and how well he looked after his people. We listened politely, and were relieved when he finally finished. But then, to our dismay, one of his stooges took the floor. Another speech. More polite listening. Then a third. Then a fourth . . .

By this time we couldn't take any more. I stood up, announced that we'd really got the message, then nodded to our fixer. The time had come to cut to the chase. It was obvious that the only thing that was going to bring about our passage out of Ajegunle was hard cash, and so the fixer handed over a fistful of notes. It wasn't much in our terms – maybe about 50 quid – but I suppose to them it was a reasonable amount of chop-chop.

The deal was done. Our hosts' penchant for public speaking seemed suddenly to disappear. We took our leave, hit the streets and got the hell out of there. I'm no eco-warrior, but I've seen some dreadful things that man has done, and Ajegunle definitely makes the top ten.

9. The Juju Men

There are two kinds of piracy in Nigeria.

The first is purely criminal. It might be driven by the fact that the people are poor, but it is essentially armed robbery on water. The looting of boats in the quarantine zone of Lagos, the problems that prevented the fishermen of Ajegunle from casting their nets further afield: these were down to attacks from pirates who had a purely criminal motivation.

But there is another side to Nigerian piracy – a political side, carried out by insurgent groups in the Niger Delta. It is an irony that one of Nigeria's biggest problems is a direct result of one of its greatest assets. Oil.

I'd seen for myself in Ajegunle that while Nigeria might be oil rich, its people are some of the poorest in the world. But that only tells half the story. Standard Bank – one of Africa's largest financial institutions – estimates that over the past 37 years Nigeria has earned $1.19 trillion in oil revenue. That's 1.9 million million bucks. Nigeria's current yearly revenue from oil is around $40 billion. On the flip side of the coin, in the 30 years between 1970 and 2000 the number of Nigerians living on less than a dollar a day increased almost five-fold from 19 million to 90 million. The average income is less than that of Senegal, but Senegal doesn't export oil – it exports fish and nuts.

Forty billion dollars a year revenue; 90 million people on

less than a dollar a day. You don't need a PhD in advanced mathematics to work out that something's happening to the dosh.

Nigeria is one of the most corrupt countries in the world. According to the Economic and Financial Crimes Commission – Nigeria's anti-corruption agency – around 70 per cent of all oil revenue is stolen or wasted. It is thought that 85 per cent of all the money made from Nigeria's oil ends up in the pockets of 1 per cent of the population. Nigeria might be a place with huge natural resources, but it's also a place where the divide between very rich and impossibly poor is massive. A study in 2003 determined the top five most corrupt public institutions in Nigeria. The list goes like this: the police, political parties, national and state assemblies, local/municipal government, federal/state executive councils. It's a list that doesn't really leave much hope for the ordinary man or woman in the street.

The Niger Delta is the main oil-producing region of Nigeria. In 2008 it produced, on average, $2.2 billion of oil every month. The federal government is officially supposed to distribute about half of the country's oil wealth among the state governors, but because of the level of corruption, this money simply does not trickle down to the people. According to a report by Human Rights Watch in 2006, the government of Rivers State was awarded an annual budget of $1.3 billion. Out of this, the state apportioned: $65,000 a *day* for 'transportation fees' for the governor's office, $10 million for catering, entertainment, gifts and souvenirs, and $38 million for two helicopters. Health services in the same period received just $22 million.

As a result, the Niger Delta suffers terrible poverty even

by Nigerian standards. Less than a quarter of its inhabitants have access to clean water and very few villages have anything like what you and I would consider to be the most basic of amenities. The oil wealth that could have been spent on health and education for the millions of impoverished citizens of the Delta has been embezzled by the various layers of political corruption. Some of the money has even ended up in the UK. In 2007 a British court froze the assets of the former governor of Delta State, James Ibori. The frozen assets were said to amount to $35 million. While he was in office Ibori's official salary was $25,000. So either he'd been saving up for 1,400 years or he had other interests.

Extreme poverty is not the only consequence of the oil industry in the Niger Delta. It has also led to a shocking level of environmental pollution. Each year about 300 individual oil spills are reported, but the World Bank estimates that the true number could be ten times that. In 2008 reported oil spills amounted to 10,000 barrels, but individual spills can be bigger even that that – in 1998 one leak released 800,000 barrels. The effect this has on the environment is devastating. People living among the oilfields are constantly breathing in methane gas; a minor leak can destroy a year's worth of food for an entire community. Oil-infected waters have destroyed the fish population and have had a devastating effect on the mangrove forests of the Delta, with dreadful consequences for wildlife and humans alike.

The more I learned about the Niger Delta, the more I realized that while Nigeria's natural resources were highly profitable for a privileged few, and of course constantly propped up by our own oil addiction, the consequences of the oil industry were very bad news for the ordinary people of Nigeria. It was in the late 1980s that the dissatisfaction with their lot felt by so many of them turned itself into a series of insurgent groups.

The first of these groups to receive widespread attention was the Movement for the Survival of the Ogoni People (MOSOP). The Ogoni are a small indigenous group of around half a million, and their homeland – which they call Ogoniland – is located in the Niger Delta's Rivers State east of the capital city of Port Harcourt. They suffered more than most when the oil workers moved into their land. In 1990 MOSOP, led by the Nigerian environmental activist Ken Saro-Wiwa, started a non-violent campaign against the government and the oil producers. MOSOP drew up an Ogoni Bill of Rights which demanded a fair share of oil revenues and a reversal of the environmental damage that had already been caused.

In 1993 MOSOP organized peaceful marches by almost half of the Ogoni population, designed to bring the situation to the attention of the international community. Soon afterwards the Nigerian government embarked upon a military occupation of the area. The following year Ken Saro-Wiwa was arrested on bogus charges. He and eight other members of MOSOP were tried in what was widely agreed to be a kangaroo court. They were found guilty and sentenced to death by hanging. On 10 November 1995 the non-violent campaigner and his eight colleagues were executed.

MOSOP continued despite their leader's death, but the Niger Delta problem gave rise to several other groups, more militant than Ken Saro-Wiwa's organization. These included the Niger Delta People's Volunteer Force, led by Alhaji Dokubo-Asari. The NDPVF threatened 'all-out war' against the government. President Obasanjo offered Asari amnesty and money in return for the NDPVF's weapons, but soon reneged on the deal. Asari was arrested and remains in prison.

The latest, and largest, of these groups is MEND – the Movement for the Emancipation of the Niger Delta. They first came to widespread public attention in January 2006 when they kidnapped four foreign oil workers. Since then they have mounted sustained attacks on oil pipelines in the Delta, their stated aim being to reduce the country's oil production to the barest minimum. They have also continued their policy of pirating foreign ships and kidnapping foreign oil workers – 'white gold' as they're referred to in the Delta. In 2006 they kidnapped 80 foreigners. Between January and July 2007 they took more than 150. In 2007 the kidnap and ransom response company ASI Global rated Nigeria as being second only to Iraq in terms of kidnap threat; in the same year, foreign oil companies removed all non-essential personnel from the region.

MEND's job is made a good deal easier by the geography of the Delta – the network of mangrove swamps, creeks and channels that make it such a good place to hide. If you have a boat, you can move around the Delta virtually unseen; and of course you can take your hostages with you. It's pirate heaven. Or hell, depending on your point of view.

MEND's attacks on oil installations and their kidnapping campaign have had a direct result on the Niger Delta's oil output, reducing it by about a third. The organization has three main demands: the release of Alhaji Dokubo-Asari from prison, the receipt of 50 per cent of the oil revenue of the Niger Delta and the withdrawal of government troops from the region. Unlike Ken Saro-Wiwa's MOSOP, MEND positions itself decidedly at the violent end of the scale, warning the oil industry of its intentions in the following terms: 'It must be clear that the Nigerian government cannot protect your workers or assets. Leave our land while you can, or die in it . . . Our aim is to totally destroy the capacity of the Nigerian government to export oil.'

And they mean it. Their attacks have become increasingly bold. I was told by one trawler owner I met in Nigeria, who wanted to remain anonymous, that some vessels in the Bight of Benin fly special flags to indicate that they have paid MEND off in order to reduce their chance of being pirated. But the militant pirates don't only attack boats. In June 2008 MEND attack vessels hit the Bonga oil platform. This platform can extract up to 200,000 barrels of oil per day, but because it lies 75 miles from the coast it was generally believed to be out of the militants' range. That one attack shut down 10 per cent of Nigeria's oil production. The Nigerian government has attempted to downplay the organization's significance since MEND first appeared by saying that it's just a criminal gang and has tried to quash it by military force. To this end, they have established the Joint Task Force – a combined force taken from the navy, the army and the police – specifically to combat crime, militancy and piracy in the Niger Delta. The JTF was dispatched to the Delta under the moniker Operation Restore Hope – ironically the same phrase the United Nations used for their activities in Somalia that ended in the disastrous Battle of

Mogadishu. But if restoring hope truly is the aim of the JTF, it has quite a job on its hands: MEND know the area around the Delta much better than the government forces; they are better equipped and very well armed. (We heard rumours of a ship run by an enterprising arms dealer that sailed in and out of the region, a kind of floating gun super-market. Whether this was true or not, I don't know, but there's certainly no shortage of weapons in that part of Africa.) And in any case, Nigeria being Nigeria, it is said that the JTF troops are far from squeaky clean. They have faced numerous allegations over the murder and rape of hundreds of civilians in areas thought to be militant strong-holds – not exactly the best way of endearing yourself to the local population. The JTF is also unpopular in certain circles because in its struggle against MEND it is seen as protecting the interests of the oil multinationals and not the Nigerian people.

Conversely, the insurgents have the support of a large proportion of the public. Their aims are the aims of the common people: an end to poverty and government corrup-tion. It is possible to buy on the beaches of the Niger Delta wooden models, about a foot long, depicting a boat with a couple of MEND militants – identifiable by a flash of red on their balaclavas – with two blindfolded *oyibos* in the back who have oil-company logos carved on their clothes. And people only sell these kidnapping mementos because there's a market for them among the locals. The Niger Delta, after all, is hardly a tourist hot spot.

It is of course the case, as happens with any such militant organization, that criminal gangs – in Nigeria they call them cults – have tried to get into the act, pirating and kidnapping for financial gain rather than political ends. MEND are savvy enough to distance themselves from such cults. In July 2007 they secured the release of a three-year-old British girl who was being held for ransom in Rivers State; in October 2008 they freed 18 oil workers who had been kidnapped for non-political reasons by people they referred to as 'sea pirates'.

In Lagos the pirates were purely criminal. From our point of view, this meant they had no reason to want to talk to us, no agenda that they wanted to promote. MEND, we thought, would be different. They had a drum to bang. They wanted their cause to gain attention. If we wanted to meet Nigerian pirates, they were our best bet; and if we wanted to contact MEND, we'd have to leave Lagos and travel south into the Delta. It wasn't a journey to be undertaken lightly, and the Nigerian authorities warned us against it. A delicate ceasefire between government forces and MEND had just collapsed, and the insurgents' policy of taking Europeans hostage meant that we would be very much in the firing line. Moreover, none of us had forgotten about Matthew Maguire and Robin Barry Hughes. They had been kidnapped by pirates five months previously and it was MEND who had claimed responsibility. The rumour was that they had specifically targeted British hostages because of a statement Gordon Brown had made in which he indicated his willingness to aid the Nigerian government should their ability to produce oil come under threat. All this meant that our plan to contact the MEND pirates was even more dangerous. But we knew that if we wanted fully to understand piracy in Nigeria, we needed to hear what MEND had to say. We needed to meet them.

So it was that we prepared to make the journey from Lagos to Port Harcourt, the capital of Rivers State, one of the nine states that make up the Niger Delta. We knew that MEND had Matthew Maguire and Robin Barry Hughes; we knew there was a possibility that they would see us as more desirable hostages. It wasn't too fanciful to believe that they would be willing to release Maguire for one of us. So it was that we forced ourselves to decide who, if push came to shove, should be the one to offer themselves up in that extreme scenario. In reality, the decision was already made for us. Everyone else in the crew had children. Everyone except the presenter. In retrospect it was a bit of a romantic notion, but I couldn't say I relished the idea of an enforced stay at the pleasure of the Movement for the Emancipation of the Niger Delta. Still, as we flew to the region that was their centre of operations, I couldn't shake the thought that it was a distinct possibility . . .

For the purposes of our investigations, we like to travel under the radar. Attract too much attention and people get nervous. Camera shy. They certainly start looking at you in a different way if they see you have security. I suppose that goes with the territory of searching out people who don't always want to be found. As we emerged from Port Harcourt International Airport, though, it was immediately clear that keeping a low profile was going to be a bit of an issue.

A team of armed police – uniformed and plain clothes, about 15 in all – was waiting for us; we were driven to our hotel by a police officer and our vehicle was flanked by police vans with wailing sirens. We cut through the thick, noisy, dirty traffic – people just got out of the way, and I would have done too – but it felt as if every man, woman and child knew we had arrived, and they stared at us as we passed through the busy streets. We couldn't have been more obvious if we'd tried. The security had been laid on at the insistence of the Port Harcourt authorities. From a safety point of view it made sense, I guess – every person with white skin in Port Harcourt is assumed to be an oil worker and is therefore a potential kidnapping victim. There are many such kidnappings a year from Port Harcourt and for us to be swiped would have been a high-profile calamity for the Nigerian authorities.

From an investigative point of view, however, it was a disaster. We were told that we couldn't go anywhere or film anything without our security team. They didn't leave us even when we arrived at our hotel. The lobby was crowded. We were later told that it was full of plain-clothes police, undercover government officials and MEND spies. Whether that's true or not I don't know, but I will say this: there were a lot of people hanging around in that lobby reading newspapers and doing not much else, and they didn't look to me like residents. I felt like I was living in a John le Carré novel. Before long, a creeping sense of paranoia started to ooze over us – a paranoia that would be with us for the rest of our stay in the Delta. I've been to some paranoid countries in my travels, places that make you feel uncomfortable for reasons you can't quite articulate. But the Niger Delta takes the cake.

MEND is a shadowy organization. Little is known about its power structure, and if its members want to hide they can easily do so in the Delta. We'd had an indication from people claiming to represent the movement before we arrived in Port Harcourt that they would be willing to meet us. But such people are by their very nature elusive. You don't just walk up to their doorstep and demand an interview. You don't summon them; they summon you. We knew we could be in for a long wait before that happened, so in the meantime we took to the street. I wanted to see the places these Nigerian pirates were known to frequent, and witness for myself some of the problems I had heard so much about.

Port Harcourt was different from Lagos. You feel even less safe walking round the town. The locals were noticeably more hostile towards white faces – you could see it in their aggressive stares. Our police escort didn't help matters because they were obviously even less trusted than the *oyibos*. This was hardly surprising: during my time in that town I saw members of the police force hitting people in the street for no apparent reason; I saw them bashing cars with their AKs. It wasn't exactly *Heartbeat*, and I have to say that when the coppers were out of sight (which didn't happen very often) I felt very, very white and very, very vulnerable. Never more so than when we were on the quayside. Bonny Island, the main terminal for all the crude oil extracted in the region, was just 40 minutes away up the creek. The waterways were filled with small elderly motorboats that ferried the locals up to Bonny Island and to the nearby villages. I didn't fancy taking my chances in one of those, not least because it was on this stretch of water that Matthew Maguire and Robin Barry Hughes had been pirated. I wondered how near or far away from us they were at that very moment, but in the Niger Delta it was impossible to know. Their location would only be known when – and if – MEND *wanted* it to be known.

Our fixer in Port Harcourt was a local independent journalist, a respected and intelligent man. He accompanied us everywhere and gave us the benefit of his knowledge. It was while I was talking to him, however, that I got one of my starkest ever insights into the difference between African culture and our own. We had driven, together with our always-present police escort, along a road that looked down into a nearby slum. This, our fixer told us, was where pirates and militants were known to live. From our vantage point on the high ground we could see that there was a shoot-out happening down below.

We turned to our police guard and asked them if I could go down to the slum and film what was going on. Predictably enough, I suppose, they shook their heads. 'No. You cannot go.'

I begged them. 'We really need to —'

Nothing doing. 'You cannot film this. You cannot go.'

I tried to talk them round. 'This is the whole reason for us being here. If we can't go and film this, what's the point?'

One of the policemen frowned at me. 'They have juju,' he said.

In West Africa, juju is a form of witchcraft. But it's not just something used to scare naughty children into good behaviour. Everyone believes in it. *Everyone*. The policemen told me that the pirates in the region had a special kind of juju that made bullets melt on contact with them. That was why they were so dangerous to approach.

I tried to keep my calm and turned to our fixer. He was a sophisticated man and I expected him to at least share my exasperation. But no. He was slowly nodding his head. 'It's true,' he told me. 'I have seen it. I have seen it with my own eyes.'

'Don't be silly, mate,' I told him. 'I've seen what a 7.62 round can do to someone and it doesn't melt on flesh and bone.'

But he was adamant. 'It does. I have *seen* it. And I will *not* go down there. You will not be able to shoot them and they will walk up to you and cut off your head with a machete.'

'I don't believe you. I want to go down there.'

'I am not going down there. *You* are not going down there. And you are not allowed to film.'

Sometimes you have to accept that you're flogging a dead horse, no matter how frustrating it might be. We weren't going down into the slum; we weren't going to get close to these gun-toting militants. And that was the end of that.

Our armed guards explained that the pirates achieved this magical effect by cutting their skin and putting some kind of leaf into their veins in order to make themselves like ghosts. And as we drove away from that shoot-out and a missed opportunity, I reflected that the fact that bullets patently did *not* melt on the skin of Nigerian pirates was actually immaterial. Our guards and our fixer believed it 100 per cent. They believed in juju in the same way a devout Christian believes in God. In a strange way that steadfast, unquestioning belief *made* it true in that the juju men reaped the benefit whether they were invulnerable to bullets or not. And it wasn't lost on any of us that if even an armed police unit was too scared to approach a shoot-out, the militants involved pretty well had carte blanche to do as they pleased. I might not have believed in juju, but it made the prospect of meeting with the juju men nerve-racking, to say the least . . .

10. A Drop in the Ocean

Our time in Port Harcourt was a frustrating one. We kept receiving emails and mobile phone calls from MEND, but at the last minute these meetings would always fall through. What we didn't know was that the militants were being heavily hit by the Joint Task Force at the time. They had other things on their minds than sitting in front of a camera for our benefit.

Constantly getting teed up and let down, though, had a bad effect on the camera crew and me. We know each other well, and we've been in dangerous places before – places where the bullets were flying – but nowhere compared to Port Harcourt for paranoia. If we *were* going to meet MEND, it would mean slipping out of our hotel room at night and trying to avoid our armed guards – an action that would probably get us arrested if we were caught. That in itself shrouded us in a sense of paranoid secrecy – the last thing any of us wanted to do was see the inside of one of the Nigerian jails, which by all accounts made Strangeways look like the Sheraton. But it was more than that. There aren't many places in the world where you're scared to leave your hotel compound, but Port Harcourt was one of them. Without wanting to sound in any way racist, in most places I'd travelled to I'd felt a vague sense of protection in being white. People might want to kill me, but the repercussions of them doing so would have been immense. You got the feeling that in Port Harcourt no one would give a shit.

Each night that we were on standby to sneak out and meet MEND, I would put calls through to two people in the UK, telling them that if I didn't call them again by a certain time they were to contact the Foreign Office immediately because it would probably mean we'd been kidnapped. Belt and braces stuff, but necessary under the circumstances. Still, not good for your frame of mind. As a result of all these strains, tensions between the crew increased. We started getting snappy with each other. It wasn't personal; it was simply something about that place.

We couldn't just stay in our hotel for days on end, though. While we waited for our meet to go ahead, we made a journey – along with our security guards / armed chaperones, of course – deeper into the Niger Delta, half because we wanted to see it for ourselves, half because we knew that this was the territory in which MEND operated and we thought our chances of catching up with them would be greater if we put ourselves where they were known to be. Ogoniland is a few hours' drive from Port Harcourt. Ken Saro-Wiwa's heartland, this was the region where oil was first tapped in the Niger Delta, and also the first region to rise up against the effects the oil industry was having on the people, their livelihoods and their environment. I was keen to see what it was like, but I could never have imagined the devastation I was about to discover.

Oil is no longer tapped in Ogoniland. The non-violent resistance of Ken Saro-Wiwa and MOSOP had the desired effect, forcing the oil multinationals to stop drilling in that region. There are still pipelines, though, and the infrastructure that goes with them. These pipelines are a target for the militants: only the day before, one of them had been blown up. The oil companies might have withdrawn from Ogoniland, but that didn't mean it wasn't still a dangerous place.

This is Africa as you'd imagine it. As our convoy drove along the mud tracks that led us deeper into Ogoniland, we passed thin men wearing ragged clothes, and nowhere did we see any signs of wealth. We stopped by a creek. There were fishing nets, wooden canoes and ramshackle huts. Progress had not come to Ogoniland, at least not to this part of it. You had the impression that the region looked much as it had done 100 years ago.

With one exception. A hundred years ago the area's natural resources had yet to be discovered, or exploited.

Our plan was to travel by boat up the creek and, unusually, our guards refused to come any further. The kidnap threat here was particularly high and I suppose they didn't want to risk it, their fully loaded AK-47s notwithstanding. Or maybe it was just because the boats all had holes in them and looked like they were about to sink. Up until now the presence of the guards had been a thorn in our side, but once we stepped into our wooden canoes and saw them and the shore ease away, we felt their absence keenly. We were about to enter the heart of the Niger Delta, and we knew that pirates, militants and kidnappers could be lying in wait around any corner, or hidden in the mangrove swamp. Not to put too fine a point on it, we were shitting ourselves.

Our guide as we slid through the water was a local man called Sonny. He sat in the back of my canoe, wearing a US Open baseball cap that looked decidedly out of place in this quiet, alien backwater. Sonny was taking us to see a damaged oil well head. It had leaked over a year ago and we were to witness the effect that leak had had.

It didn't take long for us to see what all the fuss was about.

As we paddled, I noticed a rainbow film on the oars, like the colours you see when a child blows a soap-sud bubble. This wasn't soap, however, and it wasn't child's play. Before long, you could see that the water was thick with globules of oil. You could smell it in the air too, the heavy, choking scent of crude. Here, miles from anywhere in the middle of the mangrove swamp, the air should have been clean and fresh, but instead it smelled like a petrol station. The further we went, the worse it got. If anyone had been so foolish as to light a match, God only knows what would have happened. We were warned not to use our mobile phones for fear that an electrical spark would ignite the fumes. About six months previously two guys had been killed in that way, and we were shown where the explosion had burned away a substantial part of the mangrove bushes. What a way to go. I was more than a bit worried about the wisdom of keeping the camera rolling because of the battery.

But roll we did, through the maze of dangerous swamps in the company of men we didn't know. Sonny explained to us that fish, winkles and mangrove crabs are important to the Ogoni people. It seemed they still managed to catch a small quantity of fish in these distressed waters, though it was astonishing to me that anything managed to live there. You might as well try and live in a petrol tank, and I certainly didn't see any sign of life as we continued our slow journey into the labyrinth. I didn't hear any either. It was deathly silent all around.

Sonny was a quietly spoken man who seemed friendly enough; we all knew, though, how quickly things could change. I couldn't suppress my nervousness as we continued to paddle through the polluted creek. It didn't take long for us to arrive at the well head. By now the creek was more oil than water, and our boats approached with care. It looked like an appalling piece of modern sculpture, a confusion of pipes and plumbing, surrounded by some sort of scaffolding. There would once have been a platform on top of this so that the black gold could be tapped, barrelled, put onto barges and exported. But now that the oil companies had withdrawn from Ogoniland, this was all that was left.

We circled the well head. Around us, we could see the mangrove bushes stained with oil – these are tidal waters, so when the water swells and lowers, it leaves its polluted trace on the surrounding vegetation. The fumes were chokingly thick now – they were in our throats and in our eyes – and the air itself was hot. Sonny explained that deep in the earth huge oil reserves were bursting to gush out. The only thing that was stopping that from happening was the small piece of machinery in front of us.

At least, it was *trying* to stop it from happening. Sonny pointed out the clunky network of plumbing at the top of the head. 'Can you see the oil coming up?' he asked me. 'If you look at that pipe up there, you can see something like smoke.'

I certainly could. A thick, cloudy vapour was hissing from the top of the well head – a bit like steam from a kettle, only this vapour was enormously explosive. There was also a constant, steady drip of viscous black liquid dropping into the water. The head might have been designed to keep the oil underground, but it clearly wasn't doing its job very well.

There were two possible reasons for the well head not functioning properly. The first was neglect. The oil multinationals had left the area; there was no profit to be made in maintaining what they had left behind and so it had been allowed to fall into disrepair. Not, as far as I could tell, an entirely unlikely scenario. But there was another possibility too: this head could have been one hub of an illegal trade that exists all over the world but which is prevalent in Nigeria. That trade is oil bunkering.

Bunkering is a fancy word for theft. It's big business in Nigeria – estimated to be worth $30 million a day. Looking at this leaking oil head, you could well understand why. It wouldn't be too much of a chore to bring a barge up to an outlet like this, attach a pipe to the plumbing at the top and simply tap off as much as you could carry. It appears that this is being done by all manner of people. Impoverished Lagosians can pump a little fuel into jerrycans; corrupt politicians and officials have the means to bunker oil on a rather grander scale; militants across the Niger Delta exchange bunkered oil for weapons. The bunkered oil is taken to offshore loading stations and then sold on into the world market. The International Maritime Organization estimates that about 80,000 barrels of oil were bunkered every day in 2008. Crime breeds crime, and Dr Sofiri Peterside, director of the Centre for Advanced Social Sciences in Port Harcourt, estimates that during 2008 a thousand people died in turf wars directly related to bunkering.

Sonny explained that bunkering could be done not only from a well head like this, but also from any one of the pipes that pump fuel across the region up towards Bonny

Island. All anyone needed to do was find a valve, open it and help themselves. Here on the water it was clearly more than possible that the oil dripping from this head was a result of illegal bunkering – someone had attached a pipe, taken what they wanted and failed to close up the plumbing properly.

It wasn't the sort of place you could stay for long. My eyes and throat were stinging from the fumes. The sky above was thundery and threatening. It looked like the heavens were about to open and I remember thinking that might not be a bad thing. Perhaps it would relieve us of the symptoms the oil vapour was causing.

We headed back down the creek and returned to the bank. By now any doubts we'd had about our escorts had dissipated a bit, but we were deeply shocked by what we had just seen. We loaded ourselves back into the car. Our tour of Ogoniland was not over yet – Sonny still had a few sights to show us. Although production had stopped here, there remained a huge network of pipes taking oil through Ogoniland to the terminals on the coast. Our convoy took us to the site of an old flow station and a new one. These places pump the oil offshore. We couldn't stay there long – this was an extremely dangerous place. The oil companies employ locals to protect the flow stations against oil bunkerers and militants. Ostensibly these people are employed to protect the community, but inevitably they divide it by overstepping the mark. It was just after we arrived when we received word that these locals already knew we were there and were on their way. Furthermore, they were armed. We knew that it was a very sensitive area to film, and that it was impossible to judge how our presence would be

On my way to another spill near Bodo, feeling slightly concerned about being kidnapped.

The angry villagers of Bodo speak out about the effect the presence of the oil companies has had on their livelihoods.

This villager believes that the only solution to the problem is to blow up the manifold.

God.

Governor Amaechi – or to give him his full title, the Right Honourable Rotimi Chibuike Amaechi, His Exellency the Executive Governor of Rivers State.

As requested we arrive at 7.30 in the morning, ready for our 8.00 meeting. But we were kept waiting . . .

. . . and waiting for two and a half hours . . .

. . . before finally being ushered in to see the man himself.

False alarm: we are asked to wait some more, and are offered breakfast – chilli doughnut with blancmange filling. There was also goat stew filled with bones.

The governor takes me on what is little more than a public relations tour of all the good works he has established in Port Harcourt.

He is a charming man, and genuinely popular with a lot of people, including these children we visited at a local school.

MEND – the Movement for the Emancipation of the Niger Delta. 'It must be clear that the Nigerian government cannot protect your workers or assets. Leave our land while you can, or die in it . . . Our aim is to totally destroy the capacity of the Nigerian government to export oil.'

Me in a MMEA (Malaysian Maritime Enforcement Agency) helicopter, patrolling the Malacca Straits for pirates.

From the helicopter I saw one of the nine radar stations positioned on small islands the length of the straits, which constantly scan the area for suspicious activity.

'Go go go!' Members of the MMEA board a ship and raid it for pirates as part of the training exercise.

Within minutes they have swept the ship, handcuffed the 'baddies' and have them all laid out on the deck, face down with their legs crossed.

Finally, red smoke is sent up to indicate that the ship has been secured.

The captain of the *Nepline Delima*, bearing scars inflicted by a pirate's machete.

Muhammad Hamid shows me a photo of the pirates lying face down after the boat was retaken.

Muhammad's bravery was big news in Malaysia; however, he cannot return to the sea and the job he loves.

I finally get to meet a pirate at his house in Batam. He asks to be addressed as 'Lightning Storm Across the Sea'.

With the pirates in a very small boat in the busy shipping lanes off the coast of Batam.

Storm and the other pirates explain the term 'shopping' to me.

A long walk in to 'Pirate Island', trying to avoid the highly poisonous stone fish.

Taking off the rough edges in order to make the bamboo less difficult to climb.

Being proved wrong! I witness five pirates in a tree.

Storm explains how the pirates slash the palms of any crew members who put up a fight.

We head back from the island in a torrential Indonesian rainstorm. There's no gold at the end of this pirate's rainbow.

Talking to a pirate's wife.
'He's a naughty boy!'

I meet with the pirates
for the last time.

Big business. I finally come face to face with a Somali pirate.

interpreted. Frankly, we didn't really feel like sticking around to find out. Time for a sharp exit, and on to our final destination for the day: another deserted well head, this time one which the oil companies claim to have cleaned up.

This head was on land but it looked very similar to the one we had visited in the creek. It too had oil fumes steaming, dragon-like, from its plumbing. The surrounding ground was one huge puddle of oil. 'So, as you see,' Sonny told us as we padded towards the well head, 'they have cleaned the spill. What they call "clean-up" has been done.'

It didn't look very clean to me. Oil was still leaking from the head and the surrounding space was dead and barren. Had it ever been cleaned up? Or had someone recently come along, bunkered oil and failed to seal the oil head properly? It was impossible to tell, but one thing was sure.

This place wasn't clean, and it wasn't healthy.

It was devastated.

Ledum Mitee is a lawyer and human rights campaigner in the Niger Delta, a friendly and intelligent man who received me in the yard of his Ogoniland compound. Following the death of Ken Saro-Wiwa, Mitee is the president of the Movement for the Survival of the Ogoni People. He had agreed to explain to me in more detail what it was that the inhabitants of the Niger Delta had to put up with. I asked him exactly what was threatening the survival of the Ogoni people.

'Oil was being exploited in front of people's houses,' he told me. 'In your backyard or anywhere. I grew up in a house that is about 200 metres from the nearest oil well. They spill occasionally. The only source of water that people have is stream water, and these rivers are themselves polluted. With gas flares 24 hours a day it makes it difficult for the crops to pollinate.'

The water they drank, the fish they fished for, the crops they grew – all these were being damaged by the oil industry. And I, as our fixer might have said, had seen it with my own eyes. But it wasn't just that. Ledum explained to me that the land was important to the Ogoni people not only because of what it could produce, but because of its spiritual connotations. 'It's where our ancestors live. You have the right to protect them, and if you don't, if the land is being desecrated, that portends some calamity to the community. Some forests that are sacred to the people are being felled for oil wells. We are not supposed to do that to them. The deities are annoyed.'

As Ledum spoke, I was reminded of the cultural differences that exist between the multinational oil corporations and the people whose land they are exploiting: the inhabitants of the Niger Delta were not only suffering environmentally and physically, they were suffering spiritually too.

MOSOP is a peaceful organization; Ledum Mitee is a peaceful man. I wondered what his thoughts were about MEND's less than peaceful modus operandi. He spoke frankly. 'The execution of Ken and the rest of my colleagues,' he told me, 'was intended to intimidate the rest. But it produced the opposite effect because most of those who have taken to militancy in other parts of the Delta cite our case as an example. They say, *you* were killed. *I* will not wait to be killed before we start killing.'

I asked him if he saw a direct connection between the piracy in the region, the militancy, the criminality and the pressure exerted by the JTF, the oil companies and the government. Ledum Mitee had no doubt. 'All these things are one single process. One reinforces the other.' The situation in the Niger Delta, then, was a vicious circle, and it sounded to me like it could only get worse.

I put it to Mitee that the environmental situation in Ogoniland was not just the fault of the oil companies – it was also down to the practice of oil bunkering. He agreed, and he enlightened me further on the gravity of the problem. 'There are three stages we found of bunkering. The first stage is those who cut the pipes and put it in jerrycans. Boys who are cutting the pipes in some areas and selling to the middlemen – those who have barges. And before you can be someone at that second stage, you must have a lot of connection and leverage, with armed, military people. Then you have those guys who will take it to the high seas where you have the big tankers. That is controlled by very, very important people who call the shots from Abuja. Last year, through bunkering, we lost almost $15 billion of oil.'

The bunkering of oil, it was becoming clear to me, was an illegal act on the water – yet another form of piracy, and the sort of sums Mitee was talking about were staggering. The government's own anti-corruption task force estimates that $400 billion has gone missing since oil was first discovered in the Delta. And as with so much of the corruption in Nigeria, it occurs at the highest level. You don't get the oil out into the open market without the help of people in authority. That means the government. Once it enters the world's fuel supply, there's nothing anyone can do about it – chances are that you or I have filled up our cars on illegal bunkered oil without even knowing it. You can see the attraction, both for the corrupt politicians in Abuja and for the poor of Ogoniland – if you've got gold right on your front door, chances are you're going to grab a handful.

I'd been shocked by what I had seen in Ogoniland. But as we'd been driving around our guides had told us that there was a village called Bodo on the outskirts of the area that was even worse. So the next morning we decided to take a look. In order to get to this new oil spill we needed to head further up the river. The canoes we had been in the previous day would be no good to cover that kind of distance, and so we boarded a small fleet of lifeboats with outboard motors. I say *we* boarded – in fact we were piggybacked onto the boats by our guides, who insisted that we shouldn't risk wading through that polluted river.

We sped through the confusing network of waterways. The plan was to stop off to see the oil leak, then move on into the village of Bodo itself. So it was that we moored at the edge of the mangrove swamp, alighted from our boats and set off in search of oil.

The spill that they took me to was on a much more massive scale than those I had seen the previous day. All around, the mangrove – which takes hundreds of years to grow – had been killed. The ground itself was a soggy, muddy, oily mess; you could touch it with your fingers and they would come up stained black. The closer we drew to the source of the leak, the blacker the earth became. I felt like I was sinking in a quicksand of black gold. The mud itself was hot because of the oil – so hot that it started to cook my feet. Eventually we just couldn't walk any further.

These pipes have been there for many years and they don't have an indefinite lifespan. Sooner or later, they're going to split. Bunkering is doubtless a big environmental problem in the Niger Delta, but it's not the only one: the area suffers from an ageing oil infrastructure that hasn't been maintained and is causing devastation such as that which I was looking at now. The underground pipe had obviously been leaking for a long time, and eventually the oil had spurted to the surface. It's very difficult to find the source of such a leak and it takes a long time – time during which the environmental damage accumulates. This leak had been fixed a year ago, but it was clear that its impact would last for tens, maybe hundreds of years to come. It was hell on earth, and I was shocked to learn that oil spills such as this happen, on average, once a day in Nigeria.

The boggy ground around the oil spill wasn't the sort of place you wanted to stay for long, so we returned to our boats and headed up towards Bodo. There we disembarked again. As we entered the village we received the familiar hostile looks – the fact that we had white skin naturally made the locals think that we were oil workers. Not their favourite people. When it became clear who we were, however, they grew a little less antagonistic, even eager to talk to us and explain what was happening to their home.

The villagers were angry with the oil companies and the effect their presence has had on their lives. A crowd of them gathered round me, and their spokesman spoke vehemently about the lack of compensation they had received. 'We are fed up,' he said. 'This is our river. This is our only source of livelihood. Over 80 per cent of this community depends on this river. Look at all the people – you can see that they are all hungry. If this river was OK the way it was, all these boys would be on the river struggling for their daily bread.'

I looked towards the river. The boys he was indicating weren't working – they were larking about in the filthy, oily water.

'But because they have nothing to do,' the villager continued, 'every day we fight with them that they should not commit stealing and all that.'

The story I was hearing was similar to the one I had been told in Ajegunle: because of the pollution, people were turning to crime in order to put food in their bellies.

The villager continued. 'All this militancy is attributed to it. Their pipes should be removed from our land. Our source of livelihood is destroyed now. And one of these days they will hear from us, because the solution would be to blow up the manifold. And we will. We *will*. I am saying to you we will. We are going to blow down this manifold and let the government come and kill all of us. So let them kill us with their guns instead of we die of hunger.'

Truly desperate words. It would have been easy to mistake them for mere rhetoric, but the crowd of villagers hanging round their spokesman showed no sign that they disagreed with him, and he spoke with a real passion. Part of our reason for travelling into the Delta was to try and make contact with MEND. We hadn't done that, but we had certainly learned why they exist and why they have support among certain sectors of the community. The villagers in Bodo honestly believed that the pollution was killing them. It was causing crime and misery. Under circumstances like that, it's perhaps understandable that people might want to take things into their own hands, and that their measures are likely to be extreme . . .

Bodo was an edgy place. It smelled like a refinery, and we were covered in oil. The kids offered to clean our boots for a few dollars – cheap for the kind of work they had to put in, but I still have those boots and they still reek of oil.

The day wasn't over yet. As we sped back, I was in a boat with our journalist fixer and four or five of the locals who were showing us around. Suddenly, for no apparent reason, our boat peeled off down a tributary, away from where the others were heading.

And in the Niger Delta, that's not a good thing to happen.

I felt my stomach turn to lead. *Oh fuck*, I thought to myself. *This is it. We're being taken.*

Nervous people on planes are known to look at the faces of the air stewardesses if they hit bad turbulence. If the cabin crew look nervous, they know they should panic. Similarly, I quickly glanced at our fixer, hoping to see a reassuring expression of calm. Not a bit of it. He looked as alarmed as I felt – with a sinking feeling of a lift you can't get out of that is hurtling to the ground.

'Where are you going?' our fixer shouted. 'WHERE ARE YOU GOING?'

Our guides looked blandly at us. 'Short cut,' they said.

'No,' the fixer said. '*No! No short cut.*'

By now the others were well out of sight. We were entirely under these people's control: we couldn't have escaped even if we'd tried. The only way out of that boat was into the water, and you'd have just drowned in the oil. I muttered nervously, doing my best to at least *look* calm. 'Can we just turn round?'

They looked at us like we were mad. Truth of the matter was that our boys were racing the others. But not in my head they weren't. In my head we were about to spend a few months enjoying the hospitality of the Niger Delta pirates.

There was a moment of stand-off. Our guides insisted that they wanted to take their short cut; I found myself nervously reflecting on an uncomfortable fact I had heard. Apparently, a substantial proportion of people, male and female, who are kidnapped in West Africa get raped. And – close your eyes now if you're of a squeamish disposition – not always with a penis. Bits of wood, bits of metal . . . It's a way of dominating someone. There was a good deal of buttock clenching going on. Not that that would have helped.

Eventually, our guides relented. We turned back, caught up with the others and made it to shore safely, but we'd had a quick insight into how easy it would be to kidnap someone in that network of channels. I don't think I fully relaxed until we were back in our armed convoy heading out of Ogoniland and back to Port Harcourt.

We were only in that part of the Delta for a short time, during which it was difficult to get a real handle on the ins and outs of the environmental damage that was being done there. The oil companies claim that the leakages are solely down to the mismanagement of the well heads by the many people illegally bunkering oil. It appeared to me that this was true in some places, but not everywhere, and you'd be hard pushed entirely to absolve the multinationals of blame. Whatever the truth, one thing was clear to me. The oil bunkerers were doing very nicely out of what was going on in Ogoniland; the oil companies weren't doing too badly either. The losers were ordinary citizens and the environment. Having seen this at first hand, even if I didn't agree with their methods, I could well understand why militant political groups like MEND existed.

In June 2009, a few months after I left Nigeria, one of the multinational corporations, Shell, made a payout of $15.5 million to the families of the Ogoni Nine, including Ken Saro-Wiwa's son, in settlement of a legal action in which it was accused of having collaborated in their execution. Shell did not concede or admit to any of the accusations, but by avoiding a lengthy court case they stopped the world at large becoming more aware of the environmental situation in the Niger Delta. A large proportion of that money will be used to pay the Ogoni Nine's legal costs, but a sum of $5 million has been put aside to set up a trust for educational and community projects in the Niger Delta. The trust's name is Kisi, which means 'progress'. And maybe it is progress of a kind. I can't help thinking, though, that in a country that produces $40 billion of black gold a year, $5 million is just a drop of oil in the ocean.

11. Kidnap Alley

Back in our Port Harcourt hotel, we returned to our prisoner-like existence. Subject to the whims of the MEND spokesmen, who would occasionally get in contact by phone and then let us down, we couldn't go anywhere without our armed guards, who were there for our protection but also to make sure we didn't go walkabout. We wanted to be low-profile, to melt into the background, but that was proving impossible. To make our predicament worse, we then received an official invitation to visit the governor of Rivers State early the next morning. We were bleary-eyed because we'd been up half the night waiting for phone calls from pirates. But we were also in Port Harcourt as the governor's guests and couldn't do anything without his permission. So in a way it wasn't so much an invitation as a summons.

Governor Amaechi – or to give him his full title, the Right Honourable Rotimi Chibuike Amaechi, His Exellency the Executive Governor of Rivers State – is taking a hard line on piracy. He's one of MEND's biggest adversaries, and a bit of a maverick within the Nigerian political system. The government had recently passed a law giving all kidnappers an automatic life sentence, but Amaechi himself had supported increasing that to a death sentence. The word was that he had plans to turn Rivers State from the most volatile area in the Niger Delta into a thriving megacity, with skyscrapers and a monorail. If that was the case, he certainly had his work cut out. He had a hard act to follow too. One of his predecessors, Peter Odili, faced accusations over the theft and mismanagement of billions of dollars' worth of oil revenue. However, he has since been granted immunity by a government anti-corruption investigation. I guess that's just the way it works.

Even if I resented being escorted to his offices with the kind of close protection I'd never previously had, part of me was curious to see what this optimistic hardliner was like. As we headed through Port Harcourt, we saw evidence of Amaechi cracking down on other illegal acts too. All too frequently we would pass houses – many newly built – with red marks on the door. These marks indicated that the houses had been built without planning permission, and the governor's zero-tolerance administration had ordered that they were to be knocked down. So even before we arrived I had the impression that Amaechi meant what he said.

We arrived at the governor's office, as requested, at 7.30 in the morning, ready for an 8.00 meeting, and were asked to go through the sort of security cordon you'd expect at any airport. But if Amaechi was keen to see us, as he claimed to be, he didn't have a very good way of showing it. We were kept waiting in the lobby for two and a half hours before finally being ushered in to see the man himself. It was a bit like getting in to see the pope, what with all the goons and stooges and layers of security. Amaechi was obviously a popular man, but he was only the governor of one state of one region of Nigeria. It was immediately obvious, though, that maintaining his administration required a *lot* of money – you could tell that not only from the layers of bureaucracy and security that surrounded the man, but also from the relative affluence of the building. Amaechi looked younger than I expected – all the photos and paintings of him I'd seen around the place had been retouched to make him look older and more imposing.

Amaechi wasn't quite ready to talk to us, so he offered us breakfast while we were waiting. He led us into the breakfast room, an ornate space with a large table surrounded by gaudy but not inexpensive chairs. Breakfast consisted of typical Nigerian cuisine. I wasn't a big fan of the chilli doughnut with blancmange filling; there was also goat stew filled with bones – as in many places I've been, the animal had clearly been carved with a hammer. I certainly wouldn't want to slag off the way the Nigerians eat – it's their cuisine, and they adore it. No doubt they find the idea of bacon and eggs a bit odd, but what was to their taste wasn't hugely to mine, and I'd have done anything for a bowl of cornflakes.

After hours of waiting, the moment finally arrived for us to have a bit of face time with the governor. He was a charming man, in his way. You could see how he might be a popular politician, and he smiled politely at me as I asked if I might talk to him about some of the issues he had inherited when he took over.

I asked the governor what his take on MEND was. His face became a little less smiley. 'I don't think there is anything called MEND,' he replied. 'I have not seen one.'

Really? So there was no Movement for the Emancipation of the Niger Delta?

'I've not seen one. Let one person come forward and negotiate with us. I've not seen one. I can't say whether they exist, but I've never seen one person called MEND. So far

164

the people I have been dealing with in the Rivers State have been criminals.'

So was it the governor's viewpoint that the people calling themselves MEND were using their organization as a political excuse for criminal actions?

'Yes. Ninety-nine per cent of those involved in Rivers State are criminals. Simple.'

I asked him about his support for the death penalty for acts of piracy and kidnapping. He explained to me that in Nigeria robbery attracts the death penalty. Kidnapping, from his point of view, was even worse – the robbery of a person. He believed that his calls for the death penalty were popular with the people. 'You should go to the streets,' he told me. 'The people are tired of these criminals. So it's quite popular. It may be unpopular with the NGOs, civil rights or human rights movements, but it's popular with our population.'

Amaechi had told me I should hit the streets of Port Harcourt. I wondered if he would accompany me. Ever-obliging, he agreed. 'Let's go,' he said.

The governor then took me on what was little more than a public relations tour of all the good works he had initiated in Port Harcourt. It was a curious excursion. He insisted on driving me himself, to show what a man of the people he was – it helped though that he had an armed convoy around him, with a Russian DshK heavy machine gun mounted on a pickup and 20 men with assault rifles clearing the path of traffic ahead of us. To give the guy his due, however, he didn't appear to be afraid of getting his hands dirty. As we were travelling down the highway we saw a local trying to extort 'taxes' from another driver; the driver was refusing and the extortionist had attacked him. When Amaechi saw this, he ground to a halt, jumped out and ran across the highway. 'What are you doing?' he demanded forcefully, before turning to his guards. 'Arrest that man!' he instructed. A bit later on we were in one of Port Harcourt's incessant traffic jams when we spotted a white army van going the wrong way up the road. Again, he stopped the car, jumped out and made the van turn around and travel the right way up the road, those inside apologizing to everyone as they passed.

As we toured the town righting wrongs like some kind of West African Judge Dredd, I asked Amaechi about the piracy that blighted the region. What were the reasons for it, in his view, and what could be done to stem the problem? I was half-expecting more of the hard-line dogma, but in fact he showed himself to be sensitive to the causes of Nigerian piracy. 'Poverty,' he told me. 'Most of those people who are involved in crime now used to go fishing. Now there is nowhere to fish. The military government that we had lacked the courage to enforce discipline and government control, which is what we are doing now.' But the piracy was a direct result of poverty. After all, he said, 'Who would want to carry guns and rob people at sea if they can feed themselves?' You don't take the kind of risk involved in committing acts of piracy, he maintained, unless you know you have a risk of dying of poverty.

We were given a tour around a new hospital Amaechi was building, power plants, schools and other worthy projects. I couldn't help noticing, though, that there were a lot of half-finished construction sites. When we stopped to look at one of these, Amaechi approached the Italian contractor, who happened to be on site. 'Why is this not finished?' he demanded. 'What is wrong? *Why* is it not finished?'

The contractor looked, I thought, a bit nervous. 'Do you want the real answer?' he asked. 'On camera?'

'Of course,' Amaechi stated. 'You can be honest.'

'You haven't paid me.'

That smooth smile spread over Amaechi's face once more. 'We will pay you, my friend,' he said. 'You do not need to worry about that!'

But the contractor looked worried, and I had the distinct impression that his worry derived from the fact that telling the governor of Rivers State that he was downing tools might have consequences for more than his bank balance. Maybe he just felt the same sense of paranoia that we all did in this town. I don't know.

I wasn't so naive not to realize that our excursion with Governor Amaechi was little more than a PR stunt, but even so it struck me as he walked around the town that he was genuinely popular with a lot of people. I was left to consider that I had seen a number of different sides to the same story. The political piracy, kidnapping and industrial sabotage carried out by MEND was clearly a big problem for the area. As with many militant groups who seek their ends by unacceptable means, their grievances were real. I'd met ordinary folk who sympathized with MEND because their lives, frankly, had been ruined by the awful consequences of bunkering and oil spillages. And now I'd met the administration, whose principal aim was to crush the militants and the criminality with which they were associated, and that administration had its supporters too.

The only people I hadn't managed to connect with were MEND themselves. And truth to tell, I was beginning to wonder if we ever would.

That night MEND once again told us to stand by, to wait for another call that would tell us where to go, and when. Yet again we prepared to slip away from our security under cover of night; yet again the call never came. The trouble was this: the Joint Task Force had been carrying out a sustained attack on MEND bases in the area. Either the militants thought it was too dangerous to meet us at that moment in time, or they just weren't in a position to do it. And so the following morning – exhausted and a bit demoralized – we took the decision to cut our losses in Rivers State and travel elsewhere in the Delta. If we could get closer to some MEND strongholds where the JTF *hadn't* been active, maybe we would have more luck.

The town of Warri is 95 miles from Port Harcourt in neighbouring Delta State. The security goons who had been tasked with accompanying us seemed very anxious that we should leave early, and we soon found out why that was. To get there, you need to travel up a road which has been dubbed Kidnap Alley. No prizes for guessing why. The journey from Port Harcourt to Warri takes about six hours; if we left too late, the security boys would have to come back down Kidnap Alley in the dark. Not to put too fine a point on it, they were shitting themselves at the prospect. These were burly, armed policemen – a fair indication of how dangerous the road was. While we were en route, we would occasionally have to stop by the side of the road to take a leak. Whenever that happened, the guards' paranoia increased a hundred-fold. They really didn't want to be there.

The journey was made slower by the fact that we were forever being stopped at checkpoints by local police looking for chop-chop. We managed to stream some Eddie Izzard from an iPod to the car radio – surreal stuff at the best of times, but doubly so when you're driving up Kidnap Alley. This didn't please our driver. He wanted to listen to his tribal beats – fine for 20 minutes, but six hours of it would send you east of Barking. I'd never seen our guards look so happy as when they dropped us off at our hotel in Warri. Not even a goodbye – they were instantly gone in the hope that they could get back to Port Harcourt before it was dark.

Now that we were out of the jurisdiction of Governor Amaechi we no longer had to contend with the ever-present personal security. That didn't mean, however, that we were entirely free agents. There was a heavy police presence around our hotel, and we were told in no uncertain terms that we would be stupid to leave. Travel into town, they said, and you'll get killed or kidnapped. The hotel, though, was not the sort of place where you really wanted to spend any time. When we arrived, I was greeted by the hotel owner. 'We have a big room for you, Mr Kemp,' he said, and led me proudly up.

It was a big room all right, but that was all that could be said for it. At some stage the door had been pulled off its hinges, then inexpertly replaced using screws without proper threads. I'd been given one of those plastic key cards, but there was no point because you could just open the door without it. Not that you'd want to. Inside, parts of the walls were spattered brown and red. It was either ketchup and brown sauce, or it was blood and shit. The carpet was mysteriously sticky. The shower curtain stank of mildew and there was a bucket by the toilet so that you could flush it, as the cistern didn't fill properly. There were mosquitoes everywhere and it was obvious that the bedclothes hadn't been changed in a long time – they were black with grease from other people's bodies, and there was a dent in the pillow from when it had been last used. The sort of bed that makes you itch just looking at it.

But this was our hotel and we had to make do. We once more started to put out the feelers, to make calls to contacts that we had. And then we did the only thing we *could* do. We waited.

And waited.

Confined to our hotel for our own safety, we just had to hope that the nearby MEND bases had escaped government attacks. But there was no way of knowing, and our lines of communication were worryingly silent. We waited for several days and nights, long past the time when we should have been on a plane out of there. There's only so long you can wait in a hotel room in 40-degree heat, with shit on the walls, having read the same book four times. As each day passed, it became increasingly clear that MEND were unlikely to get in touch – we could only assume that they'd been hit by the JTF – and we were going to have to bail out. It was increasingly clear that the programme we wanted to make wasn't going to happen. With the frustration of failure weighing heavy on us, we finally decided there was nothing more we could do. We would have to return to Lagos empty-handed.

Once the decision was made, we moved quickly. We

wanted to be on the next flight out of there. We packed our gear up like madmen, knowing we had to shift sharpish if we weren't going to miss our plane, and we asked our fixer to organize a couple of cars to the provincial airport nearby. Somehow he forgot, which only made our rush through the go-slows of Warri even worse, but we finally got to the airport. Strangely we were recognized – a white oil worker even came up and asked me to sign a *Gangs* book for them – but all our attention was focused on splitting. Warri, we had decided, was far too much of a worry. The queue at the airport seemed to last for ever. When the time came for me to put my hand luggage through the scanner (it was the day pack I used in Afghanistan) I saw it slip into the machine before the conveyor belt stopped. One of the security men addressed me.

'Who is your big boss?' he demanded.

By now I'd lost all patience with Nigerian bureaucracy. 'We're an autonomous organization,' I told him facetiously. 'We don't have a big boss.'

'What?' He had suddenly been joined by a number of others. 'We need to speak to your big boss.'

'We don't have one.'

'We have to know. We need chop-chop.'

I shook my head. 'There isn't any chop-chop. Can I have my bag back, please?'

'No. We need chop-chop.'

I shook my head again, then put my hand towards the machine to drag out my bag.

'If you put your hand in there,' a female security guard snapped at me, 'we chop it off.'

I froze. She half looked as if she meant it.

171

'We need chop-chop,' she insisted.

But by now I'd truly had enough. I raised my voice. 'I'M NOT PAYING CHOP-CHOP.' Everyone in the terminal must have heard me. They all looked towards me and sucked their teeth at the *oyibo* kicking up a fuss.

I looked back along the queue. Ewen, our director, was only a few positions down. 'Look,' I said. 'You want chop-chop? Ask him.' It was a bit of a three-billy-goats-gruff tactic – I felt pretty sure that Ewen in his six-foot-four Glaswegian way would make it very clear that they weren't getting any chop-chop from him either. I went through and stood back to watch the fireworks. Funnily enough, the Nigerians came off second best in that little argument. I think they'd just picked the wrong batch of exhausted, disillusioned, pissed-off foreigners to tap for cash.

We returned to Lagos, and then to London, feeling that we had failed, but maybe we were being too hard on ourselves. It was true that we hadn't managed to meet MEND or any pirates. But in our time in the Niger Delta we had certainly gained an insight into why the pirates do what they do. I couldn't condone what was happening in the Niger Delta – kidnapping, murder, acts of terrorism – but I felt that at least I could now understand why it was happening. The political piracy in the Delta and out at sea – like the criminal piracy in the quarantine zone of Lagos or the petty piracy that hits the fishermen of Ajegunle – had its origins in abject poverty and the environmental degradation that was ironically a direct offshoot of the fact that Nigeria was so oil rich. And perhaps it's fair to say that the biggest pirates in Nigeria are the people in power, those who, as Ledum Mitee had explained, made millions from selling bunkered oil on the open market.

As I think back on my time in Nigeria, I wonder if I was too harsh on it. Maybe I just saw the wrong side of the happiest country in the world. But I can't help thinking that with all that potential wealth, it should be a lot happier than it is. That annoyed me, and saddened me.

When we left, Robin Barry Hughes and Matthew Maguire were still being held somewhere in the Niger Delta. On 20 April 2009 Robin Barry Hughes was released for health reasons; Matthew Maguire was set free on 12 June 2009, having been held hostage for nine months. When we admitted we'd been in the Delta trying to find him, he told us we were mad. He probably wasn't far wrong. It wasn't long after our departure that government forces escalated attacks against militants in the Delta and a blanket ban was placed on all journalists in the area. Had we waited a couple of months, we couldn't have gone there even if we'd wanted to. And as I write this book MEND have just destroyed another pipeline in the Delta. The problems of that region are far from over.

Our global search for piracy, though, was to take us elsewhere, to the most famous pirate-infested stretch of water on the planet: the South China Sea. We had already learned that searching for pirates could take us to the most unexpected places, and none of us knew what we would find when we got there . . .

PART 3
The South China Sea

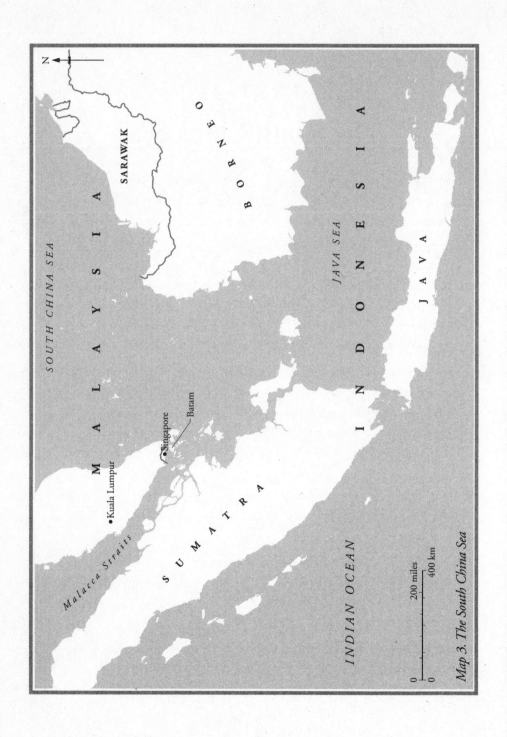

Map 3. The South China Sea

12. The Malacca Straits

In 2005 the merchant vessel *Nepline Delima* was making its way north up the Malacca Straits, a narrow stretch of water bordered by Indonesia on the west and Malaysia on the east. It was night-time when it came under attack by a ten-man group of pirates armed with machetes and machine guns.

The *Nepline Delima* was an oil tanker, carrying $12 million of oil, and a classic example of a low-freeboard vessel. Valuable and vulnerable. In this instance, however, things didn't go quite according to plan for the pirates. Their attack was thwarted by a young member of the crew. His name was Muhammad Hamid, he was just 27 years old, and his story is one of great bravery. His actions that night could certainly have got him killed, and for all he knows that may happen yet. He agreed to meet us in his small village somewhere on the Malaysian mainland, but only on the proviso that we did not reveal where this was. This young man was living, along with his family, in fear.

Muhammad explained to me what happened the night the pirates came to call. 'The captain made an announcement: "Help! Help! There are pirates on the boat! Get up, boys! Get up!" They broke into the captain's room and attacked him with a machete. The crew ran away.' As he spoke he showed me pictures of the captain, his slashed face patched up and bandaged.

The pirates chased the crew all around the boat; moments

later Muhammad could hear his friends being beaten. 'So I hid,' he told me simply. He secreted himself under the bed in his cabin. At one point the pirates, who were searching for him, entered his room and the light from their torches illuminated his knees and chest, but by some miracle they didn't see him. Knowing that the pirates must have arrived by boat, he then snuck away from his hiding place, looked over the edge of the ship and located their vessel. He climbed down the outside of the ship into their speedboat. 'When I got into the boat, I was able to cut the rope. Finally I was free. I was safe.'

Muhammad might have been safe, but his crew mates weren't. He knew he had to do something, but he had never driven a speedboat like this before. It took him ten minutes to fumble around in the darkness for the ignition button before he was able to get the boat moving. Even then, he had only the vaguest sense of where he was and, more crucially, which direction he was supposed to travel in. But luck was on his side. He travelled 50 miles, through rain-storms and high seas, to shore. He stopped a couple of times for a cigarette to calm his nerves, and who can blame him? After five hours he ran out of fuel, but managed to locate a spare canister that the pirates had stashed away.

While Muhammad was trying to find help, the crew of the *Nepline Delima* were all put into one room, where they were, quite literally, pissing themselves. They all assumed that their shipmate was dead.

Muhammad finally hit land. Immediately he alerted the powers that be and told them that there was a pirate attack occurring right now on his ship. But the authorities didn't believe him: for whatever reason, they thought at first that

Muhammad was a pirate himself. Eventually, though, they accepted his word and an operation was mounted to retake the *Nepline Delima*.

Muhammad explained to me what happened. 'The police promised them that if they surrendered, they would let them go free.' The pirates bought it, but of course the police had no intention of keeping their word. There was a six-hour stand-off, at the end of which the crew were released and the pirates arrested.

A happy ending, but there was more to this story than met the eye. It later transpired that the first officer and another member of the crew were in league with the pirates. They had delivered the coordinates of the ship for a piece of the pie. The first officer was later released, but the rest of the pirates were sentenced to seven years in a Malaysian jail. As for Muhammad Hamid, his life will never be the same. His bravery made a big splash in Malaysia, but he now feels unable to return to the job that he loves. 'If I sail again, they might just find me,' he said. He feared that the families or associates of the pirates would take revenge on him. Kill him. Hence his new life of enforced anonymity.

Muhammad was a brave man, and a lucky one. If the pirates had caught him trying to escape, chances are that he'd now be dead.

The Straits of Malacca are the second-busiest shipping lane in the world, after, believe it or not, the English Channel. Flanked by Malaysia and Singapore on the east and Indonesia on the west, it has historically been, and remains, an important channel for vessels making the profitable journey from China to India. It is also the most direct route from the bustling ports of south-east Asia to the Persian Gulf and up through the Suez Canal to Europe. Put simply, it's full of boats, and those boats are full of goods.

And this has been the case for centuries. In the days before oil became the world's most valuable commodity, spices were transported in vast quantities through the Malacca Straits and they were worth a great deal to the Europeans of the eighteenth and nineteenth centuries. Much of the European colonization of south-east Asia was driven by the desire to control the spice trade, and as the quantity of high-value shipping increased in these waters so, inevitably, did the incidence of piracy.

Pirates had roamed the Straits of Malacca long before that, however. Just as the corsairs and buccaneers had been used for political reasons as private additions to countries' naval might during the Golden Age of Piracy, so in the fourteenth century a local ruler by the name of Parameswara was able to fend off his land-hungry neighbouring rulers by keeping the pirate crews of the Malacca Straits onside. If you were to travel to the bottom of these waters, the skeletons of old ships and the watery graves of generations of sailors would be a testament to the historically turbulent nature of the South China Sea, a stretch of water that has always been feared by seamen.

The Malacca Straits and the South China Sea are no less turbulent now. In 2008 there was, on average, one pirate attack a week here. Singapore itself has the second-busiest port in the world. Each day 1,000 ships travel through its sea lanes, carrying a quarter of the world's maritime trade and a third of its oil needs. Such a high quantity of shipping, of course, presents an easy target for pirates and until recently pirate attacks were so bad that the Malacca Straits were designated a war zone by Lloyds of London, with insurance premiums to match. The truth is that if you're the owner of a merchant vessel and you choose to send your ship through the Malacca Straits instead of via a longer, and therefore more expensive, route, you're taking a gamble.

From a personal point of view, south-east Asia has a certain family resonance. My Uncle Tom was married to my nan's sister Olive. During the Second World War, as a captain in the British army, he was stationed on the island of Singapore. This was a crucial strategic location, the site of the main British military base in south-east Asia. It fell to the Japanese on 15 February 1942, in part due to a surprising tactic by the enemy. Rather than attack the island, as had been expected, by sea, they sent their troops overland across Malaysia on bicycles. What followed was a rout. The Allies were forced to surrender and Winston Churchill called it the 'worst disaster' and the 'largest capitulation' in British history. Around 80,000 Allied troops became POWs, and Uncle Tom was one of them.

I know only too well that there aren't many pleasant ways to spend a war. But if there were, several years as a Japanese POW wouldn't be one of them. Uncle Tom was set to work on the Burma Railway. Designed to link Thailand and Burma, the line was important to the Japanese precisely because without it they had to bring supplies and troops to Burma through the Malacca Straits, where they were a target for Allied submarines. Its construction came at a high price. The film *The Bridge on the River Kwai* is based around the Burma Railway, but the events of that movie are largely fictitious. The truth would be too gruelling to watch. The line became known as the Death Railway: an estimated 16,000 prisoners of war died constructing it, but that figure is dwarfed by the 90,000 Asian workers who perished.

Uncle Tom never talked to me about his time as a POW, but I subsequently heard stories. If a group of prisoners failed to lay their allotted length of track on any particular day, they'd be woken up the next morning at an irregular time. Their guards would then force them to dig a grave. When it was done, they would, at random, shoot one of the POWs dead and leave his mates to fill in the hole. After the Japanese surrender, the POWs were so emaciated that the British government did not want the public to see them in that state. Uncle Tom was sent to Canada to recover, and so he didn't see Olive until a year after he was rescued. For someone who had undergone such terrors, Uncle Tom was a lovely man. Sensitive. During his time as a POW he used to write poetry on the back of the few cardboard Red Cross boxes that got through, using blood or flower stamens as ink. But I have a childhood memory of seeing the skin on his stomach, marked and scarred from where he had been beaten with split bamboo sticks.

So it was that, as a child, this part of the world held a horrific mystery for me and I felt strange about making my first journey there. My first port of call, however, would not be Singapore but Kuala Lumpur, the capital of Malaysia. It very much feels like a city plonked in the middle of the jungle. All the time I was there I had the weird sensation that the jungle was only just being kept at bay, that given half a chance its tendrils would wrap themselves around the buildings and reclaim the land taken by the city. It was hot, cloudy and humid when I was there, with intermittent rain. And when it rained, it rained — some of the biggest thunderstorms I'd ever seen. You wouldn't want to be at sea in some of those. I liked the Malaysian people: my impression of them was that they were tough, hard-working and intelligent. Their capital city came across as a place that was thriving.

Kuala Lumpur is home to the Malaysian Maritime Enforcement Agency. The MMEA had been in existence for about four years. Its main role is to combat piracy and it has been surprisingly successful against massive odds. It comprises members of the Malaysian armed forces, and they had offered us the chance to meet one of their admirals, then join them on their patrols and training exercises.

We met the admiral on a boat patrolling the straits. He explained to me that their jurisdiction covered the eastern, Malaysian, side of the straits, which comprises about 640,000 square miles of water. Not as big as the Gulf of Aden, but still a sizeable stretch and one which includes 1,400 miles of coastline. Every month, he told me, 70,000 vessels pass through it. One of the most dangerous areas for piracy, he explained, is the southern mouth of the channel, near Singapore. This was for two reasons. First, because the channel gets narrower here, ships have to slow down to avoid collisions. And second, any vessel heading into the port of Singapore has to wait its turn. It wasn't as bad as the quarantine anchorage in Lagos, but it did mean sitting still for a while. And as I'd already learned, if a ship's sitting still, it's much easier to hit.

When it came to piracy in the Malacca Straits, the admiral knew his onions. 'There are three types of activity normally,' he told me. The first was straightforward petty theft. Opportunism. The pirates board a ship, steal whatever they can get their hands on and then disappear. The sort of thing that was happening in Lagos on a daily basis. A second, less common, pirating technique was a variation on the kidnapping theme. The pirates would commandeer the ship, then nab the captain or some of the crew and disappear with them. The ship itself would be allowed to sail free, but the hostages would be held to ransom.

The third type of piracy the admiral described to me was rather more elaborate. The pirates commandeer the ship and let the crew go. They then repaint the whole vessel, change its name and use it for their own ends. 'It becomes,' the admiral told me, 'what we call a phantom ship.' This might sound like an unwieldy operation, but there's plenty of ocean in which to hide these vessels, and it seems to be the case that they are sometimes pirated to order. Chosen like food off a menu. Indeed, according to the admiral, some of the piracy in the Malacca Straits is highly organized. Pirates have people within the harbours who have access to all sorts of crucial information – the nature of the ships' cargos, where they're going and where and when they have to slow down – so they can choose the best place to intercept them.

Sometimes shipowners fail to report piracy attacks to the authorities. This is because they don't want their insurance premiums to increase – a bit like you or I not claiming when we bump our car to avoid losing our no-claims bonus. But I had also learned from other sources that there are unscrupulous owners who are more than happy to get into bed with the pirates and take the insurance companies for a ride. In such a case, the shipowner might let the pirates know where and when to hijack his ship. He will take the insurance money, and let the pirates sell the vessel, at which point he also takes a cut of the sale. Everyone's a winner – except the insurance companies, and of course the traumatized crew . . .

The admiral also told me that he believed certain shipowners were willing to pay pirate organizations a fee to ensure their safe passage. I was reminded of the trawler owner who admitted that he paid MEND in order to sail safely round the coast of Nigeria – from what the admiral was saying, this was a fairly common practice.

The MMEA don't just patrol the Malacca Straits by ship; they also use helicopters, looking out for suspicious vessels from the air. They have their work cut out. I'd learned in Nigeria that, as a pirate, you're at a huge advantage if you have an easy waterside hideout. In the Niger Delta the massive complex of waterways provided just that. Here, the geography wasn't much different. As I joined an MMEA helicopter and we rose high above the water, I immediately got a fix on the maze of mangrove swamps that line the coast. It was a marbled landscape of thin waterways and green trees. You could hide a boat in there and never be found, no matter how many helicopters were swarming above you. The admiral had explained to me that pirates in these waters always make sure they operate relatively close to the coastline. That way, if they are observed, they can quickly get into the mangroves before the authorities have the opportunity to catch up with them. The MMEA were looking into new imaging technologies to help them see pirates in the dark and when they're under cover, but even I could tell that the most sophisticated thermal imagery would be no good in these mangrove swamps. There would be all sorts of life hidden in that foliage. Only some of it would be pirates . . .

As we flew over a fishing village called Crab Island, I asked the MMEA officers who were escorting us what sort of boats the pirates favoured. What, exactly, were the officers looking for?

'Normally they use a fast boat, a small boat that is more manoeuvrable than a ship, because you need to catch up with a big ship in order to close in and do your activity.'

Down below, I noticed such a boat and asked if we could follow it. We did so. The owners were clearly just fishing, but from that height I could see how easy it would be for them to slip into the mangrove and immediately out of sight.

'So, Ross,' the pilot said. 'You tell me. How are you going to prevent them from coming in and out? There's so many places where they can hide.'

It was impossible, I agreed. Even if you had another hundred helicopters.

The channel between Malaysia and Indonesia is particularly narrow – about ten miles at its tightest point – and this makes it even tougher to police because pirates can slip from the Indonesian coast to the Malaysian side with ease. And if I thought the Gulf of Aden was busy, I was about to have my eyes opened. The Malacca Straits were non-stop. It was obvious how pirates would be attracted to this area like bees to flowers. From the helicopter I saw one of the nine radar stations positioned on small islands the length of the straits, which constantly scan the area looking for suspicious activity. But despite this surveillance, and the military presence of the MMEA in the skies above, ships are still advised to travel through these waters at high speed in order to make them that bit less susceptible to piracy. I saw one such vessel moving at above the magic figure of 12 knots. The ship itself had a fairly low freeboard and four enormous cranes on its deck. These cranes meant that it could load and unload itself without being reliant on the infrastructure of whatever port at which it might dock. That in itself made it a very valuable piece of equipment, regardless of what sort of cargo it was carrying. If you were a pirate and came across one of these vessels, you'd see dollar signs. No wonder it was shifting.

If a ship does get pirated in these waters, the Malaysian government has the facility to react in the form of the MMEA's own elite force, who are specially trained to retake ships. I was invited to go along with this special unit on a training exercise to see just how sharp they were, and what they were capable of. These guys were well armed, carrying Heckler & Koch MP7 submachine guns, and in their black gear and balaclavas they looked impressive.

It may only have been a training exercise, but it was enough to give me an insight into just what a dangerous job these guys have. We congregated on an operations ship in the middle of the straits. This ship had been supplied to the Malaysian government by the Japanese. The Malacca Straits are particularly important to Japan. It's politically too sensitive for them to send their own navy into these waters, however, so instead they supply the Malaysians with equipment such as this. A kind of insurance premium to ensure that their shipping doesn't get hit. The Japanese, after all, for all their wealth and success, are an island race, utterly reliant on shipping for their prosperity. If Japan's shipping lines were cut off or seriously compromised, the country would soon crumble. Eighty per cent of its oil comes through these waters, and Japan lives or dies by its trade.

From the Japanese boat, along with this heavily armed task force, the camera crew and I boarded a couple of RIBs, which sped – and I mean *sped* – towards a target vessel, a tugboat which had been hijacked by 'pirates' holding the crew. As the tug came into view, I couldn't help thinking that if this were a real-life operation, if the pirates we were apprehending were real-life pirates, I'd be feeling pretty damn vulnerable. It's true that by the time this special forces unit is on its way, with a sniper in the helicopter hovering overhead for air support, the game would be up. Any right-thinking pirate would put his hands up and do the time. But there are always a few loose cannons, and if the pirates did decide to put up a fight and open fire on the SF unit, there's no doubt who'd be more vulnerable – and it wouldn't be the boys in the tug. A few GPMG rounds into the hull of that RIB and it would sink, and you'd have a pretty good chance of killing everyone on board. The sea offered the commandos no protection, and they were dangerously exposed.

We travelled at motorbike speed, covering the half-mile or so to the tug immensely quickly, our bow wave spraying into our eyes. The two RIBs took up positions on either side of the tug and the commandos boarded with a lot more speed and expertise than I did. Instantly they were swarming over the tug, shouting at each other in the international language of special forces: 'Go go go!' Within minutes they had swept the ship, handcuffed everyone and had them all laid out on the deck, face down with their legs crossed so that they could easily see if anyone was preparing to stand up. Uncross your legs and you're a threat: in a real-life situation, that would mean the commandos might get to use those MP7s. One of the crew pointed out which of the captives were pirates – as far as the guys were concerned, everyone was a potential threat until proved otherwise. Finally, red smoke was sent up to indicate that the ship had been secured.

It was a slick operation. It might only have been an exercise, but it was a crucial one for the unit if they were to keep their skills honed. This particular unit had already been called upon to intervene in genuine piracy situations 15 times, and they knew that number 16 could happen at any moment.

We returned to the Japanese ship and headed back to port, sharing snakefruit – an indigenous fruit so named because of its scaly skin – with the MMEA maritime police. As we were entering the harbour, they clocked a boat coming in from Indonesia, which they pulled over. It was a fairly big boat, about half the length of a football pitch, and shaped a bit like a junk. The unit searched the vessel and it became clear that it was totally brimful of contraband. There wasn't a single bit of unused space. All sorts of things that you or I wouldn't think of smuggling were on board: chickens, pigs, ducks and, most valuable of all, Viagra, or a version of it – a growth industry, I'm told. (There's a massive business in fake pharmaceuticals in this part of the world, and while a few fake Viagra tablets might just render someone a bit floppy, there's a much more serious side to this racket. Imagine someone with HIV taking what they think are antiretroviral drugs to keep themselves alive, when in fact it's just salt and water . . .) Smuggling between Indonesia and Malaysia is commonplace – the maritime police could have stopped any one of the ships making that short journey and had a good chance of finding someone up to no good. The crew seemed pretty matter-of-fact about being nicked; the contraband was confiscated and the skipper knew he could face a penalty of some description. I don't know what that would be, but even he looked rather as if it was all in a day's work.

13. Lightning Storm Across the Sea

The job of policing the Malacca Straits is difficult, but the actions taken by the MMEA and the Malaysian government have had an effect. Some people think that Lloyds declaring it a war zone was the catalyst that made the Malaysian authorities wake up and smell the coffee; others that they would have had to do something about it at some stage. Whatever the truth, while it is undoubtedly the case that piracy remains a problem, it has decreased in certain parts of the straits as a result of the authorities' efforts.

When I had spoken to Muhammad Hamid, however, the brave young man who had thwarted the pirate attack on the *Nepline Delima*, he had given me an interesting nugget of information. The pirates who had taken his ship came from a place called Batam, a small Indonesian island (one of the 17,500 that make up that disparate country) situated just 12 miles off the coast of Singapore. This coincided with other information we had been given. The MMEA admiral had indicated that many of the pirates had moved their field of operations further to the south-east. It struck me when he said this that the MMEA's operations had not so much *stopped* piracy, but forced the pirates to work somewhere else. There's a lot of sea out there, and there's no way you can police it all.

It made sense that Batam, positioned right at the mouth of the Malacca Straits, would be a pirate hangout. So if I wanted to get close to Indonesian pirates, that small island sounded like the place to go. On the map it looks like just a quick hop, but with 20-odd bags and all the administration that goes with taking camera equipment from one country to another, it's not like that. Flying to Singapore from Malaysia is, of course, entering a different country, as was the boat journey from Singapore to Batam. Malaysia to Singapore to Indonesia is not a straightforward trip, especially for a camera crew.

Batam is the same size as Singapore – about 275 square miles. But that's where the similarities end. Singapore is rich and bustling, thriving from its position as a major international hub and financial centre. Batam, separated from Singapore by just a few miles of water, couldn't be more different. It's a poor place, with about a fifth of the population of Singapore. Those people that have jobs work in traditional industries such as fishing and manufacturing, but the gulf between the haves of Singapore and the have-nots of Batam couldn't be more stark. The shores were lined with rickety wooden dwellings supported on stilts; across the water you could see the gleaming skyscrapers of Singapore. The poverty here wasn't as bad as that which I'd seen in, say, Ajegunle, or maybe it was just the case that there was less desperation here. In Ajegunle rubbish lined the streets; here you had the impression that people might be poor, but they were more aware of their own environment. Parts of the island have even tried to establish themselves as tourist destinations. Away from the shanties there are a few beach resorts, and of course you get a great deal more for your money than you would if you were holidaying on Singapore island.

Still, poverty is poverty. Batam might have a small holiday industry, but it also has the problems that often accompany economic deprivation. It is, for example, a well-known destination for sex tourists, especially popular with the rich of Singapore in search of a dirty weekend. There are also known to be at least ten groups of pirates operating off the island. Batam is dominated by the shipping lanes. Look out to sea and you can't help but be impressed by the massive number of enormous merchant vessels that fill the skyline. I could well believe that if you were of a piratical frame of mind, the sight of all that wealth might be too much to resist, especially if you didn't have the means of making a living any other way. Or even, to be honest, if you did . . .

My hope was that by heading to Batam we could finally come face to face with modern-day pirates. Once again we knew that our best chance of achieving our ends was by staying inconspicuous; once again we looked like being thwarted. When we arrived at our hotel there was an electronic display in the foyer with rolling news and stock market prices. I was bleary-eyed and jet-lagged, but my eyes soon opened when I saw something flash across the screen. 'Welcome to celebrity ROSS KEMP!'

I blinked, then turned to the guys. 'Did I just see that?'

'See what?'

'My name, up on that screen.'

They shook their heads. 'Don't be stupid.'

I agreed with them, perfectly willing to believe that with the jet lag and exhaustion I'd been seeing things. But then I looked up again.

'Welcome to international celebrity ROSS KEMP! Staying here for five nights only!'

I turned to the guys again. 'You saw it this time, right?'

They nodded their heads slowly. 'Yeah, we saw it.' So much for our top-secret undercover investigation.

We'd been tipped off that the pirate gangs hang around the many pool bars that line the docks, waiting for their next job. So it was that on our first night in Batam we headed down to one of these bars with a couple of local fixers. They were grubby, low-rent places, the sort of joints where you could well imagine people of a criminal tendency hanging out. Smoky. Dimly lit. While we took up residence in one of the bars, our fixers moved to a neighbouring establishment, asking questions and gently probing the locals, trying to get an in with a Batam pirate who might be willing to speak to us while we did our best to keep a low profile.

That first night, though, there was nothing doing. It was with a vague sense of déjà vu that we headed back to our hotel room empty-handed, desperately hoping that we weren't about to relive our frustrations in the Niger Delta.

That evening in the pool halls, however, paid off. As a result of our under-the-counter enquiries, one of the pirate commanders of Batam agreed to meet us. It was a turning point in our investigation. We had travelled all over the world in search of pirates. We'd witnessed acts of piracy at first hand, and we'd experienced some of the factors that led desperate people to become pirates. However, although we'd come close – agonizingly close – to meeting actual pirates, we'd always fallen at the final post. Now was our chance, and I was a little apprehensive as we drove through the busy streets of the island, dodging the traffic as we made our way, finally, to meet a pirate.

The principal mode of transport on Batam, as it is all over south-east Asia, is the 50cc motorcycle. You see them everywhere and soon get used to their constant wasp-like humming. I've seen six people on one of these things – Dad driving and the rest of the family clinging on wherever they can like a hugger-mugger version of the Royal Signals Motorcycle Display Team. There are no people carriers for the poor of Batam. The vehicle that we were following, the one that was supposed to be leading us to our pirate, was not a motorcycle but a small silver car. The irony wasn't lost on me. To find a pirate, I wasn't going to sea but following a car, weaving among the overloaded motorbikes. But as I was beginning to learn, trouble on the water is directly linked to trouble on land. In a weird kind of way, it made sense.

As we followed the vehicle – and attracted glances from the locals, for whom Europeans were clearly a curiosity – I couldn't help but feel a bit dubious that this was anything other than a wild goose chase. We'd been let down too many times before to get our hopes up.

This time, though, our local fixers were on the money.

When we were a mile from the pirate's house, we stopped filming. The conditions of our interview were, reasonably enough, that we revealed neither his identity nor his location – not that I would ever have been able to find my way back there. But, in accordance with his request, we refrained from turning on the camera again until we were inside his house. A nice house, with a four-by-four parked outside. Clean. Well kept. It was a far cry from the poor buildings and shanties you find elsewhere on the island. If the balaclava'd man sitting in front of me genuinely was a pirate, as he claimed to be, it struck me that his line of work was definitely keeping the wolf from the door. What surprised me was that this had the hallmarks of being a religious household. A piece from the Bible was displayed on one of the walls, but in the background you could hear regular calls to prayer from two nearby mosques, reminding us that Indonesia is a Muslim, not a Christian, country.

In order to keep his identity secret, our pirate insisted that we use a fake name. 'What do you want me to call you?' I asked.

He spoke an indecipherable phrase, and our translator giggled. I turned to her. 'What does he want to be called?'

'He is called Lightning Storm Across the Sea.'

Modest, huh? It sounded like a bit of a mouthful to me. 'Do you think it would be all right if we just called him Storm?' I suggested.

She nodded. 'Yes, I think so.' And so it was that I found myself sitting down with a balaclava'd pirate called Storm. Over the years I flatter myself that I've become something of an aficionado in balaclava wear for the discerning criminal. To be honest, though, I wasn't quite sure what Storm was wearing. Maybe there's not much call for such items in Indonesia, but Storm's headwear had a distinctly home-made look. I couldn't help wondering if in one of his drawers there was a jumper with an arm missing.

I didn't dislike Storm. There was a calmness about him. Perhaps that's something that comes with being at sea for a long time. I don't know, but I could tell that he wasn't shouty or showy. As I grew to know him better, I learned that although he treated us with respect, he had a ruthless side. Calculating. Mess with him while he was going about his business and you'd surely regret it. He was the leader of a small group of pirates, some of whom I would meet later. That didn't mean, though, that he was entirely autonomous. Storm admitted to me that he took orders from someone further up the line to target certain ships, and I wanted to know who that person was.

Nothing doing. 'We don't know who the boss is,' Storm told me. 'This is Mafia law.'

Either Storm genuinely didn't know, or he wasn't going to tell me his name, and I could understand why that might be the case. He wasn't referring necessarily to the Italian Mafia, but it was clear that he was a cog in the wheel of some bigger crime organization. I doubted that his bosses would have taken too kindly to their names being revealed just because Storm wanted to get on the telly.

Storm wouldn't reveal the names of his masters, but he did shed some light on how his instructions, and the information about which boat to take, filtered down to him.

'Sometimes the crew gives us information. They give us the coordinates, the location of the ship that must be attacked.'

Knowing what I knew about the *Nepline Delima*, Storm's words rang true; the MMEA admiral had also hinted at this. Inside jobs – *Treasure Island* for the twenty-first century.

Storm went on to explain what happened to a ship once he and his colleagues had taken it. 'Up to the buyer,' he said. 'If it's wanted in Europe – no problem. If it's wanted in Asia – no problem. Sometimes it can take two weeks or even a month.' Quite an operation – these guys were substantially more than hit-and-run merchants, and there was clearly a lot of money involved in what they were doing.

Storm explained that most of the time when a ship is hijacked in this way, a buyer is already lined up – they don't just do these jobs on spec. But occasionally 'they want the boat to be lost because they need the insurance money to buy another boat'.

Once the pirates had delivered their boat to its designated destination, they would catch a flight back to Indonesia as part of the deal. So far, so sneaky. But a pirated ship has a crew, even if some of them are in cahoots with the hijack-ers – they would be lightly beaten up for the sake of appearances. But what happens to them then? Storm spoke matter-of-factly. 'We tie them up, blindfold them and leave them on an island,' he said. 'Or we put them on a raft and send them away.'

It was sounding more and more like *Treasure Island* by the minute, and I was struck by the fact that some things, at least, hadn't changed all that much since the Golden Age of Piracy, when pirated crews would be left on an island as a matter of course. Nowadays it's easier to locate somebody abandoned in this way, but crews can still potentially be marooned for quite some time. I wondered what they did for food. Or did the pirates just leave them to starve?

'They're human too,' Storm replied. 'They must be fed and not left to die.' That, at least, was something.

It was clear that in Storm's line of work you needed to be armed. I wanted to know what sort of weapons he and his buddies carried. 'Machete,' he told me. 'But I don't always use it.' You can bet your bottom dollar, though, that he *threatens* to use it, and when I put that to him Storm just nodded.

My Indonesian pirate had spoken in an honest and straightforward manner about what he did and how he did it. He might have been hiding his face behind his balaclava, but I didn't have the impression that he was hiding the truth. On the contrary, he appeared, if anything, proud of his activities. He saw himself as a professional, and demanded the respect that came with it. And as a proud professional, I wondered what he thought about his more high-profile Somali cousins, the ones who had so successfully eluded us in the Gulf of Aden. Storm was rather dismissive of them.

'In Somalia they board the boat and start shooting,' he said as if that was an act of the highest foolishness. 'You don't do a job like that. The pirate from Somalia is a stupid pirate. They're not in our class. They're low class in Somalia.' Pirate envy? Storm definitely thought that he and his boys were a cut above the rest.

Storm and his comrades didn't just make their living from big hijacks and insurance jobs. Like in any business, they knew that downtime was time when they weren't earning, and so they filled up the quiet periods with an activity known as 'shopping'. Storm explained to me exactly what this was. 'That's the term used by the pirates in Batam when we board any passing ship, just take the money and go.'

Hijacking they do with the cooperation of the crew; shopping is another matter. The piratical equivalent of smash and grab, it's a lot less risky than hijacking a ship, and the rewards are potentially great – especially as you can hit more than one ship in a night. I asked him if the crews generally put up any resistance when Storm and his gang went shopping. 'Some will fight back,' he said quietly, 'but we are not afraid of them. If they want to fight, we will kill them.'

He sounded almost prosaic as he said it. Cold. There was something scary about that lack of emotion, about the fact that he wasn't trying to be the big man but was just saying it as it was.

I didn't doubt that he was telling the truth.

For whatever reason, Storm and I seemed to get along. He offered to take us out into the busy shipping lanes off the coast of Batam so that he could show me exactly how they operated and which ships made good targets. In order to do this, we linked up with another guy who wanted to give himself some sort of Dick Dastardly name – I think it was Ghost of the High Seas. More inventive than 'Mr Smith', I guess, but we tried not to show that we found their monikers amusing.

Going out to sea with a troop of balaclava'd pirates has its risks. Storm and Ghost were clearly dangerous men but I didn't feel, for the moment at least, that they were likely to give us any problems. And it wouldn't have been difficult to pick Ghost out of a line-up, even with a balaclava, because he had wingnuts which made him look like he was wearing ear defenders. The authorities, though, were a different matter. The waters of Batam were highly patrolled – if we were caught in the company of pirates, we would have a lot of explaining to do. To keep our profile lower, Storm suggested we rent a traditional fishing boat – long and low and with a small outboard motor. To be honest, the vessel wasn't really fit for the job. It wasn't much more than 15 metres in length and a couple of metres wide. Into that space we had to fit me, two pirates, someone steering, a translator and three camera crew. A boat like this simply isn't designed to come up against the wakes of the kind of shipping we were likely to encounter, and being heavily weighed down with bodies didn't help matters. We were a mismatched bunch, and trying to explain what we were doing in the shipping lanes would not, I thought, be easy. But we were in the pirates' hands and didn't have much option other than to do what they suggested.

Not long after we set sail, it started to look as if our plan wasn't going to be successful. We were way out in the Malacca Straits – land had disappeared – when one of the many patrol boats turned towards us. It was painted in brown and blue camouflage, had a distinctly military look, and appeared to have clocked us.

I felt my heart sink. Associating with pirates was undoubtedly a serious offence, and a stint in an Indonesian jail wasn't very high up the list of things I wanted to do while I was here. Fortunately for us, at the last minute the patrol boat veered away. It seemed we were of no interest to it, and we were able to continue our voyage unobserved.

We steered into the path of what looked to me like a very large vessel. I asked Storm if he would consider pirating a ship that size. He nodded his head.

'Isn't it too high?' I asked him.

'No,' he replied emphatically. 'No, this is almost perfect.' He said he would take it from behind (no sniggering at the back), which surprised me because the freeboard was at its highest there. But what surprised me even more than that was the fact that as we were bobbing around in the ocean discussing the niceties of how to hijack a ship, the ship itself was heading straight for us. Because of our perspective, it was difficult to say just how fast the vessel was travelling, but it was certainly shifting – one moment it looked far away, and the next it was almost on top of us. Its bow wave and wake were massive – for a brief moment I got an insight into the nerves you'd need to get up close to one of these things when they're moving. What was clear, however, was that this big ship simply hadn't seen us. It was on a direct collision course and was making no attempt to steer away or to alert us to its presence. The implication wasn't lost on me: if this ship couldn't see us during the hours of daylight, what kind of chance would it have at night?

Storm reiterated that he had taken ships this size. 'For shopping,' he said.

Not for hijacking, though?

'Sometimes.'

Our little boat rolled and rattled in the wake. Wouldn't they wait until it was stationary, to make life a bit easier?

No way. 'Moving. While it's moving.'

We continued our tour of the shipping lanes and before long drew up alongside another vessel, the NYK *Antares*, 300 metres long and registered in Panama. It was piled high with countless enormous, colourful shipping containers – impossible to say what it was carrying, but it certainly had a lot of stuff on board. It was, Storm told me, an ideal target for shopping. This wasn't just because of its shape and size but because, as it came from Panama, its crew would most likely be carrying American dollars. As in so many other parts of the world, in Batam the greenback talks. Ships carrying dollars run a much higher risk of hit-and-run attacks than any others. Storm estimated that there would be a minimum of $3,000 on board. Three thousand bucks would go a long way in Batam, but our pirates told us that they wouldn't be satisfied with that as a payday. 'If they are only carrying the minimum then we have to find more boats,' Storm explained. 'In one night we aim to collect $15,000 before we go home.'

Fifteen thousand dollars. Hence the smart four-by-four parked outside his house. I wondered how often they would go out shopping to swipe sums like this. 'It's difficult to say. Sometimes we go out once a month, sometimes it's two or three times a month. We usually go shopping at the beginning of the month because that's when the crew get paid.' So, if nothing else, our boys knew how to get the maximum return on their investment. There was something extremely businesslike about the way they approached all this.

Unlike the previous vessel, the *Antares* spotted us. There was a man on the bridge wing with a pair of binoculars and a radio. He clearly didn't like what he saw. The air was suddenly filled with a huge sound. Many merchant vessels have the facility to operate directional horns, a piece of apparatus that they use in an attempt to prevent piracy. If I were a pirate, I could well imagine that having that number of decibels blasted in your direction could encourage you to try your luck elsewhere. Apparently, though, they're not all that effective.

On this occasion the noise was more than enough to warn us off. If we didn't move away they could easily have sent out a distress call, and in any case, if any of the patrol ships had heard the *Antares*' horn, they could well be in the vicinity soon.

'Turn away!' Storm shouted. '*Turn away!*' There was an edge to his voice, so we made ourselves scarce.

As the day progressed, Storm and Ghost continued to

point out vessels in the Malacca Straits. There barely seemed to be any that they wouldn't consider pirating. Many of the ships they showed us had high freeboards. I'd learned in Somalia that high-freeboard boats were generally less vulnerable because it was more difficult for the pirates to use their ladders and grappling hooks to get on deck. But these Indonesian pirates seemed confident – blasé, even – that they could board such vessels with ease. What was more amazing was that they didn't use ladders *or* grappling hooks. They had a different technique – one that had been used in this region for centuries.

But there wasn't time for them to tell me about it now. The sky was darkening. Clouds gathered. We had no lights on board, and because we were so small we were not identifiable on any ship's radar. This meant we were vulnerable to collisions, so with that thought in mind we decided to call it a day, and headed back to shore.

That night there was another torrential thunderstorm. The heavens opened. It had been a long old day, a day during which I'd had a small taste of what it was like to be a pirate on the Malacca Straits. Frankly, I was very glad to return to the relative comfort of a hotel room, rather than be stuck out at sea in a tiny rickety boat, buffeted by the billowing swell of the waves, the air almost as full of water as the wide, hazardous ocean.

14. Five Little Pirates Sitting in a Tree

There are certain things you never expect to hear yourself say. 'I'm glad I've bumped into pirates' is probably one of them. But after so much time searching, so many disappointments and shattered expectations, I was pretty pleased to have made contact with some genuine Indonesian pirates, to be shown the ropes by Storm and Ghost. And as they seemed to trust us, the next day they offered to take us out to an island where they would demonstrate to us the techniques they used to board ships. Just one problem: the island to which they were taking us was one of those that they used to maroon hijacked crews. I was glad that our investigation was bearing fruit, but I think it was at the back of everyone's mind that we needed to stay on the good side of these characters if we didn't want to be marooned ourselves . . .

The pirates had said that what they were about to show us required the use of parangs – a kind of machete that is very common in that part of the world. But for some bizarre legal or health and safety reason that I still don't understand, we were informed by London that I had to supply the weapons. Fortunately, getting your hands on a parang is rather easier on Batam island than it is back home – you just walk into a hardware store and pay your money. They even did me a deal – buy two, get a third off. In Indonesia parangs are everywhere – it's a bit like buying a screwdriver.

Except, of course, that a parang can do a lot more damage than a Phillips. In any case, when we finally hooked up with our pirates again, they already had their own machetes.

Hardware sorted, it was time to leave Batam. This time the pirates sent a boat for us. We loaded up and sped towards one of the many islands that are dotted around this stretch of water. As we travelled, the horizon was dominated by the skyline of Singapore and I was reminded once more what a temptation that must be for the poor people of Indonesia. With millions of dollars' worth of goods and cash sailing out of that port, right past their front door, it's hardly surprising that some of them grab the opportunity to fill their boots. And there were hundreds of islands too. If the pirates had a fast boat, they could squirrel themselves away on one of these islands and it would be virtually impossible to find them.

We had agreed with the pirates that we wouldn't reveal the name of the island they used for their activities. When we arrived there, the tide was out so our boat had to anchor several football pitches away from the shore. As a result we had to wade in with water up to our knees – a slightly nervy process because the region plays host to stone fish, highly poisonous ceatures which are able to camouflage themselves against the underwater stones. Stepping on one of those can be at best excruciating, at worst fatal. The locals were happy to take the risk; I wore my shoes. We must have been an odd sight, and the balaclava'd pirates waiting for us on the island – five or six of them on this occasion, members of Storm's crew – knew that. They stayed firmly out of sight, behind the treeline, in case we attracted any unwanted attention.

Bamboo grows high on this island, and it was among the bamboo that the pirates were waiting for us. This was the raw material of their trade, the thing they used to board ships in the absence of ladders and grappling hooks. Armed with super-sharp parangs – which they wielded with great skill – they cut down a 40- to 50-foot high bamboo stalk, before shaving off the sharp edges to leave a perfectly smooth pole. As they worked I noticed for the first time that almost to a man the skin on their legs was covered with indentations that looked as if they had been carved away with a teaspoon. This, I was told, was a result of scratching away at mosquito bites when they were children, and it was certainly true that the mosquito population was very high.

The pirates would use a bamboo pole such as they had just prepared to rest against the side of the ship, but in order for it to stay in place they needed some sort of hook at the top. I was expecting a dedicated metal hook; in fact they used a short, strong length of a particular root, which they tied to the end of the bamboo with twine (in a delightful shade of pink) and fixed in a V-shape so it could be used to hang the whole bamboo from the railing on the edge of a ship's deck.

The pirates made their bamboo poles from scratch in minutes. In order to scale a high-freeboard boat they would need to join a few such lengths of bamboo together, so it might take a little longer. But not much. I couldn't help wondering what would happen if they were caught travelling with a piece of equipment like this. Storm shrugged. 'Before the marine police catch us,' he said, 'we throw everything overboard. Into the sea.' Which made perfect sense, of course, because all they needed to do was come back here and make another one.

It was impressive stuff, but I still couldn't quite see how anyone could shimmy up it so they offered to show me. Obviously we couldn't do it out at sea because we'd be arrested; instead they hung the bamboo pole from the branch of a nearby tree. The base of the pole was a couple of metres from the ground; the top was several metres up. If I had tried to make like a pirate and climb the bamboo, everyone would have had a good laugh and I'd have landed in a heap. Not so these guys. With his parang slung across his back, the first one shimmied up the pole in moments. Then the next. Within seconds, there were five little pirates sitting in the tree. And if they could be up a tree in seconds, they could be on the deck of merchant vessel in seconds too.

The pirates slid back down as easily as they had shimmied up. Once they were on terra firma, Storm explained to me exactly what would happen once they had boarded the vessel. 'We take our parangs,' he said. 'We look for the crew on the ship and we apprehend them. We go directly to the bridge and turn off the communications system, then we look for the captain. I tell the captain I need money and it's better for him to surrender and not fight back. If you fight back, you're going to die.'

And if the captain says no?

'Then we have to hurt them.'

Generally speaking, Storm said, it was the Russian and Korean crews who tended to put up a struggle. If this should happen, they cut their victims' hands – he demonstrated with a mock slash across his palm. 'When their hand is wounded, they start bleeding, and when they see the blood, they usually give up.' And, of course, a man with sliced-up hands is severely disabled.

But what if their hostages still fight back?

'We kill him.'

Simple as that. Indeed, simplicity was the key to the pirates' endeavours – I doubted that the techniques they had shown me had changed for hundreds of years. If it ain't broke, don't fix it. The pink twine they used to attach the hook was a modern invention, but it would have been perfectly possible to use some sort of natural cordage in its place. It also struck me that their outlay was minimal. Storm said that they tended to hire boats from local smugglers, and the rest of the equipment they need is just there for the taking, with the exception of the parangs, which can be bought cheaply from a hardware store. It's not quite like having to get your hands on a sawn-off shotgun to commit an armed robbery. Expenditure tiny; potential rewards huge. No wonder Storm and his crew were eager practitioners of their art.

Before we left the island, the pirates used their parangs to hack up the bamboo stalks and hide their tracks. They were worried about the patrol boats in the area, so we decided to call it a day. As we headed back, we encountered yet another torrential Indonesian rainstorm, one of the worst I'd ever experienced. Forging across the water back towards Batam, I couldn't have been wetter if I'd jumped in the sea. In the distance, a huge, bright rainbow shone above one of the many islands, dipping over the horizon and back down into the sea. Was there a pot of gold at the end of it? I couldn't help thinking that if you were a pirate, armed only with a piece of bamboo and a razor-sharp parang, there probably was.

*

In our minds, pirates are mysterious, romantic figures. In reality, they're just ordinary people, criminals who ply their trade at sea. As such, they have ordinary concerns, and families too. I was given the opportunity to meet the wife of one of Storm's crew. Like her husband, the pirate's wife didn't want her face shown or her name revealed. Rather than don a makeshift balaclava, however, she hid her features more elegantly using a small umbrella as we sat by the waterfront and discussed what it was like to be married to the mob.

She was a lovely girl – softly spoken, heavily pregnant and with passable, if hesitant, English. She had met her husband nine years previously and for a while they were best friends. She came from a good background and explained that her family – many of whom had died in the Bali bombings – had no idea that she was married to a pirate. They all believed he earned his living from a small shop he owned, where he sold handmade chairs. I wondered what would happen if they found out the truth.

'They ask me to divorce, maybe.'

Even though the baby's on the way?

She nodded her head.

The pirate's wife explained to me that when Storm's crew went out on a job, the wives would all spend the night together in one house, trying to sleep but more often chatting and comforting each other as they waited for their husbands to come home safely. The worst times, she said, were when the men switched off their mobile phones. Out of sight. Out of contact. But not out of mind. I could only imagine the strain they must be under, knowing that their men were out doing something so potentially dangerous, knowing that they could disappear, or die. Who would look after her then, I asked.

She gave a little laugh. 'Nobody,' she replied.

Doesn't that worry her as well?

'Yeah, I worry. I say this one already to him, but he say, "This is my life. I had this one before I see you."'

It was in his blood, she told me, to be a pirate. 'Sometimes he say, "If I have a son, I want him same like me. Be the pirate."'

And would that make her happy too?

'No. I want he be the police. Maybe this is how to stop the father being a pirate.'

This young lady was under no illusions about the reality of her husband's activities. She surely knew that he could kill people – that maybe he had already. Did that not bother her? 'This is a problem for me,' she said, 'but I cannot say anything. This is his life.'

The pirate's wife clearly worried and disapproved of her husband's nocturnal activities. At the same time she accepted that this was how he brought home the bacon. 'We eat from this job,' she said quietly. 'If he not go for working, we no have anything.'

She was very frank with me, and the more we spoke the more I realized that her life was very far from being a bed of roses. Her husband clearly liked life in the fast lane, and that wasn't limited to piracy. 'Girls, money, drugs – all the pirates same like that.' Even her husband? 'Now after married, no – but before he always drunk. If he drink, he always slap me, fight with me, hit me. After he know I'm pregnant, he change everything. But I know him. He's not a good man. He's a naughty boy.'

There was something slightly tragic about her. Without wanting to over-romanticize it, I was reminded of Carmela Soprano. She wasn't a bad person; she was just resigned to the reality of her life. She didn't want her husband to be a pirate, but she knew she couldn't change him. Maybe she didn't *want* to change him. There was a curious mixture of disapproval and acceptance, and it all came down to the age-old story. Before they got married, her husband's family gave her the third degree.

'They say, "Do you know he no go to school?"'

'I say, "Yeah, I know."'

'"Do you know he the pirate? Do you know he stay in jail before?"'

'And I say, "Yeah, I know."'

'"And you accept him?"'

'"If he accept me, I can accept everything, bad and good, from him. Because I love him."'

It was abundantly clear that this young woman was not with her husband for any reason other than love. 'For me, money not mean anything. If you have love, maybe you can have anything you want.'

And maybe you can. But as the sun went down over the seas where her husband plied his dangerous trade, I couldn't help wondering what the future held for this quietly spoken woman, pregnant by a pirate she loved and unable – perhaps unwilling – to get him to change his ways.

My time on the island of Batam was drawing to a close. But before I left I took the opportunity to meet Storm and his crew one last time. They had shown me *where* they performed their acts of piracy; they had shown me *how* they performed their acts of piracy. But so far they hadn't been too forthcoming on the whys and wherefores. We met on yet another island – the lads had even put on fresh balaclavas for the occasion – and as we sat under a tree, shading ourselves from the blistering heat of the Indonesian sun, I tried to get to the bottom of why these pirates did what they did.

'Poverty is everywhere,' Storm told me. 'We steal to eat, not to get rich.'

Really? I put it to them that when they go shopping, they can make a lot of money in one night. Storm disagreed. 'When we go shopping we find that not every ship has a lot of cash. So if we don't get much we have to do it again until we get at least $10,000 each and then we go home.'

I wasn't quite buying it. They said they only committed acts of piracy to eat, not to get rich. But that kind of money buys a lot of food. I suggested to them that it also buys cars and houses.

A beat.

An unpleasant silence.

Up until now the atmosphere between me and Storm's crew had been good. Relaxed even. This was the only time it turned. They obviously didn't like the way the conversation had gone, and suddenly the mood changed, like a cloud slipping over the sun. I knew that I couldn't afford to upset them too much – if things became nasty between us, they could just mug us, steal our camera equipment and leave us on the island.

Storm shook his head. 'No,' he said. And that was that. He didn't want to elaborate, and I certainly wasn't going to push the issue.

We'd heard rumours that there was a mythology among Indonesian pirates that they could make themselves invisible. Not normally the sort of thing you'd give credence to, but after my experiences in Nigeria I was interested to know what Storm and the crew had to say. One of the younger members, whose ears made his balaclava stick out comically, put his oar in. 'That's right,' he announced. 'We have supernatural powers. You can call it magic. We make people see other things instead of us. For example, for two months I went shopping every day and I was never caught. So I believe it.'

He spoke passionately. His mates, though, were on the verge of laughter. I asked Storm what he thought. 'I used to believe it,' he admitted. 'But then I was caught and put in jail!'

Ah.

'So I don't believe in magic any more. I use common sense now.'

Common sense sounded to me like a better strategy than mysticism. The guys told me that the brother of one of them was a member of the maritime police, and he knew full well how his sibling made his living. The two brothers had an agreement: if the copper had to nick the pirate, he would go to jail; but in the meantime he agreed not to shop him. Like I say: common sense, not magic.

Given that most of the crew didn't consider themselves to be invulnerable, however, didn't they worry that one day they'd be caught or would come to harm? 'That's always a risk in this kind of job,' one of the crew admitted. 'We don't think about life and death. We die when the time comes for us to die. That's the risk we choose to take.'

The vibe between us all had settled down now. I felt a bit more comfortable asking my last question of this gang of pirates. 'What would happen if someone tried to give away your identity? If a pirate went to the police, what would happen to him?'

A pregnant pause.

'Our law is Mafia law,' answered Ghost. 'We would kill that person.'

And as if to back him up, another repeated the words.

'Kill him,' he said.

We took our leave of the pirates. They didn't, in the end, maroon us, or rob us. They just disappeared, unrepentant and proud, ready to steal another day. I prepared to leave Batam – and south-east Asia – with the strange feeling that always accompanies meeting people like that. I knew they were criminals. I knew that what they did was wrong. I didn't condone it in any way. But when you get to know people on a personal level, you can't help but start to understand things from their point of view. Storm and his crew claimed to be driven by poverty. How true that was, I can't say. He certainly seemed to live in a nicer house than most, and he drove a decent car. The sort of sums they claimed to secure when they went shopping were substantial – enough to keep more people than just them well clear of the breadline. And though Batam was a notorious pirate hot spot, there were plenty of poor people there who *didn't* resort to illegality.

That said, Storm and his boys were hardly living a life of unparalleled luxury. If they weren't able to earn their living from piracy, what sort of life *would* they have? Indonesia is a poor country. Nearly 18 per cent of its people live below the poverty line, and nearly 50 per cent live on less than two dollars a day. It's not difficult to see why crime might thrive; and in a country that is made up of thousands of tiny islands, it's not difficult to see why a substantial proportion of that crime might take place on the water – especially in an area where they have the imposing skyline of rich Singapore to tempt them. I didn't admire the pirates for their violence, but I did have a sneaking admiration for their focus and professionalism, for making their difficult way in a difficult world.

Moreover, by their own admission, the people I had met were very much on the bottom rung of piracy. They weren't commanding multi-million-dollar ransoms like the Somali pirates, and they were being manipulated by shadowy Mr Big figures who were pocketing the real money while Storm's crew risked their lives and their liberty. It was the Mr Bigs that I really despised, not their foot soldiers.

I didn't leave Batam feeling sympathy for the pirates I had met, but I did feel I understood them. And I also understood this. Piracy at sea is not so different from criminality on land. It will exist as long as the gulf between the haves and the have-nots remains wide.

PART 4
Djibouti

15. The Pirate of Puntland

While I had been in south-east Asia, piracy off the coast of Somalia had gone off the scale. During my time on HMS *Northumberland* a delicate kind of ceasefire had existed. The warships of Operation Atalanta had refrained from storming hijacked ships; in return, the pirates had held back from killing their hostages. But since then things had changed, and they'd changed for the worse.

The *Maersk Alabama* was a 17,000-tonne American cargo ship. It was attacked by four pirates in the April of 2009, but things did not go quite according to their plan. When the pirates boarded, the captain, Richard Phillips, instructed all his crew to lock themselves in their cabins. He then offered himself to the pirates as a hostage, with the proviso that the *Alabama* was set free. The pirates put Phillips on one of the merchant vessel's bright-orange lifeboats, then sailed it to within 30 miles of the Somali coast under the constant surveillance of US warships and helicopters.

FBI hostage negotiators flew to the scene and opened up lines of communication. The pirates demanded a ransom of $2 million in return for the captain's life. The captain tried to escape by jumping into the sea. The pirates easily recaptured him – though one of them sustained an injury to his hand – and started making threats against his life. They were surrounded by the might of the American navy, including the missile cruiser USS *Bainbridge*, but that didn't seem to dampen their enthusiasm.

Days passed. The pirates ran out of food and water. They accepted supplies from the Americans, and as a result a small boat made several trips between the pirates and the *Bainbridge*. On one of these trips the pirate with the wounded hand asked for medical assistance. He was, in effect, surrendering, and he was taken back to the American warship.

That left three of them, and Captain Phillips.

Unbeknown to the pirates, a team of US Navy Seals had parachuted into the sea with inflatable boats before being picked up by the *Bainbridge*. Their orders, direct from President Obama, were to use force only if Captain Phillips' life appeared to be in imminent danger. Four days after their original attack the pirates, having run out of fuel, accepted a towline from the *Bainbridge*. That evening, however, the Seals observed a tracer bullet coming from the pirates' boat. Tracers are generally only fired in order to give the user an idea of the trajectory on which they should fire live rounds. It didn't exactly ease the tension, and the Seals used night-vision devices to see what was happening. One of the pirates, they observed, had his assault rifle pointed at the back of Captain Phillips; what was more, the Seals had a clear line of fire at all three targets.

The Seals received the order to fire. Three pirates. Three shots. That was all they needed, even though the lifeboat was being trailed at the end of a 100-foot line and presented a moving target for the sharpshooters. The pirates died instantly and the Seals rescued Captain Phillips.

The *Maersk Alabama* was the first American ship to be pirated since the Second Barbary War nearly 200 years previously, and the reaction to the death of the pirates on the Somali mainland showed the problems involved with using military force to combat piracy. A pirate holding a Greek ship went on the record as saying, 'Every country will be treated the way it treats us. In the future, America will be the one crying . . .'

Intervention by special forces led to the pirates being killed and Captain Phillips being rescued. But the good guys don't always win, no matter how highly trained they are; violence doesn't always go according to plan. This was well illustrated by an incident that occurred at practically the same time as the hijacking of the *Maersk Alabama*. This was the pirating of the French yacht *Tanit*. The *Tanit*'s skipper was a 28-year-old man by the name of Florent Lemacon, and on board were four other passengers, including his wife and three-year-old son.

Lemacon was making his way down the Gulf of Aden to the island of Zanzibar, off the coast of Tanzania. He'd been warned about the dangers, but had made the decision not to heed the advice – by all accounts he was a free spirit, determined not to allow criminal elements to stop him from going where and doing what he wanted. Good on him, I guess. They took certain precautions, such as sailing with their lights dimmed to avoid detection by pirates. They even sent a message from the middle of the ocean which read, 'We are in the middle of the piracy zone . . . the danger is there, and has indeed become greater over the past months, but the ocean is vast. The pirates must not be allowed to destroy our dream.'

Unfortunately, the pirates didn't see it quite the same way. *Tanit* was 400 miles off the coast of Somalia when it was boarded by pirates with AK-47s and held to ransom. Unfortunately for the Lemacons, they didn't have the might of an international shipping organization behind them, nor a precious cargo – at least not in monetary terms. Negotiations with the pirates broke down. On this occasion there was no suitcase full of used notes parachuted onto the deck. Instead, there was a troop of French special forces, dispatched to do what special forces do.

The commandos stormed the yacht and were engaged by the gun-toting pirates. A firefight took place, and two of the pirates were killed. But the yacht's skipper was caught in the crossfire and took a bullet in the head. Whether it came from a pirate's gun or from one of the French SF weapons isn't public knowledge. The net result was the same, though: Florent Lemacon died instantly, widowing a wife and orphaning a child.

The significance of these two events wasn't lost on me. During my stay on HMS *Northumberland* the Royal Marines had been unable to board the pirated *Saldanha* for fear that the pirates, who so far had avoided killing their hostages, would change tack. The Somali pirates certainly had the weaponry to cause a great deal of death and destruction, and if the situation on the mainland was anything to go by, they were ruthless enough to do so should they decide to. The question was this: now that foreign governments had started to retaliate, would the pirates escalate the situation? Was the body count about to start rising?

My time on *Northumberland* had been interesting but ultimately frustrating. I still felt there was more to learn about the situation in Somalia, that there was more of a story to tell. Of course, nothing had changed on the mainland – setting foot on Somali soil was still so hazardous as to make it a no-go area for Western film crews. We could, however, go back to Djibouti, the neighbouring country where we had disembarked from *Northumberland*. Which was handy, because we had an in with a fixer who was about to put a cherry on the top of the cake of our investigation.

His name wasn't Jacques, but that's what I'll call him. He was a good-looking Frenchman who ran a diving school in that tiny country. My impression was that he was a man with connections – a good pair of eyes and a brain full of local knowledge that he would share with anyone for a fee. He knew everyone, and everyone knew Jacques. Djibouti is now a military port, and while we were there a Japanese warship arrived. The commander sought Jacques out and asked if he could help him go hunting for big game. Perhaps he had mistaken Djibouti for the Serengeti.

Jacques' face was a picture. 'You are mad!' he said. 'You want to kill things? There's nothing to kill here. I can take you diving, but you cannot kill anything.' The commander was sent packing, disappointed that he wasn't able to decorate the bridge of his ship with a rhino's head; but happily Jacques was of more use to us in the hunt for our quarry. He knew people who knew people, and thought he could fix us up with a genuine Somali pirate. It was too good an opportunity to pass up.

Jacques specialized in getting people in and out of Somalia, and said that he could, in principle, get us into the piratical region of Puntland. Like everyone else we talked to, though, he qualified his statement by saying we only had a 50-50 chance of getting out alive. Camera teams, he told us, were especially at risk. If you went into Somalia as a fixer or a problem solver and got killed, chances were there would be repercussions from your murder from whoever was hiring you. But camera teams don't go into that country at anyone's behest. Nobody in Somalia is going to protect them. If we wanted to meet Jacques' pirate *in* Somalia, the only way of doing it would be to fly into a provincial Puntland airport and conduct the interview on the tarmac. That might be all right, but Jacques also told us that if we chose that option, we'd have to make sure our plane's engines were constantly turning over. Great for a quick getaway if everything went pear-shaped; impossible for our camera crew to record anything satisfactory above the sound of the engines.

We couldn't travel to meet Jacques' pirate for all these reasons. But maybe he could fix it so that the pirate could come to us. Only time would tell. Meanwhile we had another stroke of good luck.

Colonel Abshir was born in the Bari region of northern Somalia. Having passed through the Somali Military Academy, where he studied tanks, army fighting and military leadership, he became a lieutenant colonel and a high-ranking intelligence officer in the government of Siad Barré – the last Somali administration to be officially recognized by the international community. Some people branded Barré's regime a dictatorship; I could only imagine what an intelligence officer in such a regime had got up to. Barré was removed from power in a coup and died in Kenya in 1995, but former members of his government remained influential in Somali society, and Colonel Abshir was one of them. He was now part of the Puntland Private Security Consultation Organization. As such, he knew a thing or two about the pirates of Puntland. We had arranged to meet him in Djibouti, to get an insight into Somali piracy from someone on the inside.

It was a hot, dusty afternoon. Impossibly hot – the kind of heat that you know will do you damage if you stay out in it too long. We met in a room at Jacques' diving school.

As we sat down together in the blistering heat, Colonel Abshir told me of his hopes for his country. 'I was born in an independent Somalia,' he said. 'There was a central government that was governing the whole country. My only wish is to see a proper Somali central government, a government with proper institutions that safeguards law and order and wipes out the current situations of sea piracy, terrorism and other problems, and provides a proper, lasting solution for Somalia. My ambition is to have a peaceful life. For the remaining days of my life, I would like to live in Somalia with a government that offers me and my family the opportunity to get education, employment and guaranteed security for the future. I wish to have a government that is good to its neighbouring countries and the entire world. God willing, that will happen one day.'

God willing indeed. But the gulf between the Somalia of Colonel Abshir's ambitions and the one that currently existed seemed to me to be almost insurmountably wide.

I wanted to talk to the colonel about what I'd heard regarding the reasons for piracy in Somalia – the toxic waste, the illegal fishing. His answer was not quite what I expected. 'Yes,' he said, 'there is dumping of material such as nuclear waste, industrial waste, illegal fishing in our waters and other problems. However, the simple, ordinary pirate boy has no knowledge of these. It is not, as they claim, that they are patriotic and defending the fishes in our sea or against waste and other illegal activities. These illiterate pirates have no knowledge of what nuclear or industrial waste *is*. These pirates are employees, and are put to work by some individuals.'

The colonel's point was enlightening. I didn't have much doubt that the dumping of toxic waste and the illegal fishing of Somali waters had been at least a catalyst for the piracy that currently existed, but what he seemed to be saying was that it had now evolved into something more businesslike.

What of Eyl, that lawless pirate town to which the MV *Saldanha* had been taken. 'Eyl is the garage of hijacked ships,' he agreed. 'The pirate will take the kidnapped ship to Eyl because in there he will find his friends, plenty of other sea pirates who are also armed and live in Eyl.'

I asked him how he expected the use of force in the cases of the *Maersk Alabama* and the *Tanit* to affect piracy in the region. 'From now on,' he told me, 'I think that if a French or American national is taken hostage, they won't ask for a ransom. They will either give them back or treat them in the same way that their friends were treated.'

Treating them in the same way, of course, meant shooting them. I couldn't help but think that this was a more likely outcome than simply letting them go.

Abshir smiled as he spoke. It was difficult to judge quite what he thought about all this. 'The pirates,' he told me, 'are like a family, regardless of where they come from. They share a common interest.'

And family, as we know, look after their own.

Colonel Abshir revealed to me the Somali pirates were not working entirely on their own – some of them were getting outside help. 'We know that there are some nationals from Sudan, Asmara, Mombasa that are helping pirates, teaching them techniques.' (Sudan! Perhaps my slip of the tongue when I was pontificating for the chiefs of Ajegunle hadn't been so wide of the mark . . .) In fact, the problem went deeper than that. 'During the war between the two Yemens, which North Yemen won, there were many military officers from the south who were sacked from their jobs. These officers were disarmed and suffered demoralization. They were later given some small fishing boats. They used to fish in the Somali water and had a good working relationship with other Somali fishermen. We know that they are now involved in the piracy in Somalia. I have concrete evidence of a case in which some Yemeni fishermen from the former marine force of Yemen actually hijacked a ship and sold it to the Somali pirates.'

From what the colonel was saying, the problem of piracy off the coast of Somalia was more multi-layered than I had previously thought. There were the fishermen; there were the people who controlled the fishermen; there were foreigners who had been attracted to the region because of unrest in their own countries. I wondered if Abshir had any idea of the number of pirates currently operating in his country. 'Our organization,' he told me, 'has registered the number of pirates to be nearly 3,000.' This figure included both those who had actually taken part in acts of piracy as well as those who were dealers and investors. Amazingly, Colonel Abshir claimed to know exactly who they all were. 'We have registered all of them and have photographs of most of them. We also have details of their names, ethnic origins, names of their mothers and their places of birth and nationality. We monitor their activities and know their current situations – where they are and if they have left the country.'

If this was true, it was astonishing. In Nigeria and Batam the pirates were shadowy and secretive. In Somalia, apparently, the authorities had their numbers, but because of the disastrous situation in that country, they were powerless to act. 'I can't give their names at the moment,' Abshir said, 'because they are too powerful.'

I could understand that the colonel might not want to give us the names of those people he knew to be involved in piracy. That could be dangerous for his health. But I did want to know what was happening to the massive quantities of money that were being earned as ransoms for the merchant vessels taken to Eyl. 'The team on the ship share the money,' he told me, 'and the biggest share goes to the boss.' And these bosses, he said, were very, very wealthy men. 'Millionaires. *Millionaires!*'

The big question was this: how do you stop someone from becoming a pirate? 'If all the warships in the world were gathered together in the Somali sea,' he suggested, 'it's still not a solution.' My time on *Northumberland* suggested he was right. And he predicted that if things continued on their current trajectory, the situation could only get worse. 'If the international community chooses not to do anything, it is possible that these movements of piracy, terrorism, smugglers, illegal armies, drug traffickers and human rights abuses could lead to worse international security situations. Everything that is possible will happen. There could be explosions. They could explode oil tankers. They could even kill people on captured ships because the pirates now have enough money and are very rich. They might not need any more money. That is possible.'

And did the colonel have any suggestions as to how the international community could help?

'Only if they could approach the small regional administration of Puntland, offer to recruit and train one to two thousand soldiers from the Somalis in Puntland, offer proper equipment, install intelligence systems and also offer financial assistance to Puntland. I strongly believe that the budget of all that will be less than what they are now spending on a half-day. If they could make a network and launch one very successful operation against these pirates, I am sure they would be wiped out.'

Not the worst idea I'd ever heard. But as the colonel spoke I couldn't help remembering that the international community had tried to intervene in Somalia before. The result of that intervention had been the disastrous Battle of Mogadishu. I didn't doubt that Abshir's belief that piracy needed to be tackled on land, not at sea, was on the money. But having been bitten once, I can't help thinking that the international community is likely to be twice shy . . .

Colonel Abshir's take on Somalian piracy had been bleak but honest. However, I was about to get a much more personal view of the situation. Because finally, after months of searching, the call finally came in. By ways and means that I can't fully reveal, our contacts had come good. A meet had been arranged and we were about to come face to face with a genuine Somali pirate, one of the reckless individuals who wreak such havoc in the Gulf of Aden, commanding ransoms of millions of pounds, and striking genuine fear into the hearts of any ships' crews passing through that busy and important waterway.

We were told to leave the city of Djibouti and travel by boat to a secret location – a small island just off the coast and not far from Somali waters. It was early in the morning, but already the heat was intense. The waters round the island were crystalline and blue – like something out of a holiday brochure. I wouldn't recommend taking your holidays round here, though, for fear of encountering someone like the man I was here to meet. We stood on the sandy shore of that island, not knowing what to expect or even if our man was actually going to turn up for sure. After my experiences in Nigeria I was more than prepared to be disappointed yet again. Pirates, I had learned, had a way of promising one thing and doing another. Reliability was not their strong point.

But then, as I stood on the beach, a boat slid slowly into view.

It was a small boat. Old. Painted white, with an outboard motor. There were two men in it, dark-skinned and with black and white keffiyehs wrapped around their heads to obscure their faces. One of these men was our pirate. He wore a white short-sleeved shirt and dark trousers. His body was thin – slight almost. In many ways he was unremark-able to look at. Unprepossessing. As we settled down to talk on the beach, I had the impression that he was rather bemused by my interest in him and the way he made his living, as though sea piracy was rather run-of-the-mill. The norm. At the same time he seemed aware of the image that Somali pirates had around the world – especially since the hijacking of the *Tanit* and the *Alabama* – and he wanted to put his side of the story.

I asked him how he became a pirate and he explained that he used to be a fisherman. 'The community faced difficulties,' he told me, 'because the fishermen were chased away from the sea by the invasion of illegal fishing. The problem started because of the invasion and the fighting began. When they destroyed our fishing nets with fishes inside, then we started fighting them.'

Colonel Abshir had told me that the pirates of Somalia were illiterates who had no idea of illegal fishing and toxic waste. This man admitted to me that he was indeed illiterate, but he certainly knew something of the origins of piracy in the area. As he spoke, though, it became clear that it had definitely evolved into something bigger. Our pirate did not work for himself. He was bankrolled by someone further up the line. An investor. A Mr Big. When a ransom was collected successfully, he told me, the pirates would get 30 per cent, Mr Big would get 70 per cent. A disproportionate cut but still – 30 per cent of a few million goes a long way in Somalia. 'It's true,' he said. 'There are some who are very rich. Everywhere you go, people welcome you because they say you have a lot of money, and they receive you warmly.'

What did the pirates do with that sort of money?

'We use it to build houses,' he told me. 'We give half to our families and the other half we spend on our relatives, who could be in the town or the countryside.' Some of the money, he told me, he used to buy herds of camels – camel meat being much prized as a food in Somalia.

I asked our pirate to talk me through the process of capturing a ship. How did they go about it? What techniques did they use?

'We have some satellite radios that we use for communication,' he explained. 'We speak to the ship and order it to stop. If it does not stop, we open fire and eventually stop it by force. A ship carrying heavy cargo can be captured in less than five minutes. First we enter the ship and order all the persons on board to stand still. Then we anchor it. We install communication systems and communicate with the owner of the ship. We ask for the ransom money and tell them that we will hold the ship until the demand is met.'

He made it sound simple, and in a way, I suppose, it was. 'A ship has nothing to defend itself with,' he explained. 'Nothing!' I asked him what sort of weapons they used. He favoured an AK-47; others, he told me, were partial to the PKM – a Russian general purpose machine gun. Professional equipment for a professional job, most of which, he told me, came into the country from Ethiopia. But he qualified this. 'You can only use your weapon to defend against someone who attacks you. You do not need to use it for other purposes. Nobody just opens fire and wants to waste bullets.'

I thought of Storm and of his assertion that the Somali pirate is a stupid pirate. I wasn't sure I agreed. This guy sounded like he knew what he was talking about. Like he had it all worked out.

Abshir had predicted an escalation of violence, and I wondered what our pirate's take on the recent shootings aboard the *Maersk Alabama* and the *Tanit* heralded. Had the situation changed now that the Americans and French had killed Somali pirates? 'If a person enters our territory,' he said calmly, 'he won't be killed. But the French and Americans have caused problems by killing our people. Others will not be killed. We will contact their government to tell them that we have taken some of their nationals as hostages and tell them to come to Puntland to sort the matter out.' He clapped his hands together, almost as if he was relishing the prospect. It would be a brave foreign official, I thought, that would take him up on his offer . . .

I wanted to know how our man had become a pirate, how he had learned the techniques necessary to perform such audacious acts. The answer truly surprised me. 'If a person lives by the sea,' he said, 'and has sailed many times, then he can learn to be a pirate. You can learn piracy if you have your own gun and know how to defend yourself. There's nothing difficult about being at sea. If you're well trained you can do anything you want.'

But if you're well trained, that means somebody has trained you.

He nodded his head. 'Yes. I received a little training. There are about 30 schools for sea piracy in Somalia.'

Thirty schools. I had no idea if he was telling the truth, but if our pirate was alleging thirty, there's definitely more than one.

'The training takes about a year. They teach how to capture the ship, resolve the problems and how to keep the ship. They teach us about every sort of weapon – rocket-propelled grenades, anti-aircraft missiles and many other types.'

And who was it that was giving them this training?

'Our trainers are ex-marines, people who used to be in the Somali military.'

Someone, though, must be paying for all this. Our pirate nodded, before explaining that what often happens is this:

the big bosses pay for the pirates to undergo their year's training. Then, when the pirates start making money, they pay their bankrollers back. Student loans, Somalia style.

I asked him if he thought piracy would ever stop in Somalia. Again he nodded. 'If we get a proper government, then sea piracy will stop.' That, at least, seemed to be something everybody could agree on.

Our interview was drawing to a close. There was one more question I wanted to ask him. 'In other countries,' I suggested, 'you might be perceived to be criminals. How do you answer that?'

He looked genuinely astonished by the suggestion. 'Who?' he asked. 'Me? I am not a criminal and I have not committed any crime. And I've never hurt a white man.' He slapped his hands together again, as if to say that's that. But that final assertion begged the question: how many men had he hurt that didn't happen to be white?

And so our conversation came to an end. I thanked the pirate for agreeing to talk to me, and he told me that I would always be welcome in Somalia.

I appreciated the thought, and I'd never say never. But as the pirate from Puntland disappeared from view, his old white boat slipping over the horizon of that clear blue sea, I reflected on this: from what I knew about his ravaged, dangerous, violent country, I couldn't see that happening for a very long time to come.

Afterword

When I set out to investigate modern-day piracy, I didn't really know what I'd find. The things I discovered truly opened my eyes.

Piracy, it seems to me, exists for three reasons: criminal, economic and political. Sometimes the boundaries between these three reasons become blurred. Many criminals commit acts of villainy because they have an economic imperative, because they are poor. And many people are poor because of the terrible political situations in their country. What is undoubtedly the case is that it's not easy to make absolute judgements about the causes of piracy. And there are no easy solutions.

In Somalia I heard it said that piracy was the direct result of illegal fishing and the dumping of toxic waste, but it was also clear that there was a booming piratical business from which a lot of people were making a lot of money. In Nigeria there was some piracy that was clearly a direct result of economic hardship and some that was politically motivated, but on the other side of the fence there were plenty of people who saw MEND as out-and-out criminals. No doubt some of them were. The pirates of Batam claimed to go shopping simply to put food on the table for themselves and their families; while it was true that some of them drove big cars and had decent houses, you had to wonder whether they would have been forced into criminality had it not been for Indonesia's economic shape.

It was always touch and go that I would ever meet any actual pirates. I was glad I did, but in the end I was aware that the people I spoke to were little more than foot soldiers. The pirates themselves – the ones who take the risks and face the dangers – are just the tip of the iceberg. They are backed up by greater forces. The pirate from Puntland told us that 70 per cent of the takings from a ransomed ship went to these Mr Big figures, sponsors who paid for their training, expected their cut in return and had now grown filthy rich. In Nigeria small-time pirates were bunkering oil, but it was the people in authority – government ministers and wealthy businessmen – who were putting the oil onto the open market and reaping the substantial rewards. And in south-east Asia shipowners were hiring pirates to hijack their own vessels, often with the complicity of some of the crew, as part of elaborate and massive insurance scams.

Many merchant vessels around the world fly flags of convenience. This means that they originate from one country but are registered in another in order to attract a lower tax liability. When these ships get into trouble, however, they expect the maritime forces of the international community to come to their rescue. Whether you think that's acceptable or not, one thing is clear: piracy itself cannot be effectively policed. In Somalia a merchant vessel was taken from under our noses despite the impressive military presence of Operation Atalanta. If pirates don't fear a Type 23 frigate, they don't fear anything. In the Malacca Straits the efforts of the MMEA were having some effect, but the truth is that if you eliminate pirates from one stretch of water, all that happens is that they reappear somewhere else. If you look at maps indicating global piracy hot spots from year to year, you'll see that they change position, but they don't become noticeably less numerous.

Piracy, it seems to me, can't be stopped on the water. The sea is too big; the pirates' ships are too small; they can hide too easily; and once they've jettisoned the tools of their trade it's too difficult to distinguish them from fishermen. But 90 per cent of world trade travels by sea, and the problem has to be addressed. Piracy has existed ever since man first took to the water, and it would be naive to imagine we can eradicate it completely, but it's on the increase, and that worrying trajectory has to be reversed.

Maybe if we turned our eyes towards what is happening on the land, and focus on the *causes* of piracy, we might have a better chance of stopping it. Pirates aren't born at sea. They come from the land, they return to the land, and the money they spend, they spend on the land. Piracy is a seaborne menace that has its roots in poverty and political unrest on land. And as long as these continue, pirates will always take to the sea.

While people starve and governments fail their citizens, the waters of the world can never be safe.

THE FIRST CHRISTIAN HISTORIAN

As the first historian of Christianity, Luke's reliability is vigorously disputed among scholars. The author of the Acts is often accused of being a biased, imprecise and anti-Jewish historian who created a distorted portrait of Paul. Daniel Marguerat tries to avoid being caught in this true/false quagmire when examining Luke's interpretation of history. Instead he combines different tools – reflection upon historiography, the rules of ancient historians and narrative criticism – to analyse the Acts and gauge the historiographical aims of their author. Marguerat examines the construction of the narrative, the framing of the plot and the characterization, and places his evaluation firmly in the framework of ancient historiography, where history reflects tradition and not documentation. This is a fresh and original approach to the classic themes of Lucan theology: Christianity between Jerusalem and Rome, the image of God, the work of the Spirit, the unity of Luke and the Acts.

DANIEL MARGUERAT is Professor of New Testament at the Faculty of Theology of the University of Lausanne, Switzerland, and a leading scholar on the book of *Acts*. He is the author of numerous books and articles, including *Le jugement dans l'évangile de Matthieu* (2nd edn, 1995) and *How to Read Bible Stories* (in collaboration with Yvan Bourquin, 1999).

SOCIETY FOR NEW TESTAMENT STUDIES

MONOGRAPH SERIES

General Editor: Richard Bauckham

121

THE FIRST CHRISTIAN HISTORIAN

The First Christian Historian

Writing the 'Acts of the Apostles'

DANIEL MARGUERAT
Université de Lausanne, Switzerland

Translated by Ken McKinney, Gregory J. Laughery and Richard Bauckham

CAMBRIDGE
UNIVERSITY PRESS

PUBLISHED BY THE PRESS SYNDICATE OF THE UNIVERSITY OF CAMBRIDGE
The Pitt Building, Trumpington Street, Cambridge, United Kingdom

CAMBRIDGE UNIVERSITY PRESS
The Edinburgh Building, Cambridge CB2 2RU, UK
40 West 20th Street, New York, NY 10011-4211, USA
477 Williamstown Road, Port Melbourne, VIC 3207, Australia
Ruiz de Alarcón 13, 28014 Madrid, Spain
Dock House, The Waterfront, Cape Town 8001, South Africa

http://www.cambridge.org

First published 2002

Printed in the United Kingdom at the University Press, Cambridge

Typeface Times 10/12 pt   *System* LATEX 2ε [TB]

A catalogue record for this book is available from the British Library

Library of Congress cataloguing in publication data

Marguerat, Daniel, 1943–
[Première histoire du christianisme. English]
The first Christian historian: Acts of the Apostles / Daniel Marguerat; translated by
Ken McKinney, Gregory J. Laughery and Richard Bauckham
    p. cm.   (Society for New Testament Studies monograph series; 121)
Includes bibliographical references and index.
ISBN 0 521 81650 5 (hardback)
1. Bible. N.T. Acts – Historiography.   I. Title.   II. Monograph series (Society for New
Testament Studies); 121.

BS2625.6.H5513   2002
226.6′067–dc21   2002019251

ISBN 0 521 81650 5 hardback

In memory of Dom Jacques Dupont (1915–1998)

CONTENTS

PREFACE

Luke, not Eusebius of Caesarea, was the first Christian historian. In antiquity, he was the first to present a religious movement in a historiographical manner. As for all historians, the aim of Luke is identity. When he recounts the birth of Christianity, its undesirable rupture with Judaism, and then the universal adventure of the Word, the author of Acts offers the Christianity of his time, an understanding of its identity through a return to its origins.

My reading of the historiographical work of Luke combines two procedures of investigation: historical criticism and narrative criticism. I am convinced that the understanding of a biblical writing requires that it be immersed in the historical milieu of its production (this is the epistemological credo of the historical-critical method). Constantly, in the course of the study, I shall be examining the culture and codes of communication of the ancient Mediterranean world to which Luke and his readers belong. However, the author of Acts is also a storyteller; the tools of narrative criticism help to identify the strategy of the narrator, the organization of the story, and the programmatic clues for reading that he has sown in his text.

One of the insights defended in this book is that we cannot reach the theology the author has written into his work without adopting the itinerary he imposes on his readers; this itinerary is the twists and turns of the narrative. I think that narrative reading makes it possible to do justice to the thinking, often scorned by scholars, of this talented storyteller. Because he tells his story well, Luke's thinking is not systematic. In rediscovering the hidden architecture of his work, one discovers the mastery and coherence of this great historian and theologian, without whom Christianity would be ignorant of most of its origins.

This book is the translation of eleven chapters of my work *La première histoire du Christianisme (Actes des apôtres)* (Lectio Divina 180; Paris, Cerf and Geneva, Labor et Fides, 1999). Chapter 10 has been published in a slightly abridged form in David P. Moessner, *Jesus and the Heritage of Israel* (Harrisburg, PA, Trinity Press International, 1999), pp. 284–304.

Begun in November 1992 at the Graduate Theological Union in Berkeley (where I was an invited scholar), the French version was completed in June 1999 at the University of Lausanne (Switzerland). Its argumentation has profited from the questions and suggestions of countless colleagues, students and friends, many of whom are cited in the footnotes. The preparation of the book owes much to my assistant Emmanuelle Steffek, whose work was invaluable, checking the references, the bibliography, and the multiple re-drafts. The English version depends on the talent of three translators, Ken McKinney, Gregory J. Laughery and Richard Bauckham, whom I congratulate on their patience in understanding my French. I am particularly indebted to Richard Bauckham for having reread and corrected the English text, and to David Alban and Valérie Nicolet, whose competencies were precious in checking the final version. The English translation was made possible through a grant of the 'Société Académique Vaudoise', and the generosity of a donor.

I wonder if Luke benefited from as much support. I hope so.

1

HOW LUKE WROTE HISTORY

Was the first historian of Christianity a proper historian?

There is no doubt that Luke – for this is what we name the anonymous author of the third gospel and the book of Acts – intended to tell a story about the birth of Christianity. He was the first to have written a biography of Jesus followed by what was later given the title of 'Acts of Apostles' (Πράξεις ἀποστολῶν). In antiquity, this would never be repeated. The two volumes of this grand work were divided at the time of the constitution of the canon of the New Testament, before the year AD 200; the first volume was grouped with Matthew, Mark and John to form the fourfold Gospel; the second work was placed at the head of the epistles, to establish the narrative framework of the Pauline writings.

It is here, at the moment when the corpus of Christian literature begins to emerge, that Luke's writing, dedicated to the 'most excellent Theophilus' (Luke 1. 3; Acts 1. 1), was broken in two. The length of the whole is impressive. These fifty-two chapters represent a quarter of the New Testament. Modern exegesis refers to this text as Luke–Acts in order to remind readers that Acts cannot be read without remembering the gospel as Luke has written it.

Luke, then, wanted to create a history, but was he a good historian? Exegetes continue to disagree on the answer. In order to take a position in this debate one must first of all clarify what is meant by writing history and what we mean by *historiography*. It has been shown that the expectations of the reader vary according to the type of historiography adopted by the author. Paul Ricœur helps us to clarify this point by proposing a useful taxonomy. Secondly, I shall investigate the ethical rules in use in the first century. A study of the work of historians in Graeco-Roman antiquity leads us to note that historiography did not wait until the Enlightenment to be conscious of itself. Among the Greek and Roman historians there is open discussion about the notion of *truth* in history.

I intend to move forward, depending successively on the results of recent epistemological reflection as well as the deontological debates of 'the ancients' concerning historiography.

How does one write history?

Until the beginning of the nineteenth century, the question of the historical reliability of Luke's work was not even an issue. Anyone who wanted to know how the Church was born had but one place to turn: the Acts of the Apostles. This document provided what was necessary and, even more, what was to be believed. The book of Acts was both a manual of the history of Christianity and (especially) the baptismal certificate of a Church born of God.

Doubts arise

Doubts arose, however, when the data of Acts were seriously compared with the rest of the New Testament. W. Ward Gasque designates the first critic of the reliability of Acts as Wilhem Martin Leberecht de Wette (1780–1849).[1] The problem emerged when the Lucan portrait of Paul was compared with the information given in the letters of the apostle (Acts 9. 1–30; 15. 1–35 compared with Gal. 1. 13 – 2. 21). De Wette argued that Luke's information is partly false, partly miraculous and partly incomplete.

But this was only the beginning. Not long after, de Wette was followed by the wave of Tübingen-school critics (*Tendenzkritik*) who imposed their reading of a conflictual history of Christianity, where Luke played the role of mediator. Ferdinand Christian Baur (1792–1860), the brilliant initiator of this historical paradigm, situated the historian Luke at the critical moment when the state of Christianity required a synthesis between the Petrine tendency and the Pauline heritage. Baur saw in Acts

> the apologetic attempt of a Pauline author to orchestrate the bringing together and the reunion of the two parties face to face. Luke makes Paul appear as Petrine as possible and Peter as Pauline as possible, by throwing as much as possible a reconciliatory veil over the differences that, according to the unequivocal statement of Paul in his letter to the Galatians, had without a doubt separated the two apostles, and by plunging into forgetfulness what troubled the relationship between the two parties,

[1] W. W. Gasque, *History of the Interpretation*, 1989, pp. 24–6.

i.e. the hatred of the Gentile Christians against Judaism and the Jewish Christians' hatred toward paganism. This benefits their common hatred against the unbelieving Jews who have made the apostle Paul the constant object of irrepressible hatred.[2]

The advantages of the Tendenzkritik

I shall often return to the merits of the Tübingen school, which has wrongly been reduced to a Hegelian schema of thesis–antithesis–synthesis (now rejected in the historiography of ancient Christianity).[3] The major achievement of the *Tendenzkritik* was to place the framework for understanding Luke–Acts in history, and to propose a historiographical goal which aimed to fix the identity of Christianity around the end of the first century. The *Tendenzkritik* intuition was to view Luke as seeking to reconcile competing, if not antagonistic[4] values, within Christianity. This intuition should now be rethought, without oversimplification.

To return to Baur: his works functioned as a real detonator in the criticism of Luke's historiography. Many questions have arisen since then. Is it not wrong to present Peter and Paul, antagonists on the question of *kashrut* according to Galatians 2. 11–16, as like-minded? Why is no place in Acts given to Paul's virulent battle concerning the Law?[5] Paul's version of the Jerusalem assembly in Galatians 2. 6–10 (an unconditional recognition of his mission) is constantly set against Luke's conciliatory reading (compromise obtained by means of a minimal code of purity, the apostolic decree of Acts 15. 20, 29). How is one to explain the silence of Acts concerning the confessional conflicts that the letters of Paul, as well as the Johannine epistles and the Pastorals, reveal? In other words, according to Paul, Christianity's search for its identity, from the 30s to the 60s (the period covered by the narrative of Acts), was a lively conflictual debate. Yet Luke paints a picture of (nearly) perfect harmony between the apostles. For Baur, there is no doubt that 'the presentation of the Acts of the Apostles must be regarded as an intentional modification of the historical

---

[2] F. C. Baur, *Über den Ursprung*, 1838, p. 142.

[3] See especially chapters 2 'A narrative of beginnings' and 4 'A Christianity between Jerusalem and Rome'.

[4] A presentation of the work of the Tübingen school relating to the Acts may be found in Gasque's *History*, 1989, pp. 26–54. Also C. K. Barrett's 'How History Should be Written', 1986, offers an interesting evaluation of F. C. Baur's argumentation.

[5] To get an idea of the differences between Paul's account and the Lucan presentation, one should read synoptically Gal. 5. 3–6 and Acts 16. 3 (the circumcision); Rom. 3. 21–6 and Acts 21. 20–4 (the question of the Law); Phil. 3. 4–9 and Acts 23. 6; 26. 5 (the Pharisaic identity).

truth (*geschichtliche Wahrheit*) in the interests of its specific tendency (*Tendenz*)'.[6]

A gaffe on a worldwide scale

Baur then, brings Luke before the tribunal of 'historical truth', but he allows him the mitigating circumstances of being captive to a historical and theological tendency (*Tendenz*). But the most provocative expression comes from Franz Overbeck, who in 1919 referred to the work of Luke as a 'gaffe on the scale of world history'.[7] What was the mistake? According to Overbeck, Luke's sin was to have confused history and fiction, that is, to 'treat historiographically that which was not history and was not transmitted as such'. In brief, the author of Acts blended history and legend, historical and supernatural fact, in a concoction from which the modern historian recoils in distaste. Etienne Trocmé, in 1957, concedes that Luke is a 'capable amateur historian, but insufficiently formed for his task'.[8] Ernst Haenchen adds that Luke was the author of an 'edifying book'.[9]

It is unnecessary to continue.[10] The denunciation of Luke as a falsifier of history, at best naive, is forceful and scathing. Very generally speaking, the opinions of scholars are fixed along party lines: on one side the extreme scepticism of German exegesis concerning the historical work of Luke (Vielhauer, Conzelmann, Haenchen, Lüdemann, Roloff, with the exception of Hengel), and on the other side the determination of Anglo-American research to rehabilitate the documentary reliability of Luke–Acts (Gasque, Bruce, Marshall, Hemer, Bauckham).[11]

---

[6] F. C. Baur, *Paulus, der Apostel* [1845], 1866, p. 120.

[7] F. Overbeck, *Christentum und Kultur*, 1919, p. 78: 'Es ist das *eine Taktlosigkeit von welthistorischen Dimensionen*, der grösste Excess der falschen Stellung, die sich Lukas zum Gegenstand gibt' (italics mine). For understanding Overbeck and his time, one book stands out: J. C. Emmelius, *Tendenzkritik*, 1975.

[8] E. Trocmé, *'Livre des Actes'*, 1957, p. 105.

[9] E. Haenchen notes that the Lucan preface (Luke 1. 1–4) inaugurates a work in the style of Xenophon, if not a Thucydides, but the author 'lacked two requisites for such an undertaking: an adequate historical foundation – and the right readers. Any book he might conceivably offer his readers – especially as a sequel to the third gospel – had to be a work of *edification*' (*Acts of the Apostles*, 1971, p. 103). This however, does not prevent Haenchen from honouring the historiographical capacities of the author (*ibid.*, pp. 90–103)!

[10] A detailed state of research can be found in F. F. Bruce's 'Acts of the Apostles', 1985, see pp. 2575–82 or E. Rasco's 'Tappe fondamentali', 1997.

[11] The edition, in the making, dedicated to the historical roots of Acts demonstrates the Anglo-American effort to render the historicity of the Lucan narrative credible: *The Book of Acts in Its First Century Setting*; 5 vols. have appeared since 1993.

An aporia

The doubts about Luke's historiographical work have created an embarassing aporia. On the one hand, even if it is acknowledged as incomplete,[12] the information given by Acts is indispensable for anyone desiring to reconstruct the period of the first Christian generation; no biography of the apostle Paul, for example, can leave aside chapters 9 to 28 of Acts. On the other hand, suspicion about the historical reliability of the Lucan narrative inhibits a serious consideration of Luke's information.[13] Frequently the historians of early Christianity begin by questioning the historical value of Acts, only to go on, quite pragmatically, to use the data of the Lucan narrative in their research.[14]

If we wish to escape this impasse, there must be reflection on the very concept of historiography. It is symptomatic that neither Baur nor Overbeck appeals to a theory of history; both, in the direct line of positivism, identify historical truth with hard documentary facts.

Historiography and postmodernity

Since Overbeck's rationalism, in which it was thought possible to separate clearly the true and the false, reflection on the writing of history has progressed. We have become more modest and less naive over the definition of truth in history. This shift has taken place, in my opinion, in the following manner.

First, the works of Raymond Aron on the philosophy of history, Henri-Irénée Marrou on historical epistemology, and Paul Veyne on the notion of plot have destroyed the distinction between history and historiography.[15] There is no history apart from the historian's interpretative mediation

---

[12] Historians of early Christianity reproach the author of Acts for two weaknesses: (1) an exclusive attention to the creation of the communities to the detriment of their duration; (2) a fixation on the expansion of the Pauline mission toward the west (from Jerusalem to Rome) to the detriment of the other *tendencies* (especially Johannine) and the expansion toward the south (Egypt). For example, see W. Schneemelcher, *Urchristentum*, 1981, pp. 37–8.

[13] F. C. Baur was perfectly aware of the aporia: the book of Acts is 'eine höchst wichtige Quelle für die Geschichte der apostolischen Zeit, aber auch eine Quelle, aus welcher erst durch strenge historische Kritik ein wahrhaft geschichtliches Bild der von ihr geschilderten Personen und Verhältnisse gewonnen werden kann' (*Paulus* [1845], 1866, p. 13).

[14] A recent example is Etienne Trocmé in *L'enfance du christianisme*, 1997 (compare pages 70, 90, 96, 105–6 and 116).

[15] R. Aron, *Philosophie de l'histoire* [1938], 1957. H. I. Marrou, *De la connaissance historique* [1954], 1975. P. Veyne, *Comment on écrit l'histoire* [1971], 1996. Neither can one overlook the works of P. Ricœur concerning temporality and intentionality in a historical narrative: *Time and Narrative*, I, 1984.

which supplies meaning: history is narrative and, as such, constructed from a point of view. Over the multitude of facts at his/her disposal, the historian throws a plot, retaining certain facts that are judged significant, while excluding others, and relating some to others in a relationship of cause and effect. The crusades, for example, told from a Christian or Arab point of view are not the same history. Therefore historiography should not be regarded as descriptive, but rather (re)constructive. Historiography does not line up bare facts (what Baur and Overbeck called *geschichtliche Wahrheit*), but only facts interpreted by means of a logic imposed by the historian. In this operation, as Raymond Aron recognizes, 'theory precedes history'[16] or, if one prefers, point of view precedes the writing of history. The 'truth' of history does not depend on the factuality of the event recounted (even though the historian is required to keep to the facts), but, rather, depends on the interpretation the historian gives to a reality that is always in itself open to a plurality of interpretative options.[17]

Second, the works of Arnaldo Momigliano allow us not only to distinguish between Greek and Jewish historiography, but also to consider the goal of identity pursued in all historiography.[18] The past is never (at least in antiquity) explored for itself, but is recorded with a view to constituting a memory for the present of its readers. I would add that the history which any social group chooses to retain is, generally speaking, that which is required by its present, a present often fragile or in crisis. (The current revision of the theory of the sources of the Pentateuch, bringing the literary fixation of the texts down to the period of the exile will not contradict this point![19]) The history that a social group retains is rarely the history of its mistakes or its crimes, but rather the epic of its exploits and the evil of the 'others'[20] (see the Jewish–Christian relations in Luke–Acts). Such a history is the intellectual instrument by which an institution fixes its identity by considering where it has come from.

Consequently, Lucan historiography is not to be judged on its conformity to so-called *bruta facta* (always ambiguous). Rather, it must be evaluated according to the *point of view of the historian* which controls

---

[16] *Philosophie de l'histoire*, 1957, p. 93.

[17] There is a useful reflection on the spirit of the historian by P. Gibert, *Vérité historique*, 1990.

[18] Especially, A. Momigliano, *Fondations du savoir*, 1992.

[19] A. de Pury, ed., *Pentateuque*, 1991.

[20] M. Douglas describes the process by which institutions provide themselves with a historical memory: 'Institutions create shadowed places in which nothing can be seen and no questions asked. They make other areas show finely discriminated detail, which is closely scrutinized and ordered' (*How Institutions Think*, 1986, p. 69).

the writing of the narrative, *the truth* that the author aims to communicate and *the need for identity* to which the work of the historian responds.

What credentials?

This reorientation concerning historiography faces two objections.

First, what are we to do with the contradictory readings of the same facts, for example the Lucan and Pauline versions of the Jerusalem assembly (Acts 15 and Gal. 2) or the 'un-Pauline' concerns on the observance of the Torah (23. 6; 26. 5–7; 28. 17; cf. 16. 3)[21] which Luke attributes to the apostle? Are we not forced to choose between one version and the other? In the case of the Jerusalem assembly, let us avoid deciding too quickly, since we know that Paul's account in Galatians 2 is rhetorically oriented[22] and therefore one cannot claim objectivity for it. As to the theology attributed to Paul, divergence cannot be denied. We should consider that Luke's work evidences the development of Paulinism within Lucan Christianity. The book of Acts offers us privileged access to the reception of the apostle's thought in the milieu of a Pauline movement in the 80s.[23]

The second objection to the postmodern questioning of historiography can be formulated in the following manner: if historiography must be judged from a point of view that the author defends, what credentials of credibility can still be accorded to historians? How does history differ from a purely imaginary reproduction of the past? Marrou, in asking this question, leaves us with only one criterion: 'the character of reality'.[24] Although vague, this criterion is useful in distinguishing ancient historiography from the Greek novel. Contrary to what Richard Pervo

---

[21] It seems hardly compatible with the language of the apostle in his epistles that Paul declares in the *present tense* that he belongs to the Pharisaic party (Acts 23. 6), that he considers himself in conflict with Jewish theology on the question of the resurrection (26. 5–7), that he affirms that he did nothing against Jewish customs (28. 17) or that he forces Timothy to be circumcised because of fear of the Jews (16. 3).

[22] G. Betori attempts to demonstrate that the rhetorical construction of the speech, which is argumentative in Paul and narrative in Luke, destroys the statute of objectivity improperly attributed to Gal. 2 from the Tubingen school: 'Opera storiografica', 1986, pp. 115–21.

[23] If we limit ourselves to a true/false alternative, the analysis of the relationship between the Paul of Luke and the Paul of the epistles is truncated; it is the phenomenon of the reception of Paulinism that is to be evaluated in its similarities and its differences (see the subject below, pp. 56–9; 84). See also my article 'Acts of Paul', 1997. It is the same concerning the study of the Christian Apocrypha, according to E. Junod's article ('Créations romanesques', 1983, pp. 271–85), which shows that the alternative novelistic fiction/historical truth leads to a dead end.

[24] 'L'histoire se différencie de ses falsifications ou de ses sosies par ce caractère de réalité qui pénètre tout son être' (*De la connaissance historique* [1954], 1975, p. 225).

argues, it is not the narrative processes that allow us to distinguish ancient historiography from the Greek novel.[25] Rather, it is the relationship of the narrative to the *realia*. I therefore propose that we adopt the 'character of reality' as a criterion for distinguishing Lucan historiography from novel. What I mean by this is the textual presence of realities (topographical, cultural, socio-political, economic) of the world described by the narrator. I shall apply this later.

Three types of historiography

Paul Ricœur has moved the discussion one step forward by distinguishing three types of historiography.[26]

First, he identifies a *documentary* history, which seeks to establish the verifiable facts (example: how Titus took Jerusalem in the year AD 70). He then speaks of an *explicative* history, which evaluates the event from a social, economic or political horizon; it answers the question: what were the consequences of Titus' conquest of Jerusalem for Jews and Christians? Finally, Ricœur speaks of a historiography in the strong sense, which rewrites the past in the founding narratives that people need in order to construct their self-understanding. We find here again the function of memory in forming identity. It corresponds to the work of the historian who interprets the capture of Jerusalem by Roman troops as a divine sanction against the infidelity of the chosen people.

Ricœur calls this *poetic* history (in the etymological sense of *poiein*, as it appears in founding myths). Poetic history does not conform to the same norms as the other types and does not fit the criterion of true/false verification (like *documentary* history). Neither does it weigh up the diverse evaluations of an event (like explanatory history). Rather, its truth lies in the interpretation it gives to the past and the possibility it offers to a community to understand itself in the present.[27] In other words, what historiography in the strong sense recognizes as trustworthy is the self-consciousness that it offers to the group of readers.

The taxonomy is fascinating, because *it puts an end to a totalitarian definition of historiography that would allow only one sort*. Hence, there

[25] R. I. Pervo has defended the affiliation of Acts with the novelistic genre on the basis of the narrative procedures of the author, without noticing that almost all of these procedures are common to novelists and Hellenistic historians (*Profit with Delight*, 1987).

[26] P. Ricœur, 'Philosophies critiques', 1994. See also his *Critique et la conviction*, 1995, pp. 131–2.

[27] P. Ricœur defines poetic history as 'celle des grandes affabulations de l'auto-compréhension d'une nation à travers ses récits fondateurs' (*Critique et la conviction*, 1995, p. 312).

are several ways to do history, each one as legitimate as the other. If one is to do justice to the historian, one must investigate his/her historiographical aim. In particular, the recognition of the poetic dimension is very important. By validating symbolic expression in history, it frees the historian from suspicion of the symbolic as improper or deviant with regard to the ethics of historiography. On the contrary, Ricœur says, the symbolic (and I add: whether theological or not) is intrinsic to a poetic historiographical aim. Historiography, in this sense, as it lays out founding narratives, rightly derives from a need to symbolize and imagine.

One could criticize Ricœur in that the divisions between these three categories are rarely neat and tidy. This will be confirmed when I investigate the parameters to which the book of Acts responds. An attentive reading of the narrative does not lead to the understanding that there is any one pure type of historiography. Acts is sometimes historiographically poetic, while at other times it is documentary.

A poetic history

The affiliation of Acts with poetic history is attested by the way the narrator constantly has God intervening, saving or consoling his people: God communicates with the apostles through dreams or angels (5. 19; 7. 55; 9. 10; etc.); God causes the community to grow miraculously (2. 47; 5. 14; 11. 24; 12. 24); God overturns Saul on the road to Damascus in order to make him the vehicle of the Gentile mission (9. 1–19a); God provokes the meeting of Peter and Cornelius through supernatural interventions (10. 1–48); God opens the doors of prisons for his imprisoned messengers (12. 6–11; 16. 25–6) or strikes down the enemies of believers (5. 1–11; 12. 21–3), and so on. From chapter 1 where the Twelve are reconstituted after the shameful death of Judas (1. 15–26), the narrator unfolds the account of the birth of the Church, in which the principal agent in this narrative is the powerful arm of God.

A brief analysis of Acts 16. 6–10 will concretize this primary aim of the narrative. This short passage tells how the missionary itinerary of Paul and Silas was violently deflected to Macedonia. The messengers 'went through the regions of Phrygia and Galatia, having been forbidden by the Holy Spirit to speak the word in Asia'; the same Spirit 'does not allow them' to go to Bithynia, but reroutes them to Troas where, in a vision, a Macedonian begs them: 'Come over to Macedonia and help us!'[28] Such a version of the facts would be inadmissible in a documentary

[28] These verses are interesting to analyse from the point of view of the language they use for God. For this, see pp. 86–92.

history, in which concrete information about the why and how of these constraints would be required. This kind of history, however, is legitimate in a founding narrative whose goal is to show how the Spirit gave birth to the Church by miraculously guiding the witnesses of the Word. The 'poetic' of Luke's narrative is to be found in the demonstration of this divine guidance in history. Narrating the lives of the apostles then consists in reconstituting them under this sign. It means both repeating what happened (mimesis) and reconstructing it in a creative manner.

A documentary interest

On the other hand, the narrative of Acts regularly – and to our surprise – offers topographical, socio-political or onomastic notations whose narrative usefulness is not apparent on a first reading. Such a concern for detail has no equivalent in Luke's gospel. But Acts gives extraordinary attention to the area of Paul's mission, the routes followed, the cities visited, the people met, and the synagogues. For example, Luke's three verses that recount the voyage from Troas to Miletus (20. 13–15) enumerate the stops in Assos, Mytilene, Chios, Samos and Trogyllium with quasi-technical accuracy, without mentioning any missionary activity in these cities. The narrator can be incredibly precise when he describes the itinerary of the missionaries (13. 4; 19. 21–3; 20. 36–8), the choice of routes (20. 2–3, 13–15), the length of the voyage (20. 6, 15), the lodging conditions (18. 1–3; 21. 8–10), the farewell scenes (21. 5–7, 12–14), and so on. The superb chapter 27, with its account of the shipwreck, where Luke lets himself go with novelistic effects, is, at the same time, famous for the astonishing precision of its nautical vocabulary. This mixture of fiction and realism is striking when compared to the Greek novel. The latter strictly limits the presence of toponymic details or indications to their narrative potential. The apocryphal *Acts* of apostles in this respect resemble novelistic fiction rather than the documentary history of the canonical Acts. After Luke, apocryphal literature rapidly abandons historical realism.[29]

The same documentary realism applies to Luke's description of Roman institutions. The narrator seems to have perfect information concerning the administrative apparatus of the Empire. Philippi is correctly called a colony (κολωνία: 16. 12) and its *praetores* receive the name of στρατηγοί

---

[29] This is shown below, pp. 238; 249–53.

(16. 20); the officials of Thessalonica are correctly called πολιτάρχαι (17. 8); in Athens, Paul is dragged to the Ἄρειον πάγον (17. 19); in Corinth, the proconsul Gallio receives the title of ἀνθυπάτος, just like Sergius Paulus in Cyprus (18. 12; 13. 7–8). The verification of these titles, from our knowledge of Roman usage, confirms that Luke knew what he was doing when he used this vocabulary.[30]

Realistic effect?

It goes without saying that the above observations can be contradicted. The local colour of Acts could only be the narrative clothing of a fiction created by its author; the indications of factuality could be subverted and conceived in order to create the illusion of reality.[31] One branch of Hellenistic literature, paradoxography, plays precisely with this mixture of realism and fiction, the fantastic and the rational.[32] As Roland Barthes would say, Luke could then be mimicking realism with the 'realistic effect' (*effet de réel*). Yet this conclusion is not unavoidable. Against this suspicion, one could mention: (a) the different practices of the Greek novel, where there is little concern for credibility in the narrative; (b) the constant presence of the indicators of factuality throughout the narrative, which give Acts (differently from apocryphal literature) an unprecedented mixture of fiction and reality.

The case of the 'golden age' of the Jerusalem community is illuminating from this point of view. This idyllic picture painted by the author glorifies the exemplary unanimity and the sharing of possessions in the Jerusalem church (2. 42–7; 4. 32–5; 5. 12–16). This is often denounced as a product of Luke's imagination. But the example of Qumran, close both historically and geographically, proves that there is nothing improbable about a communal system of sharing possessions in Palestine in the 30s.[33] Lucan 'poetics' consists in extending to earliest Christianity generally the economic ethic that was limited to a particular group, whose memory had been magnified by tradition.

---

[30] Documented verification can be found in the second volume of *The Book of Acts in Its First Century Setting: The Book of Acts in Its Graeco-Roman Setting*, ed. David W. J. Gill and Conrad Gempf, 1994, or in J. Taylor's 'Roman Empire', 1996.

[31] An interesting study by L. C. A. Alexander concludes that only with great difficulty can the indications of factuality to Graeco-Roman historiography be trusted: 'Fact, Fiction', 1998, pp. 380–99. The author pertinently concludes that the attribution of a literary genre to Luke–Acts does nothing to solve the question of historical reliability. Ancient historiography resorts to fiction as well as (though not as much as) the ancient novel does.

[32] See the analysis in E. Gabba, 'True History', 1981, pp. 53ff.

[33] See H. J. Klauck's study, 'Gütergemeinschaft', 1989.

Fact and fiction

The conclusion to be drawn is that Acts must not be judged by the standard of documentary precision, which it only offers in a secondary fashion. To refrain from requiring historiography to reveal illusory *bruta facta* shows itself to be a mark of wisdom. Finally (and especially), it is necessary to shift the notion of truth in accordance with the historiographical aim. In this case, the truth of Luke's work is to be measured by its poetic aim (in Ricœur's terms), that is, his reading of the founding history of the Church.

I repeat that all historical work is driven by a choice of plot, a narrative setting and the effects of (re)composition. Once the necessary subjectivity of the historian in the construction of the plot of the narrative is recognized, we must abandon the factual/fictional duality as the product of an unhealthy rationalism. Again it is Paul Ricœur who teaches us to what extent the act of narrating is common to these two grand narrative types, history and fiction, which both entail a mimetic function (i.e. representation of reality).[34] The work of the historian and the work of the storyteller are not as far apart as positivism (which ignores the narrative dimension of historiography) would like to believe. There is more fiction in history than the classic historian will admit. In order to *fashion* a plot (from the Latin *fingere*, which has the same root as *fiction*), the historian works with fictional elements. The difference between a history book and a historical novel lies in the fact that the novelist exercises minimum control over the realism of the characters and plot. Yet, over and above the difference between a fictive and a historical account, it is important to point out that one who tells a *story* (*une histoire*) and one who tells *history* (*l'histoire*) share a common trait: they bring historicity to linguistic expression.[35]

Long before the notion of plot was introduced into the historiographical debate by Paul Veyne, Martin Dibelius had perceived the narrative and theological performance of Luke. This is why, in a 1948 article, he gave Luke the title *der erste christliche Historiker* (the first Christian historian), which inspired the title of the present book. He writes that Luke 'attempted to tie together what had been transmitted in the community and what he

---

[34] For what follows, I draw from P. Ricœur's 'Narrative Function', 1981.

[35] Notice the admirable way in which Paul Ricœur makes the connection: he finds 'it in the historical condition itself which demands that the historicity of human experience can be brought to language only as narrativity, and moreover that this narrativity itself can be articulated only by the crossed interplay of the two narrative modes. For historicity comes to language only in so far as we tell stories or tell history ... *We belong to history before telling stories or writing history. The game of telling is included in the reality told*' ('Narrative Function', 1981, p. 294).

had experienced himself in a meaningful context' as well as 'making visible the orientation of the events'; in short, 'from stories he made history (*aus Geschichten Geschichte*)'.[36]

Dibelius is a master of historiographical thought. He argues that it is because Luke weaves a plot, and consequently is obliged to use fictional elements, that he is a historian.

Luke: the position of a historian

What did first-century readers expect from a history book? What codes of communication linked historian and readers? What were the rules for historical writing in Luke's Roman social context?

As I said, history did not wait for the Enlightenment to think through its epistemology. Ancient authors did write about the aim of historiography: to write history is to look for the causes of events (which brings us back to the notion of plot, since it is what provides a sequence for the facts).[37] After Polybius and Cicero,[38] Dionysius of Halicarnassus wrote: 'to seek the causes of what has happened (τὰς αἰτίας ἱστορῆσαι τῶν γινομένων), the forms of action and the intentions of those who acted, and what happened by destiny' (*Roman Antiquities* 5.56.1). *Historia* means 'seeking', 'exploration'; Greek history is in search of causalities.

The pamphlet of Lucian

When we consider the ethics of the Graeco-Roman historian, the name that comes immediately to mind is Lucian of Samosata. Lucian, a rhetor, wrote the pamphlet *How to Write History* (Πῶς δεῖ ἱστορίαν συγγράφειν) between AD 166 and 168. Although this work is later than the writings of Luke, there are nevertheless strong reasons to think that this pamphlet (Lucian attacks the incompetence of the historians of his time) fixes a much earlier scholarly tradition. Lucian states: 'history has one task and one end: what is useful (τὸ χρήσιμον), and that comes from truth alone' (9). 'The historian's sole duty is to tell what happened ... This, I repeat, is the sole duty of the historian, and only to Truth must sacrifice be made (μόνη θυτέον τῇ ἀληθείᾳ). When one is going to write history, everything else must be ignored...' (39–40).

But how is one to satisfy his requirement of truth?

---

[36] M. Dibelius, 'The First Christian Historian' [1948], 1956, pp. 127 and 129.

[37] Concerning the narratological concept of plot, see D. Marguerat and Y. Bourquin, *How to Read*, 1999, pp. 40–57.

[38] Polybius, *Histories* 3.32; 12.25b. Cicero, *De oratore* 2.15 (62–3).

A code in ten rules

Willem van Unnik, depending on Lucian's *How to Write History* and Dionysius of Halicarnassus' *Letter to Pompei* (written between 30 and 7 BC), formulated the code of the Graeco-Roman historian in ten rules.[39]

The ten rules are as follows: (1) the choice of a noble subject; (2) the usefulness of the subject for its addressees; (3) independence of mind and absence of partiality, that is, the author's παρρησία; (4) good construction of the narrative, especially the beginning and the end; (5) an adequate collection of preparatory material; (6) selection and variety in the treatment of the information; (7) correct disposition and ordering of the account; (8) liveliness (ἐνέργεια) in the narration; (9) moderation in the topographical details; (10) composition of speeches adapted to the orator and the rhetorical situation.

The reader familiar with Acts immediately recognizes the significant number of these rules to which Luke adheres. It has often been said that the preface of Luke 1. 1–4 places the author within Hellenistic 'high literature'. Loveday Alexander's study shows, however, that the style of the Lucan preface is close to technical (or scientific) prose and does not imply an elite audience.[40] In any case, comparison of Luke–Acts with the list of historiographical norms confirms that the Lucan writing corresponds to standard Graeco-Roman historiography. We shall find that Luke follows eight of the ten rules: his transgression of the other two (the first and the third) points us toward the specificity of Luke's project. The instructions observed by Luke are also followed by the majority of historians of Hellenistic Judaism, especially Flavius Josephus.

The moralism of history

For the biblical author it is no surprise that the reading of a historical narrative should be profitable to the reader (rule two). It cannot be repeated enough that this is a basic characteristic of Greek and Roman historiography: history must edify and this is why it plays an important role in education. The works of Livy, Dionysius of Halicarnassus, Sallust and Plutarch illustrate the intrinsic moralism that views historiography, and

---

[39] W. C. van Unnik, 'Second Book', 1979, pp. 37–60. The references can be found here.

[40] L. C. A. Alexander has shown in an elaborate study that the style of the preface was not only specific to historical works, but also to scientific ones; the dedication to Theophilus ensures a high socio-political level for Luke–Acts within the Graeco-Roman literature (*Preface*, 1993).

not only biography, as proposing for the reader both positive and negative *exempla*. The narrative of Acts is full of just this sort of perspective. Philip, Barnabas and Lydia are positive examples, while Ananias and Sapphira, Simon Magus and Bar-Jesus are negative ones.[41]

The construction of the narrative

Good workmanship in the construction (rule four) and disposition of the narrative (rule seven) are announced in the Lucan preface: the narrative *ad Theophilum* will be set forth καθεξῆς (Luke 1. 3), *in order*. Concerning the movement of narrative and its transitions, Lucian of Samosata states:

> After the preface, long or short in proportion to its subject matter, let the transition to the narrative be gentle and easy. For all the body of the history is simply a long narrative. So let it be adorned with the virtues proper to narrative, progressing smoothly, evenly and consistently, free from humps and hollows. Then let its clarity be limpid, achieved, as I have said, both by diction and the interweaving of the matter. For he will make everything distinct and complete, and when he [the historian] has finished the first topic he will introduce the second, fastened to it and linked with it like a chain, to avoid breaks and a multiplicity of disjointed narratives; no, always the first and second topics must not merely be neighbours but have common matter and overlap. (*How to Write History* 55)[42]

This concern for *dispositio* is concretized in the careful construction of the narrative of Acts. The connections and transitions in the narrative correspond to Luke's concern that the historian 'interweave' the beginning and end of sequences in order to obtain a narrative continuity. Jacques Dupont has well illustrated this interweaving technique in Acts. The classic example is Acts 7. 54 – 8. 3.[43]

In addition, Luke has taken particular care in constructing the end of Acts, deliberately giving his narrative an open ending. I shall discuss the reasons for this later.[44]

---

[41] This common characteristic among Hellenistic and Jewish historians, as well as in Luke, has been explored by W. S. Kurz, 'Narrative Models', 1990.

[42] Most citations of Lucian of Samosata are taken from K. Kilburn's translation in the Loeb Classical Library.

[43] J. Dupont, 'Question du plan', 1984.

[44] See chapter 10: 'The enigma of the end of Acts (Acts 28. 16–31)'.

The question of sources

The gathering of preparatory material (rule five), as defined by Lucian, explains why the identification of the sources of Acts is an impossible task. What does Lucian write?

> As to the facts themselves, he should not assemble them at random, but only after much laborious and painstaking investigation... When he has collected all or most of the facts let him first make them into a series of notes (ὑπόμνημα), a body (σῶμα) of material as yet with no beauty or continuity. Then, after arranging them into order (τάξις), let him give it beauty and enhance it with the charms of expression, figure, and rhythm.
>
> (*How to Write History* 47–8)

We should notice here the three stages of composition: first, the series of notes (ὑπόμνημα), then a formless draft (σῶμα) and finally, order and style (τάξις). The existence of preparatory notes leads to the conclusion that the author puts the information from his sources into a document that he himself writes.[45] The use of these notes in the definitive text makes it intelligible that, through this double filter, the indications which would permit us to identify the author's sources have disappeared from the surface of the text. This point does not only rest on Lucian's statements; the ancient procedure of writing is described in similar terms in a letter of Pliny the Younger.[46] So we can conclude that Luke has rewritten everything, erasing the traces of the documents consulted. Yet, is it not the sign of a good writer to make what was borrowed disappear?[47]

Variety and vivacity

Rules six and eight (selection, variety and vivacity) are also clearly followed in Acts, as we can judge from the care taken by the author to vary his style and its effects.

---

[45] On the notion of ὑπόμνημα, see C. J. Thornton, *Zeuge des Zeugen*, 1991, pp. 289–96.

[46] Pliny mentions the following steps while describing the work of his uncle, Pliny the Elder: *legere* (literally: listen to the *lector*), *adnotare* (this corresponds to the ὑπόμνημα), *excerpere* (make extracts), *dictare* (*Letters* 3.5.10–15).

[47] In spite of the massive work accomplished by M. E. Boismard and A. Lamouille (*Actes des deux apôtres*, I–III, 1990), I can only agree with the position put forward by their predecessor in the same collection in 1926: 'We must conclude that all of the attempts to determine the exact sources of Acts from a literary point of view have failed. It is useless to go into the details and try to identify a source document for one part or another, because the writer has not literally reproduced his sources; he has reworked them with his own vocabulary and style' (E. Jacquier, *Actes des apôtres*, 1926, p. cxliv; my translation).

> The task of the historian is similar: to give a fine arrangement
> to events and illuminate them as vividly as possible. And when
> a man who has heard him thinks thereafter that he is actually
> seeing what is being described and then praises him – then it is
> that the work of our Phidias of history is perfect and has received
> its proper praise. (*How to Write History* 51)

Note Lucian's beautiful metaphor: the brilliance of style seeks to create in the reader a vision, 'mediated' by the word; it serves to make the event visible. The preoccupation with vivacity, the ἐνέργεια in the writing, corresponds to the function of entertainment that Richard Pervo has shown so well to be a Lucan art:[48] however, I would add, in contrast to Pervo, that to instruct through entertaining is an adage that historians and novelists share.

With Luke, the example that comes to mind is his way of handling narrative redundancy, a key element in the art of variation on a theme; a comparison of the three versions of the conversion of Paul (Acts 9; 22; 26) will show this in detail.[49]

Topographical indications

Lucian recommends moderation in topographical indications: 'You need especial discretion in descriptions of mountains, fortifications, and rivers ... you will touch on them lightly for the sake of expediency or clarity, then change the subject ...' (*How to Write History* 57). As we have seen above there is no excess in Luke with regard to itinerary details. This author, unlike the novelists, is not interested in the description of the scenery or houses.

Speeches

The composition of the numerous speeches in Acts (rule ten) has been the object of a vast number of studies. I do not intend to go over the same ground.[50] Narratively, a speech constitutes a sort of meta-narrative (a narrative about the narrative), since it allows the characters

---

[48] R. I. Pervo (*Profit with Delight*, 1987) has made the following lines from Horace, which attribute rhetorical success to him who allies seduction and instruction, the canon of novelistic narration: *Omne tulit punctum qui miscuit utile dulci, / lectorem delectando pariterque monendo* (*Ars poetica* 343–4.). However, to attribute this only to novelists is to forget the historians.

[49] Cf. chapter 9: 'Saul's conversion (Acts 9; 22; 26)'.

[50] See M. L. Soars, *Speeches*, 1994.

in the story to interpret the events narrated (e.g., Peter interpreting the intervention of the Spirit at Pentecost in 2. 14–36). In this manner, they supplement and accelerate the process of interpreting the narrative for the reader. Later I shall consider their unifying value in narration.[51]

Recall that, for the composition of his speeches, Luke has followed the famous Thucydidean dogma:[52]

> As to the speeches that were made by different men, either when they were about to begin the war or when they were already engaged therein, it has been difficult to recall with strict accuracy the words actually spoken, both for me as regards that which I myself heard, and for those who from various other sources have brought me reports. Therefore the speeches are given in the language in which, as it seemed to me (ὡς δ' ἂν ἐδόκουν μοι), the several speakers would express (τὰ δέοντα), on the subjects under consideration, the sentiments most befitting the occasion, though at the same time I have adhered as closely as possible to the general sense of what was actually said.
>
> (*Peloponnesian War* 1.22.1)[53]

Even though the τὰ δέοντα has recently been contested,[54] it seems difficult to deny that the great Greek historian justifies the retrospective reconstruction of speeches on the basis of what is appropriate for the speaker and the rhetorical situation. Polybius distinguishes himself from Graeco-Roman historians by accepting an ethic which is more strictly documentary;[55] but Lucian follows the Thucydidean rule:

> If a person has to be introduced to make a speech, above all let his language suit his person and his subject (μάλιστα μὲν ἐοικότα τῷ προσώπῳ καὶ τῷ πράγματι οἰκεῖα λεγέσθω),

---

[51] See pp. 49–59.

[52] See P. A. Stadter, ed., *Speeches in Thucydides*, 1973. J. De Romilly, *Histoire et raison*, 1967. W. J. McCoy, 'In the Shadow', 1996, pp. 3–23.

[53] Cited following Ch. F. Smith's translation in the Loeb Classical Library, 1980.

[54] S. E. Porter ('Thucydides 1,22,1', 1990, p. 142) admits that Thucydides justifies himself here for not reporting the *ipsissima verba*. Yet he considers that the liberty claimed by the historian concerns the form of the information, without affecting 'the fundamental veracity of his account'. Nonetheless, Thucydides speaks of a *reconstructed* truth, allowing the historian the right to interpret. See also the remarks of the editor, B. Witherington in *History, Literature, and Society*, 1996, pp. 23–32.

[55] For Polybius, it is necessary 'to know the speeches that have been well kept, in their truth (τοὺς κατ' ἀλήθειαν εἰρημένους οἷοί ποτ' ἂν ὦσι γνῶναι)' (*Histories* 20.25b.1).

and next let these also be as clear as possible. It is then, however, that you can play the orator and show your eloquence.

(*How to Write History* 58)

The Thucydidean rule is applied to the letter in Luke, who shows an impressive care for verisimilitude in the reconstruction of the oratory art. The language that he provides for his characters corresponds to the audiences of the speech: Peter's Greek at Pentecost (2. 14–36) is strongly Hebraized, whereas Paul's in Athens (17. 22–31) is Atticizing classical. Moreover, the narrator places in the mouths of his characters subjects and a theology suitable for the situation described (Peter at Pentecost uses the formulae of an archaic Judaeo-Christian confession of faith; Paul in Athens utilizes a missionary strategy to the Gentiles that must have been applied by Christianity in Luke's time). The preoccupation with verisimilitude has thus led the author of Acts to research, in his documentation or in his investigations in the communities, a suitable argumentation and style. What we often forget is that the composition of a narrative 'in the manner of' was a well-known exercise in ancient rhetorical schools: the *prosopopoeia*. Students were required to compose a speech from the particular point of view of a historical or mythical character, borrowing his voice and adapting it for a specified audience.[56] Luke shows himself a master of this rhetorical performance.

In summary, the speeches of the generals in Thucydides are no more simply *verbatim* than those of the apostles in Acts. The criticism that Dionysius of Halicarnassus makes of Thucydides confirms this. He does not rebuke the Athenian for the fictitious nature of his speeches, but rather for the inadequacy of the subjects he places on the lips of his heroes;[57] for Dionysius, this fault must be criticized because Thucydides is the recommended model for *imitatio* in the schools.

A laughing matter

For Lucian, rule number one for the historian is the choice of his subject. What is a 'good subject' for Graeco-Roman historians? It is sufficient to

[56] References in W. S. Kurz's 'Variant Narrators', 1997, pp. 572–3.

[57] The criticism that he addresses to the great historian for his composition of the speech that Pericles gives in Athens is symptomatic (*De Thucydide* 44–6; cf. Thucydides, *Peloponnesian War* 2.60–4). In Dionysius' view, the tone and style are inappropriate to the dissatisfaction of the crowd that blames Pericles for having led them into war: 'Pericles should have been made to speak humbly and in such manner as to turn the jury's anger. This would have been the proper procedure for a historian who sought to imitate real life' (*De Thucydide* 45). Plausibility, not documentary exactitude, is here the criterion of truth.

go through their works to find an answer to this question. The classical historian deals with political or military history, unless he undertakes an ethnographical study. He tells of the lives and the vicissitudes of the great, generals and emperors. He displays his brilliance in describing manoeuvres of conquest. He narrates battles. Lucian himself does not forgo the occasion to ridicule historians who do not know how to narrate a battle.[58]

The subject that Luke chose is by no means insignificant. He insists that 'it was not done in a corner' (26. 26), and, as soon as possible, he anchors his narrative in world history (Luke 2. 1–2; 3. 1!). However, Πράξεις, his *res gestae*,[59] are devoted neither to Alexander the Great (Callisthenes), nor to Cyrus (Xenophon of Athens), nor to the destiny of the Greeks and Barbarians (Theopompus of Chios), nor to the Romans (Sallust). It is very doubtful whether Luke's history would have impressed Lucian of Samosata. 'History was political history',[60] van Unnik maintains.

What a Greek historian would find laughable, however, fits into the direct line of another kind of historiography, the Jewish one. The historical writings of the Hebrew Bible are devoted exclusively to narrating how God intervenes in the joys and sorrows of a small people. Luke, situated at the crossroads of Hellenistic and Jewish historiography, opts for the Jewish line as far as subject matter is concerned. The Jewish historian Flavius Josephus conforms to the Graeco-Roman model in his *Jewish Antiquities*. Arnaldo Momigliano sees in Christian historiography of the fourth and fifth centuries (Eusebius, Sozomen, Socrates the scholastic, Theodoret of Cyrrhus), with its unfolding of ecclesiastic conflicts and its history of heresies, a continuation of military history.[61] Luke, while he fits into mould of the Graeco-Roman narrative procedures,[62] nevertheless makes the thematic choice of biblical historians.

---

[58] *How to Write History* 28–9.

[59] The title attributed (by Luke?) to the book of Acts, Πράξεις, corresponds to the Latin *res gestae* and aligns the Lucan work with the chronicles of important characters and peoples (according to E. Plümacher, art. 'Apostelgeschichte' 1978, pp. 513–14.)

[60] W. C. van Unnik, 'Second Book', 1979, p. 38.

[61] A. Momigliano, *Fondations*, 1992, pp. 155–69.

[62] At the end of an interesting comparison of the accounts of Greek (Herodotus, Thucydides) and biblical (Josh. 6) battles, L. C. A. Alexander concludes that there is a close proximity in Luke's style (length, characters, details) with biblical narrative: 'where there is a significant difference between the two traditions, Luke follows the biblical approach to historiography almost every time' ('Marathon or Jericho?', 1998, p. 119). The difference concerns especially the question of the authorial voice, which will be dealt with later.

A theological historiography

There is another point relating to rule three where Luke violates the *ethos* of the Graeco-Roman historians in favour of the biblical tradition: the παρρησία. This should be understood as the virtue of honesty, boldness and freedom of expression. Lucian is very aware of this requirement: a historian must be 'fearless, incorruptible, free, a friend of free expression and the truth . . . sparing no one, showing neither pity nor shame' (*How to Write History* 41) and 'a free man, full of frankness, with no adulation or servility' (61). Lucian fights for the historian's freedom of thought, which must neither flatter the great nor turn history into propaganda. Does Luke subscribe to this requirement? While he attaches great importance to the παρρησία of the apostles (which indicates their audacity in proclaiming the Word rather than their freedom of thought),[63] Luke does not display a historian's intellectual autonomy; his reading of history is a believer's reading. The first verses of Acts (1. 6–7) already indicate this: Luke understands history as a theologian, that is, as a time that belongs in advance to God. We must resist the temptation to turn the author of Acts into a Christian Thucydides; he is closer in thought to a Flavius Josephus or the authors of the books of Maccabees.

The difference between Luke and the Greek historians, biographers or novelists is obvious with regard to the *relationship to the religious*. Critical detachment is important for the Greek authors, who systematically make a point of distancing themselves from the supernatural phenomema they report to their readers.[64] In rejecting the improbable and the sensational, Polybius sets the tone: spectacular or miraculous events are tolerable only to 'safeguard the piety of the people towards the divine'.[65] Historians and novelists sometimes evoke Destiny, or the whims of the gods.[66] 'The gods

---

[63] 2. 29; 4. 13, 29, 31; 28. 31. Παρρησιάζεσθαι: 9. 27–8; 13. 46; 14. 3; 18. 26; 19. 8; 28. 26.

[64] We can appreciate Lucian's cynicism: 'if a myth comes along you must tell it but not believe it entirely (οὐ μὴν πιστωτέος πάντως); no, make it known for your audience to make of it what they will – you run no risk and lean to neither side' (*How to Write History* 60).

[65] *Histories* 16.12.9: διασῴζειν τὴν τοῦ πλήθους εὐσέβειαν πρὸς τὸ θεῖον. E. Plümacher sees in this concession of Polybius the motive for the integration of miracles in the Lucan writing of history; this total contempt for the theological foundation of Luke's venture reveals the limit of Luke's integration into a Graeco-Roman historiography, for which Plümacher argues ('ΤΕΡΑΤΕΙΑ', 1998, pp. 66–90, esp. pp. 86–8).

[66] I rely on the study of A. Billault (*Création romanesque*, 1991, pp. 103–9), who thinks that when Greek novelists deal with the gods they speak of their active presence, or of their jealousy toward humans (Chronos, Eros) or ascribe the cause of events to Fortune (τυχή). Billault notes that although the Greek novel does not ignore the religious, the divine origin of events gives no particular significance to them.

have their place' comments Loveday Alexander, 'but it is a familiar and acceptable one: divine oracles, or Fortune, may be invoked on occasion to move the plot forward; people who offend against Love are punished; a troubled heroine prays to Isis or Aphrodite for protection . . . But these coincidences are not themselves occasions for "marvelling", either by the characters in the narrative, or by its readers.'[67] Entirely contrary to this, the readers of Acts are never called on to distance themselves from supernatural manifestations, but rather to marvel at them.

Jewish historiography, Greek historiography

This is a major point at which the two historiographies part company: the Greek is critical, the Jewish is not.[68] Greek historiography has its model in Herodotus, borrowing from him the *persona* of the narrator who comments on what he reports; this authorial voice produces a distance between the facts narrated and their reception by the readers.[69] There is a fundamental epistemological difference here. Greek and Jewish historians both understand their task as a search for truth, a quest for the ἀληθὴς ἱστορίας[70] (the requirement of veracity in history is the watchword of ancient historiography); yet the former establish the plausibility of the event, while the latter expose the *truth* of the God who rules the world. Greek history is illuminating, Jewish history is confessional. This is why the intrusion of the narrator is not appropriate in Hebrew historiography. He disappears behind his words (Josephus is an exception[71]). On the contrary, the Greek perspective plays with the articulation of different points of view.

---

[67] L. C. A. Alexander, 'Fact, Fiction', 1998, p. 394.

[68] For what follows: A. Momigliano, *Fondations*, 1992, pp. 5–32.

[69] C. Calame (*Récit en Grèce antique*, 1986, pp. 71–7) distinguishes four types of intrusion by the narrator: (a) identification of the source of information; (b) judgement on the truth of the information and the credit to be given to it; (c) remarks concerning the articulation of the work; and (d) value judgement on the content of the account. The last two categories are rare. The second is the most interesting for us; for example: Herodotus' extreme reservation about what the priests of Chaldea or Egypt say. Thus, when the Chaldean priests recount that the god comes to his temple to sleep with a chosen woman, the historian of Halicarnassus comments that their words do not seem to be trustworthy (ἐμοὶ μὲν οὐ πιστὰ λέγοντες: *The Histories* 1.182.1; cf. also 6.121.1; 6.123.1; 6.124.2).

[70] In *Against Apion* (1.23–7), Josephus ratifies this aim for historiography and makes it his own; but he reproaches the Greek historians for sacrificing it in favour of a pursuit of eloquence and literary effect (1.27). Josephus frequently resorts to the term ἀλήθεια when he deals with the ethics of historiography in his prefaces: *B.J.* 1.6; 1.17; 1.30; *A.J.* 1.4; *C. Ap.* 1.6; 1.15; 1.24; 1.50; 1.52; 1.56. Diodorus Siculus speaks of ἱστορία as a 'prophetess of truth' (*Historical Library* 1.2.2).

[71] Examples abound in Josephus. *Against Apion* presents long narrative sections filled with authorial interventions. A noteworthy shift is also perceptible from 1 Macc. to 2 Macc.

Loveday Alexander has pointed out the absence of the authorial voice in Acts. She considers this to be a sign of Luke's affiliation with Jewish historiography.[72] The narrator never directly addresses the reader (intrusive narrator) in order to guide the reader's reception of the story. There is no authorial supervision regulating the reading. Direct intrusions ('intradiegetic'[73]) are limited to the dedication to Theophilus (Luke 1. 1–4) and the famous 'we-passages'.

The reading pact of Luke–Acts

The dedication to Theophilus (Luke 1. 1–4) is of interest because it creates the link between narrator and readers. Narratology uses the term 'reading pact' for these initial textual sequences in which the narrator establishes the frame of understanding for the work, thereby indicating how it should be read.[74] What signal does Luke give in his preface for the reader's benefit? It has hardly been noticed until recently that the Lucan *incipit* constructs a very particular type of reader.

Twice, the preface uses a pronoun that should alert us: 'Since many have undertaken to set down an orderly account of the events that have been fulfilled among us (ἐν ἡμῖν), just as they were handed on to us (ἡμῖν) by those who from the beginning were eyewitnesses and servants of the word...' (vv. 1–2). To whom do these two ἡμῖν refer? To the readers. The dedication, by this repeated pronoun, includes the readers in what one may well call a reading community, to which the narrator also belongs.[75] It would be a mistake to think that the reader the author hopes for comes to the text with a blank slate (a *tabula rasa* as *reader-response criticism* would have us believe). In any case, this is not Luke's intention. His dedication to an already instructed Theophilus (Luke 1. 4) sets the tone for potential readers. The pragmatic function of the dedication is therefore to open up and mark out the reading space: the narrative which follows (the gospel and Acts) takes place within a relationship composed

The latter is marked by the interventions of an intrusive narrator (cf. the long preface of 2 Macc. 2. 19–32). See also the quotations in W. S. Kurz, 'Narrative Models', 1990, pp. 179–82.

[72] L. C. A. Alexander, 'Fact, Fiction', 1998, pp. 395–9.

[73] Narrative criticism uses the term 'intradiegetic' to designate what is intrinsic to the story (for example, the 'we' of 16. 10–17, which is a collective character in the narrative) and 'extradiegetic' for what is external to the story (for example: the 'I' of Luke 1. 3 which is not a character in the narrative).

[74] The linguist Gérard Genette speaks of 'péritexte' to indicate everything that comes from the prefatory strategy of the author, that is, everything that the author places before the narrative itself in order to orient the reader (*Seuils*, 1987, p. 7).

[75] With L. C. A. Alexander, *Preface*, 1993, pp. 141–2; pp. 191–3.

of a common faith in the saving events (the 'events ... fulfilled among us') and a common adherence to a tradition ('handed on ... by those who from the beginning were eyewitnesses').

The establishment of such a reading community, without parallel in Graeco-Roman historiography, denotes again Luke's remarkable originality. He is able to draw from both the Greek historical tradition and the biblical tradition. This eclecticism strikes the reader from the very beginning of his work: after a dedication (Luke 1. 1–4) in the purest Hellenistic style, Luke passes, without transition, to a writing full of Septuagintalisms (ἐγένετο ἐν ταῖς ἡμεραῖς; 1. 4a). This combination is not just cultural, as we shall see later. It is necessary to investigate more fully Luke's orchestration of the convergence of Greek culture and ancient Jewish tradition, Rome and Jerusalem.[76]

The 'we-passages'

The 'we-passages' (16. 10–17; 20. 5–15; 21. 1–18; 27. 1 – 28. 16) have excited the curiosity of exegetes. Their main concern has been with the possibility of discovering the identity of the mysterious traveller who belongs in this way to the group of Paul's travelling companions; exegetes have hoped in this way to place the author of Acts at the side of the great apostle,[77] but to no avail. I would argue that the identification of the collective ἡμεῖς with the 'I' of Luke is inappropriate, for three reasons: (1) the authorial 'I' is not comparable with a narrative 'we'; (2) the 'I' of Luke 1 is extradiegetic, while the 'we' of the passages is attributed to a collective character within the narrative, the group of Paul's companions, which is intradiegetic; (3) differently from the 'I' of the preface, that overhangs the story, the 'we' does not directly address the reader and remains internal to the story.

I conclude that the use of ἡμεῖς is a narrative device for making the narrative credible, signalling its origin in a group to which the narrator belongs.[78] It intervenes at important moments in Paul's itinerary (Acts 16: the entry into Greece; Acts 20: the resurrection of Eutychus in Troas; Acts 21: the ascent to Jerusalem; Acts 27–8: the trip to Rome). As such, in narratological terms, the ἡμεῖς indicates the spatio-temporal and ideological

[76] See chapter 4 below: 'A Christianity between Jerusalem and Rome'.

[77] A good overview of research can be found in V. Fusco, 'Sezioni-noi', 1983, pp. 73–86 and 'Ancora', 1991, pp. 231–9. He concludes that the problem of literary source is unresolvable.

[78] On this procedure and its possible Old Testament origin, see J. Wehnert, *Wir-Passagen*, 1989.

point of view that the author has adopted.[79] The question of literary origin aside (and it is not unreasonable to think of a travel journal), it is important to notice at the pragmatic level that the narrator has four times placed himself close to his hero Paul. This proximity says much about the theological tradition in which he hopes to be recognized and about the legitimacy he claims in receiving his inheritance.

Conclusion: Luke at the crossroads of two historiographies

Luke is situated precisely at the meeting point of Jewish and Greek historiographical currents. His narrative devices are heavily indebted to the cultural standard in the Roman Empire, that is, history as the Greeks wrote it. However, contrary to the ideal of objectivity found in Herodean and Thucydidean historiography, Luke recounts a confessional history. Jacob Jervell is right to insist on this: Luke does not set out the destiny of a religious movement moving toward Rome from its origin in the Near East, but the expansion of a mission that he intends from the very start to make known as 'a history of salvation'.[80] The quest for causality which animates the Graeco-Roman historian is exclusively theological for Luke. He shows a complete lack of interest in other causes. This characteristic incontestably links Luke's narrative with biblical historiography. Judaeo-Christian *historia* has no other ambition than to point to God behind the event.

However, as I have said, a historian is guided, in the interrogation of his/her sources and the narrative reconstruction of the past, by a specific point of view. Questions of literary genre and the point of view of Luke the historian will be the subjects of the next chapter.

[79] The notion of point of view (with its geographical, cultural and ideological components) has been studied by Boris Uspensky, *A Poetics of Composition*, 1973. See also D. Marguerat and Y. Bourquin, *How to Read*, 1999, pp. 66–9.

[80] J. Jervell: 'He wanted to write history of a special sort, salvation history. He did not intend to write ecclesiastical history or the history of a religious movement, an oriental sect' ('Future of the Past', 1996, p. 110).

2

A NARRATIVE OF BEGINNINGS

What can be said about the aim of the book of Acts? Why did Luke write a follow-up to his gospel? What was his goal and what pushed him to write this grand historical work? I shall deal with these questions in two ways. First, it is important to know what the book of Acts resembles in the world of ancient literature. To what literary genre does it belong? Second, the relevance of the narrator's point of view, or his narrative intention must be considered. I shall conclude by evaluating Luke's decision to add the Acts of the Apostles to the gospel.

Seeking a literary genre

In today's context, the affiliation of the gospels with the Graeco-Roman literary genre of biography (the affinity of the gospel of Luke with the *Lives* of the philosophers is evident)[1] provokes no great difficulties. On the contrary, exegetes continue to have a hard time classifying the second part of the work *ad Theophilum*. Many suggestions have been made in an attempt to identify the literary genre of Acts, but the absence of any satisfying analogy in ancient literature makes the decision arduous.[2]

A continuation of the gospel?

Charles Talbert has proposed that one view of the Luke–Acts succession is the *Life* of a philosopher followed by the story of his disciples. Hence, the biography of the founder of the religious movement should be

---

[1] According to D. E. Aune, from a formal and functional point of view, the gospels constitute a sub-category of ancient biography (*Literary Environment*, 1987, p. 46).

[2] After a detailed criticism of scholarly propositions, A. J. M. Wedderburn concludes that it must be dismissed: 'Weil keine Zeitgenossen oder Nachfolger solche Acta geschrieben haben, ist sein Werk eigentlich ein Werk *sui generis*. Es gehört zu keiner Gattung, wenn eine Gattung per definitionem aus mehreren Werken bestehen sollte' ('Gattung', 1996, p. 319). See also C. J. Hemer, *Book of Acts*, 1989, p. 42.

followed by the story of his successors.[3] It is certainly true that the idea
of succession was cultivated by the philosophical schools in antiquity,
each one conscious of its origins. However, unfortunately, no one has
yet been able to define a 'lives of the successors' literary genre in antiquity. Talbert can only refer to the 'Lives of Philosophers' by Diogenes
Laertius, a biographical compendium of eighty-two philosophers, which
resembles more a list of succession than a narrative of origins.[4] Furthermore, the relationship between Jesus and the apostles is not presented in
successional categories, like those set out by the author of the Pastoral
letters (requirement of doctrinal integrity and faithfulness to the apostolic
tradition).

If Acts is to be understood as a sequel to the gospel, one finds closer
models by looking in the direction of the philosophical treatises (Philo's
De vita Mosis[5] or Josephus' *Against Apion*) or the double writings of the
Hebrew Bible (1–2 Samuel, 1–2 Kings, etc). However, any comparison
immediately shows the unprecedented role that the paschal turning-point
plays, as it is on this that Luke's diptych pivots (Luke 24/Acts 1), making
Acts not merely a simple addition attached to the gospel, but the story of
the agents of the Resurrected One.

An apology?

In his monumental commentary, Ernst Haenchen popularized the idea
that Acts was an *apologia pro ecclesia*.[6] He is impressed by the positive
role given to the Roman political system, and by the important section
devoted to Paul's defence before the authorities of the Empire (chs. 24–6).
Furthermore, 'when we read Acts as a whole, rather than selectively, it
is Paul the prisoner even more than Paul the missionary whom we are
meant to remember'.[7] Haenchen argues that the writing of the book has

---

[3] C. H. Talbert, *Literary Patterns*, 1974, pp. 125–40. See also 'Monograph or 'Bios'?',
1996 (where the author proposes reading Acts like 'a *bios* of a people, the church' p. 69;
thus the difference with historiography fades).

[4] See D. E. Aune's criticism, *Literary Environment*, 1987, pp. 78–9.

[5] The preface of Book 2 of *De vita Mosis* (2.1) is comparable, for it announces a sequel
devoted to what 'follows and accompanies' (περὶ τῶν ἑπομένων καὶ ἀκολούθων) the first
treatise (ἡ πρότερα σύνταξις); in fact, this sequel does not present the succession to Moses
but, rather, develops what deals with the legislation, the responsibility of the High Priest
and prophecy, while the first book was reserved for the royal and philosophical dimensions
of the character (2.2).

[6] E. Haenchen, *Acts of the Apostles*, 1971, pp. 78–81; 'Judentum und Christentum',
1968, pp. 370–4. Also H. Conzelmann, *Acts of the Apostles*, 1987, pp.192–204.

[7] This remark is from R. Maddox (*Purpose*, 1982, p. 67), who criticizes Haenchen's view,
while still maintaining Luke's political conformity: 'The proper business of Christians is to

one ultimate purpose: to plead in favour of the political correctness of Christianity. His theory has been abandoned today on the basis that the vast majority of the speeches in Acts are destined for the Jews and even when Paul is confronted by Roman authorities (Acts 18. 12–16; 24. 10–23; 25–6) it always concerns his relationship to Judaism.

C. K. Barrett offers these scathing words: '[Acts] was not addressed to the Emperor, with the intention of proving the political harmlessness of Christianity in general and of Paul in particular . . . No Roman official would ever have filtered out so much of what to him would be theological and ecclesiastical rubbish in order to reach so tiny a grain of relevant apology'.[8] If the idea that the Acts might have been a 'self-defence' file destined for the imperial authority must be abandoned – Harnack even imagined that Acts had been written by Luke between Paul's two Roman captivities and was to be used in defending him before the emperor – the apologetic question has not yet been settled. I shall return to this below.

A historical monograph?

Faced with the difficulty of finding an adequate classification for Acts, Hans Conzelmann has proposed, as a last resort, the vague category of *historical monograph*.[9] Conzelmann's view leads us to believe that Acts is a historical account with a sole theme. If this were the case, what might be the theme? If it is the lives of the apostles, one moves in the direction of biography; but Luke is hardly interested, with regard to his characters, in the elements that a biographer would retain (he leaves out the ends of the lives of Peter and Paul). If one envisions an 'ecclesiastical history' like Eusebius' work it is hardly any more adequate. Luke is clearly uninterested in the institutional continuity of the Church.[10] If it is necessary to determine the sole theme of the book of Acts, one should look in the direction of the history of mission or even better, the beginning of Christianity.

Richard Pervo, in his brilliant study, has argued for the novelistic dimension of Acts and risked the label 'historical novel.'[11] Even though

live at peace with the sovereign power, so far as possible, and not to play the hero' (*ibid.*, p. 97). This, however, is to misunderstand the Lucan hero ethic, which consists of announcing the Gospel by means of a vulnerable and threatened life (Acts 22. 17–21; 24. 10–21; 26. 19–23; cf. 7. 51–3).

[8] C. K. Barrett, *Luke the Historian*, 1961, p. 63.

[9] H. Conzelmann, *Acts of the Apostles*, 1987, p. xl.

[10] It is worth quoting Conzelmann on this subject: 'It is striking that continuity in history of the church is not located in institutions' (*Acts of the Apostles*, 1987, p. xlv).

[11] R. I. Pervo, *Profit with Delight*, 1987, pp. 115–38.

he is convincing, demonstrating the entertaining dimension of the narrative and taking down the barriers that isolate the canonical Acts from the apocryphal Acts, he nevertheless has not established the validity of the title 'historical novel'. This is because, firstly, it was not a literary genre in antiquity and, secondly, the narrative devices that Pervo puts forward do not allow one to draw any distinctions between a novelistic writing and a historiographic one, as both of these genres use them interchangeably in Hellenistic culture.[12]

An apologetic history?

I return now to the apologetic theme. A rejection of a political apology does not lead us to ignore the indisputable apologetic intentions that are found throughout the book of Acts. F. F. Bruce rightly maintains, 'The author of Acts has a right to be called... the first Christian apologist. The great age of Christian apologetic was the second century, but of the three main types of defense represented among the second-century Christian apologists, Luke provides first-century prototypes: defense against pagan religion (Christianity is true; paganism is false), defense against Judaism (Christianity is the fulfilment of true Judaism), defense against political accusations (Christianity is innocent of any offense against Roman law').[13]

But is it correct to give such an important place to apologetics in Acts? In fact, in the Lucan narrative we find speeches defending Christianity against Jewish accusations, as well as propaganda against paganism or justifying the political virginity of the Christian faith.[14] This profusion of apologetics within the narrative, however, does not yet say what might be the apologetic aim of the *narrative itself*. The decisive argument seems to be the one of the audience: who is the reader addressed by Acts? It is neither the Synagogue (that bristled at the degradation of the figure of the 'Jews' on every page), nor the Gentiles ignorant of Christianity (who got

---

[12] Pervo makes an inventory of shared episodes in the plot of Acts and the Greek novels: conspiracies, riots, imprisonments, miraculous deliverances, storms and shipwrecks, comic incidents, exotism, and so on. For a detailed critique of his proposal of a literary affiliation with Acts, see D. L. Balch's 'Genre', 1991, pp. 7–11.

[13] F. F. Bruce, *Acts of the Apostles*, 1990, p. 22.

[14] Loveday Alexander has carefully made an inventory of the different types of internal apologetics in Acts: (a) the anti-Jewish apologetic (Acts 4–5; 6–7); (b) the propaganda toward the Gentiles (14. 11–18; 17. 16–34); (c) the political apologetic (16. 19–21; 17. 6–7; 18. 12–13; 19. 35–40; 24–6); (d) an apologetic internal to the Church (15. 23–9). She concludes that these witnesses have a paradigmatic status for the reader and notes the predominance of the (a) and (c) types ('Apologetic Text', 1999).

lost incessantly in the reminiscences of the LXX). The language of Acts is *a language for the initiated*. The implied reader[15] is the Christian or an interested sympathizer, as for example, the most excellent Theophilus (Luke 1. 3–4; Acts 1. 1). Luke's apologetic is addressed to Christian 'insiders' of the movement and a circle which gravitates around it.

Gregory Sterling integrates the Acts into a literary current he titles *apologetic historiography* (in line with Manetho, Berossos, Artapanos and the *Jewish Antiquities* of Josephus).[16] The aim which links these works together is to unfold the identity of a movement by exposing its native traditions, by revealing its cultural dignity and the antiquity of its origins; the outstanding characteristic is the self-definition of the group by the means of historiography. Philip Esler has given a sociological foundation to this view by describing the programme of the author of *ad Theophilum* as a 'sophisticated attempt to explain and justify Christianity to the members of his community at a time when they were exposed to social and political pressures which were making their allegiance waver'.[17]

In a comparison of the literary modes used, to assimilate Luke–Acts with the historical works that Sterling cites seems a bit forced.[18] On the other hand, however, the advantage of Sterling's proposal is to align two characteristics of the text: an apologetic goal and a Christian readership. Furthermore, this fits nicely with what has been said in the preceding chapter concerning the identity intention of all historiographical work, specifically its defence of an identity that is threatened. Therefore, after these considerations, the *historiographical* genre, given that the boundary between historiography and ancient biography is not always clear, is the best fit for the book of Acts.

Defense and illustration of Christian faith

The failure of the various attempts mentioned above to determine the literary genre of Acts must teach us a lesson: the aim of this book does not allow itself to be confined to a narrow formulation. What was said in

[15] In narratology, the 'implied reader' is the image of the recipient of the narrative, as the text makes him appear (his presupposed knowledge) and as the narrative constructs him (his cooperation in reading the text). For further development, see D. Marguerat and Y. Bourquin's *How to Read*, 1999, pp. 14–15.

[16] G. E. Sterling, *Historiography and Self-Definition*, 1992.

[17] P. F. Esler, *Community*, 1987, p. 222. The author sees Luke–Acts as the vehicle of a sectarian Christianity that narratively constructs 'a symbolic universe, a sacred canopy, beneath which the institutional order of his community is given meaning and justification'.

[18] The apologetic of Josephus is argued and direct. Luke, however, proceeds indirectly by means of the narrative. Furthermore, motives such as universal dimension, cultural patriotism, the incomparable antiquity of the movement, the demonstration of antiquity and the total reliability of its archives find only a weak echo in Acts.

the previous chapter concerning a historiographical undertaking makes this clear. If history answers an institutional necessity to fix the memory of the past, then the ambition of the work *ad Theophilum* is to provide Lucan Christianity with an identity. In writing his diptych, the author wants to show his readers *who they are, where they come from and what formed them.* He writes to allow them to understand and speak of themselves (to others, to the Jews and the Gentiles). This identity intention, which is apologetic in the large sense, does not exclude secondary motives. The proposals elucidated above (successional, apologetical in the narrow sense, biographical, hagiographical, novelistic) represent virtualities. However, these do not acquire their pertinence unless articulated in defence and illustration of the Christian faith which overshadows them. This, in fact, was the role of schools in antiquity, according to H. I. Marrou. Read the ancient authors, read the historians, in order to understand, *via* the past, who one is.

Luke seems to be the first to have presented a religious movement in a historical mode. In any case, he was the first in the history of Christianity to recognize the need to endow the Christianity of his time[19] with a tool of self-understanding. He accomplishes this not only by the means of a history of its founder (the gospel), but also by a *history of its foundation.* Within this grand work, the gospel unfolds the biography of the Master; the Acts then present how, through successive and undesired breaks, the community of the disciples separates itself from Judaism in order to constitute progressively a Church within the Empire. I. Howard Marshall is not mistaken in concluding that linking the history of the movement to that of its founder represents a *unicum* in literature.[20]

The narratives of beginnings

What more is there to be said concerning this identity-creating narrative in order to specify its function? I propose the term *narrative of beginnings*. Pierre Gibert, in his book entitled *Bible, mythes et récits de*

[19] In my opinion, the inability of scholars to agree on a portrait of a 'Lucan church', signifies a difference from Matthew, which addresses a community whose problems and contours are easily discernible. Neither is Luke's horizon linked, like John's, to a group of churches, but rather to a Pauline movement. His work as a chronicler of Christianity is addressed to a wide public (especially to Rome?), which I shall define in what follows as 'Lucan Christianity'.

[20] 'It would seem so far that no proposal to account for Luke–Acts in terms of known genres has been successful. Even within the Christian context there is nothing corresponding to it . . . The whole work demonstrates affinities both to historical monographs and to biographies, but it appears to represent a new type of work, of which it is the only example, in which under the shape of a 'scientific treatise' Luke has produced a work which deals with 'the beginnings of Christianity' (I. H. Marshall, ' "Former Treatise" ', 1993, pp. 179–80).

commencement,[21] studies the narratives of beginnings in the Hebrew Bible. His interest is in the narratives of origin, such as the story of Adam and Eve (Gen. 2–3), Cain and Abel (Gen. 4), the calling of Abraham (Gen. 12), the crossing of the Red Sea (Exod. 14), the passing of the Jordan (Josh. 3–4), the calling of Samuel (1 Sam. 3), and so on.

For Pierre Gibert, it is clear that a narrative of beginnings is not a literary genre.[22] Rather, this term designates a function that the account receives in the anamnesis of the past. This *flashback reading* which the historian performs,[23] transforms a word into a *narrative of beginnings* by way of a strong symbolic investment. The fact that the passing of the Jordan or the calling of Abraham become narratives of beginnings is the result of the historian's decision, even if this decision comes in the course of the process of collective transmission. In doing this, it is the historian's task to confirm or revise any 'beginnings' previously established by a dominant ideology; its reading of the past will be either accepted or repudiated by the historian.

What are the parameters which transform a story into a narrative of beginnings? If I have understood Gibert's approach,[24] there are six: (1) the presence of a break which functions as an founding rupture; (2) the intervention of a supernatural dimension implying transcendence; (3) a mysterious aspect reinforced by the absence of any other witnesses (vision, divine call); (4) the event is understood by reference to an ultimate origin, to an absolute beginning; (5) the situation which is created presents something new; (6) the event inaugurates a history or a posterity.

We can see how these factors affect the narrative of Exodus 14:[25] the crossing of the Red Sea proceeds from a salvific separation, brought about by Moses' action, the scope of which leads back to the absolute beginning which is the creation of the world (separating from the original chaos in which the Egyptians are swallowed up); divine protection of the holy people opens up to the newness of a liberation, which founds a history to which the time in the desert will give form.

Acts – a story of beginnings

In my opinion, an application of this label to Acts seems productive. Let me verify the criteria.

---

[21] P. Gibert, *Bible*, 1986.   [22] *Ibid.*, pp. 245–6.
[23] '... le commencement implique toujours un après-coup, à partir duquel il est défini et légitimé' (*ibid.*, p. 50).
[24] See especially, *ibid.*, pp. 23–53.   [25] *Ibid.*, pp. 171–86.

First, the founding rupture clearly corresponds to the division between Jesus' followers and Synagogue Judaism, a theme that is mentioned in each of the twenty-eight chapters. This schism takes on the status of original separation.

Second, the implication of the transcendent is found in the many divine interventions, which not only create the unexpected (Pentecost; the call of Saul; the success of the Word with the non-Jews), but force the history to change the route of the missionaries (the meeting of Peter and Cornelius – Acts 10–11; the passage into Macedonia – Acts 16). Visions, ecstasies, prophecies, angelic appearances and earthquakes show the variety of the supernatural means which God uses to accomplish his plan.

Third, the absence of other witnesses only occurs in certain precise moments, when the supernatural dimension comes into play. Thus the miracle of tongues at Pentecost remains a mystery, since the hearers do not know why they understand the wonders of God (2. 7–13). The conversion of Saul on the road to Damascus is witnessed by his travelling companions who are either blinded to what takes place (9. 7) or are deaf (22. 9).[26] The other visions and angelic appearances take place (as is normal) without witness. Except for these particular sections, the 'beginning' of Christianity unfolds in the sight and the knowledge of many.

Fourth, the reference to an ultimate origin is interesting because it stamps a specific role on what may be referred to as the two significant matrices of the narrative of Acts: (1) the gospel of Luke and, (2) the Septuagint.[27] These two antecedent texts (in the historical and literary sense) function as norms of the theological truthfulness of the events narrated. To understand these texts as 'absolute beginnings' means to say that the narrator accustoms his readers to view them as endowed with such an authority. In other words, Luke's intensive use of the 'LXX style'[28] not only implies – as has often been affirmed – that the narrator presupposes on the part of his readers a knowledge of the Greek Scriptures, but that this very frequent usage betrays Luke's desire to accustom his readers to enter into the universe of the Greek Bible, to read it as Scripture, in short, to appropriate it. In this respect, we can speak of the gnoseological function of the narrative: it makes known to the readers a language of antiquity.[29]

---

[26] For an analysis of this motif, see chapter 9: 'Saul's conversion (Acts 9; 22; 26)', pp. 185–6; 192 n.37.

[27] The use for Acts of these two 'pre-texts' (the gospel of Luke and the LXX) as matrices has been observed by J. B. Green in his essay 'Internal Repetition', 1996, esp. pp. 290–5.

[28] The demonstration has been made by E. Plümacher in *Schriftsteller*, 1972, pp. 38–72.

[29] See L. C. A. Alexander, 'Intertextualité', 2000, pp. 201–14.

The fifth criterion (the something new) is confirmed, even though Luke shows that Christianity can appeal to the most essential Jewish traditions. Luke is conscious that the opening of the covenant to the Gentiles, (Acts 10–11) and the relocation from Jerusalem to Rome opens the way to a new and different religious movement distinct from the Synagogue. It is in his time that the rupture with Judaism will be accomplished. The God of Israel has become the God of all.

Sixth, the beginning of a posterity is evident. This posterity is especially represented by the Lucan readership. Can we see in the throng of characters of the narrative a mirror-image of this posterity? The book that we are dealing with is above all the most populated in the New Testament.

Summary. Neither a novel, biography or hagiography, nor an apology in the strict sense, the book of Acts cannot be locked into any of these categories. However, it must be acknowledged that it shares many characteristics with such literary genres. The closest categorization is a historiography with an apologetic aim, which permits Christianity both to understand and to speak itself. Its status as a narrative of beginnings assures the Lucan work a clear identity function.

The point of view of Luke the historian

With Luke's aim now clarified, the question of point of view must be dealt with. What is the theological point of view at work in his reading of history? Of and from what is Luke's theology constructed? In my opinion, five points are important:

(1)   his valorization of the world;
(2)   his sense of the resurrection;
(3)   his conception of God;
(4)   his theology of the Word;
(5)   his theology of providence.

A valorization of the world

Luke is both historian and theologian. More precisely, he is a historian *because* he is a theologian. History, for Luke, is the place where humanity and the divine meet. This conception of history is worlds apart from apocalyptic. Apocalyptic thought is structured by a strong dualism which leads it to detest the world in the name of the future Kingdom. It takes only a comparison of the status of Rome in Acts and the Apocalypse of John to be convinced. It is the goal of Paul's mission for the former and the symbol of evil for the latter. The capital of the Empire is the target of the narrative from Acts 19. 21 onwards, whereas from Revelation 13 onwards it is silhouetted behind the metaphors of evil.

Such a repulsion is foreign to Luke, who never departs from his intense admiration for the Roman Empire: its communication networks of which Paul makes use, its cities, the functioning of its institutions. Yet his admiration is not naive; for example, when necessary, he does not hesitate to lampoon unscrupulous officials (see Felix in 24. 24–6). This critical attitude however, does not change the basically positive orientation of his relation to the world. The Roman Empire is still the place where God meets, sends, illuminates and supports his messengers. Furthermore, it is here that Christianity is promised expansion, with Paul's arrival in the capital (28. 16ff.) as the pledge.

Recurrence of the resurrection in history

In having decided to show how salvation fits *into* history, Luke does not telescope time. He does not fuse his period with Jesus' time (like Mark and Matthew) or with the period of origins (there will be no return to the 'golden age' of Acts 1–5).[30] If the return of Jesus remains the horizon of history, Luke sees an open future for Christianity that will no longer be harmed by the imminent awaiting of the parousia. Once again, this perspective has little in common with the seer of Revelation, who sees history vanishing under the pressure of a terrifying and liberating future.

If history is theologically valorized in Luke's eyes, it is because he sees at work the effects of the resurrection of Jesus. The healing miracle, that is not the Spirit's working, but an act of the Name of Jesus Christ (3. 6; 4. 10, 30; 16. 18; 19. 13),[31] is the privileged vehicle of this recurrence of the resurrection in history. Peter also points out that the key to understanding the event of Pentecost is the resurrection (2. 22–36); it is also the resurrection that he announces to Cornelius (10. 37–43), and Paul will do the same in his speeches. The book of Acts is the only New Testament

[30] Luke's idealized portrait of the golden age has often been criticized. Intended for the Christianity of his time, threatened by 'savage wolves' who 'come distorting the truth in order to entice the disciples to follow them' (Acts 20. 29–30), Luke presents more a prototype for the Church than a picture full of nostalgic idealism. This prototype is destined to stimulate and encourage believers. Projected into the past, even in the frightening form of the Ananias and Sapphira story, Christian unity appears as a gift and a requirement – a gift of the Spirit inscribed in its history and attested by it.

[31] Concerning this Lucan peculiarity in miracle traditions, see my article 'Magic and Miracle in the Acts of the Apostles' (forthcoming).

book to make the resurrection a transforming agent in history. It is up to the witness to decode, in the confusion of events, the action of the God who raised Jesus from the dead.

An image of God that changes

Whoever speaks of history speaks of order, succession and calendar. This is precisely why the author of Acts will mark out his narrative by the various stages that he discerns in the progression of history: the origins (chs. 1–5), the Stephen crisis (chs. 6–7), the progress outside Jerusalem (chs. 8–12), the mission to the Jews and the Gentiles (13. 1 – 15. 35), the Pauline mission (15. 36 – 20. 38) and the martyrdom of Paul (21–8). God dictates for the dawning community a rhythmic development, which Luke wants to divide into periods.[32]

Whoever speaks of history also speaks of continuity and change. Luke's history of a dawning Christianity fits into the continuation of the history of Israel. The numerous speeches of Acts ceaselessly repeat, almost to the point of boredom, that the God of Jesus is none other than the God of the Fathers, the God of Abraham, of Isaac and of Jacob (3. 13; 7. 2–50; 13. 17–26; 22. 3; 24. 14; 26. 6–8; 28. 17). Luke, in a variety of ways, strives to mention the signs of continuity in his salvation history, whether they be of a textual order (the intensive use of the LXX), a geographical order (the emblematic role of Jerusalem as the symbol of God's faithfulness) or a personal order (the modelling of Paul on Peter).[33]

These markers of continuity must be all the more evident since Luke's narrative emphasizes *an image of God that changes and is transformed*. In spite of the use of an ancient term derived from the LXX (προσωπολήμπτης) to say it (10. 34), Luke is aware of something new when he places on the lips of Peter the assertion that God no longer 'shows any partiality' (lit. 'makes no acceptance of persons'). The holiness of the chosen people is enlarged to worldwide dimensions. It is again Peter who announces to Cornelius, that from now on 'everyone who believes in him receives forgiveness of sins through his name' (10. 43b). Luke is

---

[32] Luke's preoccupation with the periodization of history allows one to understand the calendar (unknown to the rest of the New Testament tradition) fixed by the author at the interval between Jesus and the Church: forty days of appearances of the Risen One (Acts 1. 3), then the Ascension and then Pentecost after fifty days (Acts 2. 1). Whatever the case may be with the information collected by Luke, this scanning of time is related to his vocation as a historian. Since he is devoted to telling how salvation is manifested in history, it is important for him to describe the salvific events according to the rules of historiography, in other words, to tell them, to date them and to localize them.

[33] On this process of modelling, called *syncrisis*, see below pp. 56–9 (ch. 3).

the only one in the New Testament to *narrativize* how the God of Israel becomes the God of all.

A theology of the word

The theme of Acts is neither the history of the Church, nor the activity of the Spirit, but the expansion of the Word. The real hero of the Acts of the Apostles is the *logos*, the Word. [34] The promise of the Risen One (1. 8), which overshadows the narrative, announces the mandate transmitted to the disciples and installs them as witnesses, from Jerusalem to the end of the earth.

The foundation is Christological. 'For Luke, the word of God was made flesh in Jesus, but not in John's manner: it is the word of God in the past addressed to the *prophets* and not pre-existent in heaven, which took on the body of Jesus (Acts 10. 36–7).'[35] At Pentecost (Acts 2), the Holy Spirit takes charge in creating the conditions for the diffusion of the Word. However, it seems that from this event, the apostles are less the trustees of a word to be proclaimed, than the witnesses of a Word that precedes them, the effects of which they have to recognize.[36] Clearly, Luke does not imagine the visibility of the Word without the presence of the witnesses. Yet throughout his narrative, the Word precedes them, acting on them rather than the reverse. The Word 'grows' (6. 7; 12. 24; 19. 20). The Word 'spread throughout the region' (13. 49). It is the Word that is received (2. 41; 8. 14; 11. 1; 17. 11) and that is praised (13. 48). Paul is 'possessed'[37] by the Word (18. 5). The whole conflict between the apostles and the Jerusalem authorities (Acts 3–5) plays on who controls the Word, as the narrator ironically exposes the helplessness of the adversaries to censure it (4. 1–4, 17; 5. 17–28, 40). The same situation occurs in Jerusalem (4. 23–31) and Philippi (16. 19–26): the attempts to silence the witnesses meet with the power of God that shakes the earth. Then, at the end of the narrative, Paul's imprisonment does not prevent their preaching 'with all boldness and without hindrance' (Acts 28. 31b).

Just prior to entering into the martyrdom of Paul there is a particularly striking miracle which draws attention to the Lucan conception of the Word: the

---

[34] In his commentary, M. Benéitez has rightly recognized this point: *Salvación*, 1986, see esp. pp. 483ff.

[35] F. Bovon, *Luke the Theologian*, 1987, p. 197.

[36] In a short study, Louis Panier has expressed the dynamic and propulsive character of the *logos* in Acts: 'Portes ouvertes', 1991.

[37] Συνέχεσθαι expresses for Luke the grasp, the strong mastery, the possession. He uses it in Luke 4. 38 and Acts 28. 8 for a sickness and, in Luke 19. 43 and 22. 63 for attack of enemies.

resurrection of Eutychus (20. 7–12). Bernard Trémel,[38] in a quite remarkable fashion, has exploited the symbolism of the narrative. He has shown that a liturgical setting permeates the text by means of time (the first day of the week), the presence of lamps (20. 8) and by the sharing of bread. Eutychus' fall is an exit from this symbolic space inhabited by light and life, which animates the Word preached by the apostle; the rupture with this space is signified narratively by the sleep, provoking the fall. But the Word is powerful enough to bring back to life a man who has slipped into death. Paul does not utter any therapeutic formula; he simply declares: 'do not be alarmed for his life is in him' (20. 10), and the power of the Word is enough.

The growth of the Word is co-extensive with that of the Church.[39] The same verb πληθύνω, that evokes proliferation, is used for the *logos* (12. 24) and the Church (6. 1, 7; 9. 31). The Church, for Luke, as for Paul in Romans 9. 8–9, is a *creatura verbi*; believers are defined by their acceptance of the Word (8. 14; 11. 1; 17. 11; cf. Luke 8. 13) and are called 'hearers of the Word'. Luke's text is fashioned by a theology of the fecundity of the Word, which is announced in the gospel from the parable of the sower (Luke 8. 4–8, 11–15) onwards, and which has its roots in the dynamic Old Testament concept of דָּבָר.[40]

A theology of providence

E. Käsemann brought about something of a shock in Lucan studies by claiming that Luke, a bad student of Paul, had exchanged Paul's (good) theology of the cross for a theology of glory. In support of this idea he observes that in Luke–Acts, the resurrection and not the cross occupies the central place in assuring salvation.[41] This observation is correct. Luke does have triumphalist accents, in mentioning the irrepressible growth of the Word or the Church[42] or when he narrativizes the theme of providential failure (e.g. 8. 1b–4; 25. 11 – 28. 31).[43] Yet even if his observation of a

---

[38] B. Trémel, 'A propos', 1980. It is instructive to compare Acts 20 with the *Acts of Paul*. The apocryphal story of the resuscitation of Patrocles concentrates precisely on a missing element in Luke's narrative: a therapeutic performance orchestrated by the apostle (*Acts of Paul* 11. 1–2). For further details see my article '*Acts of Paul*', 1997, pp. 169–83.

[39] The ecclesiological dimension of λόγος in Acts has been shown by J. Kodell, ' "Word of God" ', 1974.

[40] See W. Reinhardt's study, *Wachstum*, 1995, pp. 103–16.

[41] E. Käsemann, *Ruf der Freiheit*, 1972, pp. 207–22. U. Wilckens had already protested at the time against the prejudice provoked by imposing Pauline theological categories on Luke–Acts ('Interpreting', 1966, pp. 60–83).

[42] Acts 1. 15; 2. 41; 5. 14; 6. 1, 7; 9. 31; 11. 21; 12. 24; 13. 49; 16. 5; 18. 10; 19. 20.

[43] 8. 1b-4: the scattering of the Christians in Jerusalem due to persecution has a positive effect on the spreading of the Word in Samaria (8. 5) and the proclamation of salvation to the Gentiles in Antioch (11. 19–21). In 25. 11 – 28. 31 Paul's appeal to the emperor in order

divergence with Pauline soteriology is correct (Luke is clearly not Paul),[44] Käsemann's alternative proposal is unacceptable. He argues that one must choose between the Pauline paradox of life working in death (Gal. 2. 19–20; 2 Cor. 12. 9–10; Rom. 6. 6–8) or a triumphalist theology centred on the success of God. His proposal is false. The forcing of a choice between the two is misleading and must be rejected.

Lucan theology is not a theology of glory, but a theology of providence.[45] At the end of Acts, the reader cannot help but recognize the steadfastness of divine *pronoia*.[46] God always saves his own, even in the most extreme dangers, such as conspiracy, threat of death or storm. The failure of the witnesses is distressing, but it is *providential failure*[47] as it results in the expansion of their mission (8. 1–4; 16. 6–10; 25. 11).

In effect, Luke develops in his narrative a rhetoric of the Gospel's success. Even in weakness, the Word comes through and causes faith to blossom. However, this rhetoric has nothing to do with triumphalism. Success for the Word does not grow independently of the suffering of the messengers, but because of it. It is remarkable that each of the three references to the growth of the Word which I have just mentioned (6. 7; 12. 24; 19. 20) occurs narratively on the day after a crisis.[48] Threatened, beaten, betrayed, judged, imprisoned and stoned, the messengers do not ensure the advancement of the Word *in spite of* the bad things that happen to them, but *because of* them. At Lystra, where he heals a paralysed man, Paul is stoned and left for dead (14. 19). In Philippi, the evangelization of Paul and Silas fails after the exorcism of the 'pythoness' woman, but then succeeds from prison (16. 16–40). Thessalonica, Beroea, Corinth and Ephesus (Acts 17–19) are all stops where evangelization culminates in the violent rejection of the missionary.

---

to avoid a denial of justice leads the apostle to witness to the Word in the capital of the Empire.

[44] I shall later compare Luke and Paul on the question of the validity of the Law, pp. 59–64 (ch. 3).

[45] The work of D. Gerber concerning Lucan Christology also explores this path freed from Pauline pressures. This exegete refuses the alternative *theologia crucis/theologia gloriae*. Based on study of the infancy narratives, he prefers a soteriology of advent, especially bound to the earthly manifestation of Jesus ('Préparation du salut', 1991; 'Il vous est né un Sauveur', 1997).

[46] On this theme, see J. T. Squires, *Plan of God*, 1993, pp. 37–77.

[47] This is J. Zumstein's formulation in 'Apôtre comme martyr', 1991, p. 202. The theme has been developed in detail in S. Cunningham's *'Through Many Tribulations'*, 1997, pp. 186–327.

[48] 6. 7 meets the issue of the internal crisis caused by the neglect of the widows of the 'Hellenists'; 12. 24 concludes the tragic scenario of the killing of James, the imprisonment of Peter and the death of Herod; 19. 20 concludes the troubled ministry of Paul in Corinth and Ephesus.

At the risk of misunderstanding Luke's thought, the reader of Acts must not ignore this characteristic in the management of the narrative. The narrator never stops his text on the success of the preaching of Paul, but rather re-starts it, always anew, with the continuation of a voyage that becomes a path of suffering. Hence, the Acts is not yet the apocryphal *Acts* of apostles where missionary success opens pagan temples and smashes idols.[49] Luke's narrative portrays a Synagogue strongly opposing Paul's mission and Graeco-Roman cults resisting their Christian rivals (Lystra, Philippi, Athens, Ephesus). God's protection, concerning his messengers, does not spare them from either failure or humiliation or martyrdom.[50] Luke has even modelled the death of the first martyr (7. 54–60) on his version of Jesus' Passion.[51] Stephen dies not only because of his Lord, but also like him. The announcement of Paul's calling also uses a vocabulary of martyrdom rather than that of mission: 'he is an instrument whom I have chosen to bring my name before Gentiles and kings and before the people of Israel; I myself will show him how much he must suffer for the sake of my name' (9. 15–16).

Rather than a triumphal path, the route of the heralds of the Word is the road of the cross. According to Luke, this is the frame in which witness takes place.

Conclusion: the Gospel and the apostle

After having clarified the theological point of view of Luke the historian, I shall now appraise the construction of his work, in other words, his decision to write a narrative of beginnings as a sequel to the biography of Jesus. This decision, theologically, is of the utmost importance. Let us consider its import.

First, this means that Luke does not make the past sacred. In this sense, he is different from the author of the *Protoevangelium of James*. However, Luke sanctifies the continuation of the gospel, the post-paschal period. No other author in antiquity will dare to attach to the story of Jesus that

[49] This motif appears in certain apocryphal *Acts* of the second century (*Acts of John* and *Acts of Paul*) and then more frequently in the third century. In the *Acts of John*, the temple of Artemis of Ephesus tumbles down to the cries of the crowd: 'One is the God of John' (*Acts of John* 37–45, quotation 42); in the *Acts of Paul*, it is the statue of Apollos of Sidon which crumbles after Paul prays to God: '[save] us by speedily bringing down thy righteousness upon us' (*Acts of Paul* 5).

[50] The first exegete to have opposed Käsemann's view from a narrative reading of the mission in Acts is B. R. Gaventa, 'Towards a Theology', 1988, pp. 153–7.

[51] Luke's reading does not turn the Passion tradition into a *theologia gloriae*: P. Pokorný, *Lukanischen Schriften*, 1998, p. 149.

of the first Christians. In this respect, Luke writing to Theophilus moves into *terra incognita*.

The memory of the witnesses

Second, this act signifies for Luke that faith in the incarnation does not conceal the history of the communicators of faith. The memory of the Gospel cannot be understood without the apostle, nor the memory of the Master without the disciple; nor the memory of God without his witnesses. An indication of this can be found in the preface of Luke's work, which already connects salvific time with the time of testimony (Luke 1. 1–2). The historical role of the apostles after Jesus is signified from Peter's first statement onwards (Acts 1. 21–2), as well as from the first speeches of Acts, as underscored in the kerygmatic declarations with the repetitive 'we are the witnesses' (2. 32; 3. 15; 5. 32).

The theological choice of remembering the apostles, outlined in the history of Christianity, is faced with two opposing lines: a forgetting of the witnesses in a gnostic spirituality where Christianity becomes wisdom and its word the message, and at the other extremity, the hagiography of the third century where the figure of the witness hides the Christ. Contrary to the former, Luke connects the kerygma to the human mediations of God and incorporates the messengers into the message.[52] In contrast to the latter, the hagiographical drift, Luke never gives up the conviction that the apostles are witnesses, not actors in the savific drama. He does not recount their deaths.

Jesus and Paul

The writing of the double work 'Jesus + apostles' signifies that Luke is the first to formulate the basis of the Christian faith under the banner εὐαγγέλιον καὶ ἀποστολικόν, the Gospel and the apostle. He is the first to make known that an anamnesis of the founding story of Christianity must include Jesus and the apostles. He is also the first to link Jesus and Paul in the tradition. The canon of the New Testament will ratify this theological choice. C. K. Barrett, defying anachronism, concludes that 'Luke–Acts is the first New Testament.'[53] In any case, the double work *ad Theophilum* accomplishes its identity aim by gathering in one writing

---

[52] F. Bovon is very sensitive to this theme: *Evangile et l'apôtre*, 1993 and 'Structure canonique', 1994.

[53] C. K. Barrett, 'Third Gospel as a Preface', 1992, p. 1462; see also 'First New Testament?', 1996, pp. 102–3.

everything that Christianity at Luke's time should know about its past. Like a narrative catechism, Luke–Acts presents the important elements of doctrine to its readers: words of the Master, speeches of the apostles, Christian rereading of the Scriptures, the work of the Spirit. What more did the readers need?

The historical statement of this *novum* that is constituted in a Christian form as the double work *ad Theophilum* demands literary exploration. How does the unity of Luke–Acts function? This is the question that I deal with in my next chapter.

3

THE UNITY OF LUKE–ACTS: THE TASK OF READING

In writing his 'Acts of Apostles', Luke offers his readers a narrative of beginnings. This narrative of the birth of Christianity is part of a double work, which begins with the biography of Jesus. Henry Joel Cadbury was the first, in 1927, to call this 'Luke–Acts'.[1]

While it is true that this label had to wait for redaction criticism (*Redaktionsgeschichte*) to be more widely accepted in research, after Conzelmann[2] it has become (almost) compulsory. If the unity of the authorship of the gospel of Luke and Acts, affirmed by the early Church,[3] has never been seriously the subject of doubt, research is indebted to Henry Cadbury and subsequently to Martin Dibelius, for the impulse to explore the unity of the Lucan diptych on the literary and theological level.

'Luke–Acts' represents, therefore, a very recent concept in the bimillennial history of the reading of the New Testament. This concept imposed itself so rapidly in research that it can be considered today as a *fait acquis*.[4] Since the 1960s a recognition that the gospel of Luke and the book of Acts were the work of the same author and a crystallization of the same theology has been the postulate of all research on Luke's text. In doing

[1] Having used the formula 'Luke–Acts' in several articles in *JBL* in 1925 and 1926, H. J. Cadbury made it famous in his 1927 monograph: *The Making of Luke–Acts*. To justify it he depends on the Old Testament example of the two books of Samuel or Kings, but for the Lucan writings he prefers to maintain their names rather than to retitle them *Ad Theophilum I* and *Ad Theophilum II*. 'Hyphenated compounds are not typographically beautiful or altogether congenial to the English language, but in order to emphasize the historic unity of the two volumes addressed to Theophilus the expression "Luke–Acts" is perhaps justifiable' (p. 11).

[2] H. Conzelmann, *Theology of St Luke*, 1982.

[3] E. Jacquier, *Actes des apôtres*, 1926, pp. lvi–lvii.

[4] Marcel Dumais, in presenting the state of research, considers that the first established fact of the exegesis of Acts is the consideration of Luke and Acts as 'un seul livre en deux tomes' ('Bilan et orientations', 1995, p. 313). Rather than a 'fait acquis', we should speak of a heuristic proposition, always open to falsification, and especially questionable concerning its means (as I hope to show).

this, exegetes have made an important methodological decision, maintaining that a correct reading of Luke's work requires the uniting of what the canon of the New Testament has divided. This heuristic principle has been undeniably productive: it has made it possible to consider Luke in the three roles of historian, writer and theologian, across the whole range of his work.

But here is where misunderstandings arise. What is 'unity' in narrative? If unity of thought in the Pauline correspondence can be deduced from a consistent vocabulary, a uniform use of conceptual tools, and a coherence in the argumentative discussions, what can be said of narrative? Are the same indications discernible? Evidently not. A narrator does not expound his views as systematically as in an argumentative genre; ideas are transmitted indirectly through characters, or distilled in (implicit and explicit) commentaries. A storyteller like Luke does not always clearly present what he thinks. In brief, while narrativity in no way excludes coherence in the author's thought system, such coherence does not reveal itself in an argumentative type of logic. So I ask again: how do we discern the unity of thought in narrative?

Internal tensions in the work

We have recently been invited to 'rethink the unity of Luke and Acts' (from the title of a book by Parsons and Pervo).[5] These two authors have pointed out that there are internal tensions in the work; here are the major ones:

> The gospel and Acts belong to two different literary genres, the former biographical and the latter historiographical.[6]
> The gospel and Acts treat their sources differently (Dibelius in 1923 had already drawn attention to this phenomenon);[7] from a stylistic point of view, the piecemeal narrative of the gospel is not at all like the great speeches of Acts or long narrative sequences (Acts 3–5; 10–11; 13–14; 21–6).
> The reader moves from a thematic centred on the βασιλεία τοῦ θεοῦ (gospel) to a strongly Christological kerygma (Acts).

[5] M. C. Parsons and R. I. Pervo, *Rethinking*, 1993. Before them, J. M. Dawsey, 'Literary Unity', 1989; M. C. Parsons, 'Unity of Lukan Writings', 1990, pp. 29–53; and much earlier: A. C. Clark, *Acts of the Apostles*, 1933, pp. 393–405.

[6] In an attempt to overcome this obstacle (the identification of Luke and Acts as belonging to the same literary genre), R. I. Pervo wrote a provocative article: 'Same Genre?', 1989. See also M. C. Parsons and R. I. Pervo's *Rethinking*, 1993, pp. 20–44.

[7] M. Dibelius, 'Style Criticism' [1923], 1956. Dibelius concluded that the primitive kerygmatic tradition did not include any account of the apostles. J. Jervell has contested this and rightly so ('Problem of Traditions', 1972).

The duality of righteous/sinner (δίκαιος/ἁμαρτωλός), so important in the gospel (Luke 5. 32; 7. 34–5, 39; 15. 1–17; 18. 9–14; 19. 6–10), disappears in Acts.

The authority of the Torah in its entirety is maintained in Luke 16. 17; but it no longer governs the soteriology of Acts (cf. Acts 15. 10, 28–9!).

The aggressive words of the Lucan Jesus against the rich (Luke 6. 24–5; 12. 13–21; 20. 47) and the dangers of riches (Luke 12. 33–4; 16. 19–31; 18. 18–30) disappear in Acts, replaced by an ethic of sharing (Acts 2. 42–5; 4. 32–7) and a preoccupation with the privileged and persons of high rank (Acts 8. 27; 9. 36; 16. 14; 17. 34; 18. 7; etc.).

On the basis of these disparities, Parsons and Pervo invite us to separate the gospel of Luke and Acts. In their opinion, the unity of authorship is not in question, but rather the homogeneity as well as the generic or the theological. Without arguing for the divorce of the two books, they invite us to rethink the relationship between them: 'The relationships between these two books are relations *between two books*, not correspondences within a conveniently divided entirety.'[8] In my opinion, this statement is correct. It warns us of the risk involved in the axiomatic status given by research to the single entity Luke–Acts, the risk of attributing to the author of *ad Theophilum* a uniformity of thought that is found scattered through the episodes of the macro-narrative (Luke 1 to Acts 28), without any consideration for the discordances.[9] On the other hand, the proposal to separate Luke and Acts risks exaggerating the internal tensions to the detriment of the unity of the work. From a narratological perspective, one wonders if, in spite of these internal tensions, the macro-narrative provides an effect of unity for the reader and, if so, by what means.

An effect of unity

I defend the following thesis: *the narrative of Luke–Acts does aim to provide a unifying effect at the theological level; but this unity is not announced in the text; it is devolved as a task to the reader who must construct this unity in the course of reading.* A commentary: the only 'meta-discourse' that Luke presents concerning his narrative (Luke 1. 1–4 and Acts 1. 1–2) suggests that he conceived his work in two parts, since he refers to the gospel as the 'first word' (πρῶτος λόγος: Acts 1. 1a); however, this articulation does not decide the issue of coherence. The question of unity has to be resolved at the level of the narrative strategy.

---

[8] *Rethinking*, 1993, p. 126.

[9] The monographs of Robert O'Toole (*Unity*, 1984) and Donald Juel (*Promise*, 1984) run this risk.

So the writing of a double work 'Jesus and apostles' does not invite an *ad libitum* reading: by virtue of the linear disposition of the narrative, the reading of Acts presupposes the information contained in the gospel. In addition, the teleological principle of reading implies that the meaning (and unity) of a work are perceptible at its end, the moment at which the work appears in its totality. It is therefore by the device of echoes between the before and the after of the narrative that the narrator will provoke the reader to construct the unity of the narration. In practice, then, the task is to take an inventory of the signs intended to unify the world of the narrative and to assure that the end of the narrative confirms the unifying aim.

Intrinsic tensions of narrativity

I also defend the view that *the search for unity in a narrative must integrate the presence of tensions and ruptures inherent to the narrative phenomenon.*

A comment: Stephen Moore has rightly argued that tensions and shifts are intrinsic to narrativity, which rejects the systemization of argumentative discourse.[10] I would add that this characteristic is even more true for historical narration. Historical narrative is obliged to take into consideration an evolution, a story that moves forward, a project that shifts. Typical of this is the way the Lucan pneumatology differs according to the situation: the history of Israel (the prophets), the gospel (Jesus) or Acts (the apostles, then all believers).[11] The question then becomes: in a narrative assigned to recording shifts and movements, how does the narrator maintain continuity?

It is also important to think about how the narrator indicates in his account the facts that produce fresh developments. In this respect, the pivotal role that Easter plays (it is the hinge on which the Lucan diptych turns) must not be underestimated. Of all the stylistic and terminological variations between the gospel and Acts carefully observed by Albert Clark and James Dawsey,[12] some can be explained by the presence of sources, but many are due to the paschal turning point. This is the case in the use of μαθητής (qualified by a possessive pronoun in the gospel and absolute in Acts)[13] or in the diverse handling of the Christological

---

[10] S. Moore, 'Unified Narratives?', 1987.

[11] This will be examined in more detail in chapter 6: 'The work of the Spirit'.

[12] A. C. Clark, *Acts of the Apostles*, 1933, pp. 393–405. J. M. Dawsey, 'Literary Unity', 1989.

[13] Whereas in the gospel μαθητής is most often determined by a possessive pronoun (usually οἱ μαθηταὶ αὐτοῦ), the term appears in the absolute sense in Acts or it figures as an ecclesiastical designation with οἱ πιστεύοντες (exceptions: Acts 9. 1, 25).

titles between the gospel (a differentiated use) and Acts (a cumulative use).[14]

From here I shall proceed in three steps. First, an investigation of the literary clues which indicate that the narrator has the narrative entity of Luke–Acts in mind. Second, a presentation of three means by which the unification of the narrative world of Luke–Acts is provided for the reader: the prolepsis, the narrative chain and modelling. Third, an elucidation of one of the most notable theological shifts in the work *ad Theophilum*: the change in the status of the Law between the gospel and Acts. I would like to show, by this specific case, how Luke maintains the unity of his work, while nevertheless indicating the deep shift that the Christological event effects.

Luke–Acts, a narrative entity

What literary indications show that the author conceived the fifty-two chapters of Luke–Acts as a whole?

Information withheld

Surprisingly, the first indication comes from source criticism. More than once, study of synoptic parallels has shown that the narrator has deliberately withheld a motif of the gospel, in order to move it to Acts. The reason is always to create an effect later in the narrative.

During Jesus' trial before the Sanhedrin, the Markan motif of false witness concerning the destruction of the Temple and its reconstruction in three days (Mark 14. 58) has been left out by Luke (cf. 23. 66), who later brings it back at the arrest of Stephen (Acts 6. 14). Is it possible that Luke was ignorant of this criticism of the Temple in the Jesus tradition? A detail in Acts 6. 14 proves the contrary. In a subtle manner, the accusation against Stephen is not by a direct word, but a reported one: 'For we have heard him say that this Jesus of Nazareth will destroy this place and will change the customs that Moses handed on to us.' This shows that Luke is not ignorant of the origin of the criticism, but transfers it from the Master to the disciple. But why the shift? The most obvious reason is that the role played by the Temple in Acts 1–5 could not have been maintained in the

[14] The gospel of Luke offers a use of Christological titles (κύριος, διδάσκαλος, ἐπιστάτης, υἱὸς τοῦ ἀνθρώπου, χριστός) differentiated according to the characters in the narrative. The speeches in Acts accumulate these titles, reflecting a post-paschal kerygmatic concentration (for example Acts 3. 13–21!).

light of the eschatological degradation to which Mark's logion subjected the Temple.

Similarly, the suspension of the Torah of purity (Mark 7. 1–23) does not occur in Luke's work until Peter's vision in Acts 10; Luke eliminates it so as not to anticipate the removal of the barrier between pure and impure, disclosed to the apostle ('What God has made clean, you must not call profane!', Acts 10. 15).[15] A further example: the weight the narrator gives to the question of Israel's refusal, at the end of the macro-narrative (Acts 28. 16–31), leads him to abbreviate the quotation of Isaiah 6. 9–10 in the teaching in parables (Luke 8. 10b; different from Mark 4. 12 and Matthew 13. 14–15). The intention is to reserve the full version, and therefore the full weight of the prophetic text, for his final verses (Acts 28. 26–7).[16]

These three examples of withholding information show, at the very least, that the narrator envisions a plot whose completion is Acts 28 rather than Luke 24. A study of the rhetorical procedure of inclusion will take us a step further.

Significant inclusions

Inclusio, which recalls at the end an initial motif, is a rhetorical procedure used by both narrators and orators to make the unity of the subject clearer. It is a device for closing the narrative.

In this case, each of the panels of the Lucan diptych is framed by a significant inclusion. The gospel goes from the Temple, where the coming of the Saviour is announced (Luke 1. 5–25), to the Temple where the disciples await the coming of the Spirit (Luke 24. 53); in this way the narrative is anchored in the presence of God with his people, to which the symbolic meaning of the Temple refers. The book of Acts unfolds between the preaching of the Risen One about the βασιλεία τοῦ θεοῦ (Acts 1. 3) and the preaching of Paul about the βασιλεία τοῦ θεοῦ (Acts 28. 31). The essential continuity of the message is established, but completed for Paul with the reference to teaching 'about the Lord Jesus Christ' (continuity *and* displacement).

---

[15] C. K. Barrett correctly perceived this point: 'Third gospel as a Preface', 1992, pp. 1456–7.

[16] This procedure of transferring a fragment from one pericope to another has been identified by D. Hermant ('Procédé', 1997). Curiously, this exegete sees it only as gratuitous literary manipulation by the author the 'malin plaisir qu'un virtuose éprouve à exercer parfois sa virtuosité sans que personne en ait conscience' (p. 547). The examples I have just given, in addition to showing the care Luke gives to his writing, demonstrate that literary transfers can be required by the unfolding plot of the macro-narrative.

For its part the whole work is overshadowed by the narrative arc constructed by the two Lucan references to 'the salvation of God':[17] the salvation of God predicted by the Baptist with the words of Isaiah 40. 5 (Luke 3. 6: καὶ ὄψεται πᾶσα σὰρξ τὸ σωτήριον τοῦ θεοῦ) and the offer of the salvation of God to the nations (Acts 28. 28: τοῖς ἔθνεσιν ἀπεστάλη τοῦτο τὸ σωτήριον τοῦ θεοῦ, which follows the long quotation from Isaiah 6. 9–10. Between these narrative boundary-markers there is a circularity in the narrative, allowing the reader to verify the aim of Luke's narration.[18] This circularity is crystallized in a history of salvation, a salvation predicted, incarnated, announced, rejected by the majority of the Jews, and, finally, offered to the Gentiles who 'will listen' (Acts 28. 28b).

Whether through a negative means (withholding information) or a positive means (closing the narrative by inclusion), it is clear that the work addressed to Theophilus is meant to be read as a narrative entity. Furthermore, its unity must affect its aim. In practice, what means does the author employ to ensure the unity of his salvation history?

Three unifying procedures

I begin with prolepsis, which is a projection toward the future of the story. The book of Acts opens with a gigantic prolepsis, the promise of the Risen One to the Eleven: 'You will receive power when the Holy Spirit has come upon you; and you will be my witnesses in Jerusalem, in all Judaea and Samaria, and to the ends of the earth' (1. 8). The location of this announcement, at the threshold of Acts, gives it the value of a narrative programme, going even beyond Acts 28 (Rome is not yet the end of the earth). In addition to providing the reader with an outline of the narrative, 1. 8 announces the Christological engendering of the history that follows: through the joys (and especially sorrows) of the messengers, it is the story of a promise that bears fruit. Thus the prolepsis in Acts 1. 8 functions very clearly as a key to reading the whole narrative.

However, the author of Luke–Acts is fond of giving his prolepses[19] a twist that is less clear, *more elliptic.* I shall give a few examples.

---

[17] The formula τὸ σωτήριον τοῦ θεοῦ does not appear elsewhere in Luke–Acts. The third occurrence of σωτήριον in Luke's writing is Luke 2. 30 ('my eyes have seen your salvation').

[18] J. Dupont is very attentive to the importance of the inclusion procedure in Luke's double–work, especially at the conclusion of Acts; he sees 28. 16–31 as an echo of Paul's trial (Acts 21–8), but also of the speech in Antioch of Pisidia (Acts 13), the preaching of Jesus in Nazareth (Luke 4) and the infancy narratives (Luke 1) ('Conclusion', 1984).

[19] Going through the gospel in search of indicators pointing in the direction of Acts, C. K. Barrett has made an inventory of some forty-one possible references ('Third gospel

Elliptic prolepses

At the heart of the infancy narratives, Simeon's oracle combines blessing Jesus' parents (Luke 2. 34a) with an announcement to Mary which casts a shadow over the rest of the story: 'This child is destined for the falling and the rising of many in Israel, and to be a sign that will be opposed so that the inner thoughts of many will be revealed – and a sword will pierce your own soul too' (Luke 2. 34b–35a). The clash between the peace celebrated by Simeon (2. 29) and the suffering he announces leaves the prediction very imprecise: of what does the 'falling and rising' consist? When will Mary be pierced? The reader will only discover the answers by reading on.

Later, in Luke 9. 51, the great itinerary of the Lucan Jesus is introduced by a comment of the narrator which has caused continual difficulty for exegetes: 'When the days drew near for him to be taken up (τὰς ἡμέρας τῆς ἀναλήμψεως αὐτοῦ), he set his face to go to Jerusalem.' Commentators have wondered about the meaning of ἀναλήμψις, *hapax legomenon* in the substantive form, but attested in *Testament of Levi* 18. 3 and *Psalms of Solomon* 4. 18.[20] Does the term refer to the the Ascension of Jesus (supported by Acts 1. 2, 11, 22)? Or does it refer more generally to Jesus' journey up to Jerusalem and then the Passion (supported by ἀναλαμβάνω in Acts 7. 43; 10. 16; 20. 13–14; 23. 31)?[21] The plural τὰς ἡμέρας favours the latter sense, which is more extensive (cf. the singular ἕως τῆς ἡμέρας ἧς ἀνελήμφθη in Acts 1. 22). Yet the connotation of ascension is not entirely absent. The semantic decision remains open for the reader and only the narrated events, at the transition between the two parts of the work (Luke 24/Acts 1), will clarify the fulfilment of this ἀναλήμψις that in this context remains elliptic. Luke's writing, we see, uses the ambiguity of the term in order to leave the reader's decision open in Luke 9. 51.[22] As the narrative advances to Jesus'

---

as a Preface', 1992, pp. 1451–66, esp. 1453–61). From his inventory, I maintain a proleptic potential for the following references: Luke 3. 6 (Gentile mission); 4. 16–30 (Gentile mission); 7. 1–10 (Acts 10–11); 9. 52–6 and 17. 11–19 (Acts 8); 10. 11 (Acts 13. 51); 10. 19 (Acts 28. 6); 11. 49 (the apostles); 12. 8 (Acts 7. 56); 12. 11–12. (the suffering of the missionaries); 19. 45–6 (the role of the Temple); 21. 12–19 (the suffering of the missionaries); 22. 15–20 and 24. 30–1, 35 (the breaking of bread); 23. 6–12 (Acts 4. 27); 23. 34–46 (Acts 7); 23. 47 (the Christological title δίκαιος); 24. 49 (Acts 2).

[20] G. Delling, art, 'λαμβάνω κτλ', 1967 [orig. 1942], pp. 7–8; G. Friedrich, 'Entrückungschristologie', 1973.

[21] The exegetical debate is presented in G. Friedrich's 'Entrückungschristologie', 1973, pp. 70–4; the author favours reference to the Passion.

[22] I depend here upon the valuable remarks of F. Bovon in 'Effect of Realism', 1995, see p. 102; cf. *Evangile selon saint Luc*, 1996, p. 33.

exaltation, it leads not only to reducing the semantic indeterminacy, but also (and especially) to grounding the Passion–resurrection scenario in Jesus' resolution, 'setting his face' to assume a destiny which fulfils the Father's will.[23]

Fire and Pentecost

I perceive the same deliberate indeterminacy of sense in Luke 12. 49–50, in Jesus' declaration about the 'fire' he has come to throw on the earth and the 'baptism' with which he must be baptized. Seeking the exact meaning of this prolepsis leads to difficulty, as fire is a common metaphor in Judaism for eschatological judgement, as the reader is well aware from Luke 3. 9, 17; 9. 54. But the synonymous parallelism between πῦρ and βάπτισμα calls for a reference to the Holy Spirit; the Baptist's words in 3. 16 already move in this direction. It is only upon arriving at the Pentecost narrative that the reader will be able to reread Jesus' declaration and discern a prediction of the coming of the Spirit. Furthermore, this is formulated in unusual terms: the promise of the Risen One is not that the disciples will receive the Holy Spirit, but that they will be 'clothed with power from on high' (ἐνδύσησθε ἐξ ὕψους δύναμιν Luke 24. 49; cf. Acts 1. 8). Once again, the narrative contains its own keys for reading: the use of δύναμις as a metaphor for the Spirit is a Septuagintalism used elsewhere in Luke–Acts (Luke 1. 17, 35; 4. 14; Acts 8. 10; 10. 38).[24]

A deliberate uncertainty

There are other prolepses, just as elliptic, that mark Paul's destiny in the book of Acts. Acts 9. 16: 'I myself will show him how much he must suffer for the sake of my name'. Acts 13. 2: 'Set apart for me Barnabas and Saul for the work (ἔργον) to which I have called them'. Acts 21. 11: 'This is the way the Jews in Jerusalem will bind the man who owns this belt and will hand him over to the Gentiles.' In each of these three cases, the reader is condemned to uncertainty until the narrative answers the questions: what will Paul suffer for the name of Jesus? What is the ἔργον to which Barnabas and Saul are called? How will the Jews capture Paul in Jerusalem?

---

[23] The same procedure of ambiguity at the Transfiguration has led the narrator to have Moses and Elijah speak (9. 31) of the 'exodus' of Jesus rather than his departure toward Jerusalem. The point of this is to provide the ascent toward the Passion with an exodus connotation. P. Doble sees here the use of a Wisdom motif (*Paradox*, 1996, pp. 210–14).

[24] On the equivalent δύναμις/πνεῦμα, see below, pp. 119–21 (ch. 6).

One has the right to wonder why Luke does not announce things more directly. Why does he avoid speaking clearly? Here we touch on a procedure typical of our author: semantic ambiguity.[25] In fact, the potential of sense created by the ambiguity leaves indeterminate a prediction which only later will be fulfilled in the narrative. Narratologically, the function is as follows: semantic ambiguity opens in the narrative a place for uncertainty, which frustrates the reader by omitting or hiding an element that is necessary for understanding; the reader will then look, in the continuation of the narrative, for that which fills this lack of information. An elliptical or ambiguous phrase can then (though not always!) be the result of a narrative strategy intended to stimulate the reader's quest for verification.

Elliptical phrases are not the result of Luke's incompetence as a writer, but a method consciously applied to create distance between announcement and accomplishment. This procedure is of the utmost importance as it implies that the scheme announcement–accomplishment or, in other words, promise–fulfilment, belongs at the very heart of the Lucan diptych.[26] In this way the progress of the macro-narrative leads the reader to verify the reliability of the promises, and so to discern the unifying logic of the narration. By leading the reader to recognize the fulfilment of the predictions announced, the narrative functions as a site for verifying the truthfulness of divine promises.

Narrative chains

The second procedure for unifying the narrative is what I call the 'narrative chain'. These are the lines that the author draws between the two parts of his diptych, enabling the reader to gauge the continuity and progression of the narrative.

One very obvious chain is the *chain of centurions*. Three centurions appear at key moments in the Lucan narrative: the centurion of Capernaum (Luke 7. 1–10) is the first non-Jew to ask Jesus for healing; a centurion confesses his faith at the foot of the cross (Luke 23. 47); it is also with a centurion, Cornelius, that Peter experiences the bestowal of salvation on the Gentiles (Acts 10–11; 15. 7–11). This chain of centurions is not

---

[25] The question of semantic ambivalence in Luke will be dealt with in the next chapter: 'A Christianity between Jerusalem and Rome'.

[26] Although F. Bovon does not adopt the narratological perspective that is developed here, he comes to the same conclusion: 'Exegetes have too little noticed that the structure of Luke–Acts, conditioned by the motif of accomplishment in the Old Testament, is itself dominated by *an internal play of promise and fulfilment*. Nor have they remarked that this interaction functions *because of prophecies which are voluntarily ambiguous*' ('Effect of Realism', 1995, p. 101; italics mine).

a mere detail; it links three men whose faith is, in each case, exemplary. The centurion of Capernaum points out that his slave can be healed by means of Jesus' word overcoming the insuperable distance between Jew and Gentile. The example of his faith is underlined by Jesus: 'I tell you, not even in Israel have I found such faith' (Luke 7. 9b). At the cross, the soldier's declaration of faith is unique (Luke 23. 47). As for Cornelius, whose piety is strongly emphasized (pious, God-fearer, generous in his giving and constantly in prayer: Acts 10. 2), the motive behind the grace that is given to him through Peter is explained by the angel's message: 'Your prayers and your alms have ascended as a memorial before God' (Acts 10. 4b). The narrator has linked these three soldiers together by the common theme of the astonishing grace accorded to faith. This link is all the more necessary in that he needs to prepare for the rupture that is represented by the collapse of the barrier between pure and impure that separates Peter from Cornelius (Acts 10. 9–16). The chain of centurions has three effects on the level of the narrative: (a) it creates the continuity between the meeting of Peter and Cornelius and an action of Jesus; (b) it legitimates the favour of God towards Cornelius by the positive construction of the character of the 'centurion';[27] (c) it prepares for the shock of the opening up of salvation to the Gentiles.

The Damascus event

The importance given to the event on the Damascus Road in Acts is well known. It is related by the narrator (Acts 9. 1–9a), then retold by Paul before the people of Jerusalem (22. 1–21) and before Agrippa (26. 1–29). This *chain of the conversion of Saul* is initiated and prepared for, earlier, in the Gospel. Christ's declaration in Acts 9. 15 ('he is an instrument whom I have chosen to bring my name before Gentiles and kings (ἐνωπίον ἐθνῶν τε καὶ βασιλέων) and before the people of Israel') is a direct echo of Jesus' prediction to his disciples: 'they will arrest you and you will be brought before kings and governors (ἐπὶ βασιλεῖς καὶ ἡγεμόνας) because of my name' (Luke 21. 12). Earlier in the narrative, the Lucan Jesus had warned his disciples of the necessity of defending their faith: 'When they bring you before the synagogues, the rulers, and the authorities, do not worry about how you are to defend

---

[27] The positive role of the character ἑκατοντάρχης will also be assigned to the centurions who accompany the suffering Paul from Acts 21 onwards. They constantly play the role of protectors to the apostle who is threatened: 21. 32; 22. 25–6; 23. 17, 23; 24. 23; 27. 1, 6, 11, 31, 43; cf. 28. 16.

yourselves or what you are to say; for the Holy Spirit will teach you at the very hour what you ought to say' (Luke 12. 11–12).

Luke has given Saul's transformation a fundamental importance. It ensures the legitimacy of the mission outside Judaism, in continuity with the history of the fathers. Yet, by anchoring Paul's destiny prior to Acts 9 in the words of Jesus preparing his disciples for their witness and suffering, the narrator gives the Pauline mission the mark of *continuum*.

Grace and purity

The third chain: between the parables of Luke 15 and Jesus' encounter with Zacchaeus (Luke 19. 1–10), Jean-Noël Aletti detects an interesting echo consisting in the following scenario: (a) a dispute about the acceptance of sinners (15. 2) or of Zacchaeus (19. 5); (b) a soteriological declaration (15. 7, 10, 24, 32; 19. 9); (c) a manifestation of joy (15. 6–7, 10, 23, 32; 19. 6).[28] The correspondence between Luke 15 and 19 indicates that with Zacchaeus, the parabolic affirmation is both concretized and confirmed: salvation comes to sinners in spite of the protests of the righteous. The attentive reader is aware of this recurrence when this chain 'grace *versus* ritual Torah' reappears with a difference at the Jerusalem council (Acts 15). The situation of this summit meeting reduplicates in a fascinating way the situation of Luke 15: the believers in Judaea protest that one cannot be saved without circumcision (v. 1), whereas the account of the conversion of pagans by Paul and Barnabas 'brought great joy to all the believers' (v. 3). The frontline of the dispute is transferred to the very heart of the Church. This message is produced by the repetition of the scenario: the same grace prevails. James' speech confirms this: 'God *from the beginning* looked favourably on the Gentiles, to take from among them a people for his name' (15. 14).[29]

There is also a *Pentecostal chain*, which leads the reader from the prediction of imminent fire, as previously noted (Luke 12. 49), to the tongues of fire at Pentecost (Acts 2. 1–13) and the collective irruptions of the Spirit in Acts 10. 44–6 and 19. 6. The expansion of the Church is thus accompanied by the astonishing interventions of God, who shakes up his Church in order to open it to the world.

[28] J.-N. Aletti, *Quand Luc raconte*, 1998, pp. 260–3.

[29] We find here another type of relationship between Acts and the gospel. The narrative of Acts has to put into words the attitudes that in the gospel occur between Jesus and his interlocutors (in this case Jesus, Zacchaeus and the crowd). Zacchaeus becomes the prototype of the grace and acceptance that those who uphold the mission from Antioch come to Jerusalem to defend.

The effects of redundancy

The presence of narrative chains suggests that Luke is working with the effect of redundancy. While not the present subject, it would be interesting to observe the variations that the author introduces from one narrative to another.[30] Like any storyteller, Luke avoids being tedious. But what we need to notice here is the effect of the narrative chains on the reading of Luke–Acts.

(1) The phenomenon of narrative redundancy assists memorization and structures understanding. The links that the narrative chains create throughout the multi-faceted macro-narrative open up axes for reading. They mark the way. They signal the key points. From the point of view of Acts, the following motifs are indicated: the opening toward the Gentiles, the call to witness, the gift of the Spirit and the superiority of grace over the Law.

(2) The further we go in the macro-narrative, the more the redundancies abound. They multiply from Acts 10 onwards.[31] The increasingly frequent narrative repetitions evince Luke's desire that readers engage in a global reading that progressively deepens the significance of the events reported. The most impressive case is Peter's fourfold retelling of his conversion, since Acts 10. 9–29 can rightly be called the 'conversion of Peter.'[32] The apostle begins by transposing his ecstatic vision to an *ethical* level ('but God has shown me that I should not call anyone profane or unclean...' 10. 28). He then deduces that God is impartial (οὐκ ἔστιν προσωπολήμπτης ὁ θεός 10. 34), founds this *Christologically* (10. 36–43), and follows it with a *pneumatological* reading: the sending of the Spirit is a matter of God's grace (11. 17). Finally, in Jerusalem, the *soteriological* consequences are drawn (15. 9–10): if God has purified their hearts by faith, why should they be subject to the Law?[33] The narrative chain leads us from ethics to soteriology, by way of the image of God, of Christology and pneumatology, which all deepen the meaning. This path is a veritable course in dogmatics.

(3) In salvation history, God repeats himself no more than Luke does. The echoes created by the narrative chain indicate, on the one hand, the

---

[30] The three narratives of Saul's conversion (Acts 9; 22; 26) are a privileged field for studying the variations that the narrator introduces; see chapter 9.

[31] Narrative redundancy affects the following passages: 11. 1–18; 15. 7–11; 20. 18–35; 22. 1–21; 25. 10–21; 26. 2–27; 28. 17–20.

[32] On this subject, see pp. 98–102 (ch. 5) and 187–91 (ch. 9).

[33] Louis Marin has given us an unsurpassed study of the sequence from 10. 1 to 11. 18, with its multiple effects of redundancy: 'Essai d'analyse structurale', 1971. Concerning the phenomenon of redundancy in Acts 10–11, see also R. Witherup, 'Cornelius', 1993 and W. S. Kurz, 'Variant Narrators', 1997.

continuity of God's presence with his people and, on the other hand, the differences between the ways in which God is present for Jesus and his messengers. Without exception, the hermeneutical key to the narrative chain resides in a saying of Jesus (Luke 7. 9; 12. 49; 15. 7, 10, 32; 19. 9; 21. 12; Acts 11. 16). So the chain constructs a fundamental continuity of the Acts, not with Judaism,[34] but with the action of God in Jesus Christ: the continuity with Jewish tradition passes through him.

A procedure of modelling: syncrisis

Narrative repetition and echoes are the subtle ways that Luke chooses to remind the reader. He accentuates them in another procedure of rereading in which he excels: modelling, otherwise called *syncrisis*. *Syncrisis* is an ancient rhetorical device. It consists in modelling the presentation of a character on another in order to compare them, or at least to establish a correlation between the two.[35] *Syncrisis* creates a network of internal intertextuality within the Lucan work.[36] It brings together two characters of the narrative under the sign of a similar event (such as the martyrdom of Jesus and Stephen: Luke 23. 34–46 and Acts 7. 55–60) or by means of a similar narrative scenario (such as the meeting in Emmaus and the conversion of the Ethiopian: Luke 24. 13–35 and Acts 8. 26–40).[37]

The most complete example of Lucan *syncrisis* is the Jesus–Peter–Paul parallel. This has been shown many times and I shall not repeat the well-known arguments.[38] To summarize briefly: Peter and Paul heal as Jesus healed (Luke 5. 18–25; Acts 3. 1–8; Acts 14. 8–10); like Jesus at his baptism, Peter and Paul receive an ecstatic vision at the key moments of their ministry (Acts 9. 3–9; 10. 10–16); like Jesus, they preach and endure the hostility of the Jews; like their master, they suffer and are threatened

---

[34] *Pace* J. Jervell, 'Future of the Past', 1996, p. 125.

[35] A. George has devoted a beautiful study to the imposing *syncrisis* John the Baptist/Jesus around which Luke built his infancy narrative ('Parallèle entre Jean-Baptiste et Jésus' [1978], 1986). J.-N. Aletti has given a large portion of his book to the Lucan *syncrisis* (*Quand Luc raconte*, 1998, see especially pp. 69–166).

[36] On the internal intertextuality of Luke–Acts, see J. B. Green's suggestions. He parallels the inscription of the history of the Church in Jesus' history and the inscription of Jesus' history and the Church's in Israel's history. 'Internal Repetition', 1996, pp. 293–5.

[37] Other examples: the correlation of Saul's conversion (Acts 9. 3–19a) with the meeting of Peter and Cornelius (Acts 10. 1–23), and of Peter's liberation from prison (Acts 12. 12–17) with the narratives of the paschal appearances (Luke 24. 5–36).

[38] See literature on the subject: J. Dupont, 'Pierre et Paul', 1967; C. H. Talbert, *Literary Patterns*, 1974, pp. 15–23; W. Radl, *Paulus und Jesus*, 1975; R. F. O'Toole, 'Parallels between Jesus and His Disciples', 1983; S. M. Praeder, 'Jesus–Paul', 1984; D. P. Moessner, ' "Christ Must Suffer" ', 1986, J.-N. Aletti, *Quand Luc raconte*, 1998, pp. 84–103.

by death; Paul is brought before the authorities like Jesus (Acts 21–6); and like him, Peter and Paul are delivered miraculously at the end of their lives (Acts 12. 6–17; 24. 27 – 28. 6). In all of this, my interest now is solely in the effects on the reading of Luke's work. I discern three.

Action and suffering

First, the modelling of the disciples on the Master is a matter of actions (acting and suffering), not speech. The word of the witnesses does not replace or imitate Jesus' word, but rather refers to the Christological kerygma (Acts 2. 22–36; 3. 13–26; 4. 10–12; 7. 52; 10. 37–43; 13. 26–39; etc.). The gospel is the necessary presupposition for reading the speeches in Acts, but surprisingly the characters in the narrative never quote the gospel. In Acts, there are only two quotations attributed to Jesus (11. 16 and 20. 35). The first refers to Acts 1. 5 and the second is not found in the gospel. The result is that the relation of Acts to the gospel is not that of a commentary, but rather a rereading by continuation. According to the categories of Genette, one should speak of hypertextuality rather than metatextuality.[39] The book of Acts is not a *pesher* on the gospel, but recounts its after-effects in history.

A call to remembrance of the gospel

Secondly, Luke has fixed a point of departure for the *syncrisis* in an action of Christ that remedies the powerlessness of the apostles. The technique of modelling emerges for the first time at the healing of the lame man at the Beautiful Gate of the Temple (Acts 3. 1–10).

In the text of Acts 3. 1–10,[40] several linguistic signals remind the reader of the healing of the paralytic in Luke 5. 17–26: verse 6, περιπάτει (ἔγειρε καί is textually secondary), cf. Luke 5. 23; verse 7, παραχρῆμα, cf. Luke 5. 25a; verse 8a, ἔστη, cf. Luke 5. 25a, ἀναστάς; verses 8–9, αἰνῶν τὸν θεόν, cf. Luke 5. 25–6, δοξάζων/ἐδόξαζον τὸν θεόν; verse 9, πᾶς ὁ λαός, cf. Luke 5. 26a, ἅπαντας; verse 10, ἔκστασις, θάμβος, cf. Luke 5. 26, ἔκστασις, φόβος.

---

[39] G. Genette distinguishes these two varieties of intertextuality by speaking of *hyper-textuality* when a text is grafted onto another by reference or allusion. He reserves the term *metatextuality* for the explicit commentary of one text on another (e.g. *pesher*) (*Palimpsests*, 1997, pp. 5–10.)

[40] For what follows, I borrow from the analysis of G. Muhlack, *Parallelen*, 1979, pp. 27–36.

There are also more numerous and emphatic signs pointing to a correlation between this narrative and Paul's healing of the lame man at Lystra (Acts 14. 8–11): verse 2, τις ἀνὴρ... χωλὸς ἐκ κοιλίας μητρὸς αὐτοῦ, cf. Acts 14. 8; verse 4, ἀτενίσας... εἶπεν, cf. Acts 14. 9–10; verse 8a, ἐξαλλόμενος ἔστη καὶ περιεπάτει, cf. Acts 14. 10b, ἥλατο καὶ περιεπάτει; verse 9a, εἶδεν πᾶς ὁ λαός, cf. Acts 14. 11a: οἵ τε ὄχλοι ἰδόντες.

Notice how the narrative of Acts 3 is grafted onto the Christological model of Luke 5. The lame man begs for alms from Peter and John who are going to the Temple for prayers at the ninth hour (3. 3). Peter looks intently at him and declares: 'I have no silver or gold, but what I have I give to you; in the name of Jesus Christ (ἐν τῷ ὀνόματι Ἰησοῦ Χριστοῦ) of Nazareth, stand up and walk!' (3. 6). At this moment in the narrative the correlative clues begin, that is, at this precise moment when the apostles indicate what is lacking: money. This lack signals the powerlessness of the witnesses to fulfil the need expressed by the lame man. Overcoming their incapacity, the ὄνομα Ἰησοῦ Χριστοῦ becomes the operative agent of the miracle, by means of a word borrowed (partially) from the Master: 'walk!' (περιπάτει 3. 6). Peter's commentary is unambiguous: '*his name* itself has made this man strong, and the faith that is through Jesus has given him perfect health...' (3. 16). The correlative clues literally ratify what is said about the active 'name of Jesus Christ': the Risen One confirms and continues his healing activity through the mediation of the apostles. Frame, place and antagonists have changed. The reader of Acts is called to remember the gospel in order to understand that the healing at the Beautiful Gate is not an innovation, but appeals to a Christological precedent that gives it meaning.

Neither imitation nor confusion

Thirdly, I stress the fact that Luke's literary technique escapes all schematic categorizations. I have already mentioned the unobtrusiveness of the clues to the correlation between Acts 3 and Luke 5. Similarly, the suffering destiny of Peter and Paul recalls the Passion of Jesus, *without confusing the two*. This is why I hesitate to speak, even on a typological level, of a 'resurrection of Peter' (Acts 12) or of a 'Passion–resurrection of Paul' (Acts 27. 9 – 28. 6).[41] The deaths of the two heroes are evaded

---

[41] M. D. Goulder (*Type and History*, 1964, pp. 62–3.) has strongly supported a typological reading, followed by W. Radl, *Paulus und Jesus*, 1975, pp. 222–51 and J.-N. Aletti, *Quand Luc raconte*, 1998, pp. 69–103.

by the narrator (Acts 12. 17; 28. 30–1),[42] as if it is necessary not to over-shadow the only salvific death, that of Jesus. The *syncrisis* is not a copy. It brings two characters, two events closer on the basis of differentiation. It is remarkable that, on the path of identification between Christ and the apostle, Luke has not crossed the threshold that the apocryphal *Acts* of apostles have no hesitation in passing: Christ appears with the counte-nance of Paul in the *Acts of Paul and Thecla* (3. 21) and takes on the face of Thomas in the *Acts of Thomas* (151–3 and 154–5).

Luke's theology does not go this far: modelling never produces imita-tion or confusion, but always integrates the factor of difference. It points to a conformity with a founding model and a permanence of divine as-sistance to the ill-treated witnesses. It corresponds to a new development of the Old Testament typology that marks the gospel. As the Christology of the gospel is constructed with the help of typological models (Elijah-Elisha and Moses), in Acts the destiny of the witnesses is woven into a Christological typology which aligns the life of the witnesses with the message they announce.

Summary. Three procedures have been studied which demonstrate the authorial desire to lead the reader to discover the logic of the divine direc-tion of history: the elliptic prolepsis, the narrative chain and the *syncrisis*. These procedures have a common effect, in that they push the reader/hearer to survey the two panels of the Lucan diptych, to keep moving backwards and forwards within the narrative. They lead to a rereading of Acts from the gospel and to a rereading of the gospel from the point of view of the progress of the story charted in Acts. These narra-tive procedures suggest rather than impose. They evoke a Christological precedent more than they describe it. Inviting the reader to discover the logic of the divine plan of salvation, they impel him/her to weave together the connections from one end of the writing to the other. In short, they solicit him/her to unify Luke and Acts.

Permanence and suspension of the Law

I said above that tensions and new developments do not threaten the unity of the plot of a narrative. On the contrary, a captivating narrative requires

[42] Except for Peter's brief appearance at the Jerusalem council (Acts 15. 7–11), where he gives a soteriological reading of his meeting with Cornelius, he disappears from the narrative in 12. 17, according to the narrator's enigmatic and very metaphorical commentary: Καὶ ἐξελθὼν ἐπορεύθη εἰς ἕτερον τόπον ('he left and went to another place'). The classic enigma of the Lucan silence concerning the death of Paul (28. 30–1) will be dealt with in chapter 10: 'The enigma of the end of Acts (28. 16–31)'.

them. This statement must still be tested with regard to Luke's position on the Torah. The coherence of the Lucan view of Torah,[43] as one moves from the gospel to Acts,[44] does not seem clear.

Integral validity

From the gospel's point of view, the status of the Law is unambiguous: 'It is easier for heaven and earth to pass away, than for one stroke of a letter in the law to be dropped' (Luke 16. 17). Even if he is 'himself in favour of a spiritual concentration of the Law',[45] Luke does not ignore its ritual component. At the beginning of the gospel, Jesus' mother respects the Mosaic prescription concerning purification and offers the required sacrifice (Luke 2. 22–4). Luke takes over, without weakening it, the Q logion that rebukes the Pharisees for paying tithes on garden herbs instead of practising justice and the love of God, and, he adds, 'it is these you ought to have practised, without neglecting the others' (Luke 11. 42). The Lucan Jesus comments on the Torah (6. 27–42), refers a lawyer to the summary of the Law in order to receive eternal life (10. 25–8), and answers the rich man with a condensed version of the Decalogue (18. 18–20). The Law in its integrity remains in force.

Observance and rejection

What can be said of the second volume of Luke's work? The result of the analysis is double: observance and rejection. Here, as in other places, Luke differentiates. I shall put forward the two positions.

---

[43] The latest to have dealt with the question of the Law in Luke–Acts are: F. G. Downing, 'Freedom', 1984; M. Klinghardt, *Gesetz*, 1988; J. A. Fitzmyer, *Luke the Theologian*, 1989, pp. 175–202; K. Salo, *Luke's Treatment*, 1991; H. Merkel, 'Gesetz', 1996; F. Bovon, 'La Loi', 1997.

[44] The Lucan ethic of possessions poses an identical problem. After the way the Lucan Jesus curses the rich ('But woe to you who are rich, for you have received your consolation' Luke 6. 24), how are we to understand the accommodating interest of the author in the conversion of the Graeco-Roman 'women of high standing' (Acts 17. 4, 12)? Narrative criticism refuses to reduce the contradiction by means of source-critical arguments (the editor disagreeing with his sources). It observes the means the narrator employs to move the reader from the prescriptive ideal of the gospel (that the narrative never invalidates) to the lived reality in Acts; that is, from the evangelical imperative of relinquishment (Luke 12. 13–21; 18. 18–30) to the model of sharing of possessions (Acts 2. 42–5; 4. 32–7) and the realization of the presence of rich people in the community (Acts 16. 14–15; 17. 4, 12; etc.). I have developed this analysis in another study: 'Luc–Actes: une unité à construire', 1999, pp. 57–81.

[45] F. Bovon, 'La Loi', 1997, p. 208.

On the one hand, Peter's vision *opens a breach*. If God removes age-old separation between pure and impure (10. 1 – 11. 18), he invalidates the ritual Torah at a stroke. Peter at the Jerusalem council takes this to the extreme: 'why are you putting God to the test by placing on the neck of the disciples a yoke that neither our ancestors nor we have been able to bear?' (Acts 15. 10). Before this, Stephen had said, 'you are the ones that received the law as ordained by angels, and yet you have not kept it' (7. 53) and, in the synagogue of Antioch of Pisidia, Paul preached the forgiveness of sins and justification 'from which you could not be freed by the law of Moses' (Acts 13. 39). Peter and Paul (note the convergence of these authorities on the subject) declare a twofold impotence with reference to the Law: it has not been respected by Israel and it can in no way offer forgiveness.

On the other hand, the ritual law *always dictates practice*. The Paul of Acts circumcises Timothy when he makes him his collaborator (16. 3). Before the Sanhedrin, he shouts 'I am a Pharisee' (23. 6), and the reader should appreciate the weight of the present tense ἐγώ Φαρισαῖός εἰμι. Faced with the Jewish deputation in Rome, his defence is concentrated in the sweeping declaration, 'though I had done nothing against our people or the customs of the fathers' (οὐδὲν ἐναντίον ποιήσας τῷ λαῷ ἢ τοῖς ἔθεσι τοῖς πατρῴοις, 28. 17). It is surprising that, in Acts as in the infancy narratives (Luke 1–2), the author makes absolutely no criticism of Jewish rituals.

Should we conclude that, in Luke's vision, the Torah has lost its *raison d'être* for Christians of non-Jewish origin, while it maintains its authority, rituals included, for the Judaeo-Christians? A commentary by the narrator might go in this direction: Paul circumcises Timothy 'because of the Jews who were in those places, for they all knew that his father was a Greek' (16. 3b). Circumcision comes in here to seal the Jewish identity of Timothy, the 'mulatto' (Jewish by his mother and Greek by his father) who, like the Christianity of the Pauline mission, is of mixed origin. Yet this bipartite solution is not Luke's solution. The proof of this is the apostolic decree in Acts 15. 29, which imposes ritual prescriptions on Gentile Christians.

Two points of view: soteriological and historical

The Lucan position is subtle or, to be more precise, on the question of the Law, Luke combines two points of view that are not systematically related: *the soteriological aspect and the historical aspect*.

From a soteriological standpoint, the Christological event puts an end to the Law, not because God has repudiated it, but because it was proved incapable of providing forgiveness. Peter (13. 38) and Paul (22. 16) agree on this. With regard to salvation, the Law is null and void and, to express this (*pace* Vielhauer),[46] Luke uses very Pauline accents: 'by this Jesus everyone who believes is set justified' (πᾶς ὁ πιστεύων δικαιοῦται, 13. 39).

However, the historian in Luke also speaks. He is a historian of continuity, who safeguards whatever can be preserved. The Law ruled during the time of Israel, and, even if the people did not respect it, it remains these 'living oracles' (λόγια ζῶντα) (7. 38) received from God. Differently from Paul, Luke does not separate the Law from the promise. Because the function of defining the people of God (this role of providing identity as Jacob Jervell says)[47] remains attached to the Law, Luke, no more than Paul assumes the right to annul it. The Law, therefore, continues to leave its imprint on Paul's actions (circumcision: 16. 3; purification rite: 21. 20–6), certifying his irrevocable Jewishness.

The identity function of the Torah

The argument of continuity and the function of defining identity are also valid for the Church composed of Jewish and Gentile Christians that Luke has in view. The Torah remains, but it is spiritualized, summarized in its moral prescriptions: the double commandment of love (Luke 10. 27) and the second table of the Decalogue (Luke 18. 20). It is these values that Luke admires in Cornelius, the Godfearer from Caesarea: 'Your prayers and your alms have ascended as a memorial before God' (10. 4). Prayer and alms, love of God and concern for others are the basic components of a Law that does not die. For Luke, the recognition of this moral Torah defines a people recruited also from outside Judaism. This people is recognized by the 'purification of the heart' (15. 9) that Peter mentions, a purification that God offers by faith in Jesus.

---

[46] In a famous and provocative article, Ph. Vielhauer rejects the idea that the author of Acts has any truly Pauline traits ('On the "Paulinism"', 1966, p. 48). 'He presents no specifically Pauline idea.' This view (which is correct) of the theological difference between the Paul of the epistles and the Paul of Acts must today be replaced in a historical paradigm which takes account of the reception of the Pauline tradition and the school phenomenon. In other words, we should stop repeating that Luke was a (bad) student of the apostle to the Gentiles and ask why and how the missionary figure of Paul was received along a narrative trajectory (Luke–Acts, *The Acts of Paul and Thecla*), while the pastoral and institutional dimension was retained in an discursive trajectory (deutero-Pauline epistles; the Pastoral Epistles; *Correspondence of Paul and Seneca*).

[47] J. Jervell, *People of God*, 1972, pp. 141–3. However, while affirming that the Law is an identity marker of the Church because it is an '*indelebilis* character' of Israel, Jervell underestimates the Christological shift in salvation history.

It should be noted that the famous apostolic decree (15. 28–9.) adopted at the Jerusalem council imposes four prohibitions, not in the name of the Torah, but in the name of the Holy Spirit and the apostles. 'For it has seemed good to the Holy Spirit and to us . . .' This is to say that in the Christian regime the decree receives its authority not as a substratum of the Law, but as the *didache* of the apostles.

Luke the historian and Luke the theologian

What a survey of the Law throughout the work *ad Theophilum* makes clear is that *Luke the historian and Luke the theologian do not always say the same thing*. The theologian identifies the continuity in the action of God in history, while the historian is conscious that history evolves. We come back again to the difficulty noted at the beginning of this chapter: coherence is more difficult to grasp, since the mind of the author is not expressed in a systematic mode, but narratively. Should we agree with Matthias Klinghardt[48] that the solution resides in the diversity of the readership targeted by the author, that the Lucan work is open to two audiences (Jewish Christian and Gentile Christian) and each chooses their own right of way? Or should we rather say that the complete rupture between Lucan Christianity and the Synagogue confers only the value of legitimation on the attachment that the Paul of Acts shows to the ritual Torah? This second position seems to me more appropriate to the historiographical dimension of the work *ad Theophilum*.

Conclusion: Luke–Acts, a diptych

On the basis of the case of the Law, it is clear that Acts succeeds the gospel as a continuing story, with its necessary shifts. Hence the term 'diptych' is suitable for the Luke–Acts entity, if we think of two paintings joined together by a central hinge (Luke 24/Acts 1: the exaltation of Jesus). Rather than attributing to Luke a consolidated theological idea that he distributes throughout the episodes of the narrative, it is more appropriate to consider Acts as a sequel[49] (or better as an *effect of the gospel*), arranging mirror reflections from one narrative to the other, with the necessary resumptions, shifts and recompositions. The back-and-forth

---

[48] M. Klinghardt, *Gesetz*, 1988 (esp. pp. 306–9).

[49] M. C. Parsons and R. I. Pervo, *Rethinking*, 1993, p. 126: 'Literally, Acts is best characterized as a sequel.' The term 'sequel' is preferable to considering Acts a 'confirmation of the gospel' (W. C. van Unnik, 'Confirmation', 1960) or Luke a 'preface to Acts' (C. K. Barrett, 'Third gospel as a Preface', 1992).

movement from the gospel to Acts and from Acts to the gospel that this mirroring provokes is the work of reading, and it is from this work that the unity of Luke–Acts emerges.

The proposition defended in this chapter is precisely that the unity of the work *ad Theophilum* does not lie in the text, but *takes place in the act of reading*. The work of the reader is guided by a series of markers that the author has placed in the narrative (inclusions, prolepsis, narrative chains and *syncrisis*). Because Luke constantly appeals to the reader's memory, because Luke forces the reader to go back and forth between the Lucan diptych, this narrative device leads the reader to reread the gospel with Acts in mind, to seek for the hermeneutical keys to the narrative, and to discern in Acts the fulfilment of the predictions of the gospel. The Christological precedent which underpins the destiny of the apostles is constantly evoked, rather than made explicit, by the narrative of Acts. It solicits a recalling of the gospel that provokes the reader to *create* the unity of Luke–Acts. Thus the Acts of the apostles is offered to the reader as a site for verifying the promises of the gospel. Did not the author, in his preface, inform the most excellent Theophilus that his narrative would enable him to verify 'the truth (ἀσφαλεία) concerning the things about which [he] had been instructed' (Luke 1. 4)?

4

A CHRISTIANITY BETWEEN JERUSALEM
AND ROME

Luke's writing leads its reader on a geographical axis from Jerusalem, where the Infancy narratives unfold (Luke 1–2), to Rome, where Paul arrives as a prisoner (Acts 28). Narratively, Luke's plot links together Jerusalem and Rome. No one denies the theological dimension of this geography, yet questions remain. How does Luke theologically link these two great cultural and religious centres? How does he situate Christianity between Jerusalem and Rome – or, alternatively, between Israel and the Roman Empire?

Without exaggeration, one could say that the whole history of the interpretation of Luke–Acts unfolds from this problematic. Anyone who wants to establish the theological aim of Luke's writing must first determine how the author positions Christianity in relation to Judaism and in relation to the pagan world.

In my opinion, research has constantly held the relationship between Jerusalem and Rome in a positive/negative polarity. Adopting Rome would require Luke to break with Jerusalem. Alternatively, those who think he maintains an openness to Judaism assume that this position requires him to distance himself from Empire. A few examples are in order. Alfred Loisy, in his monumental commentary of 1920,[1] defended the idea of a redaction of Acts in several stages. In the end, Israel, victim of a textual revision aimed at valorizing the image of Rome, is depicted as the quintessence of evil. Ernst Haenchen also correlates the rejection of Jerusalem and an opening toward the pagans.[2] S. J. Cassidy takes the opposite view, favouring the relationship to Jerusalem in order to emphasize (in my view unduly) a critical attitude toward Rome.[3] Taking up Loisy's thesis, L. M. Wills interprets Lucan anti-Judaism as the negative side of his attachment to Rome. Luke denigrated the Jews in order to break down the

---

[1] *Actes des apôtres*, 1920. See also *Actes des apôtres avec introduction et notes*, 1925.
[2] *Acts of the Apostles*, 1971, p. 653, etc.
[3] *Society and Politics*, 1987.

relationship of Christianity with Israel and to attach it to Rome.[4] Hence, in one manner or another, the relationship with Jerusalem and Rome is understood as an 'either-or' situation. Is this alternative pertinent? The resistance which opposes the text of Luke–Acts to its application[5] invites a different line of thought.

Heuristically, I propose another paradigm, in which Jerusalem and Rome do not exclude one another, but converge to establish the identity of Christianity. I would like to show that the relationship of Christianity to Judaism is a question of identity for Christianity according to Luke just as much as is the relationship to the Roman Empire, and that the author does not simply 'accommodate'[6] the Judaeo-Christian tradition to a Graeco-Roman readership. Rather, he develops what I call a 'programme of theological integration' (I shall return to this expression) between Jerusalem and Rome.

I shall begin with an initial clue, which is the construction of the characters in the book of Acts. Lucan language will be considered next in order to examine a rhetorical process that is unique to Luke: double signification. Following this, I shall define the Lucan programme of integration between Jerusalem and Rome, bringing together Luke and his contemporary, Josephus, who has a similar project. Finally, I shall set out the consequences of the programme.

Paul, Barnabas, Timothy and others

The curious construction of certain characters in the book of Acts provides a first indication, perhaps the most evident one, of a desired linkage between Judaism and paganism. Luke, in effect, has meticulously composed the cultural and religious profile of a few key characters among the agents of the Christian mission.

Paul

Paul's case is the most blatant. The narratives of the Damascus road call him by his Aramaic name Saoul (9. 4; 22. 7; 26. 14), but this son of

---

[4] 'Depiction', 1991, pp. 631–54, esp. 652.

[5] The work published by J. B. Tyson, *Luke–Acts and the Jewish People*, 1988, presents a choice of contrasting views on the question of the relationship to Judaism; the diversity of proposed readings shows, from my point of view, that Luke's narrative resists logical alternatives.

[6] This expression comes from F. W. Danker: 'Cultural Accommodation', 1983, pp. 391–414.

Abraham is also Παῦλος (13. 9), child of the Empire, and Roman citizen. Luke has him asserting his status as a zealous Pharisee with as much force as that of being a Roman citizen (22. 28). At the crossroads of two worlds, the apostle to Jews and Gentiles belongs both to Jerusalem and to Rome. This double origin constructs Paul in accordance with the Christianity whose identity Luke establishes. It is a religion that claims its Jewish origin and seeks its place in Roman society.[7]

Barnabas

Luke has not confined this mixed cultural adherence to his most emblematic character. Barnabas, who with Paul will lead the first mission to Asia Minor and Greece (Acts 13–14), is introduced by the narrator in 4. 36: 'There was a Levite, a native of Cyprus, Joseph, to whom the apostles gave the name Barnabas (which means "son of encouragement").' At this point in the narrative of Acts – we are still in chapter 4 – there is no mention of a mission to non-Jews; but the identity of Barnabas already anticipates it, for he is of Jewish descent, a Levite, but not of Jerusalemite Judaism. Barnabas comes from the Diaspora and his Cypriot origin announces the first stage in his missionary journey with Paul: Cyprus, where the proconsul Sergius Paulus will be converted (13. 6–12). Barnabas is a transitional character on the road from Judaism to paganism, such as Luke likes to place throughout his narrative. Stephen (Acts 6–7) and the Ethiopian eunuch (Acts 8) are two examples of the same type: one is a Hellenistic Jew and the other is described as a proselyte, a reader of the Scriptures and a pilgrim to Jerusalem.

Timothy

The double cultural and religious allegiance is even clearer with the collaborator Paul chooses to replace Barnabas: Timothy (16. 1–5), the son of a converted Jewish woman and a Greek father. Notice the difference from Barnabas: the narrative of Acts has progressed since chapter 13. The legitimacy of the mission outside Judaism has just been recognized by the Jerusalem assembly (ch. 15), and, by his double affiliation, Timothy symbolizes the Church that can henceforth be born: a Church composed

---

[7] J. Roloff has well understood the ambivalence of the Lucan Paul. He is both 'der grosse Heidenmissionar und Repräsentant der legendenumwobenen Anfangsepoche der Kirche' and the 'Symbol und Garant der bleibenden inneren Kontinuität dieser Kirche mit ihren Anfängen und, darüber hinaus, mit Israel' ('Paulus-Darstellung', 1979, pp. 510–31, quotation 528–9).

of those Jews who rallied to the cause of Christ and believers of Gentile origin.[8] In every detail, the identity of Timothy coincides with that of the Church, a Church in formation, for the priority is reserved to believing Israel – the Jew first and then the Greek.

The Godfearers

The importance the author of Acts gives to the figure of the Godfearers proceeds from the same narrative strategy; for the Godfearers, who are Gentiles, live in the orbit of the synagogue, where they share the worship and the knowledge of the Scriptures.[9] Although they are situated on the side of paganism,[10] the Godfearers are representatives, like Paul, Barnabas and Timothy, of a Christianity that defines itself as related to both Jerusalem and Rome.

The cultural and religious mixing of these characters indicates a desire to hold together Jewish origin and installation in the Empire. This aim would remain anecdotal if it were limited to the narrative composition of a few figures. However it can also be perceived at the level of Lucan language, to which I now turn.

Semantic ambivalence: a Lucan rhetorical device

In the classic *The Beginnings of Christianity*,[11] Henry Cadbury makes a remark that to my knowledge has not been exploited in research. Cadbury notes that the Lucan syntax sometimes presents ambiguities that allow two possible interpretations. He wonders if these ambiguities do not reveal a literary procedure consciously used by Luke: 'Luke is apparently fond of these constructions.'[12] It seems to me that Cadbury's intuition can be expanded from the syntactical to the semantic level. Several expressions can be found in the gospel and the book of Acts that attest a process of

---

[8]   With R. C. Tannehill, *Narrative Unity*, II, 1990, p. 78.

[9]   Acts 10. 22; 13. 16, 26; 17. 4, 12, 17; 18. 4, 17.

[10]   M. J. Cook sees in the Lucan mention of the Godfearers a literary procedure aimed at introducing a narrative transitional figure between Judaism and paganism ('Mission', 1988, p. 120). J. T. Sanders reminds us that the Godfearers still belong to paganism, since, in contrast with the proselytes, they are not integrated into Judaism by conversion ('Who is a Jew', 1991, pp. 434–45, especially pp. 439–43).

[11]   'Commentary on the Preface of Luke', 1934, pp. 489–510.

[12]   I thank F. Bovon for this quotation. Cadbury makes the remark concerning the attachment of ἀκριβῶς in Luke 1. 3: 'Here also either translation is possible, since on account of its amphibolous position the word may be applied to either παρακολουθήκοτι or γράψαι. *Perhaps it goes partly with each since Luke is apparently fond of these constructions*' (italics mine) (*ibid.*, p. 504).

semantic ambivalence deliberately used by the author. The following are a few examples.[13]

The Passion narrative

In the Passion narrative (Luke 23), Luke has strongly emphasized, over against Mark, the motif of Jesus' innocence. He has his innocence declared on three occasions by Pilate (23. 4, 14, 22), then by the thief on the cross (23. 41), and then by the Roman centurion in 23. 47. In Luke the Roman centurion confesses something very different from in Mark. Where Mark writes, 'Truly, this man was a son of God' (15. 39), the centurion in Luke says, "Ὄντως ὁ ἄνθρωπος οὗτος δίκαιος ἦν' (23. 47). How is the word δίκαιος to be understood?[14] Should we interpret it in the judicial sense of innocence (Kilpatrick)?[15] Or is this a theological designation of the suffering righteous one (Karris and Doble)?[16] From a lexicographical point of view, the Greek permits both. In his commentary on Luke, J. A. Fitzmyer attributes the first sense to the tradition, but recognizes that the second is plausible at the level of Lucan redaction.[17]

I wonder if Luke consciously intended the ambiguity; for it permits the redactor to place the death of Jesus in both the Hellenistic tradition of the innocent martyr and in the Jewish tradition of the suffering righteous one.[18] At a stroke, the interpretative potential of the cross is considerably enlarged, since the meaning of the death of Jesus can be received by both the Greek and the Jewish reader. Should we then not conclude that the author intended this dual reading? The conscious character of the

[13] I have already noted the presence of semantic ambivalence: see pp. 50–1 (ch. 3).

[14] This debate is carefully laid out by P. Doble, *Paradox*, 1996, pp. 70–89.

[15] 'Hence of the two possible meanings of δίκαιος at Luke 23. 47, that of "righteous" must be rejected as being quite pointless, while that of "innocent" fits in well with the general theme of the chapter'; G. D. Kilpatrick, 'Theme', 1942, pp. 34–6, quotation p. 35.

[16] R. J. Karris: 'to translate δίκαιος in Luke 23. 47 properly, one must look to the pervasive Lucan motif of justice. From that perspective, the argument can be made that with the use of δίκαιος in 23. 47 that motif has come to a climactic expression. In the light of the Lucan motif of justice, δίκαιος should be translated as "righteous" ('Lucan View of Jesus' Death', 1986, pp. 65–75, quotation p. 73). P. Doble ascribes the theological use of δίκαιος in Luke 23. 47 to the sapiential theology of the oppressed righteous (Wis. 1. 16 – 3. 9): 'to render δίκαιος at Luke 23. 47 as "innocent" is not only to ignore Luke's consistent practice but, worse, to obscure his *theologia crucis*' (*Paradox*, 1996, p. 160).

[17] J. A. Fitzmyer, *Gospel*, 1985, p. 1520. For Fitzmyer, the shift in meaning occurs between the first stage (traditional) and the third (redactional).

[18] In the same direction, see R. L. Brawley, *Luke–Acts and the Jews*, 1987, p. 141 note 29.

ambiguity could be confirmed by the fact that the two meanings find
support in the context: the juridical sense is suggested by the insertion
of the centurion's declaration in a sequence marked, as we have seen,
by several declarations of innocence (Pilate and the thief on the cross);
the theological meaning is supported by the presence of the title 'the
righteous one' (ὁ δίκαιος) to designate the suffering Jesus in Acts (3. 14;
7. 52; 22. 14).

Paul in Athens (Acts 17. 16–34)

Since the works of Dibelius and Gärtner[19] we know that the speech of
Paul in Athens (Acts 17. 16–34), this apologetic masterpiece, is open
to a Greek philosophical and religious reading as well as to a Jewish
reading (nurtured by the LXX). The speech opens with an already ambiguous address as Paul calls the Athenians δεισιδαιμονεστέροι (17. 22);
are they 'very religious' or 'very superstitious'? The word offers the
two nuances in the Koine and I believe Luke wants to allow the reader
to choose his/her own preference. But the ambivalence of the speech
(between a Greek and a Jewish reading) depends on an expression
that I think commentators are tempted to settle too quickly. The God
that Paul proclaims in Athens created all people ἐξ ἑνός (17. 26); who is
this 'one'? Is the God of Acts 17 the Creator that Israel worships (in this
case, ἑνός is masculine and designates the one man, Adam), or is this
God the original principle in which the Stoics believe (in this case, ἑνός
is neuter)?[20]

The whole speech is open to two readings: it can be read with one or
the other hermeneutical key, according to the horizon of understanding
adopted by the reader. When the speaker declares that this God, having
populated the earth, 'defined the times (καιροί) of their existence and
the boundaries (ὁροθεσίαι) of the places where they live' (17. 26), the
καιροί can be interpreted as the seasons from a Hellenistic point of view
and the periods of history from a Jewish one; the ὁροθεσίαι represent
natural limits for the Greek and political borders for the Jew (17. 26).
In verse 29, the affirmation that God does not resemble silver, gold or
stone can fit with Jewish faith, in which all representations of the divine

---

[19] M. Dibelius, 'Paul in Athens' [1939], 1956, pp. 78–83. B. Gärtner, *Areopagus Speech*,
1955.

[20] Contrary to modern commentators, who without justification opt for the masculine
ἑνός (in the name of Paul's Jewish faith!), M. Dibelius was conscious of the ambiguity of
the expression, but he placed the problem in the textual tradition ('Paul on the Areopagus'
[1939], 1956, p. 28).

image are forbidden, but it can also be received by the Greek for whom the Living one can only be represented by a living person.[21] We are convinced by reading the admirable passage of Seneca on the refinement of the conception of God:

> Precepts are commonly given as to how the gods should be worshipped. But let us forbid lamps to be lighted on the Sabbath, since the gods do not need light, neither do men take pleasure in soot. Let us forbid men to offer morning salutation and to throng the doors of temples; mortal ambitions are attracted by such ceremonies, but God is worshipped by those who truly know Him. *(Letters to Lucilius* 15. 95.47)[22]

The apologetic of the speech is concretized in this openness of meaning, which should interrogate and provoke the reflection of the reader until Luke settles the matter. For Luke does this,[23] but only at the end (17. 31) when the call to conversion is motivated by the reference to Christ as Judge of the world. Here, the ambiguity of the speech comes up against a credal formulation: God is going 'to judge the world with righteousness through a man whom he has appointed, and of this he has given assurance to all by raising him from the dead' (17. 31b). Up to this point, philosophical monotheism and biblical faith could advance side by side.[24] In the name of what theology? In my view, it is not difficult to see Luke's signature

---

[21] Cf. H. Conzelmann, *Acts of the Apostles*, 1987, p. 145.

[22] This text is cited according the translation by R. M. Gummere, 1971, in the Loeb Classical Library. See also *Letters to Lucilius* 8.73.16. One can also find a number of Greek philosophical texts close to the categories of Acts 17 in E. Des Places, *La religion grecque*, 1969, pp. 329–61; V. Gatti, *Discorso*, 1979, pp. 68–209; E. Berti, 'Discorso', 1985, pp. 251–9.

[23] M. Dumais concludes his skilful analysis of the semantic ambivalence of the Athens speech by seeing Luke defending 'deux voies d'accès au vrai Dieu, la voie de la raison et la voie religieuse' ('Salut en dehors de la foi?', 1997, pp. 179–89, quotation p. 188). To attribute to the author of *ad Theophilum* a position of natural theology, in my opinion, is to misunderstand the statement of ἄγνοια (v. 30a) and the call to μετανοεῖν (v. 30b) clearly announced at the end of the speech. Furthermore, the study of E. Delebecque shows that the Western text has reduced the ambivalence by its Christianization of the text ('Deux versions', 1995).

[24] This understanding of intentional plurality in the readings of Acts 17 stands against the idea that Luke limited himself, in the redaction of Paul's speech, to rendering the Christian message comprehensible to an audience unaware of Israel's religious tradition (J. Dupont, 'Discours à l'Aréopage', 1984, p. 423). One must distinguish between story world and narrative rhetoric. At the level of plot (story world), the symbolic function of the meeting of the Lucan Paul with the representatives of Greek thought is undeniable; but for the reader (narrative rhetoric), the author of Acts seeks to demonstrate a possible dual way into speaking about God (on the distinction between story world and narrative rhetoric, see below, p. 104).

behind this theology of the universality of God; for Luke's God is the God of the Jew as well as the Greek – as Peter confesses, a God who 'shows no partiality' (10. 34).[25]

Acts 27–28

The last two chapters of Acts (27–8) also present several cases of semantic ambivalence. The rescue of Paul and his companions is open to two readings. It sends the biblical reader to God, the master of the waters, whom the reader knows to be the Creator of the ocean, the God of Jonah or the God behind Jesus' calming of the storm (Luke 8. 22–5). However, the hero's being saved from shipwreck does not surprise the reader of the Greek novel, where the rescue from the anger of the waters had become, since the Odyssey, a classic metaphor of divine protection of the righteous.[26] Thus in the eyes of both the Jewish and the Greek reader, the God of the ocean demonstrates the innocence of Paul by saving him from the storm. The terminology supports this dual aspect of the discourse: the abundant use of the 'saving' vocabulary (σῴζειν, διασῴζειν, σωτηρία)[27] is understandable in a maritime narrative, yet at the same time, the theological dimension goes beyond the secular meaning to transform this maritime epic into a metaphor of salvation. Hence, the announcement that 'all that were brought safely to land' (27. 44) can be understood as the happy ending of the drama, but it can also be deciphered as a parable of universal salvation.

It is the same with the meal at which Paul presides on the ship (27. 33–6). Paul takes bread, gives thanks, breaks it and begins to eat. This in turn stirs his companions to summon courage and to eat. Is this meal eucharistic? Yes and no. Here again Luke's narrative finesse is confirmed. The reader coming from the gospel will not miss the imitation of the vocabulary of the last meal of Jesus (καὶ ἔδωκεν αὐτοῖς λέγων Luke 22. 19) and also the absence of a cup (Luke 22. 17, 20), which prevents

---

[25] The same confluence of Jewish culture and Greek philosophical tradition is perceptible in two other passages of religious critique: the polemic of Stephen against the localization of God in the Temple (7. 46–50) and the critique of pagan polytheism in Lystra (14. 15–17); in both cases, the prophetic critique coincides with Greek philosophical monotheism.

[26] Material gathered by G. B. Miles and G. Trompf in 'Luke and Antiphon', 1979, pp. 259–67; D. Ladouceur, 'Hellenistic Preconceptions', 1980, pp. 435–49. Concerning the sequence of Acts 27. 1 – 28. 10, see below pp. 216–21 (ch. 10).

[27] Acts 27. 20, 31, 34, 43, 44; 28. 1, 4. This same ambivalence is found in Acts 4. 9. For a contrary opinion, see A. George, who maintains the strictly profane character of σῴζειν/σωτηρία in Acts 27–8 ('Vocabulaire de salut', 1978, pp. 307–20, esp. pp. 308–9).

the transformation of the ship's passengers into a eucharistic assembly. It is more correct to speak of a prefiguration of the Lord's supper.[28] This partial imitation favours another reading, which sees in the proposal of the meal a confirmation of Paul's status. This status has been maintained throughout the voyage: that of a wise man, educated in the ways of the divine, expert in navigation, prudent and confident, in a word, the status of a hero. Once again the procedure of ambivalence borders on metaphor.

It is no longer surprising that the ship on which Paul arrives in Puteoli carries the figurehead of the Dioscuri (28. 11). In Greek mythology, Castor and Pollux are considered to be protectors of seafaring people, but, even more, guardians of truth and avengers of perjury.[29] A small hint from the narrator: at the moment he disembarks into the heart of the Empire, Paul, the son of Israel, sails under a flag that assures the Greek reader that divine favour has been granted him.

Ambiguous terms and themes

The list of the ways in which Luke cultivates ambiguity could be extended.

Concerning the ambiguity of Luke's *terminology*: σώτηρ (saviour) is a messianic title as well as an imperial Roman one; ἐν τοῖς τοῦ πατρός μου has a double meaning in Luke 2. 49 (does the neuter article τοῖς mean 'my father's domain' or 'my father's affairs'?);[30] νόμος is ambivalent in Acts 18. 13 (either the Torah or the Roman law), and so on.

The author sometimes chooses ambivalent *themes*, or more precisely themes current in both cultures.

---

[28] After his first negative view ('Wir können freilich nicht sagen, dass Paulus ein wirkliches "Herrenmahl" oder "Abendmahl" mit dieser ganzen Schar gefeiert hat'), B. Reicke opts for a prefiguration of the sacramental meal in this sharing of the food on the ship ('Mahlzeit', 1948, pp. 401–10, quotation on pp. 408–9). Tannehill chooses: 'Paul's meal, then, is as sacramental as any other meal in Luke–Acts' (*Narrative Unity*, II, 1990, p. 335). I prefer to maintain the subtlety by which Luke lets the reader understand the eucharistic *connotation* of the meal; the reader cannot ignore it, any more than he/she can in Luke 9. 16 (the multiplication of the bread) or in 24. 30 (Emmaus). A supplementary argument: κλάσαι ἄρτον synthetically designates the Lord's supper in Luke 24. 30; Acts 2. 42, 46 and 20. 7, 11.

[29] M. Albert, *Culte de Castor et Pollux*, 1883. See also S. Geppert, *Castor und Pollux*, 1996, pp. 4–35.

[30] In an article published in 1978, H. J. de Jonge notes the semantic ambiguity of ἐν τοῖς τοῦ πατρός μου in Luke 2. 49 and attributes it to the author's conscious plan ('Sonship', 1978, pp. 317–54, see pp. 331–6).

(a) The genealogy of Jesus (Luke 3) fits into the tradition of Jewish historiography but also satisfies the Roman taste for the antiquity of a religious movement.[31] (b) The description of the ascension (Acts 1. 9–11) appeals both to the apocalyptic motif of the exaltation of the righteous and to the Hellenistic pattern of the translation of the hero to heaven. (c) The evocation of the Gentile nations in the Pentecost narrative (Acts 2. 9–11a) corresponds to the universality of prophetic eschatology, but also to the Roman ideal of the acceptance of foreign nations.[32] (d) To say that the crowd of believers had 'one heart and one soul' (Acts 4. 32a) echoes both the formula of the אֶחָד לֵב in the Hebrew Bible and the equivalent formula μία ψυχή of the Greeks.[33] (e) The description of the sharing of possessions in the Jerusalem community (Acts 4. 32–4) takes over, on the one hand, the phrasing found in Deuteronomy 15. 4 in the LXX (οὐδὲ ἐνδεής τις ἦν ἐν αὐτοῖς, Acts 4. 34), but on the other hand, takes up the slogan of the Greek ideal of friendship (ἦν αὐτοῖς ἅπαντα κοινά, 4. 32). (f) The narrator gives a dramatic turn to the narrative of the death of Herod, who 'because he had not given the glory to God' is struck by an angel of the Lord and dies 'eaten by worms' (12. 23). Luke has used, on this occasion, a *topos* of ancient literature, both Jewish and Greek, to describe the death of the tyrant.[34]

Later,[35] I shall have the opportunity to deal with the theme of the voyage, which saturates the gospel (Luke 9. 51 – 19. 28) as well as Acts (the travels of the apostles and especially Paul's). We shall see that Luke borrowed it from Hellenistic culture, where it was fashionable, calling on the reader's imagination and fashioning the image of the itinerant philosopher. However, the theme is not foreign to Jewish memory, which cultivates the remembrance of

---

[31] This need to attest the antiquity of their tradition through a genealogical derivation of origin can be found in authors of the fourth and third centuries BC (Berossos, Manetho) as well as in Flavius Josephus. See p. 80.

[32] D. Balch has expounded the Roman ideal of *oikoumenè*, that he identifies in Dionysius of Halicarnassus in the first century BC and Aelius Aristides in the second century AD ('Comments on the Genre', 1989, pp. 343–61, esp. pp. 353–60).

[33] אֶחָד לֵב Jer. 32. 39 (MT); 1 Chron. 12. 38; 2 Chron. 30. 12. μία ψυχή: Aristotle, *Nic. Ethics* 9.8; Cicero, *De amicitia* 92. See C. K. Barrett, *Acts of the Apostles*, I, 1994, p. 253.

[34] After others, O. W. Allen (*Death of Herod*, 1997) has recently traced the classical motif of the death of the tyrant in Herodotus (*Persian Wars* 4.205), Pausanias (*Description of Greece* 9.7.1–3), Polybius (*Histories* 31.9), Lucian (*Alexander the False Prophet* 59) and Diodorus Siculus (*Historical Library* 36.13) as well as the authors of 2 Chron. (21. 1–20), 1 Macc. (6. 1–13), 2 Macc. (9. 1–28) or Josephus (*B.J.* 1.70–84, 647–56; *A.J.* 12.354–9, 413; 13.301–19; 17.146–99; 19.343–50).

[35] See chapter 11: 'Travels and travellers'.

the great journeys of the past (the nomadism of the Patriarchs, the Exodus).

An ambiguous process

The recurrence of this phenomenon makes the hypothesis that the author lacks clarity dubious. Rather, I discern here the presence of a rhetorical device that Luke uses with consummate art: amphibology. This procedure of dual meaning not only indicates that the author refuses to impose one meaning; for amphibology is the literary support for polysemy. Using amphibology is the deliberate calculation of an author who has decided to suggest the double meaning of a word or an event. I stress the pragmatic effect: the ambiguity does not enforce one meaning. It challenges and intrigues. It proposes. It surprises by not limiting the sense. It is for the reader to resolve it or to continue reading the text maintaining the plurality of meanings that are suggested. Amphibology is a rhetorical device that the authors of Midrash used frequently; in the treatise *bMegilla* 14b, the deliberate use of double meaning is called *tartey machma*.[36]

Why does the author of Luke–Acts have recourse to semantic ambiguity? This linguistic procedure could be reduced to a subtle game of scrambling that Luke plays with the reader, but the examination of the duality of meaning claims attention. As we have seen, semantic duality is always constructed with the Jewish dimension, turned toward the LXX, and the Hellenistic dimension oriented to Greek philosophy or culture. The duality of meaning created by the author systematically points toward Jerusalem and Rome. I have spoken of a theological programme of integration in Luke and I shall now explain this terminology.

A theological programme of integration

The device of semantic ambivalence just described is the signature of a theology that does not seek to exclude, but to include by integration. It is here that Luke the writer is in the service of Luke the theologian. In my view, the author seeks to define Christian identity by a double demonstration, which creates strong tensions in his narrative:

---

[36] Mentioned by M. Dumais in *Le langage de l'évangélisation*, 1976, p. 94; see also pp. 335–8. J. Carmignac identified the procedure in the Qumran *pesharim* (*Textes de Qumrân*, II, 1963, p. 47).

on the one hand, he seeks the roots of the Church in Jerusalem, that is, in the continuation of a history of salvation that began with Israel; and on the other hand, God opens up to universality, where the Roman Empire represents the framework for geographical and political expansion. The two sides of the amphibology go back to the two points of reference for the identity of nascent Christianity. Luke's theological ambition even permeates his choices of writing, which hold open the continuity with Israel as well as the expansion to the nations. The phenomenon of double signification serves this theological programme, since it presents Christianity as both the fulfilment of the promises of the Scriptures and as the answer to the religious quest of the Graeco-Roman world.

Yet let us not imagine that, hidden behind the term 'integration' applied to the Lucan theological project, there is the quest for a compromise between Rome and Jerusalem, nor the idea of a synthesis favoured by the Tübingen school. With this term I would designate Luke's ambition to link Jerusalem and Rome in the definition of Christianity. Could it be said that integrating the two poles assigns each one its proper place: Jerusalem representing the past, and Rome the future, of Christianity? This verdict is historically correct, but inadequate theologically. Rather, Luke foresees a Christianity that brings together the best that Judaism and Hellenistic paganism have to offer. The quintessence of Judaism is its indefectible attachment to the Torah and its hope of resurrection. The Paul of Acts never stops repeating that this is crystallized in the Good News of Jesus (13. 32–9; 20. 27; 21. 24; 23. 6; 28. 20b). Starting from the speech to the Sanhedrin (23. 6) and continuing to the end of Acts (28. 20), by way of Paul's defence before Agrippa (26. 6–7), the line of defence constructed by Paul's speeches aims to show that 'the hope of Israel' finds in faith in Jesus its legitimate outcome. On the other hand, Luke perceives the best of what the Empire has to offer in the universality of Roman society where the promise of salvation offered to all peoples will find its place.

An Apology pro imperio

The universality of the *imperium romanum* is concretized by a culture, by a network of communication on land and sea, by the riches of the cities, by the functioning of its institutions. Concerning all this, Luke has an undeniably informed and admiring view. His information is evidenced by his concern for exactitude in toponymy and the precision with which he describes the working of the imperial institutions.[37] Luke clearly knows the workings of the Roman judicial system; he admires its effectiveness and approves the principle of equity, the *aequitas romana*.[38] This fascination, however, does not stifle his critical sense, when imperial officials are not worthy of their task.[39] But it remains necessary to see why Luke shares such admiration with his readers. This favourable judgement is not a defence of the Church. One can speak, with Paul Walaskay, of an *apologia pro imperio*,[40] if we mean by that the Lucan effort to give a positive character to his Christian readers' view of the Empire where the future of their religion will unfold.[41]

If the hypothesis defended up to this point is correct, one must conclude that Luke–Acts attempts to remove the division between Jerusalem and Rome, a division that affected a large part of Judaism (but with nuances)[42] and that the Jewish War had just aggravated. Luke shows, in his work, how the God of the people of Israel has become the God of all. The meeting of Peter and Cornelius, where the age-old barrier between pure and impure (10. 9–16) collapses, constitutes this turning point in the book of Acts. However, the author is persuaded that access to this universal God is facilitated by the universality of the Empire; his description of the success of the Pauline mission, with the exception of the Synagogue, is a promise for the future of Christianity (13. 12, 48; 14. 11–18; 16. 14–16, 29–32; etc.).

[37] See J. Taylor's synthetic study, 'Roman Empire', 1996, pp. 2436–500.

[38] The governor Festus allows Paul to profit from the principle of *aequitas* by declaring that it was not 'the custom of the Romans to hand over anyone before the accused had met the accusers face to face and had been given an opportunity to make a defence against the charge' (25. 16). This is the occasion to recall the fine, yet forgotten article by J. Dupont 'Aequitas romana', 1967, pp. 527–52.

[39] One may consult Cassidy's study, *Society and Politics*, 1987, but keep in mind that the spirit of Luke's view of the *imperium romanum* does not partake either of systematic criticism of the political authorities (which confuses the institution with the corruption of certain officials) or of naivety (which would sacrifice the moral sense). Luke shares the spirit of the age: like many others in the first century, he both admires and dreads this great organizing system of Roman power.

[40] P. W. Walaskay, '*And So We Came to Rome*', 1983. This formula has been criticized, and with good reason, for setting aside the identity goal of the narrative of Acts with regard to Lucan Christianity.

[41] Contrary to the repeated affirmations of J. Jervell (see his contribution, 'Future of the Past', 1996, p. 123), I maintain that Luke's marked taste for describing the Roman Empire and its functioning shows an interest in the *imperium romanum* that is not only documentary, but also theological.

[42] See M. Hadas-Lebel's monumental work devoted to this subject, *Jérusalem contre Rome*, 1990. G. Stemberger ('Beurteilung', 1979, pp. 338–96) also shows the variety of Jewish feelings toward Rome, going from hate in apocalyptic circles to the relative indifference of the rabbis (even the positive appreciation of Johanan ben Zakkai).

A project of Christian civilization

F. Bovon has argued that Lucan universalism is consciously built on the model of the imperial ambitions of Rome and on the Roman ideology of the gathering of all peoples.[43] The model of the Roman *concordia* would thus have allowed Luke to break with the centripetal eschatalogical universalism of Israel (i.e. focused on Jerusalem). It is true that from the birth of Jesus, during the prefecture of Quirinius (Luke 2. 2), to Paul's stay in Rome under surveillance (Acts 28. 16, 30), a conviction of Luke's is deployed, which one can gather from the formula placed on the lips of Paul: '*these things have not taken place in a corner*' (26. 26b). Sketched in filigree behind the work *ad Theophilum*, there is a project of Christian civilization encompassing what must be called Jewish antiquity and Roman modernity. From this point of view, the κυριότης of Jesus proclaims itself the counterpoint of imperial authority, while the Lucan εἰρήνη accomplishes what the *Pax romana* failed to do,[44] and Pentecost steals from Caesar the power to create unanimity among the peoples.

During the debates at the Jerusalem council on the question of the Law an argument arises which carries the day and would not leave the Greek reader unmoved: 'For it has seemed good to the Holy Spirit and to us to impose on you no further burden than these essentials...' (15. 28). What the apostles and the elders of the church of Jerusalem prescribe for their Gentile brothers thus obeys the notably Greek rule of the mean, the reasonable, the minimum necessary. The Lucan image of a universal and reasonable Christianity, universal because it is reasonable, shows itself here. It must be remembered that the Greeks and the Romans were horrified by excess, especially in religious matters. They classified as superstitious any religion that imposed upon its adepts a doctrine or a behaviour that went beyond what was reasonable. Let me quote Seneca once again, 'Although a man hear what limit he should observe in sacrifice, and how far he should recoil from burdensome superstitions, he will never make sufficient progress until he has conceived a right idea of God, regarding Him as one who possesses all things, and allots all things, and bestows them without price' (*Letters to Lucilius* 15.95.48). In fact, if one observes the reception of the text of Acts in history, one notices that it has

---

[43] 'Israel, the Church and the Gentiles', 1995, pp. 81–95.

[44] On the Lucan evaluation of the *Pax Romana*, W. M. Swartley dismisses H. Conzelmann and R. J. Cassidy, by showing that Luke does not model his εἰρήνη on that of the Empire (as the former thinks), nor set it up as a rival to the Empire (as the latter affirms), but goes beyond it, starting from an ideology of the eschatological jubilee ('Politics and Peace', 1983, pp. 18–37).

been read and brandished by theologians in search of consensus: Justin, Irenaeus, Tertullian.[45]

An open ending

The final scene of Acts (28. 16–31) illustrates, in its own way, this dimension of universality. For the moment, I will not linger over this crucial text in which Paul takes leave of his Jewish interlocutors and addresses to the readers an evaluation of his mission to Israel (vv. 25–8).[46] I will only mention the opening produced by the whole of the last scene that the author of Acts depicts before leaving his readers (28. 30–1): Paul received in his house 'all (πάντας) who came to him', announcing to them the Kingdom of God and the Lord Jesus Christ. It is not putting too much weight on πάντας, in my opinion, to say that this is an indication of the universality of the Church which Luke has in mind, a Church that is not in pure continuity with Israel. The book of Acts ends with the vision of this house of Paul where the recomposition of Christian identity is announced: it is a house, neither a Temple (place of roots) nor a Synagogue (place of refusal), but a new space, the space of the Empire, where Jews and Gentiles together are invited to unite the antiquity of the βασιλεία τοῦ θεοῦ with the newness of the Lord Jesus (28. 31). By reaching back to Adam (Luke 3. 38), the Lucan genealogy of Jesus already pointed, proleptically, to human universality.[47]

Flavius Josephus

Luke's ambition to reconcile Jewish particularism and Roman universalism is not without analogy in antiquity or even without precedent. At the same period, Flavius Josephus had the same ambition in writing the *Jewish War* and the *Jewish Antiquities*. The relationship between Luke and Josephus has produced an abundant literature, which has attempted to show the literary dependence of one on the other. I do not believe that any such dependence can be proved.[48] My interest is rather in recognizing

---

[45] A fine observation of this phenomenon of reading is found in C. K. Barrett, 'Christian Consensus', 1987, pp. 28–33.

[46] This whole scene is treated in chapter 10, pp. 205–30.

[47] M. C. Parsons and R. I. Pervo skilfully bring together Luke 3. 33–8 and Acts 17. 26–8 under the title of a universalist anthropology (*Rethinking*, 1993, pp. 96–101).

[48] The champion of this thesis was M. Krenkel, *Josephus und Lucas*, 1894. This thesis was rejected notably by H. Schreckenberg in 'Flavius Josephus', 1980, pp. 179–209.

the analogy between their apologetic purposes.[49] The points of contact are numerous.[50] (a) Both offer a definition of their religious movement by means of a historiographical work. (b) Both establish the great antiquity of their religion, a recognized criterion of prestige in Graeco-Roman culture. (c) Both claim the compatibility of their religious customs with the ethos of Roman society, allowing believers to combine their faith with allegiance to Rome. (d) Both present their God as all-powerful in the world, the supreme Providence, even in relation to the Roman authority. (e) Both wish to overcome the rupture produced between Jerusalem and Rome by the events of 70 (a more serious crisis in the case of Josephus), and to construct a work of conciliation.

The comparison can be refined even further. Like Luke, Josephus does not work only with the polarity Jerusalem–Rome. His system of thought articulates three points of reference: Jews – Romans – Greeks. For the Jewish writer, Rome constitutes a positive pole with regard to Judaism; the Greeks inherit the image of the enemy, and Josephus does not hesitate to say that they persecuted the Jews (which he does not say of the Romans). The *Against Apion* is particularly clear on this subject.[51] On the other hand, in the writings of Philo of Alexandria, Greek culture is viewed positively; it is the other peoples (λαοί) who compose the negative faction.[52] As for Luke, he makes of Paul's visit to Athens (Acts 17. 16–34) the meeting place of the Gospel and the prestigious Greek culture; but the result of the apostle's preaching is meagre and the reaction of the scholars grotesque (17. 32–4). In contrast, alongside the corrupt Roman officials (such as the governor Felix, Acts 24. 24–7), Luke is careful to depict the honest representatives of the Roman administration (Gallio in Acts 18; the tribune Lysias in Acts 21–3; the centurion Julius in Acts 27), or those interested by the new doctrine (Sergius Paulus in Acts 13; Festus in Acts 25). For Josephus, as for Luke, the future is Roman, not Greek.

---

[49] In this sense, see F. G. Downing, 'Ethical Pagan Theism', 1980–1, pp. 544–63; 'Common Ground', 1982, pp. 546–59; but especially G. E. Sterling's fine study, *Historiography and Self-Definition*, 1992.

[50] The inventory that follows is inspired by D. R. Edwards' work, 'Surviving the Web', 1991, pp. 179–201, see 201 and G. E. Sterling's *Historiography and Self-Definition*, 1992, pp. 365–9.

[51] The *Against Apion* is unsparing in its accusations against the Greeks, the mediocrity of their historiography (1.6–27) and the vulgarity of their religion (2.236–54). On the other hand, the Romans are gratified with flattering attributes: philanthropy (2.40), charity (2.57) and esteem for the Jews (2.63).

[52] This world vision is especially clear in *In Flaccum* and *Legatio ad Gaium*.

It should also be noted that the device of semantic ambivalence that has been detected in Luke is not without analogy in Josephus. The *Jewish War* offers a striking example of two speeches steeped in Hellenistic and Jewish categories.

The first speech is attributed to the author, under the walls of Jerusalem besieged by the troops of Titus. Josephus addresses himself to the besieged with a harangue linking in succession a Graeco-Roman section (5.362–74) and a Jewish section (5.375–419). The former advances rational arguments in favour of surrender and evokes Fortune (τύχη), which is on the side of Rome: 'Fortune is everywhere on their side (μεταβῆναι γὰρ πρὸς αὐτοὺς πάντοθεν τὴν τύχην) and God, who transfers the Empire from one nation to another, is now in Italy' (5.367); the second part rereads the history of Israel under the aegis of God as avenger. A mixed readership (Jewish and Roman) will be able to find itself here.

The other speech is in the mouth of Eleazar, just before the surrender of Masada. There is also here a first section that is clearly Stoic (call to freedom by the choice of a 'noble death': 7.323–36) preceding a Jewish section, where defeat is announced as a result of divine anger against the sins of the rebels of Masada (7.327–33). The difference from Luke is found in the succession of two rhetorical periods clearly stereotyped, whereas the device of semantic ambiguity consists in the simultaneity of the effects.

The God of Luke is not the God of Josephus

Clearly, the God of Luke is not the God of Josephus. He is not to be confused with πρόνοια. The relationship to Roman authority is more critical in Luke: the power of Rome is overcome by the βασιλεία τοῦ θεοῦ. The references to this at the beginning of the gospel (Luke 1. 33; 4. 43) and at the end of the Acts (28. 23, 31) encompass the whole of Luke's work. The God of Josephus, on the other hand, is much more clearly, with τύχη, on the side of Caesar.[53] But, on the whole, Luke and the Jewish historian appear as each a bearer of a religious movement that attempts to find a place in Roman society at the end of the first century. Their eminently positive relationship with the Empire leads them to Hellenize their traditions, in order to show them adequate to the religious aspirations of Roman society and to claim a place in the religious marketplace.

---

[53] Josephus' speech to those beseiged in Jerusalem should have been felt as blasphemous by the Jewish readers. For the τύχη (see also *B.J.* 2.390; 3.353; 5.412; 6.38), for Josephus, is a manifestation of the divine will and as such to be considered an instrument of God (cf. S. J. D. Cohen, 'Josephus, Jeremiah, and Polybius', 1982, pp. 366–81, see pp. 373–4.)

Inculturation: failure and success

Historically, what was the reception of these two efforts of inculturation?

In the Judaism of the first century, the position of Josephus will be challenged by Rabbinic isolationism; his ambition to reconcile Jews and Greeks seemed an accommodation in which Jewish identity was threatened with destruction. In the Christianity of the third generation, the Lucan proposal of integration into the *imperium romanum* is distinct from two other positions: submission to the political power, represented in 1 Peter, and aggressive confrontation with the world, represented by the Revelation of John.

In fact, at the moment when Judaeo-Hellenistic historiography comes to an end with Josephus, there begins with Luke the age of Christian historiography. The theological dream of Luke succeeded where that of Josephus failed; this 'success' depends on the nature of Christianity and the universality of the God it proclaims. But I would immediately add that the inculturation of Christianity in the Empire includes, according to Luke, two conditions that history has respected very poorly: one is the openness of Christianity to its religious heritage, Israel; the other is a critical acceptance of the world, made possible by that liberty of word (the παρρησία) which, in Luke's eyes, constitutes the mark of the witnesses led by the Spirit. However, we must recognize that historically the advancement of Christianity has been marked by anti-Judaism and by adaptation to the world.

Conclusion: integration of the opposing poles

The narrative construction of certain key characters in Acts, as well as the presence of a rhetorical device of amphibology from the pen of its author, allow us to conclude that there is a conscious use of double meaning in Luke. The device of semantic ambivalence that we have observed serves the theological aim of Luke–Acts; it also authorizes a reading nourished by the Jewish tradition in contact with the LXX as well as a reading oriented to the ideals of Graeco-Roman culture. It seems conclusively established that the amphibology translates, at the level of its language, Luke's theological project. This project is to integrate into the definition of Christianity, the two opposite poles, Jerusalem and Rome. Hence, in the eyes of the author of *ad Theophilum*, Christianity represents the place where the promises of salvation made to a particular people (Israel) come together with the universality of God that the Christian mission proclaims (in and thanks to the Empire). A rereading of the whole of

Luke–Acts would, I think, verify that the logic of Lucan thought, with its surprising theological choices, resides precisely in this ambition to configure Christian identity between Jerusalem and Rome.

Three consequences can be drawn from this fact. The first concerns the exegesis of Luke–Acts, the second the identity of the recipients of the writings, and the third the historiographical choices of the author.

The exegesis of Luke–Acts

The work of Luke *ad Theophilum* distinguishes itself by an effort to articulate what exegetes constantly separate: the offer of salvation to the nations and the respect for the particularity of Israel. Of this broad theological vision, Christianity from the end of the first century conserved only the first pole, adopting an admiring and pragmatic attitude to the Roman Empire; the writing to Theophilus represented for Christianity an excellent instrument of integration. However, the reading of Luke–Acts should not remain captive to this unbalanced reception of the work: Lucan theology is constructed in the tension between the two poles: Jerusalem and Rome. It remains as the testimony to a theological programme in which Christian identity is sought between the particular and the universal, its roots and its future, its tradition and its openness to the world.

The identity of the recipients of Luke–Acts

Who were the hearers/readers envisaged by Luke? The present analysis explains the difficulty felt by exegetes in defining a precise circle of recipients. An audience that was mainly Graeco-Roman is excluded by the importance given to the debate with Israel. On the other hand, the blackening of the figure of the Ἰουδαῖοι refutes the idea of a missionary appeal to the Jews. My argument has confirmed that the Lucan work implies a diversified readership (cultivated pagans, Christians, proselytes of the Diaspora), but we can now better understand why: for this readership interested in Christianity, the Lucan narrative uses as many Jewish as Hellenistic cultural elements. A 'mixed' proposal makes the Godfearers the public target of the work *ad Theophilum*; this circle represents, no doubt, an ideal image of the implied reader, but not an exclusive definition.[54] The amplitude of the Lucan narrative goes far beyond a strategy of persuasion directed only at this fringe of the Synagogue.

---

[54] This thesis is defended by J. B. Tyson in 'Jews and Judaism', 1995, pp. 19–38. In this same direction, restricting the readers of Luke–Acts to 'Christians with a Jewish background

The historiographical choices of Luke

In his theological programme of integration, Luke has enlarged the holiness of Israel to worldwide dimensions. A question arises: was the price to be paid for such an audacious theological aim too high? It led in effect to the alignment of Peter with Paul and Paul with Peter, in order to show the coherence of the Christian movement. In order to show the theological continuity between Israel and the Church, it led to bringing together the extremes of Paul and Judaism (13. 16–41; 22. 1–5; 23. 6; 26. 4–8; 28. 17); on the other hand, in order to serve the same programme of integration, the apostle to the Gentiles was drawn into the orbit of the Hellenistic religious mentality (17. 22–31). Thus, the Lucan portrait of the apostle conceals the ruptures established by Paul concerning the question of the Torah (e.g. Gal. 3. 10–13) and the question of Greek religiosity (1 Cor. 1. 18–25). Nevertheless, I would say that Pauline ruptures have not completely disappeared from Luke's writings; they have been taken within the understanding of the Torah, which is not abolished in its capacity to establish the identity of the people of God.[55]

This Lucan position regarding the Law confirms once again the theological programme that I have defined: on the one hand, the abandonment of the Torah surely signifies the apostasy from the covenant in the eyes of Jewish tradition, and the Lucan Paul cannot consent to this. On the other hand, if we can believe the sharp comments from the Gentile philosopher Celsus quoted by Origen,[56] 'to desert the Law of the fathers' is an impropriety for Graeco-Roman culture: Luke's Paul could not agree to this either. Maintaining the ancient Mosaic law (on the condition of re-centring it on the moral imperatives) therefore satisfies the programme of the Christianity configured between Jerusalem and Rome.

---

of thought', J. Jervell clearly does not give adequate attention to the implied audience, which the phenomenon of semantic ambivalence denotes ('Future of the Past', 1996, p. 125).

[55] M. Klinghardt defends the idea that the ritual law is commuted to moral law, allowing the evangelist to uphold the continued validity of the Torah in its capacity to define the people of God: *Gesetz*, 1988. Also see F. Bovon, 'La Loi', 1997, pp. 219–22.

[56] 'You have deserted the Law of your fathers', Celsus reproaches the converted Jews (Origen, *Against Celsus* 2.4); 'it is a duty to preserve what has been decided for the common good . . .; and it would be impiety to abandon the laws established in each locality from the beginning' (*ibid.*, 5.25).

5

THE GOD OF ACTS

What image of God does the author of Luke–Acts offer his readers?[1] In the small number of studies devoted to this question, the majority offer an analysis of the contents, enumerating the characteristics with which Luke adorns the God of his narrative: God as the agent of salvation history, Jesus as the mirror of the Father's action, the joy of God at the return of the lost, the God Peter discovers to be universal (Acts 10–11), the providential God of the sermon in Athens, and so forth.[2] Thus, there emerges the portrait of a God faithful to what he has promised, a God who moves toward a universal programme, and who is openly interventionist in his guidance of history.

However, this type of study, which consists in extracting from the Lucan text what it says about God, must be questioned in regard to its method. Marcel Dumais, in a recent account of the state of the research on the Acts of the Apostles, notes that an exhaustive portrait of the God of Luke remains to be painted, as research up to this point has focused on pneumatology, Christology, and the conception of history.[3] In my opinion, *such an enterprise cannot bypass the manner in which Luke, in his narrative, constructs a discourse about God.* For if one presses the text of Luke in search of his statements about God, one accumulates in effect a jumble of parables, visions, logia and trances, human discourse and angelic revelations. Semiotics, however, has taught us that form is meaning. Along

---

[1] A French version of this text appeared in: *L'Evangile exploré. Mélanges offerts à Simon Légasse*, A. Marchadour, ed., 1996, pp. 301–31. The present version of this chapter owes much to the criticisms and suggestions of the members of the Society of Biblical Literature seminar on Luke–Acts (Philadelphia, 1995), especially Robert Tannehill, to whom I owe sincere thanks.

[2] See G. Schneider, 'Gott und Christus', 1980, or *Theologe*, 1985, pp. 213–14; R. F. O'Toole, *Unity*, 1984; F. Bovon, 'God of Luke', 1995; R. L. Brawley, *Centering on God*, 1990, pp. 107–24; L. M. Maloney, *'All that God Had Done'*, 1991.

[3] 'On n'a pas encore vraiment élaboré une "théologie" lucanienne au sens premier du terme, c'est-à-dire un discours systématique sur la conception de Dieu dans l'œuvre de Luc' (M. Dumais, 'Bilan et orientations', 1995, pp. 328–9).

similar lines, narratology teaches us to distinguish the narrative authorities a narrator uses to communicate his information to readers. I shall explore this narratological approach, dealing particularly with the way the author of Acts constructs his image of God. Several works have opened up this approach.[4] How does the narrator express, throughout the narrative, the action and the word of God? How does he communicate what he knows of God and how does he make this knowledge known to his readers?

I shall proceed in two steps. First, taking a broad overview of the entire book of Acts, my aim is to observe the Lucan discourse on God; one will note that a theologically coherent narrative strategy, hardly noticed until recently, rigorously controls the statements about God in Acts and distributes them according to two quite distinct modes. Second, adopting a more syntagmatic perspective, my intention is to recognize what functions the divine interventions fulfil in the plot of the narrative; the typology that emerges from the analysis enables the identification of a triple function: programmatic, performative and interpretative. The conclusion deals with the God of Luke.

Two languages to speak of 'God'

One of the most abrupt and unpredictable turning points in the Pauline mission takes place just after the Jerusalem council. Paul has begun what we refer to as his second missionary journey (Acts 15. 36). He is travelling through Cilicia with Silas, when, one after the other, three events force him to change his itinerary: the Holy Spirit prevents (κωλυθέντες) them from going into Asia (16. 6); the Spirit of Jesus does not allow (οὐκ εἴασεν) them to go to Bithynia (16. 7); and, in a night vision, Paul sees a Macedonian pleading for him to come and help (16. 9). For the reader of the book of Acts, familiar with the language of the Septuagint, each of these interventions bears the signature of God: the intervention of the Holy Spirit (or the Spirit of Jesus: the only occurrence in Acts) and the vision are part of the traditional theophanic code. The decoding of these theophanic signs poses no problem for the reader who attributes to God the origin of the coming of the Spirit at Pentecost (2. 1–11). The only surprising thing is the rapid succession of the events, which signals an unusual pressure of God on human history.

---

[4] I refer to the statistical studies of R. L. Mowery, 'Direct Statements', 1990, pp. 196–211; 'God the Father', 1990, pp. 124–32; 'Lord, God, and Father', 1995, pp. 82–101, as well as to the contribution of K. Löning, 'Gottesbild', 1992, pp. 88–117. The clearest analysis of this narratological perspective can be found in J.-N. Aletti, *Quand Luc raconte*, 1998, pp. 19–68.

Just after the mention of this threefold redirecting of the Pauline itinerary, the first of the 'we-passages' (16. 10–17) starts, naming the invisible author of the three interventions and deciphering the underlying intention: 'we immediately tried to cross over to Macedonia, being convinced that God had called us to proclaim the good news to them' (16. 10).

This narrative sequence clearly illustrates that an investigation of the image of God in the book of Acts requires observing these two very different modes of presentation: on the one hand, explicit discourse where God is directly named (16. 10) and, on the other hand, implicit discourse where God manifests himself through theophanic mediations whose code is known to the readers (16. 6–7, 9). Both constitute the theo-logy of the book of Acts.

These two modes that Luke borrows to speak of God conform to the religious language of his time. On the one hand, for the Jewish tradition, as for the Graeco-Roman culture of the first century, the God of heaven uses intermediaries when he wants to reach people. On the other hand, Luke knows how to unfold a discourse in which God is explicitly named and called by his titles: θεός, κύριος, πατήρ. What relationship does the narrator establish between these two forms of language to speak of God (one implicit and the other explicit)?

Implicit language

The implicit language corresponds to the theophanies of the Greek Bible, the Septuagint.

God transmits his messages through angels sent to the apostles (1. 10–11; 5. 19–20), to Philip (8. 26), to Peter (12. 7–10), to Herod (12. 23), to Cornelius (10. 3–6, 22, 30–2; 11. 13–14), to Paul (27. 23–4; cf. 23. 9). God gives visions or trances to Stephen (7. 55–6), to Peter (10. 10–16; 11. 5–10), to Paul (9. 3–8, cf. 22. 6–11 and 26. 13–18; 16. 9). These visions can be apparitions of Jesus (1. 3–11; 7. 56; 18. 9–10; 22. 6–11; cf. 9. 17). There are also double visions, highly valued by the Greeks and Romans (9. 10–12; 10. 1–23). The casting of lots can also signify God's action (1. 26), but more frequently the action of the Spirit addressing the apostles (2. 1–11), Philip (8. 29, 39), Cornelius (10. 44–6; 11. 15), the community (13. 2), Peter (10. 19–20; 11. 12) or Paul (16. 6–7). We also witness wonders: earthquakes (4. 31; 16. 26), miraculous deliverances from prison (5. 19–20; 12. 6–10; 16. 26), rescue from the storm (27. 9–44). The power of the apostles also signals the divine when they heal, perform exorcisms, resuscitate the dead, punish those guilty of fraud and escape from vipers.[5]

---

[5] Healings and exorcisms: 3. 1–10: 9. 17–18; 14. 8–10; 16. 16–18; 28. 7–8. Raisings of the dead: 9. 36–42; 20. 7–12; Punitive acts: 5. 1–11; 13. 9–12; 19. 13–17. Paul escapes from

One witnesses an extraordinary diversity of means of divine intervention. Luke, in skilful management of the vocabulary, applies an adequate language for each occurrence.[6] However, one should notice that, from Luke's point of view, the greatest intervention of God in history is surely the resurrection of Jesus. It not only overshadows his narrative, but also brings the thaumaturgical power of the apostles with it: 'Jesus Christ that you crucified, God has raised from the dead' (4. 10; 2. 26–7; 3. 14–15; 13. 29–30; etc.).

This inventory of divine interferences calls for three remarks.

First, God's interventions in such remarkable diversity do not have their equal in the gospel of Luke, except at the beginning and the end: the infancy narrative (Luke 1–2) and the paschal cycle (Luke 24).[7] As soon as Jesus arrives on the scene (Luke 2. 40), he monopolizes the divine. Appearances of angels, trances and irruptions of the Spirit are reserved for him alone.[8] This impressive Christological concentration of the gospel makes way in Acts for a theology offering more balance between the poles of Christology (the resurrection kerygma and miracles), pneumatology (the launch of missions) and theo-logy (God as the agent of the history of salvation).

Second, the divine interventions are not uniformly distributed in the flow of the narrative. There is a concentration of ecstatic manifestations or collective wonders in the first section of the book (Acts 1–7), while, as the narrative reaches its culmination, the divine materializes essentially in favour of individuals, especially Paul (18. 9–10; 22. 6–11, 17–21; 23. 9; 26. 13–18; 27. 23–4; 28. 3–6). One major exception to this is the rescue at sea (27. 9–44). Does this development mean that the closer the narrative gets to the author's time, the more he has conformed the manifestation of the divine to what characterizes the period of Christianity he addresses? Whatever the case, the most spectacular epiphanies, the ones that ignited the community, are confined to the 'golden age', that idyllic period of the Church at

a viper: 28. 3–6. Healing summaries: 2. 43; 5. 12–13; 6. 8; 14. 3; 19. 11–12; 28. 9. Acts links miracles to Christology (they concretize the power of the 'name of the Lord'), rather than to theo-logy.

[6] The care with which Luke chooses a technical terminology is manifest, for example, in the diversity of his vocabulary of visions: ὁράω, ὅραμα, θεωρέω, ἀκούω, ἔκστασις, φῶς, φωνή. On the other hand, he avoids ὄναρ and ὄνειρος (dream).

[7] Trances and epiphanies abound at the beginning of the gospel: Luke 1. 11–20, 26–38, 41, 64, 67; 2. 9–14, 27 and visions return in force in the paschal cycle: Luke 24. 4–7, 31, 36–51.

[8] The only exception is the Transfiguration which narrativizes the ecstatic visions of a group of disciples (Luke 9. 28–36).

Jerusalem which Luke so admires (2. 1–11; 4. 31; 5. 15; 7. 55–6; 8. 39).[9]

Third, Luke is not reluctant to requisition for his narrative all available forms of the divine, in order to impress and convince his readers.[10] He varies the divine manifestations, sometimes according to the LXX, and at other times following Graeco-Roman tastes. However, it would be a mistake to conclude that this is opportunism. Independently of the propensity of popular Hellenistic faith for the marvellous (see the Greek novel), the Simon episode (8. 9–12, 18–24), as well as the narrative of Bar-Jesus (13. 6–11), signal that Luke lived in a world where magical practice and religious competition had set off an open debate about the proper handling of the divine. The author of Acts, for his part, clearly battles against syncretism.[11] The decisive question then becomes the interpretation of the theophanic signs. It is to this task that the author of Acts applies himself.

Explicit language

Alongside the implicit language in the narrative runs an explicit language that names God: θεός, κύριος, πατήρ.[12] As the subject of a verbal phrase, θεός appears sixty-one times in the Acts, κύριος nine times and πατήρ once.[13]

How does Luke use these divine titles as subjects? A first indication immediately attracts our attention: the massive presence of the titles in the speeches (fifty-two out of sixty-one times for θεός; four of the nine occurrences of κύριος). The explicit language for God is thus primarily a matter of speech rather than narrative style. It belongs to the rhetorical aim of the Lucan speeches, which is to interpret the action of the narrative to his readers. But to go further in the analysis: what can be said of the uses of the divine titles as subjects in narrative? The answer is enlightening: God never appears as a figure of the story world, but only in words attributed

---

[9] I shall deal later with this development of manifestations of the Spirit through the narrative of Acts, which differentiates the pneumatic experiences of the 'golden age' (Acts 1–8) and the inspiration of individuals by the Spirit (second part of Acts): see pp. 110–13.

[10] This has already been noted by F. Bovon, 'God of Luke', 1995, pp. 68–9.

[11] See my article 'Magic and Miracles', forthcoming. Luke's critical perspective on polytheism and magic has been studied by B. Wildhaber, *Paganisme populaire*, 1987, and H. J. Klauck, 'Paphos', 1994, pp. 93–108 and *Magie und Heidentum*, 1996.

[12] I shall leave aside the appended titles (ὕψιστος: 7. 48; 16. 17) which do not affect the basis of the analysis.

[13] For an inventory of these, consult R. L. Mowery, 'Direct Statements', 1990, and 'Lord, God, and Father', 1995. See also K. Löning, 'Gottesbild', 1992, pp. 95–6.

to someone.[14] Except for a few rare occasions, the narrator never directly ascribes the action of the narrative to God. In other words, God becomes a subject only in the words of a character.

It is the angel who tells Peter, struck by the vision of the menagerie descended from heaven: 'What God has made clean, you must not call profane' (10. 15). It is Peter who recognizes the mark of God in his escape from prison, first for himself ('the Lord has sent his angel and rescued me', 12. 11), then in front of the community ('[he] described for them how the Lord had brought him out of prison', 12. 17). It is Paul who says to the high priest Ananias who is going to strike him: 'it is you whom God is going to strike' (23. 3). God is designated as active subject solely in the frame of direct discourse (1. 7; 10. 15, 28; 11. 18; 12. 11; 23. 3) or in an indirect discourse introduced by a verb of communication (12. 17; 14. 27; 15. 4, 12; 21. 19)[15] or, at the most, when the narrator describes the inner conviction of a character (16. 10).[16] The only exceptions, if we set aside the introductory formula of a quotation from Scripture (13. 47), concern two summaries (2. 47 and 19. 11) and two ambiguous mentions of κύριος that could be Christological (16. 14; 21. 19).[17] This is too little evidence to contradict the overwhelming Lucan tendency to refer to God in the nominative position only in words exchanged between two characters in the story world. As R. L. Mowery has shown, the same language game takes place in the relationship between the Passion–resurrection in the gospel (Luke 22–4), which never names the divine instigator of the events, and the speeches in Acts, in which Peter and Paul constantly attribute to God the raising of Christ from the dead.[18] In the same way, Ananias has to intervene in order for Saul to hear in Damascus of 'the Lord Jesus who appeared to you on your way' (9. 17), just as Barnabas has to mediate in order that the Jerusalem community may learn 'how on the road [Saul] had seen the Lord, who had spoken to him' (9. 27).[19]

---

[14] With K. Löning, 'Von Gott ist immer nur die Rede zwischen den Figuren der erzählten' ('Gottesbild', 1992, pp. 95–6).

[15] ἀναγγέλλω (14. 27; 15. 4), ἐξηγέομαι (15. 12; 21. 19), διηγέομαι (12. 17).

[16] συμβιβάζοντες ὅτι (16. 10).

[17] In 16. 14 it is not certain if κύριος designates God (see v. 14a) or Jesus (v. 15b). It is the same in 18. 9, but there κύριος looks back to Jesus by way of v. 8.

[18] 'Lord, God, and Father', 1995, pp. 89–101. Luke designates God indirectly by a divine passive (ἠγέρθη, 24. 6, 34), by the theological δεῖ (24. 7, 26, 44) or by scriptural reference (24. 46). On the other hand, the explicit mention of God as the author of the raising of Jesus becomes a stereotype in the speeches in Acts (2. 24, 32; 3. 15, 22, 26; 4. 10; 5. 30; 10. 40; 13. 30, 33–4, 37; 17. 31; 26. 8). From the same author: 'Divine Hand', 1991, pp. 558–75.

[19] Did Saul, thrown to the ground at Damascus, see Christ? The narrator is quite discreet on this: Saul is dazzled by a light and hears a voice (9. 3–4); only Barnabas will put a name to the vision. For a further reading of Acts 9, see chapter 9: 'Saul's conversion (Acts 9; 22; 26)'.

No further examples are necessary. The point is clear: naming God is not so obvious; only the word of the witness can designate the author of the events that direct history.

Engendering the word

What is to be deduced from this sequence 'implicit statement/explicit speech'? Those familiar with the work *ad Theophilum* will remember the sequence of action and speech that is customary for this author: the event comes first, then the word which elucidates its meaning (Acts 2. 1–13 and 2. 14–36). This response is correct, but inadequate. Why precisely this preference for the order act/word? In the case that concerns us, it is difficult not to see in this relationship a trajectory proposed to the reader. Is not this passing from the implicit to the explicit, from the event to the word which awakens meaning, from the ambiguity of history to the word which names God, the scenario to which the Lucan narration invites us? In the movement of the story as it returns upon itself in order to name what it has just shown, there is an engendering of the theological word. Following the characters of the story the reader is called to identify, in the opacity of what took place, a divine logic of salvation.

In this manner, the story fulfils a teaching, not to say catechetical function, if one thinks of the most excellent Theophilus (Luke 1. 4). To follow the story, with its rhythm of veiling and unveiling, leads the reader into the process of decoding the theological meaning of the history that he/she lives, in order to apply to her/his own world (the world of the reader) the rules which govern the performance of the characters in the story world. One must read (the story recounted by Luke) in order to learn to read (one's own story). In Ricœur's terms, the catechetical function of the story occurs in the passage from *mimesis II* (the configuration of action in the story world) to *mimesis III* (the refiguration of the plot in the reader's world)[20] or, in other words, when the plot of the narrative intersects and informs the plot of the life of the reader. To read the work *ad Theophilum* is to learn to name God.

Neither Homer nor Genesis

The examination of the language required to speak of 'God' in the book of Acts reveals a systematic control on the part of the narrator, who chooses narrative language when God manifests himself by mediation,

[20] P. Ricœur, *Time and Narrative*, I, 1984, pp. 64–87.

which conceals him, and who chooses discursive language when God is mentioned by name as an agent of history. In the technical terms of narrative analysis: the implicit language is reserved for the narrator (extra-diegetic authority), while the explicit language characterizes the speech of the characters of the story (intra-diegetic authorities).[21]

This division of language lays out the problematic to which the analysis of the image of God in Acts belongs. Evidently, Luke is reluctant to describe a God metamorphosing and mixing with the affairs of people incognito, in the style of Genesis or the *Odyssey*. However, beyond respect for the holiness of God, which rejects vulgar anthropomorphisms, what role does Luke give to the discourse about God in the frame of his narrative? How does the explicit discourse that names God participate in and advance the plot of Acts? In order to deal with this problematic it is essential to proceed case by case, following the function that the statements about God exercise in the narrative. This is the subject of the inquiry.

How are the history of God and human history articulated?

It has recently been affirmed, and not without reason, that the central theme of Acts is the 'plan of God'.[22] Speaking of God in the book of Acts consists of asking how God intervenes to direct history according to his plan. How are the history of God and human history, or if one prefers, divine will and human freedom, articulated in Acts?

From the point of view of the plot of the narrative, divine interventions can have three distinct functions.[23] In some cases, they precede events and take on a *programmatic* function (in the form of a vision, a dream or an oracle), for example, when Paul is led off to Macedonia (16. 6–10). On other occasions, they exercise a *performative* function, at the moment that God intervenes by saving, punishing, or guiding the course of the events, for example, the Damascus road incident (9. 1–19a). They can also fulfil an *interpretative* function, when they are situated after the events in order to indicate their meaning or to justify them, for example, Stephen's vision (7. 55–6). I shall show how Luke artistically combines in the composition of his narrative the three functions, which together enunciate the irruption of the divine into history.

---

[21] Readers interested in the differentiation of narrative authorities should consult D. Marguerat and Y. Bourquin, *How to Read*, 1999, pp. 141–9.

[22] J. T. Squires, *Plan of God*, 1993.

[23] This taxonomy of functions has been inspired by the illuminating book of J.-N. Aletti: *Quand Luc raconte*, 1998, pp. 21–26.

The programmatic function: God precedes history

The programmatic statement, which announces and anticipates what follows in the narrative, is a narrative device of which Luke is fond; the best-known examples are the promise of the Risen One in 1. 8 and the prediction of the destiny of Paul in 9. 15–16. This type of proleptic formulation concretizes the notion of divine guidance in history that is so important for Luke.[24] The programmatic statement can be revealed in a dream, as in 23. 11, where, by a night vision, the Lord informs Paul of his future: 'For just as you have testified for me in Jerusalem, so you must bear witness also in Rome.' It can be by means of Agabus' prediction: 'This is the way the Jews in Jerusalem will bind the man who owns this belt and will hand him over to the Gentiles' (21. 11). This is again a trait that links Acts with the Greek novel. As has been shown by the study of Suzanne Saïd, dreams and predictions can fulfil a proleptic function in the novel, either by anticipation (Chariton, Achilles Tatius) or programmatically (Xenophon of Ephesus).[25]

With regard to discourse about God, three programmatic announcements (5. 38–9, 16. 10 and 27. 23–5) merit consideration: each one is attached to explicit language.

The 'Gamaliel principle'

In the Lucan narrative, the programmatic statement functions according to what, with Jean-Noël Aletti, I call the 'Gamaliel principle'.[26] Gamaliel was the Pharisee who persuaded the Sanhedrin not to mistreat the apostles by proposing the following rule, 'let them alone; because if this plan or undertaking is of human origin, it will fail; but if it is of God, you will not be able to overthrow them...' (5. 38b–39a).[27] But is there any evidence that allows one to verify that the work of the apostles is indeed 'of God'? Only the narrative of their actions allows verification that their works will not disappear and this is precisely why Luke indissolubly links the description of the plans of God with the life of the witnesses. *The Lucan narrative becomes the place of proof, the irreplaceable medium of theological verification offered to its readers.* Aletti states:

[24] The notion of providence in Hellenistic historiography and Luke has been examined by J. T. Squires, *Plan of God*, 1993, esp. pp. 103–54.

[25] 'Oracles et devins', 1997, pp. 398–403.

[26] J.-N. Aletti, *Quand Luc raconte*, 1998, pp. 58–9.

[27] This rule corresponds to a Hellenistic 'topos' as pointed out by J. T. Squires, *Plan of God*, 1993, p. 176 and note 109.

The reader must not minimize the importance of the principle of discernment, because it comes precisely from a man who does not follow Jesus. And doubtless one should add that this principle (I) renders verification necessary in some way and hence the continuation of the narrative; (II) permits the narrator not to intervene in order to support or to justify the facts; their exposition itself will be the most powerful of proofs.[28]

The interest in the Gamaliel principle, for present purposes, is that it links the recognition of the divine will with the destiny of the group who witness to Jesus. *Anyone who wants to discern the ways of God only has a narrative recounting the joys and more often the misfortunes of a group of believers. No other mirror is offered.* The reading of the narrative of Acts becomes, when one applies the Gamaliel principle, the place to perceive the ways of God. Only the Lucan narrative, as it moves forward, teaches the reader to what 'work' the Holy Spirit calls Paul and Barnabas (13. 2), or how the prophecy of Agabus will come to pass (21. 11).

The programmatic statements disseminated throughout the narrative orient the reading, functioning as 'advance' signals planted by the narrator to guide the decoding of the narrative. The prolepsis of Acts 16. 10 will help to make clear how such a signal works.

The product of a group

Acts 16. 10 belongs to the episode cited above, where two interventions of the Spirit, barring the way of Paul and Silas, precede the vision of the Macedonian's call for the help of the apostles (16. 6–9). The decoding of these divine interventions or, if one prefers, the passage from an implicit language about God to an explicit one is the product of the group in which the narrator includes himself, the group identified as 'we';[29] its interpretative work finally redirects the missionary itinerary toward Macedonia, for *'we immediately tried to cross over to Macedonia, being convinced that God had called us to proclaim the good news to them'* (16. 10). The programmatic value of this proleptic declaration cannot be doubted: the call for help by the Macedonian is understood as coming from God in order to change the direction of the diffusion of the Word toward the West. The evangelization of Macedonia begins, preparing that of Greece (Acts 17–18).

---

[28] J.-N. Aletti, *Quand Luc raconte*, 1998, pp. 58–9.
[29] I have discussed the 'we-passages' in chapter 1, pp. 24–5.

But, how can this interpretation be verified? The narrator does not require the reader to wait long: a few verses later, in Philippi, the preaching of the apostles meets the attentive ears of Lydia who '*was listening to us... The Lord opened her heart to listen eagerly to what was said by Paul*' (16. 14). A little later, the miraculous deliverance of Peter and Silas from prison (16. 25–6) confirms that the apostles' work is truly 'from God'. The Gamaliel principle has worked.

Eucharist in the storm

The term θεός appears four times in the narrative of the storm (Acts 27), whereas κύριος is absent. The fourth occurrence comes during the eucharist-type meal that Paul organizes on the ship (v. 35). The three other uses are concentrated in verses 23–5, where Paul communicates to his companions what an angel of the Lord revealed to him during a vision: 'Do not be afraid, Paul; you must stand before Caesar; and, indeed, God has granted safety to all those who are sailing with you' (v. 24).

This sequence plays a decisive role in the narrative. After the unfortunate decision of the crew (against Paul's advice! vv. 9–12) and the assault of the tempest (vv. 13–20), the apostle is presented as the (only) true hero of the narrative. 'Intimate with God and visited by him, Paul is not discouraged but inhabited by an unalterable confidence; he knows the future of things and people perfectly, reassuring his shipmates and always giving good advice. Paul dominates the storm rather than becoming its victim.'[30] This is true, but notice *how* the hero Paul is constructed by the narrator: through a speech act. Paul, in effect, is the only character in chapter 27 to act by word:[31] the centurion Julius protects his prisoner, the captain decides, the sailors panic, and the soldiers are overwhelmed by the situation. It is only to Paul that Luke gives, in three cases, words.

The first discourse (v. 10) is a warning of imminent disaster: 'the voyage will be with danger and much heavy loss'. The second reassures (vv. 21b–25), but depends on a word that is an angel's, not his own: 'For last night there stood before me an angel of the God to whom I belong, and whom I worship, and he said...' (v. 23). In this formulation, the double motif vision/hearing attests the revealed character of the apostle's knowledge. A theological reading of the event unfolds, which not only signals that the journey remains under the divine δεῖ ('*you must* stand before Caesar'),

---

[30] J. Zumstein, 'Apôtre comme martyr', 1991, p. 203.

[31] Paul's statement is signalled by speech verbs: παραινέω and λέγων (vv. 9b–10a), λέγω (v. 21), παραινέω (v. 22), παρακαλέω (vv. 33–4), λέγω (v. 35).

but also predicts its happy ending. This declaration recurs in the third intervention (vv. 33b–34) and will be concretized with the symbolic act of the meal on the morning of the landing in Malta, anticipating the giving of thanks, the εὐχαριστεῖν τῷ θεῷ (v. 35) and the end of the drama in the favourable result of the journey.

The narrative function of the Pauline discourse in the economy of Acts 27 is now clear. Coming after the dramatic report of the tempest and its consequence, the despair of the passengers (v. 20), the explicit language about God has a double effect, both revelatory and programmatic. *Revelatory* in the sense that Paul names God as the ultimate (and paradoxical) agent of the event. *Programmatic* in the sense that the apostle interprets the rescue of the ship as a gracious act belonging to the plan of God for his messenger. The divine origin of the rescue is unveiled nowhere else; but the reader of the Septuagint will verify the appropriateness of it by appealing to the theme of the Creator, master of the waters, while the reader of Graeco-Roman culture will remember the classic motif of divine protection of the innocent (the story of the viper (28. 3–6) and the brief mention of the Dioscuri (28. 11c) will justify this).[32]

Conclusion: in Acts, the proleptic announcement of the plan of God by means of a vision or a prediction serves to programme the theological reading of the narrative. Following the 'Gamaliel principle' (5. 38–9), it assigns the reader the course of day-by-day history as a place to discover and to celebrate the ways of God.

The performative function: God redirects history

Alongside the programmatic function is the performative function: the God of the book of Acts is an interventionist God. Luke describes him as continually breaking into the narrative with miracles, shaking up his community by sending the Spirit, opening prison doors, converting the persecutor of Christ, saving his messengers from all dangers, blinding charlatan magicians, striking Herod, saving the 276 passengers on a ship so that his messenger can arrive safely, and so forth. From the beginning to the end of the narrative, the God of Acts removes obstacles that hinder

---

[32] Concerning both the Jewish and Hellenistic concepts at work in the narrative of Acts 27, see pp. 72–3 and 276–8. In addition to the classic references to Jonah and Psalms, Rabbinic literature also links storms to the wrath of God, for example, in the miraculous liberation of Rabbi Gamaliel (*bBab. Mes.* 59b) or in relating the fright of Titus rocked by the waves on his return to Rome after the devastation of Jerusalem (*Aboth Rabbi Nathan* 7). I also recall that, in the Graeco-Roman pantheon, the celestial twins Castor and Pollux have the reputation of being the protectors of seafaring people, guardians of truth, and punishers of perjurers.

the success of his plan: the spreading of the Word.[33] However, as we have already seen,[34] God's protection does not shield his envoys from failure, humiliation, flagellation and martyrdom. The route of the missionaries is a 'via dolorosa'.

On several occasions, this route will be modified by the interventions of the God who redirects history. I have already established this with reference to the episode of the Macedonian (16. 6–10). I shall now deal with it in the light of three other texts: Acts 8. 26–40, Acts 9 and Acts 10–11. These will allow a closer focus on the Lucan procedure which we have already glimpsed: the (explicit) discourse of the witness always follows the (implicit) language of the narrator. *The word of the witness is an after-word, which decodes the intervention of God and names its author.* What can be said about this after-word?

A God who arranges and withdraws

The encounter of Philip and the Ethiopian eunuch (8. 26–40) is arranged by God: the angel of the Lord orders Philip to take the road from Jerusalem to Gaza, which is deserted (v. 26). Then (the second initiative) the Spirit tells him: '*Go over to the chariot and join it*' (v. 29). The reader is thus prepared for the miraculously foreseen meeting, whose outcome will follow the plan of God. Finally, the mysterious snatching away of Philip by the Spirit confirms this point of view (v. 39): 'The Spirit of the Lord snatched Philip away; the eunuch saw him no more.' The evangelist Philip has played the role God assigned to him: he can now disappear from the sight of the eunuch as well as from the narrative of Acts.[35]

This text has one striking particularity: at the beginning of the story there are two initial directions (vv. 26 and 29) and at the end a final vanishing act (v. 39), which frame the encounter. Between the two, where the essence of the story takes place (the catechism of the eunuch, his request and baptism), there is no trace of divine intervention. What does this structure signify? There are two answers.

First, the theophanic interventions provoke the incredible: a eunuch, excluded from the cult according to Deuteronomy 23. 2 LXX, is welcomed

---

[33] Remember, in my view, the theme of the book of Acts is neither the Spirit, nor the relationship with Israel (even if this question is one of identity for Lucan Christianity), but rather the expansion of the Word in the world. See pp. 37–8.

[34] See pp. 38–40.

[35] On the role played by the the eunuch in the missionary strategy that underlies the plot of Acts, see: E. Dinkler, 'ανηρ ΑΙΘΙΟΥ', 1975; C. J. Martin, 'Function', 1986; F. Scott Spencer, *Philip*, 1992, pp. 128–87.

in his desire to understand the Scriptures and to join the covenant people through baptism.[36] The massive divine manipulation (vv. 26, 29) attests that the violation of Mosaic legislation is not Christian impertinence, but the work of God.

Second, once he is in the eunuch's presence, Philip acts alone. While it is true that he is overshadowed by the injunction of the Spirit (v. 29), which signifies his empowering to witness,[37] he nevertheless acts alone. No light, no angel inspires his announcement of the 'good news of Jesus' (v. 35). No trance dictates his decision to baptize the eunuch. Philip's initiative as witness is his own. His preaching relies (v. 35) on the text of Isaiah 53. 7–8 which has just been quoted, but he witnesses on his own authority. *In Acts, God never dictates their preaching to the messengers.* His pressure on events can be forceful, but the word of the missionaries is a matter of their own responsibility.[38]

To summarize: the theophanic interventions create a totally unexpected framework in which the responsibility of the witness plays a role as he interprets the event and names its author. It all happens as if the God of Acts, having organized the encounter by supernatural means, withdraws to leave space for the witness. *History becomes salvation history only when men and women accept the role God indicates for them. But this never removes their responsibility in word or in witnessing action.* The pericope of the meeting between Peter and Cornelius and the conversion of Paul on the Damascus road also fit into this perspective.

The enormity of God's choices

In composing the narrative of the encounter of Peter and Cornelius (Acts 10. 1 – 11. 18; 15. 7–11), Luke has pushed his narrative art to its highest standard of excellence. This can be measured by the density of narrative techniques applied in the sequence: the intertwining of the paths of two persons, realized by means of intersecting discourses (10. 1–33); the visionary encounter anticipating the face-to-face encounter

[36] The ostracizing of eunuchs for reasons of ritual impurity (Lev. 21. 20; 22. 24) is confirmed by Flavius Josephus (*A.J.* 4.290–1) and Philo (*De Spec. Leg.* 1.324–5). Hope for their inclusion into the eschatological community is present in Isa. 56. 3–8 and Wis. 3. 14–15; Acts 8 belongs to this development.

[37] On the Spirit as empowering for witness in Acts, see my reflections in chapter 6: 'The work of the Spirit'.

[38] This is not the case in apocalyptic literature, where the word of the witness/seer is legitimated by the process of dictation: see 4 Ezra 14. 37–49; 2 *En.* 22. 28, and the messages entrusted to Enoch the 'scribe of justice' (*1 En.* 12. 4; 15. 1). Also Rev. 1. 19; 10. 4; 14. 13; 19. 9; 21. 5; 22. 19.

of Peter and Cornelius (10. 5–6, 22); Peter's progressive awareness of the meaning of the event evidenced by the four times that he speaks out (10. 28–30; 10. 34–43; 11. 5–17; 15. 7–11).[39]

This excellence in the construction of the narrative can be explained by the role of the pericope in the plot of the book: God lets Peter know, by a vision which mixes all sorts of animals, that he is pulling down the centuries-old barrier between the pure and the impure (10. 13–15). To legitimate the outrageousness of the divine choice, which opens the covenant to Gentiles, Luke is not reluctant to refer to supernatural means: a vision (10. 3), a trance (10. 10), a message of the Spirit (10. 19) and the descent of the Spirit himself (10. 44, 46), all of these being necessary to shatter Peter's resistance.[40]

The narrative sequence of Acts 10. 1 – 11. 18 should be compared with the narrative of Saul's conversion in chapter 9, along with its rereadings in chapters 22 and 26. The same narrative technique is at work in the construction of the story: interweaving (9. 10–17), double vision (9. 10–12), successive readings of the event by Paul (9. 20; 22. 6–21; 26. 12–23).[41]

However, bringing these two sequences together is even more necessary for reasons of thematic affinity. On both sides:

> an unheard of and staggering choice by God: Saul the enemy of Christ; Cornelius the non-Jew;
> a theophanic manifestation with no immediate follow-up, leaving the individual stunned (9. 9) or confused (10. 17);
> a new initiative of God in the sending of messengers (9. 17; 10. 17b–20) commissioned by a vision (9. 10–12; 10. 5–8);
> resistance to the divine initiative arriving where it was unexpected: from Ananias and Peter, representatives of the believing community (9. 10, 13–14; 10. 17);
> an integration into the community of the marginal person chosen by God.

[39] On narrative construction in Acts 10–11, I refer to the now classic study of R. C. Tannehill, *Narrative Unity*, II, 1990, pp. 128–45. The procedure of narrative redundancy has been studied by R. D. Witherup, 'Cornelius', 1993; C. Lukasz, *Evangelizzazione*, 1993; W. S. Kurz, 'Variant Narrators', 1997.

[40] The eloquent study of B. R. Gaventa, *From Darkness to Light*, 1986, pp. 107–25, deserves to be read concerning this chapter of Acts.

[41] On the rereading of Acts 9 in Acts 22 and 26, see chapter 10: 'Saul's conversion (Acts 9; 22; 26)'. The structural resemblance between Acts 9 and Acts 10–11 has been recognized by W. S. Kurz, *Reading Luke-Acts*, 1993, p. 131, and R. D. Witherup, 'Cornelius', 1993, pp. 62–4. Also J.-N. Aletti, *Quand Luc raconte*, 1998, pp. 42–8.

The two conclusions move toward different goals:

> Saul's vocation is revealed to Ananias, but not to Saul (9. 15–
> 16); it will be unfolded by the narrative; whereas Peter draws
> the inference of Cornelius' incorporation in the Church before
> the Jerusalem council (15. 7–11);
> Saul knows the reversal of his destiny and the persecutor be-
> comes the persecuted (9. 19b–30), while Peter's initiative is
> confirmed by the descent of the Spirit (10. 44–8).

In both cases, God turns history around by a surprising choice, which has to overcome the resistance of the Church and whose consequences for the rest of the plot are immense. As F. Bovon has said, 'Luke thus designs a new aspect of God: . . . we see constituted a God of all. The God of the fathers ceases to be the God of direct descendants only . . . Luke is the only one to express this truth *in narrative style*.'[42] But how does this theological reading work? How are these astonishing events interpreted as the coming of God to each and every person?

Here again, the passage from the implicit to the explicit is assured by the discourse of the witness. I shall show this first in Acts 10–11, before noting the presence of a similar scenario in Acts 9; 22; 26.

10.13–14   Upon the order 'Kill *and eat*', Peter answers with a pious refusal.
10. 15, 17 The declaration of the celestial voice 'What God has *made clean,
            you must not call profane*' does not convince Peter but plunges
            him into confusion.
10. 22   The messengers of Cornelius declare that a holy angel revealed
            to them that they would hear the ῥήματα (words and events)
            from Peter (differently v. 5!); but which ones?

Peter's words will progressively interpret the event:

10. 28   Peter, discovering (εὑρίσκει v. 27b) a large crowd, applies his vision
            about eating to human relations: 'God has shown *me that I should
            not call anyone profane or unclean.*'
10. 34   Peter broadens the concept of the universality of God to whoever
            practises righteousness in any nation: '*I truly understand that God
            is not* προσωπολήμπτης.'
10. 47   Peter interprets the glossolalia in the house of Cornelius as the sign
            of the Spirit authorizing their baptism.
11. 17   Peter assimilates the work of the Spirit to 'the *same gift that he gave
            us.*'

---

[42] F. Bovon, 'God of Luke', 1995, p. 78.

15. 8   Peter further extends this by the motif of the purification of the heart by faith.

In summary:

(1)   Peter passes from the implicit to the explicit by naming God; this procedure is manifest in the syntax, which makes θεός the subject of the statements in Peter's discourse;[43]

(2)   Peter's words progressively gain in theological intensity;

(3)   the theological elaboration takes place through the exchange of persons and the responsibility of the witness.

An analogous scenario can be observed in Acts 9; 22; 26:

9. 3–8   A theophanic shock throws Saul to the ground and blinds him.

9. 9   The shock utterly bewilders Saul.

9. 17   Ananias lays hands on him to heal his blindness and fill him with the Holy Spirit; but for what task?

Paul's discourse progressively interprets the event:

9. 20, 22   Saul proclaims Jesus Son of God and Messiah.

(9. 27   Barnabas tells how Saul saw the Lord who spoke to him.)

22. 14   Paul, speaking to the people of Jerusalem, rereads the event of Damascus as the will of the God of the fathers to make him a witness before all.

22. 18, 21   Paul tells how the Lord appeared to him in the Temple to send him to the nations.

26. 16–18   Paul declares before Agrippa that Jesus revealed the reason for his appearance: to send him to convert the nations to belief in him.

In summary:

(1)   Paul passes from the implicit to the explicit by naming Jesus; this procedure is manifested narratively by the increasingly active role that is given to Jesus in the dialogue with Paul (22. 10, 17–21; 26. 15–18);

(2)   Paul's vocation is affirmed more clearly in passing from 9. 15–16 to 22. 14–15, 18–21 and 26. 16–18;

(3)   the concentration on the dialogue between Paul and Jesus goes hand in hand with the progressive fading out of the role of Ananias (compare 9. 10–17 with 22. 12–16; absence in ch. 26).

The sequence of a theophany and then a discourse that explains it is clearly shown in the examples of Acts 10–11 and Acts 9; 22; 26. Is this

---

[43] This is the case in 10. 28, 34, 38, 40; 11. 9, 17; 15. 7–8.

to be viewed as a simple narrative procedure of Luke or a theological structure? I prefer the latter and now articulate why.

A discreet God

In the sequence of the theophany and the word of the witness, each element has its own function. The theophany signals that the initiative comes from God; it presents an unexpected character, sometimes outlandish in his choices, but also enigmatic, requiring the reading of a believer. It is striking that the narrator never says 'God did' or 'God said'; he lets one of the characters in the narrative say it, not without having shown, in some cases, the correct reading of the event. There is a divine discretion, which indicates the theology that Luke draws on: *a theology of the hidden God, who reveals himself by veiling himself: it is the word of the witness that must pierce the uncertainty.* This is not a theology of mystery, but a theology of revelation, which brings Luke close to the sapiential-apocalyptic tradition of the Q source.[44] The name of God is not pronounced until after the event, not immediately but by the mediation of a word that designates him.

Theocentric Christology

In the word of the witnesses, this concentration on God is connected with another phenomenon, not often mentioned: the consistent theocentrism of the speeches in the book of Acts. The theology that animates the discourses in Acts is not Christocentric, as one might expect: when Christ is mentioned, the words generally point to the action of God.[45] In Acts 2, Peter's speech celebrates the God who revealed Jesus, whose resurrection David predicted. In Acts 3, the word points to God who establishes a time of refreshing through Christ. Stephen (Acts 7) speaks of the God of Abraham, Joseph and Moses, constantly enduring the unfaithfulness of his people. In 10. 34–43, Peter announces the God who is partial to none. In Acts 13, Paul announces in Antioch the God who fulfils the promises made to the fathers in giving them judges, kings and a Saviour. In Lystra

[44] I have in mind Luke's reception of Q logia about the wisdom of God, especially Luke 13. 34–5; see also 19. 41–4 (motif of hidden/revealed) and 21. 20–4 (differently Mark 13. 14–20). On this subject see K. Löning, 'Gottesbild', 1992, pp. 100–1.

[45] Christology, in the speeches of Acts, is carried by the reference to God who raised Jesus from the dead: 2. 22–4, 32–3; 3. 13, 15, 18, 25–6; 10. 40, 42; 13. 37; 17. 31. In qualification of this fact, my colleagues in the 'Luke–Acts Seminar' (SBL Annual Meeting, Philadelphia, 1995) prefer to speak of a 'theocentric Christology' in Luke.

(Acts 14), it is the Creator God who fills people with his goodness. In Athens (Acts 17), it is God the giver of life who should not be sought among idols.

The common aim of the speeches is to promote faith in the God who has ultimately unveiled his mercy (his εὐδοκία) to Israel, according to the promises of Scripture, in the sending and resurrection of his Son. The orators of the book of Acts call for conversion, not to Christ, but to God.[46]

An ignorance which must be removed

But from what must one convert? The same term applies to Jews (3. 17; 13. 27) and pagans (17. 30): ἀγνοία. This is not ignorance, but a mistake about God. It concerns precisely the theological misunderstanding that the word of the witness must rectify. ἀγνοία is a soteriological category in Luke, characterizing both the Jewish error on the subject of the Messiah and the bewilderment of the Hellenistic religious quest, and therefore applicable to all. It must be said of all people not only that they 'know not what they do' (Luke 23. 34), but that they do not know God. The Lucan ἀγνοία, then, does not represent a passing deficiency, but rather a soteriological lack. It gives rise to the speech of the witness, with its hermeneutic of the God who reveals his eschatological action in the person of Jesus. The motif is sapiential.[47]

To summarize: with the action of Philip in Samaria (Acts 8), the conversion of Saul (Acts 9) and the encounter of Peter and Cornelius (Acts 10–11), Luke shows how God advances history by jolts, intentionally opening the word of salvation to all people. In conformity with Jewish historiography, the author of Acts describes a God who allows himself to be known, while at the same time hiding, in the events of history. 'God' does not speak, he is brought to expression by the word of the witness. This explains why Luke deploys a theology of the word; through the speeches of the witnesses, he can lift God's incognito and move from misunderstanding to knowledge. This alternation of narrative (which describes history) and speech (which deciphers the action of God within history) concretizes narratively the movement of the Lucan mission, putting in evidence the role of the confession of faith by the witness, which alone can decode the signs of the eschatological work of God in the chaos of history.

---

[46] μετανοεῖν: 2. 38; 3. 19; 17. 30; ἐπιστρέφειν: 3. 19; 14. 15; 26. 20.
[47] P. Doble has pointed this out in his study, *Paradox*, 1996, pp. 214–22.

The interpretative function: God reveals the meaning of history

Divine interventions in the book of Acts above all else serve the two functions that have just been examined: proleptic and performative. More rarely, they are placed after the events in order to justify or to confirm them or to indicate their importance. At the level of the narrative, these analepses[48] initiate a process of verification for the reader.

Retrospection

I have already noted in passing several retrospective divine irruptions. After the baptism of the Ethiopian eunuch, Philip is seized by the Spirit and disappears (8. 39). This remarkable procedure does not merely satisfy a taste for the marvellous; it confirms for the reader an otherwise surprising divine decree: the integration of a eunuch into the covenant. Another retrospective intervention is the interruption of Peter at the house of Cornelius by the irruption of the Spirit (10. 44–5); in the eyes of Peter's Jewish entourage, this noisy divine approval concretizes Peter's speech, which allows the benefit of the forgiveness of sins to pagans (10. 43), with the decision to baptize then coming to ratify the divine decree (10. 47).

In Acts 8 as in Acts 10, the theophanic intervention after the event retrospectively validates a paradoxical logic, the logic of the ways of God. Hence the transgression of limits, in which Philip and Peter participate, already initiated by the supernatural interventions, as we have seen above, is confirmed afterwards. This confirmation offers the reader the certainty that the process of the extension of the covenant is intended and accomplished by God himself through witnesses.

A logic of testimony

The vision of Stephen at his martyrdom, another validating intervention, is also at the service of a paradoxical logic: 'Look, I see the heavens opened and the Son of Man standing at the right hand of God' (7. 56).[49] But why do the heavens open? Here we must distinguish two levels.[50] At the level of

---

[48] By analepsis, I mean the return of a narrative to an element that is chronologically anterior, the inverse movement (the reference to a future event) is called prolepsis. See G. Genette, *Figures III*, 1972, pp. 90–115.

[49] See M. Sabbe, *Son of Man Saying*, 1979, pp. 241–79; R. Pesch, *Stephanus*, 1966.

[50] In what follows, I rely on the differentiation set out by S. Chatman between story and discourse; the first corresponds to the *what* of the narrative and the second to the *how*, that is the narrative rhetoric (S. Chatman, *Story and Discourse*, 1978). On the theory: D Marguerat and Y. Bourquin, *How to Read*, 1999, pp. 18–28.

the story, Stephen's vision sets in motion the murderous fury of the members of the Sanhedrin who 'cover their ears' and drag him out of the city to stone him (7. 57–8); Stephen's vision in effect announces the resurrection of the Crucified One. At the level of the narrative rhetoric, the anachronistic use of the title υἱὸς τοῦ ἀνθρώπου echoes Jesus' declaration during his trial (Luke 22. 69). However, the vision does not immediately provide its *raison d'être*. A few verses later, two of Stephen's statements reinforce the parallelism of the two martyrs: 'Lord Jesus, receive my spirit' (7. 59b; Luke 23. 46) and 'Lord, do not hold this sin against them' (7. 60b; Luke 23. 34). One can measure the extent of the paradox: the evoking of the exaltation of Jesus at the right hand of God does not help the witness to escape death, but rather leads him to it, confirming Stephen's thesis about the constant resistance of his Jewish listeners to the Holy Spirit (7. 51).

Stephen's death, which heightens the open crisis between the Jerusalem authorities and the apostles (Acts 3–7),[51] is therefore at the same time paradigmatic of the condition of the witness of Jesus. The reader now knows that proclamation of the gospel does not offer a destiny any different from that of the Master. Stephen's vision certifies the conformity of his martyrdom to the Passion of Jesus (Stephen not only dies *for* Jesus, he dies *like* him), but this effect of verification extends also to the rest of the narrative, since it sets up *a divine logic of testimony: those who proclaim the gospel must expect to suffer.*

Saul of Tarsus, who moves from the role of the persecutor to that of the persecuted, will immediately experience this (9. 19b–30). The vision of the Lord that he will receive in Jerusalem (23. 11) functions analeptically ('Keep up your courage! For just as you have testified for me in Jerusalem...') and proleptically ('you must bear witness also in Rome'). On the one hand, this message confirms the validity of Paul's two speeches in Jerusalem (22. 1–21; 23. 6), in spite of the confusion they create. On the other hand, it precedes Paul's appeal to Caesar (25. 11), inscribing it by anticipation in the plan of God.[52]

One question arises: Under the weight of divine pressure do people become puppets?

---

[51] On the rise of the crisis between the Christian community and the Jerusalem authorities in chapters 1–7, see pp. 158–64.

[52] Note the same procedure in 18. 9: the epiphany of Christ, which Paul experienced prior to his appearance before Gallio, presents two sides, one analeptic ('Do not be afraid, but speak and do not be silent'), the other proleptic ('for I am with you, and no one will lay a hand on you to harm you, for there are many in this city who are my people'). The first validates the attitude adopted by Paul up to this point, while the second outlines the programme for Paul's stay in Corinth, foreseeing the failure of the denunciation before the proconsul.

Are the witnesses puppets?

Up to this point, the divine programming of the events has appeared very strong, since it envelops (before, during and after) the events of history. By contrast, as has been noted above,[53] the responsibility of the witness in the elaboration of his testimony appears total. How does Luke handle this tension? Is the freedom of the witness only a charade?[54]

Luke offers no systematic reflection on the matter, but an observation of the narrative nevertheless provides some indications. Peter legitimizes the baptism of Gentiles at Cornelius' house by saying: 'who was I to hinder God?' (11. 17b; already 10. 47). The same verb κωλύειν was used by the eunuch in 8. 36: 'What is to prevent me from being baptized?' On the stage of the story, *the roles are clearly distributed: God takes the initiative and human action follows*. The apostles are conscious of having a place in the divine economy, which will be explained to the pagans in terms of providence (17. 26–8)[55] and to the Jews in the words of the Scriptures. In Antioch, Paul legitimizes his right to proclaim the promise of salvation to non-Jews with the help of Isaiah 49. 6: 'I have set you to be a light for the Gentiles, so that you may bring salvation to the ends of the earth' (13. 47). In Jerusalem, Paul and Barnabas present 'all the signs and wonders that *God had done through them* among the Gentiles' (15. 12), allowing James, with the help of Amos 9. 11–12, to see the opening to the Gentiles as the expression of God's unchanging will. The Scripture plays here the role of retrospective confirmation. One sees, however, that this intervention comes in secondarily, as a final authority after the theophanic signs have taken place.

This relationship between the roles of the Scriptures and the theophanic signs allows us to gauge the importance of their *retrospective* character: *they have a balancing effect in relation to the programmatic interventions, by letting the action of the witnesses take place beforehand*. Luke sets divine intrusion into history and human decision side by side, without seeing any contradiction. In two successive verses he can speak of the departure of Paul and Barnabas as a delegation of the Antiochene community (13. 3) and as a sending by the Holy Spirit (13. 4). The Spirit

---

[53] See pp. 97–8.

[54] This is at least what J. Jervell argues: 'God is the only *causa*, the motor and the driving force in history, the only master in history ... Humans are forced to bring about all the things God has foreordained' ('Future of the Past', 1996, p. 106).

[55] The Lucan understanding of the notion of providence has been illuminated by J. H. Neyrey, 'Epicureans', 1990, pp. 118–34.

does not short-circuit the human connections, but uses human mediations, which through prayer are open to his directions (13. 3).[56]

Furthermore, even resistance to the Gospel is included in God's plan, as is illustrated in a masterly way by the quotation of Isaiah 6. 9–10 at the end of the book of Acts (28. 26–7). However, from chapter 3 onwards, the narrative shows how the Jews systematically refuse to listen to the admonitions of the apostles, whether Peter, Stephen or Paul. The end of Acts does not present the liberty of the adversaries as a charade, but rather shows that Paul's failure in his mission to the Jews (a) fits into a prophetic failure at the heart of his people; and (b) serves God's plan to offer salvation beyond Israel (28. 28).[57] Perhaps it is with this principle in mind that Luke does not close off the question about Israel at the end of his work, leaving in suspense the future of the people of Abraham. With this example, we perceive how Luke succeeds in aligning the omnipotence of God and human freedom, *without the one eliminating the other, without providence crushing the individual's responsibility.* Human freedom remains, a freedom even to say no.

Conclusion: the God of Luke

I shall now bring together, in conclusion, three characteristics of the God of Acts, which have been explained in the course of this chapter: the non-obviousness of God, the interaction of the human and the divine, and the irony of God.

The non-obviousness of God

In Acts God is never immediately evident. The author uses two languages to speak of God: one (implicit) refers to God through theophanic signs; the other names God explicitly, but it only enters the narrative through the words of believers. A theology of the hidden God permeates the narrative: the way to this God is encumbered by misunderstanding (ἀγνοία) and requires the mediation of a revelatory word. God comes to the world through the words of his messengers. In recounting the story of God, the

---

[56] On the theme of mediations in Luke's theology, one should consult the inspiring study of F. Bovon, 'Importance of Mediations', 1995, pp. 51–66.

[57] Attention must be paid to the commission given to the prophet in the introduction to the quotation of Isa. 6. 9–10 (28. 26a): 'Go to this people and say ...' This mention, unique in the quotations of Isa. 6. 9–10 in the New Testament, aligns Paul's mission with that of the prophet by assimilating his failure in the mission to the Jews to Isaiah's failure. Paul's inability to assemble Israel around the name of Jesus thus belongs retrospectively in a tradition attested by the Scripture. The study of this text will be continued on p. 221.

author of Acts has no other means at his disposal than to recount the story of his messengers.

Interaction of human and divine

Luke's God redirects history in order to inscribe it in his plan, which is to disseminate the offer of salvation to all. The initiative to change the direction of history is always in God's hands, the witness's responsibility is to enter into his logic of salvation. Yet for Luke, human freedom, even when it resists these divine intrusions, is never abrogated. This explains the astonishing dialectic of the narrative of Acts, where the divine and the human constantly meet and mix in varying mediations, in order to transform history into salvation history.

Irony of God

Every page of the book of Acts displays the irony of God. If humans remain free to act, they ignore the consequences. Neither Gamaliel, when he pleads in favour of the liberation of the apostles, nor the magistrates of Philippi, when they imprison Paul and Silas, nor even Claudius, the tribune, when he takes Paul to Caesarea under escort, realize their collaboration with the divine plan. The irony of God consists in integrating even the actions of his enemies in order to make them contribute to the advancement of the Word 'to the ends of the earth' (1. 8).

6

THE WORK OF THE SPIRIT

Within the New Testament no one knew better than Luke how to recount the work of the Spirit. He has given the Spirit such central importance that Eugène Jacquier in 1926 writes: 'The Acts are, so to speak, the Gospel of the Spirit.'[1] This designation, as we shall see in what follows, is only partially justified.

In saying that the work of the *pneuma* is unfolded here in such a central way does not necessarily mean that the rest of the New Testament is silent with regard to the Spirit. Along with the author of Luke–Acts, Paul and John are the two other New Testament theologians who develop a pneumatology. Briefly, Pauline thought situates the Spirit, on the one hand, as the foundation of faith ('No one can say "Jesus is Lord" except by the Holy Spirit', 1 Cor. 12. 3), and, on the other hand, as the norm for Christian existence, through 'the law of the Spirit' (Rom. 8). The evangelist John develops his pneumatology in the framework of the farewell speeches: the Paraclete actualizes Jesus' teaching (14. 25–6); he reveals the Son (15. 26–7), and leads to the fullness of the truth (16. 13–15); he has a word function. In the Acts of the Apostles, we never encounter the idea that the Holy Spirit provokes faith, or that he glorifies the Son. On the other hand, Luke continually shows the Spirit taking hold of communities, directing the apostles, inciting actions, speaking, ordering, forbidding, and so on. What is the profile of the Spirit according to Acts? What are the distinctive features and what features are close to Paul's or John's understanding?

Recounting the work of the Spirit

The uniqueness of Luke's point of view is precisely that he *recounts* the work of the Spirit in history. Paul argues, at least in the Corinthian crisis. The Johannine Jesus explains, in a discursive manner, the relationship

---

[1] *Actes des apôtres*, 1926, p. cvii.

that links him to the Spirit. Luke does not explain the Spirit, he shows him at work. He does not discuss the Spirit; he shows him in action. Luke never explains his conception of the Spirit (taken straight from, in my opinion, the Old Testament), and this oversight irritates theologians who conclude 'that he does not possess a very elaborated or meditated pneumatology'.[2] This is, however, a misunderstanding of the potential of a narrative theology, the result of not having looked for the codes. The role of the exegete today is to assemble the evidences scattered throughout the narrative and to elucidate the underlying theological structure – while respecting the constraints that narrativity imposes on reflection, admitting the shadows, welcoming the tensions, without forcing it into a logical type of discourse. Luke has used the only tool available to the narrator who wishes to establish a role: he has made the Spirit 'a character'[3] of his narrative, much like Paul, Stephen or Lydia, even though he accords the Spirit an eminent place in the hierarchy of characters. This means that Luke presents less a concept than a *pragmatic of the Holy Spirit*.

There is no question here: this operation is not theologically innocent. To draw the Spirit into the scene of the narrative is to enrol in the programme a God who intervenes in human affairs. The pragmatic of the Spirit translates and inspires an experience of the Spirit. In his own way, Luke rejoins the situation of the first Christians, practical theologians, indwelt by the Spirit, living by him, committed to proclaiming the kerygma rather than to advancing a teaching about the Spirit.[4]

This study will unfold in six steps. After examining the occurrences of the *pneuma* in the narrative, I shall then turn to the ecclesiological dimension, the function of the Word, the dynamic of unity, the question of whether the Spirit is free or captive, and, finally, I shall conclude with the Lucan pragmatic of the Spirit.

The Church between fire and the Word

The presence of the Spirit is striking in the work *ad Theophilum*: one hundred and six mentions of the Spirit in the Lucan diptych, seventy

---

[2] E. Trocmé, 'Saint-Esprit', 1969, p. 21.

[3] W. H. Shepherd has given this title to his dissertation (*Narrative Function*, 1994).

[4] Concerning Luke's pneumatology, see H. von Baer, *Heilige Geist*, 1926; G. Betori, 'Spirito', 1987; F. F. Bruce, 'Holy Spirit', 1973, pp. 166–83; M.-A. Chevallier, 'Luc et l'Esprit Saint', 1982, pp. 1–16; J. D. G. Dunn, *Baptism*, 1970; A. George, 'Esprit Saint', 1978, pp. 500–42; H. Giesen, 'Heilige Geist', 1983, pp. 19–42; G. Haya Prats, *Force de l'Eglise*, 1975; J. H. E. Hull, *Holy Spirit*, 1967; O. Mainville, *Esprit*, 1991; E. Schweizer, art. 'πνεῦμα', 1968, pp. 404–15; J. B. Shelton, *Mighty*, 1991; M. B. Turner, 'Jesus and the Spirit', 1981; 'Power From on High', 1996. For the state of research: F. Bovon, *Luke the Theologian*, 1987, pp. 198–238, 417; O. Mainville, *Esprit*, 1991, pp. 19–47.

of which are in Acts. This represents 28 per cent of the occurrences in the New Testament.[5] Marcel Dumais concludes that, 'the term and the theme of the Spirit are omnipresent in the Lucan work'.[6] But can one be so sure? To my surprise, a verification of the statistics ends up contesting this affirmation: Luke distributes the references to the *pneuma* in a quantitatively unequal manner throughout the twenty-eight chapters of Acts and even more surprisingly, he does so in a qualitatively unequal manner as well. A demonstration is merited, since one suspects that in an analysis of narrative discourse the silences are as revealing as the words. Wolfgang Iser, the narratologist, has pointed out that the gaps play a part in communication as well as the text itself.[7]

I shall adopt, in order to frame the statistical research, a non-original division structuring the narrative into four sections: the golden age of the community of Jerusalem (1–7), the Peter cycle (8–12), Paul's mission (13–20), the martyrdom of Paul (21–8). Both the anthropological and the demonological usage of *pneuma* have been excluded.[8]

During the golden age (seven chapters): twenty-three occurrences.

Here the Spirit is primarily the Spirit of prophecy given to the community at Pentecost (1. 5, 8; 2. 4, 17–18) or later (4. 31; 5. 32); also the Spirit which animates community mission (5. 39) and which it is futile to resist (7. 51). *Pneuma* can also be the Old Testament Spirit of prophecy (1. 16; 4. 25). He fills the seven Hellenist deacons (6. 3) or Stephen (6. 5, 10; 7. 55), and empowers his word.

In the Peter cycle (five chapters) eighteen occurrences.

In eleven cases the Spirit descends on a community and produces ecstatic or prophetic manifestations (8. 15, 17, 18, 19; 9. 31; 10. 38, 44, 45, 47; 11. 15, 16). In two cases, a man is said to be full of the Spirit: Paul (9. 17) and Cornelius (11. 24). In five cases, the Spirit intervenes directly in the life of an individual: he speaks to Philip (8. 29) and takes him away (8. 39); he speaks to Peter (10. 19; 11. 12) and expresses himself through Agabus (11. 28).

During the Pauline mission (eight chapters): fifteen occurrences.

Ecstatic community intervention recedes: the disciples (13. 52), the home of Cornelius (15. 8), Ephesus (19. 2a, 2b, 6). The immediate intervention of the Spirit in the lives of individuals is dominant: the Spirit sends (13. 4); he fills Paul (13. 9); he causes decisions to be taken (15. 28; 19. 21); he destroys plans

---

[5] Mark in comparison has 23 occurrences of the term πνεῦμα, Matthew 19, and the Pauline corpus 120. For the statistics, see A. George, 'Esprit Saint', 1978, pp. 501–27.

[6] M. Dumais, 'Bilan et orientations', 1995, p. 329.

[7] These gaps are points of indeterminacy of sense (W. Iser, *Act of Reading*, 1978, pp. 182–203).

[8] Acts 8. 7; 16. 6, 18; 17. 16; 18. 25; 19. 12, 13, 15, 16; 23. 8, 9. The case of 23. 9 is debatable, but the absence of the article with πνεῦμα leaves the reader in doubt whether the Spirit of God is intended (the semantic ambiguity is what Luke wants). Furthermore, the text adopted here is that of Nestle–Aland (27th edn); the Western textual variants in 15. 29 and 19. 1 are not considered.

(16. 6, 7); he binds Paul (20. 22); he speaks (13. 2; 20. 23); he appoints bishops (20. 28).

During the martyrdom of Paul (eight chapters): three occurrences.

The Spirit expresses himself only through Paul (21. 4, 11) and the Scripture (28. 25).

What conclusions should be drawn from this inventory of the functions of and references to the *pneuma* in Acts?[9]

First, the Spirit reaches only believers. Whether groups or individuals, only the followers of Jesus or the holy men of Israel are touched. It is not the *pneuma* who stops Saul on the Damascus road (Acts 9), nor is it the *pneuma* who inspires Julius the centurion to protect Paul (Acts 27). The Spirit acts in and for the believing community.

Second, the number of references to the Spirit diminishes as the narrative advances. One notices this at first glance in comparing the twenty-three occurrences in the golden age (seven chapters) to the three occurrences in the martyrdom of Paul (eight chapters). The golden age (Acts 1–7) appears as the period in which the progress of Christianity is the result of intensive miraculous activity of the Spirit. The frequency is slightly diminished in the cycle of Peter (Acts 8–12), where the Gospel passes beyond the frontiers of Judaism, becoming open to Gentiles. This opening to the Gentiles is concretized during the Pauline mission (Acts 13–20), where the narrative brings to the fore the interaction of characters around Paul and the way in which the Spirit brings about this interaction. The almost absent *pneuma* in the martyrdom of Paul is quite astonishing: no trace of the Spirit of God between chapters 22 and 27 where we have the apology of Paul in front of the people of Jerusalem (22), in front of the Sanhedrin (23), and in front of Agrippa (26). I conclude that the Spirit in Luke is an inaugurating Spirit, the agent of beginnings, of the creation of communities, and the impulse that gives birth to Churches.

Third, the ecstatic community outpourings recede in favour of a personal intervention. The Spirit's manifestations, then, are not uniform from one end of the narrative to the other. Strongly ecclesial in origin, his action focuses more and more, yet not exclusively, on those who serve the Word. This development is clear if one compares the forms of intervention. From the golden age to the martyrdom of Paul the number of community interventions decreases from eighteen to none. From the cycle of Peter to the mission of Paul, the number decreases from eleven to four. However, this

---

[9] One would have hoped for more methodological rigour in the research of W. H. Shepherd, *Narrative Function*, 1994. The author investigates neither the frequency of references throughout the narrative, nor the silences of Luke concerning the *pneuma* (for example, in the miracle narratives).

sliding from the collective toward the individual is also part of the movement from the ecstatic in the direction of the activity of the Word. This
is also partially related to the evolution of the narrative itself. But it is
clear enough to render unlikely the idea that the author of Acts projects
in his narrative the spiritual experience of the Christianity of his time.[10] It
is more pertinent to take into consideration the following fact: Acts 1–7
corresponds to a story of beginnings, whereas the Pauline period (Acts
13–20 and 21–8) brings one chronologically closer to the post-apostolic
period, the time of Luke. In this case Luke could have, at the end of the
narrative, conformed the emergence of the Spirit to the forms he observed
in the Christianity of his time. I conclude that the charismatic communal
outpouring does not appear to be, from Luke's point of view, the privileged channel of the Spirit. The Spirit is diverse. Luke's narration begins
at Pentecost, in fire and loud noise; it ends with the figure of the prisoner
Paul preaching in Rome (28. 30). The author unfolds his story of the
Church between fire and the Word. But, between these two milestones in
the narrative, the history of salvation progresses, and with it the modes of
Spirit intervention develop. The Church is always led by the Spirit, but
the breath of God does not act in identical ways from one end to the other
in Acts.[11]

*Fourth, the narrative moves forward with a growing personalization
of the Spirit.* The increase in personal interventions makes him appear,
more and more, like a sort of *deus ex machina* abruptly breaking in to
modify the course of history. The Spirit's personalization is growing; he
is more clearly, towards the end, the grammatical subject of the phrase
which names him. In 16. 7, he is even called 'the Spirit of Jesus'. In
preparation here, obscurely, is a line that will conclude with the well-
known trinitarian developments. Are these abrupt irruptions of the Spirit
into the life of the individual cause for fearing for the liberty of the
individual? The question of the intervention of the divine breath in the
sphere of human responsibility must be reserved for later. Having covered
the question of the occurrences of the Spirit in Acts, I shall now turn to
the question of the relation of Spirit and Church.

The Spirit builds the Church

Luke's narrative shares with Mark and Matthew the declaration of the
Baptist who humbles himself before Jesus: 'I baptize you with water. . .

[10] This is the thesis of J. Borremans, 'Esprit Saint', 1970.
[11] This trait has been pointed out in the analysis (unfortunately non-systematic) of
G. Haya Prats, *Force de l'Eglise*, 1975.

He will baptize you with the Holy Spirit and fire' (Luke 3. 16; Mark 1. 8; Matt. 3.11). However, Luke's work is the only one where Christ takes up this word and addresses it to his audience as a promise of the Father: 'John baptized in water, but you shall be baptized with the Holy Spirit not many days from now' (Acts 1. 5). The book of Acts opens with the promise of the coming of the Spirit on the disciples which is realized at Pentecost. Lohse appropriately speaks of this narrative as the front porch, 'a great porch at the beginning of the history of the Church, that the reader must pass through in order to enter into universal history'.[12] Pentecost is the founding event. According to Luke, one cannot be unaware that the Church is not born from humanity, but from the breath of God.

When Luke places the Spirit's irruption at the beginning of his history of the Church, he expresses a conviction shared by the whole of primitive Christianity: the pouring out of the Spirit was a post-paschal reality; it is not the work of the earthly Jesus, but of the risen Christ (John 15. 26; 16. 7; 20. 22, Gal. 4. 6; 2 Cor. 3. 17: cf. Matt. 28. 19–20). Jesus himself seems to have spoken little of the Spirit and did not give him to his disciples. This historical fact is confirmed by the hesitation of the first Christians to project their charismatic experience into the gospels.[13] *Before Easter, Jesus is the sole bearer of the Spirit*. In his gospel, Luke accentuates this exclusive bond between Jesus and the Spirit, on the one hand, by the motif of the virgin birth (1. 35) and, on the other hand, by quoting Isaiah 61. 1 in the programmatic sermon in Nazareth ('The Spirit of the Lord is upon me', 4. 18). Jesus comes from the Spirit and is inhabited by the Spirit.[14]

However, Easter and Jesus' ascension initiate a change. Jesus' absence is now the rule (Acts 1. 11) and the Spirit comes upon believers. As the apostle Peter says in explaining the event of Pentecost to the people of Jerusalem: 'Being therefore exalted at the right hand of God, and having received from the Father the promise of the Holy Spirit, he [Jesus] has poured out this that you both see and hear' (2. 33). This formulation is nevertheless curious. Did Jesus not already possess the Spirit? Yes, but it is with the Spirit destined for believers that Christ is now endowed. In

---

[12] 'ein grosses Portal am Anfang der Kirchengeschichte, durch das der Leser schreiten und Eingang in die Weltgeschichte finden soll' (E. Lohse, 'Pfingstberichtes', 1973, p. 190).

[13] E. Schweizer, art. 'πνεῦμα', 1968, pp. 404–5.

[14] It is important to affirm the double relation of *pneuma* with the Lucan Christ, as both a product of the Spirit and a master of the Spirit; to accentuate exclusively Jesus' mastery over the Spirit, as Schweizer does, leads to a one-sided reading of Jesus as an archetype of the charismatic believer, to the detriment of his unity (so J. D. G. Dunn, *Jesus and the Spirit*, 1975). M. B. Turner is correct in opposing this view ('Jesus and the Spirit', 1981).

this conception of the Spirit, as both attributed to Jesus and destined for believers, Luke with no confusion, marries two Jewish scriptural traditions. One endows the Messiah with the Spirit (Isa. 11. 2; 42. 1; 61. 1); and the other attributes the Spirit to the regenerated people of God (Num. 11. 29; Ezek. 39. 29; Joel 3. 1).[15] In fact, Acts 2. 33 articulates in the same declaration: resurrection of Jesus, divine promise of the Spirit and his being poured out on believers. Odette Mainville, the author of an important monograph on the Spirit in the work of Luke, even sees this as 'the key to the interpretation of the pneumatology of Luke'.[16]

The Spirit as witness

Luke, then, is to be situated with the first Christians and their conviction that Christ is the mediator of the Spirit. However, he attributes to the *pneuma a precise function*: 'But you will receive power when the Holy Spirit has come upon you; and you will be my witnesses in Jerusalem, in all Judaea and Samaria, and to the ends of the earth' (Acts 1. 8). The Spirit is a power; he enables the disciples to be witnesses of Jesus, from Jerusalem to the ends of the earth. What is of interest in this programmatic verse is that it locates the origin of the venture of Christian mission in the founding gift of the Spirit. In this sense, it is incorrect to say that the Spirit makes the witness possible, and better to say that he *is* the witness. *The gift of the Spirit is the power to witness to Jesus.* The entire unfolding of the mission in Acts confirms this function of the Spirit as the enabling power to witness.

Using his tradition, Luke edited the Pentecost narrative (2. 1–13) in a way that evokes the great theophanies of the Old Testament, but especially the gift of the Law at Sinai.[17] The Spirit is both visible and audible: the sound of the tempest, the flames of fire that come down on each of the Twelve, the noise that arises from the many languages being spoken! It is likely that Luke has rewritten a narrative that was centred on speaking in tongues and has transformed it into an event of universal communication; 'to speak in other languages' (λαλεῖν ἑτέραις γλώσσαις v.4b) might be a rereading of an original expression known to the first Christians: 'to speak in tongues' (λαλεῖν γλώσσαις Acts 10. 46; 19. 6; 1 Cor. 12. 30; 13. 1; 14. 2, 39). Whatever the case, in its present state, the text describes this

[15] M.-A. Chevallier has traced these scriptural trajectories in ancient Judaism: *Souffle de Dieu*, 1978, pp. 44–76.

[16] *Esprit*, 1991, p. 15.

[17] Exod. 19. 8, 16–19 LXX and its rereadings in *Mekhilta Exod.* 2. 20 and *Midrash Deut.* 33. 2. This is set forth in J. Potin, *La fête juive*, I, 1971, pp. 299–322.

miracle: the Twelve lose their Galilean particularism and become the core of the universal Church (vv. 6–11).[18] Luke hardly considers that the gathering crowd, made up of Jews and proselytes residing in Jerusalem, might understand the Aramaic of the disciples. On the contrary, what is important for him is that this microcosm, this kaleidoscope of nations, a nucleus of the Church, announces the great acts of God to the whole world. From its birth, the Church created by the Spirit has three distinctive features: (a) it is a missionary community, not by vocation but by definition; (b) everyone in the community receives the Spirit, a sign of the eschatological times, in order to testify; (c) the Church comes from and cannot understand itself without Israel.

Pentecost unfolds

When he accentuates a significant event, Luke tends to multiply the reminders in the flow of the narrative; this is evident in the summaries of Acts 2–5; or again in the vocation of Paul, which is repeated three times (Acts 9; 22; 26). This procedure of recurrence[19] also affects Pentecost. Luke shows how, in order to enlarge the Pentecostal nucleus to worldwide dimensions, the Spirit pushes the community *in spite of itself to go beyond* the boundaries of Israel, to go beyond the limits of the Law, to exceed the boundaries of Asia to arrive in Rome, the world's centre. At the occasion of each of these advances, a reminder of the first Pentecost echoes clearly or vaguely.

First, Samaria is won over, evangelized by Philip (Acts 8) and the Samaritans 'receive the Holy Spirit' from the hands of Peter and John (8. 17). But the decisive opening to the Gentiles comes with the encounter of Peter and Cornelius, a narrative superbly recounted by the author of Acts (10–11), which should be referred to as the conversion of Peter rather than of Cornelius.[20] Enduring two assaults from God, through an ecstasy and then by a message of the Spirit, Peter has to come to grips with the unbelievable: the Holy Spirit falls on the house of Cornelius, incorporating

---

[18] The identity of the group assembled at Pentecost is not clear (2. 1). It is tempting to imagine a large assembly of the one hundred and twenty believers in 1. 15, but, in my opinion, this is not Luke's view. The group at Pentecost is the former reconstituted circle of the Twelve (1. 23–5), in whose name Peter will speak out (2. 14–37). Luke does not skip over the stages of salvation history.

[19] Luke's usage of the procedure of recurrence will be examined with regard to the three variants of the conversion of Saul. See chapter 9, especially. pp. 183–6.

[20] Cornelius receives an answer (10. 4), but nothing in the narrative indicates a change on his part. In this encounter between two worlds, the central character is Peter, whose resistance God progressively breaks down (10. 9–33, 44–8), in order to lead him to abandon the ceremonial Torah that dictated the barriers between pure and unpure (10. 9–16).

the Gentiles into the community, but at the same time destroying the centuries-old barrier that separated the Gentiles from the people of God. Faith in Christ no longer passes by way of the Torah. As Peter would tell the story, in a beautiful exercise in theological reading of reality:

> As I began to speak, the Holy Spirit fell on them just as on us at the beginning. And I remembered the word of the Lord, how he said, 'John baptized with water, but you shall be baptized with the Holy Spirit.' If then God gave the same gift to them as he gave to us when we believed in the Lord Jesus Christ, who was I that I could withstand God? (11. 15–17)

After this second Pentecost, the Spirit continues to direct the progress of the Church. The selection of Barnabas and Paul for the first missionary activity to the Gentiles is ordered by the Spirit (13. 2). Paul and Silas' leaving Asia is provoked by the Spirit who blocks all other paths, forcing them to go towards Europe (16. 6–10). A pouring out of glossolalia of the Pentecostal type takes place in Ephesus around Paul (19. 6). Then the apostle to the Gentiles, who understands that he is 'bound in the Spirit', sets off for Jerusalem, where the long route to martyrdom that would lead him to Rome begins. In each of these hinge episodes, where salvation history moves to a higher level, it is the Spirit that pulls the believing community ahead in order that the plan of God can be accomplished.

Faith precedes

This rapid overview of the role of the Spirit in the structure of the book of Acts allows me to show, from Luke's point of view, how *the Spirit brings about the birth of the Church*. He founds the Church as a group that by definition is missionary, promised to universality. He animates and makes the Church grow (9. 31), by giving to each believer the power to witness to Jesus. This short summary in 9. 31 is instructive in that it speaks of the Church (ἐκκλησία) which grows 'built and moving forward by the fear of the Lord and the encouragement (παράκλησις) of the Holy Spirit'. While the first factor in the edification of the people of God (the fear of the Lord) is typically Old Testament, the second (the Spirit) is a Lucan innovation. The Spirit is not at the origin of individual faith, which is born from listening to the Christological word, but he is at the origin of testimony. This succession, particularly clear in the evangelization of Samaria (compare 8. 5–6, 12 and 8. 14–17),[21] already appeared in the promise made by the Risen Christ to his disciples (1. 8). The disciples'

---

[21] It is after having believed Philip's preaching (8. 5–6) and having been baptized (8. 12) that the Samaritans receive the Spirit (8. 14–17); it is true that the episode of the visit of

faith, which emerges from their close relationship with Jesus, precedes the vocation to be witnesses and to receive the Spirit. This pattern illustrates the condition of every believer: differently from Paul, the author situates faith exclusively in relation to Christ, while missionary activity is the Spirit's realm.

'They spoke the Word of God with boldness'

How is the Spirit of testimony concretized? What does it produce? There is one episode, in this first section of Acts where Luke describes the model community in Jerusalem, that answers these questions. In chapter 4 the Christians are exposed to the hostility of the Jerusalem authorities, who have Peter and John arrested and brought before the Sanhedrin. How does the community react when the two apostles are released from prison (4. 23–30)? They do not simply break out in praise; they do not pray for their own comfort. They pray for the continuation of the missionary witness; they ask their Lord to be able to proclaim the Word 'with all boldness' (the term παρρησία implies both courage to speak and freedom of speech); they ask God to stretch forth his hand 'to heal, and signs and wonders are performed through the name of your holy servant Jesus' (4. 30). At the end of the prayer, the earth trembles. The earthquake is a sign of fulfilment, as 16. 6 also points out. Consequently, Luke continues, 'they were all filled with the Holy Spirit and spoke the Word of God with boldness' (v. 31). Note that the fulfilment concerns the witness, but not healings. The request to speak the Word with παρρησία is answered, corresponding to the promise made by Jesus to his disciples to grant them the Spirit's assistance in case of persecution (Luke 12. 12). The conclusion is significant: the connection is made between the Spirit and preaching, not between the Spirit and miracles. I shall return to this later.

A work of the Word

Scholars have for a long time pointed out this peculiarity of Luke's pneumatology: for Luke, the Spirit always has, in one way or another, something to do with *the proclamation of the Word*.[22] He is a Spirit of prophecy.

Peter and John poses the question of the relationship between the baptism and the coming of the Spirit. I shall investigate this later (see pp. 126–7). One finds the same linear succession between the mention of faith and the outpouring of the Spirit concerning Cornelius (10. 2, 44) and the Ephesians (19. 1–2, 6).

[22] H. von Baer, *Heilige Geist*, 1926, pp. 90ff; E. Schweizer, art. 'πνεῦμα', 1968, pp. 406–13; G. Haya Prats, *Esprit*, 1975, pp. 93–116; H. Giesen, *Heilige Geist*, p. 39;

We have seen this in the founding event of Pentecost: Peter's speech makes it clear that the irruption of the Spirit is a prophetic event (2. 17–18), with the help of quotations from Joel 2 and Numbers 11. 29: 'Yes, on my menservants and my maidservants, in those days I will pour out my Spirit'; and Luke adds 'and they will prophesy' (2. 18). The Spirit does not lead to ecstasy, but to the communication of a word. In the events that echo the first Pentecost, glossolalia is commented on in the same manner, whether it is in the house of Cornelius ('For they heard them speaking in tongues and *extolling God*', 10. 46) or in Ephesus ('They spoke with tongues and *prophesied*', 19. 6). The gift of the Spirit is a communicable word.

The relationship between the Spirit and preaching is confirmed here and there in the rest of the work. It is 'filled with the Spirit' that Peter speaks to the people of Jerusalem (4. 8). Wisdom and the Spirit give Stephen's word its irresistible force (6. 10); it is the same for Barnabas in Antioch (11. 24).

Luke shares with Judaism this idea that the Spirit is essentially *a spirit of prophecy*.[23] Already in the Infancy narratives, the prophetic dimension of the Old Testament (e.g. Luke 1. 46, 67; 2. 25–7) and the prophetic inspiration of the Baptist (Luke 1. 15, 17) have been stressed. The Lucan description of Jesus does not refute this insistence on the spirit of prophecy.[24] The Spirit's work is a work of the Word, and to speak 'boldly in the name of Jesus' (Acts 9. 27) must be considered as the sign *par excellence* of the Spirit.

Spirit and miracles

What then can be said about the link Paul makes between miracles and the Spirit's work (1 Cor. 12. 9–10; etc.)? We encounter a famous *quaestio*

O. Mainville, *Esprit*, 1991, pp. 284–318. G. Betori has devoted an article to this subject correctly perceiving this in the function of the announcement of salvation, the centre of Lucan pneumatology ('Spirito', 1987, p. 419).

[23] G. W. H. Lampe has shown that the substance of Luke's pneumatology is derived from the Old Testament, in opposition to the Hellenistic affiliation preferred by the history of religions school ('Holy Spirit', 1955, pp. 159–200). See for example M. A. Chevallier, *Souffle de Dieu*, 1978, pp. 21–35 and 44–73; this study shows how the Jewish tradition never separated from the prophetic dimension of the Old Testament *ruaḥ*; dominant in the orthodox current at the end of the first century, it is present in Qumran (in spite of its stress on the Spirit's ethical function in believers), and in Philo (in spite of the rise of an anthropological dualism of a Platonic type). The fundamental conviction remains that the *pneuma prophètikon* was the prerogative of the prophets, that it is extinguished today, and that it is awaited as the sign of the world to come.

[24] Different from Matt. (12. 28), Luke does not explicitly attribute to the Spirit the origin of miracles (Luke 11. 20). Cf. A. George, 'Esprit Saint', 1978, pp. 515–18.

disputata. An attentive reading of Luke–Acts leads the reader to the conclusion that the author avoids all explicit links, as in Acts 4. 29–31. Luke's gospel never associates Jesus' thaumaturgical activity with the *pneuma*. In Acts, the miracles of Jesus (2. 22), Peter (4. 7), Stephen (6. 8), Philip (8. 10) or Paul (19. 11) are all attributed to 'power' (δύναμις) but never to the Spirit. This fact has led E. Schweizer, in his classic article on the Spirit, to conclude that Luke limited the Spirit's work exclusively to prophetic preaching, with no relationship to miracles.[25]

With its radicality, this thesis leads to a theological aporia: if miracles are not the work of the Spirit, in Luke's eyes, where do they originate? In order to nuance Schweizer's judgement I shall put in evidence three arguments: the dynamic of the word, thaumaturgical power, and the concept of δύναμις.[26]

Firstly, the word is accompanied by *visible signs*; this dynamic conception of the word is typical of the Hebrew Bible, and Luke is sensitive to it: see the summaries (Acts 2. 42–7; 4. 32–5; 5. 12–16) as well as 6. 8; 11. 24; 13. 12, and so on.

Secondly, *the common conviction of all early Christianity* is that miracle-working power is a product of the Spirit. This is confirmed in the programmatic preaching in Nazareth (Luke 4. 16–21), where the quotation of Isaiah 61. 1–2. ('The Spirit of God is upon me') fits into the framework of a messianic theology of the Jubilee, which takes into account the liberation of captives, the healing of the blind and the liberation of the oppressed (v. 18).[27] Similarly, in Peter's speech at Cornelius' house, he explains significantly 'how God anointed Jesus of Nazareth with the Holy Spirit and with power; how he went about doing good and healing all that were oppressed by the devil' (Acts 10. 38); the activity of the healer is concretized with the anointing of the Holy Spirit and of power. These two terms appear here in conjunction.

Thirdly, the term 'power' (δύναμις), present in Acts 10. 38, can also be used *to designate the Spirit*. This is the case in Luke 1. 35; 24. 49; Acts 1. 8. The two terms are linked in Acts 1. 17; 4. 14; and Acts 10. 38. Could this proximity of language imply a proximity of the Spirit and miracles?[28]

These observations nuance Schweizer's diagnosis, which remains fundamentally correct. Even if Luke is not a stranger to the pneumatological origin of the power to heal, he still basically maintains that the Spirit's

---

[25] Art. 'πνεῦμα', 1968, p. 407.

[26] In what follows, I agree with the conclusions of F. Bovon, *Luke the Theologian*, 1987, pp. 213–14.

[27] With M. B. Turner ('Jesus and the Spirit', 1981, pp. 14–22), who refutes the thesis of the exclusive concentration of Lucan pneumatology on the prophetic word.

[28] Note for example the affair of Elymas Bar-Jesus the magician (Acts 13. 9–11), denounced and punished with blindness by Paul; how can one separate, in the action of Paul 'filled with the Spirit' (v. 9), the act from the word, the exorcism from the prophecy?

work is prophetic. Why? In my view, this phenomenon does not come from Luke's desire to restrict the Spirit to the domain of the word, but it emanates from an unshakeable decision to attach miracles to Christology. One of the recurrent formulae in Acts is 'the name of the Lord (Jesus Christ)'. It is the name of the Lord that saves (2. 21; 4. 12; 10. 43; 22. 16). It is in the name of the Lord that the believer is baptized (2. 38; 8. 16; 10. 48; 19. 5).[29] It is also the name of the Lord that heals (3. 6, 16; 4. 10, 30; 16. 18; 19. 13). Luke is uncompromising on this theological point: the 'signs and wonders' that astonish the populations of the Mediterranean basin from the beginnings of Christianity do not originate with some religious hero, even one greatly inspired; they are *the work of the Christ*, and the sign of the presence of the Risen One among his own.[30] This Christological intransigence makes for a deficiency in Luke's pneumatology. I think, however, that this was of little importance in his eyes.

The inquiry that I have just pursued concerning the spirit of prophecy allows us to discover two new features of the Spirit in Luke–Acts. Firstly, the Spirit is not at the disposal of the Church; he is requested in prayer and received as a gift. Secondly, the work of the Spirit is essentially a work of the Word, which places Christians in the line of the prophets. The Spirit is at the service of the expansion of the Word. It is the Word, not the Spirit that Luke says grows (Acts 6. 7; 12. 24; 19. 20). I concur with F. Bovon who remarks, 'Luke, with Paul, refuses to place the Spirit in the forefront. It is the Word, stimulated and accompanied by the Spirit, which is the most important.'[31] Here we have a thoroughly Johannine motif.

This is why it is unwise to entitle Acts, the 'gospel of the Holy Spirit'. In that case, one sees only the vehicle and forgets what it transports. The book of Acts narrates the progression of the Word, encouraged by the Spirit and made effective through him.

The Spirit and unity

The progress of the Word, triumphant despite resistant confrontation, is what the author of Acts wishes to recount. The first part of his book is

[29] See the study of M. Quesnel on the formula 'in the name of': *Baptisés*, 1985, pp. 79–119.

[30] The question of miracle and its ambiguity will be dealt with in D. Marguerat, 'Magic and Miracles in the Acts of the Apostles' (forthcoming).

[31] *Luke the Theologian*, 1987, p. 238. B. Gillièron says well: 'L'Esprit au service de la parole', *Saint-Esprit*, 1978, p. 119. I have shown above that Luke unfolds a theology of the word in Acts (pp. 37–8).

devoted to the life of the community in Jerusalem up to the moment when it breaks apart as a result of Jewish pressure. Chapters 1 to 7 are marked by editorial notes that, without exception, insist on the growth of the community. Around the Twelve, there are one hundred and twenty believers (1. 15), then three thousand at Pentecost (2. 41), then five thousand at Peter and John's arrest (4. 4). Other indications and a rich quantitative vocabulary[32] also express the pleophoric dimension of Christianity's golden age. Without a doubt, this miraculous growth is the signature of the Spirit.

Parallel to this quantitative data, Luke, in his story of beginnings, also includes other information: the original community was one. The unity of the Twelve is already accentuated in 1. 12 and 2. 1. However, the three summaries are the privileged place where the *unity of the Church* is emphasized. The first summary (2. 42–7) has programmatic value; it sets forth the theme of the communion of believers, with its spiritual and material composition: 'They devoted themselves to the apostles' teaching and fellowship, to breaking of bread and prayers' (2. 42). We should notice the multiplicity of verbs in the imperfect, which indicates the enduring quality of the community. It is the same in the second summary (4. 32–5), which develops the theme of sharing possessions, and in the third (5. 12–16), which presents healing activity.

The ethical concretization of the Spirit

The three great summaries are full of the vocabulary of unity: they were together (2. 46; 5. 12), they were of one heart and soul (4. 32), they shared according to the needs of all (2. 45), so that no one was needy (4. 34).

What is the relationship with the Spirit? At first glance, the text presents none. Once again, Luke is not a systematician; his discourse is not argumentative, but narrative, and it is important therefore to search for his codes. This must be done by viewing the before and after of this episode, examining the macro-narrative as it unfolds. Let me explain.

Where is the first summary placed (2. 42–7)? In a way, it concludes the long Pentecostal sequence, that includes the account of the event, Peter's speech and the reaction of the people; verse 42 goes on without any transition, whereas the beginning of chapter 3 marks a break (the place changes in 3. 1). Luke conceived as a whole the Pentecostal sequence from 2. 1 to

[32] The multitude (πλῆθος): 2. 6; 4. 32; 5. 14, 16; 6. 2, 5). Many (πολύς): 1. 3; 2. 40, 43; 4. 4, 17, 22; 5. 12; 6. 7. To increase (πληθύνω): 6. 1–7; 7. 17. To add (προστίθημι): 2. 41, 47; 5. 14. Big (μέγας): 2. 20; 4. 33a, 33b; 5. 5, 11; 6. 8; 7. 11, 57, 60. There are thirty-two occurrences of πᾶς and five of ἅπας in chapters 1 to 7 to express totality.

2. 47, culminating with the summary. This literary composition requires interpretation in terms of its theological effects and, in my opinion, the conclusion is necessary: the outpouring of the Spirit reaches its climax in the unification of the believing community.[33] Even if we refuse to see, in the Spirit, the new Torah regulating Christian existence and Pentecost functioning as a new Sinai revelation, it remains true that *the irruption of the breath of God creating the Church finds its ethical concretization in the unity of the believers.* Edgar Haulotte, who has accomplished a fine reading of Acts, has spoken well of 'life in communion, the ultimate phase of Pentecost.'[34]

The result is even clearer with regard to *the second summary* (4. 32–5). As we have seen above, the endowment of the Spirit (4. 31) applies to the Word. After the positive model of the sharing of possessions (4. 32–3), there is the famous (and terrible) negative example of Ananias and Sapphira (5. 1–11). Since they sold a piece of property for the benefit of the community and without saying so retained a part of the sum, Ananias and Sapphira are unmasked by Peter and struck down at his feet. The sentence of death that eliminates them is carefully justified: 'Ananias, why has Satan filled your heart to lie to the Holy Spirit and to keep back part of the proceeds of the land?' (5. 3). I propose the following reading of this text:[35] the crime is not in financial withholding, but in offending against the principle of sharing everything in common (4. 32). Ananias and Sapphira have not sinned against morality, but against the Spirit in his function of constructing unity. Acts 5, then, is the figure of original sin in the Church, which introduces the Christian community to the realm of the equivocal. The reader learns how the Church, in its origin, was directed by the Spirit while also being exposed to Satan and how God has (terribly) protected it from the attacks of Evil.

A dimension of sanctification

I shall conclude on the question of unity. The three successive summaries of Acts 2–5, as well as the drama of Ananias and Sapphira, show an active Spirit at work in producing communion (κοινωνία) in the believing community. The construction of the narrative leads to this inevitable conclusion: in the eyes of Luke, the unity of the first Christians concretizes

[33] With E. Lohse, 'Pfingstberichtes', 1973, p. 188.

[34] This is the title of his article: 'La vie en communion, phase ultime de la Pentecôte', 1981. A more detailed text can be found in E. Haulotte, *Actes des apôtres*, 1977, p. 545.

[35] For a fuller, more detailed exposition than can be undertaken here, the reader should consult chapter 8 'Ananias and Sapphira (Acts 5. 1–11): the original sin'.

the action of the *pneuma*. These considerations should provide a deterrent to the endless discussions of the absence of 'the sanctifying Spirit' in the pneumatology of Luke.[36] While it is true that Luke does not focus on the future of believers in the new life, his insistence on naming the κοινωνία in the number of *notae ecclesiae* (2. 42) signals, to those who wish to hear, that this theologian is not indifferent to the path the Spirit traces in the heart of the converted.

If we return to Acts 5, yet from another angle, the narrative creates a question. The Spirit appears dangerously linked to the Church and dangerously linked to the ministry of the apostles. Is the Spirit free or captive to the institution?

Free or captive Spirit?

In addition to Acts 5, two other texts sharpen the question concerning the freedom of the Spirit: the episode in Samaria (8. 14–17), where, after Philip's visit, Peter and John arrive to confer the Spirit by the imposition of hands, and the episode in Ephesus (19. 1–7), where Paul comes to baptize and to transmit the Spirit to the disciples of John, who had only received John's baptism. In both cases, a first baptismal rite is downplayed in contrast to the benefit of the imposition of hands by an apostolate, which then gives the Spirit. The suspicion that the Spirit is being tamed by the apostolate cannot be ignored. Käsemann has notoriously maintained just this, denouncing this institutional regulation of the Spirit as proto-catholic. Is Luke, then, the forerunner of *Una sancta catholica*?[37] It has also often been asked if the author envisaged or even reflected on two baptisms, one in water and the other in the Spirit.

Up to this point, it is the Spirit who has been the guide of mission, the leader of the apostles, the one who chooses those to be sent out; it is the Spirit who transports Philip to Samaria and converts Peter in Cornelius' house, and it is the Spirit who binds Paul and blocks his route; with this mass of evidence it is hard to imagine that the Spirit is at the apostles' disposal, let alone that the Spirit is in their control. It is rather the contrary. The apostles appear to be controlled by the Spirit, the strategist of universal mission. Do Ananias and Sapphira and the episodes of Samaria and Ephesus constitute three disturbing exceptions?

[36] One is reminded of this refrain in Lucan research by M. Dumais, 'Bilan et orientations', 1995, p. 350.

[37] E. Käsemann supports this thesis in his article 'Johannesjünger', 1964, pp. 158–68: '*Lukas hat Geschichte übermalt und konstruiert, um die* Una sancta apostolica *gegenüber dem Zugriff der Gnostiker und Häretiker seiner Tage zu verteidigen*' (p. 168).

Two different discourses

In order to be sure, it is important to return to the 'Gentile Pentecost' (Acts 10–11). Luke attaches tremendous significance to the meeting of Peter and Cornelius. The comparison is instructive, as in this account the order of events is reversed: the Spirit's falling on the house of Cornelius precedes any sacramental intervention (10. 44–8), and the baptismal rite only ratifies a decision, already taken in heaven, to incorporate the Gentiles. Peter says, 'who was I that I could hinder God?' (11. 17). Later at the Jerusalem assembly, Peter has to justify his action before the others. His terminology is not the usual: 'God who knows the human heart, testified to them by giving them the Holy Spirit, just as he did to us. . .' (15. 8). The verb 'witness' (μαρτυρεῖν) belongs to mission vocabulary, and is ordinarily applied to the apostles that the Resurrected One has made his witnesses: 'and you will be my witnesses (μάρτυρες) in Jerusalem, in all Judaea. . .' (1. 8). In this case, God is the witness.[38] The reversal gives rise to thought as, on both occasions, the Holy Spirit is linked with testimony.

Concerning the Spirit of testimony, then, Luke is capable of maintaining *two different discourses*. On the one hand (Acts 1. 8), the Spirit is the power to witness which the Risen One gives to his people, and which makes them the instruments of God. On the other hand (Acts 15. 8), the Spirit precedes believers and provokes the events through which God makes his plan known. In other words, the Spirit leads faithful believers into missionary activity, but he also gives rise to events which the believers are invited to read theologically in order to perceive the will of the Lord. Therefore, the Spirit sets in place a relationship between theology and practice that is more complex than first suspected.

The Spirit, the pledge of God's consent

The account in Samaria (8. 14–17) fits into the same perspective. Philip proclaimed Christ to the Samaritans, who believed and were baptized (8. 12). When the apostles in Jerusalem hear of this, they delegate Peter and John, who then go and lay hands on the Samaritans, who receive the Holy Spirit; for the Spirit had not come upon any of them, says the narrator (8.16). It is important to note that the rite of imposing hands is preceded

---

[38] The same verb μαρτυρεῖν is applied to God who witnesses to his grace by granting a miracle-working activity to Paul and Barnabas (14. 3); but in line with his distinction between the Spirit of prophecy and the power to do miracles, Luke does not mention the Spirit in this case.

by a prayer 'for them that they might receive the Holy Spirit' (8. 15). The character of gift is explicitly maintained. Furthermore, the question that governs the narrative is neither ministerial nor sacramental.[39] Peter and John do not question the content of Philip's preaching, nor even the validity of his baptism. The evangelization of Samaria is the first extension of the Gospel outside Jerusalem and its Judaean environment. The geographical expansion promised by the Risen One (1. 8) now begins to take place, but the passage must still be ratified, and this is the role of the Spirit.

The action of Peter and John does not indicate any deficiency in Philip's mission. They come from Jerusalem – for in Luke's construction of the narrative, everything originates from Jerusalem, the city where salvation was concretized, and all must be legitimized by the church of Jerusalem. Peter and John come from the mother church, stretching out their hands so that the Spirit can descend in Samaria. The reference 'and they received the Holy Spirit' (8. 17) signals that *the Lord gives his consent to this missionary expansion.*[40] In other words, God 'testifies' to Philip's mission and leads the Jerusalem church to agree with it as well. A significant detail in the composition is that Luke does not forget to mention the return of the apostles to Jerusalem (8. 25).

Baptism and Spirit

The episode in Ephesus (19. 1–7) requires clarification. What is the relation, in Luke's thought, between *baptism and the coming of the Spirit?* Paul arrives at Ephesus and realizes that the believers know nothing about the Holy Spirit. They acknowledge having received the baptism of John, which is a baptism of conversion. At this point, the apostle then baptizes them 'in the name of the Lord Jesus', laying hands on them, and the Spirit is manifested by speaking in tongues. Here again, in my opinion, this is more to affirm the superiority of Christian baptism over John's baptism than to rectify a deficient institutional situation.

---

[39] With H. Steichele, 'Geist und Amt', 1976, pp. 185–203, esp. 199–203. A different view is expressed by M. Quesnel, *Baptisés*, 1985. L. Hartman is right when he sees in this rite a concretization of the link with the origin, that is, Jerusalem: 'Lukas will die wachsende Kirche an den Ausgangspunkt des Zeugnisses, Jerusalem, binden, gerade deshalb, weil der Schritt nach Samarien der zweite auf dem in 1, 8 angegebenen Weg ist' (*Namen*, 1992, p. 129).

[40] In the same sense: M. Gourges, 'Esprit des commencements', 1986, pp. 376–85; however, the distinction proposed by the author between a 'peaceful Spirit' linked to baptism and a 'shattering Spirit' of the eschatological type cannot be maintained for Lucan thought.

To be too precise regarding the link between baptism and the Spirit in Luke's thought (he could be reflecting an ecclesiastical practice) runs the risk of doing violence to a theology unfolded in narrative which escapes systematizing. It is however, I believe, possible to advance three proposals. (1) The baptism in the name of Jesus and the coming of the Spirit are *linked*; the interventions that have been mentioned, either solicit these links (8. 16–17; 10. 47), or affirm them (19. 5–6); the Christian condition cannot exist without the coming of the Spirit on the believer. (2) Baptism and the Spirit are linked, but *distinct*: the baptismal terminology is never applied to the Spirit, and baptism is never qualified as a 'gift';[41] time can separate baptism and the coming of the Spirit, and, normally, the first precedes the second (exception: 10. 44). (3) Luke *does not differentiate between two baptisms*, one in water and the other in the Spirit.[42] He links, rather, water baptism with the forgiveness of sins, while the coming of the Spirit depends on the laying on of hands.[43]

The imposition of hands provokes the Spirit's intervention. History teaches us that this Lucan conception has functioned as a guarantee for some perverse uses. However, it must be immediately noted that the narrative of Acts provides sufficient protection against such deviations. If Luke recognizes that the imposition of hands is tied to a minister, instituted by the Church, willed by God, and wholly devoted to the Word, the giving of the Spirit remains God's doing. One can only wait for it and pray that this grace be given.[44] Simon the magus learns this the hard way, as his attempt to buy the gift is met with apostolic outrage (8. 18–24). The Spirit in the Acts is a free Spirit. He may be threatened, but he is free.

---

[41] The vocabulary linked with the Spirit (receive, give, be filled, gift) is never applied to baptism; God is the giver of the Spirit, the Church through its missionaries is the agent of baptism.

[42] M. Quesnel, *Baptisés*, 1985, pp. 179–95, has defended the thesis that the book of Acts distinguishes two types of baptismal rite: the Judaeo-Christian baptism 'in the name of Jesus Christ' (2. 38; 10. 48), which dispenses pardon for sin and the Spirit, and the pagan-Christian baptism 'in the name of the Lord Jesus' (8. 16; 19. 15), which has propaedeutic value without conferring the Spirit. Without drawing a conclusion with regard to Luke's Christian usage, one must realize that this idea must be abandoned at the level of the book of Acts. Luke never draws attention to the terms of a confession of faith or to the mode of the rite of baptism. Luke is not so much preoccupied with the ritual or doctrine of baptism; he is, rather, interested in the access to it (τί κωλύει: 8. 37; 11. 17) and in divine approval of it as evidenced by the irruption of the Spirit. Only this (not the rite) commands the descent of the *pneuma* according to Luke (2. 38–9; 9. 17–18; 10. 44; 19. 6).

[43] F. Bovon, *Luke the Theologian*, 1987, p. 235.

[44] The coming of the Spirit in response to prayer is a Lucan axiom. It is confirmed even in Jesus' baptism (Luke 3. 21, the editor adds that Jesus was 'in prayer' before receiving the Spirit). It is also confirmed in the coming of the Spirit at Pentecost (cf. 1. 14) and in Cornelius' house (10. 4, 31).

Conclusion: a pragmatic of the Spirit

How should we evaluate the strengths and weaknesses of Luke the theologian's enterprise in his narrative presentation of the Spirit's work?

No New Testament author expresses as strongly as Luke the founding role of the Spirit, who builds the Church as a missionary community and gives it its unity. Luke does not see the Spirit as the source of faith, but sees him taking hold of believers, in response to their prayer, in order to integrate them into the witness to Christ. No other New Testament author so boldly involves the Spirit in history, going as far as to interpret the setbacks of the apostles as the movement of the breath of God (16. 6–7; 20. 22). Luke draws back neither from the diversity nor from the materiality of the Spirit's interventions.

We perceive nevertheless the limits of Luke's reflection on the subject. These limits are dictated, at least in part, by the constraints of narrativity. By telling the work of the Spirit, rather than talking about him, he offers his readers *a pragmatic of the Spirit*. In vain, one waits for an elucidation with regard to the discerning of spirits, such as both Paul (1 Cor. 14) and the Johannine tradition (1 John 4. 1–6) offer. The relationship between baptism and the coming of the Spirit on the believer are not easily identifiable. The Lucan fixation on the Spirit of prophecy flows directly from the Old Testament, in a way that might be described as naive. We find no equal to the grand Pauline theme of the Spirit's participation in the regeneration of the believer. Luke is less interested in the sanctification of the person than in the sanctification of the world. The individual is of interest to him in the sense that he/she participates in the great universal mission.[45]

The reader of Acts is not directed to reflect on the Spirit but to live from him and to discern his path throughout history. For the command of the Risen One to his disciples to be witnesses in all the earth (1. 8) is not already accomplished for Luke. Acts ends like an open book: Rome, where the narrative concludes, is not 'the end of the earth'. We notice here that Luke's eschatology is not an affair of the calendar, but of geography.[46] In this sense, the sphere of the Word is the world and the Church is *en route* to a universal horizon.

---

[45] O. Mainville, who highlights Luke's fixation on the function of witness linked to the Spirit, reaches the same conclusion: 'L'Esprit, dans la perspective de Luc, est davantage fonctionnel que relationnel' (*Esprit*, 1991, p. 339).

[46] M.-A. Chevallier points correctly: 'Je risque l'idée qu'il y a pour Luc une eschatologie d'ordre géographique, une eschatologie qui reste encore à réaliser sous l'impulsion de l'Esprit' ('Luc et l'Esprit Saint', 1982, p. 7).

7

JEWS AND CHRISTIANS IN CONFLICT

The question of the relationship between Jews and Christians has become a point of tension in the exegesis of Luke's work. The unusual vehemence with which this debate is conducted stems from its background: the reassessment of the Jewish–Christian relationship after the Shoah. In this context, biblical scholars rushed in to review the image of Judaism conveyed by the New Testament texts: in which cases is anti-Judaism a fact internal to the Scriptures and in which cases is it a perverse effect of the reading of the Scriptures?[1] But the focusing on Luke–Acts can be explained by a fact peculiar to Luke's work itself: of all the New Testament writings, Luke–Acts presents not the most negative image of Judaism[2] but the most difficult to grasp.

A contaminated debate

The fifty-two chapters of history from Luke 1 to Acts 28 lead the reader from the Temple in Jerusalem, at the beginning of the gospel, to Rome, where the book of Acts ends. What kind of relationship does Christianity have with Judaism? Is the movement from Jerusalem to Rome a symbolic shift? Has the God of Luke turned his back on Judaism in order to adopt Rome and pagan Christianity? Or does Christianity construct itself, on the contrary, in close continuity with the tradition of the fathers?

[1] With regard to Acts, M. Selvidge concludes that the work is indeed guilty: the verbal violence that is used would legitimate the crushing of all opposition to Christian truth ('Aetiological Legend', 1986). On the other hand, C. A. Evans exonerates Luke from this suspicion, arguing that the Lucan denunciation of Jewish responsibility in the death of Jesus does not stem from anti-Semitic sentiments, but is an integral part of the kerygma ('Jewish Rejection?', 1990). The contradiction is only apparent, as M. Selvidge deals with the pragmatic effect of the text, while C. A. Evans treats the theological structure of the work.

[2] N. A. Beck in *Mature Christianity* (1985, pp. 207, 241) presents the opposite view: 'The anti-Jewish polemic in Acts ... is the most ... destructive of Judaism in all the New Testament documents.' What is one to think of the Matthean anti-Judaism (Matt. 21. 33 – 22. 8; 27. 25)?

It is true that the reader could be surprised by the anachronism of the question. In fact, between the 30s and 60s, that is, at the level of the *story* recounted by the book of Acts, Christianity and Judaism do not constitute two separate entities, either theologically or sociologically. Christianity is at best a variant of Judaism, recognized as a 'sect' within the Jewish diversity (Acts 24. 4, 14; 28. 22), similar to the Sadducean party or the Pharisaic circles (the same term αἵρεσις designates them in Acts 5. 17; 15. 5; 26. 5). However, the question becomes pertinent at the level of the *narration* of the story, that is, in Luke's time, in the 80s. The Christianity that he addresses lives separated from the 'synagogues of the Jews' (Acts 13. 5; 14. 1; 17. 1, 17), even when relations have not been severed and the debate remains open to a certain degree (I shall come back to this later).

The study will be difficult, the path ahead having many exegetical obstacles and the debate contaminated by heavy ideological options. I am indebted to Simon Légasse for this description of the ethic of the exegete, made with lucidity and intellectual honesty: 'to look at the texts as they are, in order to rediscover them in all their crudeness. It is only in putting all the "cards on the table", by clarifying the situation without apologetic camouflage, that we can, I think, extricate the essential message from its contemporary husk, and then try to live it today.'[3]

Following this wise ethical counsel, the path I propose consists of five steps. The first presents the exegetical disagreement; I shall then present a hypothesis in order to overcome the blind alley created by the conflicting readings. This hypothesis will be developed through three successive inquiries that will examine the schema of rupture between Paul and the Synagogue, the evolution of the role of Jewish actors in the gospel and Acts, and, finally, the outcome of open crisis with Judaism in Acts 21–8. A conclusion draws together the results.

Israel, a two-sided face

What is Christianity's relationship to Judaism in Luke–Acts? To pose such a question plunges us into the exegetical conflict which for thirty years has presented two entirely contradictory readings. Each has been developed with equal talent.[4]

---

[3] S. Légasse, 'Antijudaïsme', 1972, p. 417. G. Wasserberg shows that 'antijudaism' is an inadequate term to use for Luke–Acts (*Aus Israels Mitte*, 1998, pp. 16–30).

[4] The compilation edited by J. B. Tyson, *Luke–Acts and the Jewish People*, 1988, gives an excellent presentation of the discordant readings. For the state of the question, see

The story of a double failure

On the one hand, Luke–Acts is read as a story of a double failure: neither Jesus nor the apostles were able to convince Israel that God had opened a breach in salvation history. No other New Testament writing charges the Jews as dramatically with the responsibility of the death of Jesus. After Pentecost, Peter (Acts 3. 14–15; 4. 27) and then Stephen (Acts 7. 51–3) denounce the Jews as the murderers of Jesus. Immediately after his conversion, Paul is threatened with death by his co-religionists of Damascus (9. 23); and, despite his incessant efforts to convince his brothers, 'the Jews' do not hesitate by any means, legal or illegal, to attempt to kill him,[5] going so far as to intend to lynch him in front of the Temple in Jerusalem (21. 27–36). The end of Acts then resounds like the farewell to an Israel immured in its obduracy; salvation goes to the Gentiles because the Jews refused it (28. 28). The outcome of this reading: the chosen people become the enemies of God. Repeatedly hardhearted, Israel is dismissed from salvation history because of its unbelief.

Until the 1970s this reading constituted the consensus among exegetes. Such a reading, centred on E. Haenchen's monumental commentary,[6] basically corresponds to a traditional reception of Luke–Acts in history, which played a powerful role in the establishing of Christianity's legitimacy in the face of Israel. This position has been, from time to time, defended (yet nuanced) by those who, following Augustin George,[7] refuse to see the condemnation of Israel as a global condemnation of the whole people. On the other hand, this reading is given a stronger form by John C. O'Neill, Jack Sanders, Michael Cook and Heikki Räisänen.[8]

J. B. Tyson, *Images of Judaism*, 1992, pp. 10–16, and *Luke, Judaism and the Scholars*, 1999; H. Merkel, 'Israel im lukanischen Doppelwerk', 1994, pp. 371–82; F. Bovon 'Retrospect and Prospect', 1992, pp. 186–90, and *Luc le théologien*, 1988, pp. 342–61.

[5] Acts 13. 45, 50 (the Jews of Pisidean Antioch insult Paul and Barnabas, then plot to provoke their expulsion); 14. 2–5 (violence against the apostles); 14. 19 (stoning of Paul); 17. 5–8 (incitation to riot and the denunciation of Jason); 17. 13 (stirring up of the crowd); 18. 6, 12–13 (insults and the denunciation of Paul); 23. 12–22 (plot against Paul); 24. 1–8 (denunciation before Felix); 25. 5 (ambush). The presence of a *pattern*, 'missionary action/opposition (most often Jewish)/expansion of mission' has been inventoried in L. M. Wills, 'Depiction', 1991, pp. 631–54, especially pp. 634–44.

[6] E. Haenchen, *Acts of the Apostles*, 1971. In the same line: H. Conzelmann, *Theology of St Luke*, 1982, pp. 145–8; J. Gnilka, *Verstockung Israels*, 1961, pp. 130–54; S. G. Wilson, *Gentiles*, 1973, pp. 219–38; R. Maddox, *Purpose*, 1982, pp. 31–65.

[7] A. George, 'Israël', 1978, pp. 87–125.

[8] J. C. O'Neill, *Theology of Acts*, 1970, pp. 77–99; J. T. Sanders, *Jews*, 1987; 'Jewish People', 1988, pp. 51–75; 'Who Is a Jew?', 1991, pp. 434–55; M. J. Cook, 'Mission", 1988, pp. 102–23; H. Räisänen, 'Redemption', 1991.

Reversing the paradigm

The consensus then fell to pieces. The first attack came in 1965 from Jacob Jervell, in a study with the programmatic title 'The Divided People'.[9] According to Jervell, Luke–Acts does not orchestrate the triumph of Gentile Christianity on the ashes of Jewish history, but sets out the story of the tearing apart of Israel. It is not because of the failure of the Jewish mission that the Gentiles receive the promises, but rather as the result of its partial success!

Thus the Church does not constitute a 'new Israel' that replaces the old; it continues the 'old Israel for whom the promises are fulfilled, since a great portion of the people have been converted'.[10] Since 1965, the thesis of the Norwegian exegete has been amplified, and hardened as well, by scholars such as David Tiede, Donald Juel, Robert Tannehill, Robert Brawley and David Moessner.[11] This rereading of Luke–Acts witnesses to an impressive reversal of the paradigm; there is a switch from negative to positive in the relationship of Christianity and Judaism in order to show that instead of rejecting the Jews and severing Gentile Christianity from Israel, Luke on the contrary sets out to attach it to Judaism.[12]

Reread in this way, Luke–Acts shows that the offer of salvation to the pagans is to be understood as the fulfilment of the Scriptures; Simeon, for example, welcomes such a view in the early stages of the gospel: the revelation to the Gentiles will be the 'glory of your people Israel' (Luke 2. 32 quoting Isa. 42. 6; 49. 6). The prophetic Scriptures that Luke uses as proof of fulfilment constantly remind his readers of this fact. The author

[9]   Article published in *Luke and the People of God*, 1972, pp. 41–74. More recently, see the article: 'Future of the Past', 1996.

[10]   'Divided People', 1972, p. 51: 'The author sketches a picture of Israel for whom the promises are fulfilled; he does not show us a new Israel arising out of the rejection of the old, but he speaks of the old Israel for whom the promises are fulfilled, since a great portion of the people has been converted.'

[11]   D. L. Tiede, *Prophecy and History*, 1980, and 'Glory to Thy People Israel', 1988, pp. 21–34; D. Juel, *Promise*, 1983; R. C. Tannehill, 'Tragic Story', 1985, pp. 69–85, and 'Rejection', 1988; R. L. Brawley, *Luke–Acts and the Jews*, 1987. D. P. Moessner, 'Ironic Fulfillment', 1988.

[12]   R. L. Brawley concludes his book *Luke–Acts and the Jews*, 1987, in these terms: 'Therefore the standard paradigm for understanding Luke's view of the relation between Christianity and Judaism should pivot 180 degrees. That is, rather than setting Gentile Christianity free, Luke ties it to Judaism. And rather than rejecting the Jews, Luke appeals to them...' (p. 159). We can measure the frontal opposition with the most trenchant representative of the other opinion, J. T. Sanders: 'the author of Luke–Acts does view the Jewish people *generally* as opposed to the purposes of God, as unable to understand their own scriptures, and as both foreordained to reject and willfully rejecting their own salvation' ('Who Is a Jew?', 1991, p. 436).

of Acts insists on the fact that the Christian community in Jerusalem is composed of 'thousands of believers... among the Jews and all are zealous for the law' (Acts 21. 20). The first Christians according to Acts 1–5 live around the Temple and understand themselves as a part of Israel, like Paul, who does not cease to demonstrate his scrupulous obedience to the law of Moses (16. 3; 21. 20–6; 24. 14) and to claim his Jewish identity: 'I am a Jew, born in Tarsus in Cilicia' (Acts 22. 3). Finally, one can mention the forgiveness offered to the Jews, which punctuates the missionary speeches (2. 37; 3. 19; 7. 60; 13. 38–9), just as Jesus, having deplored the fate of Jerusalem (Luke 23. 28), offers his forgiveness on the cross (23. 34).[13]

Two irreconcilable readings

Which reading should one choose? It is clear that the choice adopted by the exegete has enormous repercussions on the Jewish–Christian dialogue. On the one hand, the Jewish people are excluded from the promises and Christianity claims to be the new Israel; Luke–Acts expresses the violence that separated Church and Synagogue in the first century. On the other hand, Judaism and Christianity are joined in a relationship of substantial continuity that makes the birth of Christianity 'the final chapter in the history of Israel';[14] the rupture between Church and Synagogue is deplored as an undesirable theological distortion of Luke's point of view. An outside observer might wonder if the opposing parties have indeed read the same text of Acts.

An internal tension in Luke–Acts

In attentively reading the text of Luke–Acts, I have come to a troubling conclusion: both readings are defensible. Each has good arguments for its position. The two readings, like any reading, select certain features of the text, while leaving others aside. To put it briefly, the first reads Luke–Acts according to a logic of narrative order (from Jerusalem to Rome), while the latter relies on the figurative level of meaning (the construction of the characters in the narrative). But I insist: each of the paradigms has something in the text to rely on. Must we then opt, according to taste, for our own ideological leanings and choose the Luke that suits us?

[13] This aspect has been underlined by F. J. Matera, 'Responsibility', 1990, pp. 77–93.

[14] I take up an expression of J. Jervell, who thinks that the author of Luke–Acts 'writes the final chapter in the history of the people of God, Israel, from Jesus to Paul in Rome' ('Future of the Past', 1996, p. 110).

My hypothesis is rather that we do not have to choose one *over* the other. I think that the impasse can be overcome if we try to accept the reading of one *and* the other as they signal that Judaism, in Luke's work, cannot be reduced to a simple equation. In other words, the conflict of interpretation that has raged for thirty years does not simply reveal the whim of exegetes cultivating their disagreements! The fact that we can develop two divergent readings of Luke–Acts, in a convincing manner, testifies to a tension that belongs to the writing itself. Each of the readings holds to one of the poles and tends to turn a blind eye to the other. *The two images in tension which appear when we juxtapose the readings are each a component of Luke's work.*[15] Therefore, I propose not to *reduce this tension*, for example by resorting to a tradition/redaction stratification,[16] but to *interpret it theologically, since it is constitutive of the image of Judaism in Luke.*

A first indication

A first indication perhaps weighs in favour of exploring this hypothesis. If Luke simply envisaged installing the Church in the place of Israel, if he had only wanted to present a pro-Christian and anti-Jewish God, why did he bother to compose such a complex narrative? Why insist on the conversion of Jews in the Diaspora? In the narrative of Acts, why does Luke reduce the evangelization of the Gentiles to derisory unimportance? The only details given are at Lystra (14. 8–18) and Athens (17. 16–34).[17] On the other hand, if Christianity was only a pure continuation

[15] J. B. Tyson deserves the credit, as the first to propose a reading of Luke–Acts that attempts to integrate the two antagonistic images of Judaism (*Images of Judaism*, 1992): 'It is incorrect to maintain that Luke is simply pro-Jewish or simply anti-Jewish. He is both' (p. 188). According to Tyson, the narration has an apologetic aim, which takes the reader from a fusional relation with Israel (Luke 1–2) to the heinous rejection of the Jews (Act 28). Tyson is correct in considering the narrative strategy, and on a number of points of detail my own research agrees with his, even if my final result is very different. Furthermore, Tyson's analysis is handicapped by the postulate that the implied reader of Luke–Acts (who is also, if I have understood correctly, the historical reader: cf. p. 182) is a Godfearer. See my criticism on this subject below at note 74.

[16] So D. Slingerland who opposes a pro-Jewish tradition covering the essential part of Acts 1–8 with the massive anti-Jewish tendency of the Lucan redaction which dominates the second part of the book ('Composition', 1988, pp. 99–113). In his time, A. Loisy also proposed to resolve the tension in the same manner, but in the opposite sense: Luke succumbed to a pro-Jewish manner of his time, 'distorting' the story by making it harsher in regard to Israel than in the tradition he received (*Actes des apôtres*, 1920, pp. 104–21, esp. pp. 114–15). Whatever the sources of Acts, the problem of the theological coherence of the work is in no way resolved through literary criticism.

[17] The relationship with Israel is the *cantus firmus* of the Acts of the Apostles. One cannot ignore this paradox: the whole book of Acts is oriented toward the Gentile mission;

of the history of Israel, why did Luke so blacken the image of the Jews, turning them into the villains of the story, by obsessively returning to their antagonism toward the apostles (Acts 3–5), Stephen (Acts 7), the Christians in Jerusalem (Acts 8), Peter (Acts 12) and Paul (Acts 13–26)?[18]

The difficulty with my hypothesis is that it must show why, according to François Bovon's formulation, the gospel of Luke and Acts are, of all the New Testament books, the works 'the most open to universalism and the most favorable to Israel'.[19] However, it is not enough simply to establish that Luke holds one view and then its opposite concerning the Jewish question. Exegetes should not push Lucan thought into incoherence unless they can prove that it merits such a fate. I shall demonstrate that the Jewish identity in Luke's work has two opposite faces, one affecting the other, one connected to the other in such a way as to form with Christianity a relationship in which continuity and discontinuity are mixed. The question of the image of Judaism is posed here in a very different manner from that in the gospels of Matthew and John, in which the image is homogeneous.[20] *The work of Luke does not offer a uniform image of Judaism, but two faces diametrically opposed. It is with the aid of these two parameters, continuity and discontinuity, that Luke evaluates the relationship between Church and Synagogue for the Christianity of his time.*

What can be the coherence of such a dialectic? I shall attempt to articulate it, by examining the schema of rupture between Paul and the Synagogue.[21] This is my first investigation.

nonetheless, it devotes much the greater part of the narration to depicting the Jewish rejection of Christian preaching. J. B. Tyson has seen this correctly in 'Problem of Jewish Rejection', 1988.

[18] M. J. Cook rightly notes that the narrator adopts the Christians' point of view and not that of the Jews. He seeks to awaken the sympathy of the reader for the persecuted missionaries rather than for the Jews irritated by these intruders. 'Mission', 1988, pp. 102–3.

[19] F. Bovon, 'Retrospect and Prospect', 1992, p. 189.

[20] Concerning the Matthean image of Judaism, see D. Marguerat, *Jugement*, 1995, pp. 237–407 and pp. 575–80. F. Vouga recently attempted to clear the gospel of John of the accusation of anti-Judaism: 'Antijudaïsmus im Johannesevangelium?', 1993.

[21] In my opinion, in order to be faithful to its objective, the exegesis of Luke–Acts must satisfy two methodological conditions: (1) Since the gospel and Acts constitute a literary and theological entity, the reading of Acts must consider the interpretative models set forth in the gospel, as well as the play of similarities and differences between the two writings. (2) Lucan theology being of a narrative type should be perceived where it presents itself, that is, not in systematic declarations, nor in a priori argumentation, but in the arrangement of the narrative, in its repetitions, its turning points, its 'flash-backs', its emphases. These two heuristic principles are established in the now classic work of R. C. Tannehill, *Narrative Unity*, 2 vols., 1986 and 1990. G. Wasserberg has recently put them to work in his excellent dissertation: *Aus Israels Mitte*, 1998.

A prophetic model of rupture

One may begin by observing the way in which Luke ends his work. The
final scene of the book of Acts (28. 16–31) puts Paul on stage, arriving
in Rome as a prisoner. The apostle hurries to meet the Jewish delegation,
and he assures them that he 'had done nothing against our people or the
customs of our fathers' (28. 17). Later the apostle preaches, but those who
hear are divided: some are convinced and others are not (28. 24). Then
Paul proclaims the famous saying of Isaiah 6. 9–10: 'Go to this people and
say, "You will indeed listen, but never understand, and you will indeed
look, but never perceive. For this people's heart has grown dull..."'
(28. 26–7). The apostle concludes by announcing that the salvation of
God has been sent to the Gentiles, who will listen (28. 28).

The composition of this scene is not surprising to the reader of Acts.
On his arrival in a city, Paul begins by addressing his Jewish brothers,
but, confronted by lack of success, he turns to the Gentiles, who receive the Gospel with joy. This is a scenario that Luke has reproduced
from the beginning of the Pauline mission (Acts 13) with a regularity
that borders on monotony. In Antioch of Pisidia (13. 42–52), in Iconium
(14. 1–7), in Thessalonica (17. 1–9), in Beroea (17. 10–14), in Corinth
(18. 1–10), in Ephesus (19. 8–10), the same schema is repeated: Paul
announces the Word in the synagogue, but he is thrown out more or
less violently. However, the scenario in Rome presents two variations
that distinguish it from the stereotype. The *first* is that the preaching of
Paul in Rome is not totally rejected, but received in a diversity of ways
(I shall come back to this ἀσυμφωνία of 28. 25[22]). The *second* variation is that the encounter takes place in two stages: the hearers are first
interested in knowing more about Paul's sect (28. 22) and then are divided between sceptics and believers (28. 24). Jacques Dupont's study,
which is now a classic concerning the conclusion of Acts, has shown
that this same schema (initial interest, then a change of attitude) has
already appeared earlier in the narrative, at the outset of the Pauline
mission.[23]

Antioch of Pisidia: the rupture

During the sermon at the synagogue of Antioch of Pisidia (13. 12–52),
which inaugurates Paul's mission with Barnabas, one observes the same
procedure. *First stage*: Paul preaches, rereading salvation history from

[22] See pp. 221–6 (ch. 10).
[23] J. Dupont, 'Conclusion', 1984, pp. 486–9.

the lineage of David, and ends with a call to accept the 'justification that you could not find in the law of Moses' (13. 38: the vocabulary is very Pauline!). 'Many Jews and devout proselytes' (13. 43) are interested; they ask the missionaries to come back. *Second stage*: the following Sabbath, before 'the whole city,' gathered to hear the word of the Lord (13. 44), the Jews, 'blaspheming . . . contradict Paul and Barnabas'. Paul declares that he will then turn to the Gentiles and bases this mandate on the prophecy of Isaiah 49. 6: 'I have set you to be a light for the Gentiles, so that you may bring salvation to the ends of the earth.' In reaction, the Jews incite a riot in the city, resulting in the expulsion of Paul and Barnabas (13. 50).

It is worth examining this rupture closely since it establishes precisely what Jervell denies exists: a causal relation between the Jewish refusal and the extension of the preaching to the Gentiles.[24] I shall now analyse in successive steps the causes of the rupture, the justification that Paul offers, and the forms of the breach.

1. What are the *causes*? The crisis is not set off at the Christological reading of Psalm 2, as one might expect (13. 33), but at the sight of 'the whole city' assembled around the missionaries (13. 44) and their success (13. 48). Who forms this assembly? Certainly, πᾶσα ἡ πόλις (13. 44) does not indicate that the crowd was completely Jewish. The narrator had already noted the mixed nature of the crowd: both at the exordium of the homily (13. 16: ἄνδρες Ἰσραηλῖται καὶ οἱ φοβούμενοι τὸν θεόν; cf. v. 26) and upon leaving the synagogue (13. 43: πολλοὶ τῶν Ἰουδαίων καὶ τῶν σεβομένων προσηλύτων). The opposition between the Jews (οἱ Ἰουδαῖοι) and the crowds (οἱ ὄχλοι), which verse 45 sets up, makes clear that the latter are composed of Godfearers or persons not belonging to the Synagogue and, in any case, Gentiles. Luke says that the Jews who saw the crowds were filled with ζῆλος: this term in the LXX can designate both, negatively, jealousy and, positively, zeal for God.[25] The meaning 'holy zeal' could be suitable here, as in Acts 5. 17, but in any case it leads to an aggressiveness toward the Christian missionaries. One should not reduce the Jewish reaction to a manifestation of simple jealousy when confronted with the success of their rivals.[26] Rather than contenting himself with this trivial approach, Luke indicates at what precise point the conflict breaks out: it is the diffusion of the 'Word of

[24] 'Divided People', 1972, pp. 55–6 and 62.
[25] The philological study of B. J. Koet (*Five Studies*, 1989, pp. 102–5) leads him to retain this positive sense for 13. 45, which is philologically correct, but is contrary to the narrative context.
[26] So M.-J. Buss, *Missionspredigt*, 1980, p. 135.

the Lord' to the Gentile crowd that seems intolerable to the Antiochean Jews.[27]

2. How does Paul *interpret* the refusal of the Antiochean Jews (13. 46–7)? The apostle mentions that the Word should *first* be addressed to them; the priority of Israel is therefore respected, but the πρῶτον maintains the extension that the hearers contest. Paul then affirms that rejecting this word is the same as judging oneself 'unworthy of eternal life' (13. 46). Consequently, Israel severs itself from a grace that it believed it possessed. The quotation of Isaiah 49. 6 then signals that the universal offer of salvation, in the face of which the Jews become indignant, is nonetheless in accord with the direction of Scripture.

3. How does the rupture *take place*? The gesture of Paul and Barnabas in shaking the dust from their feet upon leaving the city that has expelled them is well known (13. 51); but what is the meaning of this rite? Jesus prescribes it to the Twelve (Luke 9. 5) and to the Seventy-two (Luke 10. 11), as a testimony against a city that did not welcome them. The author of Acts will later attribute a similar gesture to Paul before he breaks with the synagogue in Corinth (18. 6),[28] but, in this case, the apostle offers the interpretation: 'Your blood be on your own heads! I am innocent. From now on I will go to the Gentiles.' This is the meaning that is to be kept in mind: the rite of shaking the dust off the feet does not bring a curse; it places the guilt of the rejection on the Jews and absolves Paul from any responsibility for the rupture. It is the more surprising after this crisis that one learns that in the next town, Iconium, Paul and Barnabas go to the 'synagogue of the Jews' (14. 1) where the same thing begins again: conversion of Jews *and Greeks*, provoking Jewish anger, which stirs up the city against the apostles. Later, in Corinth, as we have just seen, Paul swears a second time that 'from now on I will go to the Gentiles' (18. 6) . . . but the first name of a convert in what follows is Crispus, an official of the synagogue (18. 8).

What do these reversions mean? Does Luke seek to describe an impulsive Paul, regretting afterwards his fits of anger? Or is he simply satisfying

[27] G. Wasserberg notes that Luke does not mention the openness of Paul's preaching to 'all the city' (13. 44) until after the συναγωγή has been disbanded (13. 43a); the theological succession 'the Jew first and then the Gentile' has been respected narratively (*Aus Israels Mitte*, 1998, p. 315).

[28] There is a divergence between 13. 51 where the dust is shaken from the feet and 18. 6 where the clothes are shaken (same verb ἐκτινάσσεσθαι). R. L. Brawley sees an identical function signifying rupture, but with a progression from the clothes (Paul leaves the synagogue of Corinth, but not the city) to the feet (the messengers leave Antioch); *Luke–Acts and the Jews*, 1987, p. 73.

the constraints of a Pauline mission *pattern*?[29] The answer, it will be argued, lies deeper. In fact, it leads to the very heart of the Lucan conception of the people of God. According to Luke, the Gentiles do not replace Israel in the plan of God but, on the contrary, they join the people of God and enlarge it to worldwide dimensions. This is why Paul continually returns to the synagogue, and this is why his sermon, at the end of Acts, still addresses the Jews (28. 17–28). Not only has this extension of Israel to the nations been prophesied (13. 47), but for Luke the Gentiles joining the ranks of the chosen people do not deprive Israel of anything. What is at stake is nothing less than the fulfilment of the prophecies, from which the chosen people are in process of removing themselves.

A symbolic rupture

Is this gesture of rupture by Paul and Barnabas symbolic of the deteriorating relationship between the Christian missionaries and the Synagogue or is its validity limited to Antioch, as Tannehill argues?[30] Its symbolic value seems preferable for three reasons: (a) the repetition of the orientation to the Gentiles in 18. 6 and 28. 28 gives emphasis to the Lucan presentation of Paul's mission, and centres on it a fundamental structure; (b) the scenario in two stages gives the Jewish decision at Antioch a definitive character;[31] (c) Luke has placed in the gospel, for the attention of the reader, an interpretative model of the scenario in two stages, whose function is also programmatic: the preaching of Jesus at Nazareth.

Many commentators have already linked the beginning of Jesus' ministry (Luke 4. 16–30) with that of the Pauline mission (Acts 13. 13–52).[32] Both occur in the same place: a synagogue. Both express, at first, the same interest on the part of the hearers: they admire. And there is, at a

---

[29] Paul's three announcements to turn toward the Gentiles, after (partial or total) rejection of his preaching, mark the apostle's mission and signal the three centres of his missionary activity: Asia Minor (13. 46), Greece (18. 6) and Rome (28. 28). The return to the synagogue that follows the first two announcements has been interpreted very differently: (a) as a mechanical application of a narrative stereotype (!) (J. B. Tyson, 'Jewish Public', 1984, pp. 574–83); (b) as a clue to the continued mission to Israel, even after Rome (R. C. Tannehill, 'Rejection', 1988, pp. 98–101); (c) as the proof that Paul never rejected Israel (R. L. Brawley, *Luke–Acts and the Jews*, 1987, pp. 69–78); (d) as the demonstration of Israel's recidivism in the refusal of the Gospel (J. T. Sanders, 'Jewish People', 1988, pp. 71–5).

[30] R. C. Tannehill, 'Rejection', 1988, p. 89.

[31] E. Richard has identified in the structures in two stages a Lucan literary procedure, through which the author confirms the validity of a fact: *Acts 6,1–8,4*, 1978, pp. 214–29.

[32] Here again J. Dupont led the way: 'Conclusion', 1984, pp. 502–8. The literary comparison between the two texts has been done by W. Radl, *Paulus und Jesus*, 1975, pp. 82–100.

second stage, the same rejection: Jesus just escapes being killed. How does this text function as a model? First, because the opposition Israel versus nations is reworked by the example of the graces offered to the Gentiles through Elijah and Elisha (4. 24–7);[33] as he likes to do, Luke composes a scene, in which he anticipates a truth yet to come, which is Israel's rejection of the Word and its reception by the nations. Second, the episode functions as a model because the fate of Jesus is interpreted with the aid of the motif of the prophet rejected by his own.[34] Thus Luke sets up a prophet typology, which will function as a central category of his Christology. It is part of the destiny of the prophet, as in Jesus so too in Paul, to be rejected by his own.[35] But it is not for the prophet, neither for Jesus nor for Paul, to reject this people.

This Deuteronomistic model of the rejected prophet has its rules as David Moessner has shown:[36] the prophet has to warn the people of God, to keep them alert and to threaten them. This is not so that the people should be cursed, but because they are in danger and the prophet struggles to keep them alive. The prophet does not declare that God has abandoned his people; he has not, and this is precisely why he struggles to change their behaviour. The rhetorical effect of the word of judgement in Isaiah 6. 9–10 at the end of Acts (28. 26–7), as I shall show later,[37] fits into the same perspective.

My first demonstration has produced the following results: Paul's re-action to the crisis, set off by his mission to the non-Jews, is twofold: he claims the support of the Scriptures for his action, and he refuses to align himself with a rupture that is not his responsibility. The rupture the Synagogue desired leads Luke to reinforce the signs of theological continuity: the granting of salvation to the Gentiles does not occur over and against Israel; it does not replace the promises made to Israel. The universality of

---

[33] Cf. J. B. Tyson, *Images of Judaism*, 1992, pp. 59–62.

[34] Concerning the programmatic role of Luke 4. 16–30 in the Lucan work, J. T. Sanders seems more correct than R. L. Brawley. The latter denies all prefiguration of the rejection of the Gospel in the Nazareth episode. He sees only an affirmation of Jesus' prophetic identity (his rejection confirms ironically his status as a prophet): *Luke–Acts and the Jews*, 1987, pp. 6–27. J. T. Sanders accounts better for the historico-salvific anticipation to which Luke is devoted ('Jewish People', 1988, pp. 72–4).

[35] L. T. Johnson has paid a good deal of attention to the carrying over of the prophetic typology of the gospel of Luke into Acts; that is, from Christology to the figure of the apostle (*Literary Function*, 1977, pp. 15–126).

[36] D. P. Moessner shows how Luke fashions both Jesus and Paul with the help of the Deuteronomistic model of the prophet announcing unrelenting judgement against the people of God and then being rejected by his own; he aligns Luke 11. 37–54; 13. 31–5; 19. 11–27; and 21 with Acts 13. 40–6; 18. 6 and 28. 25–8 ('Paul in Acts', 1988, pp. 96–104).

[37] See pp. 149–51.

salvation is born in the very history of Israel, finding there both its source and legitimacy (13. 32–9); however, this opening is paradoxically put into action by the Jewish refusal of the Christian mission. This consideration leads me to my second inquiry: the evolution of the Jewish actors in the narrative.

The turning-point of history

Jack Sanders has identified the phenomenon which well explains the difficulty we have in grasping the image of Judaism in Luke: Acts does not represent one view of the Jews, but two. The first is discursive, the second is narrative.[38] The two views do not overlap. The first appears in the kerygmatic sections of the missionary speeches (Acts 2. 36; 3. 14–16; 4. 10; 5. 30; 7. 52; 10. 39; 13. 27–8) and points out the guilt of the Jews in the murder of Jesus. The second view is unfolded by the narrative, which from chapter 2 to chapter 28 brings the Jewish authorities or the Synagogue into conflict with the Christian missionaries, a conflict that both separates and unites them at the same time.

Is it possible to harmonize these two views? In Sanders' perspective, it is conceivable by reducing the narrative to the discursive: 'By the end of the Acts the Jews have *become* what they from the first *were* . . .', namely, obstinate to the purposes of God.[39] The other paradigm for reading Luke also postulates the homogeneity of the two views, but in the opposite way, through aligning the discursive with the narrative. In this perspective, the constant return of Paul to the Synagogue confirms the priority of Israel in salvation history, a priority that both Peter (3. 26) and Paul (13. 46) recognize; the rejection of the Christian missionaries does not call this into question. David Tiede writes that Acts throughout remains 'a story of God's determined purpose to redeem Israel and even to restore Israel's glory of bringing the light of God's reign to the Gentiles'.[40]

On the discursive plane, we can agree with David Tiede that the denunciation of the Jewish responsibility in the death of Jesus is limited to the first part of Acts (up to chapter 13), that it exonerates the non-Jerusalemites of direct guilt (cf. 10. 39; 13. 27), and that its conformity

---

[38] 'Jewish People', 1988, pp. 56–73; *Jews in Luke–Acts*, 1987, pp. 37–83.

[39] The quote continues, 'for what Jesus, Stephen, Peter and Paul say about the Jews – about their intransigent opposition to the purposes of God, about their hostility toward Jesus and the gospel, about their murder of Jesus – is what Luke understands the Jewish people to be in their essence' (*Jews in Luke–Acts*, 1987, p. 81).

[40] 'Glory to Thy People Israel', 1988, p. 34.

to the Scriptures supports an offer of pardon[41] (2. 36–7; 3. 17–19; 4. 12; 5. 31; 13. 38–9).[42] On the other hand, however, one must recognize that the *inclusio* of Luke 2 and Acts 28, so important to Tiede,[43] does not lead the narrative back to its point of departure. From one end of Luke's narrative to the other, history advances, actors develop, and points of no return are passed. The episode at Antioch of Pisidia has already shown us that the relationship between the Synagogue and the Christian missionaries fluctuates; there are times of acceptance and times of rejection. What is one to think about the role of Jewish actors from the beginning of the gospel to the end of Acts? Does it remain constant? If it develops, the question is why?[44]

A path through the gospel of Luke

As one investigates the gospel of Luke in search of the relationship between Jesus and the Jewish people, it is not advisable to become focused on the specific figures of the scribes or the Pharisees; their hostility arises early on (5. 21) and is continuous. In my view, Luke's use of the terms ὄχλος (crowd) and λαός (people) offers a more adequate image of the whole of Israel.[45] The result of a statistical analysis concerning this point is unexpected. It corresponds exactly to the incident at the synagogue in Nazareth (Luke 4. 16–30), to which I alluded in reference to Acts 13, and which Luke has consciously conceived of as a miniaturized presentation of his gospel. For the totality of the gospel, one finds a scenario in two stages: in a first stage, the mass of the people differ from their leaders and support the action of Jesus; at the end of the gospel, the crowd rejoins its leaders and turns against the man of Nazareth. This calls for a closer examination.

The people's favourable response to Jesus is frequently noted in the narrative;[46] it is contrasted with the negative response of the leaders (Luke

---

[41]   With S. G. Wilson, 'Jews and the Death of Jesus', 1986, pp. 155–64, esp. pp. 158–9.

[42]   The only exception is Stephen's speech, where the call to repentance and the offer of forgiveness are replaced by the prayer of the martyr requesting pardon for his executioners (7. 60).

[43]   'Glory to Thy People Israel', 1988; but read the pertinent response in D. P. Moessner, 'Ironic Fulfillment', 1988.

[44]   For what follows, see J. B. Tyson, 'Jewish Public', 1984, and *Images of Judaism*, 1992, pp. 42–180; L. Gaston, 'Anti-Judaism and the Passion Narrative', 1986; J. T. Sanders, *Jews in Luke–Acts*, 1987, pp. 155–299; R. L. Brawley, *Luke–Acts and the Jews*, 1987, pp. 84–154.

[45]   J. B. Tyson ('Jewish Public', 1984, pp. 576–7.) and R. L. Brawley (*Luke–Acts and the Jews*, 1987, p. 133) have been sensitive to the active and interventionist role of the Lucan crowds, who are not restricted to being witnesses of the event, but provoke it.

[46]   Luke 4. 42; 5. 1, 15, 26; 6. 17–19; 7. 16–17; 8. 4, 19; 9. 43; 10. 39; 15. 1–2; 18. 43.

5. 21, 26; 13. 17; 15. 1–2). It was the same for John the Baptist: Luke points out that 'all the people' listened, while the Pharisees and lawyers rejected his baptism (7. 29–30). Even in Jerusalem, the popular support that Jesus receives temporarily protects him from the attacks of his enemies (19. 48; 20. 19, 26; 22. 2). Judas has to wait for the moment far from the crowds to hand over his master (22. 6). Clearly, there is empathy between Jesus and the people.

Yet, before Pilate the same crowd cries out: 'Away with him' (αἶρε τοῦτον, 23. 18). Allied with its leaders, the people confirm the guilt of Jesus (23. 4–5, 13) and request his death (23. 21–3). What has happened? Luke gives no explanation.[47] He limits himself to dating the historical turning point at Jesus' arrest (22. 47).[48] In using the cumulative designation 'the chief priests, the leaders and the people' (23. 13), he signals that all Israel unites against the Nazarene. Does the gesture of repentance by those at the cross (23. 48: they 'return home, beating their breasts') suggest that the crowd's agreement was only due to the manipulative pressure of the leaders? This is possible. Whatever the case, the drama has been completed. It is in conformity with this unified solidarity against Jesus that Peter and Stephen will remember, without any distinction among the people of Jerusalem, this Jesus '*you* have killed' (Acts 3. 15; 4. 10; 7. 52). One finds a similar agreement when Paul lists the authors of Jesus' death, grouping the people and its leaders: οἱ κατοικοῦντες ἐν Ἰερουσαλὴμ καὶ οἱ ἄρχοντες αὐτῶν (13. 27).

A path through Acts

What about Acts? Statistical comparison shows an interesting change in vocabulary between the beginning and the end of the narrative. The terms ὄχλος and λαός abound in the first chapters of Acts in order to designate the hearing, the harmony, and the veneration that the people of Jerusalem share for the first community grouped around the apostles.[49] This vocabulary clearly diminishes by the end of Acts.[50] On the contrary,

[47] On this subject, see J. B. Tyson's 'Jewish Public', 1984, p. 579. H. Merkel: 'So sehr Lukas also die Beteiligung des Volkes am Tod Jesu hervorhebt, so wenig klagt er es oder beschuldigt es' ('Israel', 1994, p. 394).

[48] L. Gaston also notes the crowd's astonishing turnabout at Jesus' arrest which Luke sets out clearly by substituting for the παραγίνεται Ἰούδας εἷς τῶν δώδεκα καὶ μετ' αὐτοῦ ὄχλος of Mark 14. 43 – the formulation ἰδοὺ ὄχλος, καὶ ὁ λεγόμενος Ἰούδας εἷς τῶν δώδεκα (22. 47), which puts the ὄχλος to the fore and 'seems to mean the people of Israel as such' ('Anti-Judaism and the Passion Narrative', 1986, p. 145).

[49] Acts 2. 47; 3. 9, 11, 12; 4. 1, 2, 10, 17, 21; 5. 12, 13; etc. (λαός), 1. 15; 6. 7 (ὄχλος).

[50] λαός appears twenty-nine times between Acts 2 and 12, seven times between chapters 13 and 19 and only eleven times in the remainder of Acts. There are

the term 'Jew', which is practically absent in the first eight chapters (cf. 2. 5, 11), is used frequently from chapter 12 onwards, with the connotation being always more negative: from 12. 3 onwards, the formula οἱ 'Ιουδαῖοι becomes the stereotyped designation of the opposition of Israel to the preaching of the Gospel (12. 11; 13. 50; 14. 2, 4, 5, 19; etc.). At the end of Acts, οἱ 'Ιουδαῖοι is the symbol of opposition to the Gospel.[51]

This is not to say that the Christian missionaries' contentions with Judaism only begin in Antioch of Pisidia (Acts 13). But during the golden age, which has been called 'the Jerusalem spring' (chs. 2–5), the hostility the apostles encounter is confined to the circle of leaders (high priest, elders, scribes, Sadducees), whereas the people 'held them [the apostles] in high esteem' and 'more than ever believers were added to the Lord, great numbers of both men and women' (Acts 5. 13–14). At the beginning of Acts, the same rupture as we have seen in the gospel separates the people from their leaders. Fear of the crowds is a protection for the apostles against the fury of the Sanhedrin (5. 26). Not the crowd, but the Sanhedrin are blamed for the crisis that destroys the harmony: the execution of Stephen (6. 9–15; 7. 54–60). The disciples' destiny is being modelled on that of their Master. This is explicitly declared in the prayer of the community (4. 27–30).[52] The disciples cannot hope for a better fate than that of their Master (Luke 12. 8–12).

At the other end of the narrative, the climate has completely changed. Paul is seized in the Temple (!) by the Jerusalem crowd, dragged out, and escapes only through the intervention of Roman police (21. 26–33). One must note the symbolic meaning of the action of the furious crowd: after having ejected Paul (21. 30)[53] from the Temple which had been the centre

five occurrences of ὄχλος in Acts 1–11, twelve occurrences in 13 to 19 and five in 20 to 28.

[51] The figure of the Jews has been reworked narratively by Luke in order to take on the hostile pole in the network of characters in the narrative (on this narrative procedure: J. A. Darr, *Character Building*, 1992). However, it is true that the construction of this anti-hero character is not as massive as M. J. Cook and J. T. Sanders claim: (a) Luke can use it together with the mention of the Jews converted by the apostles' preaching; cf. for example 13. 43, 45; (b) the behaviour of the Jews of Cyprus (13. 5), Derbe (14. 2), Beroea (17. 10; by comparison with 17. 13!) and Ephesus (18. 19–20) is not hostile; (c) in Corinth, Ephesus, Jerusalem and Caesarea, it is the political apparatus that takes over Paul's case (however, the civil servants are, in fact, instrumentalized by the Jews: 18. 12–13; 19. 33; 21. 30–6; 14. 1–9, 27). See also H. Merkel's 'Israel', 1994, pp. 393–4.

[52] Concerning the progressive rise of hostility of the Jewish authorities toward the apostles in Acts 2–5, see chapter 8, 'Ananias and Sapphira (Act 5. 1–11): the original sin' (esp. pp. 161–2.

[53] We must also note the irony of the narrator simmering beneath the accusation that strikes the apostle: 'This is the man who is teaching everyone everywhere against our people, our law and this place; more than that, he has actually brought Greeks into the Temple and

of life for the first Christians (2. 46), they close the doors. The cry that had decided the fate of Jesus is again repeated: 'Remove this individual from the earth' (Αἶρε ἀπὸ τῆς γῆς τὸν τοιοῦτον 22. 22; cf. Luke 23. 18). As is well known, the narrator has carefully modelled the martyrdom of Paul on the Passion of Jesus.[54] Has the same coalition formed itself again as in the days of Jesus' Passion? Has Israel again united itself against the Nazarene? Everything makes one think so, but this is not the case.

From idyll to hysteria

Prior to further investigation, it is important to ask of Acts the same question posed to the gospel: at what moment does the story turn? What makes the relationship between Judaism and Christianity move from idyll to hysteria? The book of Acts is more explicit than the gospel on this point.

The *first break* goes back to the Stephen affair (6. 8 – 8.1). Accused of slandering the Temple and the Law, Stephen is led before the Sanhedrin, who, after hearing him, stone him. His speech is a summary of sacred history, from Abraham to Solomon, centred on the question of where God should be worshipped.[55] God promised Abraham that his people would come back after the exodus to worship in Israel's land (7. 7); but the construction of the Temple by Solomon was an error, for 'the Most High does not dwell in houses made with human hands' (7. 48). Stephen's contention concerns the confinement of God to Israel.

The *second break* occurs with the encounter of Peter and Cornelius. Luke has developed this into a highlight of his work (10. 1 – 11. 18). The baptism of Cornelius does not take place without the powerful intervention of God, which obliges Peter and convinces the Church of the

---

has defiled this holy place' (21. 28). Not only the apology of chapter 22 will allow Paul to claim his unshakeable fidelity to the Torah (22. 3); but the rereading of the Damascus event will culminate in an order addressed to Paul by Christ to '*get out* of Jerusalem quickly' for 'I will send you far away to the Gentiles' (22. 18, 21). In other words, Paul does not seek so much to *introduce* a Gentile into the Temple as to follow his vocation of *getting out* of the Temple to go where the Gentiles are.

[54] Paul, like Jesus, finds himself alone before people who desire his death. Paul appears before the Sanhedrin, before the Roman authority and before King Agrippa (Acts 21. 40 – 26. 32), just as Jesus appeared before the Sanhedrin, before Pilate and before Herod (Luke 22. 66 – 23. 25). The actors are the same. There is the same open defiance between the Jewish nobles who demand the head of the accused (Luke 23. 2; Acts 24. 2–9) and the Roman authorities who consider the victim innocent (Luke 24. 14–15, 22; Acts 25. 25; Acts 26. 31–2). The evidence has been assembled by W. Radl, *Paulus und Jesus*, 1975, pp. 169–251; see also J. B. Tyson's *Death of Jesus*, 1986, pp.114–41.

[55] See E. Richard, *Acts 6,1–8,4*, 1978, pp. 259–74. In his narrative overview of the book of Acts, G. Wasserberg minimizes the criticism of the Temple in Stephen's speech, considering that the rupture with Israel does not come until Acts 10–11 (*Aus Israels Mitte*, 1998, pp. 248–50).

immensity of the event: for the first time, a non-Jew is admitted into the covenant. Luke shows how God directed the course of events: (a) by an appearance to Cornelius (10. 3–6); (b) by a vision given to Peter (10. 10–16), destroying the ancient barrier between pure and impure; (c) by a revelation of the Spirit to Peter (10. 19–20); (d) by a second Pentecost in Cornelius' house (10. 45–6). Nowhere else does the book of Acts invest such a concentration of the supernatural in one event. The narrative touches on a point that is extremely sensitive to Luke.

The revelation given to Peter can be summarized in these words (10. 34): 'I truly understand that God shows no partiality' (οὐκ ἔστιν προσωπολήμπτης ὁ θεός). This is not to say that the status of Israel is abolished, but its holiness is no longer exclusive, being now enlarged to include all believers. An undeniable innovation comes into the picture here, even though the old term προσωπολήμπτης, derived from the LXX, is required to express it.[56] Peter explains the unbelievable turn of events: 'God has shown me that I should not call anyone profane or unclean' (10. 28). The recentring[57] of salvation history on the event of Jesus, already announced in Peter's speech in Jerusalem in 4. 12, receives its ethical corollary here. Paul will link it to the theme of universality in Antioch of Pisidia: God chose him to bring 'salvation to the end of the earth' (13. 47). The 'Jews' in the book of Acts will fiercely oppose this widening of the promises made to the chosen people.

I can now conclude my second investigation. The same development brings together the Acts of the Apostles and the gospel of Luke and aligns the fate of the witnesses with the destiny of their master: the growing opposition that the word of Jesus meets. Wherever it may be, witness arouses hostility, not only from the Jews, but principally from them. The heart of the conflict is the revelation that with Jesus' resurrection, the holiness of Israel includes all men and women who believe.

If we consider this development of the role of the Jewish actors, it seems that the die is cast and that Luke, with regard to the image of Judaism, endows the book of Acts with the same profile as the gospel: having

---

[56] It is striking to note the lack of weight given to this text in the reflection of those who hold to a continuity paradigm (Jervell, Tiede, Tannehill, Brawley); it is indubitable that Luke has made it a turning point in his salvation history. This is attested by the care given to the composition of 10. 1 – 11, 18, especially since the overthrow of the concept of purity is not supported by any scriptural citation in the Lucan text (with J. B. Tyson, *Images of Judaism*, 1992, pp. 119–25)! See F. Bovon's treatment of this text in 'Tradition et rédaction', 1987.

[57] To indicate the Christian rupture with Israel, D. Gerber speaks of the 'end of a belonging' (the end of the exclusiveness of the chosen people) and Christological 'recentring' ('Luc et le judaïsme', 1993, pp. 63–5).

begun in euphoria, the encounter ends in hatred. Is this what happens? No. The expected scenario does not turn out exactly according to these norms. Luke is more subtle. The way that Paul's passion resembles that of Jesus no doubt reflects Luke's desire to demonstrate the repetition of the phenomenon of rejection.[58] The chosen people no longer want Jesus or his messengers. However, in reading closely the last chapters of Acts, one can also notice the difference from the narrative of the Passion, as Luke is careful to leave open cracks in the wall of hostility. Jewish hardness is not as massive as it was with Jesus; there are openings. In this image of Judaism, which gradually grows darker as the narrative of Acts advances, there are signs which finally allow us to glimpse the fact that, in Luke's eyes, the debate does not end with a closed door. I discern two cracks and shall now devote my third inquiry to exploring them.

Openness and closure (Acts 21–28)

The question with which I am concerned here is how Luke composes the image of Judaism at the end of his work. The conclusion of a literary work is clearly a strategic position, for it is at this point, when the narrative comes to an end, that the narrative world displayed by the author rejoins the world of the readers. So the question is: what image of the relationship between Christianity and Judaism, what hope, what regrets, will the reader take away as he or she leaves the narrative world and rejoins their own?

The cracks

I mentioned two cracks. I see the first where Luke comes to the end of the story. Four Pauline apologies mark the last section of Acts: before the people of Jerusalem (ch. 22), before the Sanhedrin (ch. 23), before the governor Felix (ch. 24) and before King Agrippa (ch. 26). The accusation of the Jerusalem leaders is invariable: 'We have found this man a pestilent fellow, an agitator among all the Jews throughout the world' (24. 5; cf. already Luke 23. 5). If the indictment is clear, Paul's defence is less so, as he does not respond to the charge. Paul never seeks to clear himself of the accusation of troublemaking. His only argument, his only plea, is to affirm his Jewishness. 'I am a Jew . . . brought up at the feet of Gamaliel, educated strictly according to the law of the fathers' affirms Paul in Jerusalem (22. 3). 'I am a Pharisee, a son of Pharisees . . .' he declares before the Sanhedrin (23. 6). Again, before Felix, Paul confesses, 'I worship the

---

[58] On the procedure of *syncrisis* that is at work here, see above, pp. 56–9.

God of the fathers, believing everything laid down according to the law or written in the prophets' (24. 14). And before Agrippa: 'Now, I stand here on trial on account of my hope in the promise made by God to our fathers' (26. 6).

In Rome, the apostle will repeat that if he wears chains it is because of the hope of Israel (28. 20). What does this hope affirm? It affirms that Israel is destined to be the light to all nations, bearer of justification for all, just as the raising of Jesus from the dead attests (13. 37–9). In other words, even before the representatives of the Roman authorities, who have to decide on his life, it is to Judaism, and again to Judaism, that Paul appeals in order to certify that the mission in which he participates has its origins in the Word of the God of the fathers.[59]

Here is the crack: going against those who repudiate him, Paul claims his adherence to the holy people and the tradition of the fathers, but his protest is not without echo. In his (useless) attempt to convince the Sanhedrin (ch. 23), Paul addresses the Pharisees who form the assembly with the Sadducees: 'Brothers, I am a Pharisee, a son of a Pharisee, I am on trial concerning the hope of the resurrection of the dead' (23. 6). This statement creates a confusion in the assembly since the Sadducees do not believe in the resurrection. The result: 'certain scribes of the Pharisees' group stood up and contended, "We find nothing wrong with this man. What if a spirit or an angel has spoken to him?" (23. 9). This is most unusual. Not only does Paul affirm that he is a Pharisee, but the other Pharisees recognize him as one of their own and join King Agrippa in his defence.

Why does Luke refer to this incident? I shall not deny the narrator's playful mischief in composing the incident. The hero's play on words renders this conclusion even more likely. The common conviction of the resurrection of the dead, that Paul puts forward in order to set himself up as the victim of the Sanhedrin's hostility (23. 6), is no longer a hope as in Pharisaic piety. Rather, it belongs to history. Is Luke's desire merely to be ironical about the dissentions among the Jews, who are incapable of forming a unified front against Paul? On the contrary, I believe that once again he is sincerely seeking to clarify the following: the Christian faith,

---

[59] A. Loisy commented: 'on ne doit pas conclure que le christianisme soit une religion étrangère au judaïsme ou même anti-juive. C'est, si j'ose dire, la vraie religion juive' (*Actes des apôtres*, 1920, p. 939). In my view, Loisy describes more exactly the Lucan point of view than R. L. Brawley who formulates the same truth in the opposite direction: 'the persecution [of Paul] has a relatively positive function, namely, to demonstrate *how Jewish the Christian Paul is*. In four apologetic speeches Paul claims Pharisaic faithfulness to the law and the Scriptures, and he justifies his preaching as true to Jewish tradition' (italics mine) (*Luke–Acts and the Jews*, 1987, p. 81).

expounded by Paul, represents the best that Judaism has to offer; and, for Luke, the best it offers is surely the Pharisaic piety.[60] There are Pharisees in Jerusalem, Luke writes, who agree with this idea.

The end of Acts

In my opinion, there is a further crack at the end of Acts (28. 17–31), as the apostle encounters the Jewish delegation in Rome. This text, whose understanding is much debated, is perhaps the most difficult passage in Acts. For Luke, in the masterly conclusion of his narrative, demonstrates a subtlety that too rigid a reading scheme cannot perceive. In this case, both the paradigm of continuity (which plays down the final rupture between Paul and Judaism) and the paradigm of rupture (which gives finality to Israel's rejection without respecting Paul's openness: 28. 30) fail to grasp the full scope of the scale of the conclusion of Acts. This passage is the witness *par excellence* to Luke's ambivalence about Israel, which I have been trying to demonstrate from the beginning of this chapter. The last scene of Acts has both signs of closure and signs of openness. I am anticipating here the results of my detailed study of Acts 28. 16–31 in chapter 10.[61]

I begin with the signs of *closure*. The weight of Isaiah's word of judgement (Isa. 6. 9–10), which punctuates the mixed reaction of the Roman Jews to Paul's preaching (28. 24–7), must not be underestimated for the five reasons summarized in the following: (1) the author has truncated this quotation in Luke 8.10 (differing from Mark 4.12) in order to reserve it for the end of his work. (2) The division of the Jewish group (its ἀσυμφωνία, v. 25) is opposed to the massive agreement of the prophet Isaiah, Paul and the Holy Spirit, concerning the word of judgement. (3) The words of Isaiah are interpreted by verse 28 which affirms

---

[60] Throughout the narrative of Luke–Acts, the figure of the Pharisees goes through a curious evolution that testifies to the nuanced perception of the relationship of Judaism and Christianity which permeates the work of Luke. Adversaries at the outset of the gospel (Luke 5. 21), the Pharisees are exonerated from responsibility for Jesus' condemnation by the passage that does not mention them among the actors of the Passion (Luke 22–3). More than once in Acts, they are the defenders of the apostles, who are tormented by the Jewish leaders (Acts 5. 33–9; 22. 3; 23. 1–10). At the climax of this evolution, Paul appeals to the Pharisaic ideology (23. 6). Concerning the image of the Pharisees in Luke–Acts, one should consult: J. B. Tyson, *Death of Jesus*, 1986, pp. 64–72; R. L. Brawley, *Luke–Acts and the Jews*, 1987, pp. 84–106; J. T. Sanders, *Jews in Luke–Acts*, 1987, pp. 84–131 and J. A. Darr, *Character Building*, 1992, pp. 85–126. G. Wasserberg (*Aus Israels Mitte*, 1998, pp. 179–89) correctly notes the ambivalence of these characters in Luke–Acts, owing to the closeness that Luke ascribes to Pharisaism and Christianity concerning resurrection.

[61] For the justification of my reading, the reader can refer to pp. 223–30.

the sending of the salvation of God to the Gentiles, who will accept it in contrast to Israel's rejection. (4) From one end of Acts to the other, one can see the shift between Peter's speech in Jerusalem, proclaiming a promise destined 'for you, for your children, and for all who are far away' (2. 39), and Paul's speech in Rome, concluding that 'this salvation of God has been sent to the Gentiles; they will listen' (28. 28). (5) This declaration of verse 28 takes up the preceding statements of 13. 46 and 18. 6, but its place at the end of the work gives it a definitive character.[62]

It is difficult to deny that, from the point of view of the author of Luke–Acts, a period in salvation history comes to an end: the nations will henceforth accept what Judaism did not want and Luke's Christianity lives from this reality. Through a tragic irony, the majority of Israel has confirmed that it rejects what is in reality the fulfilment of its expectation. Concerning Judaism, it is the hour of neither triumph nor curse, but a recognition of failure. Paul recognizes that the word of Isaiah is fulfilled in the present circumstance: 'This people's heart has grown dull' (28. 27a). The Christianity that Luke addresses most probably no longer exercises an active mission to the Jews.[63]

However, this same passage also presents signs of *openness*. First, the Jewish deputation in Rome is not completely closed off by refusal, but is divided (28. 24). If Paul failed to convince Israel, if the hope of uniting Judaism around Jesus is lost, the promise to convince some that the 'light for the revelation to the Gentiles is the glory of Israel' is not abandoned.[64] A second sign of openness is that just as the prophet does not curse the people of God, but calls them to change, so the apostle Paul presented by Luke is shown in these last verses as preaching the Kingdom of God to

---

[62] R. C. Tannehill underestimates the rhetorical function of the end of the work when he aligns 28. 28 with the two preceding statements (13. 46 and 18. 6). He thinks that the cycle 'rejection of the Jews/Paul's return to the synagogue' will resume after chapter 28, as it resumed after Antioch of Pisidia and after Corinth (*Narrative Unity*, I, 1986, pp. 350–1). The *inclusio* between Acts 28. 28 and Luke 3. 6 is a supplementary indication of the conclusive character of this declaration.

[63] The deliberate blackening of the 'Jews' in Acts makes Brawley's thesis improbable. He thinks Luke's work constitutes a call to the Jews (*Luke–Acts and the Jews*, 1987, p. 159: 'Luke appeals to them'). For Luke, the dialogue between Christianity and Israel must be preserved, but his book is clearly for internal use only.

[64] The words of H. Conzelmann remain true: 'We can say that the Jews are now called to make good their claim to be "Israel". If they fail to do this, then they become "the Jews". For the individual the way of salvation is open, now as always. The polemic is at the same time a call to repentance; the continual reminder that the Church is grounded in redemptive history prevents the connection with Israel from ever being forgotten' (*Theology of St Luke*, 1982, p. 145).

'all who (πάντας) came to him' (28. 30). With regard to the Jews, this πάντας[65] does not close the door, but leaves it open.

The time of universal mission, which is inaugurated and legitimated by Acts 28, envisages the individual conversion of Jews to Christianity; the conversion of 'all the people' is postponed to the end times, as certain *logia* (Luke 13. 34–5; 19. 41–4; 21. 24b; cf. Acts 3. 21) could be understood.[66] The conclusion of Acts, then, while sealing the end of a period (and the end of a hope) yet refusing to break off the dialogue with Israel, crystallizes the position that Luke has unceasingly defended throughout his work. Had Luke wanted to leave the 'Jewish file' open at the end of his grand narrative, he would not have gone about it any differently.[67] In fact, that is exactly the way he does go about it! However, if the composition of this passage indicates the subtlety of his position concerning Judaism, it also reveals the difficulty. How can he hold to a universalism and maintain an openness to Jewish particularity at the same time? The question merits further attention in my conclusion.

Conclusion: continuity *and* rupture

My initial question was: what image of the Jewish–Christian relationship is presented in the work of Luke? I have defended the idea that the two readings, which quarrel over the interpretation of Luke–Acts, fail to capture Luke's theological project, which refuses to be imprisoned by either continuity or discontinuity. The seemingly contradictory indications present throughout the text actually help to overcome the impasse, thereby crediting Luke with a larger theological vision. His achievement consists in placing Christianity at the intersection of the continuity and the rupture with Israel,[68] or if one prefers, *Luke has attempted precisely to*

---

[65] The universality of πάντες has been defended by V. Stolle, *Zeuge als Angeklagter*, 1973, pp. 86–7 and H. Hauser, *Abschlusserzählung*, 1979, pp. 107–10.

[66] F. Mussner ('Apokatastasis', 1961, pp. 233–4) and V. Fusco ('Future of Israel', 1996, pp. 10–15) argued for this reading. H. Merkel has rallied to their position with this formulation, 'Ein Theologe, der wie Lukas so stark an der Kontinuität der Heilsgeschichte interessiert war, hätte sich selbst aufgegeben, wenn er Israel aufgegeben hätte' ('Israel im lukanischen Doppelwerk', 1994, p. 397).

[67] In a study whose exegetical finesse merits more attention by scholars, B. Wildhaber notes this, 'Et le récit [des Actes] finalement de s'achever sur un simple refus de conclure, mais qui, de fait, cache une ultime ouverture, et, de par sa formulation paradoxalement apophatique, marque un point de non retour: μετὰ πάσης παρρησίας ἀκωλύτως (Ac 28,31)' (*Paganisme populaire*, 1987, p. 75).

[68] A good synthesis by C. K. Barrett: 'Luke ... means to say to Judaism both Yes and No. Neither his Yes nor his No is as sharp as Paul's Yes and No, but they are not unrelated to them ... The Old Testment is right, of course; but it must be rightly understood. Judaism

unite what his exegetes seek to separate in his work. Everything leads one
to think that the Christianity of which Luke writes, around the 80s, constitutes an entity severed from Judaism. Luke's Christianity has abandoned
any idea of converting all Israel and is aware that its vast majority is made
up of Gentiles. Under such circumstances, why is there this ambivalent
approach to the Christianity–Judaism relationship?

I shall attempt to respond to this question with five points.

(1) An unresolved tension. Luke does not seek to inspire in his readers,
with the help of a reactionary ideology of fusion with Israel, nostalgia
for a time passed: Acts clearly draws the sympathy of its readers towards
the missionaries, who are malevolently persecuted. When Luke writes
of the progressive deterioration of the relationship with the Synagogue,
he does not encourage his readers to cut themselves off from an 'Israel
murderer of Christ': in the narrative, the break always stems from a Jewish
decision, never from Christian initiative. Between the openness to Israel,
the promises of which the Church fulfils, and the violent rupture that
separates them, Luke–Acts ends in an unresolved tension (28. 16–28).[69]
For Luke, this tension is inherent in the very identity of Christianity and
its original rupture.

(2) Reinforcing consciousness of identity. While presenting this image of the past, Luke seeks to reinforce the consciousness of identity
in the Christianity of his time. How? The fifty-two chapters of history laid out in Luke–Acts show where Christian roots lie: in the story
of a chosen people and in their Scriptures. Simultaneously, they attribute to Judaism the responsibility for a separation from which the
Christian movement is born. In following the narrative from Jerusalem
to Rome, the reader is not encouraged to repudiate his or her origin,
but rather to rediscover it as a lost origin. Only the memory of this
firm attachment gives sense to Christian identity.[70] This dialectic of
continuity and discontinuity suggests that Luke's vision of Judaism
does not lack aggressivity (see the figure of the Ἰουδαῖοι), but neither

is the heir of the Old Testament; but to fulfil itself it must become Christian' ('Attitudes to
the Temple', 1991, pp. 366–7).

[69] I share R. C. Tannehill's opinion. *Narrative Unity*, II, 1990, pp. 352–3.

[70] On this point, I disagree with J. B. Tyson, for whom Luke 1–2 represents an image of
the Jewish past that is to be rejected. In Tyson's view, the reader is identified as a Godfearer
(*Images of Judaism*, 1992, pp. 42–55, 181–3). I object to this interpretation: (a) Temple piety
as depicted in the infancy narratives is anachronistic for the narrator (who writes after 70)
as well as for the reader; (b) the ideal nature of the narrative, so beautifully portrayed in
Rembrandt's paintings, lends itself more to the evocation of roots to be rediscovered than
to the exhibition of a past to be repudiated; (c) the religious past of the Godfearer is to be
sought in paganism rather than in Judaism.

is it a denigration (Wills) nor a demonstration of the inferiority of Judaism.[71]

(3) The triumph of God. Luke's work does not culminate with the assessment that the story of the Jesus movement in its relation to Israel is a 'tragic story' (Tannehill). Once again, in Rome, Luke's Paul protests against the ejection that his fellow Jews so desire, but, at the same time, he works at integrating the Gentiles into the people of God. Luke sees the triumph of God in this act! The famous apostolic decree of 15. 28–9 is representative of the Christianity that Luke has in mind, a reasonable and universal Christianity, breaking with the exclusivity of Israel, yet whose faith and practice inherit the quintessence of 'the religion and ethic of Judaism, with just enough of its practice to show continuity'.[72] On the question of Israel's future, Luke is ignorant of the promise in Romans 11. 25–9; but the book of Acts does not end with a logic of closure and several indications in the gospel (Luke 13. 34–5; 19. 41–4: 21. 24b) ring out like an echo, a distant echo, of the apocalyptic hope of the apostle to the Gentiles. In his own way, Luke could also signify here (*pace* Vielhauer) his dependence on Paul.

(4) A wide horizon. It is tempting to see in the historical figure of the Godfearers the missing link between Israel and Gentile Christianity. Some have thought that Luke would argue in their favour (Jervell)[73] or that his work was addressed to this group (Tyson).[74] Even if the role that Luke makes this transitional figure play is undeniable (the Ethiopian eunuch, Cornelius), the Church is not merely an enlarged Synagogue.

---

[71] L. M. Wills thinks that the negative portrayal of the Jews as troublemakers in Acts aims to disparage them, with the double goal of 'deconstructing' the relationship of Christianity with Israel and linking them to Roman society ('Depiction', 1991, p. 652); concerning the first point, my study contradicts his conclusion.

[72] I quote C. K. Barrett, 'Luke–Acts', 1996, p. 95.

[73] J. Jervell defended the idea that Acts told the story of the extension of salvation from the Jews to the Godfearers and not to the Gentiles, and then 'the church is very much like the synagogue, where you find the same two groups' ('The Church of Jews', 1988, p. 14). But were not the Godfearers in any case Gentiles? (see the useful update of this subject in J. T. Sanders' 'Who is a Jew?', 1991, esp. pp. 439–51).

[74] In spite of Tyson's demonstration in *Images of Judaism*, 1992, it does not appear that the Godfearers hold the key to Luke's ambivalence with regard to Judaism: 'If one intent of the implied author is to wean the implied reader away from Judaism and convince him/her to accept the Christian message, the ambivalence in Luke–Acts in regard to the images of Judaism can be understood' (p. 183). As to the identity of the Godfearers, we can note: (a) that it does not coincide with the identification of Theophilus in Luke 1. 4 (Christian catechesis); (b) that the text of Luke–Acts is clearly more open (what is the interest of the Godfearer in the episode in Lystra (Acts 14) or the one in Athens (Acts 17)?). Concerning the strategy of the work, the image of Judaism in Luke 1–2 is not repulsive, and Acts 28 culminates in the opening of the universal mission rather than in the closing of the Jewish file. G. Wasserberg (*Aus Israels Mitte*, 1998, pp. 42–54) confirms this point of view.

This would limit the horizon of his work by reducing the victory of God, in the evangelization of the Gentiles, to a plea for the integration of the fringes of Judaism.

(5) The universality of the holy people. What vision of the Church lives in the work *ad Theophilum*? Luke has a vision of the people of God in which Jew and Gentile coexist, a vision of the universality of the holy people in which each one opens up to God by confessing his/her errors. I think that Christianity for Luke resembles the school of Tyrannus of Ephesus (19. 9) or the house of Paul in Rome (28. 16, 30–1). After the Synagogue severed its ties with the apostle, he reconstituted a community in these places, a community in which the two poles of the kingdom of God and the Lordship of Jesus Christ (28. 23, 31) are both expressed and in which 'both Jews and Gentiles heard the Word of the Lord' (19. 10; 28. 30). In Luke's time, this vision was already utopian. However, Luke's dream remains to this day an inheritance to be rediscovered, in so far as one allows his theological programme its force, which is to reconcile and not to exclude, to maintain and not to destroy the relationship with Israel, in both its continuity and its discontinuity.

8

ANANIAS AND SAPPHIRA (ACTS 5. 1–11): THE ORIGINAL SIN

The story of the judgement of God on Ananias and Sapphira (Acts 5. 1–11) is the most tragic episode in the book of Acts. The Lucan art of dramatization reaches the height of *pathos*: the tragic end of Ananias struck down by Peter's accusing word, his rapid burial, then the arrival of Sapphira ignorant of the dramatic event, her open lie followed by her death, announced with a tone of black humour (5. 9b). The pragmatic effect sought by the narrator is apparent in the text itself: 'great fear seized all who heard of it' (5. 5, 11). This is a story that is meant to provoke fear.

It must be said that the story, situated in the idyllic picture of the first Christian community which unfolds in chapters 2 to 5, strikes the reader with a narrative shock. What is the intention of the author of Acts? The violence to the reader is also theological: how can one justify the tragic disproportion between Ananias and Sapphira's crime and the sanction that strikes them? How can the absence of the typically Lucan offer of conversion (μετάνοια) be explained? Can Lucan ecclesiology endure this dualist vision of a pure community from which the sinner is excluded by death?

Furthermore, from an author with a reputation of aiming to soften the internal conflicts of the Church (6. 1–6; 15. 7–35), the brutal emergence of this crisis comes as a surprise. The punishment of the magician Bar-Jesus (13. 6–12), which constitutes the analogy of the present narrative in the context of the modelling of Paul on Peter, concludes less tragically with his blinding. The story of Acts 5 presents itself as both a rupture in the depiction of the 'golden age' of Christianity (chs. 2–5) and as an anomaly in the theology of Luke.

No help from source criticism

In its effort to understand these odd features, research has turned to source criticism, attempting to unravel what originates with the redactor and what was inherited from tradition. The results have produced an even more profound perplexity.

Scholars have rushed to attribute the substance of the narrative to a source, with the exception of verse 4. It is not necessary to repeat here the arguments that are well known and convincing.[1] From the time of Ernst Haenchen, verses 7–11 have been most often considered as the redactor's extension of the primitive story;[2] but this hypothesis is not convincing, for, as the parables show, redundancy is also characteristic of popular rhetoric. If the narrative received by Luke had already envisioned the couple,[3] the redaction of verses 7–11, in which the scenario of guilt and death is repeated with Sapphira, has in any case been carefully attended to by Luke with the goal of ensuring a dramatic climax to the story.

The text is constructed like a diptych, whose two panels – one centred on the man (vv. 1–6) and the other on the woman (vv. 7–11) – correspond. Comparison of verses 2 and 8, 3 and 9a, 5a and 10a, 5b and 11[4] shows that, from the first to the second portrait, the narrator has orchestrated an intensification of the scenario culminating with the fear that seizes 'the whole church' (5. 11).

A methodological resort to the dialectic tradition/redaction does not resolve the theological embarrassment for the reader. On the contrary, it leads to the conclusion that Luke not only agrees to accept the story into his work, but even accentuates its dramatic effect! It becomes, in the light of this, even more intriguing to know what interest is guiding the author here.

Five readings of the text

In reading through the commentaries on Acts 5, one is struck by how this theological embarrassment has led scholars to appeal to a hermeneutical canon outside the text of Acts.

---

[1] They can be found in G. Schneider, *Apostelgeschichte*, I, 1980, pp. 369–72.

[2] E. Haenchen, *Acts of the Apostles*, 1971, p. 241. For opposing views, see G. Schneider, *Apostelgeschichte*, I, 1980, p. 371; R. Pesch, *Apostelgeschichte*, 1986, p. 196; and J. Jervell, *Apostelgeschichte*, 1998, pp. 197–8.

[3] This is the literary thesis held by R. Pesch, *Apostelgeschichte*, I, 1986, p. 196; B. Prete, 'Anania e Saffira', 1988, p. 483; J. Jervell, *Apostelgeschichte*, 1998, pp. 197 and 199. One could critique this thesis by appealing to Luke's partiality for pairing a man and a woman (the centurion and the widow in Luke 7; Jairus and the woman in Luke 8; the Samaritan and the two sisters in Luke 10; etc.), but the insistence of the author on the presence of women does not authorize source criticism to attribute to him every mention of feminine presence!

[4] Ananias does not speak (2), whereas Sapphira lies publicly (8); Ananias is accused of lying to the Spirit (3), Sapphira of tempting it (9b); Peter does not announce the death of Ananias (4), but does announce Sapphira's (9b); the husband listens, falls and dies (5a), the wife falls 'immediately' and dies (10a); the rumour spreads in 11 to 'the whole church'.

The reading of the Fathers is dominated by a dogmatic (an elaboration of the doctrine of the Trinity), ethical (the rejection of greed) or institutional (an exaltation of Peter's power)[5] quest.

Modern exegesis has deployed five kinds of reading, each resorting to an external hermeneutical canon.

(a) An *aetiological* reading perceives in the story of God's judgement on Ananias and Sapphira the legendary response provided for the anxiety of the first Christians faced with the destiny of those who have died before the parousia. The interpretative model is 1 Thessalonians 4. 13–17.[6]

(b) A *Qumranian* reading views this as a punishment for disciplinary fraud in the giving of possessions to the community (5. 3–4);[7] the interpretative model is found in the regulations of the Qumran sect: 1 QS 6. 24b–25 and CD 14. 20–1.[8]

(c) A *typological* reading discerns in this event the theft of something sacred. Its model is the fraud of Achan (Josh. 7).[9]

(d) An *institutional* reading attributes to the text the function of legitimizing a sacred rite of excommunication, as in 1 Corinthians 5. 13 and Matthew 18. 15–17.[10]

(e) For the *salvation-history* reading, the crime of Ananias and Sapphira is not moral, but theological. It blocks the action of the Spirit in directing salvation history (Acts 1. 8).[11]

In contrast to all these readings, I shall adopt an interpretative criterion intrinsic to the narration, seeking the point of view constructed by the

[5] For a history of interpretation, see P. B. Brown's thesis, 'Meaning and Function', 1969, pp. 51–92.

[6] This is the hypothesis formulated by P. H. Menoud, 'Mort d'Ananias et Saphira', 1950. M.-E. Boismard and A. Lamouille take it up again in *Actes des deux apôtres*, II, 1990, p. 165.

[7] J. Schmitt, 'Contributions', 1957; E. Trocmé, *'Livre des Actes'*, 1957, pp. 197–9; M. Klinghardt, *Gesetz*, 1988, pp. 57–9. Concerning the Qumranian model, B. J. Capper ('Interpretation', 1983) postulates a legal regulation for entry into the community. The two phases are illustrated in 5. 4a. The novice is required to give a declaration of surrendering all possessions to the community which is then concretized by a ritual of entry.

[8] 'If one of them has lied deliberately in matters of property, he shall be excluded from the pure Meal of the Congregation for one year and shall do penance with respect to one quarter of his food' (1QS 6. 25). '[Whoever] deliberately lies in a matter of property... and shall do penance for six days' (CD 14. 20). Texts translated by G. Vermès, *Dead Sea Scrolls*, 1995.

[9] This reading is the most widespread and is defended with fervor by B. Prete, 'Anania e Saffira', 1988, see pp. 480–1.

[10] C. Perrot, 'Ananie et Saphire', 1981; G. Schille, *Apostelgeschichte*, 1983, p. 151. G. Lüdemann accepts this meaning for tradition; *Frühe Christentum*, 1987, p. 71. According to S. Meurer, Acts 5 challenges the Church's use of punitive justice which is reserved for God alone (*Recht im Dienst*, 1972, pp. 83–92).

[11] See especially P. B. Brown, 'Meaning and Function', 1969, pp. 200–14.

author in the organization of the narrative. We know that in the reception of a tradition, a narrative theology resorts to two procedures. On the one hand, intervention in the text (I shall return to the interpretative gloss in v. 4 later) and, on the other hand, placement in the context. I shall follow the latter, which has received little attention when considering Acts 5. 1–11. My aim is to illuminate the intention that controls the Lucan narrative. What is the narrative strategy into which Acts 5. 1–11 fits, and what indications for understanding has the author placed in the narration for the reader? In other words, how did Luke programme the reading of Acts 5. 1–11 in the organization of his text?

The narrative structure of Acts 2–5

The first sequence that emerges in reading is Acts 4. 32 – 5. 11. This unit contains a summary (4. 32–5), centred on the sharing of possessions in the Jerusalem community, to which is attached two incidents: the example of Joseph called Barnabas (4. 36–7), who sells a field and brings the money to the apostles, and the example of Ananias and Sapphira (5. 1–11), who also sell a piece of property, but withhold a part of the money before laying it at the feet of the apostles. The summary and the two incidents are welded together by the same 'economic' vocabulary;[12] the Lucan redaction of the summary must be responsible for this terminological harmonization. The result, after the summary which presents (in the imperfect of duration) a principle of the sharing of possessions among the first Christians, is that the two incidents (presented in the aorist) each concretize an application of the principle of sharing.

After the panoramic horizon of the summary, the field of vision is restricted to an actualized example (Barnabas), and then a counter-example (Ananias and Sapphira). Should we conclude with Dibelius that 4. 36–7 presents a positive example and 5. 1–11 offers a negative one?[13] The idea is not wrong, but it must not be forgotten that the story of Ananias and Sapphira is not the final point in the narrative; Luke's story continues with a new summary (5. 12–16), which does not pick up the theme of sharing possessions, but rather relates the 'many signs and wonders'

---

[12] Πιπράσκειν (4. 34; 5. 3); πωλεῖν (4. 37; 5. 1); πρὸς τοὺς πόδας τῶν ἀποστόλων τιθέναι (4. 35, 37; 5. 2); ὑπάρχειν (4. 34; 5. 4) χωρίον (4. 34; 5. 3, 8); φέρειν (4. 34, 37; 5. 2); τιμή (4. 34; 5. 2). I shall return later to the decisive recurrence of the non-economic term καρδία (4. 32; 5. 3, 4).

[13] M. Dibelius, 'Style Criticism' [1923], 1956, p. 9.

accomplished among the people through the hands of the apostles (5. 12). This summary emphasizes the miraculous to such a degree that 'they even carried out the sick into the streets, so that Peter's shadow might fall on some of them as he came by' (5. 15). This new summary selects the miraculous dimensions of the story of Ananias and Sapphira, which is then amplified in order to describe a vast healing activity (5. 15–16).[14]

Placed between two summaries, one devoted to the theme of sharing possessions (4. 32–5), and the other to the miraculous activity of the apostles (5. 12–16), the story of Acts 5 responds to the narrator's dual interest. This then means that the sequence of 4. 32 – 5. 11 is too narrow a literary frame from which to discern the narrative project of the author. A wider scope of vision, that of Acts 2–5, is necessary.

A rhythmic narrative

Acts 2–5 is a literary sequence with recognized limits: it opens with Pentecost (2. 1–13) and closes before the Hellenists' complaint (6. 1–6). This literary unit, devoted to the 'golden age' of the first Christian community, is marked by three major summaries: 2. 42–7; 4. 32–5 and 5. 12–16. The first summary (2. 42–7) concludes Peter's speech at Pentecost (2. 14–36) followed by the conversion of the three thousand (2. 37–41). Few have noticed that this summary forms an inclusio with the last verse of chapter 5: πᾶσάν τε ἡμέραν (2. 46, καθ' ἡμέραν) ἐν τῷ ἱερῷ καὶ κατ' οἶκον (2. 46, ἐν τῷ ἱερῷ τε κατ' οἶκον) οὐκ ἐπαύοντο (2.46, προσκαρτεροῦντες) διδάσκοντες (2. 42, τῇ διδαχῇ) καὶ εὐαγγελιζόμενοι τὸν Χριστόν Ἰησοῦν (cf. 28. 31). On the basis of its form (synthethic description of the life of the community in the durative imperfect) and its narrative function (conclusive recapitulation marking a pivotal point in the narrative), therefore, 5. 42 deserves to be aligned with the three major summaries.

In between the first summary 2. 42–7 and the conclusion 5. 42, it appears that the narrative is not only punctuated by the summaries, but it is governed by a recurring schema that presents in succession the following elements: summary – event (scene) – interpretation (speech) – contrasted effect. This schema, with variants, is repeated four times in the narrative according to the following outline.

---

[14] Concerning this subject, see the commendable study of S. J. Noorda, 'Scene and Summary', 1979.

Summary	Event (scene)	Interpretation (speech)	Contrasted effect
2. 42–7	3. 1–10	3. 11–26	4. 1–3
			4. 4
	4. 5–7	4. 8–12	4. 13–22
			4. 23–31
4. 32–5	4. 36–7 and 5. 1–10		5. 5b, 11
5. 12–16	5. 17–21a		
	5. 21b–26	5. 27–32	5. 33
			5. 34–40
5. 41–2			

The *first summary* (2. 42–7) describes the unanimity of believers as the effect of the Spirit of Pentecost. On the one hand, the miraculous activity of the apostles (τέρατα καὶ σημεῖα, cf. 2. 19) provokes the religious fear of all (φόβος). On the other hand, ecclesial unity is concretized in the community of possessions. The event which follows, a healing at the Beautiful Gate of the Temple (3. 1–10), exemplifies the miraculous activity. Peter's speech interprets it as a sign of the efficacy of the name of Jesus (3. 16). The effect of the speech on the priests and Sadducees is negative (they imprison Peter and John, 4. 1–3), but it is positive on the crowd and five thousand are converted (4. 4).

A new event takes place in 4. 5–7 with the interrogation of the apostles by the Sanhedrin, followed by Peter's speech (4. 8–12), again provoking a contrasted reaction. The Sanhedrin deliberates (4. 13–22) and commands the apostles no longer to pronounce or to teach in the name of Jesus. Conversely, the gathered community prays to its Lord, and, as the community prays that σημεῖα καὶ τέρατα be accomplished in their midst, the place is shaken and all the believers are filled with the Holy Spirit (4. 30–1).

The *second summary* (4. 32–5) links up with the theme of sharing possessions, left suspended since 2. 44–5. As I have mentioned, this theme is condensed into two events: the act of Barnabas (4. 36–7) and the counter model of Ananias and Sapphira (5. 1–11). The sole effect is to provoke fear (φόβος) in all those who hear the news and in all the ἐκκλησία (5. 5b, 11). However, the place has changed. We are no longer in the Temple, nor before the Sanhedrin, but within the closed context of the community. What follows in the narrative will return to the exterior.

The *third summary* (5. 12–16) abandons the theme of sharing possessions only to intensify the miraculous activity of the apostles (σημεῖα καὶ τέρατα πολλά: 5. 12). These signs and wonders, which take place 'through the hands of the apostles' (5. 12a), answer the clear request of the community, who had prayed to the Lord to stretch out his hand 'to heal' and to accomplish 'signs and wonders' (4. 30). A thematic continuity with the story of Ananias and Sapphira is clear: holy fear (cf. 5. 11) keeps the crowds away from the apostles (5. 13), but provokes the conversion of 'great numbers of both men and women' (5. 14). The sick arrive in masses, hoping to be healed by the shadow of Peter, and 'they were all cured' (5. 16). Without a doubt, from the first to the third summary, the narrative accelerates and, in this escalation of success, the sequence 4. 32–5. 11 has played a determining role.

The events also gain in gravity. The success of the apostles excites the jealousy of the Sadducees (4. 17), who again have the apostles incarcerated. However, this new imprisonment is interrupted by the miraculous deliverance by an angel of the Lord (5. 17–21a). After the grotesque interval of the pursuit of the apostles . . . who are teaching in the Temple (5. 21b–26!), Peter's speech to the Sanhedrin culminates in the announcement of the exaltation of the Crucified One (5. 31). Again, opinions are divided: some wish to put the apostles to death (5. 33), while others decide to free the apostles, convinced by Gamaliel's argument: 'keep away from these men and let them alone; because if this plan or this undertaking is of human origin, it will fall; but if it is of God, you will not be able to overthrow them – in that case you may even be found fighting against God!' (5. 38–9).

A double gradation

Finally, what is the plot of the macro-narrative of Acts 2. 42 – 5. 42? It recounts *how the Spirit of Pentecost seized the first Christian community, grouped around the apostolic nucleus, in order to constitute and expand it in an open crisis with the Jewish religious authorities.* From chapter 2 to chapter 5, a double gradation takes place. On the one hand, the believing community grows in numbers (2. 41; 4. 4; 5. 14) and the thaumaturgical activity of the apostles builds in intensity (2. 43; 3. 7–8; 4. 33; 5. 12–16). On the other hand, in contrast to the success of the community with the Jewish crowds, the confrontation with the authorities of the people progressively intensifies (4. 3; 4. 18; 5. 33; 5. 40–1); it reaches its climax in the stoning of Stephen (7. 54–8), which the desire for his death mentioned in 5. 33 already anticipates.[15]

The conflict arises specifically between the Christian group and the Sadducean aristocracy, overshadowed by the figure of the High Priest. Territorially, it takes place between the Temple (crystallization of the Sadducean power) and the Sanhedrin (where the Jewish officials have the right to forbid preaching). The growing crisis between the Christian group and the Sadducean leaders has all the characteristics of a territorial quarrel,[16] aiming to determine who possesses the theological authority at the centre of Israel's religion. Gamaliel's compromise does not prevent the apostles from being beaten nor from once again being prohibited from preaching (5. 40). This Sadducean victory is nevertheless a Pyrrhic victory. Verse 42 indicates at once that the spread of the Word is irresistible: 'every day in the Temple and at home they did not cease to teach and proclaim Jesus as the Messiah'.

At this juncture, it must be clearly said, and this will be fundamental to the interpretation of the text, that the sequence 4. 32 – 5. 11 *does not fit into the growth of Jewish hostility*. On the other hand, the decisive role that it does play in the success of the community is attested by the religious fear that surrounds it like an aura (5. 5b, 11) and by the excess of the miraculous attested in the third summary (5. 12–16).

A reading centred on the community

What consequences can now be drawn for the understanding of 4. 32 – 5. 11? I see four.

(a) The sequence belongs to the macro-narrative which is entirely dedicated to showing *the marvellous growth of the community*, in spite of and through the opposition that binds it to the Jewish people. The narrator contrives to contrast a unified Christian community (2. 42–7; 4. 23–35; 5. 12b) with the hostile (4. 1–3, 17; 5. 17–18, 33, 40), helpless (4. 13–17, 21) or divided Jewish authorities (5. 21b–26, 33–9). On the one hand, there is harmony and, on the other, division and hatred. What

---

[15] The double gradation in Acts 2–5 corresponds to a narrative technique that is frequently used in Acts: redundancy underlines the motif, while escalation heightens the dramatic effect. Hence, the incidences of imprisoning the apostles are repetitive and become more serious on each occasion (4. 3; 5. 18). In the same manner, the signs of divine favour on the community are repeated with growing intensity (3. 6–7; 4. 8; 5. 12–16; 5. 19). Concerning this, see A. J. Walworth, *Narrator of Acts*, 1984, pp. 158–72, especially pp. 168–72.

[16] This idea is borrowed from R. C. Webber's socio-rhetorical considerations ('Why Were the Heathen?', 1992). His analysis makes clear the fact that the narrator, while presenting the apostles as victims, does not remove their provocative role.

is at stake in this confrontation is not the need to ensure an adequate management of the community, but to know – to use Gamaliel's words – if the Church is 'of God' (ἐκ θεοῦ 5. 39).[17] The reader knows this is the case since Pentecost, but, at the level of the story, Israel must still learn it. What I have elsewhere called the 'Gamaliel principle' is placed into the narrative; hence the narrative is given the means of verification.[18] What attests the existence ἐκ θεοῦ? In this context, it is the growth of the community: 'day by day the Lord added to their number those who were being saved' (2. 47). There is no doubt that from Luke's perspective the mission's success depends on one factor alone: the fellowship of the believers. The summaries continually repeat this (2. 46–47a and 47b; 4. 32 and 33; 5. 12b and 14). Thus the fellowship of believers is viewed as an almost ontological quality of the Church. It constitutes in Acts 2–5 the essential factor in the missionary expansion.

(b) The theme of conflict, which runs through the macro-narrative, characterizes the external threat represented by the animosity of the leaders of Israel. Acts 5. 1–11 is unique in bringing up *a conflictual problematic internal to the community*. The link is provided by the dimension of mission. What is at stake in the conflict set off by Ananias and Sapphira's deception is the effect of the community on the λαός (5. 12). The community in 5. 1–11 is then not considered from the angle of how it handles discipline, but from the perspective of its power of missionary expansion. This point weighs against a Qumranian or institutional reading.

(c) The conclusion of the narrative mentions for the first time in Acts (with the exception of the gloss presented in the so-called Western tradition, D, in 2. 47), the term ἐκκλησία (5. 11). It occurs after this twenty-two times, and is applied essentially to the local community. Contrary to many commentators,[19] I do not think that Luke, who handles his vocabulary very well, accidentally chose the first occurrence of this theologically loaded terminology;[20] for if, at the level of the story, ὅλην τὴν ἐκκλησίαν designates the gathered community in Jerusalem, the narration of Acts 2–5 presents it as the archetype of all Christian communities. ἐκκλησία here designates the community of Jerusalem as a prototype of the eschatological community of salvation. This theological sense is also shown in the

---

[17] 'The Ananias story reveals an important side of this κοινωνία; it is not just a community of friends, but an enterprise of divine character... This expresses a central idea for Luke. It is the climax of ch. 4 as is phrased by Peter and John in 4. 19... Furthermore it is the climax of ch. 5 as phrased by Gamaliel in 5. 38f.' (S. J. Noorda, *Scene and Summary*, 1979, pp. 481–2).

[18] See above, pp. 93–4 (ch. 5).

[19] Most recently, J. Jervell, *Apostelgeschichte*, 1998, p. 198.

[20] With G. Lüdemann, *Early Christianity*, 1989, p. 64.

use of the term in 8. 1, 3 and 9. 31. If this is the case, we must be attentive to the function of our narrative in the acquisition of this new title. Acts 5. 1–11 recounts *how the community of believers, which up to this point is labelled with the indeterminate term* πλῆθος *(4. 32; cf. 5. 14; 6. 2), acquires the status of the assembly of the people of God* (ἐκκλησία). This status is acquired through the action of God's judgement, which excludes from the assembly those who are not 'of one heart and soul' (4. 32).[21] The problematic of the text, from the point of view of the narrator, who is responsible for the title ἐκκλησία in 5. 11, is ecclesiological rather than soteriological. Whatever the meaning of the text in the tradition, it does not lend itself, from Luke's perspective, to an aetiological reading.

(d) The succession summary – event (scene), found three times in 2. 42–5. 42, implies rhetorically that the scene illustrates and concretizes, in the life of the community, the thesis set forth in the summary. Luke has introduced in the summary 4. 32–5 two elements absent in the two scenes, 4. 36–7 and 5. 1–11. On the one hand, the selling of possessions seeks to eliminate poverty within the community (4. 34) and, on the other hand, the 'feet of the apostles' function as a centre of distribution according to the needs of each (4. 35).[22] The decision of Ananias and Sapphira is thus oriented toward the needs of others and toward the construction of a loving community. The summary places their crime in *the ethical perspective of the sharing of possessions*, rather than in the register of a sacrilegious offence pertaining to holy possessions, as the typological reading based on Joshua 7 would infer.

The community, the Spirit and the Word

The stupor of readers faced with the brutality of the story (two terrifying deaths and the absence of an offer of repentance) is heightened in the writing of the account: this writing, very factual, lacks any emotional dimension. Narrative rhetoric does not express any compassion or state of mind. Robert O'Toole, with regard to this, writes of 'shock therapy'.[23] The formula is nice, but from what is it necessary for the reader to be healed? What does shock-writing seek to make the reader aware of? Three answers are possible (not exclusive in my opinion): breaking the law of the group, the crime against the Spirit and the terrible efficacy of the Word.

---

[21] Sr Anne-Etienne and C. Combet-Galland, 'Actes 4, 32–5, 11', 1977, pp. 548–9.

[22] This has been well pointed out by F. W. Horn, *Glaube und Handeln*, 1983, pp. 46–7.

[23] R. F. O'Toole, ' "You Did Not Lie to Us" ', 1995, p. 19: 'a kind of "shock therapy" '.

A violation of loyalty

The pattern 'summary (4. 32–4) – example (4. 35–6) – counter-example (5. 1–11)' makes it clear that Barnabas complies with the law of the group concerning the sharing of possessions, while the couple betray it. Similar schemas are not unknown. Bruce Malina's works in cultural anthropology have formalized them.[24]

Malina has detected in first-century Mediterranean societies the existence of fictive family cells, that is, groups where individuals pledge themselves to a common solidarity similar to the ties of a clan, yet without being blood related. These groups, constructed on a philosophical and/or religious ideology, offer the individual protection against the social environment in exchange for unfailing loyalty. Five characteristics denote their identity: loyalty and confidence toward the group, the preservation of the common conviction toward the exterior world, an open house to all members, the obligation to take care of the needs of one another and the consciousness of sharing the same destiny. Honour and shame are dispensed according to the respect or transgression of the collective rules.

Josephus described Essene groups in the cities of Syro-Palestine who lived out an ideal derived from Qumran and correspond to this portrait. The Pythagoreans, if one follows the account of Iamblichus, formed communities where 'all things were common' (*Vit. Pyth.* 167–9). Josephus compares the Essenes with the Pythagorean cells (*A.J.* 15.371). I can affirm, then, that the model circulated. It must be said that the sharing of possessions was part of a friendship ideal, implanted in Greek culture in earlier centuries. The first literary trace of it can be found in Aristotle: 'The proverb "all is common among friends" is exact; it is in communion that friendship exists' (*Nicomachean Ethics* 8.11).[25] The author of Acts wanted to make it known to his readers that the original community, the church of Jerusalem, fulfilled the ideal of sharing which was current in the culture at that time. The portrait of this community corresponds almost exactly to the model that Malina draws: the believers are loyal to the group

---

[24] B. J. Malina, *Anthropology*, 1986. See also B. J. Malina and J. H. Neyrey, 'Honor and Shame', 1991.

[25] The formula 'all is common among friends' is repeatedly in evidence among the Greek writers (Plato, *Lysis* 207–8; Menander, *Adelphes* 9; Plutarch, *De fraterno amore* 20) as well as Latin ones (Martial, Cicero, *De off.* 1.16.51, Seneca, *De beneficiis* 7.4.1). The reader of the first century will have recognized this in Luke's writing in Acts 4. 32: '*everything they owned was held in common*', but instead of attributing this to friends, it is important to note, the author attributes this communion to 'the whole group of those who believed' moved by the Spirit of Pentecost. Concerning this hellenistic *topos*, see above, pp. 73–5 (ch. 4).

and its recognized leaders (2. 42; 4. 23–4; 5. 12); the converted welcome each other into their homes (2. 46; 5. 42; 10. 6; 12. 12; 16. 15; etc.); they provide for the needs of each other: 'no one claimed *private ownership of any possessions*' (4. 32, 35); the consciousness of an identical destiny is present (4. 23–31).

In returning to Acts 5, the pertinence of Malina's model becomes obvious. The Lucan rhetoric, as we have seen, fixes attention on the destiny of the community rather than on the psychology of individuals. It is especially impressive to note how efficiently the narrator has programmed, by the ordering of the text, a reading perspective that is strictly interior to the community. The reader is installed within the circle of the community, where he/she enters with Ananias (v. 2b), where others enter (vv. 7, 10b) and some leave (vv. 6, 10b), where also the steps of those who approach are heard (v. 9b). The event takes place within the community and all the information given to the reader comes from within. It is within that he/she learns from Peter's lips that the property sold is real estate (χωρίον: vv. 3b, 8). In contrast, the reasons for the misappropriation, exterior to the circle of the community, remain obscure to the reader, just as Sapphira coming from outside is ignorant of all that has happened within (v. 8).

The horizon of the narrative is thus limited to the community assembly, which is perhaps a cultic assembly (the period of three hours mentioned in v. 7 marks the time of Jewish ritual prayer which the Christians attend; cf. 2. 46; 3. 1). This internal horizon will only be superseded at the end (v. 11) in order to indicate that a great fear seized 'the whole *ekklesia* and all who heard of these things'. This crossing of the geographical fence of the narrative serves, as we have seen, its pragmatic effect.

Along the same lines, we can note the insistence of the narrative on the motif of removing the body: ἐξενέγκαντες ἔθαψαν (vv. 6 and 10b), with which both tableaux are completed. This motif, secondary in the destiny of individuals, becomes of first importance when it is a matter of designating the exclusion of the guilty from the community, carried out by the young members responsible for tasks of service (νεώτεροι νεανίσκοι). This is the case here. The repeated removal of bodies shows that we have here a concretization of the slogan of the Deuteronomist: 'You shall purge the evil from your midst' (Deut. 13. 6, 12; 17. 7, 12; 19. 19; 21. 21; 22. 21, 24; 24. 7; cf. Acts 3. 23).[26] This measure corresponds, in the strict sense, to excommunication.[27]

---

[26] This has been clearly pointed out by G. Schneider, *Apostelgeschichte*, I, 1980, p. 372.

[27] According to H. Havelaar, the whole narrative should be seen as 'a highly stylized form of excommunication' ('Hellenistic Parallels', 1997, p. 81). In my opinion, the

The role of the apostles

The community emphasis is not contradicted by the narrative treatment of the figure of the apostles. Peter, whose thunderous word dominates the account, is not fashioned into an individual hero. His prophetic discernment unmasks the hidden motives (vv. 3, 9a), but the reader has learned previously that the powerful word of the apostle is the work of the Spirit (4. 8). Peter performs the theological reading of the deception by situating it in the context of the combat of God and Satan (vv. 3, 9a), but he does not pronounce any sentence (cf. also 13. 1). He predicts the imminent end of Sapphira (v. 9b), but does not sentence her to death. Peter's task, as the only Christian orator until Acts 7 (Stephen), the omniscient spokesman for the apostles, never goes beyond the status of a mediator indwelt by the Spirit (4. 31).

The placing of gifts given to the community 'at the feet of the apostles' (4. 35, 37; 5. 2) may reflect an ancient custom. It expresses submission to the power of the apostles as those sent by God to the community.[28] Feet function as a symbol of power (1 Sam. 25. 4; 2 Sam. 22. 39; Ps. 8. 7; Luke 7. 38; 8. 35, 41; 17. 16; Acts 22. 3). Against Käsemann's accusation of early catholicism in Luke, one must recognize that the judgement of God which kills the couple is not a tool in the hands of Peter or the community; this epiphany of divine power comes on the community to protect it.

The focus on the development of the community

Holding on to the idea of protection: the theme of the narrative is the protection of a community threatened in regard to its own rule (4. 32). Luke is not unfolding the drama of the salvation of the individual made vulnerable by an act of treason. Rather, he relates how the original community, threatened in its confrontation with Israel, was saved from division by the efficacious judgement of God. Such a concentration, on the trajectory of the Church to the detriment of the history of the individual, does not come as a complete surprise for the reader of Acts. The work *ad Theophilum* is centred on salvation history rather than the destiny of individuals.[29]

---

excommunication only punishes the violation of the sacred (see D. Marguerat, 'Ananias et Saphira', 1993, pp. 57–8).

[28] I. Goldhahn-Müller rightly emphasizes the mediating and instrumental role of Peter: *Grenze*, 1989, pp. 159–61; against G. Schille, who sees here the combat of the θεῖος ἀνήρ against Satan (*Apostelgeschichte*, 1983, p. 148).

[29] J. Roloff rightly notes: 'Dieser Ausrichtung auf das Ganze der Gemeinde entspricht ein auf den modernen Leser geradezu provozierend wirkendes Desinteresse am individuellen Schicksal der Betroffenen' (*Apostelgeschichte*, 1981, p. 92). We know that the author of Acts leaves a number of questions open, for example, the individual's access to faith.

Luke is interested in the individual only as an instrument of divine action (Peter, Philip) or as a paradigm of martyrdom (Stephen) and testimony (Paul). Ananias and Sapphira serve here as a demonstration of the action of God, who makes of the community threatened by an internal crisis his *ecclesia*.

It is instructive to compare this text with another excommunication, coming from the Pythagorean group as seen by Iamblichus. The excluded one is given back the possessions offered at his entering the community: 'If they were rejected, they received double their property, and a tomb was raised for them by the auditors as if they were dead' (*Pythagorean Way of Life* 17.73).

One is immediately struck by two differences. On the one hand, the Pythagorean group organizes a fake burial, while the Lucan account states the fact rather than a metaphor of death. On the other hand, in Acts, the exclusion of the guilty one is not the work of the community, but of God. This aspect needs to be explored in further detail.

A crime against the Spirit

This narrative belongs to a literary genre of which ancient literature, both biblical and non-biblical, offers numerous examples: the judgement of God.[30] The main characteristic of this literary genre is to set forth the offence of the guilty and to attribute his/her punishment to divine disapproval. When the Jewish tradition appeals to the judgement of God (Gen. 19; Lev. 10. 1–5; Num. 14; Josh. 7–8; 2 Sam. 6. 3–10; 1 Kings 13–14; Isa. 62. 8–11; Ezek. 11; 2 Macc. 3; *Ber.* 5b; *bBer.* 62b; *Sifre Numb.* 28. 26; etc.), the transgressor is usually destroyed; before God, it is a question of life and death. So Judas, the traitor (Acts 1. 18), and Herod, the sacrilegious (Acts 12. 20–3), die. Graeco-Roman literature also has narratives in which lying and perjury toward the gods are punished by death;[31] but these cases are rare and even rarer are cases of immediate violent death.[32] Gerd Theissen has tightened the definition of the literary

---

[30] See the dossier compiled by L. Tosco, *Pietro e Paolo*, 1989, pp. 55–120 and A. Weiser, *Apostelgeschichte* 1981, pp. 139–42. One may add to this list, in the primitive Christian apocryphal literature, *Acts Pet.* 5. 15; *Acts Thom.* 6; *Acts John* 41–2, 86.

[31] The inventories drawn up by L. Tosco (*Pietro e Paolo*, 1989, pp. 84–9) and H. Havelaar ('Hellenistic Parallels', 1997, pp. 67–71) mention Herodotus, Plutarch, the stelae of Epidaurus, Lucian of Samosata, Diodorus Siculus, etc.

[32] H. Havelaar concludes his passage of Graeco-Roman quotations and votive inscriptions with this point: 'Divine punishment, as such, is widespread indeed but does not usually consist of a sudden, otherwise completely inexplicable death' ('Hellenistic Parallels', 1997, p. 72). His comparative study brings out the absence of any mediation (illness for example)

form by placing the present narrative in the category of 'miracles relative to a norm' (*Normenwunder*), or more precisely, of punitive miracles, in which 'a verdict is confirmed by a miracle'.[33] Such miracles are rare in the New Testament: the cursing of the fig tree (Mark 11. 12–14, 20–1), the punishing of Simon the magician (Acts 8. 18–24) and Elymas (Acts 13. 8–12). What is the function of a *Normenwunder*? Its function is both didactic and paraenetic. Theissen's classification has the merit of making one ask: *what norm did Ananias and Sapphira transgress*?

Commentators have not missed the opportunity to note a shift in the text between verse 3 and verse 4.[34] This tension denotes the presence of a literary seam that is attributed to the redactor. The complicated sentence, in Greek, can be literally translated: '[Your possession] remaining does it not remain yours and what has been sold, was it not in your possession? [What happened] that you placed this matter in your heart? You have not lied to men, but to God.' We can note the shift: in verse 3, the lie to the Holy Spirit consists in the diverting (νοσφίζεσθαι) of a part of the price of the field; verse 4 abandons the apodictic tone for a more casuistic one and emphasizes that Ananias remained completely free in the use of his possession, both before the sale (οὐχὶ μένον σοὶ ἔμενεν) and after (πραθὲν ἐν τῇ σῇ ἐξουσίᾳ ὑπῆρχεν).[35] In my opinion, the reading that Rudolf Pesch proposes is adequate, as it situates the crime at the meeting point of verse 3 and verse 4. A commitment was not forced but, when made, it had to be total. Ananias' sin was the lack of a whole-hearted commitment.[36]

It is not entirely certain that the gloss of verse 4, as it is said, legitimates the possibility of misappropriation, which would reduce Ananias' deception to a simple concealment. To reduce the crime to a sin of hypocrisy leads to an underestimation of the pejorative force of νοσφίζεσθαι, which

or any explanation (other than the effect of the word of Peter) in the case of the double death in Acts 5.

[33] G. Theissen, *Wundergeschichten*, 1974, pp. 114–20; quotation p. 117.

[34] Cf. H. Conzelmann, *Acts of the Apostles*, 1987, pp. 37–8. For the discussion, see G. Schneider's *Apostelgeschichte*, I, 1980, pp. 374–5. Against this view, see R. Pesch, *Apostelgeschichte*, I, 1986, p. 196.

[35] The syntax of the passage is difficult. Despite the proposals for correcting it, it is necessary to see in χωρίον and not in τιμή (3b) the subject of ἔμενεν and ὑπῆρχεν; οὐχ should not be read as οὐχί; and μένον can only be translated as 'remaining'. From a semantic point of view, the two parts of 5. 4a are redundant. See the detailed discussion in P. B. Brown, 'Meaning and Function', 1969, pp. 97–102.

[36] R. Pesch, *Apostelgeschichte*, I, 1986, p. 198: 'Weil Hananias nicht sein ganzes Herz an Gott ... gehangen hatte.' Pesch attributes this half-heartedness to the traditionally divisive role of Satan, which works against the totality of the commitment required by the *pneuma* (cf. p. 202).

signifies in Koine Greek,[37] as well as in the three biblical occurrences of the term,[38] 'to set aside', 'to take away', 'to misappropriate for one's benefit'. The redactional gloss of verse 4 simply certifies that nothing forced Ananias to offer this gift. Peter's double rhetorical question only serves as a reminder of the rule: the one who shares does it freely.[39]

Two fullnesses that exclude each other

The text invites us to go yet another step with an unusual formulation which Peter uses for Ananias, διὰ τί ἐπλήρωσεν ὁ Σατανᾶς τὴν καρδίαν σου, ψεύσασθαί σε τὸ πνεῦμα τὸ ἅγιον (v. 3). Peter's word establishes the truth by unmasking, behind Ananias' lie, the strategy of another power, the anti-God. The two last references to Satan in the Lucan narrative go back to the Passion: in Luke 22. 3, Satan 'enters into Judas' and, in Luke 22. 31, he 'demands' the disciples in order to 'sift' them (this refers to their testing by their Master's death). Here, Satan 'fills the heart' of Ananias, which recalls Luke 22. 3, where he enters 'into Judas'. But, above all, this unusual phrase is the opposite of what the reader has just read in 4. 31: ἐπλήσθησαν ἅπαντες τοῦ ἁγίου πνεύματος. The semantic affinity of πίμπλημι (4. 31) and πληρόω (5. 3) is too forceful to be ignored. The text then offers two fullnesses which oppose and exclude one another: one is the work of the Spirit, which leads them to speak the word of God with confidence (4. 31), and the other is the work of Satan, which leads to keeping a part for oneself. Satan has taken over the territory that should be the Spirit's: the heart of the believer.

Ananias' crime is a crime against the Spirit. Ananias becomes the instrument of Satan in his combat against the Church.[40] Satan has turned Ananias against the work of the Spirit and this opposition can only be swallowed up in death (Luke 12. 10). Peter's speech says nothing less: it is not to humans but to God that Ananias has lied (v. 4b). The crime is not ethical; the lie is not denounced as hypocrisy, but as deception toward

---

[37] C. Spicq, *Notes de lexicographie*, 1978, p. 584. The criminal meaning is attested in the commercial papyri as well as in the writing of Philo (*De vita Mos.* 1.253; *Legatio ad G.* 199), Josephus (*B.J.* 5.411; *A.J.* 4.274) and Plutarch (*Lucullus* 37.2).

[38] In Josh. 7. 1, it designates the theft by Achan of a part of the spoils of Jericho. In 2 Macc. 4. 32, it qualifies the act of Menelaus' theft of the golden vases in the Temple. In Titus 2. 10, it is the misappropriation of the possessions of the master by a slave that is intended.

[39] The pressure of the Qumran model is strong in M. Klinghardt's interpretation, who, against verse 4, supports the idea of an obligatory renunciation of possessions in the Jerusalem community in the same manner as the Essene sect (*Gesetz*, 1988, pp. 58–9).

[40] With J. Roloff, *Apostelgeschichte*, 1981, p. 94.

God. By opposing the direction of the Spirit, Ananias and Sapphira have destroyed the ἄπαντα κοινά of 4. 32. This results in endangering the whole community, and, because it no longer responds to the ideal of 'one heart and one soul' (4. 32–3), its missionary efficacy is threatened. The couple, who have excluded themselves from ecclesial solidarity, *wound the communitarian ideal*. Far from resolving this crisis by founding an ecclesiastic jurisdiction of excommunication, the text shows the Spirit exercizing its role as the 'infallible guarantor of communion within the community'.[41]

The efficacy of the Word

The third feature of which this shock-writing aims to make the reader aware is the terrifying efficacy of the Word. The pragmatic effect of the narrative is to provoke φόβος (vv. 5b, 11), holy fear. The reader knows from the first summary that fear is the human reaction to the epiphany of divine power and, at the same time, that it is a powerful vehicle of advancement of mission (2. 43; cf. 4. 33). Furthermore, the narrative gives this holy fear a very precise origin: it seizes 'all who heard these things' (vv. 5b, 11). Before moving on too quickly this remark should be carefully pondered. Why does the narrator feel the need, on two occasions, to describe the effect of the news on 'all who hear'? It is almost as if Luke places in the text the emotion that he wishes to provoke in his hearer/reader. If Luke is trying to provoke fear in his reader, what is the object of such fear? Fear of the terrible judgement of God? Fear of the power of the Spirit? I would rather say: fear of the power of the Word.

What has been said so far about the Spirit must not obscure the fact that nowhere in the text is the πνεῦμα the direct agent of the action. On the contrary, from one end to the other, the account is composed of words and sayings. Like that of Ananias, Sapphira's offence is a crime of lying (vv. 3b, 8b); Ananias dies upon hearing Peter's words (ἀκούων τοὺς λόγους τούτους, v. 5a); 'all who heard' are frightened (vv. 5b, 11). The triple mention of ἀκούειν should arrest our attention: here the word of truth causes death (v. 5a), there it provokes a holy fear (vv. 5a, 11). The word heard has the power of life and death. This is what the narrative offers to be 'heard (!)'.

It is clear that a *theology of the Word* is at work in the text, privileging hearing over vision (which we previously detected as a typical Lucan

41 A. Marc, 'Esprit saint dans les Ecritures', 1997, p. 151.

insistence).[42] From Acts 2. 37 onwards, faith is announced as the fruit of hearing the word; this theme flows through chapters 2 to 5, where the faith of new converts results from the preaching of the apostles (4. 4; 5. 5, 11, 20) and where the gift of the Spirit is concretized in the boldness given to Christian preaching (4. 31). The conclusion of the sequence confirms the link between *pneuma* and *logos*. The activity of the community animated by the Spirit is a verbal activity: διδάσκειν and εὐαγγελίζεσθαι (5. 42). Furthermore, the hostility of the Jewish authorities consists in trying to silence the apostles (4. 17; 5. 28, 40).

What is important to Luke is not to instil a 'terror of the sacred',[43] but to narrate how a hindrance to the advancement of the Word was powerfully removed. Rendered vulnerable in its missionary efforts by an act that injured its unity, the community is not left to itself. Just as God powerfully deals with the jailing of the apostles by liberating them to preach (5. 20), so he is also at work here in a terrifying way, with regard to an obstacle that stood in the way of the spreading of the Word.

An original sin

From reading the commentaries it has become common to view the fraud of Ananias and Sapphira as merely repeating the theft of Achan (Josh. 7), who diverted a part of the plunder taken at Jericho, which should have been 'put into the treasury of the house of the Lord' (6. 24). Discovered after Israel's defeat at Ai, the thief of the forbidden goods (חמר) was stoned by the people and burned with his whole family (7. 24–6). This typological parallel goes back to the Church Fathers, who compared the fraud of Ananias with Achan's profane use of holy goods.[44]

A dubious association

The association is ancient, but dubious, since the differences with Achan's misfortune are considerable. Such differences are notable with regard to the crime as well as to the punishment and the actors in the drama. (1) *The*

---

[42] See chapter 2, pp. 37–8.

[43] According to A. Mettayer's formula, 'Terrorisme du sacré', 1978, p. 415. The author is right in saying that the text is structured by a play of antitheses (life/death, Spirit/Satan, truth/lie, constraint/freedom, etc.); but he wrongly concludes that Acts 5 ascribes to the Church the power to manage these oppositions.

[44] So in John Chrysostom (*Acts of the Apostles, Homily* 12), Jerome (*Letter* 14), Asterius (*Homilies against Cupidity*), Caesarius (*Fourth Dialogue*) and Oecumenius in his *Commentaria in Acta apostolorum* in the sixth century. See the documentation assembled by P. B. Brown, 'Meaning and Function', 1969, pp. 56–7.

offence: Achan steals the forbidden loot, while the couple in Acts 5 keep a part of an offering freely given. (2) *The judgement*: the people become the executor of God's judgement on Achan and his family, whereas Peter does not pronounce any sentence. (3) *The actors*: while Achan was eliminated with 'his sons and daughters, with his oxen, donkeys and sheep, and his tent and all that he had' (Josh. 7. 24), Acts 5 does not simply swallow Sapphira up with her husband; the text aims to demonstrate her own culpability (v. 8); a man/woman duality is deployed, which structures the text in two tableaux attracting the reader's attention.

One may object that a typological reading does not require a perfect repetition of one text in another, but the taking over of a significant structure. This objection is correct. But precisely on what elements is the association based? Among the analogies, beside the common use of the rare verb νοσφίζεσθαι (Josh. 7. 1 LXX and Acts 5. 2, cf. also 2 Macc. 4. 32), we might think of the motif of the purification of the people: the elimination of the guilty family in Joshua 7, the double funeral in Acts 5. However, one must admit that in comparing the differences, the weight of the analogies is weak. It is further diminished if we consider that the meaning of νοσφίζεσθαι used here is perfectly accessible from the Koine, without having to refer to Joshua 7. One may think that this is hardly useful since establishing the meaning of νοσφίζεσθαι from the Koine Greek does not exclude a link with Joshua 7. However, on the contrary, this is vital, in the sense that this typological affiliation to the story of Achan forces exegetes to postulate for Ananias and Sapphira an initial offering of their possessions, which makes νοσφίζεσθαι the diminution of possessions already renounced.[45] Yet the Lucan text offers no support for such speculations. To hang the thesis of a typological borrowing from Joshua 7 solely on the verb νοσφίζεσθαι is an acrobatic operation with dubious effects.

This explains why other commentators see here a repetition, not of Achan's crime, but rather of the temptation of Jesus. To the axis baptism–temptation of Jesus (Luke 3. 21–2; 4. 1–13) corresponds an axis Pentecost–Acts 5, marked by the same bipolarity: the Spirit descends, then he is victorious over Satan.[46] This theological structure may

---

[45] Cf., for example, D. P. Seccombe: 'The story only makes sense if the couple had previously declared their intention to donate the land to the community' (*Possessions*, 1982, p. 212). The Church Fathers already assumed that Ananias had vowed a donation (Chrysostom, *Homily* 12; Augustine, *Sermo* 27; Jerome, *Ep.* 8 *ad Demetrium*; Gregory the Great, *Ep.* 33 *ad Venantium*).

[46] A. Weiser, *Apostelgeschichte*, 1981, p. 146; R. Pesch, *Apostelgeschichte*, I, 1986, p. 204.

be implied by Luke, but it must be acknowledged that it is not explicit in the narrative organization of Acts 2–5.

The 'symphony' of the couple

On the contrary, a curious feature of the narrative orients the reading toward another horizon: the insistence on the complicity of Ananias and his wife (συνειδυίης καὶ τῆς γυναικός: v. 2). This shared knowledge is explicitly confirmed by the response given to Peter's interrogation (v. 8). The apostle returns again to this theme by asking Sapphira: 'how is it that you have agreed together (συνεφωνήθη ὑμῖν) to put the Spirit of the Lord to the test?' The cascade of the three occurrences of σύν (vv. 1, 2 and 9), with the use of the two verbs of collusion (σύνοιδα and συμφωνέω), is striking. Ananias and Sapphira join together and this joining in complicity divides them from the solidarity of the community.[47] As accomplices in the fraud, the couple have formed a party against the ecclesial group, and for the communion of believers they have substituted their own connivance.[48] Does not this criminal alliance open up another possibility? Does not the collusion of the original couple (the first couple in Acts) bring to mind another original couple?

The analogy that comes to mind is *the account of the fall* (Gen. 3). Analysis of the narrative context has shown that the drama of Acts 5 constitutes the first crisis in the history of Christian origins. The reference to Genesis 3 is supported by a constellation of features: (1) the destruction of the original harmony (καρδία καὶ ψυχὴ μία: 4. 32); (2) the figure of Satan, which in Jewish tradition is generally perceived behind the serpent; (3) the origin of the error situated in the sin of a couple; (4) the lie to God (Gen. 3. 1; Acts 5. 4b); (5) the expulsion at the end of the narrative (cf. Gen. 3. 23).

This phenomenon is found in a completely different context, in an apocryphal writing, in the Greek *Acts of Andrew*, where the narrative of the fall is reread with a marked insistence on the agreement between Adam and Eve.[49] This text, dated between 150 and 200, relates the success

---

[47] Luke is not indifferent to the particle σύν: in Acts 28. 25, it is the 'a-symphony' (ἀσύμφονοι) of the Jewish opponents of Paul that will symbolically signify the failure of the apostolic proclamation to Israel (see below, pp. 149–51 ch. 11).

[48] I. Richter Reimer, in a feminist perspective, imagines Sapphira as the victim of a passive complicity in the criminal acts of her husband (*Women*, 1995, pp. 1–29). Her reading is no more convincing than that of the ecclesiastical tradition when it deduces from Gen. 3 the guilt of Eve by exonerating Adam from his responsibility.

[49] I am indebted to my collegue Jean-Daniel Kaestli for this comparison. His competence in extra-canonical literature has, more often than once, been of great help.

of the preaching of Andrew before Maximilla, the wife of the proconsul Aegeates, who subsequently refuses her husband's attentions. Full of grief and anger, Aegeates throws the apostle into prison; Andrew will die as a martyr on a cross. The manner in which Andrew describes his decision and the consequences to Maximilla is very interesting from the point of view of the present concern. 'Just as Adam died in Eve through consenting to that agreement (συνθέμενος τῇ ἐκείνῃ ὁμολογίᾳ), so I now live in you, who keep the Lord's commandment and give yourself over the dignity of your (true) being.'[50] The verb συντίθημι signifies agree with, consent to (*Acts of Andrew* 3. 1; 17. 1; 42. 3; 49. 3; 53. 7: 58. 2: 62. 2). In this case, the sin of Adam is to have consented to the positive declaration (ὁμολογία) of Eve.

Furthermore, Andrew says to Maximilla:

> I rightly see in you Eve repenting and in myself Adam being converted: for what she suffered in ignorance you, whose soul I address, are restoring through being converted: and what the mind suffered which was brought down with her and estranged from itself, I am putting right with you, who know that you yourself are carried on high ... what she refused to obey, you have obeyed. That to which he consented (συνέθετο), I have avoided. That by which they were led astray, we have recognized. For it has been ordained that we should correct the error made by each of them through improving ourselves.   (*Acts Andr.* B 5).

The 'conversion' of Andrew and Maximilla concerns the sin of conjugal agreement of Adam and Eve. The error of the original couple, 'error committed by each of them', Andrew and Maximilla are going to resist. Maximilla is in a position not to repeat the sin of Eve: 'For Maximilla, the servant of the Lord, by not giving him her consent (συντιθεμένη) to deeds that are alien to her, will enrage the enemy who is in him [Aegeates] to whom he belongs' (*Acts Andr.* B 13). We can see that the agreement, as in Acts 5, is reciprocal: attributed as much to Adam, as to Eve.

This parallel sheds new light on the typology used in the narrative: the offence of Ananias and Sapphira is viewed as *the repetition of the original sin of Adam and Eve.*[51] To lie to the Spirit constitutes, in the narration

---

[50] *Acts Andr.* B 7. This citation is found on page 411 of *New Testament Apocrypha,* II, ed. W. Schneemelcher, 1975 [German edition, 1964].

[51] In opposition to my reading hypothesis, R. F. O'Toole, in an article published in 1995, raises the following difficulties: (a) the absence of a verbal connection between Acts 5 and Gen. 3; (b) the differences between the two accounts (Gen. 3 offers no parallel to the role of Peter, or to the lie and death of the couple) ('You Did Not Lie to Us', 1995, pp. 201–2).

of Acts, the original sin in the Church. The conclusion of Acts 5 is the following: the *ekklesia* is a community whose members are fallible, but whose project of unity is protected by the judgement of God.

An ethic of sharing

By identifying the crime of Ananias and Sapphira as an injury against the work of the Spirit, my interpretation joins the salvation-history reading mentioned above.[52] It remains, however, to develop a dimension of the text of which this reading takes no account: the nature of the fraud. The accursed couple's crime is financial. The reader of the work *ad Theophilum* is warned about the Lucan sensitivity concerning the power of money. It runs throughout his gospel, from the denunciation of the pride of the rich in the Magnificat (Luke 1. 53) to the praise of the offering of the widow just before the Passion (21. 1–4).[53] Acts continues this line in Acts 1 by relating the curse, attached to the 'wages of unrighteousness' that Judas had gained by his treason (1. 18).

A crime of money

It is not by chance that the two crises that happen during the 'golden age' of Christianity, according to Luke, both originate in economic affairs: the offence of Ananias and Sapphira and the recrimination of the Hellenists when faced with the prejudice toward their widows (6. 1). By taking over the traditional narrative of the death of Ananias and Sapphira and by placing it in this strategic position in the narration, Luke wants to inform his readers that *the original sin in the Church is a sin of money*. The relationship of believers to their possessions takes on an eschatological dimension. Luke had already made this known in the two first summaries, where the Holy Spirit urges a sharing of possessions which accomplishes both the Deuteronomic requirement that poverty disappear among the people of God (4. 34 cites Deut. 15. 4) and the Greek ideal of friendship ἅπαντα κοινά: 2. 44; 4. 32).

The observation is correct, but, as has already been said concerning Josh. 7, this is to ignore the rules of typological interpretation by requiring a strict correspondence between the two texts. In this situation, the similarity of the literary genre (story of beginnings) and plot (transgression of the social code guaranteed by God and the punishment of the couple) suffices to identify a procedure by which the narrator appeals to the memory of Gen. 3. This is different from the *Acts of Andrew*, where the author mentions it explicitly.

[52] See pp. 168–70 above.

[53] Luke 1. 53; 3. 11; 4. 16–20; 6. 24–5; 12. 13–21; 16. 13, 19–31; 18. 18–30; 20. 47; 21. 1–4; Acts 1. 18; 2. 44–5; 4. 33–4; 8. 26–39; 13. 1, 7–12; 17. 4, 12. Concerning this theme see P. F. Esler, *Community*, 1987, pp. 164–200.

Spirit and money go hand in hand in Luke[54] who does not subscribe in any sense to a (anti-biblical) dichotomy between 'material things' and 'spiritual things'. One of the morals of the story is that money can kill one who is attached to it.

An ontological dimension of the Church

The punishment of Ananias and Sapphira demonstrates that this sharing of goods cannot be reduced to a philosophical ideal, albeit a Greek one, or to a romanticism of love. The altruistic management of possessions is, so to speak, an ontological dimension of the Church. Having wealth establishes a responsibility toward the poor which God the judge sanctions. In light of the judgement of Ananias and Sapphira, a prefiguration of eschatological judgement, the ethic of sharing possessions becomes extremely serious. Mammon (Luke 16. 13), the destroyer of life, is also a destroyer of the Church.

It is in this perspective that we must understand the redactional addition of verse 4, which nuances the imperative character of 4. 32, 34 (the renunciation of one's goods is not obligatory, but voluntary) and which reframes Peter's criticism in 5. 3 (the crime is having lied about the totality of the commitment). It is also worth noting that after the attribution of the sin to Satan in verse 3, verse 4 returns to an ethic of individual responsibility. Why this redactional corrective? Friedrich Wilhem Horn is correct in seeing a paraenetic effect here:[55] by maintaining the freedom of the gift and by highlighting the responsibility of the individual, Luke adds to the eschatological threat an exhortative dimension intended for his affluent readers. If the judgement of God on the accursed couple belongs to the time of origins and as such is not repeatable, the call to share one's possessions remains.

Conclusion: an original sin in the Church

The narrative of the death of Ananias and Sapphira, whose theological violence has perturbed exegesis since the Church Fathers, has produced an infinite number of readings. The thesis defended in this chapter is that Luke's use of this tradition, which on more than one point is a shock to his theology, can be perceived from an observation of the narrative strategy

---

[54] A nice formulation from J. Jervell, *Apostelgeschichte*, 1998, p. 195: 'Geld und Geist sind für Lukas ein wichtiges Thema.'

[55] *Glaube und Handeln*, 1983, pp. 47–9.

deployed in chapters 2 to 5. The study of the plot of the macro-narrative shows that what is at stake here is not the internal administration of the community, but rather its expansion, animated by the Spirit, through a confrontation with the Jewish authorities.

A comparison with the apocryphal *Acts of Andrew* leads to the conclusion that the typological model is not to be found in the offence of Achan (Josh. 7), but rather in the transgression of Adam and Eve (Gen. 3). Luke has included in his work, though not without resistance and corrective gloss, a narrative which he uses to expose the original sin in the Church. The story of Ananias and Sapphira takes place in the narrative sequence of Acts 2–5, which can be qualified as a story of origins, similar to Genesis 1–11. The literary genre of a story of origins explains both the marvellous dimension of the narration (the irresistible expansion of the Church) and its tragic side (two stunning deaths for which the narrator shows no compassion).

The author of Luke–Acts has situated this account in an ecclesiological perspective rather than a soteriological one. He does not unfold the drama of individual salvation, but magnifies the power of the Spirit and his work in spreading the Word. However, even if the theme of Acts 5. 1–11 is the original injury of the community, Luke's social concern could not ignore the fact that the first sin in the Church was a financial crime.

9

SAUL'S CONVERSION (ACTS 9; 22; 26)

'The historian's sole task is to tell the facts just as they have occurred.' This injunction is from the famous second-century rhetor, Lucian of Samosata,[1] whom I have cited more than once for his valuable theorizing of ancient historiography. In this case, this very simple prescription aims to guarantee the objectivity of the historian in the face of the risks of pressures or flattery toward the addressees, but it reflects well enough the requirement of accuracy which was made of Graeco-Roman historiography.

How would Lucian have reacted to reading the three accounts of Saul's conversion as presented by the book of Acts? Each time there is the 'same' episode of Saul blinded on the Damascus road, falling to the ground, then receiving the revelation of God's surprising choice of him. However, between the first narration of the event in chapter 9, and the two autobiographical repetitions in speeches by Paul[2] (Acts 22. 1–21 and 26. 1–23), the variations are considerable. This combination of repetition and variation is a testing ground for the exegesis of the book of Acts. When a scholar responds to the question why there are three accounts of Saul's conversion, one is able to identify the methodological orientation that governs his/her work. The biopsy is infallible. I shall immediately warn the reader that this book will not break the rule.

My intention is to re-examine this classical question by adopting a narratological point of view. In other words, my interest is in discussing the effect sought by the narrator in this multiplication of narratives. The question of the compatibility of Luke's narration and Paul's accounts

[1] *How to Write History*, 39.
[2] The hero of the second part of the book of Acts is called Saul (his Aramaic name) by the narrator until 13. 9 where he makes a change to Paul (his Greek name); this substitution corresponds to the orientation of the Pauline mission, which, from chapter 13, includes non-Jews. In this chapter, I shall use both names, depending on whether I am discussing Acts 9 or Acts 22 and 26.

(Gal. 1. 13–17; 1 Cor. 9. 1) is beyond the scope of my research.[3] Rather, I shall ask why Luke wanted his readers to view the Damascus road event three times, much in the manner of a tourist guide programming two additional visits to a site already visited.

A revealing site of reading

In fact, the narratives of Saul's encounter with the Risen One on the Damascus road are a test case which reveals the relation that the exegete has with the text.[4] Source criticism explained the excess of narratives by postulating Luke's use of several sources (Spitta; Wendt; Hirsch).[5] In one manner or another, scholars either condemn the inexactitude of Acts 9 or attribute the variants in Acts 22 and 26 to a defective memory of Paul.[6] However, since the works of Cadbury and Dibelius have drawn attention to Luke's own literary creativity,commentators most often identify a traditional narrative behind Acts 9, from which the narrator has developed two redactional variants in Acts 22 and 26.[7] Some commentators

---

[3] One should keep in mind that Luke's narration follows the pattern of a story of conversion (of which the story of Joseph and Aseneth gives an idea), while Paul's discourse is governed by the apologetic rhetoric of Gal. 1.

[4] Among the studies devoted to this issue: E. Hirsch, 'Drei Berichte', 1929, pp. 305–12; H. Windisch, 'Christusepiphanie', 1932, pp. 1–23; D. M. Stanley, 'Paul's Conversion', 1953, pp. 315–38; C. Burchard, *Dreizehnte Zeuge*, 1970; S. Lundgren, 'Ananias', 1971, pp. 117–22; K. Löning, *Saulustradition*, 1973; V. Stolle, *Zeuge als Angeklagter*, 1973, pp. 155–212; O. H. Steck, 'Formgeschichtliche Bemerkungen', 1976, pp. 20–8; R. F. O'Toole, *Christological Climax*, 1978; C. W. Hedrick, 'Conversion/Call', 1981, pp. 415–32; N. A. Beck, *Lukan Writer's Stories*, 1983, pp. 213–18; J. Calloud, 'Sur le chemin de Damas', 1985, pp. 3–29; 1985, pp. 40–53; 1985, pp. 21–42; 1986, pp. 1–19; R. F. Collins, 'Paul's Damascus Experience', 1986, pp. 99–118; G. Lohfink, *Conversion de saint Paul*, 1967; S. R. Bechtler, 'Meaning of Paul's Call', 1987, pp. 53–77; J. J. Kilgallen, 'Paul before Agrippa', 1988, pp. 170–95; D. Hamm, 'Paul's Blindness', 1990, pp. 63–72. According to narrative criticism: B. R. Gaventa, *From Darkness to Light*, 1986, pp. 52–95; C. J. LaHurd, *Author's Call*, 1987, pp. 182–229; R. W. Funk, *Poetics of Biblical Narrative*, 1988, pp. 156–61, pp. 204–6; M. E. Rosenblatt, 'Under Interrogation', 1988, pp. 92–123; 'Recurring Narration', 1990, pp. 94–105; R. D. Witherup, 'Functional Redundancy', 1992, pp. 67–86; W. S. Kurz, *Reading Luke–Acts*, 1993, pp. 26–7, 125–31; S. Reymond, 'Expérience du chemin de Damas', 1993; 'Paul sur le chemin de Damas', 1996, pp. 520–38.

[5] Recently, B. Witherington has revived this ancient thesis by affirming the traditional originality of the three variants. In his scenario, Acts 22 is a condensation from the apostle Paul, while Acts 26 telescopes the facts – in the memory of Paul or the work of Luke ('Editing the Good News', 1996, p. 339).

[6] The state of research can be found in G. Lohfink, *Conversion de saint Paul*, 1967, pp. 39–57.

[7] This literary verdict is based on the redactional origin of the Lucan speeches (and hence of Acts 22 and 26) argued by M. Dibelius, ('Conversion of Cornelius' [1947], 1956, pp. 110–11; 'Speeches in Acts' [1949], 1956, pp. 182–3). The one exception to this consensus has been voiced by T. L. Budesheim, 'Paul's Abschiedsrede', 1976, pp. 9–30, who

understand this as stylistic variation.[8] Others ascribe to the redactor's careless inattention to narrative discrepancies the fact that in one place Saul's companions are said to hear the voice but see nothing (9. 7) while in another they see the light and hear nothing (22. 9); or that in one place they remain standing (9. 7), while in another they fall to the ground along with Paul (26. 14).[9] The merit of redaction criticism lies in having perceived that 'this technique of repetition is one to which Luke always resorts when he wants to impress something specially upon the reader' (E. Haenchen).[10] The unresolved question is: why is the repetition combined with so much diversity?

To my knowledge, the first exegete to move away from this line of questioning, which focused on the genealogy of the text, was David Stanley in his article 'Paul's Conversion in Acts: Why the Three Accounts?' (1953). His formulation deserves to be quoted: 'The triple narrative of that supremely critical hour in a life fraught with crises deserves to be studied from another aspect: the function assigned to it in the exposition of this theme by the author of the book of Acts'.[11]

Anticipating more recent research, Stanley was framing the problem in narratological terms and asking how this tripling of the narrative actually functions within the overall plot of the book of Acts. I would like to broaden the question: how should one evaluate the interplay of repetition and variation in Acts 9, 22 and 26? Can one explain, from a narrative point of view, the variations of Acts 22 and 26 compared with Acts 9? Luke was certainly aware that the differences among his three narratives were not just matters of detail; if he was not counting on the forgetfulness of his reader, what means has he provided for the reader to put up with such variation?

First, a panoramic view of the three narratives will enable us to detect their unvarying core, to determine their status, and the function of each. Second, I shall undertake a detailed examination of each of the three. Third, a conclusion will produce some considerations for the significance of the Damascus road event in the plot of Acts.

---

ascribes Acts 22. 1–21 to the tradition and sees in Acts 9 a Hellenized adaptation due to the redactor's pen; prior to that, D. M. Stanley had adopted a similar though less clear-cut position ('Paul's Conversion', 1953, pp. 325–28).

[8] F. F. Bruce, *Acts of the Apostles*, 1990, p. 232; A. Weiser, *Apostelgeschichte*, 1981, pp. 219–22; C. W. Hedrick, 'Conversion/Call', 1981, pp. 427–32; R. Pesch, *Apostelgeschichte*, I, 1986, p. 302.

[9] H. Conzelmann, *Acts of the Apostles*, 1987, pp. 72–3; G. Schneider, *Apostelgeschichte*, II, 1982, p. 22.

[10] *Acts of the Apostles*, 1971, p. 357.   [11] 'Paul's Conversion', 1953, p. 315.

The question of the multiplication of accounts is an interesting one to raise in the work of Luke, since the phenomenon of repetition of a narrative episode is produced several times. The Ascension narrative is related in two variants (Luke 24. 50–1; Acts 1. 9–11). The events surrounding the meeting between Peter and Cornelius are related as many as three times between Acts 10 and 11, and once again at the Jerusalem assembly (15. 7–11). The 'apostolic decree' promulgated by this same assembly (15. 20), regulating the communion among Christians originating from the Jerusalem and Antioch missions respectively, is duplicated in 15. 29 and in 21. 25. The narrative of Saul's conversion is thus not the only one to undergo such multiplication.

One can broaden these findings by observing that, besides single episodes, the reader of Acts frequently sees the repetition of narrative scenarios. Chapters 2 to 5 present, four times over, the same threefold structural pattern: an event (Pentecost for example) is followed by an interpretative speech by Peter, and is then followed by a contrasting effect upon the audience. On one side there is the opposition of religious leaders, on the other, the support of the people (2. 1–41; 3. 1 – 4. 4; 4. 5–31; 5. 17–40). From chapter 13 onwards, the Pauline mission is governed by the following well-known scheme: Paul preaches in the synagogue, but as he faces the violent rejection of his message, he addresses the Godfearers and the Gentiles who welcome the Word (13. 42–51; 14. 1–6; 17. 1–9, 10–13; 18. 1–7, etc.). More widely, the modelling of Paul on Peter, which leads the narrator to ascribe to Paul similar activities to those of Peter (but generally more impressive), comes out of the rhetorical device of *syncrisis*.[12]

In summary, the repetition of narratives of the same event concretizes a phenomenon of narrative redundancy which the author of Acts uses more intensively than any other writer of the New Testament. Why has Luke given so much weight to redundancy?[13]

The poetics of biblical narrative has been studied by Robert Alter (1981) and Meir Sternberg (1987).[14] Both writers are sensitive to the phenomenon of narrative redundancy. Their work has the advantage of going beyond the negative evaluation of redundancy maintained by classical literary criticism. For these authors redundancy is not understood as excess, as a superfluous insistence, or as a rhetorical ornament. It was form criticism that taught us to speak of 'doublets'. R. Alter and M. Sternberg treat redundancy on the basis of a theory of communication which considers this process to be a way of ensuring the reception

---

[12] For an examination of this device see pp. 56–9.

[13] The classical reference for the study of literary redundancy is the article of S. R. Suleiman, 'Redundancy', 1980. On the importance of repetition in ancient rhetoric, see H. Lausberg, *Handbook*, 1998, pp. 384–92. On redundancy in the New Testament and Greek rhetoric, see E. A. Nida, J. P. Louw, A. H. Synman and J. V. W. Cronje, *Style and Discourse*, 1983, pp. 22–3. For oral rhetoric, see P. J. Achtemeier, 'Omne Verbum Sonat', 1990.

[14] R. Alter, *Art of Biblical Narrative*, New York, 1981; M. Sternberg, *Poetics*, 1987.

of the information by reducing, as much as possible, the ambiguities of meaning. Retelling is indispensable in order to counter difficulties which constitute 'all the turbulence or defaults in the system which interfere with the faithful transmission of the signals'.[15] The theoreticians of computer science have thus opened the way towards an evaluation of redundancy as a means to ensure optimal communication between narrator and narratee. In the case of Lucan redundancy, rather than a literary gimmick or a mannerism of the writer Luke, or even a regrettable lack of imagination, I prefer to speak of a mode of composition typical of the book of Acts.[16]

The choice of this procedure denotes a narrative strategy and this strategy serves a theological aim. I think Luke's theology, which constantly attempts to articulate continuity *and* movement, identity *and* change (between the Old and the New, between Jesus and the apostles), has found in this procedure of repetition an appropriate literary mediation. For repetition is never exactly the return of the same. It is 'ce lent parcours du discours en quête de sa vérité' (this slow journey of the discourse in quest of its truth; M. de Certeau). With its interplay of similarities and dissimilarities, redundancy signals the presence of the same when things change, or, if one prefers, signals the difference when things repeat themselves. In other words, I think that a theological dialectic of identity and difference is communicated through a literary interplay of similarity and dissimilarity.

One example: the journey constitutes the formal structure of the life of Luke's Jesus just like that of the life of Paul in Acts: the same itinerary, the same hostility, the same Passion, while on the other hand nothing is exactly the same for both Jesus and Paul. The disciple is not confused with the Master.[17]

A series of three narratives

Meir Sternberg has examined the various factors which comprise the rhetoric of informational redundancy within biblical narration.[18] Besides verbatim repetition (e.g. in the prediction–fulfilment scheme),

---

[15] J. Lyons, *Semantics*, I, 1977, p. 44. J. C. Anderson lists seven functions of redundancy: (1) to highlight attention; (2) to fix in the mind; (3) to emphasize the importance; (4) to create expectations; (5) to cause reassessment; (6) to unify disparate elements; (7) to build patterns of association or draw contrasts (*Matthew's Narrative Web*, p. 44).

[16] R. C. Tannehill, 'Composition', 1984, pp. 217–40, see esp. pp. 237–40.

[17] For more detail on this example, see chapters 3 (pp. 56–9) and 11 (pp. 233–4 and 253–4).

[18] M. Sternberg, *Poetics*, 1987, pp. 387–93.

Sternberg identifies *five types of possible variation* within a framework of repetition: (1) amplification; (2) suppression; (3) interpolation; (4) grammatical transformation (e.g. turning active into passive); (5) substitution. Among the factors leading to variation, Sternberg mentions change in the source of information, that is, modification of the point of view adopted between the first narration of an event and the following ones; I shall return to this point later, as it is important for my case. For now, I shall apply Sternberg's taxonomy to the three narratives.

The play of variations

Sternberg's taxonomy is valuable when comparing the three variant narratives of Paul's conversion, since one meets in each case the five types mentioned. The dialogue between Jesus and Saul is characterized by word for word repetition : 'Saul, Saul, why do you persecute me?' (He said to me:) 'I am Jesus [the Nazarene], whom you are persecuting' (9. 4–5; 22. 7–8; 26. 14–15). *An unvarying kernel*, maintained from one narrative to the next, thus focuses on the identification dialogue that follows the shock of encounter.

Variations must be assessed from Acts 9, the first account. Comparing the structure of the three narratives will allow a better grasp of the function of the shifts.

Acts 9. 1–25	Acts 22. 1–21	Acts 26. 1–23
I. vv. 1–2: Introduction. Saul, persecutor of Christians	I. vv. 1–2: Captatio	I. vv. 1–3: Captatio
II. vv. 3–7: Epiphany of Christ (with dialogue)	II. vv. 3–5: Paul, a Jew and persecutor of Christians	II. vv. 4–8: Paul Pharisee
III. vv. 8–9: Apparition's effects upon Saul	III. vv. 6–11: Epiphany of Christ (with dialogue)	III. vv. 9–11: Paul, persecutor of Christians
IV. vv. 10–16: Ananias' vision (Saul's calling)	IV. vv. 12–16: Encounter with Ananias and baptism of Paul	IV. vv. 12–18: Epiphany (Paul's calling)
V. vv. 17–19a: Mandate to Ananias and baptism of Saul	V. vv. 17–21: Ecstasy in the Jerusalem Temple (Paul's calling)	V. vv. 19–23: Effect. Paul, witness for Christ, and persecuted.

VI. vv. 19b–25: Effect.
Saul, witness for
Christ, and threatened
with death.

(9. 26–30: conspiracy	(22. 22: death shouts	(27–28: voyage to
against Saul)	from the crowd)	Rome)

I shall first look at chapter 9. After an introduction describing Saul's persecution plan (9. 1–2), the epiphany of Christ (vv. 3–9) is followed by an appearance of the Lord to Ananias (vv. 10–16), and then by the fulfilment of his mandate to heal and to baptize (vv. 17–19a). The effect is unexpected: Saul, the persecutor, becomes the persecuted witness of Christ in Damascus and Jerusalem (vv. 19b–30). Saul's change from persecutor to persecuted concretizes the overturning of his identity at Damascus and this is why commentators are wrong to break off the narrative at verse 19b, rather than continuing on to verse 30.[19]

A synoptic comparison of the narrative of Acts 9 with its autobiographical counterparts in chapters 22 and 26 allows a series of structural modifications to appear. I shall list them later.

The *amplifications* touch on several motifs: Paul's past as a Pharisee is introduced in 26. 4–8; his activity as a persecutor of Christians is amplified and aggravated in 22. 3–5 and 26. 9–11. The factor of *suppression* applies to the role of Ananias, whose vision is suppressed in chapter 22, and disappears totally from chapter 26. The persecution experienced by Saul (9. 19b–30) has no equivalent in chapter 22.

Within the speech of chapter 26, an *interpolation* has Paul's vocation announced to Paul himself during the course of the epiphany (26. 16–18: 'for I have appeared to you for this purpose'), whereas in chapter 9 Saul's vocation is communicated to Ananias alone, after the shock on the Damascus road (9. 15–16: 'he is an instrument whom I have chosen').

---

[19] The narrative caesura in 9. 19a is still defended by L. T. Johnson, *Acts of the Apostles*, 1992, p. 161; the only thing that speaks for it is a slight break between 9. 19a and 19b (ἐγένετο δέ), whereas 9. 31 represents a much clearer break, through the insertion of a narrative summary and the disappearance of the character Saul from the narrative until 11. 25. But especially the sequence 9. 1–30 is clearly identifiable by the inclusion effect orchestrated by the narrator between 9. 1–2 and 9. 26–30: (a) the journey from Jerusalem to Damascus (9. 1) is reversed in the form of a flight from Damascus to Jerusalem (9. 25–6); (b) Saul the persecutor (9. 1) becomes Saul the persecuted (9. 29); (c) the enemy of the Way (9. 2) speaks in the name of the Lord (9. 27–8); (d) the murderous intent toward Christians (9. 1) is transformed into a brotherly relationship (9. 30). Elsewhere a parallelism of motifs can be detected between 9. 19b–25 and 26–30, which function like twin narratives, rather than between 9. 13–25 and 26–30 (contrary opinion in D. Gill, 'Structure', 1974, pp. 346–8).

A comparison of 9. 6 (λαληθήσεται σοι) with 22. 10 (εἶπον) allows us to see a *grammatical transformation*, where Saul moves from a passive role in 9. 6 ('you will be told') into an active one in 22. 10 ('and I said').[20]

Finally, the speech in chapter 22 culminates in a scene of trance in the Jerusalem Temple (22. 17–21), unknown to the reader of Acts 9, and this scene serves as a *substitution* for the persecution narrative in 9. 19b–30.

Notice, in addition to this, that the character of Saul's travelling companions is subject to all the types of change. Suppression: they progressively lose their importance from Acts 9 to Acts 26 (compare 9. 16–17 with 26. 14a). Interpolation: the narrative mentions them sometimes after the dialogue (9. 7–8; 22. 9–10), sometimes before (26. 14). Transformation: in chapter 9 they hear the voice without seeing anybody (9. 7), while in chapter 22 they see without hearing (22. 9); as the Christophany occurs, sometimes they stand speechless (9. 7: εἱστήκεισαν ἐνεοί), sometimes they fall to the ground (26. 14: πάντων τε καταπεσόντων ἡμῶν εἰς τὴν γῆν).

How should one interpret this play of variations? To what narrative constraints does it respond? What design does it reveal? The literary and thematic shifts that one notices between the narrative of Acts 9 and its repetitions in the autobiographical discourses of Paul (Acts 22 and 26) are generally explained by their different places in the plot of Acts (R. C. Tannehill) or by the change of audience (B. R. Gaventa). Personally, I think of the status and function of the three narratives in the narration of Luke–Acts from the point of view of their effect on the reader; in other words I am interested in the change of narrator from one version to the other (this is the question of status) and I investigate the rhetorical effect of the redundancy on the reader (this is the question of the pragmatic function of the narrative).

The differentiation of points of view

Among the factors making for variation within redundancy, Sternberg mentions a change in the source of information involving a change of point of view.[21] That is exactly what is going on here: Acts 9 emanates from the narrator who recounts it in the third person; Acts 22 and Acts 26 are instances of autobiographical discourse with an inside view, where Paul is speaking about himself, using 'I'. From this observation W. S. Kurz has derived a key for understanding the relationship among the

---

[20] *Pace* R. D. Witherup ('Functional Redundancy', 1992, p. 70), who does not perceive any grammatical transformation between the three narratives, I do see in this mutation of the λαληθήσεται (9. 6) into εἶπον (22. 10) a modification of this type, consciously playing on the two synonymous terms.

[21] *Poetics*, 1987, pp. 380–2.

three narratives of Saul's conversion: variations from one narrative to the next may be explained by the 'influence of variant narrators'.[22] While emanating from the same author (Luke as the first narrator), the three narratives do not have the same status within the narration of Acts: Acts 22 as well as Acts 26 are attributed by the author to Paul (the second narrator). To put it another way, the three variants emanate from the same 'voice' (the narrator), but the enunciator within the narrative varies.[23] Acts originates from the first narrator, the omniscient narrator; the discourse in the third person grants the text (narratively speaking) an objective status that the first-person discourse of Paul does not have. Acts 9 is not only first in the unfolding of the narration; it is first in the hierarchy of narrative authorities.[24] In keeping with Genette's vocabulary: the enunciator of Acts 9 is extradiegetic (the narrator), while the enunciator of Acts 22 and 26 is intradiegetic (Paul, a figure internal to the narrative). Acts 22 and 26 are thus presented as retrospective readings of the Damascus road event, attributed by the narrator to his main character.

This attention given to the differentiation of enunciators sheds new light on the competitive character of the three narratives. In regard to its informative value, within the narrative, Acts 9 emanating from the ominiscient narrator towers above Acts 22 and Acts 26. The three accounts do not work together according to the principle of a 'coinciding of narrative points of view',[25] but, on the contrary, according to the principle of differentiation of points of view. The narrative device distinguishes the objective and earlier point of view of the omniscient narrator (Acts 9) from the subjective and later point of view of the speaker, Paul, in Acts 22 and 26.

Effects on the reader

Four consequences may be drawn from this discovery. (1) Having been forewarned about the difference between the enunciators, the reader will

---

[22] W. S. Kurz, *Reading Luke–Acts*, 1993, p. 125.

[23] I borrow these categories from G. Genette, *Figures III*, 1972, pp. 225–67. For a commentary on them, see D. Marguerat and Y. Bourquin, *How to Read*, 1999, pp. 102–20.

[24] According to S. Chatman, in the case of a conflict between the ideology of the narrator and that of a character, the narrator's point of view (unless he is unreliable) 'tends to override the character's' (*Story and Discourse*, 1978, p. 156). Such a supremacy of the narrator's version in cases of discrepancy is confirmed by M. Sternberg, *Poetics*, 1987, pp. 75–6, 130, 245–6, 380–2, 389–91, 413–8, 432–3, and G. W. Savran, *Telling and Retelling*, 1988, pp. 13–15.

[25] According to R. D. Witherup ('Functional Redundancy', 1992, p. 74, cf. note 19; cf. also pp. 84–5), who in my view is wrong to overemphasize the coincidence of the three narratives, when their competitive character precisely brings out their profound divergences.

not be surprised when the successive reports of the Damascus road event present divergences among themselves (this was the case between 10. 9– 16 and 11. 5–10, when Peter recounts his ecstasy). (2) The reader, confronted after Acts 9 with two speeches in the first person, will not be surprised at the gradual disappearance of secondary characters (Ananias and the travelling companions) in favour of an increased focalization on the character of Paul, reaching its peak in the speech before Agrippa.[26] (3) The supremacy of the narrator's account (Acts 9) over the retrospective speeches of Paul serves here as a literary mediation for the theological precedence of the intervention of God over the subjective appropriations of this event (the same thing can be said if one compares 10. 1–23 with the autobiographical discourses of Cornelius and Peter in 10. 24– 33; 11. 4–17). (4) The succession of the three versions is presented to the reader as 'a road to re-reading the initial Pauline experience, which is gradually understood... according to the rhythm of his missionary life'.[27]

What conclusion is required? The author of Acts was not content with simply juxtaposing three competing versions of the Damascus road event. The differentiation of narrative authorities which he has provided makes plausible for the reader the reception of three divergent versions of one and the same event. Behind this composition of a Pauline discourse intended for the Jews of Jerusalem (Acts 22) or for a political elite (Acts 26), one finds again Luke's skilful use of *prosopopoeia* to which I have already referred.[28] Recomposing a story from one character's particular point of view is a well-known exercise among the rhetorical schools of antiquity. It consists of composing a speech from the particular point of view of a historical or mythical figure, and adapting it to a specific audience.

[26] Concerning the intervention of the travelling companions and of Ananias, which occupies twelve verses in chapter 9 (9. 7–8, 10–19), there remains in chapter 26 only a half verse (26. 14a). The progressive disappearance of secondary characters between the first and the third narrative, and the concomitant ascension into prominence of the figure of Saul, have been carefully noted by R. D. Witherup ('Functional Redundancy', 1992, pp. 77–80), who speaks of 'literary rheostat' in order to describe this dialectical regulation of the narrative. The focalization on the figure of Paul in Acts 22 and 26 has been analysed by W. S. Kurz, *Reading Luke–Acts*, 1993, pp. 129–30. The principle of focalization as a position relative to the story, that is, external or internal to the story, is described by S. Rimmon-Kenan, *Narrative Fiction*, 1983, pp. 74–7. In the case of the contrasting development of secondary characters and of Saul, this author speaks of a movement of narrative 'acceleration and deceleration' (*Narrative Fiction*, 1983, p. 56). These categories have been well used by M. E. Rosenblatt in his dissertation, 'Under Interrogation', 1988, pp. 92–123, esp. pp. 102–9.

[27] S. Reymond, 'Paul sur le chemin de Damas', 1996, p. 521.

[28] See pp. 17–19. References may be found in W. S. Kurz, 'Hellenistic Rhetoric', 1980, p. 186 and D. E. Aune, *Literary Environment*, 1987, pp. 125–8.

Quintilian, the theoretician of Roman rhetoric, recommends this exercise as *utilissima exercitatio*, because 'it is highly profitable for poets and *future historians*'.[29] After the composition of the missionary preaching of Peter and Paul, the composition of the discourses of Acts 22 and 26 provides a supplementary proof of this mastery.

As a result, the three narratives are not to be compared on the same plane. The logic of the presentation of the event in each case is derived from the point of view of the one expressing himself therein. Yet this logic is also bound up with another factor, which has not yet been mentioned: the function of each narrative within the plot of the book of Acts. The examination of the narrative context of each one should provide the clues.

The function of the three narratives

Acts 9 must not be considered in isolation. The conversion of Saul on the Damascus road is part of a sequence that begins in chapter 8 with the persecution of the Jerusalem church following the martyrdom of Stephen (8. 1–3). The movement of the Christian diaspora to Samaria (Acts 8) extends to the conversion of Cornelius (Acts 10), which inaugurates the access of non-Jews to salvation. Acts 9 comes at the climax of a series of conversions (Simon, then the Ethiopian eunuch, then Saul) which show how God has widened the circle of the elect; the decisive step will be made in the encounter of Peter and Cornelius (cf. 10. 34–6).[30] The theme that dominates the plot is not the exemplarity of the converts' faith (neither Simon nor Saul are examples).[31] The common theme is God's surprising initiative in the choice of converts: Simon the greedy magician, the mutilated Ethiopian excluded from the covenant, Saul the persecutor, Cornelius the impure one. Each episode within Acts 8 to 11 confronts divine initiative (8. 4–8; 8. 26; 9. 3–12; 10. 1–23) with the believers' reactions, which vary from prophetic lucidity (8. 20–3) to obedience (8. 27a),

---

[29] *Institutio oratoria* III.8.49 (italics mine). Also read IX.2.29–32.

[30] The plot structure in Acts 8–9 has been carefully analysed in the study of S. Reymond; she ably shows how Saul's conversion both continues and overshadows the conversions in chapter 8 ('Expérience du chemin de Damas', 1993, pp. 18–86). Similar attention to narrative progression from Acts 8 to Acts 11, concerning conversion, characterizes the research done by B. R. Gaventa, *From Darkness to Light*, 1986, pp. 52–129. The greatest merit of these two studies is to break up the narrative isolation to which most commentators subject Acts 9 by comparing it with Acts 22 and 26.

[31] I agree on this point with R. D. Witherup, 'Functional Redundancy', 1992, p. 73; and yet the Lucan insistence on the theme of conversion cannot exclude a paradigmatic connotation underlying the narrative.

and embarrassment (9. 13–4, 26; 10. 17).[32] Acts 9 is thus inserted within a context that articulates both God's surprising initiatives in the enlarging of the community and the believers' reactions.

In Acts 22 and Acts 26, the subjective recomposition of the Damascus event occurs within a speech; here the important step is to ascertain the rhetorical aim the narrative ascribes to the speech. Acts 22 is Paul's final speech to the people of Jerusalem, after a Jewish plot forced him out of the Temple and closed its gates (21. 30: notice the symbolic weight of this closing of the Temple!). Saved from lynching by the Roman police (21. 31–6), Paul makes his ἀπολογία (22. 1). The result will be the crowd's shouting for his death: 'Remove him from the earth' (αἶρε ἀπὸ τῆς γῆς τὸν τοιοῦτον, 22. 22), resounding like an echo of the roar of the crowd against Jesus (αἶρε τοῦτον, Luke 23. 18). *The rhetorical function of Paul's speech is to defend himself against the charge of breaking with 'the people and the Law and this place'* (21. 28).[33] Arising from this charge, Paul's autobiography dramatically addresses his 'brothers and fathers' (22. 1) in order to convince them 'in the Hebrew language' of the apostle's Jewishness.

While Acts 22 defends Paul before his fellow Jews, Acts 26 justifies him before the other pole of the book of Acts: Graeco-Roman culture. In the presence of King Agrippa and his court (25. 23), Paul 'transculturates' the event of his conversion so that it may be grasped by a literate audience; such a meticulous care for inculturation will lead the narrator to formulate the paradox of verse 14, where Jesus addresses Saul 'in the Hebrew language' (Luke historicizes) and yet utters a proverb that is known solely from Hellenistic literature: 'It is hard for you to kick against the goads' (Luke actualizes). One must be attentive to the status conferred on Agrippa by the exordium of the speech: 'You are especially familiar with all the customs and controversies of the Jews' (πάντων τῶν κατὰ Ἰουδαίους ἐθῶν τε καὶ ζητημάτων: 26. 3). The rhetorical aim of the speech is determined: *Jewish hostility toward the apostle (26. 19–21) will be presented as a matter of internal controversy, a ζήτημα, in which Paul is being unjustly prosecuted.*[34]

---

[32]   J. T. Squires has just shown again the narrative coherence of the sequence, Acts 8. 4 – 12. 25, constructed on the theme of the opening of mission to non-Jews: 'turn to the Gentiles' ('Function', 1998).

[33]   Except for the accusation concerning his profanation of the Temple, already refuted in an explicit commentary of the narrator in 21. 29, the speech utilizes the biographical material in order to refute the charges levelled against Paul. See the analysis by F. Veltman, 'Defense Speeches', 1978, pp. 253–4.

[34]   B. R. Gaventa sees rightly when she refuses to include the *captatio benevolentiae* in 26. 3a (the appeal to Agrippa's knowledge as to ἔθη καὶ ζητήματα) within the register of flattery, but sees the formulation of the *status causae* as Paul wants to define it: 'Paul

I will summarize. For his readers, Luke has justified in two ways the variations he introduces within the three versions of the Damascus road event. On the one hand, he varies the speakers between Acts 9 and Acts 22–26. On the other hand, he explicitly designates the Pauline speeches as apologies (22. 1; 26. 1), thus determining for them a rhetorical aim which authorizes the speaker, within the canons of Graeco-Roman rhetoric, to bend the facts in favour of the thesis he defends. By twice introducing a speech for the defence, an ἀπολογία, Luke thus authorizes the Paul he is describing to invest his own subjectivity as an orator in the argumentative use of his life story.

I have thus specified the status and the function of each account within the narration of Acts. It is important now to examine the specific interpretation that the Damascus event receives in each version. It is to this task that the second part of this chapter will be devoted.

What is specific to each narrative

Each version has its specific theological theme: for Acts 9 it is the Church; for Acts 22 it is the Judaism of Paul; for Acts 26 it is Christology.

Acts 9: the ecclesial mediation

The narrative of Acts 9. 1–30, at least when considered as a whole down to verse 30, is dominated by *the reversal of Saul's identity*. From being the persecutor with schemes of killing (9. 1–2), Saul becomes the persecuted one, threatened with death (9. 23–9). From being a foe to the disciples (9. 1), he becomes a master of disciples (9.25: οἱ μαθηταὶ αὐτοῦ). From being a denier of Christ (9. 1), Saul becomes a preacher of the Messiah (9. 22; 9. 20). Brought to a halt by the Lord, Saul with his plans is utterly broken.

The Christophany on the Damascus road (9. 3–9) has the effect of reducing Saul to nothingness. How does this reversal take place? Whereas verses 1 and 2 present Saul as an active subject (Σαῦλος is the subject of virtually all verbs: ἐμπνέων, προσελθών, ἠτήσατο, εὗρη, ἀγάγῃ), the shock disempowers him: the light that encircles him (περιαστράπτω) makes him fall to the ground (vv. 3–4); from then onwards, the verbs characterizing him are in the passive (ἀνάστηθι, v. 6; λαληθήσεται, v. 6; ἠγέρθη, v. 8), or, when they are in the active voice, they denote either an action undergone by him (ἤκουσεν, v. 4;[35] εἰσελθε, v. 6;

is about to present a defense of himself as the victim of an intramural quarrel regarding resurrection from the dead, and thus the appeal to Agrippa's knowledge serves to introduce the lines of Paul's defense' (*From Darkness to Light*, 1986, pp. 78–9).

[35] Saul is less the subject of the act of seeing than the recipient of an aural phenomenon which he is given to perceive.

δεῖ ποιεῖν, v. 6; χειραγωγοῦντες, v. 8) or an absence of action (οὐδὲν ἔβλεπεν, v. 8; μὴ βλέπων καὶ οὐκ ἔφαγεν οὐδὲ ἔπιεν, v. 9). The significant accumulation of three negatives in verse 9 (neither seeing, nor eating, nor drinking) draws the final conclusion from this experience of shock, not through an image of fasting, but through a figure of nothingness and death.[36]

From this point the narrative is going to work out the reconstruction of Saul. *The Damascus road event here manifests itself as a destruction of his persecution plan and a reconstitution of his identity.* The new identity is not one that he acquires for himself (9. 1–2), but is a received identity; this new identity is referred to by the Lord in verse 15: 'This one is an instrument of election to carry my Name before the Gentiles, the kings and the children of Israel.' The statement of identification takes place in a dialogue between Christ and Ananias, in the context of a vision ('The Lord said to him in a vision', v. 10). Here Ananias is representative of the Christian community at Damascus (τις μαθητής, v. 10). This visionary dialogue with the Lord constitutes the originality of Acts 9, later abandoned in the autobiographical speeches. It sets the figure of Ananias in the forefront. Such insistence is all the more striking since the encounter with Christ has isolated Saul from his companions in order to make him the sole recipient of the word of Jesus: the companions perceive a voice, but do not know where it comes from (v. 7).[37] But the dialogue with Ananias confers on him a decisive role in the revelatory process. This calls for four comments.

First comment: the dialogue with Ananias is a prophetic call narrative.[38] It faithfully follows the typical structure of a call narrative in the

---

[36] The enigmatic mention in 9. 9 has given rise to multiple interpretations: an effect of the psychological shock (F. F. Bruce, *Acts of the Apostles*, 1990, p. 323); the preparation for receiving revelation according to Exod. 34. 28; Deut. 9. 9; Dan. 9. 3; *2 Bar.* 9. 2, etc. (L. T. Johnson, *Acts of the Apostles*, 1992, p. 164); a pre-baptismal fast in the sense of *Didache* 7.4; Justin, *Apol.* 1.61 (H. Conzelmann, *Acts of the Apostles*, 1987, p. 72). We see that interpretative models are constantly being sought outside the text, while the text itself seeks primarily to pinpoint the negativity of that time when Saul's identity is being suspended before it is reconstituted. Is this an image of a re-creation *ex nihilo*?

[37] Rather than saying that Saul's companions benefit from hearing but are deprived of sight (9. 7), it is preferable to say that they are made unable to identify the voice; therefore revelation eludes them. S. R. Bechtler is sensitive to the privilege reserved to Saul: 'The limited participation in the event by Saul's companions as described in 9:7 guarantees the objective nature of the event itself, but this event was revelatory only for Saul' ('Meaning of Paul's Call', 1987, p. 56). The motif stays the same in chapter 22 (Paul is the only beneficiary of revelation), but the mode changes: the companions hear nothing (22. 9); actually, for Paul, the apparition is essentially visual in chapter 9, auditory in chapter 22.

[38] In his Ezekiel commentary, W. Zimmerli (*Ezechiel 1–24*, 1969, pp. 16–21) has shown the connection between Acts 9. 3–9 and prophetic call narratives. He recognizes that the Old Testament two distinct types of this genre: the one is structured by the scheme divine calling – mandate – objection – overruling of the objection and sending out (Jer. 1. 4–10; Exod. 3;

Old Testament literature, according to Norman Habel's study.[39] Habel identifies six motifs that make up the structure of a prophetic call narrative: (1) confrontation with the divine; (2) introductory word; (3) commission; (4) objection; (5) reassurance; (6) sign. The dialogue with Ananias fulfils the first five motifs (1) v. 10a; (2) v. 10b; (3) vv. 11–12; (4) vv. 13–14; (5) vv. 15–16); the sixth element is lacking. One should especially notice that while Saul has a purely passive role in this operation, Ananias on the contrary is made a *mediator* in the reconstitution of Paul's identity. His initial readiness for this role is made clear by his response to the divine calling: ἰδού ἐγώ (v. 10).[40]

Second comment: verses 10 to 16 do not present a vision, but the vision of a vision. Ananias learns in a vision that Saul himself has had a vision (εἶδεν, v. 12), which reveals Ananias coming to restore his sight. Ananias' mediatorial function is now signified by the invitation to a healing gesture whose symbolic dimension shines through:[41] the blinding/recovery sequence in the vision stands for a theological illumination; the 'vision' (v. 12) Saul has in prayer already anticipates this. But one should be attentive to this device of embedded visions; it is unknown in Jewish literature with the exception of Josephus (*A.J.* 11.8.4–5), and within Graeco-Roman literature it indicates the divine programming of events.[42] The device of double vision represents a strong irruption of the divine into the course of events, since not only is a prediction made, but its fulfilment is anticipated and visualized. The reader is therefore not surprised to see Ananias

Judg. 6; 1 Sam. 9–10; Ezek. 1–2); the second includes a theophanic vision (Isa. 6; 1 Kings 22. 19–22). O. H. Steck has objected that the first type is in fact identifiable, but in 9. 10–16, while the constitutive elements of the second type are lacking here ('Formgeschichtliche Bemerkungen', 1976).

[39] N. Habel, 'Form and Significance', 1965, pp. 297–323. A more recent study by W. Vogels, 'Récits de vocation', 1973, pp. 1–24, confirms his findings, even though Vogels describes the six motifs slightly differently. I owe these references to the article by R. F. Collins, 'Paul's Damascus Experience', 1986, pp. 115–16.

[40] The scheme is well known in the Hebrew Bible: Gen. 22. 1–2, 11–12; 1 Sam. 3. 4–14; *Jub.* 44. 5; 4 Ezra 12. 2–13; etc.

[41] Interpreting the passage from blindness to light symbolically as the granting of a revelation is a common feature of both New Testament tradition and Hellenistic Judaism (Philo, *Virt.* 179; *Jos. Asen.* 8. 10; 15. 13; *Odes Sol.* 14. 18–19); it is also frequent in Luke–Acts (Luke 2. 30; 4. 18; 24. 16, 31; Acts 9. 8, 18, 40; 13. 11; 26. 18; 28. 27). The symbolic value here has been well perceived by D. Hamm ('Paul's Blindness', 1990), who connects it with the metaphorical vocabulary of Isaiah (6. 9–10; 40. 3–5; 42. 16; 49. 6; 59. 9–10). One should nevertheless note that this dimension remains covert in this case, and is unfolded by the narrator in its full value only in 26. 18.

[42] We owe the classical inventory of attestations of double visions in ancient literature to A. Wikenhauser, 'Doppeltraüme', 1948, pp. 100–11. One should add here the references to fictional literature gathered by R. I. Pervo, *Profit with Delight*, 1987, pp. 73 and 164, note 85.

balk at such a *theological forcing of history*. Within the scenario of the prophetic call, this is the typical moment for the objection.

Third comment: Ananias' objection bears neither on his own capabilities, nor on the mandate proposed to him; its bearing is upon Saul's identity: 'Lord, I have heard from many about this man, how much evil has done to your saints in Jerusalem; and here he has authority from the chief priests to bind all who call upon your Name' (vv. 13–14). How should we understand this objection? How can we understand that Ananias still considers Saul as an enemy, while the enemy has just been brought down by the Christophany on the Damascus road? To think of this reminder of Saul's past evildoing as an attempt to underline the importance of his conversion amounts to reducing the narrator's work to the banal. Rather, the narrator uses a narrative device which consists of ascribing to the reader a position superior to that of a character in the narrative.[43] In this case, Ananias trails behind the reader at the level of his information: his reaction is invalidated by the Damascus road event (9. 3–9). Ananias ignores the action of Christ, and this confers on his objection *the status of resistance* to the action of Christ.[44] In other words, Ananias' reaction, on the one hand, demonstrates that Christ has anticipated his reaction by his intervention upon Saul, but, on the other hand, casts the disciple in the role of an opponent[45] whose objection the Lord must overcome.

[43] J. Calloud notices this effect of the narrative when he comments: 'Ananias is late according to the course of the narrative' ('Sur le chemin de Damas', 1985, p. 13). The narrative device has been described by M. Sternberg, who distinguishes three positions of the reader in relation to the characters in the narrative; from the viewpoint of the knowledge communicated to him or her, the reader may be ascribed by the narrator a position that is superior, equal or inferior to the character (*Poetics*, 1987, pp. 163–72). Here, a superiority in knowledge in relation to Ananias is clearly being constructed; this narrative strategy draws attention not to Saul's past as a persecutor (the reader knows this) but to the consequences of the delaying effect applied to the representative of the Damascus disciples (See D. Marguerat and Y. Bourquin, *How to Read*, 1999, pp. 71–2).

[44] It is significant that the *Acts of Paul*, while maintaining his status as a church mediator, have totally immunized him from all resistance. Without yet taking a position on the literary relationship between the Acts of Luke and the *Acts of Paul* (see my article: 'Acts of Paul', 1997), I would note that the one who introduces Paul into the community on the occasion of his conversion is none other than Jude, the brother of the Lord (*Acts of Paul*; cf. Schneemelcher, *New Testament Apocrypha*, II, Appendix, p. 388). Theologically, could one imagine a better intermediary? This holy character, entirely different from the humble Ananias, does not lay on hands or confer baptism; his role is that of an initiator into 'the sublime love of the faith' and a prophet capable of judging the converted worthy to minister the word. See W. Rordorf, 'Paul's Conversion', 1997, p. 139.

[45] The term 'opponent' is understood here in the sense of the actantial model of A. J. Greimas, *Sémantique structurale*, 1986, pp. 172–91, esp. p 180. Greimas distributes the constitutive functions of a narrative performance into five positions: sender – addressee – object – helper – opponent. The opponent is the one who attempts to hinder the realization of the narrative performance.

Fourth comment: Christ overcomes the resistance of Ananias by revealing the new identity he confers upon Saul. I have already cited verse 15: Saul must bear his Name,[46] a formula which refers to public testimony before a universal audience (Gentiles, kings and children of Israel).[47] But now, and this is a new surprise in the narrative, Ananias' intervention with Saul is therapeutic and baptismal (9. 18). No mention is made of the mandate to the person chiefly concerned: Saul. Not to be missed in passing is the narrative strategy which makes Saul the victim of a withholding of information – a patent strategy, since it unfolds in the sight and knowledge of the reader. It has a triple effect.[48] On the narrative level, it keeps the reader attentive: when will Saul have the right to this information? On the theological level, the strategy shows, once again, the priority of Christ with regard to the direction of his Church, 'It is I who will show him what he must suffer for the sake of my Name.' On the level of the story, it permits Luke's account of Saul's progressive attentiveness to his vocation as witness and primarily as suffering witness; for the 'making' for which Saul is enlisted (9. 6: ὅ τί σε δεῖ ποιεῖν) is to be a 'suffering' (9. 16: ὅσα δεῖ αὐτὸν... παθεῖν). The narrative must progressively unfold the necessity of the passion of Paul.[49]

I shall now assemble the results gained from the preceding comments.

Beverly R. Gaventa[50] has proposed that Acts 9 illustrates the motif of 'the overthrow of an enemy' as a result of God's power. The theme of the enemy overthrown is without doubt one connotation of the narrative. However, it seems to correspond to the tradition received by Luke rather than to his own reading of the event, since the way he manages his narrative stresses God's initiative in history and the resistance of the community of disciples (in addition to Ananias, see vv. 26–7). Christ triumphs over

---

[46] The confessional and missionary dimension of this expression has been shown by G. Lohfink, 'Meinen Namen', 1990, pp. 213–21.

[47] As C. H. Hedrick notices, Acts 1. 8 and 9. 15 mention both Jewish and Gentile missions, but in reverse order ('Conversion/Call', 1981, pp. 420–1). The sequence of 9. 15 (Gentiles–kings–children of Israel) anticipates the development of the plot of Acts by emphasizing Paul's testimony before the pagan world (cf. 28. 28!).

[48] S. Reymond, 'Paul sur le chemin de Damas', 1996, pp. 527–8

[49] The prolepsis consisting of the statement of Saul's missionary call is intended 'for the reader who is led by this to continue his reading in order to verify the accomplishment', according to S. Reymond, 'Expérience du chemin de Damas', 1993, p. 71. This narrative prolepsis takes up a previous prolepsis, which is the itinerary of the apostolic witness stated in the promise of the Risen One in 1. 8; it receives from there a first confirmation, though in anticipation. J.-N. Aletti notices an identical function for the proleptic statements in Luke 1–4: 'Les prolepses formulées par les voix angéliques ont donc pour fonction de donner, dès le départ, au récit lucanien, son caractère gnoséologique' (*Art de raconter*, 1989, p. 72). The narrative institutes then, in its very writing, the revelatory function it means to exercise.

[50] B. R. Gaventa, *From Darkness to Light*, 1986, p. 66.

the enemy without any problem, but he goes to a great deal of trouble in persuading his own!

This theme corresponds well with the continuation of the narration of Acts in chapters 10 and 11, where God will have to break down resistance in order to extend the benefit of salvation to non-Jews; yet this resistance will not come from Cornelius, but from Peter and from the Jerusalem church who stumble over the time-honoured division of clean and unclean (10. 14–16, 28–29, 34–36; 11. 1–3). Luke illustrates God's difficulty in accomplishing this new turn of salvation history by setting up a cascade of supernatural interventions centring around Peter and Cornelius: an apparition to Cornelius (10. 3–6), then a vision of Peter (10. 10–16), followed by a revelation of the Spirit to Peter (10. 19–20), and finally a second Pentecost in the house of Cornelius (10. 45–6). Such a concentration of the marvellous is without equal in the book of Acts, signalling the importance of a new turn, the recognition of God's universality (10. 34).[51] Yet the theme of a divine forcing of history, catching the Church unaware, is already being prepared in Acts 9, as we have just seen. In other words, Saul's conversion in Acts 9 is interpreted as the mighty act of Christ who turns his enemy around, but must also convert his own Church with regard to Saul's new identity; Saul is to become the agent of the universal mission. *The strategy of the narrative in Acts 9 then designates as its dominant theme the establishing of an ecclesial mediation in the transformation of Saul.*[52]

But what becomes of the Damascus road event when Paul carries out his autobiographical reinterpretation? We shall discover a response with a rapid survey of chapters 22 and 26.

---

[51] The importance of chapters 10–11 within the plot of the book of Acts is clear when one examines Luke–Acts from the perspective of Jewish–Christian relations. For more on this subject, see pp. 130–6 and 145–7.

[52] The role of mediation in Luke's thought has been shown by F. Bovon (*New Testament Traditions*, 1995, pp. 51–66). Luke does not seek to oppose divine intervention and human mediation, but rather aims to show in what ways the divine requires human mediation for its manifestation. The narrative of Acts 9 fully fits within this perspective. Thus it is strange to affirm that the presence of Ananias 'was to serve as a witness to the fact that Paul was called without mediation of man' (S. Lundgren, 'Ananias', 1971, p. 122). Even though it is obvious that the Damascus event in Acts functions as an accreditation of Paul, Luke could not endorse this antithesis between divine legitimation and human testimony. We find the same error of perspective in J. Jervell, who erases the mediation of Ananias: 'Die paulinischen "Akkreditive" kommen nicht aus Jerusalem, sondern aus dem Damaskusgeschehen...Paulus ist nicht von Menschen oder durch Menschen ausgesandt' ('Paulus in der Apostelgeschichte', 1986, pp. 378–92; I quote from p. 379; see note 15!).

Acts 22: the affirmation of Jewishness

I have already mentioned the narrative situation of the speech before the people of Jerusalem: the accusation to which Paul falls victim (21. 28), the eviction from the Temple, the lynching from which the Roman police save him (21. 32).

Luke accumulates the signs of Paul's Jewishness: he speaks in Hebrew (21. 40), near the Temple, and addresses his 'brothers and fathers' (22. 1). The formula in verse 3 ἐγώ εἰμι ἀνὴρ 'Ιουδαῖος is not just a declaration of his identity; it constitutes rather *the theological thesis of his speech, unfolding Paul's uninterrupted faithfulness to the Jewish tradition.* Everything points to this faithfulness: his curriculum vitae focused on his training in the school of Gamaliel (v. 3), the legality of the proceedings when he persecuted the Damascus Christians (v. 5), his relationship with the 'brothers' in Damascus (v. 5: these ἀδελφοί are not Christians, but Jews). Ananias is not presented as a disciple (the reader holds this piece of information from Acts 9)[53] but as 'a devout man according to the Law, well spoken of by all the Jews who lived there' (v. 12); therefore Ananias' greeting Σαοὺλ ἀδελφέ suggests that it be understood in terms of Jewish brotherhood. This remodelling of Ananias' identity is dictated by the rhetorical purpose of the speech: for Paul to receive his call from a Jewish dissident would not fit the rhetorical situation of his speech.

Ananias' role is also entirely remodelled since he is not essentially the restorer of Saul's integrity, but the interpreter of his calling: 'The God of our fathers appointed you to know his will, to see the Just One and to hear a voice from his mouth; for you will be a witness for him to all people of what you have seen and heard' (vv. 14–15). One notices here that the Christological reservation of chapter 9 ('I myself will show him...', 9. 16) has disappeared, the progression of the narrative having made it superfluous.

It is especially noteworthy that one has moved from the Christo-centric formulation of Acts 9 (Saul, persecutor of Jesus, called upon to bear his Name) to a theocentric formulation, deeply rooted in the Old Testament.[54] The threefold formula (know/see/hear) by which

---

[53] When one compares 9. 10–16 with the information in chapter 22, Ananias' intervention is reduced to a minimum; the reader knows neither why Ananias pays a visit to Saul (22. 13), nor how he comes to know of Saul's calling (22. 14–15). We have here an obvious sign that Luke, in chapter 22, recomposed the event by taking into account the memory of his reader/hearer, and therefore the divergences between the narratives did not escape his notice. I agree with C. W. Hedrick, 'Conversion/Call', 1981, p. 426.

[54] W. S. Kurz notices the passage from a Christocentric perspective in Acts 9 to theocentric language in Acts 22, but he explains it by the passage from an objective point of view (omniscient narrator) to the subjective point of view of the 'Jewish Paul' revealed in chapter 22; the latter is discredited as emanating from an 'unreliable' narrator (*Reading*

Saul's call is announced (γνῶναι τὸ θέλημα αὐτοῦ, ἰδεῖν τὸν δίκαιον, ἀκοῦσαι φωνὴν ἐκ τοῦ στόματος αὐτοῦ 22. 14) piles up Septuagintalisms that make Paul's apostolic call into an expression of his Jewish identity. One gauges, once more, Luke's skill in handling language, but, I repeat, such a language performance does not merely signal the adaptation of Paul the orator to his Jerusalem audience. *The purpose that permeates the speech is to interpret the Damascus road event as a fulfilment of the apostle's Jewishness.*

Bringing this statement of Saul's calling (22. 14) together with the autobiographical preamble in verse 3 (πεπαιδευμένος κατὰ ἀκρίβειαν τοῦ πατρῴου νόμου ζηλωτὴς ὑπάρχων τοῦ θεοῦ) will show how much the orator tends to establish a flawless continuity between his past life and his present situation, as far as zeal for God and relation to the Torah are concerned.[55] With this goal in mind, Luke has totally reorganised the Damascus narrative, removing the means that brought about Saul's meeting with Ananias and also the preaching of Saul in this city. This permits him to link together four moments: the Jewish education of Saul, the Christophany at Damascus, the oracle of Ananias and the sending by the Risen One in the Temple.[56] This particular sequence of events confirms that Paul's apology works to refute the accusation of anti-Judaism brought against him at the beginning of the riot (21. 28): the encounter with the Risen One in Damascus and then in the Temple does not pit Paul against 'our people, the Law and this place'. Rather, it is the means by which the God of the fathers leads him to the heart of his Word.

This Lucan effort to actualize the Damascus event from the communication situation of Paul's speech reaches its *climax* in the scene of the vision in the Temple (22. 17–21). One must take full notice of the fact that this scene does not represent a secondary appendix to the encounter on the Damascus road; on the contrary, within the narrative scenario of 22. 1–21, the vision in the Temple constitutes the *climax* of the speech, since it gives ultimate confirmation to Paul's calling. The choice of the Temple is certainly in line with the fundamental theological function of

---

Luke–Acts, 1993, pp. 130 and 129). This is to misunderstand the rhetorical purpose of the speech in Acts 22, whose argumentative strategy aims to *establish* Paul's Jewishness rather than to discredit it in the eyes of the reader.

[55] 'Luke knows no break in Paul's attitude to the law' (E. Haenchen, *Acts of the Apostles*, 1971, p. 625).

[56] M. E. Rosenblatt, in her article 'Recurring Narration', 1990, has brought out magnificently how Luke has recomposed the narrative of the Damascus road in Acts 22 according to several narrative devices: play with temporality, change of point of view, acceleration and deceleration in the unfolding of the narrative.

the holy place in Luke's work, from the infancy Gospel onwards.[57] The fact that Paul is praying in the Temple (προσευχομένου μου, 22. 17) underlines once more his loyalty to the Jewish tradition and the piety associated with it.[58] Yet ironically, it is within this Temple, from which the Asian Jews have just evicted him (21. 30), that Paul in prayer hears Christ enjoining him to leave Jerusalem 'because they will not accept your testimony about me' (22. 18). Again, one must take full notice of the *double provocation* that Luke, in composing this scene, aims at Paul's Jerusalem audience. First of all, the κύριος who appears in the Temple is not God, but Jesus (despite a, perhaps intentional, syntactical ambiguity);[59] Jesus, whom Paul's interlocutors have rejected, is publicly affirmed as the Lord of the Temple, with features that assimilate him to God. Secondly, the addition of verses 17 to 21 transfers from Ananias (9. 10–16) to Paul the literary form of a prophetic call narrative. The traditional sequence of commission (v. 18) – objection (vv. 20–1) – reassurance (v. 21) now involves Paul directly.[60] Yet the command to mission is paradoxical for it consists in leaving Jerusalem as soon as possible in view of the refusal of his testimony[61]! This is what happens presently: at this point in the narrative of Acts, Paul is about to leave Jerusalem in order to go to Rome.

I shall sum up my reading of chapter 22. The theme here is no longer the reversal of Saul's identity and the request for ecclesial mediation

---

[57] M. Bachmann, *Jerusalem und der Tempel*, 1980; F. Weinert, 'Meaning of the Temple', 1981; A. Casalegno, *Gesù e il tempio*, 1989.

[58] O. Betz privileges this interpretation in his article: 'Vision des Paulus', 1970, pp. 113–23. According to Betz, an apostolic legitimation located in Damascus, rather than in Jerusalem, would have been deemed radically insufficient from a Jewish point of view.

[59] The syntactical connection of αὐτόν in v. 18 is not clear; should we link it with θεός in v. 14a or, by way of the αὐτοῦ in v. 16b, to τὸν δίκαιον in v. 14b? Even though the chain of occurences of αὐτός (vv. 14b, 15a, 16b) favours the second solution, the ambiguity is not entirely removed; could Luke be exploiting it on purpose, within his theocentric perspective?

[60] Unlike R. F. Collins ('Paul's Damascus Experience', 1986, pp. 115–8), I think that Acts 22, and not Acts 26, fits the structure of a prophetic call narrative according to the criteria of N. Habel as sketched above (p. 193). Indeed, out of a total of six motifs, Acts 26 includes only the first three, whereas Acts 22 presents motif 1 (divine confrontation) in vv. 6–7a; motif 2 (introductory word) in vv. 7b–8; motif 3 (commission) in vv. 14–15, with confirmation in v. 18; motif 4 (objection) in v. 19–20; motif 5 (reassurance) in v. 21; motif 6 (sign) is to be found in v. 16, where the baptism no longer concretizes Saul's healing (9. 18), but becomes the sign testifying to his missionary calling (the immediate succession of vv. 14–15 and 16 provokes this reinterpretation of the baptismal act).

[61] There is a good formulation by J. Roloff on the polemic character of the process: 'Hier entpuppt sich die scheinbare Selbstverteidigung als Angriff von unerhörter Radikalität: Der von den Juden verworfene Jesus erscheint am heiligen Ort und spricht das Verwerfungsurteil über sein Volk aus, das Paulus nun am gleichen heiligen Ort öffentlich verkündigt' (*Apostelgeschichte*, 1981, p. 320).

in that transformation, but rather the orthodoxy of Paul's religion. His conversion is being invoked at the symbolic moment of the break with Jerusalem, interpreting this break as an event that was not desired by Paul, but especially contesting Jewish criticism by indicating how much the new turn in the apostle's life is in fundamental continuity with his Jewishness. What is the significance of Paul's biography and his conversion in this argument? The thesis of the speech (22. 19–20) is that this should suffice to convince the reader that Paul's message does not proceed from anti-Jewish hatred, but from an impeccable and fanatical zeal for the God of the fathers; such zeal has not ceased to inhabit Paul from his youth onwards.

Acts 26: the power of the Risen One

The apology before Agrippa, like chapter 22, is governed by *prosopopoeia*. The interpretation of Saul's conversion obeys the same rules of narrative composition that we have just uncovered in the previous speech. There are five of them: focalization, inculturation, variation, actualization and narrative setting.

First of all, the *focalization rule*. The move to autobiographical discourse centred on the apostle's 'I' lays maximum stress on the role of Saul and diminishes the secondary roles correspondingly (down to the complete disappearance of Ananias).[62] The focus placed on Saul's role in the future leads the writer to enlarge the wording of the mandate given by Christ (vv. 16–18), quoted by Paul in a way that contrasts absolutely with the absence of any commission addressed to Saul in Acts 9.[63] In opposition to Acts 9, here 'Paul's commission derives exclusively from the heavenly Jesus.'[64] The complete disappearance of any intermediary brings Saul and the Kyrios into unmediated relation.

The *inculturation rule*: addressing a Hellenistic audience of a high cultural level, the speech explains its meaning (v. 14a) or transposes it into Graeco-Roman categories (vv. 14b, 18, 21–3).[65] The non-Semitic

---

[62] Cf. above pp. 187–9 and p. 186 n. 26.

[63] C. W. Hedrick thinks that the progressive unveiling of Saul's commission results from an effect of narrative suspense: the commission is indicated to Ananias (9. 15–16), then alluded to by Barnabas before the apostles (9. 27); Saul is informed about it secondhand by Ananias (22. 14–15), and the Kyrios refers to it in 22. 17–21. 'It is not until 26:16–18 that the suspense is broken and Luke finally tells his (impatient) reader exactly what the Lord said to Paul on the road to Damascus' ('Conversion/Call', 1981, p. 427).

[64] S. R. Bechtler, 'Meaning of Paul's Call', 1987, p. 72.

[65] Verse 14a specifies that Jesus expresses himself 'in the Hebrew language'. Verse 14b cites a proverb known since Aeschylus (*Ag.* 1624), but only in Hellenistic literature (see

proverb of verse 14b ('It hurts you to kick against the goads'), brings out with greater power the futility of the struggle, while qualifying Paul's missionary activity retroactively (Acts 13–25) as divinely ordained.[66]

The *variation rule*: just as the prophetic call scenario, with its typical moment of the recipient's objection, has been transferred from Ananias (9. 10–16) to Saul (22. 18–21), the topic of light has been metamorphosed and displaced. The encounter on the Damascus road is no longer the luminous shock throwing Saul to the ground (9. 3–4); it is an intense illumination (περιλάμψαν με φῶς, 26. 13) preparing Saul to 'open the eyes' of the people of Israel and of Gentiles in order to 'convert' them 'from darkness to light' (ἐπιστρέψαι ἀπὸ σκότους εἰς φῶς, 26. 18). This extention of the φῶς metaphor from theophanic language to the vocabulary of mission (26. 18) coincides with the application to Paul of Isaiah 49. 6, to which the narrator already referred in 13. 47: 'I have set you to be a light for the Gentiles' (τέθεικά σε εἰς φῶς ἐθνῶν).[67] No longer is Saul overwhelmed by the light; in Acts 26 he is reinterpreting this numinous encounter as a prophetic call to become himself a light, that is, a bearer of salvation beyond Israel.[68] The inclusion of his missionary activity within the conversion narrative aims to reinforce the credibility of his testimony before Agrippa.

The *actualization rule*: the end of the speech (26. 22–3) joins Paul's present situation by interpreting his testimony 'to the small one as well

L. Schmid art. 'κέντρον', 1965, pp. 663–8). Verse 18 describes Paul's mission in three statements whose wording corresponds with the vocabulary of Hellenistic Judaism (cf. Col. 1. 12–14; 1 Thess. 2. 12; 1 Pet. 5. 10). E. Haenchen has noted the many Atticisms that permeate the speech (*Acts of the Apostles*, 1971, pp. 681–94), and J. C. Lentz has shown how Luke in Acts 26 portrays Paul as a 'man of virtue' according to the canons of Graeco-Roman culture (*Luke's Portrait of Paul*, 1993, pp. 83–91).

[66] The application of the proverb is debated: does it refer to the inefficiency of Saul's persecuting activity in the past or the impossibility of retreating from his calling in the future? Most commentators lean toward the second solution. Using psychological categories, S. Reymond opts for the first solution, seeing here the trace of Saul's struggle against his own violence (26. 9–11), which only God's intervention through the appearance of Jesus is able to oppose ('Expérience du chemin de Damas', 1993, p. 126).

[67] On this mutation of the theme of light between Acts 9 and Acts 26, see the article by D. Hamm, 'Paul's Blindness', 1990, pp. 66–7. R. F. O'Toole thinks that the new mode of being of the resurrected Jesus has influenced this imagery of the light illuminating Saul with brightness (*Christological Climax*, 1978, p. 58); the insistence of chapter 26 upon the vision (26. 16, 19) might corroborate that point of view.

[68] 'The primary purpose of this address to Agrippa is to induce him to see in Paul a prophet', as D. M. Stanley categorically affirms ('Paul's Conversion', 1953, p. 334). In fact, as demonstrated many times, the statement of Saul's commission in vv. 16–18 evokes at the same time Ezekiel's call (reminiscences of Ezek. 1. 28; 2. 1, 3 in vv. 16 and 17), Jeremiah's commission (verbal similarities between Jer. 1. 7–8 and v. 17), and the mission of Isaiah's Servant (Isa. 42. 6 is virtually quoted in v. 18). This is demonstrated by R. F. O'Toole, *Christological Climax*, 1978, p. 67.

as to the great one' (μαρτυρόμενος μικρῷ τε καὶ μεγάλῳ, v. 22) as a concretization of the calling received on the Damascus road. In other words, the very wording of the speech before Agrippa confirms the call that Paul received.

Finally, the *rule of narrative setting*. Agrippa, who is the narrative addressee of the speech in Acts 26, has been presented as a special-ist in Jewish customs and controversies (26. 3).[69] The speech is going to demonstrate skilfully that Jewish hostility toward Paul is a matter of internal controversy, and furthermore, unjustified controversy; for the charge against Paul consists in nothing other than that which makes up the heart of the Jewish hope, that is, the resurrection of the dead (26. 6–8). The whole speech is governed rhetorically by the promise–fulfilment scheme as signified by the *inclusio* of verses 6–8 and verse 23:[70] the Jewish hope in the resurrection of the dead (vv. 6–8) finds its fulfil-ment in the resurrection of the Messiah (v. 23). The encounter on the Damascus road is exhibited accordingly as evidence for the resurrection of the dead, a 'heavenly vision' of the Risen One (26. 19) from which Paul could not escape.[71] One cannot help but think that Luke, theologically speaking, forces the argument. Summarizing the Jewish faith as believ-ing in a promise (ἐπ' ἐλπίδι τῆς εἰς τοὺς πατέρας ἡμῶν ἐπαγγελίας, v. 6; cf. already 23. 6) is plausible; but that this promise should be reduced to the resurrection of the dead (26. 8) is only acceptable for Pharisaic piety. Moreover, to construe the Christian kerygma as amounting to resurrection faith is typical of Luke, but the speech as-similates without nuance the Pharisaic belief and the Christian faith in the resurrection (compare 26. 8 and 26. 23!). From this stand-point, a Jew opposing the Christian proclamation of the Risen One places himself in contradiction with his own tradition. One touches here on Luke's effort, not to put Judaism on trial, but to show the in-comprehensiblity of the denial of continuity that opposes Judaism to Christianity.

To sum up, in this speech the Damascus road event acquires an argumen-tative function which differs from both Acts 9 and Acts 22. The vision

[69] Cf. p. 190.

[70] I agree with this structural observation by B. R. Gaventa, *From Darkness to Light*, 1986, p. 80. This inclusion concretizes the rhetorical purpose of the apology before Agrippa: Paul's innocence is established by the fact that he preaches nothing else but that which Israel expects.

[71] A. Barbi has well seen that within the perspective of Acts 26. 23, the universal mission is signalled as a post-resurrection activity of Christ, as already stated by 3. 26 and 5. 31: 'Paolinismo', 1986, pp. 471–518, see p. 506.

of the Risen One becomes a powerful event to which one cannot show disobedience. This is dramatized through the insistence on Saul's past as a persecutor (26. 9–11) coupled with the fact that he offers no resistance (26. 19). Yet, on the one hand, the uniqueness of the event is devalued, since it is aligned with other visions promised to Paul (26. 16b). On the other hand, the encounter with the Risen One plays the essential role of justifying the call to evangelize the Gentiles[72] and that not because of its theophanic dimension (9. 3–8), nor by virtue of its conformity with the Law (22. 14–16), but because the resurrection of the Messiah fulfils the prophecies (26. 23; cf. 26. 27).

Conclusion: an enlightening role in Acts

The comparative study of the three narratives of Saul's conversion at Damascus is impressive because it renders particularly visible the literary work of the author of Acts who decided to give the episode a key role in his narrative. The recomposing of the event in Acts 9, 22 and 26 is part of a logic that depends both on the enunciator of the discourse (the narrator or Paul) and on the rhetorical purpose of the discourse. Acts 9 emphasizes ecclesial mediation; Acts 22 Saul's Jewishness; Acts 26 the legitimation of the Gentiles.

Also important is the issue of how narrative redundancy functions within the plot of the book of Acts: from chapter 9 to chapter 26 a broad narrative arc is put in place. The history of the Gentile mission unfolds entirely within the space defined by this enlightening event; correlatively, the narrator makes the conversion of Saul function as a hermeneutical key when he narrates the expansion of the Church outside Judaism, on the one hand to point out the origin of this movement (Acts 9), and on the other hand in order to reread it theologically (Acts 22; 26).

Why does Luke consider the Damascus road event a major fact? Beyond the exaltation of the figure of Paul and his leading role in the growth of the Christian movement, I discern two reasons. The first is that this event serves to sharpen the profile of Christian identity in its twofold relation of continuity with and difference from Judaism; the call of Paul is not

---

[72] Saul's identity as established by the Risen One is to be ὑπηρέτης καὶ μάρτυς (v. 16), and within this phrase καί has an epexegetical value. The vision of the Risen One culminates not in the prerogative of a spiritual experience, but in a state of subordination to a Word to be told, that will conform Paul to the suffering destiny of his Master (26. 21–3). On this theme, see the work of S. Reymond, 'Expérience du chemin de Damas', 1993, pp. 131–7.

presented to the readers as a model of conversion to be imitated,[73] but as the emblematic illustration of the fact that through this very break the Christian faith retains a basic faithfulness to the God of the fathers. The second reason is that the Damascus road event allows the author of Acts to unfold the theological theme that he cherishes above all else; this theme is *the power of the Risen One as a transforming force within history*. The common theme of the three variant accounts of Saul's conversion is to show how Saul was violently seized by the exalted Christ, whom he had made his enemy, and how he was called to proclaim his Name among Jews and Gentiles. In the end, the consequence that Paul draws from this missionary path unfolds in the conclusion of Acts (28. 16–31), to which the next chapter is devoted.

[73] This observation does not exclude the possibility that a conversion narrative might echo the religious experience of the readers. In his dissertation, C. J. LaHurd has noted the possible 'ritual impact' of such narratives setting forth a rite of passage accessible to the reader (*Author's Call*, 1987, pp. 182–229).

10

THE ENIGMA OF THE END OF ACTS
(28. 16–31)

The way the book of Acts ends is surprising. This enigmatic conclusion has resisted centuries of enquiry. At the end of his work, Luke presents the activity of Paul, a prisoner, in the capital of the Empire. After the troubled voyage from Caesarea, Paul settles in, accompanied by a guard (28. 16). After this there is the theological debate with the delegation of Roman Jews (28. 17–28), and the book ends with the apostle evangelizing in the imperial city (28. 30–1). Considering the importance of the end of a literary work, and the effect the last image may have on the reader or hearer before leaving the narrative world, Luke's choice is perplexing.

The first difficulty is not what the narrative conclusion affirms, *but what it does not.* Why does Luke remain silent about the appeal to Caesar, which represents the avowed motive for Paul's transfer to Rome (28. 19)? The ending of Acts comes after the interminable wait for the apostle's trial, which is announced continually throughout the book (23. 11; 25. 11–12; 26. 32; 27. 24), but never occurs; it disappoints the expectation of the reader. One can understand why this expectation has intrigued exegetes, from the early Fathers onwards.[1] Why did Luke remain silent about the outcome of the trial, whether favourable (the release of the apostle) or not (the death of Paul)? Has Luke kept silent intentionally, or was he not able to say more?

A second difficulty concerns the theological debate which is the essence of the conclusion (28. 17–28): what is the verdict concerning *the relationship between Judaism and Christianity*? A third difficulty concerns the final image (28. 30–1): what significance should be given to this summary, which holds Paul's evangelistic preaching in Rome, as it were, *suspended in time*?

These three questions will guide my reflection. I shall begin by situating my entry into the problematic of the ending of Acts and then I shall identify

---

[1] A survey of research can be found in H. J. Hauser's *Abschlusserzählung*, 1979, pp. 1–3, and a more detailed survey in C. J. Hemer, *Book of Acts*, 1989, pp. 383–7.

the emergence, in Graeco-Roman literature, of what I call a 'rhetoric of silence', paying particular attention to Graeco-Roman historiography.[2] This will lead to its deployment in Acts 27–8. These results will allow me to deal with the question of the relation between Judaism and Christianity, and with the final verses of the book, concluding with a synthesis on the effect of the ending.

The problematic of the ending of Acts

The dissatisfaction felt at the end of Acts has engendered two types of hypothesis, one historical and the other theological.

Historical criticism: an unwarranted ending

Historical criticism assigns the premature conclusion of the work to a material cause. It was because of lack of papyrus, or an abandoned project for a third volume (Spitta, Zahn) or even that Luke had come to the end of his documentation (Cadbury, Harnack, Hemer).[3] One has even thought that the author had nothing more to say and that Paul lived out the rest of his life in oblivion.[4] In a more subtle manner, J. Roloff uses the reference in *1 Clement* 5 to 'jealousy and treachery' as the origins of persecutions against 'the highest and straightest pillars' (Peter and Paul) to suppose that the martyrdom of Paul was linked with Christian intrigues that Luke is not authorized to mention.[5] What these historical hypotheses have in common is that they all postulate the unintentional ending of Acts: Luke's failure to reveal the fate of Paul is attributed to constraint, ignorance or imposed muteness. The possibility that the author of Luke–Acts might have intended such a conclusion is rejected in the name of

[2] For my reading of Greek and Latin texts I am indebted to the exchanges with my colleagues of Graeco-Roman literature, Claude Calame (University of Lausanne) and Adalberto Giovannini (University of Geneva); their help was both scholarly and friendly.

[3] H. J. Cadbury hypothesizes that Luke's sources gave no detail on this point: *Making of Luke–Acts*, 1958, p. 321. Harnack thought that Luke at the end of Acts had come up to his own time: *Beiträge*, 1911, pp. 65–9; his position is unlikely considering the early date that it imposes on the editing of the Acts, but has been taken up with slight modifications by C. J. Hemer (*Book of Acts*, 1989, pp. 388–410).

[4] C. K. Barrett, 'End of Acts', 1996, p. 550.

[5] *Paulus-Darstellung*, 1979, pp. 510–31, esp. pp. 522–4. See also P. W. Walaskay, '*And So We Came to Rome*', 1983, pp. 18–22. The hypothesis of a Christian conspiracy against Paul goes back to O. Cullmann, *Saint Pierre*, 1952; it is based on a risky interpretation of ζῆλος καὶ ἔρις (*1 Cl.* 5.5), which are considered to be technical terms for a fratricidal conflict, on the basis of resemblance to Phil. 1. 15.

literary propriety or by virtue of the reader's right to further historical information.

By checking the whole work *ad Theophilum*, however, we find that Acts 28. 16–31 is certainly not a precipitated ending.[6] On the one hand, Paul's apology before the Jewish deputation in Rome (28. 17–20) recapitulates the long history of judicial conflict with the Jews, which occupies the last section of the book (21. 27 – 26. 32). On the other hand, Paul's dialogue with the Jews in Rome (28. 17–28) takes up and hardens a scenario already set up at the inauguration of his ministry in the synagogue of Antioch of Pisidia (13. 14–48): Paul begins by preaching to the Jews, but, with their rejection, he announces the transfer of the Word to the Gentiles.[7] Furthermore, by his choice of vocabulary, Luke has brought together the end and the beginning of Acts, as well as the beginning of his gospel.[8] The many connections the author creates between the end and the beginning of his work confirm the deliberate character of this ending.

Theological criticism: censuring the author

Following Dibelius' works, *theological criticism* has assessed the full range of the literary and theological choices that are at the origins of Luke's historiography; the end of Acts is seen as the result of a theological strategy. It is asserted that the programme of the Resurrected One to make witnesses to the end of the earth (ἔσχατον τῆς γῆς, 1. 8) is completed with Paul's arrival in Rome.[9] It is thought that Acts has

[6] In his now classic work, J. Dupont has shown this well: 'Conclusion', 1984, pp. 457–511, esp. pp. 483–511.

[7] In particular, Dupont demonstrates that ἰδοὺ στρεφόμεθα εἰς τὰ ἔθνη (13. 46b) forms an inclusio with τοῖς ἔθνεσιν ἀπεστάλη τοῦτο τὸ σωτήριον τοῦ θεοῦ (28. 28), by way of 18. 6: ἀπὸ τοῦ νῦν εἰς τὰ ἔθνη πορεύσομαι. Announced twice, the decision to turn to the pagans receives added weight and finality at the end of Acts ('Conclusion', 1984, pp. 486–90).

[8] The expression βασιλεία τοῦ Θεοῦ, which summarizes Paul's preaching (28. 23, 31), corresponds with that of the Resurrected One at the beginning of the Acts (1. 3). The rare expression σωτήριον τοῦ Θεοῦ (28. 28) is present in the beginning of the gospel story (Luke 2. 30; 3. 6), where it is already close to the announcement of the division of Israel faced with the revelation of universal salvation (Luke 2. 34; 3. 7–9). The inclusio between the end of Acts and the Simeon episode is theologically exploited by D. L. Tiede: 'The ending of the narrative of Acts 28 is, therefore, not the end of the story, but it is a resumption of the themes sounded in Simeon's oracles' ('Glory to Thy People Israel', 1988, pp. 21–34, quotation p. 29).

[9] Ph. H. Menoud, 'Plan des Actes', 1975, pp. 84–91, see p. 86. H. Conzelmann: 'Der sowohl geographisch wie theologisch bedeutsame "Weg" der Apg führt nach Rom als dem endgültigen Ziel' ('Geschichtliche Ort', 1974, p. 224).

been engendered by a theology of the Word so that, for Peter (12. 17) as well as for Paul, the biography of the witness gives way before the expansion of the Christian mission.[10] E. Haenchen popularized the view of Luke as an apologist. He argues that it would have been prejudicial to the image of Rome to conclude the narrative with Paul's execution on the order of the Emperor.[11] It is undeniable that the Lucan theology of the Word and the apologetic aim played a part here.[12] But we must note that: (1) Rome did not coincide with the ἔσχατον τῆς γῆς (the end of the earth) of Acts 1. 8[13] and the programme of the resurrected Jesus was not accomplished at 28. 31; (2) the end of Acts does not recount the arrival of the Word in Rome (it is already there: 28. 15), but it does recount the apostle's arrival; and (3) if Luke had wanted to make the figure of the witness disappear behind the advance of the mission, why is there such a focalization on the person of Paul (from 15. 36 onwards)?

In my opinion, the theological criticism stops too soon. It continues to think that the author of Acts ended his work *because he did not want to say more*, whether it be to obey a theological programme or to spare the political power. Just like historical criticism, theological criticism cannot imagine the rhetorical function of an ending deliberately left open, an ending that intentionally plays on the silence. Literary criticism, however, makes us attentive to the phenomenon of narrative conclusion, to its characteristics, its orchestrated abundance and its programmed silence.[14] Narrative criticism invites us to develop our evaluation of this ending from factors that are immanent in the text.

---

[10] M. Dibelius defended the idea that Luke anticipates the account of Paul's martyrdom in the farewell discourse to the Ephesian elders (20. 22–5), with a view to freeing the conclusion of his work for another theme: the perpetuity of the Word ('Speeches in Acts', 1956, pp. 155–65).

[11] *Acts of the Apostles*, 1971, pp. 731–2. To my knowledge, the proposal that Luke censored the martyrdom of Paul (executed by order of Nero), with a view to ensuring Christanity the favour of the Romans, was first formulated by K. Schrader, *Apostel Paulus*, V, 1836, pp. 573–4.

[12] The formulation of Bengel continues to be true: '*Finis libri/Paulus Romae/Victoria Dei verbi.*'

[13] On this point, W. C. van Unnik seems to have said what is essential: 'Ausdruck', 1973, pp. 386–401. Notwithstanding *Ps. Sol.* 8. 16, Rome does not represent the end of the earth – but from a Roman point of view, qualifies as the centre of the world from which all land routes emanate to explore the Empire. Luke is surely not insensitive to this.

[14] My theoretical references for a study of narrative closure in literature include: F. Kermode, *Sense of an Ending*, 1977, and *Genesis of Secrecy*, 1979; B. H. Smith, *Poetic Closure*, 1968; R. Blau Du Plessis, *Writing beyond the Ending*, 1985; A. Kotin Mortimer, *Clôture narrative*, 1985; C. Cazale Bérard, ed., *Fine della storia*, 1993; K. Stierle and R. Warning, *Ende*, 1996.

The example of Mark

Within the frame of the New Testament, the abrupt ending of the gospel of Mark is instructive,[15] even if by contrast. Christianity in the second century could no longer tolerate the end of Mark being 16. 8 (see Mark 16. 9–20) any more than it could the closure of Acts at 28. 31 (see *Acts of Paul* 11); however, the two cases are very different on the point that is of interest here. In effect, the end of Mark is considered unfinished only when compared with Matthew 28 and Luke 24. But, the lack of fulfilment at the end of Acts appears to derive from elements internal to the work: Luke has Paul's death announced to him (20. 25, 38), and repeats this announcement for the reader in terms that harmonize it with the Passion of Jesus (21. 11; cf. Luke 18. 32). Paul's appearance before Caesar is demanded by the apostle (25. 11), confirmed by Festus and Agrippa (25. 12; 26. 32), sealed by the Lord (27. 24) and recalled by Paul as the goal of his voyage (28. 19). We must conclude that, from chapter 20 to 28, the author of Acts methodically builds an expectation in the reader which he finally fails to satisfy. Is this inadvertent? Or is it because he forgets? Is there a shift in strategy? The qualities of Luke's writing have appeared too many times throughout this study for the theory of a mistake to be credible. It is my opinion that Luke in chapters 27–8 organizes a concerted displacement of the reader's expectation, which he has methodically built up to that point. In matters of narrative strategy, the author of Acts is no novice.[16]

John Chrysostom

Surprisingly, we return here to an intuition about the present text offered by St John Chrysostom in his *Homilies on Acts*. His commentary makes use of terms that a narratologist today would not reject:

---

[15] I refer the reader first of all to the excellent book by J. L. Magness, *Sense and Absence*, 1986, pp. 83–5.

[16] One thinks of the narrative shock which the drama of Ananias and Sapphira represents (5. 1, 11), rupturing the ideal communion of the original community (chs. 2–6), or again of the reversal that Saul's conversion represents (ch. 9) after the negative presentation of this character in 7. 57 – 8. 3. But the clearest example of this process of deferred expectation that Luke imposes on the reader is Paul's constant returning to the synagogue, despite his stated decision to turn to the Gentiles (cf. 13. 46 and 14. 1, 18. 6 and 18. 19: concerning the sequence of 28. 28 and 28. 30b: see below). We have the feeling that, far from being just a display of skill, this narrative strategy is taken into the service of an obvious theological intention.

'The author [i.e. Luke] brings his narrative to this point, and leaves the hearer thirsty so that he fills up the lack by himself through reflection. The outsiders [i.e. non-Christian writers] do the same; for, knowing everything wills the spirit to sleep and enfeebles it. But he does this, and does not tell what follows, deeming it superfluous for those who read the Scripture, and learn from it what it is appropriate to add to the account. In fact, you may consider that what follows is absolutely identical with what precedes.   (*Homily on Acts* 15: *PG* 60, p. 382)

According to Chrysostom, the incomplete ending of Acts: (1) is the effect of a literary strategy well attested in non-Christian literature; (2) aims to activate the reader's reflection; (3) requires the gap to be filled by extrapolation from the preceding narrative.

The first assertion requires verification before one can engage with the others: by ending a literary work without telling his readers everything, does Luke conform to a pattern known in Graeco-Roman literature? One may note that John the evangelist has done it by resorting to the literary topos of 'more than can be said' ('Jesus did many other signs before his disciples, which are not written in this book', John 20. 30).[17] What about the author of Acts? One should ask about the literary conventions that regulated the conclusion of a work in antiquity.

A rhetoric of silence

What rules in antiquity governed the conclusion of literary works? A brief glance at the research shows that the question has been hardly touched, while studies on the *prooemia* are abundant. Ancient rhetoricians dealt much more with the beginning of a work than its ending.

The classic reference is found in Aristotle's *Poetics*: the end 'is that which is, necessarily or as a rule, the natural result of something else but from which nothing else follows ... Well constructed plots must not therefore begin and end at random, but abide by the formulae we have stated.'[18] In other words, by this double constraint, the conclusion results necessarily from the plot and the plot leads necessarily to its conclusion. Is this always the case? Clearly, not!

---

[17] This motif is found in Sir. 43. 27; 1 Macc. 9. 22; Justin, *Apol.* 1.31, 48, 54; Lucian, *Dem.* 67; etc. (numerous examples collected by W. Bauer, *Leben Jesu*, 1909, pp. 364–5).
[18] *Poetics* VII. 5–7 (1450b).

The example of Homer

J. L. Magness has listed ancient works that violate the Aristotelian rule of narrative closure.[19] The *Iliad* and the *Odyssey* top the list. Both Homeric works end, from the point of view of the plot, by a coming to rest: the *Iliad* closes with Achilles giving Hector's corpse back to Priam and with the funeral laments of the Trojans (*Il.* 22.405–515);[20] the *Odyssey* terminates with Ulysses triumphing over the revolt in Ithaca and his return home (*Od.* 23.248–96). These conclusions are preceded, in the body of the work, by an announcement of developments not recounted: the reader is left under the impact of the prediction, made several times, of the death of Achilles and the fall of Troy; in the *Odyssey,* Tiresias predicts that Ulysses will have to leave Ithaca again on a new journey (*Od.* 11.119–37). Identifying this procedure of open closure is of paramount importance, since Homer in antiquity was the source of all culture and the model for all literature. Not only do other authors adopt this pattern of narrative suspension (the most frequently cited example is Virgil's *Aeneid*),[21] but the post-Homeric tradition produced many works presented as a 'sequel' of Homer.[22]

With some exaggeration, Magness draws conclusions as to the frequency of narrative suspension in the ending of ancient works. His observations nevertheless uncover the rhetorical power of a non-narrated ending, the power of the unsaid which leads readers to supply the outcome of the story through their own reflection. Is it, then, legitimate to speak of a rhetoric of silence, when so far we have limited ourselves to a few instances of narrative suspension? Even without the further attestations I shall supply, the pertinence of the term seems established by the fact that ancient rhetoric is far from insensitive to the effect of silence.

[19] *Sense and Absence*, 1986, pp. 55ff. Concerning the end of Acts, the hypothesis of a literary usage has been suggested (following Chrysostom!) by as astute a precursor as H. J. Cadbury, *Making of Luke–Acts*, 1958, pp. 321–4.

[20] The study of the ending of ancient works is made difficult by the frequent ignorance of research as to the primitive ending of the work; glossed endings abound. Concerning the *Iliad*, the termination at Book 22 is only a likely hypothesis (summary of the discussion in J. L. Magness, *Sense and Absence*, 1986, pp. 28–30).

[21] The *Aeneid* finishes with the murder of Latin chief Turnus, whom Aeneas finishes off in a burst of anger. This ending is problematic, as underlined by the last verse of Virgil (12.952): '*Vitaque cum gemitu fugit indignata sub umbras*' ('and life with a groaning fled indignant under the shadows'). Now, one encounters in the body of the narrative (12.808–40), under the guise of an agreement between Jupiter and Juno, a prediction of Aeneas' marriage with princess Lavinia; that union is a portent of the peace concluded with the Latins and the founding of a new race, concretized by the founding of Rome.

[22] See P. Salat, 'Fin de l'Enéide', 1984, pp. 11–18.

With this in mind, I shall now follow the reflections of two masters in rhetoric, Pseudo-Longinus and Quintilian.

The effect of silence

In the *Treatise of the Sublime*, Pseudo-Longinus asserts that the first of the five sources of the sublime is nobility of the soul (μεγαλοφροσύνη): 'The sublime is the echo of the greatness of the soul' (IX.2). Surprisingly, the example proposed is an instance of silence, namely the appearance in the Nekyia of Ajax, who refuses to answer Ulysses' questions. 'Thus even without voice, the naked idea, by itself, sometimes wins admiration solely through nobility of soul, just as, in the Nekyia, the silence of Ajax is great and more sublime than any speech' (IX.2). The silence of Ajax functions as a perceptible experience of μεγαλοφροσύνη; as such it expresses nothing, yet it expresses the absolute.[23]

Quintilian encourages the orators to opt for a final summary (ἀνακεφαλαίωσις) at the end of the speech (*Institutio oratoria* VI.1); and Luke conforms to this at the end of his work. But Quintilian is not insensitive to the rhetoric of the unsaid. In Book II of the *Institutio oratoria*, he elaborates on the virtue of not telling everything.

> In painting, what is attractive is the face as a whole; yet, if Apelles represented Antigone only in profile, it was in order to conceal the ugliness of her gouged out eye. What then of speaking? Are there not there also some details to be concealed, whether they must not be shown, or whether they cannot be expressed suitably? This is what Timanthes, a native of Cythnos, did, I believe, in the picture that won him the victory over Colotes of Teos. In the sacrifice of Iphigenia, he painted a sad Calchas, a yet sadder Ulysses and gave to Menelaus the maximum affliction that can be rendered by art; having exhausted all the signs of emotion, not knowing how to render the facial expression of the father appropriately, he veiled the father's head and left it to everyone to use their own imagination (*et suo cuique animo dedit aestimandam*).   (II.13.12–13)

[23] In his *Life of Apollonius of Tyana*, Philostratus is not far from Pseudo-Longinus when he describes the pious respect with which the disciples of Pythagoras surround the transmission of the words of the master: 'And all the revelations of Pythagoras were considered by his fellows as as laws, and they honoured him as though he had been a messenger of Zeus, training themselves to the silence that is fitting before the deity; for they heard many divine and secret revelations, which it would have been difficult to keep to themselves if they had not begun by learning that silence is also word (καὶ τὸ σιωπᾶν λόγος)' (*Life of Apollonius of Tyana*, 1.1).

Quintilian provides an important indication of a concerted recourse to the unsaid, in order to appeal to the imagination of the reader.

The examples invoked thus far come from the tragic poets and the Hellenistic novel. What about historiography, on which Luke–Acts is primarily modelled? Two ancient theoreticians of historiography can provide us with information at this point: Lucian of Samosata (c. 120–180), to whom we return once more, and Dionysius of Halicarnassus (end of the first century BC).

Lucian of Samasota: the freedom not to say

In his treatise *How to Write History*, Lucian expatiates on how a historian ought to begin and to construct his work, not on how he ought to end it. Is this an indication of the freedom left to the author in concluding a work? Whatever the case, Lucian deals with silence in an apology for brevity, in which he defends the idea that 'one should touch lightly on facts that lack interest or value, and dwell on those of importance; nevertheless, there are many which one can pass over in silence' (56). This plea for freedom and discernment on the part of the historian leads to the conclusion that the scenario Luke adopts to end Acts results from a deliberate choice, applying the recognized freedom of the historian to say or not to say. One can note therefore, that the author of Acts chose to close his work by presenting the preaching of Paul in Rome (28. 30–1) and that this short summary, often considered insignificant by commentators, receives by its position *in fine* a strategic importance that has to be interpreted. But if Lucian's observations help us understand why Luke has chosen to say certain things, they do not indicate his reasons for *not saying* certain things.

Blame and praise in Dionysius of Halicarnassus

The writings of Dionysius of Halicarnassus, especially his *On Thucydides* and his *Letter to Pompeius*, are more explicit.[24] According to Dionysius: 'The first duty, and perhaps the most necessary one for all historians, is to choose a beautiful subject, pleasant to the readers' (*Ep. ad Pomp.* 3.767). The second duty is to determine 'where to begin' and 'how far one must go' (*Ep. ad Pomp.* 3.769). Herodotus is cited as a model because he begins

---

[24] For studies of literary criticism in Dionysius of Halicarnassus, I have consulted the following: M. Egger, *Denys d'Halicarnasse*, 1902; W. Rhys Roberts, *Dionysius of Halicarnassus*, 1901; S. F. Bonner, *Literary Treatises*, 1969.

by indicating the cause of the hostilities between Greeks and Barbarians and 'proceeds until he has shown the punishment and vengeance exercised upon the Barbarians' (*Ep. ad Pomp.* 3.769). Dionysius privileges a return at the end to the theme that constitutes 'the beginning and the end' of the work of Herodotus (καὶ ἀρχὴ καὶ τέλος ἐστὶ τῆς ἱστορίας, *Ep. ad Pomp.* 3.767).

Thucydides, on the other hand, is a target for criticism. Not only does he fail to begin in the appropriate manner (*De Thuc.* 10.338), starting as he does with the decline of the Greeks, but he does not bring his work to a suitable end. Even though he has promised to 'recount everything', he concludes with the narrative of the battle of Cynossema in the twenty-first year of the war: 'It would have been better, having related everything, to end the history with the most admirable event and the one that would be listened to with the most delight: the return of the fugitives from Phyle, which was for the city the beginning of the recovery of freedom' (*Ep. ad Pomp.* 3.771). Quite apart from the bad taste that presenting the Greeks in a position of weakness constitutes for Dionysius, we should hold onto the thematic *inclusio* which the beginning and the ending of the historiographical work should present.[25] As we have seen above,[26] in the correspondences between Acts 28 and Luke 2/Acts 1 Luke is not to be faulted.

What about the works Dionysius criticizes? We know that Thucydides did not have time to finish the *Peloponnesian War* and botched the ending; one can sense this from the absence of speeches, which Xenophon already felt to be a deficiency. The case of the *Histories* of Herodotus is more promising. They conclude in Book 9 with a perfectly symbolic event: the defeat of Xerxes' troops at Sestos and the destruction of the bridges over the Hellespont, the same ones that had allowed Persian troops to invade Greece (9.114–20). After victory, in an act that seals the Persian defeat, the Athenians on their return home take away the cables of the bridge in order to consecrate them to their gods (9.121). The author concludes by recalling a saying of Cyrus, who had once enjoined the Persians to withdraw into their territory and to renounce invading others in order to preserve their autonomy.[27] Dionysius of Halicarnassus is right:

---

[25] Dionysius reproaches: 'Thucydides has not begun his history where one ought to, and he has not adapted to it the suitable end; by no means the least part of a good arrangement is to begin where there should be nothing before, and to end where nothing is left to be desired' (*De Thuc.* 10.830). About Xenophon, on the other hand, he appreciates the fact that 'everywhere, he has begun and ended in the most suitable and appropriate manner' (*Ep. ad Pomp.* 4.778).

[26] See pp. 206–7.

[27] The saying attributed to Cyrus is after all perfectly Greek: 'In soft countries, he said, soft men are usually born; and it does not belong to the same soil to produce admirable fruit and valiant men of war. The Persians agreed; they withdrew, acceding to the opinion

Herodotus closes on a theme which is fundamental to him, the theme of the limit; the ὕβρις of the Persians who started the war had consisted precisely in violating the limit in order to demand earth and water from the Greeks. But what Dionysius has not noticed is the lack of completion in this ending. Herodotus announced three woes to the Athenians: Darius, Xerxes, Artoxerxes (6.98).[28] His work ends under the reign of Xerxes; the prediction of the third woe remains like a shadow over the future, as an unfulfilled threat, with the saying of Cyrus, the violation of which is denounced as insanity, hanging over it. The unsaid allows Herodotus to suspend the conflict between (Greek) culture and barbarism at a point of great fragility: respect for a limit. The prediction of the three woes is a portent that the limit will not hold.

A literary convention

What shall we conclude? The attestation of narrative suspension in the ending, both in Homer and in that great master of historiography Herodotus, is impressive, when one realizes the considerable role played by these works in ancient culture. The identification of a rhetoric of silence in poetry, theatre, Hellenistic novel and historiography leads to the conclusion that it existed as a literary convention. Nor was this unknown to the Hebrew Bible.[29] Everything leads one to think that the author of Acts made use of this model.

The effect of this convention may be summed up in three points:

1. The rhetorical device takes the form of narrative suspension whereby the author, by failing to bring certain narrative data to their resolution, *prevents the closure of the narrative world for the reader* (thus Thucydides as read by Dionysius of Halicarnassus).

2. Closure must be achieved by the reader, who, in order to satisfy the need for completion, is tempted to finish the story *in consonance with its plot* (*Odyssey, Aeneid,* Herodotus's *Histories*).

expressed by Cyrus; and they chose to be masters even though they lived in an infertile land, rather than being slaves to someone else while cultivating luxuriant plains' (9.122).

[28] The earthquake that struck Delos is interpreted by Herodotus in these terms: 'It seems to me that this wonder was sent by God as a portent of the evil to come among humans. For in three generations, those of Darius, son of Hystaspes, Xerxes, son of Darius and Artoxerxes, son of Xerxes, more woes came on Greece than during the twenty generations that preceded Darius...' (6.98).

[29] P. Davies observed that the second book of Kings ends with a narrative suspension through the symbolic scene of Jehoiachin's release (25. 27–30); he has not been able to show that Luke has drawn direct inspiration from that ending in his composition of Acts 28 ('Ending', 1982/3, pp. 334–5).

3.   The narrative, even without closure, may end up with a scene (*Odyssey, Aeneid*) or a declaration (Herodotus) that functions as a metaphor or a synecdoche and implies the unwritten outcome of the narrative.[30]

Let us return now to the book of Acts. I have said that it contains two announcements for which the narrative offers no fulfilment: Paul's appeal to Caesar and the testimony to the Risen one 'as far as the ends of the earth' (1. 8). According to what has just been said, one must ask: are there clues in the body of the book which allow the reader to bring these announcements to their completion? I shall begin with the appeal to Caesar, reserving the second motif for the last section.

Acts 27–28 and the displacement of the reader's expectation

Paul, in order to escape the schemes of his adversaries, employs his right of Roman citizenship: he appeals to the imperial judicial court (25. 11). This announcement marks out the end of the book of Acts: it is predicted by God (23. 11), communicated by Paul (25. 11), sanctioned by the governor Festus (25. 12, 25), recognized by King Agrippa (26. 32) and confirmed by an angel during the storm (27. 23). With all the clarity one could wish, Luke has prepared his readers for the apostle's appearance before Caesar. But when the moment is approaching, the author of Acts devotes fifty-nine verses (27. 1–28. 15) to narrating the commotions of the trip to Rome, with abundant detail on the navigational manoeuvres to which there is no equivalent in Greek literature. Considering the strategic position of this narrative (just a few lines from the end!), the voyage to Rome has a delaying effect, which must have a specific function with regard to the reader's expectation. What is that function?

A salvific operation

Since Ulysses and the *Odyssey*, the Greek novel had made the sea voyage into the classic locus of the hero's quest for identity; in this context the symbolic ordeal takes the form of a rescue from the powers of evil.[31] Exegetes have pointed out how the ambivalence of the vocabulary of rescue

---

[30] I have borrowed categories from F. Kermode, *Genesis of Secrecy*, 1977, p. 65. W. Iser speaks of the 'gaps' of the text as an indispensable factor in the act of reading; meaning arises both from what is said and from the reader's projection on the unsaid, so that the silence of the text is not to be considered as an absence of meaning, but as an invitation to find the missing elements through projection ('Interaction', 1980, pp. 106–19).

[31] See my chapter 11: 'Travels and travellers'.

(σῴζειν, διασῴζειν, σωτηρία)[32] makes the sea epic into a metaphor of salvation. It is also clear that the last two chapters of Acts are organized according to a two-part scheme: the tableau of Acts 27. 1 – 28. 10, devoted to the Gentiles, finds its counterpart in the scene of Acts 28. 17–31, devoted to the relation with Judaism. The narrative conclusion of 27. 44 ('And thus it happened that all were brought safely (διασωθῆναι) to the land') must be read in that perspective: the rescue of the passengers of the ship prefigures the salvation of all the nations of the earth, which is already anticipated by the quasi-Eucharistic meal over which Paul presides aboard ship (27. 33–7).[33]

Paul plays the leading role in this operation of salvation. Visited by God, endowed with an unshakeable confidence, equipped with an infallible foreknowledge of the future and of people, the apostle to the Gentiles, with his imposing presence and his wisdom, dominates the surging storm.[34] The divine visitation (27. 23–4) interprets the rescue of the ship as a grace granted to Paul (κεχάρισταί σοι ὁ Θεός), making the apostle a mediator of salvation for his 276 fellow passengers. The reader knows that Paul is not guilty of the crimes of which he is accused by the Jews: Luke has made declarations of innocence into a leitmotiv of the last section of the work (18. 14–15; 20. 26; 23. 3, 9; 24. 12–13; 25. 18, 25; 26. 31–2). However, on the narrative plane, the pagans have yet to be assured of it. It is for them that the marvellous rescue in Acts 27 manifests the intervention of the God who is Lord of the waters,[35] in

[32] Acts 27. 20, 31, 34, 43, 44; 28. 1, 4. *Pace* A. George, who maintains the strictly profane character of σῴζειν/σωτηρία ('Vocabulaire de salut', 1978, pp. 307–20, see pp. 308–9).

[33] In her excellent article devoted to the voyage to Rome, S. M. Praeder rightly maintains the Eucharistic character of the meal, implied by the mimesis of the vocabulary from which Luke constructs the narrative of the Last Supper of Jesus (cf. Acts 27. 35 and Luke 22. 19); however, I think the absence of the distribution of the bread is intentional. Luke avoids assimilating the crew of the ship to a Christian assembly. Praeder also notes the universalistic aims of the meal, concretized by the unusual abundance of categories of totality in this passage: 27. 33, 35, 36, 37, cf. 27. 24, 44 ('Sea Voyages', 1984, pp. 683–706, esp. pp. 697–700); see also 'Narrative Voyage', 1980, pp. 126–42.

[34] Paul gives navigational counsel (27. 9–10); he comforts (27. 21–6); he benefits from an angelic visitation (27. 23–4); he forestalls the crime of the sailors' flight (27. 31); he celebrates a quasi-Eucharistic meal (27. 35); his presence saves the life of the prisoners (27. 43). Haenchen concludes the following from the Pauline episodes in Acts 27, which he views as redactional additions: 'In this way Chapter 27 is fitted into the final section of the book, which again shows Paul the prisoner as the focal point of the action: he, the prisoner, saves them all!' (*Acts of the Apostles*, 1971, p. 709). On the victorious figure of the apostle undergoing trial, see the study of J. Zumstein, 'Apôtre comme martyr', 1980, pp. 371–90 or *Miettes exégétiques*, 1991, pp. 183–205.

[35] In addition to Old Testament tradition (mainly Jonah and Psalms), see Luke 5. 4–8; 8. 22–5. Rabbinic literature also ties storms to the wrath of God, for example, in the miraculous deliverance of Rabbi Gamaliel (*bBab. Mes.* 59b) or in relating the terror of Titus

favour of his witness; for them providence attests to the innocence of Paul.

G. B. Miles and G. Trompf have shown that protection from the peril of the waves is also, in Greek literature, a classic motif of divine protection of the just.[36] Hence, for the Jewish as well as for the Greek reader, the God of the ocean acquits the apostle in the eyes of the pagan world! It is tempting to conclude, with these two authors, that since the apostle has been found guiltless by divine intervention, recounting his appearance before a human court of justice, even an imperial one, would become superfluous.[37] There are nevertheless two observations which prevent me from adopting this conclusion.

Divine favour for Paul

First, the Malta episode (28. 1–10) and the end of the voyage (28. 11–16) present *a chain of arguments attesting divine favour toward Paul.* (1) The apostle's immunity to the viper's bite leads the 'Barbarians' in Malta to abandon their idea that 'Justice' (Δίκη) was pursuing a criminal (28. 4); Paul is therefore innocent. (2) Moreover, they regard him as a god (28. 6b) – Luke does not bother to correct that assessment (contrary to 14. 14–18), for the Barbarians are allowed to voice in an aberrant form a verdict which is substantially correct![38] (3) The healing of 'all the other' (οἱ λοιποί) inhabitants of the island leads to a profusion of honours showered upon Paul and his companions (28. 10). (4) Through the ensign of the Dioscuri (28. 11) under which the ship sails, Paul's arrival in Puteoli bears the signature of his innocence: the twin sons of Zeus were known not only as protectors of seafaring people, but as guardians of truth and

---

shaken by the waves on his return from Rome after the sack of Jerusalem (*Aboth Rabbi Nathan* 7).

[36] G. B. Miles and G. Trompf, 'Luke and Antiphon', 1976, pp. 259–67; G. Trompf, 'On Why Luke Declined to Recount', 1984, pp. 225–39. Their thesis has been refined and expanded by D. Ladouceur, 'Hellenistic Preconceptions', 1980, pp. 435–49.

[37] 'Luke and Antiphon', 1976, p. 265: 'Paul was put to the last test by forces and exigencies far more dreaded than the requirements of a human law court, and since he had been found guiltless, what need was there to recount the outcome of his appeal?'; cf. also p. 267.

[38] J. Roloff ignores this narrative effect when he compares the Malta episode with the one in Lystra (ch. 14) and ascribes to a 'naiv-unreflektierte Paulusverehrung' the lack of a challenge to the flawed theology of the people of Malta, which regrettably assimilates the apostle to a god (*Apostelgeschichte*, 1981, p. 366). But the narrator is more subtle! He leaves this judgement standing, which the reader knows to be wrong, but which testifies to a contextualized version of the recognition of the apostle's status. Luke is a master of the reconstruction of local colour. R. I. Pervo (*Profit with Delight*, 1987, pp. 70ff.) has grasped well the Lucan taste for exotic colouring.

the punishers of perjury.[39] To sum up: storm, shipwreck, and being bitten by the viper in Malta are a number of trials, which function as an ordeal; Paul's innocence is repeated, crystallizes in a chain of signs adapted to the pagan world, but is inappropriate for the dialogue with Judaism.

An inverted trial

Secondly, Luke in Acts 28. 17–28 does indeed set up a trial situation. However, the roles are reversed. Let us look at the first interview (28. 17–22). Paul is a prisoner, but he is the one who summons others to his own dwelling (28. 17a). The Roman Jewish deputation, which on the narrative plane inherits the role of the accusers, is installed as the court before whom Paul pleads his innocence (28. 17b–20); these judges – who are impartial since no rumour concerning Paul has reached them (28. 21) – ratify Paul's innocence. At the second interview (28. 23–8), Paul keeps the initiative, but the issue has changed: the debate is no longer about the apostle's innocence, but about the culpability of the Jews before the Gospel (28. 23). Paul interprets the audience's divided reaction to his preaching by means of the word of judgement from Isaiah 6. 9–10 (28. 25–7). The role reversal is then complete. The accusers are first judges, then judged. In accordance with the Holy Spirit (28. 25), the accused wields the word of judgement: 'The heart of this people has grown thick, they have become hard of hearing with their ears, and they have veiled their eyes, lest they should see with their eyes, and hear with their ears ...' (28. 27).

Installing a change of roles

I wrote earlier of the reader's expectation being displaced by the author. This device now appears more clearly. When Luke methodically constructs the expectation of Paul's trial, this is not in order to censor it at the last moment for the sake of political decency. Luke transforms the journey to Rome into a providential manifestation of Paul's innocence in the eyes of the pagan world, which the Maltese ratify with their barbaric naivety (28. 1–10). The image of the apostle arriving in Rome as a distinguished visitor, welcomed by a Christian delegation (28. 15), settled into the liberal status of the *custodia militaris* (28. 16, 30),[40] receiving crowds

---

[39] See D. Ladouceur, 'Hellenistic Preconceptions', 1980, pp. 443–8 and H. J. Klauck, *Magie und Heidentum*, 1996, pp. 132–3 (who quotes the Homeric *Hymn* 33).
[40] On this topic see the study by H. W. Tajra, *Trial*, 1989, pp. 179–81.

of people at home (28. 17, 23, 30) – this glowing image[41] is not designed to spare the imperial justice, but rather to effect an exchange of roles. The prisoner reaches the capital and stays there with the authority of one who will not be judged, but will deliver a judgement. The function of the sequence in Acts 27. 1 – 28. 16 is to prepare for this reversal. This does not occur, however, without a paradox: this man, the bearer of a word of judgement, is in chains (28. 16b).

All this being said and done, why is there no mention of the outcome of the trial? If Luke's silence is neither ignorance nor political prudence, what is the reason? My opinion is that Luke, through the effect of judicial reversal, reinterprets a fact that his readers well remember: the execution of the apostle in Rome, perhaps at the close of his trial.[42] This subtle game with the memory of the reader is signalled by the reference to the limited length of the apostle's stay in Rome (v. 30: διετία), whose result the reader does not have to learn. But Luke depends on this memory in order to invert the roles. It is not the apostle to the Gentiles, but the chosen people in Rome who are judged. The reluctance of the author of Acts to recount the death of witnesses also has an effect, more probably than a resemblance between the death of Paul and the resurrection of Jesus, as some have suggested.[43] If the rhetoric of silence incites the reader to conclude the narrative in accordance with the plot, one can understand the means that Luke has given his readers to guide them in the task of completion. Death is indeed announced (20. 35, 38; 21. 11), but the narrative, which delays long over the firmness of the Pauline witness before those who exercise the Roman power (chs. 21–6) and over his confidence in the midst of the storm (ch. 27), implies that the witness will face death without faltering.[44]

[41] On the social image of Paul in Acts, in addition to the above cited monograph by Pervo, see also J. C. Lentz, *Luke's Portrait of Paul*, 1993 (although skimpy on Acts 27–8).

[42] The hypothesis of the death of Paul in Rome has sufficient support from literary and archaeological data (cf. G. Lüdemann, *Frühe Christentum*, 1987, pp. 274–6).

[43] While the tradition of the early Church was content to tell of the martyrdom of Peter and Paul, Acts lets both of them depart in the same manner, without relating their deaths. Beforehand, both are the object of a miraculous deliverance (12. 6–11; 28. 31b). This silence concerning the death of two witnesses has been seen in a typological perspective by M. D. Goulder, who sees here the recurrence of the death–resurrection cycle of Jesus (*Type and History*, 1964, pp. 34–51, esp. 36–9). W. Radl and J.-N. Aletti agree with this interpretation (I deal with the question on pp. 58–9), but this is to confuse the shipwreck with the death of Paul and to forget the secondary position of the witness before the Master (cf. 27. 24, 34–5; 28. 23, 31); the absence of resurrection vocabulary in chapter 12 and 27–8 does not support this interpretation either.

[44] This is essentially the image of the courageous witness that, according to R. C. Tannehill, the reader is invited to carry from Acts 27 to the suspended ending of Acts 28 (*Narrative Unity*, II, 1990, p. 355).

Positively, it is important for the author of Acts to install the image of Paul preaching at the end (28. 30–1), for it is by this remembrance and this activity that the world of the narration and the world of the reader are, in his view, linked together. We shall also see that the second prediction left open in the book of Acts, namely the testimony of the Risen One to the ἔσχατον τῆς γῆς (1. 8), towers above this final summary, in which it finds a kind of anticipatory fulfilment. I shall come to this, but only after dealing with the theological dispute in 28. 17–28.

The last theological disputation (28. 17–28)

Instead and in place of Paul's defence before the imperial tribunal the reader is present at the apology of Paul before the representatives of the Jewish community. In accordance with the norm invoked by Quintilian and Dionysus of Halicarnassus (see above, pp. 212–16), the conclusion of Acts resumes the fundamental theme of the work. It delivers the author's theological diagnosis about the relation between Church and Synagogue. My interest, at this point, is not to return to the fundamental question of the relation between Judaism and Christianity. I have already devoted a whole chapter to this question.[45] Rather, I shall examine the conflict between Paul and the Jews, at the point when Luke brings Paul's ministry to an end. The quote from Isaiah 6. 9–10 functions as the hermeneutical frame for this final theological dispute.

I have just noted the structure of reversal governing the passage; it is now necessary to observe the outcome of this reversal.

Shifts of meaning

The argumentative scenario of this final debate between Paul and his tradition of origin is remarkably constructed. Two interviews bring the prisoner apostle together with the Jewish deputation in Rome, probably composed of synagogue leaders. From the first (28. 17–22) to the second (28. 23–8), the author orchestrates a series of thematic shifts, in a crescendo that culminates in the hard word of judgement of Isaiah 6. There are five shifts.

(1) The first shift: one passes from Paul's dispute (v. 19a) to that of the Church (22b: the same verb is used, ἀντιλέγεσθαι). (2) Paul transfers the debate about 'this sect' (v. 22) to the proclamation of the Kingdom (v. 23). (3) Paul passes from the proclamation of the Kingdom (v. 24) to

---

[45] See above, chapter 7: 'Jews and Christians in conflict' (pp. 129–54).

the history of salvation (vv. 25–7). (4) The Jewish deputation is invited to pass from knowledge of the debate about the Church (vv. 22b) to another knowledge dealing with salvation for the Gentiles (v. 28a: the same term is used, γνωστόν). (5) Paul passes from the solidarity with Israel ('I have done nothing against the people or the customs of the fathers', v. 17) to distancing himself ('The Holy Spirit was right in saying to *your* fathers through the prophet Isaiah', v. 25).

These five shifts attest the reorientation of salvation history (v. 28) effected through Paul's destiny and the acceptance of his message. The first interview allows the apostle to present his apology. One may note that the modelling of Paul's martyrdom on the passion of Jesus is reinforced (vv. 17–18),[46] and that the speech points toward a validation of suffering in the name of Israel's hope (v. 20). His exculpation by the Roman authorities points to the Jewish responsibility in his present situation, but Paul defends himself against any hint of anti-Judaism in the clearest of terms: it is because of *the hope of Israel* that he wears his chains (v. 20). This hope in the promises made to the fathers, if it has as its primary objective the resurrection of the dead (26. 6–7), finds its concretization in the intervention of God in Jesus (cf. Luke 2. 37).[47] The group understands very well, since its answer (vv. 21–2) transfers the question from the person of Paul, who was not controversial in Rome, to 'this sect', which is known to be 'contested everywhere'. The second interview (28. 23–8) begins with Paul's testimony about the Kingdom of God: his proclamation is Christological (περὶ τοῦ Ἰησοῦ) and is argued from the Scriptures (Moses and the Prophets). According to a stereotype in Acts, present already in the Pentecost narrative (2. 12–13), the hearers are divided in their reactions: some are convinced and others 'do not believe' (v. 24). Thus Paul sees, in the failure of his preaching, the fulfilment of the word of the Holy Spirit, written in Israel's past in Isaiah 6. 9–10. Consequently, the Jewish deputation is called to realise that salvation, destined for the Gentiles, would from now on be addressed to them with success: 'this salvation of God has been sent to the Gentiles; they will listen' (v. 28).

[46] S. M. Praeder notes the three points which differentiate Paul's apology in 28. 18–20 from Acts 21. 18–26, 32, bringing Paul's martyrdom closer to the trial of Jesus before Pilate according to Luke 23. The three points are giving into the hands of the Romans (Luke 18. 32–3; 20. 20; 23. 1), the Roman desire to free him (Luke 23. 16, 20, 22), and the Jewish opposition to this liberation (Luke 23. 18, 21, 23). Paul's insistence on his innocence finds its parallel on the lips of Jesus in Luke 23. 15 and 23. 22 ('Narrative Voyage', 1980, p. 161).

[47] Cf. Kl. Haacker, 'Bekenntnis', 1985, pp. 437–51. Behind this apology, W. Stegemann assumes a Lucan response to the reproaches addressed by Judaism to Christianity: *Zwischen Synagoge und Obrigkeit*, 1991, pp. 180–6.

To what *theological result* does Paul's aborted dialogue with the Jews of Rome lead? In my view, Luke proceeds in an ambiguous manner, as he does often in the crucial passages of his work, and I will summarize his reading of the event in two terms: *an opening* and *an acknowledgement of failure.*

An opening...

First, the most surprising observation is that in spite of the chilling judgement of Isaiah 6. 9–10, neither Paul's discourse (according to Luke) nor the discourse of the narrator concludes by closing the door to Judaism. Luke does not, as in other places, point to the Jewish group as a united front in hostility (13. 45) or in opposition (18. 6). He notes a division in the audience between those 'convinced' (ἐπείθοντο) and the unbelievers (28. 24); there is no reason to doubt that πείθομαι represents believing adherence to Paul's preaching.[48] The text stresses not that the Jews could believe (the reader knows this already), but division in the audience, which it describes by the unexpected term 'a-symphony' (ἀσύμφωνοι, 28. 25a). At this final moment, this separation takes on a symbolic value: the recognition of the Kingdom of God in Jesus brings disunity among the Jewish people. It makes sense, therefore, to see in the inclusivity of Paul's hospitality (ἀπεδέχετο πάντας, v. 30) an invitation to include Jews as individuals among those to whom Christian preaching is addressed. Paul's preaching mentioned at the end overcomes the opposition λαός/ἔθνη, which dominated verses 25–8, to recapitulate the universality of the addressees of the Christian mission.[49] To this indication of openness, one must add the rhetorical function of the word of judgement in the Old Testament, as recalled by D. Moessner: 'Isa. 6. 9f. does not foreclose the future by a condemnation, but forcefully exhorts to an ultimate repentance.'[50] V. Fusco has also insisted on the fact that the accusation of hardening is a deuteronomist

[48] The pair πείθομαι/ἀπιστέω (28. 24) is the equivalent of the couple πιστεύω/ ἀπειθέω that Luke uses in 14. 1–2.

[49] It is worth noting that the Jews' exit from the narrative, arranged by the Byzantine text (gloss of v. 29), was precisely not intended by the narrator. The gradation that he arranged between the three successive audiences (v. 17: τῶν Ἰουδαίων πρώτους; v. 23: πλείονες; v. 30: πάντας) culminates in universality. Luke did not 'write off' Israel in his work. E. Haenchen's formula 'Luke has written the Jews off' does not apply to the received text ('Book of Acts', 1978, pp. 258–78, quotation p. 278).

[50] D. P. Moessner, ('Paul in Acts', 1988, pp. 96–104). F. Bovon has proposed to read in καὶ ἰάσομαι αὐτούς of v. 27c the hope of such a repentance ('"How Well the Holy Spirit Spoke"', 1995, p. 47). But it must be noted that, after μήποτε, the future is equivalent to a subjunctive aorist (Blass–Debrunner–Rehkopf, 442,2d).

theologoumenon that (1) is not to be confused with a sentence of rejection; (2) leaves open the possibility of a future enlightenment by a salvific intervention of God.[51] The τοῦτο τὸ σωτήριον τοῦ Θεοῦ of verse 28 confirms the salvific connotation of the end of the text of Isaiah. The signs of an opening are then perceptible, but I must admit, they are hesitant.

... and an acknowledgement of failure

Second, as a counterbalance to the opening, the acknowledgement of failure is presented with gravity. Against the 'a-symphony' of the chosen people, stands the impressive agreement between Isaiah, Paul and the Holy Spirit (28. 25). The passing of salvation to the pagans, as prompted by Israel's refusal announced in 13. 46 and 18. 6, is now sealed by the apostle's last word to Judaism, which is a single last word (ῥῆμα ἕν, 28. 25), and is at the same time the last word of Paul in Acts. Despite the desire that the theologian might have, it is not reasonable to trivialize this final fact by inferring, as earlier in Acts, that Paul will proceed without changing his preaching to Israel despite the resistance he confronts.[52] The conclusive word of the apostle in verse 28 not only evokes the possibility of the Gentiles' hearing, but opposes this future hearing (ἀκούσονται) with the past non-hearing of Israel. The end of verse 28 stresses this opposition by the position of the καί, emphasizing the pronoun αὐτοί: 'they' (the Gentiles) in contrast to 'you' (Israel) will listen. Since verse 25, the argument has moved from the individual (v. 24) to the collective level of λαός/ἔθνη; the destiny of Israel in its totality is opposed to the attitude of the Gentiles, with the intention of disqualifying the chosen people. Even if the conversion of

---

[51] V. Fusco, 'Future of Israel', 1996, pp. 1–17, see pp. 6–8.

[52] R. L. Brawley postulates that, for Luke, the preaching to Israel will proceed without change; he bases this on the resumption of the evangelization of the Jews, after Paul's resolution to turn to the Gentiles, in 13. 46 and 18. 6 ('Paul in Acts', 1984, pp. 129–34 or *Luke–Acts and the Jews*, 1987, pp. 68–78). The same trivialization of the conclusive aspect of Acts 28 is found in R. C. Tannehill's *Narrative Unity*, II, 1990, pp. 350–1; B. J. Koet's *Five Studies*, 1989, pp. 119–39; R. F. O'Toole, *Treatment of Jews*, 1993, pp. 547–9 (with reference to Exod. 32. 9; Isa. 63. 10; 2 Chron. 36.16). Arguments against this reading: (1) the strategic choice of the conclusion prevents it being seen as the repetition of the scenario in 13. 46 and 18. 6; (2) there is a gradual process, both geographical and chronological, from Asia (13. 46) (future στρεφόμεθα) to Greece (18. 6), then to Rome (28. 28) (present γνωστόν ἔστω ὑμῖν); (3) the author holds back the citation of Isa. 6. 9–10, which he shortens in 8. 10 (cf. Mark 4. 12), in order to give it *in extenso* in the narrative conclusion. G. Wasserberg correctly insists on the summarizing character of the Isa. 6. 9–10 quotation at the end of the book (*Aus Israels Mitte*, 1998, pp. 101–3; pp. 109–12; p. 115).

individuals within Judaism is envisaged and sought (v. 30: πάντες), the hope of unifying the Jewish people (v. 26: λαός)[53] around Jesus is lost.

Paul is aligned with the prophet

In this way Luke places the rupture between Church and Synagogue under the sign of historico-salvific continuity. But, this rupture is no triumph. It sanctions the failure of the apostolic preaching to convince Judaism that in Jesus the 'hope of Israel' is manifested. This theological dimension of failure comes from a fact little noticed up to now: Luke is the only New Testament author who cites Isaiah 6. 9–10 including the mandate given to the prophet: 'Go to this people and say....' (28. 26). Is this a concern for scriptural exactitude?[54] I am inclined to say that the beginning of the quotation is important to Luke because it makes it possible to align Paul with the mandate given to the prophet. The motif of the sending of the prophet reminds the reader of the repeated references to Paul's vocation, cast in the language of the prophetic vocations (22. 21; 26. 17; cf. 9. 15).[55] Consequently, a similar failure of preaching establishes, under the protection of the Spirit, a continuity between representatives of God. The apostle takes on and duplicates in the face of Israel the prophet's failure; he borrows the prophet's voice (Paul does not *speak* in vv. 26–7, but he *makes* the prophet *speak*)[56] in order to attest to the continuity of refusing God's offer all through the history of salvation. This drama welds the past to the present and places the Christian preacher and the prophet side by side. Moreover, the quotation of Isaiah presents the refusal of Israel as the result of an act of God. It is finally to God that the mystery of the hardening of the people is returned.

[53] Similarly, see now J. B. Tyson, *Images of Judaism*, 1992, pp. 174–8, and 'Jews and Judaism', 1995, pp. 36–7. For a different opinion, see H. van de Sandt, 'No salvation', 1994, pp. 341–58, esp. pp. 357–8.

[54] T. Holtz thinks it probable that Luke verified the citation in a codex of the LXX; *Alttestamentlichen Zitate*, 1968, pp. 33–7.

[55] H. van de Sandt had identified, as I have, this parallelism between the sending of the prophet and the mission of Paul, but he attributes it to the taking over of a structure found in Ezek. 2. 3–5; 3. 4–7 ('No Salvation', 1994, pp. 348–50). See also D. P. Moessner, 'Paul and the Pattern of the Prophet', 1983, pp. 203–12, and *Lord of the Banquet*, 1998, pp. 114–30, pp. 296–307.

[56] F. Bovon was aware of this effect of 'going back', which the procedure of quotation produces: ' "How Well the Holy Spirit Spoke" ', 1995, pp. 43–50, esp. pp. 44 and 48–9.

A sketch of a response

Rather than ending on a tragic verdict, the book of Acts – and this fact is of the utmost importance theologically – closes with an unresolved tension between the promise intended for Israel and the historical turning that signifies its refusal.[57] How can one explain that in treating a theme so fundamental for him, Luke ends his narrative with so ambivalent a position? We could, like V. Fusco, distrust the arguments *ex silentio* and collect indications throughout the gospel attesting the Lucan conviction of a future salvation of Israel.[58] But, again, Luke is too skilful a narrator to have bungled the end of his work by forgetting to mention the future of Israel. In my opinion, the unresolved tension of Acts 28 signals that Luke does not have a definitive solution concerning the destiny of Israel. There are only sketches of a response. The narrator wanted to leave the readers to form their own opinion by posing two correlates that he did not link systematically. On the one hand, the 'salvation of God' is to be understood in the Church as open to both Jews and Gentiles. On the other hand – a distant echo of Romans 9–11 may be heard here – the promises of the faithfulness of God to his people Israel are not annulled.

However, the last word of the narrator is to be sought in the concluding summary of verses 30–1. I must now decipher the meaning of this epilogue – which has nothing to do with an appendix, theologically speaking, since it develops the idea of a universal opening under the sign of the fulfilment of prophecy (28. 28 quotes Isa. 40. 5).

Paul the exemplary pastor (28. 30–31)

In the typology of narrative closure devices discussed above,[59] the openended conclusion implies the unwritten outcome of the narrative by means

---

[57] R. C. Tannehill judiciously concludes from the paradox Luke poses between the scriptural promises intended for Israel and the historical experience of its refusal to see in the Christ the accomplishment of the hope of Israel: 'The resulting tension, especially apparent in the tension between the promise in the Antioch sermon and the bitter words at the end of Acts, is not resolved in the narrative' ('Rejection', 1988, pp. 83–101, quotation p. 101; also *Narrative Unity*, II, 1990, p. 352. Against this author ('Rejection', p. 93), I maintain that the final scene of Acts is not 28. 17–28, but 28. 30–1, and that consequently the work of Luke does not culminate in the tragic irony of the elected people denying the promise that is destined for them, but in the announcement of salvation open to the nations (see R. C. Tannehill, 'Tragic Story', 1985, pp. 69–85).

[58] V. Fusco evokes the prophetic sayings of Luke 13. 34–5; 19. 41–4; 21. 24b (should we add Acts 3. 21–3) concerning the future salvation of Israel and affirms that Acts 28. 25–8 only mentions the 'near future' ('Future of Israel', 1996, see pp. 9–15). But the weight of the conclusion of Acts makes such a solution unlikely, which further highlights the new situation created by the repeated refusal of the Gospel as it is developed in the narrative of Acts.

[59] See pp. 210–16.

of a concluding scene functioning as metaphor or synecdoche. This is undeniably the case with the final summary presented in 28. 30–1.

A paradigmatic goal

The redaction of this short summary shows how subtly Luke can use language. First, Paul's activity in Rome is chronologically limited: 'He lived there two whole years' (v. 30a). The aorist ἐνέμεινεν and the temporal indication διετίαν ὅλην signal a period that is over, beyond which readers should use their own information and other narrative data. The summary has the biographical goal of closing the activity of the hero of Acts. At the same time, the picture has a paradigmatic purpose. The syntactic construction, an imperfect indicative (ἀπεδέχετο, v. 30b) followed by a chain of participles (κηρύσσων, διδάσκων, v. 31), creates an effect of duration and exemplariness. This construction is typical of the summaries of Acts (2. 42, 45–7; 5. 16; 8. 3; 12. 25; 15. 35; 18. 11; 19. 8–10; etc.), which describe the ideal and permanent state of the Christian community and its mission.[60] The unlimited openness of Pauline evangelization is attested by the πάντας ('he received all who came'), and Paul's three audiences are recapitulated: Jews, Gentiles and Christians. The end of the book mentions all three of them (28. 17, 23; 28. 28; 28. 15).

This summary confirms the traits that Luke, since chapter 9, has not ceased to ascribe to that figure he reveres above all others: Paul the ideal pastor and the model of the persecuted Christian. In the imperial capital, Christianity, like the apostle,[61] will now find its 'home'.[62] At the centre of the Empire, where the Roman power resides, Paul preaches the power of God's rule.[63] His teaching holds together two entities that

---

[60] 'His theme of unstoppable growth and spread of God's Word no matter what the human opposition, plays itself out to the very end of his narrative' (W. S. Kurz, *Reading Luke–Acts*, 1993, p. 109). V. Fusco has seen that the conclusion of Acts escapes an exclusively biographical interest as well as a strictly symbolic reading ('Progetto storiografico', 1986, pp. 145–8).

[61] Luke was certainly not insensitive either to the fact that the Hellenistic novels (as in the pattern of the *Odyssey*) frequently conclude with the hero's homecoming, or that coming to Rome represented a climax in the life of the great philosophers (see *The Life of Apollonius of Tyana* by Philostratus).

[62] The work of Luke transfers the reader from Jerusalem to Rome and from the Temple (Luke 1–2) to home (Acts 28). The symbolic connotation of Paul's 'home' (28. 16, 30) is still to be specified. V. K. Robbins sees an indication of the social context of the author, which he describes in 'Social Location', 1991, pp. 305–32, esp. p. 330: 'Paul, like the Christian movement, has a rightful home within the Roman Empire'; See also J. H. Elliot's 'Temple versus Household', 1991, pp. 211–40.

[63] S. J. Cassidy is (overly?) aware of the implicit criticism of the Roman state in the final summary (*Society and Politics*, 1987, pp. 130–5 and 167–70).

are no longer to be dissociated: the βασιλεία τοῦ Θεοῦ⁶⁴ and the Lord Jesus Christ (v. 31). The apostle in chains testifies with a total freedom of speech (παρρησία), which is the effect of the Spirit, and without hindrance (ἀκωλύτως), which represents a promise for the future. The theological overtones of this description of the material condition of the apostle, prisoner but free, should not be underestimated.⁶⁵ In the form of an ideal picture of the Pauline past, Luke draws up an agenda for the future.

Rejoining the world of the readers

But to whom does this agenda apply? Who must carry it out? For what category of readers is Paul set up as an exemplary pastor? The answer to these questions depends on a detail in the text which might appear trivial at first sight, which is why exegetes have not devoted much attention to it. In Acts 28. 16, Luke specifies that on 'our' arrival in Rome, Paul was allowed to 'stay at his own place (καθ' ἑαυτόν) with the soldier who was guarding him'. A similar specification returns unexpectedly in the final summary: Paul 'dwelt for two whole years at his own expense (ἐν ἰδίῳ μισθώματι)...' (28. 30). Whatever the exact sense of the rare term μισθώμα – payment, and by extension rent, personal financial means⁶⁶ – this note, in conjunction with the καθ' ἑαυτόν in verse 16, stresses the missionary's material autonomy. The portrait of the ideal pastor, which carried already an indication of the audience (v. 30b) and the summary statement of the message (v. 31), is now completed by a technical point about the external condition of missionary work.

In this miniature portrait of the missionary, in my view, Luke's interest in the perpetuation of the Pauline tradition of evangelism is manifest. One can go further. The marked interest in the Pauline mission makes it clear

⁶⁴ βασιλεία τοῦ θεοῦ is a synthetic expression of the content of Paul's preaching (Acts 19. 8; 20. 25) and the message of Jesus (Luke. 4. 43; 8. 1, etc.; Acts 1. 3). The Christological shift is remarkable if one compares 28. 31 and Acts 1. 3. J. Jervell is mistaken on this point: 'Die christliche Botschaft ist also eine durchaus jüdische Angelegenheit' (*Apostelgeschichte*, 1998, p. 626).
⁶⁵ The semantic ambivalence of ἀκωλύτως, which is both juridical (the absence of physical restraint) and theological (sign of the unstoppable action of God) has been shown by D. L. Mealand, 'Close of Acts', 1990, pp. 583–97, see pp. 589–95.
⁶⁶ C. Spicq decides with hesitation for 'rent' (*Lexique théologique*, 1991, pp. 1040–1). D. L. Mealand has clearly opted for the technical sense 'payment of rent' ('Close of Acts', 1990, pp. 583–7). For more on this term, consult H. J. Hauser, *Abschlusserzählung*, 1979, pp. 153–7.

why this ending seems suspended in time. Around the 80s, when Luke was writing, the memory of the apostle was celebrated in Pauline circles. The groups of evangelists, who would go on to conquer the Empire, were recruited in these Pauline circles. Luke, this great traveller and disciple of the apostle to the Gentiles, fascinated by the founding of the communuties, was clearly close to the evangelists of the Pauline tendency. Maybe he himself was one. One indication could lead in this direction. In contrast to the constant movement of the apostolic mission in Acts, Paul in Rome remains sedentary; he does not go out to others, they come to his house (v. 30b). Maybe he was under constraint? Maybe this new sedentary mode of mission corresponds to the conditions of evangelization in Lucan Christianity. Whatever the case, it is of the bearers of the Pauline inheritance that Luke is thinking as he writes this final summary through which the narrative world rejoins the readers' world.[67] There was no question of ending with a celebration of the past, however glorious. The final image of Paul the evangelist, as Luke takes his leave, requires reconstituting in the life of readers.

Conclusion: the power of the end

The end of a literary work possesses a peculiar power over its readers. The end of the book of Acts intrigues. However, it has become clear that this enigmatic character does not result from the inability of exegetes to discern the significance of the text. A rhetorical procedure attested in Graeco-Roman culture, identified as 'narrative suspension', allows the author of the Acts consciously to use silence and ambivalence in composing the end of his monumental work. This surprising narrative choice concretizes the theological challenge that the author of the Acts has imposed on himself: to assign to Christianity the new place that the Pauline mission has won for it – the Roman Empire – but at the same time to lead Christianity back to its Jewish roots. This intention is implicit in Luke's management of the Pauline heritage. Luke wishes to reinterpret the memory of the apostle's martyrdom, by inverting the

---

[67] It is not unimportant that the third and last 'we-sequence' in the book of Acts ends precisely . . . in Rome (27. 1 – 28. 16), indicating that the entry into the imperial capital was a collective entry of the apostle and his companions. Independent of the (hazardous) presence of a source, the end of this sequence favours my hypothesis of Lucan interest in the perpetuation of the Pauline mission. In the narrative, the 'we' points to the existence of a group: are not the Pauline evangelists called precisely to identify themselves with the historical group around the apostle? In this case, they are literally guided to Rome by the narrative. (On this question see pp. 24–5.)

structure of the expected trial (Acts 27–8), and to ensure the perpetuation of his missionary work in the present.

An open programme

For Luke, Paul's final theological debate with Judaism ends neither in the cursing of Israel nor in a trivialization of its refusal.[68] With the apostle's arrival in Rome, a new step is taken in the history of salvation, which marks the failure of the hope for the conversion of the entire Jewish people. However, the narrative is intentionally ambivalent, informed by a theology which refuses to decide on the future of the relation between Church and Synagogue. The same device of openness characterizes the final scene of Paul evangelizing Rome (28. 30–1). This portrayal of the ideal pastor points to the men and women, with Luke or close to him, who through their missionary engagement, perpetuate the memory of the apostle to the Gentiles. In this way, they were associated with the witness of the Risen One 'to the ends of the earth' (1. 8) – a programme which remains open. The summary offers an anticipation of it, as it waits to be reconstituted in the life of the reader at the moment when he or she finishes the reading of the book.

[68] The first position is held by J. T. Sanders, 'Jewish People', 1988, pp. 51–75 (the Church breaks away from Judaism); the second is maintained by J. Jervell, *People of God*, 1972, pp. 41–4 (the Church is the continuation of Israel converted to Christ).

11

TRAVELS AND TRAVELLERS

> When your eyes are sated with the spectacle of things above and
> you lower them to earth, another aspect of things, and other-
> wise wonderful, will meet your gaze. On this side you will see
> level plains stretching out their boundless expanse, on the other,
> mountains rising in great, snowclad ridges and lifting their peaks
> to heaven... You will see the ships seeking the lands they ig-
> nore; you will see that no enterprise rejects human audacity, and
> you will be, in these attempts, both spectator and participant.
>
> Seneca, *To Marcia on Consolation* 18, 4–7

One of the characteristics of the end of the twentieth century was the
extraordinary development of the travel industry: modes of transport,
communication channels and the tourist market. Travelling is no longer
the impossible dream. This revolution in mobility is not without parallels in history. Of course, there was the fifteenth century with its great
maritime conquests (the Indies, America). Earlier, the crusades had stimulated curiosity in the Orient. Another period, less known, but just as
influential in the launching of travel was the turn of the Christian era
in the Roman Empire. There are numerous indications which lead us to
believe that the Mediterranean populations of this period were fascinated
by travel.

An effect of globalization

Historians agree in describing the Roman Empire as a world in which,
everywhere, interest in unknown worlds, the development of the means of
communication, and the stability assured by the *Pax Augustana* come together to intensify exchange.[1] Land and sea routes are travelled especially

---

[1] In addition to L. Casson's classic work, *Travel*, 1974, see also T. Kleberg's *Hôtels*, 1957;
G. Marasco, *Viaggi*, 1978; G. Camassa and S. Fasce, eds., *Idea e realtà*, 1991; J.-M. André

by the professionals of travel seeking adventure and profit (soldiers, merchants, artists, adventurers, peddlers, missionaries), and less frequently by occasional travellers (cultivated intellectuals, tourists, sick persons seeking healing). 'The Roman Empire laws created a world-wide political system of communication and trade.'[2] Latin pragmatism and the Stoic doctrine of the *cosmopolis* both contributed to this increase in travel and to the effect of 'globalization' which followed at the turn of the Christian era.

We should not exaggerate: in spite of facilitated conditions, travel remained dangerous.[3] Other than the professionals, few people travelled. Yet this elitist character of travel favours it culturally, as the Greek novel attests: because there is risk, travel is attractive. Lucian of Samosata (second century) is a good witness to this mood: 'The motive and purpose of my journey lay in my intellectual activity and desire for adventure, and in my wish to find out where the end of the ocean was, and who the people were that lived on the other side' (Lucian of Samosata, *A True Story* 1.5). What a wonderful invitation to travel!

It is likely that Luke himself was a traveller. Loveday Alexander has attempted to reconstruct the 'mental map' of the author of Acts based on his vocabulary of travel. She concludes, after examining the riches of the maritime vocabulary and the frequent coastal references, that in differentiation from Paul in his epistles, the narrator of Acts is familiar with sea transport.[4]

The explosion of curiosity about unknown lands, which can be dated from the third century BC, with its enlargement of the *oikoumene* under the reign of the Ptolemies, generated the appearance of an important body of travel literature. The discovery of hitherto unknown lands and peoples, stimulated in the cultivated elite a taste for the foreign. The intermingling of people, the cosmopolitanism of the great Mediterranean cities, and the influx of non-Greeks into the ports made the foreigner seem less dangerous. A way of viewing the world begins to set in; the attraction of open horizons little by little takes over from closed-mindedness, which for a long time had been associated with the

---

and M.-F. Baslez, *Voyager*, 1993. Useful compilation of texts by F. Meijer and O. van Nijf: *Trade*, 1992. An echo of historians' reflections is presented in B. M. Rapske, 'Travel and Shipwreck', 1994, pp. 1–47.

[2] J.-M. André and M.-F. Baslez, *Voyager*, 1993, pp. 165f.

[3] Still at the beginning of the second century, Pliny the younger opposes the safety of the 'homeland' to the 'lodging of the quasi-traveller' (*Letters* 6.19).

[4] L. C. A. Alexander, 'Narrative Maps', 1995; also by the same author: ' "In Journeyings Often" ', 1995, esp. pp. 25–31.

Greek mindset.[5] The social life of citizens (religious groups included) became used to coexistence with 'outsiders'. The *Barbarian* remained an object of fantasy, but difference attracts and the taste for exotic ways grows.

It is true that the Greek imagination had something to nourish itself in the epic narratives of the *Odyssey*, which are just one long invitation to the adventure of travel, and the fabulous descriptions of the *Histories* of Herodotus. The new literature that emerges in Graeco-Roman culture (I shall return to this later) is made up of tourist guides for the traveller, stories of travel, accounts of exploration, lives of itinerant wise men, and so on. Everything encourages us to think that the Greek, the Roman or the Ephesian of the first century had abandoned the image of a closed society. The culture which nurtured the authors and readers of the New Testament is steeped in the spirit of travel.

Travellers in Luke's writings

In no part of the New Testament is the reader more powerfully exposed to the world of travel than in the works *ad Theophilum*. It is an understatement to say that the author of Luke–Acts appreciates the travel theme. It would be closer to the truth to speak of a Lucan obsession with travel and travellers.

Already in Luke's gospel (Luke 9. 51 – 19. 28),[6] the importance given to Jesus' journey from Galilee to Judaea is unusual within the Synoptic tradition. This long peregrination of the Lucan Jesus finds its counterpart in the itinerary of the Pauline mission in Acts; the orientation towards Rome covers a third of the narrative. Announced in Paul's decision (Acts 19. 21), the choice of Rome as destination is validated by a vision in 23. 11 ('Just as you have testified for me in Jerusalem, so you must bear witness also in Rome'), confirmed during the storm ('Do not be afraid, Paul; you must stand before Caesar . . .' 27. 24), and fulfilled in 28. 14. Such a mirror effect, from Jesus to Paul, is not theologically irrelevant for Luke's work. He shapes the fate of the disciple according to that of the Master

---

[5] On the image of the foreigner in Greek culture and its transformation in the Hellenistic period, see M.-F. Baslez's, *Etranger*, 1984; and the contributions assembled in R. Lonis' *Etranger dans le monde grec*, 1988–92.

[6] The end of the central section of the gospel of Luke is not easily identified; between 19. 10 and 19. 48 many breaks have been proposed. I consider 19. 29–48 to be a transitional passage, delaying the entry into Jerusalem by a series of approaches (19. 29, 41). On this question, see A. Denaux, 'Delineation', 1993, pp. 357–92.

and, in both cases, the voyage leads the hero to his death.[7] From the point of view of narrative strategy, this procedure of *syncrisis*[8] indicates that the author is able to confer on the travel motif a structuring function in the narration.

His interest in travel reaches its fullest development in the second part of the work *ad Theophilum*. Itinerancy is not limited to Paul. All readers observe that the narrative world of Acts is peopled with travellers: the pilgrims in Jerusalem for Pentecost (2. 9–11), the exiled members of the Jerusalem community going from place to place (8. 4), Philip, the evangelist of Samaria (8. 5), the Ethiopian eunuch on the road from Jerusalem to Gaza (8. 26–8), Peter, who 'went here and there' (9. 32) before disappearing from the narrative by going 'to another place' (12. 17), Aquila and Priscilla, emigrants from Rome to Corinth, where they welcome Paul (18. 2–3), and many others. In brief, in Acts, the Word travels and makes people travel.

A narrative theme of primary importance

Where does this Lucan fascination for travel and travellers originate? However one answers the question of the sources of Acts, there is no doubt that the author's received traditions contained the travel motif. Like the travels of Jesus, apostolic itinerancy was a fact of the tradition. The first Christians had preserved the memory of an epic at the beginning. But nothing obliged Luke to make this an omnipresent theme of his narrative. The partial fading of the travel motif in the apocryphal *Acts* of apostles (as we shall see later) proves that Luke was not constrained to make geographical mobility a narrative theme of utmost importance. The narrative fixation on travel is, then, the author's choice.

In my opinion, this Lucan emphasis accords with the marked interest of Graeco-Roman society in those who travel. Contrary to the repeated affirmation that the travel theme emigrated from the Greek novel to the Acts of the Apostles,[9] I think that travel was a motif much more widespread in Hellenistic culture and endowed with an astonishing range of connotations. To explain the primordial role of the journey, it is not enough to invoke Abraham's nomadism (Gen. 12–13), the migration of Jacob's

---

[7] W. Radl has minutely compared Luke 9. 51 and Acts 19. 21–2 from the perspective of a typological relationship between Jesus and Paul (*Paulus und Jesus,* 1975, pp. 103–26).

[8] The rhetorical procedure of *syncrisis* has been presented in chapter 3: 'The unity of Luke–Acts: the task of reading'.

[9] R. I. Pervo has popularized this idea in his brilliant work, *Profit with Delight,* 1987.

sons to Egypt (Gen. 45–50) or the people of Israel's wanderings in the desert.[10] The Israelites always feared the sea; they remember that Jonah's flight was a fiasco and hope that at the end of history, the sea will no longer exist (Rev. 21. 1b). Nor is it sufficient to correlate Luke–Acts with the Greek novel or the *Lives* of the philosophers. In the world of the first century, the theme of travel constitutes a product for universal consumption, as is seen in the travel literature of this period. There it becomes clear that the idea of travel does not evoke everywhere the same expectations, the same voracity or the same fantasies. On which fund(s) of imagination about travel does Luke draw when he portrays his heroes as travellers? On which cultural representations does he graft his text?

My query can be defined as historico-literary. I shall deliberately leave aside genetic questions, for example, the origin of the 'we-sequences' (16. 10–17; 20. 5–15; 21. 1–18; 27. 1 – 28. 16)[11] or the literary links (which, in my view, cannot be found) between Luke and any Greek author. My intention is rather to situate the work addressed to Theophilus within the Graeco-Roman culture of travel which both the author and his readers inhabit. I wonder if, within this culture, one can identify patterns of the travel narratives, preconstructed representations, which might have inspired the author. One question progressively, during the course of my research, imposed itself: did the author of Acts merely pander to the taste of a readership fascinated by exoticism? Or did his theological instinct prevent him from simply 'surfing' on a trendy theme?

The present study will begin by specifying the narrative function of the journey theme in Acts. The second part will examine how the journey motif fits literarily into Hellenistic culture; criteria will be established, which will allow us to classify the abundant Graeco-Roman travel literature.[12] The third step will be to indicate the cultural matrix that animates the Lucan representation of the journey. The conclusion is on the memory of travel.

[10] So J. J. Navone, 'Journey Theme', 1972, pp. 616–19. He remarks with pertinence: 'the pervasive character of the journey motif in Luke–Acts is *one of the more intriguing aspects of Luke's theology*' (p. 616). The journey motif does not appear frequently in the writings of Hellenistic Judaism: see the journeys of Tobias in *Tobit* 6–7; 10–11, or of Joseph in *Jos. Asen.* The same scepticism is found in A. Denaux, 'Old Testament Models', 1997.

[11] With regard to this question, which scholars have not satisfactorily resolved, compare the contrasting views of J. Wehnert, *Wir-Passagen*, 1989, and S. E. Porter, 'We-Passages', 1994. I have put forward a narrative approach in chapter 1: 'How Luke wrote history' (see pp. 24–5).

[12] This aspect of my study is much indebted to the discussions and the friendly collaboration of Claude Calame of the Faculté des Lettres of the University of Lausanne. I mention this interdisciplinary exchange with much gratitude.

The narrative function of travel in the book of Acts

In his gospel, Luke narrates a journey (9. 51 – 19. 28). This is what A. D. Baum calls an 'integrated subgenre', a secondary element allied to the overall genre of the gospel.[13] In Acts, on the other hand, the author has given the role of a literary macro-structure to the journey motif. What I want to point out is that the journey is not only a recurring theme in the narrative, but it exercises a structuring and unifying function in the plot of the book of Acts. This macro-structure is signalled throughout the narrative by six indications.

First indication: Acts 1. 8b. The proleptic function given in the narrative to the promise of the Resurrected One confers on the geographical itinerary the value of a narrative programmme: 'you will be my witnesses in Jerusalem, in all Judaea and Samaria, and to the ends of the earth'. Witness and journey come together here, one being the mediation of the other. Clearly, the goal indicated (the ἔσχατον τῆς γῆς) is not Rome, where the Lucan narrative ends;[14] but the narrator has carefully reoriented the itinerary of Paul's mission in the direction of Rome, from 19. 21. Note that a similar rupture occurs in Luke 9. 51, where the geographical destination indicated for Jesus' journey (Jerusalem) is coupled with an objective that overlaps it: the ἀνάλημψις, that is, the elevation of Jesus at the Ascension (see Acts 1. 2, 11, 22; same word in 10. 16).[15] The suffering to come already comes within the horizon of the exaltation of the Lord.

Similarly, the declaration of the Risen One in Acts 1. 8b takes on an 'eschatological' dimension, since it goes beyond the Roman conclusion of the narrative by assigning to the Christian mission the task of going to the end of the earth. The Lucan narrative fits into this project, which remains open in the eyes of Luke, and for which the first period of the Church offers a partial and paradigmatic fulfilment. It is important to note here that, at the threshold of the narrative of Acts, the reader learns that the status of witness is linked to an itinerary which can be called limitless.

Second indication: the recurring link between mission and itinerancy. The link presented in Acts 1. 8b is repeated throughout the narrative.

---

[13] A. D. Baum, *Lukas als Historiker*, 1993, pp. 178–98.

[14] I have argued for a non-confusion between the promise of the Resurrected One in Acts 1. 8b and the geographical programme of Acts: see my article 'Magic and Miracles in the Acts of the Apostles' (forthcoming).

[15] On the ambivalent reading of ἀνάλημψις, see above pp. 50–1, and E. Mayer's *Reiseerzählung*, 1996, pp. 69–89.

Every missionary call is linked with an indication of movement: Philip in Samaria (Acts 8. 4–5, 26, 40); the vocation of Saul (9. 15, 28); Peter (10. 20, 23); Saul and Barnabas (11. 25–6); Paul and Barnabas (13. 2–4); the second missionary journey of Paul (15. 36–40); the last missionary journey of Paul (19. 21; 20. 22–3; 23. 11; 27. 24). A close examination shows that the link between missionary witness and itinerancy is embedded by the narrator in even the slightest details: Saul's conversion stops the apostle on the road to Damascus (9. 3a), then sets him back on the road (9. 8b, 25); the decisive meeting of Peter and Cornelius, orchestrated by God, creates coming and going between Caesarea and Joppa (10. 8–9, 17, 20, 23–5).

Third indication: the plurality of the travellers. Rosa Söder has noted that, in distinction from the apocryphal *Acts* of apostles, where the interest of the narrator is fixed on a personality and his travels, the journey theme in Acts is distributed among several characters.[16] It is only in chapter 13 that Paul and his companions, then Paul alone, become the exclusive vehicles of the mission. The narrative of Acts is not devoted to only one travelling hero; for Luke, to receive the call to spread the Word is to move and to cover territory.

Fourth indication: the itineraries. In distinction from the apocryphal *Acts* of apostles, where the motif of travel is of minor interest, and where the literary function seems essentially to connect the episodes,[17] the journey in the plot of Luke's Acts plays a very important role. Sometimes the author almost completely obscures the idea of movement, as in Acts 2–7 (the golden age of the Jerusalem community) and in Acts 24–6 (Paul is immobilized in the fortress in Caesarea), while, on the other hand, he frequently focuses on a journey and makes mobility the very theme of the narrative; this procedure comes in brief passages that function like summaries.[18]

[16] R. Söder, *Apokryphen Apostelgeschichten* [1932], 1969, p. 50.

[17] R. Söder is wrong at this point. She attributes a constitutive role to the journey motif in the apocryphal *Acts* of apostles: 'nimmt man sie heraus, zerfällt die ganze übrige Geschichte' (*Apokryphen Apostelgeschichten* [1932], 1969, p. 36). Differently from the Greek novels where the journey is a necessary ingredient in the plot, the heroes of the apocryphal Acts travel little (*Acts of Peter* 5; *Acts of Thomas* 3; 16–17; 68–71), or travel plays only a weak role (*Acts of Paul*; *Acts of Andrew*; *Acts of John*). See J.-D. Kaestli's criticism in F. Bovon *et alii*, *Actes apocryphes*, 1981, p. 64.

[18] 1. 8b (from Jerusalem to the extremity of the earth); 9. 1–9 (from Jerusalem to Damascus); 11. 19–20 (from Jerusalem to Antioch); 13. 4–6 (from Antioch to Cyprus); 13. 13–14. (from Cyprus to Antioch in Pisidia); 14. 21–6 (from Lystra to Antioch); 15. 3–4 (from Antioch to Jerusalem); 15. 41 – 16. 1 (from Antioch to Lystra); 16. 4–12 (from Lystra to Philippi); 17. 1, 10, 14–15 (from Philippi to Athens); 18. 18–23 (from Corinth to Ephesus); 19. 21–2 (from Ephesus to Jerusalem); 20. 1–6 (from Ephesus to Troas); 20. 13–16

A remark made by Martin Dibelius permits us once more to stress: the text of Acts presents a multitude of geographical names that have no repercussions on the narrative development, but only indicate the itinerary.[19] This is the case with, for example, 20.

13–15: 'We went ahead (προέρχεσθαι) and set sail (ἀνάγεσθαι) for Assos, intending to take Paul on board (ἀναλαμβάνειν) there; for he had made this arrangement to go by land (πεζεύειν) himself. When he met us (συμβάλλειν) in Assos, we took him on board and went to Mitylene. We sailed (ἀποπλεύεσθαι) from there, and on the following day we arrived opposite (ἄντικρυς) Chios. The next day we touched at (παραβάλλεσθαι) Samos and the day after that[20] came to Miletus.' A reading of this passage shows the extent and diversity of Luke's travel vocabulary, especially in his use of maritime language (here and 20. 6; 21. 1–3; 27. 1–44; 28. 11–13). This richness has no parallels in the novelistic literature of travel. The conclusion must be that inscribing the apostolic mission in the geography of the Empire takes on for Luke an importance that faithfulness to his sources and the necessity for narrative transitions, do not, by themselves, explain.

Fifth indication: the realism of the journey. Scenes of farewell, departure, meeting, choice of land or walking itineraries, stayovers, length of the journey, composition of the group of travellers, entry into cities, lodging conditions, navigational technique, behaviour in the face of dangers at sea – all these concrete parameters of travel unfold in the narrative of Acts. It is no exaggeration here to see the decision of the author, who could have excluded these travel details as Paul of Tarsus did in his epistles.[21] We must give Luke credit for interest in and (practical?) knowledge of travel customs.

Sixth indication: the precedent in salvation history. It is noteworthy that after the geographical stability of the first six chapters of Acts, in

---

(from Troas to Miletus); 21. 1–8 (from Miletus to Caesarea); 21. 15–17 (from Caesarea to Jerusalem); 23. 31–3 (from Jerusalem to Caesarea); 27. 1–44 (from Caesarea to Malta); 28. 11–15 (from Malta to Rome). To this inventory, one can add 14. 22, where the distress of the itinerant missionary is interpreted theologically (also see 9. 16 after 9. 15).

[19] M. Dibelius, *Studies in the Acts*, 1956, p. 199. L. C. A. Alexander has taken up the toponomy of Acts in 'Narrative Maps', 1995, esp. pp. 46–8.

[20] The manuscript D carries: 'after remaining at Trogyllion'.

[21] To be convinced, and by examining only the Pauline section of Acts, it is enough to compare the restraint of the apostle concerning his travels (1 Thess. 2. 17 – 3. 5; Phil. 4. 10–16; 2 Cor. 7. 5–7; 13. 1–3; Rom. 15. 22–9) with several passages of Acts: 20. 36–8; 21. 5–7, 12–14 (farewells); 13. 4; 16. 6–12; 19. 21; 20. 2–3, 13–15 (itinerary choices); 19. 21–3; 20. 6, 16; 28. 12 (stopovers); 20. 6, 15 (length of travel); 13. 4; 20. 3–6 (composition of the group); 18. 1–3; 21. 8–10 (lodging conditions); 27. 1 – 28. 13 (nautical technique). A detailed comparison of Pauline and Lucan toponymics can be found in L. C. A. Alexander's 'Narrative Maps', 1995, pp. 20–2 and 31–45.

Jerusalem, the impulse to mobility is set going by a persecution related to Stephen's martyrdom (7. 54 – 8. 4). But what is contained in the speech of Stephen which exasperated the Sanhedrin? Stephen offered a reading of the history of the fathers, from Abraham's call to leave his country to Solomon's construction of the Temple *via* the sojourn in Egypt and the Exodus (7. 2–53). The continuous theme of the discourse is none other than the wandering of the people led by their God; it culminates in the prohibition on localizing God 'in houses made with human hands' (7. 48; cf. 49–50). In other words, from the point of view of the plot, Stephen's speech gives theological legitimacy to the itinerancy of Christian mission.

I have noted six indications that signal the narrator's interest in travel as such: the programmatic significance of 1. 8b, the link between witness and travel, the plurality of the travellers, the thematizing of movement, the attention paid to the *realia* of travelling and the anchoring in salvation history. The encompassing and recurrent character of the journey motif indicates that we have here a literary macro-structure, which places travel at the very core of the plot. To be specific, the book of Acts is not a 'travel narrative', but a narrative of the apostolic *praxeis*, whose witness to Christ is unavoidably mediated by itinerancy. The reader of Acts knows that the Master, between Galilee and Judaea, provided the model for this journeying.

However, if we compare Philip's itinerant mission (8. 5, 26, 40) with Saul's conversion on the Damascus road (9. 3) or the documented precision of the itineraries, we notice that the use of the travel motif draws on a wide variety of significations and symbols. From what domain of significations does the author of Acts draw? Furthermore, can we define a literary genre of 'travel narrative'?

Images of travel in Graeco-Roman culture

Homer and Herodotus powerfully informed the Greek imagination concerning the journey. If the historian of Halicarnassus is recognized as the father of Hellenistic historiography and ethnography, Homer's work incontestably played the role of archetype in Greek travel literature. On the one hand, the *Odyssey* offers the first literary declaration of a (fictional)[22] travel narrative. On the other hand, the use of Homeric poetry as a school

---

[22] The debate about the historicity of the Homeric journeys began in antiquity. Strabo, in the prolegomena to his *Geography* (1.2.9), mentions the polemic on this subject by two Alexandrian geographers, Eratosthenes and Hipparchus ('As a skilful artist which melts with gold and silver, so he [the poet] added to the true peripateiai a fabulous element'). On

manual in antiquity guaranteed the perpetuation of the model up to the Christian era. As the oldest and best-known writing, how does the epic of Ulysses function as a model? One can already detect here the ingredients that will orient the subsequent literature and explain readers' interest in travel narratives.

(a) The Homeric text presents long geographical descriptions (Strabo will give Homer the title, 'the first geographer'); but this geography has a social or, rather, anthropological objective.[23] The main intention is not to describe the places, but to present the manners and customs that allow readers to situate themselves by differentiation. Exoticism fits into this perspective on identity. The image of the other provides an image of oneself.

(b) The narrator's point of view is always situated; it is from his categories and his value system that the other is evaluated and judged.[24]

(c) The journey to the edge of the world (the *eschatiai*) gives rise to a reflection on civilization. In the face of barbarian extreme, the Greek traveller is led to question himself concerning the progress and deficiencies of his own culture.[25]

(d) The *Odyssey* sets in place the structure of the *nostos*, which is a circular journey. In this case it is the heroes' return home from the war of Troy. This structure of the return home is found in the Greek novel which will add to it the motif of separation; love takes on the role of the compulsion to be reunited.

The descendants of Homer turn out to be numerous. The geographical dimension is taken up in the form of travel itineraries (the *Periplus*), while Porphyry and the Pythagoreans submit the Homeric text to an allegorical reading (the journey of the soul). The exploration narratives are clearly modelled on Herodotus. Historians and poets commemorate the era of the founders of colonies. In the biographies of their masters, the great philosophical schools (Platonic, Pythagorean, Cynic) cultivate the initiatory value of itinerancy. There is no Greek novel that does not tell of the travels of its heroes.[26] Finally, in the Roman period, the attraction of the far distant creates a flow of literature, where there is in various proportions a mixing of the data at the writers' disposal, the power of their imagination, and their personal memories. The travel motif becomes the bearer of strong symbolic connotations, which deal with the discovery of

this subject see G. Chiarini, 'Nostoi e labirinto', 1985, pp. 11–35; S. Saïd, 'Homère', 1992, pp. 5–83.

[23] I draw on the pertinent remarks by C. Jacob, *Géographie*, 1991 ('L'*Odyssée* apparaît ainsi comme l'un des textes fondateurs de l'anthropologie grecque . . .'), quotation p. 30.

[24] When he comes to the island of the Cyclops, Ulysses announces to his companions that he will 'go and find what manner of people live here. Are they violent and barbarous, without justice? Or are they hospitable and godfearing?' (*Od.* 9.172–6).

[25] On the island of the sun (*Od.* 12.260–453), it is Ulysses' companions who behave as savages, massacring the sun god's cattle, which then brings down the anger of the gods on them, materialized by a storm from which only Ulysses escapes.

[26] For further detail, see below pp. 241–6.

the other, the quest for knowledge, the flight of the imagination and the course of life.

How to classify?

Can we classify this proliferation of literature, which deals, in various ways, with the travel theme? We have already understood that the Greek novel exercises no monopoly over this theme. Frankly, none of the attempts to identify a literary genre which could be called 'journey narrative' have succeeded.[27] The most we can do is to follow Thornton, who proposes to differentiate between travel journal, travel chronicle and travel narrative (*Reisetagebuch, Reisebericht, Reiseerzählung*).[28] This classification is made according to the degree of literary elaboration. Fragments of travel journals have come down to us, such as the journal of Theophanus, dated between AD 317 and 323, which relate, in a terse manner, itineraries, halts, distances covered and purchases of the group.[29] It is not out of the question that the author of Acts had access to such a document, which could be called a proto-narrative, about Paul's expeditions. Beyond this raw material, the chronicle is a more elaborate narrative, written after the trip either to preserve the memories or to act as official archives; the *Periplus* of Hanno the Carthaginian on the coast of West Africa, probably from the sixth century BC, is one of the oldest preserved. The third group (and here we see the limitation of the proposed classification) comprises all the literary uses of the travel motif (real or fictive).

My proposition is to adopt as the criterion the function accorded in the writing to the travel motif, which leads to a taxonomy of six categories: the itinerary, the founding of a colony, the journey of exploration, the novelistic journey, the itinerancy of the philosopher and the path of initiation. These six encompass all of Graeco-Roman literature about travel. The order adopted implies a degree of decreasing materiality, and, symmetrically, an increasing order of symbolization; it leads from cartographic inventory to the journey of the soul.

[27] See K. Berger, 'Hellenistische Gattungen', 1984, pp. 1274–81; from the same author, *Formgeschichte*, 1984, pp. 276–7. The absence of any formal criterion is also striking in A. D. Baum, *Lukas als Historiker*, 1993, pp. 155–77.

[28] C. J. Thornton, *Zeuge des Zeugen*, 1991, pp. 295–9. His classification allows a distinguishing of the *Periplus* (second category), but groups all the rest of the literature in a third group.

[29] L. C. A. Alexander drew my attention to this text published under the title P. Ryl. 616–51 in *Catalogue of the Greek and Latin Papyri in the John Rylands Library Manchester*, C. H. Roberts and E. G. Turner, eds., IV, 1952, pp. 104–57. The document is commented on by L. Casson, *Travel*, 1974, p. 177, pp. 190–3.

(a) *The Periplus.* At a practical level, the *Periplus* describe itineraries, while the *Periegeseis* offer the equivalent of tourist guidebooks.[30] The oldest are from Ctesias of Cnidus (fifth century BC) and Eudoxus of Cnidus (fourth century BC), and the most famous is the *Description of Greece* by Pausanias (second century BC). These practical guides written for the traveller leave little space for feelings. Their aim is pragmatic. The reader is educated by ethnographic notes or reminders of history. The coastal *Periplus* of the Greeks find their counterparts in the *Itineraria romana*, the routes known from the first century onwards. Initially, they were to help travellers and merchants, indicating the main roads and stopovers; but, during the Empire, they were destined for a growing public of armchair tourists, who used these guides to give themselves an imaginary trip around the Mediterranean.[31]

(b) *The founding of colonies ('ktiseis').* Whether the colonization is of political-religious order or whether it takes the form of a military expedition, the foundation account harks back to the pioneers who were at the origin of the *apoikia* (migration). Troy, Carthage, Thera, Cyrene, Taranto are among the cities whose founding accounts commemorate the circumstances of the separation from the motherland (often a social tension),[32] and especially the action of the gods in leading the colonists in their enterprise.[33] There is a process of 'hero-making' at work in this rereading of the past, where myth and history intertwine and fact and legend interweave.[34]

(c) *The journey of exploration.* A curiosity for new worlds and an appetite for discovering unknown customs are at the origin of the narratives of exploration. The classic point of reference is Herodotus of Halicarnassus and his *Historiae*. The perspective adopted is ethnographic, not to say ethnocentric; for if these writings have the merit of contextualizing foreign cultures (Egyptian, Libyan, Mesopotamian, etc.), reality is perceived through a Greek/Barbarian dualism which structures the world-view.[35] Christian Jacob speaks of a 'rhetoric of alterity' to describe Herodotus' manner of shaping the singularity of non-Greek usages

---

[30] See G. Marasco, *Viaggi*, 1978, pp. 85–91; M.-F. Baslez, *Etranger*, 1984, pp. 255–60. A good overview of this literary genre can be found in O. A. W. Dilke, *Maps*, 1985, esp. in his chapter 6.

[31] Aelius Aristides, a second-century orator, offers a good example of travel through reading in his *Oratio* XLIV.

[32] See F. Trotta, 'Madrepatria', 1991, pp. 37–66, esp. pp. 43–4.

[33] Documents gathered by F. Létoublon, *Fonder une cité*, 1987.

[34] Hero-making and symbolization through narrative have been analysed by C. Calame in his remarkable study, *Mythe et histoire*, 1996.

[35] See the remarks of M.-F. Baslez, *Etranger*, 1984, pp. 254–60.

in his ethnographic description.[36] In reaction to this, from the second century BC, several non-Greek writers borrowed the literary genre established by Herodotus in order to present their own culture and its past, exploiting this literary form to their own advantage and with apologetic aims.[37]

Agartharchides of Cnidus (second century BC), with his periplus *Events in Europe, Events in Asia*, and *On the Erythraean Sea*, is a good example of this exploration of alterity, where observation gives place to the fantastic as soon as it approaches the *eschatiai*.[38] There, at the extreme of what we call narratives of exploration, we can place the narratives of utopian journeys where attraction of the imaginary asserts itself. Among these pioneers of science fiction, we find Euhemerus of Messena (around 300 BC) and his wonderful island of Panchaea, where the Greek gods live like humans; at the same period, Hecateus of Abdera imagines his enigmatic Hyperboreans and Jambulus recounts his fictive expedition to the seven islands of the sun; the romance of Alexander draws on the journey of Onesicritus to India to encounter the wisdom of the Gymnosophists; around AD 180, Lucian of Samosata offers a pastiche by editing his pseudo-'True Story'.[39] Originating in the philosophical tradition (Plato and Atlantis), this utopian novel quickly acquires a social-critical dimension, using the fictional narrative to describe truly alternative societies.[40] The favourite destination of these utopian voyages is the island on which the traveller (preferably shipwrecked) disembarks.[41]

(d) *The novelistic journey.* It is understandable that comparative literary studies began by comparing the work *ad Theophilum* and the Greek novel. For in the novel, as in Acts, travel is an indispensable ingredient

---

[36] *Géographie*, 1991, pp. 64ff.

[37] I mention Berossus and his *Babyloniaka*, Manethon and his *Aigyptiaka*, and the historiographers of Hellenistic Judaism (Demetrius, Artapanus, Eupolemus and Josephus). On this subject, see G. E. Sterling, *Historiography and Self-Definition*, 1992.

[38] See below, pp. 251–2, the example taken from the description of the pillage of the Ichthyophagi in the treatise *On the Erythraean Sea*.

[39] Plato, *Timaeus* 24e–25d; *Critias* 113d–121c. Onesicritus: see Strabo, *Geography* 15,1,63–5. Euhemerus and his *Sacred Record*; see Diodorus Siculus, *Historical Library* 5. 41–3. Jambulus: see Diodorus Siculus, *ibid.*, 2. 55–60.

[40] On the utopian literature, which constitutes a *novum* in the Hellenistic travel literature, see H. Kuch's study, 'Funktionswandlungen', 1989, pp. 52–62. C. Mossé, 'Utopies égalitaires', 1969. R. Villgradter, F. Krey, eds., *Utopische Roman*, 1973, esp. pp. 45–68.

[41] An example of this enthusiasm for utopia: the popular story called 'Account of the Shipwreck' (also called 'The Island of the Serpent'), as originally from Pharaonic Egypt, where the shipwrecked man is instructed by a god-serpent about divine mysteries and magical practices (published by E. Lefebvre, *Romans et contes égyptiens*, 1949, pp. 29–40).

in the narrative plot. It is the journey that separates the heroes, furthers their quests and orchestrates the final reunion, as we see in Chariton's *Chaereas and Callirhoë*, Achildes Tatius' *Leucippe and Cleitophon* or the *Aethiopica* of Heliodorus. Longus' *Daphnis and Chloe* is an exception, because the journey is interior.[42] By showing how the hero survives in a hostile world, the novel joins the daily experience of the reader and offers a place of identification. The travel novel is close to the narrative of exploration, especially in its geographical digressions,[43] even if its motivation for movement is not the same: travelling serves the quest of the hero, who must overcome trials inflicted on him, most often by Destiny.[44] Nevertheless, the two categories share a taste for the exotic and the capacity to broaden the reader's horizon of experience; both participate in a form of cultural expansionism.[45] Travel functions here as a resonance chamber for human existence: as a factor that separates the heroes, it also makes their reunion possible, as embodied in the inevitable happy ending expected by the reader.[46]

(e) *The itinerancy of the philosopher or the missionary.* 'It was typical of a philosopher or miracle-worker to be itinerant.'[47] Rosa Söder's statement corresponds to the picture given by the first missionary aretalogies and the *Lives* of philosophers: philosopher and healer are itinerants. Whether it be Pythagoras described by Iamblichus or by Diogenes Laertius, or Apollonius of Tyana related by Philostratus, both practised the nomadism of sages. Actually, their itinerancy has more than one function: on the one hand, it is an instrument in their quest for knowledge; and on the other hand, it allows the diffusion of their doctrine and the implementation of their miraculous abilities.[48] Even more

---

[42] On the Greek novel, in addition to the classical studies of E. Rhode and B. E. Perry, see the excellent collective work plublished by H. Kuch, *Antike Roman*, 1989; B. P. Reardon, *Courants littéraires*, 1971, pp. 309–403; T. Hägg, *Novel in Antiquity*, 1983; N. Holzberg, *Antike Roman*, 1986; R. I. Pervo, *Profit with Delight*, 1987, pp. 86–114; M. Fusillo, *Naissance du roman*, 1991; F. Létoublon, *Lieux communs*, 1993; G. F. Schmelling, ed., *Novel*, 1996.

[43] P. Grimal shows that, differently from the exploration narrative, the novel does not describe the barbarian world, but uses it as a narrative framework in order to contrast with it the Hellenism of the heroes: 'Formation', 1992, p. 14.

[44] The role of the religious in the novel has been studied (in a minimalistic sense) by I. Stark, 'Religiöse Elemente', 1989, pp. 135–49.

[45] This expression comes from A. Billault, *Création romanesque*, 1991, p. 284; concerning the journey, see pp. 191–9.

[46] Following H. Kuch, the 'happy end' was 'jedenfalls gattungsverbindlich schon für die Reiseromane aus der Anfangsphase des Romangenus. Von weiter und gefärlicher Fahrt, auf die sich die Autoren begeben haben wollten, kehrten sie alle ohne Ausnahme wohlbehalten zurück' (H. Kuch, 'Funktionswandlungen', 1989, p. 76).

[47] R. Söder, *Apokryphen Apostelgeschichten* [1932], 1969, p. 35.

[48] So M. Sassi, 'Viaggio', 1991.

fundamentally, itinerancy becomes an ideal where the alterity and the freedom of the sage is asserted to the world. A symbolism is announced here that my last category will develop: the initiatory significance of the journey.

(f) *The path of initiation.* The metaphorization of the path[49] is exploited by the authors for whom movement becomes an image of the search for the True and the Beautiful. The erotic quest is diverted here into a philosophical register and becomes a desire for truth. It seems that this symbolism of the path goes back to Hesiod (*Works*, 287–8), who poses the duality of the flat path leading to evil and the difficult path leading to virtue. Following this line of symbolism, we find Pindar and his rich metaphor of the path[50] or Theocritus, whose Seventh Idyll allegorizes the scenario of the journey in the name of a poetry of inspiration. The final point of this trajectory is the celestial journey of the visionary and the transports of the soul.[51]

The interest of this taxonomy is to bring clarity to the vast field of significations in Hellenistic literature from which the travel theme draws. However, one must keep in mind that the six categories mentioned above are not entirely distinct from each other. A partial overlapping has appeared between narrative of exploration and the novel; the same could be said of philosophical itinerancy and the path of initiation. When the author of the *Acts of Andrew and Matthias* (a second-century apocryphal narrative) relates the journey of his heroes to the country of the cannibals, he exploits both the taste for the exotic, cultivated by the utopian journey of exploration, and the attraction to adventure stimulated by the novel.

Nevertheless, the classification adopted shows that the travel motif is perceived in various ways according to the literary corpus that uses it, whether it constitutes the theme of the account (our first categories) or the frame of the action (last categories). The *Periplus* respond to the material needs of the traveller. The narrative of founding a colony invokes the conquest of unknown lands and cultural expansion. In the narrative of exploration, travelling awakens curiosity for the exotic. For novel readers, the journey is a synonym for risk and the quest for happiness. For the *Lives* of the philosophers, travel fits into the perspective

---

[49] On the symbolic connotations of the path in Greek literature, the best study remains O. Becker's *Bild des Weges*, 1937. See also B. Snell, *Découverte* (1946), 1994, pp. 315–31.

[50] O. Becker, *Bild des Weges*, 1937, pp. 50–100.

[51] C. Kappler differs by proposing to include all accounts of heavenly voyage in the definition of apocalyptic. C. Kappler, ed., *Apocalypses et voyages*, 1987. For the gnostic trajectory, see K. Rudolph, 'Gnostische Reisen', 1994, pp. 493–503.

of communication of knowledge. Finally, the path may be a place of initiation.

The semantics of the journey in the book of Acts

To which field of the imagination of the journey is the reader of Acts invited? I shall formulate at once the result to which my examination of the Lucan narrative has led me: the semantics of journey that emerges from Acts does not coincide with any of the categories mentioned above. In other words, the author of Acts can, certainly with different emphases, nevertheless draw widely from the whole of the 'journey' theme as it is deployed in Hellenistic culture. The journey is therefore a polyvalent theme in Acts. This is not surprising if one remembers the role matrix that the *Periplus* of Ulysses played in Graeco-Roman culture. Ulysses' journeys express different facets of the theme, which Greek literature will take up more selectively later: exploration, cultural expansion, danger, initiatory quest. Yet Ulysses' itinerancy is not that of a philosopher, but of a human.[52]

This result must now be established in detail.

The narrative of Christian conquest

The first analogy suggested by comparing the travel literature and the book of Acts concerns the narratives of the founding of colonies (the *ktiseis*). At first sight, the dissemination of the Word from Jerusalem and the colonization of a region from a city correspond to close, if not similar themes. The care the author of Acts takes from 19. 21 onwards to point the itinerary toward Rome, the unrelenting progression of the narrative in this direction from 23. 11, and the dramatization of the final voyage (27. 1 – 28. 13) reveal that Rome represents the goal of a strategy of missionary conquest. We should remember that, if the decision goes back to Paul (19. 21), it obeys the vocation received at Damascus (9. 15). As for the completion, the ending of Acts is eloquent: the apostle prisoner can proclaim there the βασιλεία τοῦ θεοῦ and the Lord Jesus Christ (28. 31a); the universality of his audience (πάντας τοὺς εἰσπορευομένους πρὸς αὐτόν, 28. 30) is the pledge, in the eyes of Luke, of another universality, still to come, the Christian universality.[53] The prediction heard at Damascus about Paul's vocation to the Gentiles is fulfilled (cf. 9. 15 and 28. 28).

---

[52] This point of view is defended by P. Scarpi, *Fuga*, 1992, pp. 150–215.
[53] I have defended this reading above, pp. 223–4 and 227.

Numerous affinities

However, the correspondence with narratives of the founding of a colony go far beyond thematic affinity. F. Trotta has identified six traditional motifs in founding narratives:[54] (1) the reasons for leaving (often a στάσις, social tension between two groups); (2) the search for a leader who maintains good relations with the motherland; (3) the consultation of an oracle; (4) the preparations for departure; (5) the journey; (6) the disembarkation (reconnaissance of the region and conflict with the native population). Trotta stresses the decisive role of the third motif: consulting an oracle is an obligatory step in any colonizing enterprise.[55] It can take the form of permission to leave, of a saying to be interpreted in the right manner, or of a precise indication of the site to be colonized. Without this oracular direction, the expedition is destined to fail. For proof, we can cite the fate of Dorieus. Herodotus tells of his misadventures, after landing in Libya without having asked at Delphi for the help of Apollo.[56] The historian of Halicarnassus, in both of his two divergent versions of the founding of Cyrene by Battus and his companions (*Histories* 4.145–58), underlines the decisive role of the oracle of Delphi.[57]

The crucial narrative function of the oracle of Delphi in Herodotus' text has been clearly brought out by Claude Calame: 'In the course of the Herodotian narrative, the oracle contributes in some way to determining the action. It is the oracle that orients the action by assigning it a goal and a limit.'[58] In semiotic language, Apollo assumes the position of 'Dispatcher of the action' and the head of the colonial expedition becomes the 'operating Subject'. Pindar[59] subscribes to this position in his lyric narration of the foundation of Cyrene (the colonial expedition fulfils an

---

[54] 'Madrepatria', 1991, pp. 43–50.

[55] For what follows, see *ibid.*, pp. 45–6.

[56] *Histories* 5.42. Dorieus, son of the king of Sparta, but excluded from the throne, goes to Libya to found a colony under the direction of guides from Thera. But he has not consulted the oracle of Apollo in Delphi. For Herodotus, this explains the fact that the Spartans, after having ejected the natives, are forced to go home after two years.

[57] Herodotus relates successively a version from Thera, where the invitation to found a city in Libya is formulated by the Pythia on the occasion of a sacrifice in Delphi, then a version from Cyrene, more social, according to which the colonization was entrusted to the bastard Battus when he went to consult the oracle of Delphi about his stuttering. See C. Calame, 'Mythe, récit épique et histoire', 1988, pp. 107–16. On the same subject: J. Kirchberg, *Funktion der Orakel*, 1965, pp. 51–8.

[58] 'Mythe, récit épique et histoire', 1988, p. 120. From the same author, see *Mythe et histoire*, 1996, pp. 145–53. Another analysis of the Herodotian mantic is in E. Lévy, who insists on the responsibility of the individual in the interpretation of the oracle ('Devins et oracles', 1997).

[59] *Pythian Odes* IV, see V and IX.

oracle of the Pythia, which itself fulfils a prediction of Medea); but Pindar specifies that the Pythian oracle was αὐτόματος (*Pythian Odes* IV.60), that is, it was spontaneously emitted, anticipating the whole project of colonization. In the book of Acts, the narrative function of divine predictions is no longer in need of demonstration (1. 8; 1. 16; 9. 15–16; 13. 2; 16. 6–10; 21. 11; 27. 25; etc.).[60] Two nocturnal revelations reaffirm the divine will concerning Rome as the destination (23. 11; 27. 24). But if one looks again at the six traditional motifs identified by Trotta, it appears that the end of Acts puts them all in place. (1) *Departure*: it is provoked by a conflict between Paul and the Jewish authorities (21. 17 – 25. 12). (2) *The leader*: Paul, the Damascus road convert, incarnates the theological link between Judaism and Christianity. (3) *The oracle*: divine revelations play a role similar to that of the Pythian oracle, except that their interpretation is not disputable from the narrator's point of view. (4) *The preparations for the journey*: they are briefly mentioned (27. 1–2). (5) *The journey* is related at great length in 27. 3–44. (6) *Disembarkation*: the welcome in Rome is ambivalent: positive on the part of the 'brothers' (28. 14–15), negative on the part of the majority of the Jewish delegation (28. 24).

Acts 16

Acts 28 is not the only section of the narrative concerned with such a correspondence. The similarity is evident if we examine in detail the narrative of the evangelization of Philippi (16. 6–40). The journey follows an internal crisis of the church (15. 5–21), whose resolution is concretized in the sending out of Paul and Silas (15. 22–41). The preparations include the choice and the circumcision of Timothy (16. 1–3). The destination is announced by a triple divine intervention (16. 6–9), concluded by a vision given to the leader and requiring interpretation (16. 10). Then there is a brief description of the journey (16. 11). The entry into Philippi (16. 12), Alexander the Great's capital, represents the first Pauline breakthrough into mainland Greece.[61] After the conversion of Lydia, which can be compared with a fourth intervention of God ('The Lord opened her heart to listen eagerly to what was said by Paul', 16. 14b), the 'conflict with the natives' breaks out when the apostle exorcises the slave-girl. The crisis,

---

[60] See J. T. Squires, *Plan of God*, 1993, pp. 121ff.

[61] Neither the geopolitical importance of this expedition nor the irony of the 'inverted colonization' in this emblematic city would have escaped the Greek reader: from Asia Minor to mainland Greece, this is the inverted trajectory of the *apoikia* that Paul and his companions follow.

dragged into the marketplace (16. 19), results in the imprisonment of the missionaries and their miraculous deliverance.[62] Is not the church in Lydia's house, where Paul and Silas take leave of the 'brothers' (16. 40), comparable to a colony? If so, we cannot repress the impression that the narratives of the founding of a colony function in the background of the episode as a preconstructed model especially directed to the reader.

The ending of Acts

Finally, one gets the impression that, as in the accounts of *ktiseis*, Luke at the end of his book (28. 16–31) recounts how Christianity freed itself from its birthplace, Jerusalem, in order to acquire its new place, the Empire, as concretized by its capital. This literary pattern leads us to understand the definite orientation of the narrative in the direction of Rome. However, the traditional model of founding narratives is modified. Luke's geography is theological: Rome is not a colony, but the new centre of diffusion for the Gospel. The welcome of the 'brothers' (28. 14–15) replaces the native hostility, the role of refusal having passed to the Jewish delegation that met the apostle. Paul's statement in 28. 28 signals that after this repeated refusal by Judaism, a page turns in Christian evangelism; but relations with the 'mother religion' (in absence of a mother land) are not yet terminated.[63]

A novel of adventure and exploration

Richard Pervo has skilfully compared the Acts of the Apostles and ancient novels as narrative entertainment. His argument relies on the similar literary and rhetorical procedures used in both: juxtaposition of scenes, suspense, burlesque, pathos, humor, irony, and so on.[64] Danger at sea is a subject appreciated by Greek novelists and their readers,[65] and Luke was not insensitive to this; he did, however, prefer the storm (ch. 27)[66] to attacking pirates, which was another success of the novel genre.

[62] The various aspects of this captivating scene cannot be dealt with here. I. Richter Reimer brings together the two figures of Lydia and the slave-girl under the theme of the liberation of women (*Women*, 1995, pp. 175–94). H. J. Klauck has analysed the confrontation to pagan religiousity (*Magie und Heidentum*, 1996, pp. 77–87). On the reasons for this exorcism, see my article 'Magic and Miracles in the Acts of the Apostles' (forthcoming).

[63] Concerning the opening of the 'Israel file', at the end of Acts, see pp. 221–6.

[64] R. I. Pervo, *Profit with Delight*, 1987, pp. 12–85.

[65] See F. Létoublon, *Lieux communs* 1993, pp. 64–5, pp. 175–80 and A. Billault, *Création romanesque*, 1991, pp. 195–97.

[66] Among the novels: *Aethiopica* V.22.7; V.27.1–7: *Leucippe and Cleitophon* III.1–5; *Satyricon* 114–15; *Chaereas and Callirhoë*. III.3 The model can be found in the *Odyssey*

Where Pervo is not convincing is in his attempt to classify Acts under the label (unknown in antiquity) of 'historical novel';[67] for the procedures he highlights are not absent from Graeco-Roman historiography, and they do not provide a pertinent criterion of distinction from historical monographs. I shall pursue this point in order to show how the narrative of Acts differs from the novelistic journey and is closer to the narrative of exploration developed by geographers and Hellenistic historians. My demonstration deals with three points.

The realism of the journey

The first point is *Luke's realism in narrating the journey.* This is shown concretely in the precision of the itineraries and the often detailed explanation of the means of travel. I have already noted this. Such documentary care is completely alien to the Greek novel, which only mentions such details for the sake of their narrative potential; its concern for verisimilitude is weak. Yet if we turn to the apocryphal *Acts* of apostles, we immediately perceive that they follow the track of the novel; I have already pointed out the virtual absence of the journey motif from the *Acts of Peter, Acts of Thomas* and *Acts of John.*[68] As for the *Acts of Paul and Thecla*, brief notices[69] allow us to understand that movement is not a motif that the author has narrativized. Furthermore, differently from the canonical Acts, it is impossible to reconstruct geographically the route of the apostle in this writing.

Leucippe and Cleitophon, the novel of Achilles Tatius, offers a fascinating parallel to the shipwreck narrative in Acts 27: the same narrative tension, the same use of nautical jargon to increase the pathos of the scene, the same happy ending for the hero of the account (III.1–5). In a more compact style, Luke is as gifted as a Tatius. However, this (unique) parallel *a contrario* draws attention to the itineraries in the Acts of the Apostles that are less narrativized. What can be concluded about Luke's

---

Book 5 (narrator) and Book 7 (taken over by Ulysses). For a detailed comparison, motif by motif, between Acts 27 and the Greek novel, see S. M. Praeder, 'Narrative Voyage', 1980, pp. 227–56.

[67] R. I. Pervo, *Profit with Delight*, 1987, pp. 115–35. I have defended this critique in chapter 2: 'A narrative of beginnings' (see pp. 28–9).

[68] See above, p. 237, n. 17.

[69] These accounts are extremely concise, without comment on or even description of the movement: Titus 'followed the royal road which leads to Lystra' (*Acts of Paul* 3); Paul 'came into Antioch' (26); Thecla 'left for Myra' (40); Thecla 'went to Iconium' (62). Itinerancy serves as a loose link between the scenes which, beyond geography, can be read separately without problem.

writing? Such a concern for documentary precision is clearly closer to the *Periplus* and the narrative of exploration than to the novel. The concern with detail and the credibility of the narrative signal the intention of historiographical documentary.

As to *the origin of the Lucan documentation*, one may hesitate. If we refuse to make Luke an eyewitness of the events he recounts,[70] we might think of the author's experiential and book-learned knowledge of travel; or, according to Roland Barthes' formula, should we speak of a literary construction with an 'effet de réel' (realistic effect)? Whatever the origin, *the theological effect* of this documentary concern should not be neglected: it indicates a positive relationship with Roman society, which is translated into a confidence (not without criticism)[71] in its institutions, a knowledge of the efficiency of its network of communication, and the possibilities of movement it offers. Luke is content to present a world where travel is possible, where words and people circulate, where in spite of the risks and thanks to the providence of God, missionaries arrive safely at their destinations. It is in this world that Christianity, which is only at the beginning of its expansion, is encouraged to live and to spread in all directions.

Attraction to the exotic

The second point of my demonstration is *attraction to the exotic*.[72] Several scenes in Acts clearly lend themselves to an interest in the exotic, which the literature of exploration had planted in the minds of its readership.

Agartharchides' treatise, *On the Erythraean Sea*[73] provides a good example of the Graeco-Roman readership's attraction to the *eschatiai*. During his periplus, the author descibes the tribe of the Ichthyophagi (Photius 449a.30–451a.46; Diodorus 3.15–22), a clan that has 'neither cities, nor fields, nor the basic rudiments of technical imagination' (Photius 448b.31).

The absence of socialization, together with the adoption of animal postures, indicates a state of primitive humanity for the Greek mind. 'They go about entirely naked as do their women; procreation of children is done in common, like herds of cattle' (Diodorus 3.15; Photius 449a.25–6). 'Besides the physical perception of pleasure and pain, they have not the least notion of good and evil' (Diodorus 3.15,1–2; Photius 449a.31). Evidently, for Agartharchides, the clan of the Ichthyophagi corresponds to the golden age, before the arrival of civilizing heroes; but this golden age is described with

[70] This view is still maintained by B. M. Rapske, 'Travel and Shipwreck', 1994.

[71] R. J. Cassidy has (too) forcefully demonstrated this point in his study, *Society and Politics*, 1987. On the problematic of relations with the Empire, see chapter 4: 'A Christianity between Jerusalem and Rome'.

[72] This point has been brought out by R. I. Pervo, *Profit with Delight*, 1987, pp. 69–72.

[73] The text is transmitted by Photius, *Bibliotheca*, 441a–460b and by Diodorus Siculus, *Historical Library* 3.11–48. On the author, see A. Dihle, 'Hellenistischen Ethnographie', 1962; H. Verdin, 'Agartharchide de Cnide', 1990; C. Jacob, *Géographie*, 1991, pp. 133–46.

envy, because it has a consciousness of happiness that civilization no longer possesses. 'Whereas the way of life we are used to consists as much in the superfluous as in the necessary, the Ichthyophagi of whom I have spoken have excluded ... all that is useless, and they lack nothing necessary' (Photius 451b.11ff.).

This is a beautiful expression of the Hellenistic nostalgia that is often present when historiographers describe the lands and the people of the ends of the earth. On these geographical borders, we can say that we are also at the borders of narratives of exploration and literature of utopia.

Let us return to the narrative of Acts: several accounts evoke the magic of the borders. The meeting of Philip with the Ethiopian eunuch (8. 26–40) echoes, for the reader, the wonders of Ethiopia and the court of Candace. The baroque scene at Lystra (14. 11–18), where Barnabas and Paul are confused with Zeus and Hermes (whom the crowd acclaims in the Lycaonian language! 14. 11), corresponds to the astonishment of the Greek tourist faced with the strange customs of Barbarians.

The height of the picturesque is reached in 28. 1–10, on the isle of Malta (an island is the favourite location of utopian novels). The Maltese (explicitly called βάρβαροι by the narrator, v. 2) welcome Paul and his shipwrecked companions; faced with the miracle of the viper that spares the apostle, they cry out: 'he is a god!' (28. 6). Differently from the episode in Lystra (14. 14–15), Luke does not correct the false confession of the Maltese. Why this difference? In my opinion, Luke plays on the strangeness of the location. The narrative function of the episode, within the plot of Acts 27–8, is, on the one hand, to sanction the innocence of the apostle as shown by the saving of the ship, and, on the other hand, to prefigure the welcome Christian missionaries receive in distant lands.[74] While the delegates of the Jews err (28. 24–5), the reaction of the islanders, aberrant in its formulation, is correct in its attitude; in their categories, they perceived that the apostle was a medium of the divine.[75] Luke here connects with the contemporary attraction for remote lands, the borders, the ends of the earth. Is this not the lure already active in the programmatic statement in 1. 8b? In this sense, the episode in Malta anticipates, in a narrative manner, the ἔσχατον announced in 1. 8b as the limit of the missionary witness.

[74] See above pp. 218–19 and 253–4.

[75] Surprisingly, modern tourists visiting Malta are shown the cave where Paul stayed during his evangelization of the Maltese. Luke's account of the journey to the *eschatiai* has been transformed into a founding narrative ... which witnesses to the permeability of the travel literature!

The geographical itinerary of Acts

My third point is the *geographical itinerary of Acts*. As I have said, the novel inherits the structure of the Homeric *nostos*: the resolution of the plot entails the reunion of the lovers and their return home. Luke–Acts, however, does not offer the circularity of a return to Jerusalem. If the itinerary of Peter brings him back to the holy City (Acts 15. 7–11), Paul's route moves the centre of the Word towards the West. The ending of the work *ad Theophilum* is left open, its geographic movement indisputably centrifugal:[76] from Jerusalem (Luke 1–2; Acts 1) to Rome (Acts 28), the displacement is irreversible, geographically as well as symbolically. The break with this constitutive feature of the novel is clear, even though it is not out of the question to think that Rome, henceforth, represents for Luke, the new 'house' that Christianity is called to inhabit. Yet the consonance with other corpora (narratives of exploration and the founding of colonies) is only the more apparent.

In summary, three characteristics emerge that bring together Acts and the narratives of exploration: there is the documentary concern, the tendency to utopian escape when the narrator describes the border lands, and the geographical movement of the narrative. Structurally, Luke thus rejoins the tradition of the ethnographic narrative in the shadow of Herodotus.

Itinerancy, the claim to universality

What is the function of itinerancy in the *Lives* of ancient philosophers? At the end of a study, in which she outlines the quest for knowledge attached to *theoria* (the observation of things), Maria Sassi develops, in a captivating manner, the theme of universality linked to the nomadism of the philosopher.[77] Since he is no longer a citizen of one place, the wandering sage is a citizen of the *cosmos*. The Cynics (Diogenes of Sinope) developed this status of the sage as *cosmopolitès*, members of the universal homeland (cf. Plutarch, *Lives of Illustrious Men* 1. 6). Socrates, in the *Republic* (496c), claims that exile is a condition for engaging in philosophy freely. As a citizen of nowhere, the philosopher can be the messenger of a wisdom destined for all.

Can the itinerancy of the apostles in Acts be compared with that of the Cynics or the Pythagoreans? At one point, their itinerancy converges

---

[76] Here I rejoin a remark of L. C. A. Alexander, ' "In Journeyings Often" ', 1995, p. 23.
[77] M. M. Sassi, 'Viaggio', 1991, pp. 27–8.

with that of the wandering sages: the claim to universality. Going back and forth across Asia and Greece, profiting on land and sea from the protection of their Lord, the missionaries of the Gospel bear witness to the widespread power of their God. It is not a status of exile that brings them universality, but the never failing protection of the God they proclaim. The βασιλεία τοῦ θεοῦ that the Christian missionaries preach (8. 12; 19. 8; 20. 25; 28. 23, 31) reaches out to the whole world, which means to the borders of the Roman Empire. The area they cover in the book of Acts bears witness to this territorial claim. It is clear that the author of Acts is not indifferent to the instrument of propaganda that the network of roads and maritime routes represents. To travel is to claim a territory for the Word.[78] To travel, to speak to all, concretizes the revelation given to Peter: 'I truly understand that God shows no partiality' (10. 34).

The figure of the wandering philosopher forces us back to the Lucan Jesus in order to understand how the expression 'travel narrative' (*Reisebericht*), applied to Luke 9. 51 – 19. 28 (if I am not mistaken) first by Schleiermacher, is inappropriate. Strictly speaking, the Jesus of the third gospel does not travel. Luke wishes to describe him as an itinerant sage, in the manner of the Hellenistic masters, but not as a traveller, in the manner of Paul and the missionaries of Acts. This is proved by the impossibility of reconstructing Jesus' geographical itinerary (Wellhausen concluded Luke's geographical incompetence)[79] and the author's emphasis on the journeying of the master rather than on the destination of his journeys.[80]

The path, a course of initiation?

The metaphor of the path is abundantly present in Greek literature, as the image of a crossroads (Hesiod or the fable of Prodicus), or as a place of inspiration (Pindar) or further, as a path of initiation (Theocritus).[81] The metaphorization of the path is also widespread in the world of religions; within Hellenistic Judaism, Philo uses it in an ethical as well as a soteriological manner.[82]

---

[78] V. K. Robbins defended the idea of the Lucan claim to an 'area of activity' in the Empire for Christianity ('Mixed Population', 1991). But I am inclined to think this claim was less symbiotic and more aggressive, as D. R. Edwards holds in his article in the same volume: 'Surviving the Web', 1991.

[79] J. Wellhausen, *Evangelium Lucae*, 1904, p. 46. The only episodes clearly localized are 9. 52–6; 18. 35–43 and 19. 1–10. D. P. Moessner has drawn attention to the hiatus between the form and content of the 'travel narrative' (*Lord of the Banquet*, 1998, pp. 14–20).

[80] Cf. 4. 43 and the Christological use of πορεύεσθαι in 9. 51, 53, 56, 57; 13. 33; 17. 11; 22. 22.

[81] See the bibliography in note 49 above.

[82] W. Michaelis, art. ὁδός, 1967, pp. 42–65; on Philo, pp. 60–5.

Does Acts work with an initiatory concept of the path? The text that comes to mind is Paul's conversion at Damascus (Acts 9). Four indications could tend in this direction.

Firstly, the narrative expressly mentions that Saul was on the road (ἐν δὲ τῷ πορεύεσθαι, 9. 3); his travelling companions are literally co-travellers (συνοδεύοντες, 9. 7). This emphasis is maintained in the two autobiographical repetitions by Paul in 22. 6 and 26. 13.

Secondly, the narrative composition of the sequence in 9. 1–30 asserts a reversal of Saul's status within an unchanged geographical course. Saul goes to Damascus to bring the disciples he would have captured (9. 1–2) to Jerusalem. After the epiphanic shock on the road to Damascus, Saul indeed returns to Jerusalem (9. 25–6). However, his status is reversed: the enemy of Jesus has become his zealous disciple; the persecutor has become persecuted; the tormentor of the disciples has made disciples himself (9. 25a: οἱ μαθηταὶ αὐτοῦ). The road to Damascus was a place of radical change, giving the ex-Pharisee a new identity.

Thirdly, for the first time in Acts, the absolute use of ὁδός to designate the Christian Way emerges (9. 2; cf. 19. 9; 22. 4; 24. 22). Perhaps this link is not accidental.

Fourthly, in its recurrence within the book of Acts (cf. Acts 22 and 26), Saul's conversion on the Damascus road plays a theologically crucial role. It allows Luke to mark the continuity between the old and the new people that God assembles, and to affirm that God himself is at work in this new direction of salvation history. In the manner of the *Lives* of philosophers, it also allows a remembrance of the mysterious events by which Saul of Tarsus became the apostle to the Gentiles, object of veneration within the Pauline movement in which Luke is situated.

Finally, in Acts 9, the hints of a symbolism of a path of initiation are very weak. However, it is probable that, given its presence in the culture, it has infiltrated the reception of the text during the centuries of reading. But, it is important to note that Paul's initiation is not that of Apollonius; the latter consists in the confirmation and deepening of a (neo-Pythagorean) wisdom already acquired; the divine wisdom of Apollonius is acquired, for the narrator, from the beginning of the book and the philosopher's famous visit to the hill of the Brahmans (3. 11–16), the climax of his journey to India, leads him to verify what he already knows.[83] On the

---

[83] ' "And what do you think we know more than yourself?" "I", replied the other, "consider that your lore is profounder and much more divine than our own; and if I add nothing to my present stock of knowledge while I am with you, I shall at least have learned that I have nothing more to learn" ' (Philostratus, *Life of Apollonius of Tyana*, 3.16, translation F. C. Conybeare, in the Loeb Classical Library, 1949).

other hand, Paul's initiation does not result from a progressive acquisition of wisdom, but from a powerful act of Christ that overcomes him and reverses his destiny.

Conclusion: the memory of a time when the Word travelled

The narrative world of Acts is peopled by travellers. The choice to make the itinerancy of the apostles (which is traditional) a narrative theme of the utmost importance is a decision of the author of Acts. We can, I think, imagine that Luke is familiar with sea travel and used to coastal itineraries, delighting in describing the ambiance of travel, its departures and arrivals, its trips, its farewell and reunion scenes. Writing in a Graeco-Roman society where travel was cherished, in reality or by reading, he exploited all the potentialities of this theme for his readers who were eager for adventure. Already in Luke's gospel, Jesus takes on the characteristics of an itinerant sage.

In fact, at this time, the journey was a widespread motif in a vast field of literature, from the practical guides for travellers (the *Periplus*) to the *Lives* of wandering philosophers, passing by way of the narratives of exploration and founding of colonies. The path also lends itself to the symbolism of the path of initiation. Certainly, the Greek novel does not hold a monopoly on the travel theme; furthermore, it is with the narratives of exploration and the founding of colonies, that the Acts of the Apostles has its closest ties. Here, travelling becomes, by turns, the vector of a missionary strategy, or the assertion of a reconnaissance of the Roman Empire, or the occasion of a claim to universality, or even, on the road to Damascus, the place of a founding experience.

However, it is probable that Luke is the witness to a practice in decline. The end of Acts leaves the reader with a description of a sedentary Paul in Rome (28. 30–1). The ministries that appear promising for the future of Lucan Christianity are those highlighted in the Pastoral epistles, elders and deacons; the time is near when the *Didache* will cast a shadow over the itinerant prophets. Therefore, Luke celebrates the memory of a time when the Word circulated and moved men and women toward one another. It was a time when witness was allied with the magic of far-off lands.

BIBLIOGRAPHY

Abbreviations for journal titles and book series follow S. Schwertner, *Internationales Abkürzungsverzeichnis für Theologie und Grenzgebiete*, 2nd edition, Berlin, Walter de Gruyter, 1992.

Primary sources

Carmignac, J. *et alii, Les textes de Qumrân traduits et annotés*, Paris, Letouzey et Ané, vol. I, 1961; vol. II, 1963.

Lagrange, M. J., *Introduction à l'étude du Nouveau Testament*, vol. I. *Histoire ancienne du canon du Nouveau Testament*, Paris, Gabalda, 1933.

Maier, J., *Die Qumran-Essener: Die Texte vom Toten Meer*, 3 vols. (UTB 1862, 1863 and 1916), Munich, Reinhardt, 1995 and 1996.

Meijer, F. and van Nijf, O., *Trade, Transport and Society in the Ancient World. A Sourcebook*, London-New York, Routledge, 1992.

Migne, J.-P., *Patrologia graeca*, Paris, 1857–66.

Philonenko, M. and Dupont-Sommer, A., eds., *La Bible. Ecrits intertestamentaires* (La Pléiade), Paris, Gallimard, 1987.

Roberts, C. H. and Turner, E. G., eds., *Catalogue of the Greek and Latin Papyri in the John Rylands Library Manchester*, vol. iv, Manchester, Manchester University Press, 1952.

Schneemelcher, W., ed., *New Testament Apocrypha* [vol. I, 1963; vol. II, 1964], 2nd edition, Philadelphia, Westminster, 1975.

Vermès, G., *The Dead Sea Scrolls in English*, 4th edition, Sheffield, Sheffield Academic Press, 1995.

Secondary works

Achtemeier, P. J., 'Omne Verbum Sonat: The New Testament and the Oral Environment of Late Western Antiquity', *JBL* 109, 1990, pp. 3–27.

Albert, M., *Le culte de Castor et Pollux en Italie*, Paris, 1883.

Aletti, J.-N., *L'art de raconter Jésus Christ*, Paris, Seuil, 1989.

Quand Luc raconte. Le récit comme théologie (Lire la Bible 115), Paris, Cerf, 1998.

Alexander, L. C. A., *The Preface to Luke's Gospel* (SNTS.MS 78), Cambridge, Cambridge University Press, 1993.

'Acts and Ancient Intellectual Biography', in B. W. Winter and A. D. Clarke, eds., *The Book of Acts in Its First Century Setting*, vol. I: *The Book of*

Acts in Its Ancient Literary Setting, Grand Rapids, Eerdmans and Carlisle, Paternoster, 1993, pp. 31–64.

' "In Journeyings Often": Voyaging in Acts of the Apostles and in Greek Romance', in C. M. Tuckett, ed., *Luke's Literary Achievement* (JSNT.SS 116), Sheffield, Sheffield Academic Press, 1995, pp. 17–49.

'Narrative Maps: Reflections on the Toponymy of Acts', in M. D. Carroll, D. J. A. Clines and Ph. A. Davies, eds., *The Bible in Human Society. Essays in Honour of J. Rogerson* (JSOT.SS 200), Sheffield, Sheffield Academic Press, 1995, pp. 17–57.

'Fact, Fiction and the Genre of Acts', *NTS* 44, 1998, pp. 380–99.

'Marathon or Jericho? Reading Acts in Dialogue with Biblical and Greek Historiography', in D. J. A. Clines and S. D. Moore, eds., *Auguries. The Jubilee Volume of the Sheffield Department of Biblical Studies* (JSOT.SS 269), Sheffield, Sheffield Academic Press, 1998, pp. 92–125.

'The Acts of the Apostles as an Apologetic Text', in M. J. Edwards, M. Goodman and C. Rowland, eds., *Jewish and Christian Apologetic in the Graeco-Roman World*, Oxford, Oxford University Press, 1999, pp. 15–44.

'L'intertextualité et la question des lecteurs. Réflexions sur l'usage de la Bible dans les Actes des apôtres', in D. Marguerat and A. Curtis, eds., *Intertextualités. La Bible en échos* (Monde de la Bible 40), Geneva, Labor et Fides, 2000, pp. 201–14.

Allen, O. W., *The Death of Herod. The Narrative and Theological Function of Retribution in Luke–Acts* (SBL.DS 158), Atlanta, Scholars Press, 1997.

Alter, R., *The Art of Biblical Narrative*, New York, Basic Books, 1981.

Anderson, J. C., *Matthew's Narrative Web: Over, and Over, and Over Again* (JSNT.SS 91), Sheffield, JSOT Press, 1994.

André, J. M. and Baslez, M. F., *Voyager dans l'antiquité*, Paris, Fayard, 1993.

Anne-Etienne, Sr and Combet-Galland, C., 'Actes 4, 32 – 5, 11', *ETR* 52, 1977, pp. 548–53.

Aron, R., *Introduction à la philosophie de l'histoire*, 14th edition, Paris, Gallimard, 1957.

Aune, D. E., *The New Testament in Its Literary Environment*, Philadelphia, Fortress Press, 1987.

Bachmann, M., *Jerusalem und der Tempel. Die geographisch-theologischen Elemente in der lukanischen Sicht des jüdischen Kultzentrums* (BWANT 109), Stuttgart, Kohlhammer, 1980.

Balch, D. L., 'Comments on the Genre as a Political Theme of Luke–Acts: A Preliminary Comparison of Two Hellenistic Historians', *SBL.SP* 1989, Atlanta, Scholars Press, 1989, pp. 343–61.

'The Genre of Luke–Acts: Individual Biography, Adventure Novel, or Political History?', *Southwestern Journal of Theology*, 1991, pp. 5–19.

'Attitudes toward Foreigners in 2 Maccabees, Eupolemus, Esther, Aristeas, and Luke–Acts', in A. J. Malherbe, F. W. Norris and J. W. Thompson, eds., *The Early Church in Its Context. Essays in Honor of E. Ferguson* (NT.S 90), Leiden, Brill, 1998, pp. 22–47.

Barbi, A., 'Il paolinismo degli Atti', *RivBib* 48, 1986, pp. 471–518.

Barrett, C. K., *Luke the Historian in Recent Study*, London, Epworth, 1961.

'Acts and Christian Consensus', in P. W. Bøckman and R. E. Kristiansen, eds., *Context. Festschrift P. J. Borgen*, Trondheim, Tapir, 1987, pp. 19–33.

'Attitudes to the Temple in the Acts of the Apostles', in W. Horbury, ed., *Templum Amicitiae. Essays in Honour of B. Lindars* (JSNT.SS 48), Sheffield, JSOT Press, 1991, pp. 345–67.

'The Third Gospel as a Preface to Acts? Some Reflections', in F. Van Segbroek *et alii*, eds., *The Four Gospels 1992. Festschrift F. Neirynck*, vol. II (BEThL 100), Leuven, Peeters, 1992, pp. 1451–66.

The Acts of the Apostles, vol. I (ICC), Edinburgh, Clark, 1994.

'How History Should Be Written', in B. Witherington, ed., *History, Literature, and Society in the Book of Acts*, Cambridge, Cambridge University Press, 1996, pp. 33–57.

'Luke–Acts', in J. Barclay and J. Sweet, eds., *Early Christian Thought in Its Jewish Context*, Cambridge, Cambridge University Press, 1996, pp. 84–95.

'The End of Acts', in P. Schäfer, ed., *Geschichte – Tradition – Reflexion. Festschrift M. Hengel*, vol. III, Tübingen, Mohr, 1996, pp. 545–55.

'The First New Testament?', *NT* 38, 1996, pp. 94–104.

Baslez, M.-F., *L'étranger dans la Grèce antique*, Paris, Belles Lettres, 1984.

Bauer, W., *Das Leben Jesu im Zeitalter der neutestamentlichen Apokryphen*, Tübingen, Mohr, 1909.

Baum, A. D., *Lukas als Historiker der letzten Jesusreise*, Wuppertal and Zurich, Brockhaus, 1993.

Baur, F. C., *Über den Ursprung des Episcopats in der christlichen Kirche*, Tübingen, Fues, 1838.

Paulus, der Apostel Jesu Christi [1845], 2nd edition, Leipzig, Fues, 1866.

Bechtler, S. R., 'The Meaning of Paul's Call and Commissioning in Luke's Story: An Exegetical Study of Acts 9, 22, and 26', *Studia Biblica and Theologica* 15, 1987, pp. 53–77.

Beck, N. A., *Mature Christianity*, Selinsgrove, PA, Susquehanna University Press 1985.

'The Lukan Writer's Stories about the Call of Paul', *SBL.SP* 1983, Chico, Scholars Press, 1983, pp. 213–18.

Becker, O., *Das Bild des Weges*, Berlin, Weidmann, 1937.

Benéitez, M., *Esta salvación de Dios (Hech 28,28)*, Madrid, UPCM, 1986.

Berger, K., *Formgeschichte des Neuen Testaments*, Heidelberg, Quelle und Meyer, 1984.

'Hellenistische Gattungen im Neuen Testament', in W. Haase, ed., *ANRW* II, 25.2, Berlin, de Gruyter, 1984, pp. 1274–81.

Berti, E., 'Il discorso di Paolo agli Ateniesi e la filosofia greca classica', *Archivio di Filosofia* 53, 1985, pp. 251–9.

Betori, G., 'Gli Atti come opera storiografica. Osservazioni di metodo', in Pontificio Istituto biblico di Roma, *La storiografia nella Bibbia. Atti della XXVIII settimana biblica*, Bologna, Dehoniane, 1986, pp. 115–21.

'Lo spirito e l'annuncio della parola negli Atti degli Apostoli', *RivBib* 35, 1987, pp. 399–441.

Betz, O., 'Die Vision des Paulus im Tempel von Jerusalem. Apg 22,17–21 als Beitrag zur Deutung des Damaskuserlebnis', in O. Böcher and K. Haacker, eds., *Verborum Veritas. Festschrift G. Stählin*, Wuppertal, Brockaus, 1970, pp. 113–23.

Billault, A., *La création romanesque dans la littérature grecque à l'époque impériale*, Paris, Presses Universitaires de France, 1991.

Blau Du Plessis, R., *Writing beyond the Ending*, Bloomington, Indiana University Press, 1985.

Boismard, M.-E. and Lamouille, A., *Les Actes des deux apôtres*, 3 vols. (EtB NS 12–14), Paris, Gabalda, 1990.

Bonner, S. F., *The Literary Treatises of Dionysius of Halicarnassus. A Study in the Development of Critical Method*, Amsterdam, Hakkert, 1969.

Borremans, J., 'L'Esprit Saint dans la catéchèse évangélique de Luc', *Lumen Vitae* 25, 1970, pp. 103–22.

Bossuyt, P. and Radermakers, J., *Témoins de la Parole de la Grâce. Actes des apôtres*, 2 vols., Bruxelles, Institut d'Etudes Théologiques, 1995.

Bovon, F., *Luke the Theologian: Thirty-Three Years of Research (1950–1983)* (Princeton Theological Monograph Series 12), Allison Park, Pickwick, 1987.

'Tradition et rédaction en Actes 10, 1 – 11, 18', in *L'œuvre de Luc* (LeDiv 130), Paris, 1987, pp. 97–120.

Luc le théologien. Vingt-cinq ans de recherche (1950–1975), 2nd edition, La Monde de la Bible 5, Geneva, Labor et Fides, 1988.

L'évangile selon saint Luc 1, 1 – 9, 50 (CNT IIIa), Geneva, Labor et Fides, 1991.

'Studies in Luke–Acts: Retrospect and Prospect', *HThR* 85, 1992, pp. 175–96.

L'évangile et l'apôtre. Le Christ inséparable de ses témoins, Aubonne, Edition du Moulin, 1993.

'La structure canonique de l'évangile et de l'apôtre', *Cristianesimo nella storia* 15, 1994, pp. 559–76.

New Testament Traditions and Apocryphal Narratives (Princeton Theological Monograph Series 36), Allison Park, Pickwick, 1995.

' "How Well the Holy Spirit Spoke through the Prophet Isaiah to Your Ancestors!" (Acts 28:25)', in *New Testament Traditions and Apocryphal Narratives* (Princeton Theological Monograph Series 36), Allison Park, Pickwick, 1995, pp. 43–50.

'Israel, the Church and the Gentiles in the Twofold Work of Luke', in *New Testament Traditions and Apocryphal Narratives* (Princeton Theological Monograph Series 36), Allison Park, Pickwick, 1995, pp. 81–95.

'The Effect of Realism and Prophetic Ambiguity in the Works of Luke', in *New Testament Traditions and Apocryphal Narratives* (Princeton Theological Monograph Series 36), Allison Park, Pickwick, 1995, p. 97–104.

'The God of Luke', in *New Testament Traditions and Apocryphal Narratives* (Princeton Theological Monograph Series 36), Allison Park, Pickwick, 1995, pp. 67–80.

'The Importance of Mediations in Luke's Theological Plan', in *New Testament Traditions and Apocryphal Narratives* (Princeton Theological Monograph Series 36), Allison Park, Pickwick, 1995, pp. 51–66.

L'évangile selon saint Luc 9, 51 – 14, 35 (CNT IIIb), Geneva, Labor et Fides, 1996.

'La Loi dans l'œuvre de Luc', in C. Focant, ed., *La Loi dans l'un et l'autre Testament* (LeDiv 168), Paris, Cerf, 1997, pp. 206–25.

Brawley, R. L., 'Paul in Acts: Lucan Apology and Conciliation', in C. H.Talbert, ed., *Luke–Acts. New Perspectives from the SBL Seminar*, New York, Crossroad, 1984, pp. 129–34.

Luke–Acts and the Jews. Conflict, Apology, and Conciliation (SBL.MS 33), Atlanta, Scholars Press, 1987.

Centering on God. Method and Message in Luke–Acts, Louisville, Westminster/John Knox, 1990.

Breytenbach, C., *Paulus und Barnabas in der Provinz Galatien. Studien zu Apostelgeschichte 13f.; 16,6; 18,23 und den Adressaten des Galaterbriefes* (AGJU 38), Leiden, Brill, 1996.

Brown, P. B., 'The Meaning and Function of Acts 5:1–11 in the Purpose of Luke–Acts', Dissertation, Boston University, 1969.

Bruce, F. F., 'The Holy Spirit in the Acts of the Apostles', *Interpretation* 27, 1973, pp. 166–83.

'The Acts of the Apostles: Historical Record or Theological Reconstruction?', in W. Haase, ed., *ANRW* II, 25.3, Berlin and New York, de Gruyter, 1985, pp. 2569–603.

The Acts of the Apostles. The Greek Text with Introduction and Commentary, 3rd edition, Grand Rapids, Eerdmans and Leicester, Apollos, 1990.

Budesheim, T. L., 'Paul's *Abschiedsrede* in the Acts of the Apostles', *HThR* 69, 1976, pp. 9–30.

Bultmann, R., *L'histoire de la tradition synoptique*, French translation, Paris, Seuil, 1973.

Burchard, C., *Der dreizehnte Zeuge*, FRLANT 103, Göttingen, Vandenhoeck und Ruprecht, 1970.

Buss, M. F. J., *Die Missionspredigt des Apostels Paulus im Pisidien Antiochien*, FzB 38, Stuttgart, Katholisches Bibelwerk, 1980.

Cadbury, H. J., *The Making of Luke–Acts* [1927], 2nd edition, London, Macmillan, 1958.

'Commentary on the Preface of Luke', in F. J. Foakes Jackson and K. Lake, eds., *The Beginnings of Christianity*, vol. II, London, Macmillan, 1934, pp. 489–510.

Calame, C., *Le récit en Grèce antique*, Paris, Kleinsieck, 1986.

'Mythe, récit épique et histoire: le récit hérodotéen de la fondation de Cyrène', in C. Calame, ed., *Métamorphoses du mythe en Grèce antique*, Geneva, Labor et Fides, 1988, pp. 105–25.

Mythe et histoire dans l'antiquité grecque. La création symbolique d'une colonie, Lausanne, Payot, 1996.

Calloud, J., 'Sur le chemin de Damas. Quelques lumières sur l'organisation discursive d'un texte, Actes des apôtres 9, 1–19', *SémBib* 37, 1985, pp. 3–29; 38, 1985, pp. 40–53; 40, 1985, pp. 21–42; 42, 1986, pp. 1–19.

Camassa, G. and Fasce, S., eds., *Idea e realtà del viaggio*, Genova, ECIG, 1991.

Capper, B. J., 'The Interpretation of Acts 5. 4', *JSNT* 19, 1983, pp. 117–31.

Casalegno, A., *Gesù e il tempio*, Brescia, Morcelliana, 1984.

Cassidy, S. J., *Society and Politics in the Acts of the Apostles*, Maryknoll, Orbis Books, 1987.

Casson, L., *Travel in the Ancient World*, London, Allen & Unwin, 1974 (2nd edition Baltimore and London, Hopkins, 1994).

Cazale Bérard, C., ed., *Fine della storia e storia senza fine* (Narrativa 4), Paris, Nanterre, Université Paris X, 1993.

Chatman, S., *Story and Discourse*, Ithaca, Cornell University Press, 1978.

Chevallier, M.-A., 'Luc et l'Esprit Saint', *RSR* 56, 1982, pp. 1–16.

Souffle de Dieu. Le Saint-Esprit dans le Nouveau Testament, vol. I, Paris, Beauchesne, 1978.

Chiarini, G., 'Nostoi e labirinto. Mito e realtà nei viaggi di Odisseo', *Quaderni di Storia* 21, 1985, pp. 11–35.

Clark, A. C., *The Acts of the Apostles*, Oxford, Clarendon, 1933.

Cohen, S. J. D., 'Josephus, Jeremiah, and Polybius', *History and Theory* 21, 1982, pp. 366–81.

Collins, R. F., 'Paul's Damascus Experience: Reflections on the Lukan Account', *Louvain Studies* 11, 1986, pp. 99–118.

Conzelmann, H., 'Der geschichtliche Ort der lukanischen Schriften im Urchristentum', in G. Braumann, ed., *Das Lukas-Evangelium* (WdF 280), Darmstadt, Wissensch. Buchgesellschaft, 1974, pp. 236–60.

The Theology of St Luke, London, SCM Press, 1982.

Acts of the Apostles: A Commentary on the Acts of the Apostles (Hermeneia), Philadelphia, Fortress Press, 1987.

Cook, M. J., 'The Mission to the Jews in Acts: Unraveling Luke's "Myth of the Myriads"', in J. B. Tyson, ed., *Luke–Acts and the Jewish People. Eight Critical Perspectives*, Minneapolis, Augsburg, 1988, pp. 102–23.

Crum, W. E., 'New Coptic Manuscripts in the John Rylands Library', *BJRL* 5, 1920, pp. 497–503.

Cullmann, O., *Saint Pierre, disciple, apôtre, martyr*, Neuchâtel and Paris, Delachaux et Niestlé, 1952.

Cunningham, S., *'Through Many Tribulations'. The Theology of Persecution in Luke–Acts* (JSNT.SS 142), Sheffield, Sheffield Academic Press, 1997.

Danker, F. W., 'Graeco-Roman Cultural Accommodation in the Christology of Luke–Acts', *SBL.SP* 1983, Chico, Scholars Press, 1983, pp. 391–414.

Darr, J. A., *On Character Building. The Reader and the Rhetoric of Characterization in Luke–Acts*, Louisville, Westminster/John Knox, 1992.

Davies, P., 'The Ending of Acts', *ET* 94, 1982/3, pp. 334–5.

Dawsey, J. M., 'The Literary Unity of Luke–Acts: Questions of Style – a Task for Literary Critics', *NTS* 35, 1989, pp. 48–66.

De Jonge, H. J., 'Sonship, Wisdom, Infancy: Luke 2,41–51a', *NTS* 24, 1978, pp. 317–54.

Delebecque, E., *Les deux Actes des apôtres* (EtB NS 6), Paris, Gabalda, 1986.

'Les deux versions du discours de saint Paul à l'Aréopage (*Actes des apôtres* 17, 22–31)', in *Etudes sur le Grec du Nouveau Testament*, Aix-en-Provence, Publications de l'Université de Provence, 1995, pp. 231–48.

Delling, G., art. 'λαμβάνω κτλ.', *TDNT* 4, Grand Rapids, Eerdmans, 1967, pp. 5–155.

Denaux, A., 'The Delineation of the Lucan Travel Narrative within the Overall Structure of the Gospel of Luke', in C. Focant, ed., *The Synoptic Gospels. Source Criticism and the New Literary Criticism* (BEThL 110), Leuven, Peeters, 1993, pp. 357–92.

'Old Testament Models for the Lukan Travel Narrative', in C. M. Tuckett, ed., *The Scriptures in the Gospel* (BEThL 131), Leuven, Peeters, 1997, pp. 271–305.

De Pury, A., ed., *Le Pentateuque en question*, 2nd edition (Monde de la Bible 19), Geneva, Labor et Fides, 1991.

De Romilly, J., *Histoire et raison chez Thucydide*, Paris, Belles Lettres, 1967.

La Guerre du Péloponnèse, vol. I, 5th edition, Paris, Belles Lettres, 1981.

Des Places, E., *La religion grecque. Dieux, cultes, rites et sentiments religieux dans la Grèce antique*, Paris, A. et J. Picard, 1969.

Dettwiler, A., *Die Gegenwart des Erhöhten. Eine exegetische Studie zu den johanneischen Abschiedsreden (Joh 13,31–16,33) unter besonderer Berücksichtigung ihres Relecture-Charakters* (FRLANT 169), Göttingen, Vandenhoeck und Ruprecht, 1995.

Dibelius, M., *Studies in the Acts of the Apostles*, London, SCM Press, 1956.

'Paul in Athens' [1939], in *Studies in the Acts of the Apostles*, London, SCM Press, 1956, pp. 78–83.

'Paul on the Areopagus' [1939], in *Studies in the Acts of the Apostles*, London, SCM Press, 1956, pp. 26–77.

'Style Criticism of the Book of Acts' [1923], in *Studies in the Acts of the Apostles*, London, SCM Press, 1956, pp. 1–25.

'The Acts of the Apostles in the Setting of the History of Early Christian Literature', in *Studies in the Acts of the Apostles*, London, SCM Press, 1956, pp. 192–206.

'The Conversion of Cornelius' [1947], in *Studies in the Acts of the Apostles*, London, SCM Press, 1956, pp. 109–22.

'The First Christian Historian' [1948], in *Studies in the Acts of the Apostles*, London, SCM Press, 1956, pp. 123–37.

'The Speeches in Acts and Ancient Historiography' [1949], in *Studies in the Acts of the Apostles*, London, SCM Press, 1956, pp. 138–85.

Dihle, A., 'Zur hellenistischen Ethnographie', in *Grecs et Barbares* (Entretiens sur l'antiquité classique 8), Geneva, 1962, pp. 205–39.

Dilke, O. A. W., *Greek and Roman Maps*, London, Thames and Hudson, 1985.

Dinkler, E., 'Philippus und der ANHR ΑΙΘΙΟΨ (Apg 8,26–40). Historische und geographische Bemerkungen zum Missionsablauf nach Lukas', in E. E. Ellis and E. Grässer, eds., *Jesus und Paulus. Festschrift W. G. Kümmel*, Göttingen, Vandenhoeck und Ruprecht, 1975, pp. 85–95.

Doble, P., *The Paradox of Salvation. Luke's Theology of the Cross* (SNTS. MS 87), Cambridge, Cambridge University Press, 1996.

Douglas, M., *How Institutions Think*, London, Routledge & Kegan Paul, 1986.

Downing, F. G., 'Ethical Pagan Theism and the Speeches in Acts', *NTS* 27, 1980/1, pp. 544–63.

'Common Ground with Paganism in Luke and Josephus', *NTS* 28, 1982, pp. 546–59.

'Freedom from the Law in Luke–Acts', *JSNT* 22, 1984, pp. 53–80.

Dumais, M., *Le langage de l'évangélisation*, Tournai, Desclée and Montreal, Bellarmin, 1976.

'Le salut universel par le Christ selon les Actes des apôtres', *SNTU* A 18, 1993, pp. 113–31.

'Les Actes des apôtres. Bilan et orientations', in ACEBAC, *'De bien des manières'. La recherche biblique aux abords du XXIe siècle* (LeDiv 163), Montreal, Fides and Paris, Cerf, 1995, pp. 307–64.

'Le salut en dehors de la foi en Jésus-Christ?', *Eglise et Théologie* 28, 1997, pp. 161–90.

Dunn, J. D. G., *Baptism in the Holy Spirit*, London, SCM Press, 1970.

Jesus and the Spirit, London, SCM Press, 1975.

Dupont, J., 'Aequitas romana. Notes sur Actes 25,16', in *Etudes sur les Actes des apôtres* (LeDiv 45), Paris, Cerf, 1967, pp. 527–52.

'Pierre et Paul dans les Actes', in *Etudes sur les Actes des apôtres* (LeDiv 45), Paris, Cerf, 1967, pp. 173–184.

'La conclusion des Actes et son rapport à l'ensemble de l'ouvrage de Luc', in J. Kremer, ed., *Les Actes des apôtres. Traditions, rédaction, théologie* (BEThL 48), Gembloux, Duculot and Leuven, Leuven University Press, 1979, pp. 359–404, or in *Nouvelles études sur les Actes des apôtres* (LeDiv 118), Paris, Cerf, 1984, pp. 457–511.

'La question du plan des Actes des apôtres à la lumière d'un texte de Lucien de Samosate', in *Nouvelles études sur les Actes des apôtres* (LeDiv 118), Paris, Cerf, 1984, pp. 24–36.

'Le discours à l'Aréopage (Ac 17, 22–31), lieu de rencontre entre christianisme et hellénisme', in *Nouvelles études sur les Actes des apôtres* (LeDiv 118), Paris, Cerf, 1984, pp. 380–423.

Edwards, D. R., 'Surviving the Web of Roman Power: Religion and Politics in the Acts of the Apostles, Josephus, and Chariton's *Chaereas and Callirhoe*', in L. C. A. Alexander, ed., *Images of Empire* (JSOT.SS 122), Sheffield, Sheffield Academic Press, 1991, pp. 179–201.

Egger, M., *Denys d'Halicarnasse. Essai sur la critique littéraire et la rhétorique chez les Grecs au siècle d'Auguste*, Paris, Picard, 1902.

Elliott, J. H., 'Temple versus Household in Luke–Acts. A Contrast in Social Institutions', in J. H. Neyrey, ed., *The Social World of Luke–Acts*, Peabody, Hendrickson, 1991, pp. 211–40.

Emmelius, J. C., *Tendenzkritik und Formengeschichte. Der Beitrag Franz Overbecks zur Auslegung der Apostelgeschichte im 19. Jahrhundert* (FKDG 27), Göttingen, Vandenhoeck und Ruprecht, 1975.

Esler, P. F., *Community and Gospel in Luke–Acts. The Social and Political Motivations of Lucan Theology* (SNTS.MS 57), Cambridge, Cambridge University Press, 1987.

Evans, C. A., 'Is Luke's View of the Jewish Rejection of Jesus Anti-Semitic?', in D. D. Sylva, ed., *Reimaging the Death of the Lukan Jesus* (BBB 73), Frankfurt, Hain, 1990, pp. 29–56.

Fitzmyer, J. A., *The Gospel according to Luke X–XXIV* (AB 28A), New York, Doubleday, 1985.

Luke the Theologian. Aspects of His Teaching, New York, Paulist Press, 1989.

Friedrich, G., 'Lk 9,51 und die Entrückungschristologie des Lukas', in P. Hoffmann, ed., *Orientierung an Jesus. Festschrift J. Schmid*, Freiburg and Basel, Herder, 1973, pp. 48–77.

Funk, R. W., *The Poetics of Biblical Narrative*, Sonoma, CA, Polebridge, 1988.

Fusco, V., 'Le sezioni-noi degli Atti nella discussione recente', *BeO* 25, 1983, pp. 73–86.

'Progetto storiografico e progetto teologico nell' opera lucana', in Pontificio Istituto biblico di Roma, *La storiografia nella Bibbia. Atti della XXVIII settimana biblica*, Bologna, Dehoniane, 1986, pp. 123–52.

'Ancora sulle sezioni-noi degli Atti', *RivBib* 39, 1991, pp. 231–9.

'Luke-Acts and the Future of Israel', *NT* 38, 1996, pp. 1–17.

Fusillo, M., *Naissance du roman*, Paris, Seuil, 1991.

Gabba, E., 'True History and False History in Classical Antiquity', *JRS* 71, 1981, pp. 50–62.

Gärtner, B., *The Areopagus Speech and Natural Revelation* (ASNU 21), Lund, Gleerup and Copenhagen, Munksgaard, 1955.

Gasque, W. W., *A History of the Interpretation of the Acts of the Apostles*, 2nd edition, Peabody, Hendrickson, 1989.

Gaston, L., 'Anti-Judaism and the Passion Narrative in Luke and Acts', in P. Richardson, ed., *Anti-Judaism in Early Christianity*, vol. I, Waterloo, W. Laurier University Press, 1986, pp. 127–53.

Gatti, V., *Il discorso di Paolo ad Atene: Storia dell'interpretazione – esegesi – teologia della missione e della religioni*, Parma, 1979 (Brescia, Paideia, 1982).

Gaventa, B. R., *From Darkness to Light. Aspects of Conversion in the New Testament*, Philadelphia, Fortress Press, 1986.

'Towards a Theology of Acts. Reading and Rereading', *Interpretation* 42, 1988, pp. 146–57.

Genette, G., *Figures III*, Paris, Seuil, 1972.

Seuils, Paris, Seuil, 1987.

Palimpsests. Literature in the Second Degree (Stages 8), Lincoln, University of Nebraska Press, 1997.

George, A., 'Israël', in *Etudes sur l'œuvre de Luc* (Sources bibliques), Paris, Gabalda, 1978, pp. 87–125.

'L'Esprit Saint dans l'œuvre de Luc', *RB* 85, 1978, pp. 500–542.

'Le parallèle entre Jean-Baptiste et Jésus en Luc 1–2', in *Etudes sur l'œuvre de Luc* (Sources bibliques), Paris, Gabalda, 1978, pp. 43–65.

'Le vocabulaire de salut', in *Etudes sur l'œuvre de Luc* (Sources bibliques), Paris, Gabalda, 1978, pp. 307–320.

Geppert, S., *Castor und Pollux. Untersuchung zu den Darstellung der Dioskuren in der römischen Kaiserzeit*, München, 1996.

Gerber, D., 'La préparation du salut d'après Luc 1–2', thèse de doctorat, Université de Strasbourg, 1991.

'Luc et le judaïsme', *Cahier biblique* 32, Foi et Vie, Paris, 1993, pp. 55–66.

'Il vous est né un Sauveur', thèse d'habilitation, Université de Strasbourg, 1997.

Gibert, P., *Bible, mythes et récits de commencement* (Parole de Dieu), Paris, Seuil, 1986.

Vérité historique et esprit historien. L'historien biblique de Gédéon face à Hérodote, Paris, Cerf, 1990.

Giesen, H., 'Der Heilige Geist als Ursprung und treibende Kraft des christlichen Lebens', in *Glaube und Handeln*, vol. II, Frankfurt, Lang, 1983.

Gill, D., 'The Structure of Acts 9', *Bib* 55, 1974, pp. 346–8.

Gill, D. W. J. and Gempf, C., eds., *The Book of Acts in Its First Century Setting*, vol. II: *The Book of Acts in Its Graeco-Roman Setting*, Grand Rapids. Eerdmans and Carlisle, Paternoster, 1994.

Gilliéron, B., *Le Saint-Esprit, actualité du Christ*, Geneva, Labor et Fides, 1978.

Gnilka, J., *Die Verstockung Israels. Isaias 6,9–10 in der Theologie der Synoptiker* (StANT 3), Munich, Kösel, 1961.

Goldhahn-Müller, I., *Die Grenze der Gemeinde* (GTA 39), Göttingen, Vandenhoeck und Ruprecht, 1989.

Goulder, M. D., *Type and History in Acts*, London, SPCK, 1964.

Gourgues, M., 'Esprit des commencements et esprit des prolongements dans les Actes. Note sur la 'Pentecôte des Samaritains' (Ac 8, 5–25)', *RB* 93, 1986, pp. 376–85.

Green, J. B., 'Internal Repetition in Luke–Acts: Contemporary Narratology and Lucan Historiography', in B.Witherington, ed., *History, Literature, and Society in the Book of Acts*, Cambridge, Cambridge University Press, 1996, pp. 283–99.

Greimas, A. J., *Structural Semantics: An Attempt at Method*, Lincoln, University of Nebraska Press, 1984.

Sémantique structurale: recherche de méthode (Coll. Formes sémiotiques), Paris, Presses Universitaires de France, 1986.

Grimal, P., *Romans grecs et latins*, La Pléiade, Paris, Gallimard, 1958.

'Essai sur la formation du genre romanesque dans l'antiquité', in *Le monde du roman grec* (Etudes de littérature ancienne 4), Paris, Presses de l'Ecole normale supérieure, 1992, pp. 13–19.

Haacker, Kl., 'Das Bekenntnis des Paulus zur Hoffnung Israels nach der Apostelgeschichte des Lukas', *NTS* 31, 1985, pp. 437–51.

Habel, N., 'The Form and Significance of the Call Narratives', *ZAW* 77, 1965, pp. 297–323.

Hadas-Lebel, M., *Jérusalem contre Rome*, Paris, Cerf, 1990.

Haenchen, E., 'Judentum und Christentum in der Apostelgeschichte', in *Die Bibel und wir*, Tübingen, Mohr, 1968, pp. 338–74.

The Acts of the Apostles: A Commentary, Philadelphia, Westminster Press, 1971.

'The Book of Acts as Source Material for the History of Early Christianity', in L. E. Keck and J. L. Martyn, eds., *Studies in Luke–Acts. Essays Presented in Honor of P. Schubert*, 3rd edition, London, 1978, pp. 258–78.

Hägg T., *The Novel in Antiquity*, Oxford, Blackwell, 1983.

Hamm, D., 'Paul's Blindness and Its Healing: Clues to Symbolic Intent (Acts 9; 22 and 26)', *Bib* 71, 1990, pp. 63–72.

Harnack, A., *Beiträge zur Einleitung in das Neue Testament*, vol. IV. *Neue Untersuchungen zur Apostelgeschichte und zur Abfassungszeit der synoptischen Evangelien*, Leipzig, Hinrichs, 1911.

Hartman, L. O., *Auf den Namen des Herrn Jesus. Die Taufe in den neutestamentlichen Schriften* (SBS 148), Stuttgart, Katholisches Bibelwerk, 1992.

Haulotte, E., *Actes des apôtres. Un guide de lecture* (Suppl. Vie chrétienne 212), Paris, 1977.

'La vie en communion, phase ultime de la Pentecôte. Actes 2, 42–47', *Cahiers bibliques* 19, Foi et Vie, Paris, 1981, pp. 69–75.

Hauser, H. J., *Strukturen der Abschlusserzählung der Apostelgeschichte (Apg 28,16–31)* (AnBib 86), Roma, Biblical Institute Press, 1979.

Havelaar, H., 'Hellenistic Parallels to Acts 5,1–11 and the Problem of Conflicting Interpretations', *JSNT* 67, 1997, pp. 63–82.

Haya Prats, G., *L'Esprit, force de l'Eglise* (LeDiv 81), Paris, Cerf, 1975.
Hedrick, C. H., 'Paul's Conversion/Call: A Comparative Analysis of the Three Reports in Acts', *JBL* 100, 1981, pp. 415–32.
Hemer, C. J., *The Book of Acts in the Setting of Hellenistic History* (WUNT 49), Tübingen, Mohr, 1989.
Hermant, D., 'Un procédé d'écriture de Luc: le transfert', *RB* 104, 1997, pp. 528–56.
Hirsch, E., 'Die drei Berichte der Apostelgeschichte über die Bekehrung des Paulus', *ZNW* 28, 1929, pp. 305–12.
Holtz, T., *Untersuchungen über die alttestamentlichen Zitate bei Lukas* (TU 104), Berlin, Akademie-Verlag, 1968.
Holzberg, N., *Der antike Roman*, Munich and Zurich, Artemis, 1986.
Horn, F. W., *Glaube und Handeln in der Theologie des Lukas* (GTA 26), Göttingen, Vandenhoeck und Ruprecht, 1983.
Hull, J. H. E., *The Holy Spirit in the Acts of the Apostles*, London, Lutterworth, 1967.
Hurtado, L. W., 'Convert, Apostate or Apostle to the Nations: The "Conversion" of Paul in recent Scholarship', *Studies in Religion* 22, 1993, pp. 273–84.
Iser, W., *The Act of Reading: A Theory of Aesthetic Response*, London, Routledge, 1978.
'Interaction between Text and Reader', in S. R. Suleiman and I. Crosman, eds., *The Reader in the Text*, Princeton, Princeton University Press, 1980, pp. 106–119.
Jacob, C., *Géographie et ethnographie en Grèce ancienne*, Paris, Colin, 1991.
Jacquier, E., *Les Actes des apôtres* (EtB), Paris, Gabalda, 1926.
Jeandillou, J.-F., *L'analyse textuelle*, Paris, A. Colin-Masson, 1997.
Jervell, J., *Luke and the People of God. A New Look at Luke–Acts*, Minneapolis, Augsburg, 1972.
'The Divided People', in *Luke and the People of God. A New Look at Luke–Acts*, Minneapolis, Augsburg, 1972, pp. 41–74.
'The Problem of Traditions in Acts', in *Luke and the People of God. A New Look at Luke–Acts*, Minneapolis, Augsburg, 1972, pp. 19–40.
'Paulus in der Apostelgeschichte und die Geschichte des Urchristentums', *NTS* 32, 1986, pp. 378–92.
'The Church of Jews and Godfearers', in J. B. Tyson, ed., *Luke–Acts and the Jewish People. Eight Critical Perspectives*, Minneapolis, Augsburg, 1988, pp. 11–20.
'The Future of the Past: Luke's Vision of Salvation History and Its Bearing on His Writing of History', in B. Witherington, ed., *History, Literature, and Society in the Book of Acts*, Cambridge, Cambridge University Press, 1996, pp. 104–26.
Die Apostelgeschichte (KEK), Göttingen, Vandenhoeck und Ruprecht, 1998.
Johnson, L. T., *The Literary Function of Possessions in Luke–Acts* (SBL.DS 39), Missoula, Scholars Press, 1977.
The Acts of the Apostles (Sacra Pagina 5), Collegeville, Liturgical Press, 1992.
Juel, D., *Luke–Acts. The Promise of History*, Atlanta, John Knox, 1983.
Junod, E., 'Créations romanesques et traditions ecclésiastiques dans les Actes apocryphes des apôtres', *Gregorianum* 23, 1983, pp. 271–85.

Kaestli, J. D., 'Les scènes d'attribution des champs de mission et de départ de l'apôtre dans les Actes apocryphes', in F. Bovon *et alii*, ed., *Les Actes apocryphes des apôtres*, Geneva, Labor et Fides, 1981, pp. 249–64.

Kappler, C., ed., *Apocalypses et voyages dans l'au-delà*, Paris, Cerf, 1987.

Karris, R. J., 'Luke 23.47 and the Lucan View of Jesus' Death', *JBL* 105, 1986, pp. 65–74.

Käsemann, E., 'Die Johannesjünger in Ephesus', in *Exegetische Versuche und Besinnungen*, vol. I, Göttingen, Vandenhoeck und Ruprecht, 1964, pp. 158–68.

Der Ruf der Freiheit, 5th edition, Tübingen, Mohr, 1972.

Kermode, F., *The Sense of an Ending*, London, Oxford University Press, 1966, repr. 1977.

The Genesis of Secrecy. On the Interpretation of Narrative, Cambridge, MA. and London, Harvard University Press, 1979.

Killgallen, J. J., 'Paul before Agrippa (Acts 26,2–23): Some Considerations', *Bib* 69, 1988, pp. 170–95.

Kilpatrick, G. D., 'A Theme of the Lucan Passion Story and Luke 23,47', *JThS* 43, 1942, pp. 34–6.

Kirchberg, J., *Die Funktion der Orakel im Werke Herodots*, Göttingen, Vandenhoeck und Ruprecht, 1965.

Klauck, H. J., 'Gütergemeinschaft in der klassischen Antike, in Qumran und im Neuen Testament', in *Gemeinde. Amt. Sakrament*, Würzburg, Echter, 1989, pp. 69–100.

'With Paul in Paphos and Lystra. Magic and Paganism in the Acts of the Apostles', *Neotestamentica* 28, 1994, pp. 93–108.

Magie und Heidentum in der Apostelgeschichte des Lukas (SBS 167), Stuttgart, Katholisches Bibel Werk, 1996.

Kleberg, T., *Hôtels, restaurants et cabarets dans l'antiquité romaine*, Uppsala, Almqvist et Wiksells, 1957.

Klinghardt, M., *Gesetz und Volk Gottes. Das lukanische Verständnis des Gesetzes nach Herkunft, Funktion und seinem Ort in der Geschichte des Urchristentums* (WUNT 2,32), Tübingen, Mohr, 1988.

Kodell, J., ' "The Word of God Grew" '. The Ecclesial Tendency of ΛΟΓΟΣ in Acts 1,7; 12,24; 19,20', *Bib* 55, 1974, pp. 505–19.

Koet, B. J., *Five Studies on Interpretation of Scripture in Luke–Acts* (SNTA 14), Leuven, Peeters, 1989.

Krenkel, M., *Josephus und Lucas. Der schriftstellerische Einfluss des jüdischen Geschichtsschreibers auf den christlichen nachgewiesen*, Leipzig, 1894.

Krieger, K. S., *Geschichtsschreibung als Apologetik bei Flavius Josephus* (TANZ 9), Tübingen, Francke, 1994.

Kristeva, J., Σημειωτική. *Recherches pour une sémanalyse*, Paris, Seuil, 1969.

Kuch, H., 'Funktionswandlungen des antiken Romans', in H. Kuch, ed., *Der antike Roman*, Berlin, Akademie-Verlag, 1989, pp. 52–81.

Kurz, W. S., 'Hellenistic Rhetoric in the Christological Proof of Luke–Acts', *CBQ* 42, 1980, pp. 171–95.

'Narrative Models for Imitation in Luke–Acts', in D. L. Balch, E. Ferguson and W. A. Meeks, eds., *Greeks, Romans, and Christians. Essays in Honor of A. J. Malherbe*, Minneapolis, Fortress Press, 1990, pp. 171–89.

Reading Luke–Acts. Dynamics of Biblical Narrative, Louisville, Westminster/ John Knox, 1993.

'Effects of Variant Narrators in Acts 10–11', *NTS* 43, 1997, pp. 570–86.

Ladouceur, D., 'Hellenistic Preconceptions of Shipwreck and Pollution as a Context for Acts 27–28', *HThR* 73, 1980, pp. 435–49.

LaHurd, C. J., *The Author's Call to the Audience in the Acts of the Apostles*, Dissertation, Ann Arbor, University of Michigan Press, 1987.

Lampe, G. W. H., 'The Holy Spirit in the Writings of Luke', in D. E. Nineham, ed., *Studies in the Gospels. Essays in Memory of R. H. Lightfoot*, Oxford, Blackwell, 1955, pp. 159–200.

Lanczkowski, G., *et alii*, art. 'Geschichte/Geschichtsschreibung/Geschichtsphilosophie', *TRE* 12, 1984, pp. 569–698.

Lausberg, H., *Handbook of Literary Rhetoric: A Foundation for Literary Study*, Leiden, Brill, 1998, pp. 384–92.

Lefebvre, G., *Romans et contes égyptiens de l'époque pharaonique*, Paris, Adrien-Maisonneuve, 1949.

Légasse, S., 'L'"antijudaïsme" dans l'évangile selon Matthieu', in M. Didier, ed., *L'évangile selon Matthieu. Rédaction et théologie* (BEThL 29), Gembloux, Duculot, 1972, pp. 417–28.

Lentz, J. C., *Luke's Portrait of Paul* (SNTS.MS 77), Cambridge, Cambridge University Press, 1993.

L'Eplattenier, C., *Les Actes des apôtres*, Geneva, Labor et Fides, 1987.

Létoublon, F., *Fonder une cité*, Grenoble, Ellug, 1987.

Les lieux communs du roman. Stéréotypes grecs d'aventure et d'amour (Mnemosyne Supp. 123), Leiden, Brill, 1993.

Lévy, E., 'Devins et oracles chez Hérodote', in J. G. Heintz, ed., *Oracles et prophéties dans l'antiquité. Actes du Colloque de Strasbourg 15–17 juin 1995*, Paris, De Boccard, 1997, pp. 345–65.

Lohfink, G., *La conversion de saint Paul* (Lire la Bible 11), Paris, Cerf, 1967.

'Meinen Namen zu tragen... (Apg 9,15)', in *Studien zum Neuen Testament* (SBAB 5), Stuttgart, Katholisches Bibel Werk, 1990, pp. 213–221.

Lohse, E., 'Die Bedeutung des Pfingstberichtes im Rahmen des lukanischen Geschichtswerkes', in *Die Einheit des Neuen Testaments*, Göttingen, Vandenhoeck und Ruprecht, 1973, pp. 178–92.

Loisy, A., *Les Actes des apôtres*, Paris, Nourry, 1920.

Les Actes des apôtres. Traduction nouvelle avec introduction et notes, Paris, Rieder, 1925.

Loncke, J., 'Liber Actuum apte vocatur Spiritus Sancti Evangelium', *Collectiones Brugenses* 42, 1946, pp. 46–52.

Löning, K., *Die Saulustradition in der Apostelgeschichte* (NTA 9), Münster, Aschendorff, 1973.

'Das Gottesbild der Apostelgeschichte im Spannungsfeld von Frühjudentum und Fremdreligionen', in H. J. Klauck, ed., *Monotheismus und Christologie. Zur Gottesfrage im hellenistischen Judentum und im Urchristentum* (QD 138), Freiburg, Herder, 1992, pp. 88–117.

Lonis, R., *L'étranger dans le monde grec*, 2 vols., Nancy, Presses Universitaires, 1988 and 1992.

Lüdemann, G., *Das frühe Christentum nach den Traditionen der Apostelgeschichte*, Göttingen, Vandenhoeck und Ruprecht, 1987.
    Early Christianity according to the Traditions in Acts: A Commentary, London, SCM Press, 1989.
Lukasz, C., *Evangelizzazione e conflitto. Indagine sulla coerenza letteraria e tematica della pericopa di Cornelio (Atti 10,1–11,18)* (EHS.T 484), Bern, Lang, 1993.
Lundgren, S., 'Ananias and the Calling of Paul in Acts', *ST* 25, 1971, pp. 117–22.
Lyons, J., *Semantics*, vol. I, Cambridge, Cambridge University Press, 1977.
MacDonald, D. R., 'Luke's Eutychus and Homer's Elpenor: Acts 20,7–12 and *Odyssey* 10–12', *Journal of Higher Criticism* 1, 1994, pp. 5–24.
Maddox, R., *The Purpose of Luke–Acts*, Edinburgh, Clark, 1982 (repr. 1985).
Magness, J. L., *Sense and Absence. Structure and Suspension in the Ending of Mark's Gospel* (SBL Semeia Studies), Atlanta, Scholars Press, 1986.
Mainville, O., *L'Esprit dans l'œuvre de Luc*, Montréal, Fides, 1991.
    'Le péché contre l'Esprit annoncé en Lc 12,10, commis en Ac 4,16–18: une illustration de l'unité de Luc et Actes', *NTS* 45, 1999, pp. 38–50.
Malina, B. J., *Christian Origins and Cultural Anthropology*, Atlanta, John Knox, 1986.
Malina, B. J. and Neyrey, J. H., 'Honor and Shame in Luke–Acts: Pivotal Values of the Mediterranean World', in J. H. Neyrey ed., *The Social World of Luke–Acts*, Peabody, Hendrickson, 1991, pp. 25–65.
Maloney, L. M., *'All that God Had Done with Them'. The Narration of the Works of God in the Early Christian Community as Described in the Acts of the Apostles*, New York and Bern, Lang, 1991.
Marasco, G., *I viaggi nella Grecia antica*, Roma, Ateneo-Bizzarri, 1978.
Marc, A., 'L'Esprit Saint dans les Ecritures. Ananie et Saphire (Ac 5,1–11): 'Mentir à l'Esprit Saint'. L'Esprit Saint, un juge mortel?', *Théophilyon* 2:1, 1997, pp. 149–75.
Marguerat, D., 'L'œuvre de l'Esprit. Pratique et théologie dans les Actes des apôtres', in P. Gisel, ed., *Pratique et théologie. Volume publié en l'honneur de Claude Bridel* (Pratiques 1), Geneva, Labor et Fides, 1989, pp. 141–61.
    'Ananias et Saphira (Actes 5,1–11). Le viol du sacré', *Lumière et vie* 215, 1993, pp. 51–63.
    ' "Et quand nous sommes entrés dans Rome". L'énigme de la fin du livre des Actes (28,16–31)', *RHPhR* 73, 1993, pp. 1–21.
    'La mort d'Ananias et Saphira (Ac 5,1–11) dans la stratégie narrative de Luc', *NTS* 39, 1993, pp. 209–26.
    'The End of Acts (28,16–31) and the Rhetoric of Silence', in S. E. Porter and Th. H. Olbricht, eds., *Rhetoric and the New Testament. Essays from the 1992 Heidelberg Conference* (JSNTS 90), Sheffield, Sheffield Academic Press, 1993, pp. 74–89.
    'Juifs et chrétiens selon Luc–Actes', *Bib* 75, 1994, pp. 126–46.
    Le jugement dans l'évangile de Matthieu, 2nd edition (Monde de la Bible 6), Geneva, Labor et Fides, 1995.
    'Le Nouveau Testament est-il anti-juif? L'exemple de Matthieu et du livre des Actes', *RTL* 26, 1995, pp. 145–164.

'Saul's Conversion (Acts 9–22–26) and the Multiplication of Narrative in Acts', in C. M. Tuckett ed., *Luke's Literary Achievement* (JSNT.SS 116), Sheffield, Sheffield Academic Press, 1995, pp. 127–55.

'Entrer dans le monde du récit. Une présentation de l'analyse narrative', *Transversalités*. *Revue de l'Institut catholique de Paris* 59, juillet–septembre 1996, pp. 1–17.

'Juifs et chrétiens selon Luc–Actes', in D. Marguerat, ed., *Le déchirement. Juifs et chrétiens au premier siècle* (Monde de la Bible 32), Geneva, Labor et Fides, 1996, pp. 151–78.

'Le Dieu du livre des Actes', in A. Marchadour, ed., *L'évangile exploré. Mélanges offerts à Simon Légasse* (LeDiv 166), Paris, Cerf, 1996, pp. 301–31.

Le Dieu des premiers chrétiens, 3rd edition (Essais bibliques 16), Geneva, Labor et Fides, 1997.

'*Actes de Paul* et Actes canoniques: un phénomène de relecture', *Apocrypha* 8, 1997, p. 207–24.

'Le premier historien du christianisme (Luc–Actes)', *Cahier biblique* 36, Foi et Vie, Paris, 1997, pp. 19–34.

'Magie, guérison et parole dans les Actes des apôtres', *ETR* 72, 1997, pp. 197–208.

'The *Acts of Paul* and the Canonical Acts: A Phenomenon of Rereading', *Semeia* 80, 1997, p. 169–83.

'Voyages et voyageurs dans le livre des Actes et dans la culture gréco-romaine', *RHPhR* 78, 1998, pp. 33–59.

La première histoire du christianisme (Actes des apôtres) (LeDiv 180), Paris, Cerf and Geneva Labor et Fides, 1999.

'Luc–Actes entre Jérusalem et Rome. Un procédé lucanien de double signification', *NTS* 45, 1999, pp. 70–87.

'Luc–Actes: une unité à construire', in J. Verheyden, ed., *The Unity Luke–Acts* (BEThL 142), Leuven, Peeters, 1999, pp. 57–81.

'The Enigma of the Silent Closing of Acts (28,16–31)', in D. P. Moessner, ed., *Jesus and the Heritage of Israel*, Harrisburg, Trinity Press, 1999, p. 284–304.

'Magic and Miracles in the Acts of the Apostles', in T. Klutz, ed., *Magic in the New Testament World* (JSNT.S) (forthcoming).

Marguerat, D. and Bourquin, Y., *How to Read Bible Stories. An Introduction to Narrative Criticism*, London, SCM Press, 1999.

Marin, L., 'Essai d'analyse structurale d'Actes 10,1 – 11,18', in R. Barthes *et alii*, eds., *Exégèse et herméneutique*, Paris, Seuil, 1971, pp. 213–38.

Marrou, H. I., *De la connaissance historique* [1954], 6th edition (Points H 21), Paris, Seuil, 1975.

Marshall, I. H., 'Acts and the "Former Treatise" ', in B. W. Winter and A. C. Clarke, eds., *The Book of Acts in Its First Century Setting*, vol. I: *The Book of Acts in Its Ancient Literary Setting*, Grand Rapids, Eerdmans and Carlisle, Paternoster, 1993, pp. 163–82.

Marshall, I. H. and Peterson, D., eds., *Witness to the Gospel. The Theology of Acts*, Grand Rapids-Cambridge, Eerdmans, 1998.

Martin, C. J., 'The Function of Acts 8,26–40 within the Narrative Structure of the Book of Acts. The Significance of the Eunuch's Provenance for Acts 1,8c', Dissertation, Duke University, 1986.

272   Bibliography

Matera, F. J., 'Responsibility for the Death of Jesus according to the Acts of the Apostles', *JSNT* 39, 1990, pp. 77–93.

Mayer, E., *Die Reiseerzählung des Lukas (Lk 9,51–19,10): Entscheidung in der Wüste* (EHS.T 554), Frankfurt and Bern, Lang, 1996.

McCoy, W. J., 'In the Shadow of Thucydides', in B.Witherington, ed., *History, Literature, and Society in the Book of Acts*, Cambridge, Cambridge University Press, 1996, pp. 3–23.

Mealand, D. L., 'The Close of Acts and Its Hellenistic Greek Vocabulary', *NTS* 36, 1990, pp. 583–597.

Menoud, Ph. H., 'La mort d'Ananias et de Saphira (Actes 5,1–11)', *Mélanges M. Goguel, Aux sources de la tradition chrétienne*, Neuchâtel, Delachaux et Niestlé, 1950, pp. 146–154.

'Le plan des Actes des apôtres', in *Jésus-Christ et la foi*, Neuchâtel, Delachaux et Niestlé, 1975, pp. 84–91.

Merkel, H., 'Israel im lukanischen Doppelwerk', *NTS* 40, 1994, pp. 371–382.

'Das Gesetz im lukanischen Doppelwerk', in K. Backhaus, ed., *Schrift und Tradition. Festschrift J. Ernst*, Paderborn, Schöningh, 1996, pp. 119–33.

Mettayer, A., 'Ambiguïté et terrorisme du sacré: analyse d'un texte des Actes des apôtres (4,31–5,11)', *Sciences religieuses/Studies in Religion* 7, 1978, pp. 415–24.

Meurer, S., *Das Recht im Dienst der Versöhnung und des Friedens* (AThANT 63), Zurich, Theologischer Verlag Zurich, 1972.

Michaelis, W., art. 'ὁδός', *TDNT* 5, Grand Rapids, Eerdmans, 1967, pp. 42–114.

Miles, G. B. and Trompf, G., 'Luke and Antiphon: The Theology of Acts 27–28 in the Light of Pagan Beliefs about Divine Retribution, Pollution, and Shipwreck', *HThR* 69, 1976, pp. 259–67.

Moessner, D. P., 'Paul and the Pattern of the Prophet like Moses in the Acts', *SBL.SP* 1983, Chico, Scholars Press, 1983, pp. 203–12.

'The Christ Must Suffer': New Light on the Jesus–Peter, Stephen, Paul Parallels in Luke–Acts', *NT* 28, 1986, pp. 220–56.

'Paul in Acts: Preacher of Eschatological Repentance to Israel', *NTS* 34, 1988, pp. 96–104.

'The Ironic Fulfillment of Israel's Glory', in J. B. Tyson, ed., *Luke–Acts and the Jewish People. Eight Critical Perspectives*, Minneapolis, Augsburg, 1988, pp. 35–50.

Lord of the Banquet. The Literary and Theological Significance of the Lukan Travel Narrative [1989], 2nd edition, Harrisburg, Trinity Press, 1998.

Momigliano, A., *Les fondations du savoir historique*, Paris, Belles Lettres, 1992.

Monsarrat, V., 'Ac 3,1–4,22', *ETR* 53, 1978, pp. 259–67.

Moore, S., 'Are the Gospels Unified Narratives?', *SBL.SP* 1987, Atlanta, Scholars Press, 1987, pp. 443–58.

Mortimer, A. K., *La clôture narrative*, Paris, Corti, 1985.

Mossé, C., 'Les utopies égalitaires à l'époque hellénistique', *Revue Historique* 241, 1969, pp. 297–308.

Mowery, R. L., 'Direct Statements Concerning God's Activity in Acts', *SBL.SP* 1990, Atlanta, Scholars Press, 1990, pp. 196–211.

'God the Father in Luke–Acts', in E. Richard, ed., *New Views on Luke and Acts*, Collegeville, Liturgical Press, 1990, pp. 124–32.

'The Divine Hand and the Divine Plan in the Lukan Passion', *SBL.SP* 1991, Atlanta, Scholars Press, 1991, pp. 558–75.

'Lord, God, and Father: Theological Language in Luke–Acts', *SBL.SP* 1995, Atlanta, Scholars Press, 1995, pp. 82–101.

Muhlack, G., *Die Parallelen von Lukas-Evangelium und Apostelgeschichte*, Frankfurt, Lang, 1979.

Mussner, F., 'Die Idee der Apokatastasis in der Apostelgeschichte', in H. Gross and F. Mussner, eds., *Lex Tua Veritas. Festschrift H. Junker*, Trier, Paulinus, 1961, pp. 293–306.

Navone, J. J., 'The Journey Theme in Luke–Acts', *Bible Today* 58, 1972, pp. 616–19.

Neyrey, J. H., 'Acts 17, Epicureans, and Theodicy. A Study in Stereotypes', in D. L. Balch, E. Ferguson and W. A. Meeks, eds., *Greeks, Romans and Christians. Essays in Honor of A. J. Malherbe*, Minneapolis, Fortress Press, 1990, pp. 118–34.

Neyrey, J. H., ed., *The Social World of Luke–Acts*, Peabody, Hendrickson, 1991.

Nida, E. A., Louw, J. P., Snyman, A. H. and Cronje, J. V. W., *Style and Discourse, with Special Reference to the Greek New Testament*, Cape Town, Bible Society, 1983.

Noorda, S. J., 'Scene and Summary. A Proposal for Reading Acts 4.32–5.16', in J.Kremer, ed., *Les Actes des apôtres. Traditions, rédaction, théologie* (BEThL 48), Gembloux, Duculot and Leuven, Leuven University Press 1979, pp. 475–83.

O'Neill, J. C., *The Theology of Acts in Its Historical Setting*, 2nd edition, London, SPCK, 1970.

'The Connection between Baptism and the Gift of the Spirit in Acts', *JSNT* 63, 1996, pp. 87–103.

Overbeck, F., *Christentum und Kultur*, ed., C. A. Bernoulli, Basel, Schwabe, 1919 (repr. 1963).

O'Toole, R. F., *Acts 26. The Christological Climax of Paul's Defense* (AnBib 78), Roma, Biblical Institute, 1978.

'Parallels between Jesus and His Disciples in Luke–Acts. A Further Study', *BZ* 27, 1983, pp. 195–212.

The Unity of Luke's Theology. An Analysis of Luke–Acts (GNS 9), Wilmington, DE, Michael Glazier, 1984.

'Reflections on Luke's Treatment of Jews in Luke–Acts', *Bib* 74, 1993, pp. 529–55.

'"You Did Not Lie to Us (Human Beings) but to God" (Acts 5,4c)', *Bib* 76, 1995, pp. 182–209.

Panier, L., 'Portes ouvertes à la foi. La mission dans les Actes des apôtres', *Lumière et vie* 205, 1991, pp. 103–21.

Parsons, M. C., 'The Unity of Lukan Writings: Rethinking the *Opinio Communis*', in N. H. Keathley, ed., *With Steadfast Purpose. Essays in Honor of H. J. Flanders*, Waco, Baylor University, 1990, pp. 29–53.

Parsons, M. C. and Pervo, R. I., *Rethinking the Unity of Luke and Acts*, Minneapolis, Fortress Press, 1993.

Perrot, C., 'Ananie et Saphire. Le jugement ecclésial et la justice divine', *L'année canonique* 25, 1981, pp. 109–24.

Pervo, R. I., *Profit with Delight*, Philadelphia, Fortress Press, 1987.

'Must Luke and Acts Belong to the Same Genre?', *SBL.SP* 1989, Atlanta, Scholars Press, 1989, pp. 309–16.

Pesch, R., *Die Vision des Stephanus*. *Apg 7,55–56 im Rahmen der Apostelgeschichte* (SBS 12), Stuttgart, Katholisches Bibel werk, 1966.

Die Apostelgeschichte (Apg 1–12) (EKK 5.1), Zurich, Benziger and Neukirchen, Neukirchener, 1986.

Die Apostelgeschichte (Apg 13–28) (EKK 5.2), Zurich, Benziger and Neukirchen, Neukirchener, 1986.

Piégay-Gros, N., *Introduction à l'Intertextualité*, Paris, Dunod, 1996.

Plümacher, E., *Lukas als hellenistischer Schriftsteller* (StUNT 9), Göttingen, Vandenhoeck und Ruprecht, 1972, pp. 38–72.

art. 'Apostelgeschichte', *TRE* 3, 1978, pp. 483–528.

'ΤΕΡΑΤΕΙΑ. Fiktion und Wunder in der hellenistisch-römischen Geschichtsschreibung und in der Apostelgeschichte', *ZNW* 89, 1988, pp. 66–90.

Pokornỳ, P., *Theologie der lukanischen Schriften* (FRLANT 174), Göttingen, Vandenhoeck und Ruprecht, 1998.

Porter, S. E., 'Thucydides 1,22,1 and Speeches in Acts: Is There a Thucydidean View?', *NT* 32, 1990, pp. 121–42.

'The We-Passages', in D. W. J. Gill and C. Gempf, eds., *The Book of Acts in Its First Century Setting*, vol. II: *The Book of Acts in Its Graeco-Roman Setting*, Grand Rapids, Eerdmans and Carlisle, Paternoster, 1994, pp. 545–74.

Potin, J., *La fête juive de la Pentecôte* (LeDiv 65), Paris, Cerf, 1971.

Powell, M. A., *What Are They Saying about Acts?*, New York, Paulist Press, 1991.

Praeder, S. M., 'The Narrative Voyage: An Analysis and Interpretation of Acts 27–28', Dissertation, Graduate Theological Union, Berkeley, 1980.

'Acts 27,1–28,16: Sea Voyages in Ancient Literature and the Theology of Luke–Acts', *CBQ* 46, 1984, pp. 683–706.

'Jesus–Paul, Peter–Paul, and Jesus–Peter Parallelisms in Luke–Acts: A History of Reader Response', *SBL.SP* 1984, Chico, Scholars Press, 1984, pp. 23–39.

Prete, B., 'Anania e Saffira (At 5,1–11). Componenti litterarie e dottrinali', *Riv Bib* 36, 1988, pp. 463–86.

Quesnel, M., *Baptisés dans l'Esprit. Baptême et Esprit Saint dans les Actes des apôtres* (LeDiv 120), Paris, Cerf, 1985.

Radl, W., *Paulus und Jesus im lukanischen Doppelwerk. Untersuchungen zu Parallelmotiven im Lukasevangelium und in der Apostelgeschichte* (EHR 23, T49) Bern and Frankfurt, Lang, 1975.

Räisänen, H., 'The Redemption of Israel: A Salvation-Historical Problem in Luke–Acts', in P. Luomanen, ed., *Luke–Acts. Scandinavian Perspectives*, Helsinki, Finnish Exegetical Society, and Göttingen, Vandenhoeck und Ruprecht, 1991, pp. 94–114.

Rapske, B. M., 'Acts, Travel and Shipwreck', in D. W. J. Gill and C. Gempf, eds., *The Book of Acts in Its First Century Setting*, vol. II: *The Book of Acts in Its Graeco-Roman Setting*, Grand Rapids, Eerdmans and Carlisle, Paternoster, 1994, pp. 1–47.

Rasco, E., 'Le tappe fondamentali della ricerca sugli Atti degli Apostoli', *Gregorianum* 78, 1997, pp. 5–32.

Reardon, B. P., *Courants littéraires grecs du IIe et IIIe siècles après J.-C.*, Paris, Belles Lettres, 1971.

Reicke, B., 'Die Mahlzeit mit Paulus auf den Wellen des Mittelmeers Act. 27, 33–38', *ThZ* 4, 1948, pp. 401–10.

Reinhardt, W., *Das Wachstum des Gottesvolkes*. *Biblische Theologie des Gemeindewachstums*, Göttingen, Vandenhoeck und Ruprecht, 1995.

Reymond, S., 'L'expérience du chemin de Damas. Approche narrative d'une expérience spirituelle', Diplôme de spécialisation en sciences bibliques, Université de Lausanne, 1993.

'Paul sur le chemin de Damas (Ac 9, 22 et 26). Temps et espace d'une expérience', *NRTh* 118, 1996, pp. 520–38.

Rhys Roberts, W., *Dionysius of Halicarnassus. The Three Literary Letters*, Cambridge, 1901.

Richard, E., *Acts 6,1–8,4. The Author's Method of Composition* (SBL.DS 41), Missoula, Scholars Press, 1978.

Richter Reimer, I., *Women in the Acts of the Apostles: A Feminist Liberation Perspective*, Minneapolis, Fortress Press, 1995.

Ricœur, P., 'The Narrative Function', in J. B. Thompson, ed., *Hermeneutics and the Human Sciences*, Cambridge, Cambridge University Press, 1981, pp. 274–96.

Time and Narrative, 3 vols., Chicago and London, University of Chicago Press, 1984.

Du texte à l'action. Essais d'herméneutique, vol. II, Paris, Seuil, 1986.

'Philosophies critiques de l'histoire: recherche, explication, écriture', in G. Floistad, ed., *Philosophical Problems Today*, vol. I, Dordrecht, Kluwer, 1994, pp. 139–201.

La critique et la conviction, Paris, Calmann-Lévy, 1995.

Rimmon-Kenan, S., *Narrative Fiction: Contemporary Poetics*, New York, Methuen, 1983.

Robbins, V. K., 'Luke–Acts: A Mixed Population Seeks a Home in the Roman Empire', in L. C. A. Alexander, ed., *Images of Empire* (JSOT.SS 122), Sheffield, Sheffield Academic Press, 1991, pp. 202–21.

'The Social Location of the Implied Author of Luke–Acts', in J. H. Neyrey, ed., *The Social World of Luke–Acts*, Peabody, Hendrickson, 1991, pp. 305–32.

Roloff, J., 'Die Paulus-Darstellung des Lukas. Ihre geschichtlichen Vorausetzungen und ihr theologisches Ziel', *EvTh* 39, 1979, pp. 510–31.

Die Apostelgeschichte (NTD 5), Göttingen, Vandenhoeck und Ruprecht, 1981.

Rordorf, W., 'Nochmals: Paulusakten und Pastoralbriefe' [1987], in *Lex orandi – Lex credendi* (Paradosis 36), Freiburg CH, Universitätsverlag, 1993.

'Paul's Conversion in the Canonical Acts and in the *Acts of Paul*', *Semeia* 80, 1999, pp. 137–44.

Rosenblatt, M. E., 'Under Interrogation. Paul as Witness in Juridical Contexts in Acts and the Implied Spirituality for Luke's Community', Dissertation, Ann Arbor, University of Michigan Press, 1988.

'Recurring Narration as a Lukan Literary Convention in Acts: Paul's Jerusalem Speech in Acts 22,1–22', in E. Richard, ed., *New Views on Luke and Acts*, Collegeville, Liturgical Press, 1990, pp. 94–105.

Rudolph, K., 'Gnostische Reisen: im Diesseits und ins Jenseits', in G. Sfameni Gasparro, ed., Ἀγαθὴ ἐλπίς. *Studi religiosi a onore di U. Bianchi*, Roma, Bretschneider, 1994, pp. 493–504.

Sabbe, M., 'The Son of Man Saying in Acts 7,56', in J. Kremer, ed., *Les Actes des apôtres. Traditions, rédaction, théologie* (BEThL 48), Gembloux and Leuven, Duculot, 1979, pp. 241–79.

Saïd, S., 'Homère, l'*Odyssée*, chants 5–13', in D. Alexandre *et alii*, eds., *L'autre et l'ailleurs*, Paris, 1992, pp. 5–83.

'Oracles et devins dans le monde grec', in J. G. Heintz, ed., *Oracles et prophéties dans l'antiquité. Actes du Colloque de Strasbourg 15–17 juin 1995*, Paris, De Boccard, 1997, pp. 367–403.

Salat, P., 'La fin de l'Enéide', in A. Montandon, ed., *Le point final*, Faculté des Lettres et Sciences humaines de l'Université de Clermond-Ferrand II, Nouvelle série, 20, Clermond-Ferrand, 1984, pp. 11–18.

Salo, K., *Luke's Treatment of the Law. A Redaction-Critical Investigation* (AnASU 57), Helsinki, Suomalainen Tiedeakatemia, 1991.

Sanders, J. T., *The Jews in Luke–Acts*, London, SCM Press, 1987.

'The Jewish People in Luke–Acts', in J. B. Tyson, ed., *Luke–Acts and the Jewish People. Eight Critical Perspectives*, Minneapolis, Augsburg, 1988, pp. 51–75.

'Who Is a Jew and Who Is a Gentile in the Book of Acts?', *NTS* 37, 1991, pp. 434–55.

Sassi, M. M., 'I viaggio e la festa. Note sulla rappresentazione dell'ideale filosofico della vita', in G. Camassa and S. Fasce, eds., *Idea e realtà del viaggio*, Genova, ECIG, 1991, pp. 17–36.

Savran, G. W., *Telling and Retelling. Quotation in Biblical Narrative*, Bloomington, Indiana University Press, 1988.

Scarpi, P., *La fuga e il ritorno. Storia e mitologia del viaggio*, Venice, Marsilio, 1992.

Schille, G., *Die Apostelgeschichte des Lukas* (ThHNT 5), Berlin, Evang. Verlagsanstalt, 1983.

Schmelling, G. F., ed., *The Novel in the Ancient World*, Leiden, Brill, 1996.

Schmid, L., art 'κέντρον', *TDNT* 3, Grand Rapids, Eerdmans, 1965, pp. 663–68.

Schmitt, J., 'Contributions à l'étude de la discipline pénitentielle dans l'Eglise primitive à la lumière des textes de Qumran', in *Les manuscrits de la Mer Morte, Colloque de Strasbourg 1955*, Paris, 1957, pp. 93–109.

Schneemelcher, W., 'Die Apostelgeschichte des Lukas und die Acta Pauli', in W. Eltester and J. L. Martyn, eds., *Apophoreta. Festschrift E. Haenchen* (BZNW 30), Berlin, Töpelmann, 1964, pp. 236–50.

Das Urchristentum (Urban-Taschenbücher 33), Stuttgart, Kohlhammer, 1981.

Schneider, G., *Die Apostelgeschichte*, vol. I (HThKNT 5.1), Freiburg, Herder, 1980.

'Gott und Christus als Kyrios nach der Apostelgeschichte', in J. Zmijewski and E. Nellessen, eds., *Begegnung mit dem Wort. Festschrift H. Zimmermann* (BBB 53), Bonn, Hanstein, 1980, pp. 161–174.

Die Apostelgeschichte, vol. II (HThKNT 5.2), Freiburg, Herder, 1982.

Lukas, Theologe der Heilsgeschichte (BBB 59), Bonn, Hanstein, 1985.

Schrader, K., *Der Apostel Paulus*, vol. V, Leipzig, 1836.

Schreckenberg, H., 'Flavius Josephus und die lukanischen Schriften', in W. Haubeck and M. Bachmann, eds., *Wort in der Zeit. Festschrift K. H. Rengstorf*, Leiden, Brill, 1980, pp. 179–209.

Schweizer, E., art. 'πνεῦμα', *TDNT* 6, Grand Rapids, Eerdmans, 1968, pp. 404–15.

Scott Spencer, F., *The Portrait of Philip in Acts* (JSNT.SS 67), Sheffield, Sheffield Academic Press, 1992.

Seccombe, D. P., *Possessions and the Poor in Luke–Acts* (SNTU B 6), Linz, 1982.

Selvidge, M., 'The Acts of the Apostles: A Violent Aetiological Legend', *SBL.SP* 1986, Atlanta, Scholars Press, 1986, pp. 330–40.

Sheeley, S. M., *Narrative Asides in Luke–Acts* (JSNT.SS 72), Sheffield, Sheffield Academic Press, 1992.

Shelton, J. B., *Mighty in Word and Dead. The Role of the Holy Spirit in Luke–Acts*, Peabody, Hendrickson, 1991.

Shepherd, W. H., *The Narrative Function of the Holy Spirit as a Character in Luke–Acts* (SBL.DS 147), Atlanta, Scholars Press, 1994.

Slingerland, D., 'The Composition of Acts: Some Redaction-Critical Observations', *JAAR* 56, 1988, pp. 99–113.

Smalley, S. S., 'Spirit, Kingdom and Prayer in Luke–Acts', *NT* 15, 1973, pp. 59–71.

Smith, B. H., *Poetic Closure. A Study of How Poems End*, Chicago, University of Chicago Press, 1968.

Snell, B., *La découverte de l'esprit*, Combas, L'Eclat, 1994.

Soars, M. L., *The Speeches in Acts. Their Content, Context, and Concerns*, Louisville, Westminster/John Knox, 1994.

Söder, R., *Die apokryphen Apostelgeschichten und die romanhafte Literatur der Antike* [Stuttgart, Kohlhammer, 1932], Darmstadt, 1969.

Spicq, C., *Notes de lexicographie néo-testamentaire* (OBO 22/2), Fribourg, Editions Universitaires and Göttingen, Vandenhoeck und Ruprecht, 1978.

Lexique théologique du Nouveau Testament, Fribourg, Editions Universitaires and Paris, Cerf, 1991.

Squires, J. T., *The Plan of God in Luke–Acts* (SNTS.MS 76), Cambridge, Cambridge University Press, 1993.

'The Function of Acts 8, 4–12, 25', *NTS* 44, 1998, pp. 608–17.

Stadter, P. A., ed., *The Speeches in Thucydides*, Chapel Hill, University of North Carolina Press, 1973.

Stanley, D. M., 'Paul's Conversion in Acts: Why the Three Accounts?', *CBQ* 15, 1953, pp. 315–38.

Stark, I., 'Religiöse Elemente im antiken Roman', in H. Kuch, ed., *Der antike Roman*, Berlin, Akademie-Verlag, 1989, pp. 135–49.

Steck, O. H., 'Formgeschichtliche Bemerkungen zur Darstellung des Damaskusgeschehens in der Apostelgeschichte', *ZNW* 67, 1976, pp. 20–8.

'Prophetische Prophetenauslegung', in H. F. Geisser, et alii, eds., *Wahrheit der Schrift – Wahrheit der Auslegung. Eine Zürcher Vorlesungsreihe zu G. Ebelings 80. Geburtstag*, Zurich, Theologischer Verlag, 1993, pp. 198–244.

Stegemann, W., *Zwischen Synagoge und Obrigkeit. Zur historischen Situation der lukanischen Christen* (FRLANT 152,) Göttingen, Vandenhoeck und Ruprecht, 1991.

Steichele, H., 'Geist und Amt als kirchenbildende Elemente in der Apostelgeschichte', in J. Hainz, ed., *Kirche im Werden*, Munich, Paderborn, 1976, pp. 185–203.

Stemberger, G., 'Die Beurteilung Roms in der rabbinischen Literatur', in W. Haase, ed., *ANRW* II, 19.2, Berlin and New York, de Gruyter, 1979, pp. 338–96.

Sterling, G. E., *Historiography and Self-Definition. Josephus, Luke–Acts and Apologetic Historiography* (NT.S 64), Leiden, Brill, 1992.

Sternberg, M., *The Poetics of Biblical Narrative*, Bloomington, Indiana University Press, 1987.

Stierle, K. and Warning, R., *Das Ende: Figuren einer Denkform*, Munich, Fink, 1996.

Stolle, V., *Der Zeuge als Angeklagter. Untersuchungen zum Paulusbild des Lukas* (BWANT 102), Stuttgart, Kohlhammer, 1973.

Suleiman, S. R., 'Redundancy and the "Readable Text"', *Poetics Today*, 1:3, 1980, pp. 119–42.

Swartley, W. M., 'Politics and Peace (Eirene) in Luke's Gospel', in R. J. Cassidy and P. J. Scharper, eds., *Political Issues in Luke–Acts*, Maryknoll, Orbis Books, 1983, pp. 18–37.

Tajra, H. W., *The Trial of St. Paul* (WUNT 2, 35), Tübingen, Mohr, 1989.

Talbert, C. H., *Literary Patterns. Theological Themes, and the Genre of Luke–Acts*, SBL.MS 20, Missoula, Scholars Press, 1974.

'The Acts of the Apostles: Monograph or "Bios"?', in B. Witherington ed., *History, Literature, and Society in the Book of Acts*, Cambridge, Cambridge University Press, 1996, pp. 58–72.

Talbert, C. H., ed., *Luke–Acts. New Perspectives from the SBL Seminar*, New York, Crossroad, 1984.

Tannehill, R. C., 'Israel in Luke–Acts: A Tragic Story', *JBL* 104, 1985, pp. 69–85.

'The Composition of Acts 3–5: Narrative Development and Echo Effect', *SBL.SP* 1984, Chico, Scholars Press, 1984, pp. 217–40.

The Narrative Unity of Luke–Acts. A Literary Interpretation, Minneapolis, Fortress Press, vol. I, 1986; vol. II, 1990.

'Rejection by Jews and Turning to Gentiles: The Pattern of Paul's Mission in Acts', in J. B. Tyson, ed., *Luke–Acts and the Jewish People. Eight Critical Perspectives*, Minneapolis, Augsburg, 1988, pp. 83–101.

Taylor, J., 'The Roman Empire in the Acts of the Apostles', in W. Haase, ed., *ANRW* II, 26.3, Berlin and New York, de Gruyter, 1996, pp. 2436–500.

Theissen, G., *Urchristliche Wundergeschichten* (StNT 8), Gütersloh, Mohn, 1974.

Thornton, C. J., *Der Zeuge des Zeugen. Lukas als Historiker der Paulusreisen* (WUNT 56), Tübingen, Mohr, 1991.

Tiede, D. L., *Prophecy and History in Luke–Acts*, Philadelphia, Fortress Press, 1980.

' "Glory to Thy People Israel": Luke–Acts and the Jews', in J. B. Tyson, ed., *Luke–Acts and the Jewish People. Eight Critical Perspectives*, Minneapolis, Augsburg, 1988, pp. 21–34.

Tosco, L., *Pietro e Paolo ministri del giudizio di Dio. Studio del genere letterario e della funzione di At 5,1–11 e 13,4–12* (Riv Bib Suppl. 19), Bologna, Dehoniane, 1989.

Trémel, B., 'A propos d'Ac 20,7–12: puissance du thaumaturge ou du témoin?', *RThPh* 112, 1980, pp. 359–69.

Trocmé, E., *Le 'livre des Actes' et l'histoire* (EHPhR 45), Paris, Presses Universitaires de France, 1957.

'Le Saint-Esprit et l'Eglise d'après le livre des Actes', in S. Dockx, ed., *L'Esprit Saint et l'Eglise*, Paris, Fayard, 1969, pp. 19–44.

L'enfance du christianisme, Paris, Noêsis, 1997.

Trompf, G., 'On Why Luke Declined to Recount the Death of Paul: Acts 27–28 and Beyond', in C. H. Talbert, ed., *Luke–Acts. New Perspectives from the SBL Seminar*, New York, Crossroad, 1984, pp. 225–39.

Trotta, F., 'Lasciare la madrepatria per fondare una colonia. Tre esempi nella storia di Sparta', in G. Camassa and S. Fasce, eds., *Idea e realtà del viaggio*, Genova, ECIG, 1991, pp. 37–66.

Tuckett, C. M., ed., *Luke's Literary Achievement. Collected Essays* (JSNT.SS 116), Sheffield, Sheffield Academic Press, 1995.

Turner, M. B., 'Jesus and the Spirit in Lucan Perspective', *TynB* 32, 1981, pp. 3–42.

'Power from on High. The Spirit in Israel's Restoration and Witness in Luke–Acts', *Journal of Pent. Theol*, SS 9, Sheffield, Sheffield Academic Press, 1996.

Tyson, J. B., 'The Jewish Public in Luke–Acts', *NTS* 30, 1984, pp. 574–83.

The Death of Jesus in Luke–Acts, Columbia, SC, University of South Carolina Press, 1986.

'The Problem of Jewish Rejection in Acts', in J. B. Tyson, ed., *Luke–Acts and the Jewish People. Eight Critical Perspectives*, Minneapolis, Augsburg, 1988, pp. 124–37.

Images of Judaism in Luke–Acts, Columbia, SC, University of South Carolina Press, 1992.

'Jews and Judaism in Luke–Acts: Reading as a Godfearer', *NTS* 41, 1995, pp. 19–38.

Luke, Judaism, and the Scholars. Critical Approaches to Luke–Acts, Columbia, SC, University of South Carolina Press, 1999.

Tyson, J. B., ed., *Luke–Acts and the Jewish People. Eight Critical Perspectives*, Minneapolis, Augsburg, 1988.

Uspensky, B., *A Poetics of Composition. The Structure of the Artistic Text and Typology of a Compositional Form*, Berkeley, University of California Press, 1973.

Van de Sandt, H., 'Acts 28,28: No Salvation for the People of God?', *EthL* 70, 1994, pp. 341–58.

Van Unnik, W. C., 'The "Book of Acts", the Confirmation of the Gospel', *NT* 4, 1960, pp. 26–59.

'Der Ausdruck "ΕΩΣ ΕΣΧΑΤΟΥ ΤΗΣ ΓΗΣ" (Apostelgeschichte 1,8) und sein alttestamentlicher Hintergrund', in *Sparsa Collecta*, vol. I (NT.S 29), Leiden, Brill, 1973, pp. 386–401.

'Luke's Second Book and the Rules of Hellenistic Historiography', in J. Kremer, ed., *Les Actes des apôtres. Traditions, rédaction, théologie* (BEThL 48), Gembloux, Duculot and Leuven, Leuven University Press 1979, pp. 37–60.

Veltman, F., 'The Defense Speeches of Paul in Acts', in C. H. Talbert, ed., *Perspectives on Luke–Acts*, Danville, Association of Baptist Professors of Religion and Edinburgh, Clark, 1978.

Verdin, H., 'Agatharchide de Cnide et les fictions des poètes', in *Purpose of History. Studies in Greek Historiography from the 4th to the 2nd Centuries B.C.* (Stud. Hellenist. 30), Leiden, Brill, 1990, pp. 1–15.

Veyne, P., *Comment on écrit l'histoire* [orig. 1971] (Points H 226), Paris, Seuil, 1996.

Vielhauer, Ph., 'On the "Paulinism" of Acts', in L. E. Keck and J. L. Martyn, eds., *Studies in Luke–Acts*, Nashville, 1966, pp. 33–50.

Villgradter, R. and Krey, F., eds., *Der utopische Roman*, Darmstadt, Wissenschaftliche Buchgesellschaft, 1973.

Vogels, W., 'Les récits de vocation des prophètes', *NRTh* 95, 1973, pp. 1–24.

Von Baer, H., *Der Heilige Geist in den Lukasschriften* (BWANT III,3), Stuttgart, Kohlhammer, 1926.

Vouga, F., 'Antijudaismus im Johannesevangelium?', *ThGl* 83, 1993, pp. 81–89.

Walaskay, P. W., *'And So We Came to Rome'. The Political Perspective of St Luke* (SNTS.MS, 49), Cambridge, Cambridge University Press, 1983.

Walworth, A. J., 'The Narrator of Acts', Dissertation, Southern Baptist Theological Seminary, 1984.

Wasserberg, G., *Aus Israels Mitte – Heil für die Welt* (BZNW 92), Berlin, de Gruyter, 1998.

Webber, R. C., ' "Why Were the Heathen So Arrogant?" The Socio-rhetorical Strategy of Acts 3–4', *BTB* 22/1, 1992, pp. 19–25.

Wedderburn, A. J. M., 'Zur Frage der Gattung der Apostelgeschichte', in P. Schäfer, ed., *Geschichte – Tradition – Reflexion. Festschrift M. Hengel*, vol. III, Tübingen, Mohr, 1996, pp. 303–22.

Wehnert, J., *Die Wir-Passagen der Apostelgeschichte. Ein lukanisches Stilmittel aus jüdischer Tradition* (GTA 40), Göttingen, Vandenhoeck und Ruprecht, 1989.

Weinert, F., 'The Meaning of the Temple in Luke–Acts', *BTB* 11/3, 1981, pp. 85–9.

Weiser, A., *Die Apostelgeschichte Kapitel 1–12* (ÖTBKNT 5.1), Gütersloh, Mohn, 1981.

Die Apostelgeschichte Kapitel 13–28 (ÖTBKNT 5.2), Gütersloh, Mohn, 1985.

Wellhausen, J., *Das Evangelium Lucae*, Berlin, Reimer, 1904.

Wikenhauser, A., 'Doppelträume', *Bib* 29, 1948, pp. 100–11.

Wilckens, U., 'Interpreting Luke–Acts in a Period of Existentialist Theology', in L. E. Keck and J. L. Martyn, eds., *Studies in Luke–Acts. Essays Presented in Honor of P. Schubert*, 3rd edition, London, 1978, pp. 60–83.

Wildhaber, B., *Paganisme populaire et prédication apostolique* (Monde de la Bible 15), Geneva, Labor et Fides, 1987.

Wills, L. M., 'The Depiction of the Jews in Acts', *JBL* 110, 1991, pp. 631–54.

Wilson, S. G., *The Gentiles and the Gentile Mission in Luke–Acts* (SNTS.MS 23), Cambridge, Cambridge University Press, 1973.

'The Jews and the Death of Jesus in Acts', in P. Richardson, ed., *Anti-Judaism in Early Christianity*, vol. I, Waterloo, W. Laurier, 1986, pp. 155–64.

Windisch, H., 'Die Christusepiphanie vor Damaskus (Act 9, 22 und 26) und ihre religionsgeschichtlichen Parallelen', *ZNW* 31, 1932, pp. 1–23.

Winter, B. W. and Clarke, A. C., eds., *The Book of Acts in Its First Century Setting*, vol. I: *The Book of Acts in Its Ancient Literary Setting*, Grand Rapids, Eerdmans and Carlisle, Paternoster, 1993.

Witherington, B., 'Editing the Good News: Some Synoptic Lessons for the Study of Acts', in B. Witherington, ed., *History, Literature, and Society in the Book of Acts*, Cambridge, Cambridge University Press, 1996, pp. 335–44.

Witherington, B., ed., *History, Literature, and Society in the Book of Acts*, Cambridge, Cambridge University Press, 1996.

Witherup, R. D., 'Functional Redundancy in the Acts of the Apostles: A Case Study', *JSNT* 48, 1992, pp. 67–86.

'Cornelius Over and Over and Over Again: "Functional Redundancy" in the Acts of the Apostles', *JSNT* 49, 1993, pp. 45–66.

Zimmerli, W., *Ezechiel 1–24* (BK 13,1), Neukirchen, Neukirchener, 1969.

Zumstein, J., 'L'apôtre comme martyr dans les Actes de Luc. Essai de lecture globale', *RThPh* 112, 1980, pp. 371–90; also in *Miettes exégétiques* (Monde de la Bible 25), Geneva, Labor et Fides, 1991, pp. 183–205.

INDEX OF PASSAGES